PSYCHODYNAMIC PERSPECTIVES ON

RELIGION SECT AND CULT

Edited by
DAVID A. HALPERIN

John Wright • PSG Inc
Boston   Bristol   London
1983

Library of Congress Cataloging in Publication Data
Main entry under title:

Psyschodynamic perspectives on religion, sect and cult.

  Bibliography: p.
  Includes index.
   1.   Religion--Addresses, essays, lectures. 2.   Cults--
Addresses, essays, lectures. 3.   Cults--Psychological
aspects--Addresses, essays, lectures. 4.   Psychology,
Religious--Addresses, essays, lectures. I.   Halperin,
David A.
BL50.P69 1983   291'.01'9   83-1260
ISBN 0-7236-7029-3

Published simultaneously by:
John Wright • PSG Inc, 545 Great Road, Littleton,
Massachusetts 01460 U.S.A.
John Wright & Sons Ltd, 823–825 Bath Road,
Bristol BS4 5NU, England

Printed in the United States of America.

International Standard Book Number: 0-7236-7029-3

Library of Congress Catalog Card Number: 83-1260

In memory of my father, Isaac Hirsh Halperin,
who helped me to understand the differences
between religion and cult. *Ave Atque Vale.*

CONTRIBUTORS

JOHN G. CLARK, Jr, MD
Assistant Professor of Psychiatry
Harvard Medical School
Cambridge, Massachusetts
Chairman, Executive Committee
American Family Foundation
Weston, Massachusetts

PHILIP CUSHMAN, MA
Director, Cult Prevention Program
Bureau of Jewish Education
San Francisco, California

ALEXANDER DEUTSCH, MD
Associate Clinical Professor of Psychiatry
New York University
    School of Medicine
Chief, Out-Patient Psychiatry
Cabrini Medical Center
New York, New York

KATHERINE P. EWING, PhD
Harper Instructor in the College
The Pritzker School of Medicine
University of Chicago
Chicago, Illinois

JOHANNES FABIAN, PhD
Professor of Anthropology
University of Amsterdam
Amsterdam
The Netherlands

ARTHUR N. FRAKT, JD
Dean
Loyola University College of Law
Los Angeles, California

MARVIN F. GALPER, PhD
Clinical Psychologist
San Diego County Medical Health
San Diego, California

KEVIN GARVEY
Writer, Journalist
Carlisle, Pennsylvania

CARL GOLDBERG, PhD
Department of Psychiatry
Albert Einstein College of Medicine
    of Yeshiva University
New York, New York

DAVID A. HALPERIN, MD
Assistant Clinical Professor
    of Psychiatry
Mount Sinai School of Medicine of
    the City University of New York
Consulting Psychiatrist
Cult Hotline and Treatment Program
    of Jewish Board of Family and
    Children's Services
Cult Information and Treatment
    Program of Westchester Jewish
    Community Services
New York, New York

CARL A. HAMMERSCHLAG, MD
Chief of Psychiatry
Phoenix Indian Medical Center
Phoenix, Arizona

L. D. HANKOFF, MD
Chairman, Department of Psychiatry
Elizabeth General Hospital
Elizabeth, New Jersey
Clinical Professor of Psychiatry
S.U.N.Y. College of Medicine
Stony Brook, New York

SAUL V. LEVINE, MD
Chairman and Professor
Department of Psychiatry
University of Toronto
Toronto, Ontario
Canada

ZVI LOTHANE, MD
Assistant Clinical Professor
    of Psychiatry
Mount Sinai School of Medicine
    of the City University of New York
Training Analyst
Institute for Psychoanalytic Training
    and Research
New York, New York

vi

ARNOLD MARKOWITZ, MSW
Coordinator
Cult Hotline and Treatment Program
Jewish Board of Family and
　Children's Services
New York, New York

PETER A. OLSSON, MD
Associate Clinical Professor
　of Psychiatry
Baylor College of Medicine
Houston, Texas

MORTIMER OSTOW, MD
Sandrow Visiting Professor of
　Pastoral Psychiatry
Jewish Theological Seminary
New York, New York

ROBERT J. PRESTON
Writer
Phoenix, Arizona

JAMES REBHAN, MSW
Assistant Director
Stuyvesant Residence Club
Jewish Board of Family and
　Children's Services
New York, New York

FRANCES M. SCAVULLO, CSW
Department of Psychiatry
St. Lukes-Roosevelt Hospital Center
New York, New York

J. LEE SHNEIDMAN, PhD
Professor of History
Adelphi University
Garden City, New York

CONALEE LEVINE-SHNEIDMAN, PhD
Private Practice
New York, New York

MOSHE HALEVI SPERO, MA
Chairman
Department of Individual and
　Social Behavior
Notre Dame College of Ohio
Cleveland, Ohio

VANESSA WEBER, BA
Graduate Student
Union Theological Seminary
Graduate Student
Columbia University School of
　Social Work
New York, New York

CONTENTS

viii

P R E F A C E

From the dawn of history onward, mankind has always had its religion, its supernatural beings and its gods. Whether the form has been of a pantheon of gods or spirits who dwell everywhere or the monotheistic beliefs that have come in the last 2500 years of civilization, man has always believed in the existence of such a being or beings and has guided his life in accord with the beliefs attributed to the wishes of such beings.

Whatever the essence of religion may be, and there are many essences that have been described, it has been universal among man and his society from probably before recorded time. What has varied from place to place and culture to culture have been the forms of worship and of belief, not the essential religious belief. Thus religion, in its appeal to the human being, seems to strike a deep cord in the psychological make-up of man as well as in his societies and varying cultures.

Within the framework of religion and its organizations that serve religious practices, organized religion has at times been coterminous with the temporal power of a society, at other times completely separate from it and many times coequal with it. Civilizations have waxed and waned but the variety of religious practices and religious organizations have gone on. Many religious institutions have survived when the temporal power with which they originated has perished and been replaced. At other times, the religious organization has itself disappeared as the temporal power has disappeared.

There are probably many reasons, cultural, social, economic, and most of all psychological, that have provided for the enduring place of religion, religious beliefs and religious organizations within the society of man. The interest of people in their religion and their religious organizations has also waxed and waned but never disappeared over the course of time. Some eras have been periods of exacerbation of interest and attachment to religion in its organized form while other eras, times of political, social and economic upheaval, have often been associated with a diminution of such interest. Regardless, however, of the interest or power of religion and its organizations, there have always been within any given religious group, leaders of greater fervor and greater impact who have gathered about them followers. Together they establish variations of the religious practices currently in existence, modifying them by their own personal interpretations. At times such cults or sects have captured large followings within existing religious organizations, while at other times the followers have been few. Many sects or cults die out when the inspired leader vanishes from the scene, while others have survived and flourished often after the loss of the founding leader.

Cults and sects are marked by the particular enthusiasm, fervor and often blind commitment of the leader and its followers to the particular form of teaching being provided. History has been marked by clashes between temporal powers and sect groups, and by clashes between organized religions and deviant sects or cults. History has particularly been marked by clashes between great religious groups; ie, the Crusades in which the Christians attempted to overcome the Moslems, or by the spread of Islam by the Moslem groups coming across Northern Africa into Spain until their advance was halted there.

History has also been marked by quarrels, battles and fights between different groups within each large religious branch, clashes that continue to the present time. Within Islam, clashes between Shi-ite and Sunni sects date back centuries and continue to the present time as evidenced by what has been happening in Iran, Iraq and much of the Arabian peninsula. Within the Christian world clashes between Protestant and Catholic and between their varying branches also date back many centuries. Even up to the present time in Northern Ireland, the bitterness is tinged with clash between Catholic and Protestant. Within a branch of Christianity, the Catholic church, there are as many variations and varieties of Catholicism practiced as there are national churches. The Irish Catholic is a different religious group than the Italian Catholic, who in turn is different from the Latin American Catholic. All are united within the framework of the Catholic church, but the attitudes of the followers are as much nationally determined as church determined.

Attempts at arriving at the essence of religion have been myriad. Depending upon the particular point of view of the interpreter, the essence is described as spiritual which is then attempted to be defined. Psychologists and psychoanalysts have looked to a continuation of man's infantile dependence, transformed in the adult to a regressive dependence on a presumed higher being who maintains a parental role in the spiritual realm. Students of culture have insisted upon the ethical and moral qualities of religious tenets as conveying the essence of religion and serving to guide mankind in his behavior toward one other and toward the rest of the world. William James in his *The Varieties of Religious Experience* in 1902 defined the essence of the religious experience as involving the realm of affect or emotion in contrast to the intellectual qualities of science. He felt that religion's appeal lies in that very call upon emotion of which science is devoid by its nature.

Whatever its appeal, there is no doubt that man has always been drawn toward religion, and the religious leader who founds a cult or sect often appeals particularly to the young and perhaps the troubled in spirit. That such individuals exist in greater numbers at times of political, social and economic upheaval seems also true, so that there have been varying periods in the history of nations when sects have flourished and other times when they have diminished in prominence. We seem, in this present post-World War II era, to be in one of those periods of economic, social and political upheaval that often follows great catastrophies. It is an era in which there seems to have been a great number of cults or sects developing in this country and in other countries of the world, which have attracted followers from a variety of walks of life, often to the dismay of their families and friends. This book is an effort to study, mostly from a psychological point of view but also from an anthropologic, sociologic and historical point of view, some of the factors that play into religious revival, cult and sect formation and the attraction that they have for so many people.

The early portion of this book deals with historical examples of religious innovation, cult and formation and the historical context in which they occur. The impact of the society and culture on such religious practices and of such religious practices on the society and culture are reported in fascinating detail. The study of such histories shows once again the truth of Santayana's dictum that "those who do not know history are doomed to repeat it." The history of religious sect formation in this country 150 years ago shows developments that parallel our own times and provide an interesting lesson for us. Studies of the philosophic backgrounds of various currents of thought trace these back many centuries and show how ideas persist and recur in varying forms and in present day guises. The historical parallel section takes us up to the present time to the Jonestown incident, showing the impact of a cult leader on his followers and of the nature of the followers who are drawn to such a cult leader, following him to their ultimate demise.

The second section of the book contains interesting and important studies on the nature of cult affiliation and religious identifications in the present-day world and in various levels of society. These range from drug groups through the high tech areas, to the psychoanalytic movement and to middle-class group Jewish cultures.

The final section considers a problem peculiar perhaps to our time of cult involvement by so-called "alienated" youth, brain-washing techniques that seem to capture the minds of such youth and the attempts of family and friends to remove them. Such removal involves not only psychological issues, but also ethical issues and, of course, legal issues. All of these are addressed in chapters in this last section.

The main emphasis in the book is from the psychological side which is appropriate since, above all, religion is a psychological matter as regards the individual, even though society may have its organized religions which serve to perpetuate and transmit the values of that particular society. The role of a student of psychology is to consider the individual, his beliefs, his needs, his yearnings which are the most important subject matter of scientific study. It is to this end that this book is dedicated. I congratulate the editor and authors on their contributions and thoughtful efforts at advancing knowledge in an important, and often neglected, area.

Edward D. Joseph, MD
Professor of Psychiatry
The Mount Sinai School of Medicine
Past President, International
Psycho-Analytical Association
President-Elect, American
Psychoanalytic Association

ACKNOWLEDGMENTS

I should like to acknowledge my profound debt to my wife and family, whose understanding, interest and concern supported me in completing this book, and whose patience allowed me to desert them and pursue what often seemed to be an unending task.

I should like to extend my deep appreciation to those many friends who bore with me through interminable discussions, and, whose suggestions, questions, and criticisms bore fruit in this volume. I should also like to express my appreciation to the Department of Psychiatry of the Mount Sinai School of Medicine and to Aaron Stein, MD, and the other members of the Division of Group Psychotherapy for their stimulation and interest. Above all, I should like to express my appreciation to the Jewish Board of Family and Children's Services and to the Westchester Jewish Community Services for affording me the opportunity and privilege of working with the individuals and their families whose deep human dilemmas stimulated me throughout the production of this book. Finally, I should like to express my appreciation to Alexander Wolf, MD, for having fostered my interest in groups, both benign and malignant.

Editor's Note: The chapters in this book represent the contributors' efforts to approach extraordinarily complex issues. Their conclusions and views may differ. As editor, I have not conducted independent research to confirm or disprove any of the contributors' statements or reports.

INTRODUCTION

T he attempt to separate the true from the false prophet and differentiate between the charismatic religious leader and the mountebank preying on the
credulous is as old as civilization. Hippocrates (460–377 BC) noted in his *On the
Sacred Disease:*

> They who first referred this disease to the gods, appear to me to have been just
> such persons as the conjurors, purificators, and charlatans now are, who give
> themselves out for being excessively religious, and as knowing more than other
> people.

Euripides, in his play, *The Bacchae,* described the destructive effects of cultic
fanaticism. Caelius, a Roman physician and contemporary of Galen, described
both the perils of excessive religiosity and psychotic episodes in which Roman
women threw themselves into the sea to be reborn as Aphrodite. Catullus, the
Latin poet, strikes an intense and disconcertingly contemporary note in his poem
Number 63 as he deals with the theme of self-destructive cult affiliation. In the
poem, Attis leaves his conventional home in Rome to pursue the strange new
gods of the East. Arriving at the sanctuary of the goddess, Cybele, on Mt. Ida in
Phrygia (now Turkey), he castrates himself in an act of symbolic identification
with the goddess. The poem ends with Attis's recognition of his alienation from
his home:

> Homeland, hearth, friends, parents, shall I be gone from you all?
> Shall I be gone from the streets, the halls, the places where the young men meet?

And, with the poet's recognition of the power of self-destructive cultism:

> Attis with the scream of a madman fled to the forest
> And there for ever and ever all his life's course
> He was a slave.
> O Holy Mother Lady of might. . .
> Grant that this house where I dwell
> May never know the madness thou canst send
> Drive other men to frenzy drive other men insane.

And, yet, the Gallae (capons)—the priests of Cybele— were a common sight on
the streets of Rome.

Celsus, a Roman historian, describes a "prophet" of second century in Phoe-
nicia and Israel with:

> There are many who prophesy at the slightest excuse for some trivial cause both
> inside and outside temples. . . . It is an ordinary and common custom for each to
> say: "I am God (or a son of God, or a divine Spirit). And I have come. Already the
> world is being destroyed. And you, O men are to perish because of your ini-
> quities. But I wish to save you. And you see me returning again with heavenly
> power. Blessed is he who has worshipped me now. . . . " Having brandished
> these threats they then go on to add incomprehensible, incoherent and utterly
> obscure utterances, the meaning of which no intelligent person could discover;

for they are meaningless and nonsensical, and give a chance for any fool or sorcerer to take the words in whatever sense he likes (Jonas, 1963, p 104).

Simon Magus was the most famous of the "prophets" and false messiahs described by Celsus. The early Church Fathers considered him to the arch-heresiarch (they also granted him a dubious immortality in naming the practice of buying and selling Church office—simony). Simon Magus's career provides intriguing parallels to those of modern cult leaders. Although Simon may have converted to the Church, he continued to preach as an independent messiah—granting Jesus the role of being a precursory incarnation of Simon himself. His message was distinctive in his considering:

> A woman called Helena whom he said he had found in a brothel in Tyre and who according to him was the latest and lowliest incarnation of the fallen "thought" of God, redeemed by him and a means of redemption for all who believed in them both (Jonas, 1963, p 105).

Simon is reputed to have died during a final act of "levitation." His career was notable for his use of showmanship and abstract theological speculations to confirm a rather earthy venality. His title, Magus, suggests a focus on religion as magic and on the religious leader as the Magus, the Magician. He presents, in this regard, a profound parallel to the leaders of more contemporary cults.

Simon Magus arose out of a cultural context which presented an extraordinary diversity of religious and cultic groups. His theological speculations were allied to those of the Gnostics. The Gnostics were widespread groups which proliferated primarily within the ranks of the early Christians during the first two centuries of the common era. Gnostic sectarians were found within Jewish and, later on, in Islamic groups, as well. The Cathari (see Chapter 3) may be considered a late medieval manifestation of gnosticism. Whatever the epiphenomena of their theologies, the Gnostics present a complex welter of the spiritual, the unreal, the progressive, the eccentric and the pathological. The strictures of the Church Fathers against these groups were not simply the product of their zealousness and the desire to impose a rigid authoritarian orthodoxy but a recognition of the self-destructive potential of these groups. Gnostic groups may be characterized by three criteria:

1) A sharply graded hierarchy composed of followers (credentes among the Cathari) and a hierarchial elect (perfecti among the Cathari). It is only to this elect that the arcanae—the secrets—were revealed. In mainstream religious groups the "truth" is not treated as magic to be entrusted only to the elect. Not surprisingly, gradations develop within the hierarchy, itself, whose very development is inherent in a theology that treats "knowledge" as reserved only to the few. This pattern of a hierarchial access to knowledge is paralleled within many modern cults or cult-like organizations who create level upon level of "awareness."

2) A focus on the unearthly with an immanent sense of man as having fallen from a higher spiritual realm to this alien, material world. In its radically emphasizing a sense of original sin as a fall from "spiritual heights," the material world becomes a mere pollutant. Within modern groups, this sense of alienation has been reinterpreted in very literal terms leading to speculations that mankind, itself, is derived from beings residing originally on another planet. And, cults have been formed around leaders entrusted with revelations by inhabitants of flying saucers, etc.

3) A pervasive sense of an imminent Armageddon—that the Apocalypse is at hand. The imminence of this "threat" then justifies the search for salvation through a magical solution that will presumably preserve the spiritual elect who will then reign in a "new age" as the world's spiritual (and temporal) rulers. It is not accidental that today's cult members are the first generation to have grown up under the threat of nuclear war. The presence of apolcalyptic scenarios in groups as diverse as the Unification Church, People's Temple, Transcendental Meditation, Jehovah's Witnesses and Seventh Day Adventists underlines the importance of the apocalypse in the formation of new religions and in their continuance (see Chapter 14).

Different Gnostic groups differed in their emphasis. But, the very striking parallels between these groups of the late Roman Empire and modern cult groups (without the presence of any formal continuity, albeit some late Victorian groups adopted the Gnostics as their spiritual mentors and these may have been influential in the formation of the ideology of modern cult groups) demonstrate that both Gnostics and modern cults met and meet deep psychic needs. The emergence of the Gnostics and of the modern cult groups may reflect parallel deficits in the broader society. Indeed, certain periods have been both spiritually creative and particularly fecund in the creation of cults. The late Roman Empire was such a time. The Great Awakening of the 1840s in this country is a more contemporary example (see Chapter 4). The question that arises is whether the "greening" of America during the 60s and the subsequent rise of prominence of "cults" and/or new religions is part of another Great Awakening or simply the reflection of transient adjustment problems within the American imperium?

The aftermath of the Vietnam war within the United States has been a period of soul-searching. It has been a period in which the "state religion" of a liberal, humanistic democracy with its progressive expectations and rationalistic ideology seems less valid after having expressed itself in a frustrating war and within an economy marked by stagnation. This has expressed itself in a revival of religious traditionalism (see Chapters 17 and 18). However, the question that faces the mental health profession is not simply whether or not the rise of cults and "new religions" is just the institutionalized expression of disillusionment with established forms, and one which will ultimately disappear; rather, the question is what will the mental health professional offer in the here and now to those individuals who affiliate with these groups and to their families.

Society's concern with self-destructive cultism is not new. It is not an attempt to limit the freedom of religious expression. It is a recognition that it is an appropriate task for both the broader society and for the mental health professional to protect those individuals whose credulity borders on the pathological and whose naivete leaves them ill-equipped to resist both group and individual pressures. The presence of skeptical and overly relativistic attitudes toward both religion and any intense religious involvement intensifies the difficulties inherent in this task.

Freud tended to regard any intense religious longings or concern as pathological. His antagonism toward organized religion which he expressed in *Totem and Taboo* and *Civilization and Its Discontents* with its denigration of any intense religious feeling may underlie the continuing distance between the mental health professional and religion. For the mental health professional, it may be difficult to appreciate that intense religious feelings may be healthy efforts toward integration which may confirm the individual's autonomy. The raison d'etre of

Psychodynamic Perspectives on Religion, Sect and Cult lies in helping the mental health professional to differentiate between the individual's longing for transcendence and those groups which may exploit this spiritual quest. Above all, if the mental health professional can examine and respect the individual's spiritual concerns, he will be better able to help the individual and family to deal with those groups that coat their venality with a facade of spirituality.

The consideration of religions—old/new—or of cults—benign/destructive— must not restrict itself to exaggerating the restrictive, the deceptive, or the purely pathological. New religious groups may give voice to forces that are otherwise incapable of expressing themselves. Much as traditional religion has provided a national organizing force in Poland, cult-like groups have created a sense of peoplehood in the persecuted American Indian (see Chapter 5). It is a part of the ambivalent legacy of the Zealots and Masada (see Chapter 1). Perhaps, it is not accidental that in those communities of the Diaspora in which support for the pseudomessiahs, Sabbatai Zvi and Jacob Frank, was strongest that Zionism found its first support.

What is a "cult"? Criteria may be either too restrictive or too inclusive. Not all cult-like groups necessarily meet all criteria. Margaret Thaler Singer (1980) has defined the "destructive" cult as an organization in which:

1. A leader claims divinity or special relationship with God.
2. A leader who is the sole judge of a member's actions or faith.
3. Totalitarian governance.
4. Totalistic control over the member's daily lives.
5. Exclusivity and isolation.
6. Development of deep emotional dependence.
7. Prohibition of critical analysis and independent thinking.
8. Utilization of methods of ego destruction and mind control.
9. Exploitation of a member's finances.
10. Underemployment and exploitative working conditions.

Not all cult groups meet these criteria. The individual's actual relationship to the group (especially if he has achieved a position of responsibility) may allow considerable latitude. Moreover, exclusivity and isolation refer to the nonworking portion of the member's lives, since members are encouraged to associate with nonmembers to raise money or proselytize (Shapiro, 1977). But their relationship in this context does not really admit to any dialog between member and nonmember (a factor of considerable divisiveness in the relationship of a member and his family).

Eccentricity of belief is not a factor to be included in the definition of a destructive cult. The means by which adherence to and conformity with a belief system is maintained is the central concern. As has been noted, the formation of novel religious groups may allow ideas to be expressed, although the actual group itself may not provide the form in which they will be ultimately realized. Hence, the Millenarians and Levellers of the English Revolution of the 1650s with their belief in political equality and the Great Awakening which expressed itself in both the creation of Christian Science, Mormonism, and the Temperance Movement, foreshadowed the suffragettes. Some of the new religions are a response to the permissiveness of our current society and may well reflect an appropriate impatience with the failure of "liberal" orthodoxies.

In defining the differences between an intensive normative religious affiliation and adhesion to a cult, we must examine the implications of cult affiliation. A healthy religious affiliation confirms the individual's autonomy by providing him with an integrated, internalized ability to judge and explore the moral implications of his acts and those of others. Within a cult, this ability is lost. The prerogative to explore the moral implications of behavior is externalized and displaced onto the cult leader. Above all, a healthy normative religious affiliation provides for a sense of continuity between generations. Its very rituals confirm the individual's living with autonomy and dignity. However, within a cult, rituals do not confirm the individual's autonomy. Marriage is arranged, with limited choices. It does not mark a rite of passage out of the home but rather a rite of initiation which serves to confirm the individual's increased commitment to the group (hence, the prolonged engagements of members of the Unification Church).

Religion in our society places the individual within a total framework but it does not demand a totalistic preoccupation. It confirms the individual's reliance on others, allows his participation in this world, and respects the possibility of his participation in the next. Above all, it respects and preserves the observing ego. The cult experience dissociates the individual's autonomy by encouraging self-denigration, self-contempt and self-criticism. Any continuities which might enable the individual to preserve his autonomy are depicted as evil, "satanic," or selfish. Religion confirms the superego as an active but not punitive part of the personality. The cult experience denies the validity of the observing ego and sponsors the delegation of the superego to a "deified" figure who is then granted totalistic control over the personality. Hence, the ease with which cults legitimize the use of deceptive/idealistic titles, concealing any association with their "religious" sponsor.

Mere eccentricity of belief does not make a group into a cult. The belief system of a cult (unlike that of a religion) centers on confirming the authority of its leader. The cult has its origin and often its end in the life of its leader. Thus, the intensity with which it demands that the individual surrender any competing authority/autonomy. It is hardly surprising then that many cults draw their organizational pattern and theology from a sense of apocalypse, since even the "deified" leader must die (see Chapters 14 and 16). Thus, the apocalyptic end of Jonestown becomes more understandable when its total identification with its leader is considered.

The cult differs from the sect in its totalistic preoccupation with its leader. Within a sect, the theology of the parent groups retains its ability to restrain any excesses on the part of sect leader. Within sects, the leader is usually not granted infallibility over every aspect of the member's lives and authority is delimited by dogma. While the sect leader may live in a grandiose manner, the individual's privations and loss of autonomy are less complete. Moreover, within the sect, the leader as well as the individual member are bound by the group's ideology. Within a cult, responsibilities descend and privileges ascend leading to the creation of a closed system based on the "installation of guilt for doubt and coercion for faith" (R.T. Barnhouse, personal communication, 1980).

Having defined the differences between cults and other religious groups, let us examine the role of the mental health professional in working with the cult member and his family. Three broad areas of concern arise: 1) Is cult affiliation a question of religious preference? Does it reflect group pressures and/or brainwashing? 2) Is cult affiliation a reflection of severe individual psychopathology?

Of temporary vulnerability? 3) May cult affiliation be therapeutic?

These important concerns are explored within Section Two and Section Three of this book. All of the contributors to *Psychodynamic Perspectives on Religion, Sect and Cult* respect the individual's right to accept unusual belief systems. Their concern for the individual expresses itself in an appropriate regard for the conditions in which an individual makes a decision with lifelong implications. These complex issues and the treatment approaches that have been found to be useful form the body of Section Three. As Levine (1980) has noted, the cult member and his family require responsible and sympathetic professional intervention. While cult affiliation may at times be therapeutic, cults subject to the eccentric and capricious whim of the cult leader are not therapeutic communities. The contributors to this book are united in their interest in sponsoring responsible and compassionate treatment for the individual—to help him realize his potential within whatever context or confines he chooses to realize his goals and aspirations, although they may wonder, as did William Butler Yeats (1916), that:

> The ceremony of innocence is drowned;
> The best lack all conviction, while the worst
> Are full of passionate intensity.
>
> Surely some revelation is at hand;
> Surely the Second Coming is at hand.
> The Second Coming! . . . .
> And what rough beast, its hour come round at last,
> Slouches toward Bethlehem to be born?

BIBLIOGRAPHY

Catullus GV: in Copley FO (ed and trans): *The Complete Poetry*. Ann Arbor, MI, 1964.
Euripides: The Bacchae. circa 408 BCE.
Hippocrates, in Ehrenwald J: *The History of Psychotherapy*. New York, Jason Aronson, 1976.
Levine S: Cults and mental health: Clinical conclusions. *Can J Psych* 1980;25.
Jonas H: *The Gnostic Religion*. Boston, Beacon, 1963.
Shapiro E: Destructive cultism. *Family Physician* 1977;15:2:80–3.
West LJ, Singer MT: Cults, quack and nonprofesional psychotherapies, in Kaplan H, Freedman A, Sadock B (eds): *Comprehensive Textbook of Psychiatry III*. Baltimore, Williams and Wilkins, 1980.
Yeats WB: The second coming, in Allt P, Alpach RK (eds): *Complete Poems*. (Variorum Edition) New York, Macmillan, 1968, p 401.

SECTION ONE

HISTORICAL PARALLELS

CHAPTER

1

Religious Innovation
in the Jewish Revolt Against Rome

L. D. HANKOFF

FAITH AND COMMITMENT
IN FIRST-CENTURY PALESTINE

In the pages that follow I will be making an inquiry into the nature of religious change and religious innovation among the Jews of first-century Palestine. In the period leading up to the great war of the Jews against their Roman overseers, the events and popular movements went far beyond the religious dimension. It may be seen, however, that the thread of a new religious philosophy runs through the entire insurgency movement from its historical beginnings to the last dying gasp of resistors. Furthermore, it was the opinion of our major source of information, Flavius Josephus, that a change in traditional religious ideas was basic to the rebel movement. In this chapter I will consider the social and psychological meaning of religious innovation and the manner in which it related to the turbulent events of the time. In order to understand the individuals and groups involved in religious innovation and the associated ideological and social movements, it is necessary to consider several background areas. First, the historical events need to be considered in some detail because of their complexity and the light which these events shed on the nature of evolution among the various religious and political factions. Second, as background it is necessary to understand the established Jewish religious groups and their orientations. Third, I will present what can be gleaned concerning the basic aspects of ideological transmission, conflict, and domination in the first century AD. From the vantage point of this fund of information, I will inquire into the new groups which sprang up, their interaction, and the social and psychological aspects of their existence and evolution.

Historical Background

The century in which Christianity was founded was a tumultuous one for the people living in Palestine and a period of radical change for the Jews and the

1

Jewish religion of the time. Flavius Josephus, our most significant direct source on this period, was born in 37 AD and lived through the events leading to the destruction of the Second Temple in 70 AD as well as a reorganization of the Jewish faith which followed the catastrophic war with the Romans.

The war or revolt of the Jews against the Romans, which lasted from 66 to 74 AD is described by Josephus as "the greatest not only of the wars of our own time, but, so far as accounts have reached us, well nigh of all that ever broke out between cities or nations" (*J.W.* 1.1).* In the culminating event, the siege of Jerusalem, the number of dead is given as 1,100,000 (*J.W.* 7.420).

Josephus argued that the catastrophe was avoidable and that the key factor in its consummation was an intemperate change in Jewish religious philosophy. He summarizes, "Here is a lesson that an innovation or reform in ancestral traditions weighs heavily in the scale leading to the destruction of the congregation of the people" (*Ant.* 18.9).

In providing the Emperor Titus with the authoritative account of the war (*Life* 363), Josephus began his history with the events surrounding the rise of the Maccabees stemming from the persecution of the Jews by the Seleucid king Antiochus IV who captured Jerusalem in 168 BC (*J.W.* 1.32). Antiochus IV who called himself Epiphanes, the god manifest, and was nicknamed Epimanes, the madman, instituted a course of fiendish persecution and attempted to impose pagan practices on the Jews. The Maccabee uprising followed.

When the Maccabee revolt against the Seleucid Greeks progressed and the prospect of an independent statehood became a serious reality, the religion was confronted with the issue of its own theocracy after nearly half a millenium of subjugation. During the rise of the Maccabees, a group of committed, highly traditional Jews designated as the Hassidists (Hasideans) or Pietists had joined in the revolt against the Greeks but had resisted any compromise with their religious standards. As a result they were slaughtered when they refused to fight on the Sabbath. The Hasmoneans put aside such pietistic restrictions and developed their religious and secular practices in an effective pragmatic fashion. The critical condition leading to the uprising of the Maccabees against Antiochus IV was not simply one of oppression and resistance. The social and cultural influences of the time may well have been more significant than the open and sadistic repression by the ruler of the time.

The trend of Hellenization had been set in motion by the appearance of Alexander the Great in Palestine in 331 BC. The Greeks brought with them their culture and the opportunity to join in a world of enlightenment that the barbarians were expected to welcome avidly. The influences of Hellenism were quite apparent in Palestine as the youth of all strata flocked to participate in Greek culture. The games, arts, science, and literature of the Greeks became the standard to be achieved. As the current of Hellenization took hold, the committed Jews were aware of its influence on religious practices and the conflict was joined. An ideological competition between the beckoning blandishments of Hellenism and the commitment to traditional Judaism dominated the day.

In 167 BC the father of the Maccabee brothers, Mattathias, established the theme of the resistance by publicly assassinating a Jew practicing Hellenistic idolatry. His act signaled the transition from ideological to physical conflict. His act was by no means a unique one in the history of religious controversy among

---

*Abbreviations for the works of Flavius Josephus: *J.W.*, *The Jewish War*; *Ant.*, *Jewish Antiquities*.

the Jews. It resonated with the act of Phineas in the camp of the Hebrews in the desert (Numbers 25.7–8) as well as other traditional defenders of the faith in its purity and intactness. Following the initial stunning victories of Judas Maccabee, son of Mattathias, in 165–163 BC, over two decades of shifting conflict between the Jews and the Seleucid forces ensued before a Hasmonean dynasty and an independent Judea emerged in 142 BC (Schurer, 1961, p 61).

The Hasmoneans were thereafter established as both princely and priestly leaders, but peace never came to the new nation. Both external incursions and internal rivalries led to recurring hostilities. In 129 BC the ruling John Hyrcanus, the grandson of Mattathias, forceably converted the Idumaeans in an extension of the earlier ideological conflict between paganism and Judaism (Ant. 13.257, 15.254). Open civil war between Hasmonean brothers Aristobulus II and Hyrcanus II broke out in 69 BC, and the power of Rome in the person of Pompey settled the quarrel by subjugating the nation anew in 63 BC (Schurer, 1961, pp 100–101). Under the Romans, the Idumaean family of Herod, later to be called "the Great," moved into power and eventually supplanted the Hasmonean dynasty entirely. Palestine was now a tributary of Rome and under the oversight of the Roman governor of Syria (Schurer, 1961, p 102). Herod the Great was made king of Palestine by the Emperor Augustus in 30 BC (J.W. 1.392) and thereafter conducted an enormous program of building throughout the country, including the reconstruction of the Temple.

When Herod died in 4 BC, resentment toward him and his Roman patrons was intense but had been held in check by Herod's powerful grasp. Disturbance broke out upon the death of Herod, and several opposition leaders sprang up with aspirations to the throne (J.W. 2.56–60). These uprisings were suppressed, but events continued to goad the Jews to revolution. When a census was undertaken by Quirinius in 6 AD as a basis for taxation, armed resistance again flared. The Roman authority in Palestine was exercised through the procurators or local governors who were often callous or antagonistic to the religious needs of the Jewish citizens, and a series of incidents inflamed the populace. With the appointment of Antonius Felix as procurator (52–60 AD) matters went "from bad to worse" (Ant. 20.160). Felix was particularly profligate in his private life and blood-thirsty in his administrative affairs. Whereas previous uprisings had been sporadic, "under Felix rebellion became permanent" (Schurer, 1961, p 228). Under the last procurator, Gessius Florus (64–66 AD) only a spark was needed to set off a total conflagration. Following some public mockery of his policies, Florus sent a cohort of soldiers to plunder a portion of Jerusalem. Widespread fighting occurred throughout Palestine as well as in the Diaspora.* A group of Roman soldiers was cut down in Jerusalem. In 66 AD, the governor of Syria, Cestius Gallus, dispatched a legion and many supporting troops to quell the disturbances in Judea. The Jews scored a decisive victory over the forces of

---

*Jewish communities outside of Palestine, ie, the Diaspora or Dispersion of the Jews, formed a considerable minority in the Roman world. Jewish settlers were to be found in the remotest Greek and Roman colonies, beyond the Euphrates, and in the Crimean peninsula (Dubnov, 1967, vol 1, p 811). The main concentration of the Diaspora in the first century was in the eastern Greek-speaking half of the Roman empire (Greece and Asia Minor). In addition, there were heavy concentrations of Jews in central Italy and in Babylonia (Aharoni and Avi-Yonah, 1968, map 238). During the war with the Romans, Diaspora Jews were involved in violent clashes as a result of their own revolutionary actions or in reaction to anti-Semitic mob attacks. Among the sites of violence were Alexandria, the Libyan city of Cyrene, and the Syrian cities of Antioch and Damascus (Dubnov, 1967, vol 1, pp 813–816). In the city of Rome itself, the Jewish community apparently escaped open violence during the war.

Cestius at Beth-horon. With this accomplishment, the rebel or zealot movement among the Jews was now in ascendancy, and any voices of conciliation were ignored. The various rebel groups in Jerusalem began contending for dominance. During this period, Menahem, the leader of the faction called the Sicarii, attempted to extend his power base and was killed by rivals (*J.W.* 2.444). Following Menahem's death, a group of Sicarii led by Eleazar ben Yair slipped out of Jerusalem to the security of the mountain fortress of Masada (*J.W.* 2.447).

The Emperor Nero assigned the task of pacifying Judea to his experienced general Vespasian, who mustered an army of 60,000 men. His first campaign was in the Galilee where he besieged the fortress of Jotapata which was commanded by our historian Josephus. Jotapata fell, followed by the towns of Tarichea, Gischala, and Gamala, the entire north being subdued by 67 AD (Schurer, 1961, p 257).

Vespasian and his son Titus then moved their army to headquarters in Caesarea to prepare for the siege of Jerusalem. There they learned that Nero had committed suicide on June 9, 68 AD, and the campaign was suspended. On July 1, 69 AD Vespasian was declared emperor, and the task of invading Jerusalem was turned over to Titus. In Jerusalem all rebel factions vented their fury on those suspected of pacifist or pro-Roman leanings. The rebel groups encouraged the general populace to join the resistance against Rome (*J.W.* 4.126), and open fighting between the pro- and antiwar groups broke out in Jerusalem (*J.W.* 4.131). The attack by the Zealots on the uncommitted Jerusalem population is described by Josephus as "the first step toward the city's ruin" (*J.W.* 5.3).

Several high priests and large numbers of their followers were slaughtered by Idumaeans and Zealots in a melee. The priests had urged moderation, and the leading priest Ananus was viewed by Josephus as dedicated to maintaining peace (*J.W.* 4.320). Josephus points to this act, the murder by Jews of a high priest "in the heart of Jerusalem," as the beginning of the capture of the city (*J.W.* 4.318).

The siege of Jerusalem joined the two forces in a ferocious battle which ended on September 26, 70 AD with the total destruction of the city and most of its population. All that remained for the Romans now was the mopping up operation and the great triumphal procession in Rome of the victor and his captives. Masada held out until 74 AD when its 960 Sicarii defenders destroyed themselves.

The Three Philosophies

Josephus describes the three sects, or philosophies as he termed them, which dominated the Jewish religion of his day. The Pharisees contended with the Sadducees for leadership of the main mass of the Jewish people although, for the most part, it was a peaceful competition. A third group of ascetic retreatists, the Essenees, were a significant philosophical position but a relatively minor political influence in terms of historical events and the postwar regrouping of the scattered elements of religious thinkers and leaders. Josephus describes the three philosophies in some detail and alludes to them in all four of his works. The sects were very much a part of everyday life. At age 16 Josephus systematically studied the three groups and arrived at a viewpoint of his own (*Life* 11). Although his understanding of Judaism is superficial (Thackeray, 1929, p 76), his view of the religious currents is a significant window on his psychology as well as that of other urbane Jewish citizens of the Roman empire of that day.

The Sadducees, or Zedukim as they were called in Hebrew, traced their origin and name to the first high priest under King Solomon, Zadok. Accordingly, their allegiance centered about the hereditary strain of high priests (Zeitlin, 1954;

Finkelstein, 1962, vol 2, pp 762–779). The Sadducees represented orthodoxy, opposed any innovation in the law, and accepted the Torah in specific literal terms.

The power of the Sadducees was consolidated during the Hasmonean dynasty when the high priest was given religious and secular responsibility, in effect attempting rule of Palestine as a theocracy. In taking a strict fundamentalist approach to the law, the Sadducees denied the essence and content of the oral law which was the basis for Pharisee practice and philosophy. Josephus emphasizes that the Sadducees maintained strongly a doctrine of free will and regarded the body as the repository of the soul which perishes with it (J.W. 2.165–166; Ant. 18.16–17).

The Sadducees were heavily represented in the upper classes and derived their prestige from their priestly role and land ownership. Ironically, their patrician background was associated with a relative lack of education and orientation toward learning. The Sadducees are described by Josephus as boorish and rude in their behavior (J.W. 2.166). This characterization of the wealthy Sadducees must at first appear incongruous, but it was apparently accurate. The patricians may have been versed in the language and style of the privileged classes yet steeped in materialism and dedicated to individual concerns which perpetuated ignorance.

The Pharisees, or Perushim as they were called in Hebrew, were separatists. The name is variously ascribed to the fact that they separated themselves from other Jews by their use of the oral law which modified and extended the legal restraints of the Pentateuch (Zeitlin, 1954). Finkelstein has emphasized that there was no derogatory sense implied in the origin of the name and that it had merely emphasized their separation from impurity and defilement (Finkelstein, 1962, vol 1, p 76). The label of separatists emphasized the concern of the Pharisees for purity in the various substances and foodstuffs with which they had to deal. Their concern for this issue led them to develop numerous detailed restrictions and regulations in their dealing with other Jews who were not as concerned with ritual purity and tithing as were the Pharisees. Still another origin given for their name is from the Hebrew root parosh, meaning to interpret, pointing to their main attribute as interpreters of the law (Waxman, 1960, vol 1, p 56).

The Pharisees, like the Essenees, were the spiritual descendants of the Hassidists. Their numbers were drawn largely from the plebians with particular predominance among the Jerusalemites (Finkelstein, 1962, vol 2, p 633).

The distinction between the views of the Pharisee and Sadducee was not an absolute one, and there is evidence of exchanges of admiration and respect between the two sects. It is known, for example, that Sadducee women were guided by Pharisee tradition with regard to menstrual impurity (Finkelstein, 1962, vol 2, p 637). The leaders of the two groups were probably on good terms, sat together on the Sanhedrin, and often were in agreement on the practical bent of Pharisee interpretation in relation to temple worship (Waxman, 1960, vol 1, 58).

The Essenees Accounts of this fascinating group of ascetics have been left by Philo of Alexandria, Pliny, and Josephus. All describe the Essenees with sympathy. They were a group who showed great attachment for each other, living communally, sharing all of their belongings, and behaving in a most intimate and supportive manner to all members of their sect. Josephus describes with apparent admiration the fact that most of them disdained marriage and regarded "women's wantonness" as being such that "none of the sex keeps her plighted troth to one man" (J.W. 2.121). They lived without money in the pure atmosphere of the mountains facing the Dead Sea (Pliny 5.73). Josephus notes that they dressed in white, emphasized purity and bodily cleanliness, and were apparently rewarded by their ascetic practices with long life (*J.W.* 2.123, 151).

Because of their faith, the Essenes were unafraid of any danger and easily able to triumph over pain. "Death, if it come with honor, they consider better than immortality . . . they cheerfully resigned their souls, confident that they would receive them back again" when faced with torment and tested to surrender their faith (*J.W.* 2.153). As a result of their immersion in holy works and acts, Josephus notes, the Essenees were able to foretell the future (*J.W.* 2.159). Three instances are cited in which Essenee predictions come true.

Competing orthodoxies   The three philosophies, the practices and theologies of the Pharisees, Sadducees, and Essenees, cannot be considered new or upstart religions. All were essentially traditional in their practices and consistent with the main stream of Judaism of the time. All three sects were unquestioned in their attachment to the faith and acceptability by the religious leadership. In contrast, other groups in the first century AD were considered much less acceptable, even heretical, in relation to the core religious beliefs of the Jews. The Samaritans, for example, were a group who separated themselves from the Jews on the basis of a belief in the holiness of Mount Gerizim near Shechem. The Samaritans rejected prophetic literature which affirmed the holiness of the Jerusalem temple. Their hatred for the Jews often led to acts of violence between the two groups (Baron, 1952, vol 2, pp 26–35). The Idumaeans were the lusty dwellers of the deserts of Edom in southern Palestine who had been converted to Judaism forcibly by the Hasmoneans. The Idumaeans in the era of the Second Temple were still regarded by some as uncertain in their religious status as Jews because their original conversion had been an involuntary one.

The main division between the Sadducees and Pharisees appears to have sharpened with the Hasmonean dynasty. Earlier, as resistance to the danger of Hellenization or assimilation to Greek culture took form, a group of staunch defenders of the Jewish faith, law, and tradition emerged. These were the Hassidists (Hasideans) or Pietists. The Hassidists showed a willingness to die for the cause of their faith and an expectation of reward and resurrection after death. This doctrine of the resurrection of the dead and the immortality of the soul finds its earliest expression by the prophet Isaiah writing in the eighth century BC. This theme was embraced by the Hassidists who were prominent by the time of the Maccabean uprising. The Hassidists became the basis for the Pharisaic theology which took its completed form during the development of the Hasmonean dynasty (Finkelstein, 1962, vol 2, pp 742–747).

The fortunes of the Pharisees are closely linked with the Hasmonean dynasty. During the reign of Queen Alexandra, who came to power in 78 BC, her piety and concern for the details of the law reflected that of the Pharisees and, while she ruled the country, the Pharisees ruled her (*J.W.* 1.107; *Ant.* 13.405).

The expectation of resurrection or immortality in relation to Hassidic–Pharisee belief was of great importance in the minds of Jews participating in popular uprisings. For example, when Herod the Great became terminally ill in 4 BC, learned Jews discussed the need to resist the pagan practices of the Herodian leadership. They bolstered the resistors with the pronouncement that if they were killed by the government soldiers, the resistors would attain immortality as a result of their deeds (*J.W.* 1.650). On another occasion, in 40 AD the Romans in Palestine bringing statues of the Emperor Caligula to be erected in the Temple were astonished at the multitude of Jewish men, women, and children who presented themselves calmly resigned to die to prevent the desecration (*J.W.* 2.197).

The conflict between the Pharisees and Sadducees revolved around the very issue of resurrection. The Pharisees were absolutely confident of a universe ruled by God, while the Sadducees questioned such a doctrine and denied the claim of a world to come. In their belief in the resurrection and immortality of the soul, the Pharisees were consistent with a theology which viewed the works of man as transient and the works of God as eternal. While Rome at that time was referred to as the *urbs aeterna,* the epithet eternal among the Jews was reserved for God (Heschel, 1966, p 123). The doctrines of the Pharisees also had far-reaching effects on the spread of Judaism. To the pagans, the Pharisees' doctrine of the world to come was a powerful attraction. The non-Jew, as well as the Jewish non-Pharisee, was often drawn to this group which seemed so totally secure in its doctrine of resurrection and a world to come.

Messianic Themes

The belief in an ultimate era of peace in a world ruled by God is a recurrent theme in Jewish religious philosophy. The prophet Isaiah in the eighth century BC gave his vision of the world worshiping the one God at the end of days when the wolf would lie down with the lamb. Isaiah spoke of a leader from the stock of Jesse, ie, David (Isaiah 11.1-10). The theme of a messianic era appears in other ancient eschatologies. The mythologies of the ancient world regularly described golden ages which preceded the one of mankind.*

The term messiah refers to the anointed condition, such as that of a king or priest, which conferred a divine status in the time of the First Temple (Zeitlin, 1954).

The repeated setbacks of the Jewish people and their subjugation within the various empires were woven into the messianic hope. Domination by a foreign power was interpreted as a divinely imposed penalty and a test or trial for the people to endure. The hope existed that the trial would end, the people found worthy, and the rule of God ushered in.

The lineage of David was looked upon as the source of messianic fulfillment through all of the dark days of the succeeding conquerors of the Jews. The writer of Psalm 139 expressed the hope that the seed of David would establish a throne for all generations. The messianic tradition elaborated a theme in which a Davidic leader would initiate a cycle of war leading to a world monarchy and universal peace embracing all people (Radin, 1915, p 75). Through the various eras of privation and domination, no actual member descended from David arose to make political pretensions, and during the period of the fourth and third centuries BC family records became lost so that descent from David became all but impossible to prove (Radin, 1915, p 73). The Maccabees, a non-Davidic dynasty, paid homage to the tradition, and we find in I Maccabees the dying Mattathiah expressing his faith in the everlasting kingdom of David (2.57). The Gospels of the New Testament trace the descent of Christ from David (Matthew 1.17; Luke 3.31).

Along with the Messiah ben David, rabbinic tradition spoke of a messiah descended from the tribe of Joseph, the Messiah ben Ephraim (Baron, 1952, vol 2, p 251; Zeitlin, 1954). The Messiah ben Ephraim was described as warrior who

---

*These bygone idyllic eras were a natural template for a messianic era of the future. The text of a speech by an Egyptian sage Ipuwer is suggested as such an expression of messianic hopes (Breasted, 1959, p 211). Ipuwer, at about 2000 BC, describing the disarray and deterioration at his time in Egyptian history, looks to a future when a new leader will arise and order will be restored (Pritchard, 1969, p 441-444). It is unclear, however, whether the reformist ideology of Ipuwer can be equated with a messianic tradition.

would be killed in battle in preparing the way for the Messiah ben David.

A cataclysmic or apocalyptic vision was often associated with the ushering in of the messianic age. The gigantic struggle of Gog and Magog was to precede the coming of the Messiah (Ezekiel 39.1-6). Various extraordinary natural phenomena were expected to occur. Even the name of the messiah was known, traceable to various biblical references. Among the names of the future messiah were Son of Man, Menahem (comforter), David, and Tzemah (shoot) (Patai, 1979, pp 17-20).

In considering the messianic themes of the first century AD, it is important to note that, theologically, the belief in resurrection and the immortality of the soul need not be closely bound up with messianic thinking. The messianic predictions took highly concrete and specific form, often with the expectation of an immediate cataclysm and rule on earth by the messiah. The more general beliefs in resurrection and the immortality of the soul represented a philosophy of ultimate outcome. At times, of course, messianic expectations and belief in resurrection were combined in one prediction.

The intensity of messianic expectations and movements in the first century AD is a matter of scholarly disagreement. Zeitlin (1954) argues for a relative lack of importance of messianic movements during the period preceding the war with the Romans. The Jews believed, during the time of the Maccabees, that God would strengthen them and help them against their enemies, but this was not an equivalent to the messianic expectation. Baron (1952, vol 2, p 61), however, is of the opinion that "most Jewish groups in the declining Second Commonwealth cherished the belief in the almost immediate coming of the redeemer." Baron cites Josephus on an Egyptian false prophet (*J.W.* 2.261, *Ant.* 20.169), about 58 AD and Theudas (*Ant.* 20.97), about 44 AD, as well as John the Baptist as evidence of messianic thinking. Zeitlin (1954) makes the point, however, that only a small and isolated group whom he calls the Apocalyptists believed firmly in an imminent messiah. Zeitlin states that the Apocalyptists were a relatively insignificant group of Pharisees. The Apocalyptists were opposed to terrorist methods, although they agreed with the Fourth Philosophy of Judah the Galilean (i.v.) in their hatred of the Romans and their rejection of Jewish leaders who obeyed the Romans (Zeitlin, 1954). They were the forerunners of Christianity. Following the destruction of the temple in 70 AD, as might be expected, messianic hopes were prominent among the Jews, which may account for the confusion over earlier conditions. Zeitlin further notes that ideas of resurrection, the future world, and revelation are stressed in the Mishnah (written after the destruction) but that nowhere does it mention the messiah.

As might be expected both messianic claimants and prophets often met with violent ends at the hands of the ruling powers. John the Baptist, who was beheaded about 29 AD, made no messianic claims but did see himself as the forerunner of the messiah (Baron, 1952, vol 2, p 62). The Egyptian false prophet and the "impostor" Theudas both came to swift ends at the hands of the procurators of Judaea.

The messianic themes took various forms. The activists who were already willing to take arms against Roman military power envisioned a great war. The rebel leader Menahem may have thought himself a forerunner of the messiah (Baron, 1952, vol 2, p 58). The violent end of a leader such as Menahem arrayed in the temple in royal robes (*J.W.* 2.444) did not spell the end to messianic hopes but rather was woven into a prophecy of defeat as part of the unfolding of a divine plan with the Messiah ben Ephraim as the fallen predecessor of the Messiah ben David.

A brief reference in Josphus to Jesus as the messiah (*Ant.* 18.63) has been the subject of enormous study. The *Testimonium Flavianum* was undoubtedly doctored by later interpolators, but a core of an original reference by Josephus appears likely (Thackeray, 1929, pp 125–148). Additional sources point to an original wording by Josephus in which he states that Jesus was "perhaps" or "thought to be" the messiah (Pines, 1971, p 26).

Perhaps one of the most unexpected sources of messianic hopes is that associated with the Emperor Nero (Radin, 1915, pp 294–299). Following his suicide in 68 AD, amidst the general public rejoicing were many who honored his statues and predicted his return. Twenty years later, according to Suetonius, a young man appeared among the Parthians claiming to be Nero (*Nero* 57.2). Earlier in his reign, astrologers had predicted that he would rule the East, specifically Jerusalem (*Nero* 40.3). The expectation of a universal ruler with ties to Judea was current in the Roman world at midcentury (Tacitus, *History* 5.13).

Instruments of Change

The three Jewish religious philosophies of the first century AD coexisted and competed with each other for the allegiance of the Jews of Palestine. In so doing the sects utilized the time-honored approaches to changing young and old minds. Lifton (1969) has categorized the general approaches to changing people as coercion, exhortation, therapy, and realization. In various forms, all of these approaches are to be found in the first-century AD world.

As was noted the three sects had their roots in earlier ideological conflicts, particularly that of Hellenism versus Judaism. The Seleucid era had left the issue of Hellenization indelibly in the Jewish mind. The distinction between those who embraced and those who rejected or accommodated to Helenization was clearly appreciated. In time, the struggle with Rome brought other ideological conflicts. A significant contest developed between those willing to accommodate to Roman domination and those rejecting it. The rivalry drew on political, religious, and social issues, and the contending sides used all means, fair and foul, to win others to their cause.

Hankoff (1979) has described the dynamics of attitudinal change through conflict and proposed that a basic template is discernible through many levels of the biological system from the interpersonal through the international sphere of conflict. The ideological conflict is joined when two sides enter into competition for the allegiance of a third party. The contending sides utilize various means to change the third party in their favor. The contending sides present their ideology or belief system in ways designed to convert or proselytize the third party.

The individual faced with the two contending systems experiences their difference or incongruity as cognitive dissonance and may develop a sense of conflict and the need for resolution of this dissonance (Festinger, 1957). The individual confronted with conflicting ideas must resolve the difference; reject the new ideas or change the old ideas.

The contending sides tend to heighten their efforts in the face of ideological challenge. The need to proselyize increases in the presence of a conflicting ideology which challenges the validity of one's own. Festinger describes the proselytizer as needing to redouble his efforts when the challenge to his belief system is clear-cut or more threatening. This tendency for the ideological conflict to spiral in the face of challenge is to be noted in the developments leading up to the destruction of Jerusalem in 70 AD. Those favoring resistance to Rome attempted to influence the less radical segments and progressed in their approaches to more aggressive means. The instruments of argument and exhortation gave way to more coercive means and finally terrorism was widely employed (i.v.).

Education and change   Under less radical conditions, the main agency of change for the individual is the educational system. Among the Jews of Palestine in the first century AD, we know that the educational process was intense and highly developed. The Pharisees provided an elaborate and effective educational experience for their children and followers (Baron, 1952, vol 2, pp 274–280). The Jews were a highly literate people, probably the most literate of any ancient group of the time (Diringer, 1967) and intensely aware of the value of literacy. Written material of wide distribution dates back through nearly the entire first millenium BC. There was open disdain for those whose education was inferior or incomplete. The *am ha-aretz* or common people of the land were that large segment not fully involved in Jewish learning, considered ignorant people, and suspect in their practices and purity in the view of the Pharisees.

The educational system of the Pharisees is reflected in the Talmud which addresses problems of pedagogy in considerable detail. Emphasis was placed on a well-organized rather than an ingenious student. The student was directed to learn with body and soul the details of the law, instruction beginning with the third book of the Pentateuch, Leviticus. An outline of the curriculum by talmudic authority suggested that a boy begin the Bible at 5, study oral law at 10, and at 15 begin his own interpretation of traditional sources (Baron, 1952, vol 2, pp 275, 421). An autobiographical account by Josephus that he began to study the three philosophies on his own at age 16 is thus not inconsistent with the scholarly expectations of the day (*Life* 10).

Adult education was as important as pedagogy, and an observant Jew was expected to commit part of every day to study. While the Pharisee tradition emphasized education for the rank and file, ie, the plebian followers of the religion, the Sadducees, drawn from the patricians and landowners, were much less oriented toward learning and were suspect in terms of their commitment to learning (Baron, 1952, vol 2, p 276). Many talmudic references attest to the attachment of the poorer classes to religious learning and the apparent disinterest of the upper classes.

Written materials, books, pamphlets, and documents, were prepared specifically in the service of an ideological objective by competing factions. Anti-Semitic attacks were countered with writings such as that of Josephus, *Against Apion,* and of Philo of Alexandria, *In Flaccum.*

Explanatory treatises were used for political purposes. About 10 BC Alexander, son of Herod the Great, accused of conspiring against his father, developed four books in his own defense (*J.W.* 1.498). The books described the work of Alexander's enemies and were designed to persuade Herod that Alexander was a faithful and dutiful son. Alexander's mother, Mariamme I, had a special place in the affections of Herod and this gave Alexander an advantage. Alexander's efforts failed, however, to stem the current of accusations in the complicated and tangled family of Herod the Great. Alexander was executed by Herod in 7 BC.

Letter-writing was used as a means of public influence in the ancient world. Letters to individuals were written with the intention or direction to the reader that they be communally shared. The letters of Paul of Tarsus were intended for use by an entire community of Christian believers (Doty, 1973). In addition to letters, the importance of pamphlets is evident in the development of early Christianity. The New Testament is, in effect, a collection of religious pamphlets and letters which were utilized to develop and influence support for the new religion, particularly among the early target population of Jews.

The use of written materials was studied and applied with skill. Documents were circulated and notices placed in an effort to influence the general population or segments of it. The Romans circulated handbills as a technique of propaganda. When Octavian and Marc Antony entered into armed conflict, Octavian secretly sent people into Antony's camp disguised as traders who mingled with the soldiers and distributed handbills directing them to the cause of Octavian (Appian, 1968, vol 4, p 13; Hall, 1923, p 75).

The two historical works of Josephus, the *Jewish War* and *Antiquities,* reflect his political purposes which are often complex and indirect. In providing a detailed account of the war for the emperor, his patron, it is clear enough which side will be found the most honorable. On the other hand, having the close attention of his Roman patron, Josephus sought to advance other causes. He puts the Pharisees in a favorable light and gives the Jewish advocates of conciliation a fair hearing (Neusner, 1973). It has been argued that Josephus was anxious to support the survival of Judaism in Palestine and persuade the Romans that there were Jews whom they could use in a reconstruction era (Moehring, 1975). Another motive attributed to Josephus in his account of the war is that of preventing further hostilities in the Diaspora. By emphasizing Roman might and the extent of the war damage, Josephus may have hoped to dampen rebellious Jewish activity elsewhere in the Empire (Zeitlin, 1969; Shutt, 1961, p 41; Thackeray, 1929, p 29). The Jewish population outside of Palestine numbered several million, and the possibility of uprisings by Jews in response to the events in Palestine was a very real one. Disturbances in several cities outside of Palestine occurred, and some Palestinian Jews had even considered a plan of a food blockade of the city of Rome (Baron, 1952, vol 2, p 91).

Swaying the masses   Exhortation, then as now, was the readily available instrument of human change directed at the crowd. The ability to sway an assembled group was highly prized, and Josephus records long verbatim speeches by the various figures in his histories. These include speeches of Herod, Titus, Agrippa I, Eleazar at Masada, and Josephus himself. While it is likely that these reported speeches are highly stylized by the author, the portrait of a persuasive public speaker is a recurring and important theme in the framework of ideological conflict in the age of Josephus (Thackeray, 1929, p 41).

Josephus was aware that oratorical abilities could work for both good and evil and often portrays troublemakers as the most effective persuaders. He describes one "knave with an instinct for introducing disorder into grave matters" (*Life* 135) and another "rascal naturally gifted for creating great disturbances" (*Ant.* 17.325).

In his own crowd performances, Josephus used theatrical maneuvers to gain sympathy. When early in his career he was accused by the Galileans of betrayal to the Romans, he affected an appearance of pitiful and defenseless innocence. He changed into torn black clothing, suspended his sword from his neck (*Life* 138–139), sprinkled ashes on his head, and kept his hands behind his back (*J.W.* 2.601). Upon seeing the crowd, he fell on his face and wept. Needless to say his performance was successful in convincing the crowd of his innocence. Later in the Jotapata cave when Josephus tried to dissuade the 40 men from suicide, he describes his oratorical gestures in detail. He addressed one in familiar fashion by his name, looked another intently in the eyes, clasped the hand of another, and entreated a fourth (*J.W.* 3.385).

The skillful orator accompanied his words with demonstrations of his message. When Herod presented himself to the Emperor Augustus in an effort to reestablish his power base, he came dressed as a commoner without his diadem and in a subservient and restrained manner (*J.W.* 1.387). In a different mood, when Herod was summoned to the Sanhedrin to account for his summary execution of Hezekiah the brigand, he arrived with an escort of his troops, clothed in purple, and with his hair carefully arranged (*Ant.* 14.171, 173). His appearance was designed to intimidate the Sanhedrin and to convince them that he had both the authority to execute Hezekiah and the power to defy the court. He subsequently made good his avoidance of punishment.

On the occasion when King Agrippa II rushed to Jerusalem to stem the growing tide of rebellion, Agrippa carefully staged his oratorical setting. He placed his sister, Queen Bernice, on a high palace roof where she could be seen by the crowd (*J.W.* 2.345). As he conducted his lengthy and detailed speech, he reached a climactic point in which he announced that the rebellious faction would have to proceed without his leadership if it persisted in its efforts. At this point he burst into tears as did Bernice from her vantage point, the two being in full view of the crowd below (*J.W.* 2.402). From our knowledge of Bernice's conduct of her personal affairs, it is likely that her tears were a theatrical demonstration for purposes of Agrippa's oratory.

Josephus describes these various efforts at presenting visual accompaniment to oratory in clear fashion, and it is evident that these were often deliberate, carefully thought out arrangements, much as a theater director might arrange his props and stage directions. Menahem, leader of the Sicarii, making a public appearance to enhance his following and power, arrayed himself "in royal robes" and was attended by a large following of armed men, giving the impression of a powerful ruler with his entourage (*J.W.* 2.444).

During his career in the Galilee, Josephus was the object of a plot to be attacked by a rival, Jonathon, when he was unarmed. Confronting Jonathon before a large crowd of Galileans, Josephus dramatically produced the letters which laid bare the plot (*Life* 255, 260). He then read aloud parts of the letters which illustrated the duplicity of Jonathon and roused the crowd to his side, preventing further hostile acts by Jonathon and his colleagues.

Another dramatic scene narrated by Josephus involved the father of Herod the Great, Antipater. On an occasion when the Roman emperor had questioned his loyalty and motives, Antipater "stripped off his clothes and exposed his numerous scars which he had received during the course of the many battles which he had fought in the service of the Romans" (*J.W.* 1.197). Antipater accompanied this demonstration with protestations of his loyalty and counter-accusations against those who had questioned his steadfastness in the Roman cause. The end result of Antipater's effective speech was his being appointed the governor of all Judea on that occasion (*J.W.* 1.200).

Opposing armies often used propagandistic means to secure desertions among their enemies. This was especially the case when the troops of an army were drawn from differing ethnic groups with tenuous allegiances. When the Hasmonean king Alexander Jannaeus fought the Seleucid governor Demetrius III, about

88 BC, both armies had Jews and non-Jews. Before the battle, both leaders issued proclamations inviting desertions from the opposing forces (*J.W.* 1.93).

When Herod the Great was consolidating his strength around 39 BC, he encamped outside the walls of Jerusalem where his opponent Antigonus was based (*J.W.* 1.295-296). To diminish the resistance, Herod had heralds patrol the walls and proclaim his mission of serving the people and offering full amnesty to all. Antigonus issued counter-exhortations. Josephus himself functioned as such a herald for the Romans in the final siege of Jerusalem in 70 AD. As a Roman collaborator, Josephus passed about the walls speaking "in their native tongue" to his fellow countrymen and urging surrender (*J.W.* 5.361-419).

Nor was desertion limited to mercenaries or renegades. Even the disciplined Roman troops had their share of desertions, and propagandistic advantage might be sought from them. In the siege of Jerusalem in 70 AD, the city appeared impregnable to some of the attackers who deserted to the Jewish side. Dio Cassius reports that the Jews treated them kindly in order to demonstrate their existence and to encourage more potential Roman deserters (*Epitome* 65.5.3).

Conversion and coercion   The religious ideals and practices of Judaism spread by propaganda and by example to a considerable segment of the pagan population. Large numbers of Gentiles adopted Jewish customs, and formal conversions were commonplace. In the first century AD the interest of Romans in Judaism reached a degree of official concern. In 19 AD the Emperor Tiberius "ordered the whole Jewish community to leave Rome" (*Ant.* 18.83), in reaction to the proselytizing of a Roman lady of high rank, Fulvia, and the exploitations of worshippers by Jews and priests of the goddess Isis (Radin, 1915, pp 305-313).

Under the Emperor Claudius, around 41 AD, the Jews of Rome had so increased in number that he forbade them to hold meetings, according to Dio Cassius (*History* 60.6.6). Suetonius reports an expulsion of the Jews of Rome by him (*Claudius* 25.4); Radin, 1915, p 314). Even after the war and the disarray among the Jews, the attraction of Judaism for the Romans persisted. Domitian, around 95 AD, executed many Romans for atheism, ie, the drifting into Jewish ways (Dio Cassius, *Epitome* 67.14.2).

While Jewish doctrine spread via written documents and active efforts of preachers, more coercive approaches were also used. Conversion by sword was the approach to the Idumaeans who were Judaized by the Hasmoneans under Hyrcanus in 129 BC (Radin, 1915, p 157; *Ant.* 13.257, 15.254). A similar act of forced conversion and circumcision of the Eturaeans of northern Galilee was carried out in 103 BC when that territory was conquered during the reign of the son of Hyrcanus, Aristobulus I (*Ant.* 13.318). The practice of forced conversion, or at least of forced conformity to Jewish religious law, was still present in the time of Josephus, who speaks of an incident in 67 AD when two nobles from Trachonitis seeking asylum among the Jews of the Galilee were threatened with circumcision under compulsion. Josephus intervened to prevent the citizens from enforcing the covenant on the refugees (*Life* 112-113). It may be evidence of the reaction to past Judaizing that in the Edict of Antoninus (reigned 138-161 AD) the Jews of Rome were restored to the previous religious freedom except that circumcision had to be confined to their own children and never applied to a foreign convert (Gibbon, n.d., vol 2, p 5).

We have seen that conversion to Judaism might take place under the extreme condition of the choice between death or conversion to Judaism. However, there were other forms of duress and subtle coercion that were applied and led to conversion to Judaism under conditions which obviously were not wholly voluntary. In the case of individuals wishing to marry into the Jewish nobility or seeking a favorable marriage in terms of political or material gain, a non-Jew might be faced with the insistence that he convert in order that the marriage be consummated. When King Agrippa I was given his rulership by the Emperor Claudius, he arranged for his sister Drusilla to be married to Azizus, king of Emesa (*Ant.* 20.139). Emesa (modern Homs) was a city in Syria, north of Damascus, and it is stated that Azizus consented to be circumcised in order to be married to Drusilla. This same Drusilla subsequently deserted her circumcised husband for the Roman procurator Felix, thus deserting her faith and her legal husband.

A remarkably parallel sequence of events occurred with the sister of Drusilla, Bernice. She married Polemon, king of Cilicia, who was circumcised for the purpose. She subsequently deserted him, relieving him of a marriage to a licentious woman and the faith which had been forced on him (*Ant.* 20.145–147). The circumcisions of Azizus and Polemon, brothers-in-law of Agrippa I, are clear evidence of politically motivated conversions. Agrippa II had little involvement with the faith of his fathers but made consistent efforts to be identified with Judaism and the maintenance of its holy places (Schurer, 1961, p 240).

While proselytes might arrive in the ranks of Judaism from the two extremes of coercion or honest and sincere attraction, an entire range and variety of proselytes apparently existed during the first century and the period before and after the rise of Christianity. Moore (1966, vol 1, pp 323–353) in viewing this variety of conversions has labeled those whose motives were ulterior as "counterfeit converts" (p 336). The Talmud, discussing the problem of proselytes of uncertain motives, mentions several specific, apparently unfamiliar, types. There were the lion proselytes, individuals who were converted to Judaism out of fear of divine wrath such as the Samaritans, mentioned in II Kings 17.25. Dream proselytes were those who converted in response to a dream or the advice of a dreamer. The proselytes of Mordecai and Esther, so called, were those who sought Judaism as an expedient in a time of threat (*Esther* 8.17). Perhaps the most common proselyte of ulterior motives was the love proselyte, the individual who became a Jew because of marital needs. The validity of such conversions was debated in the Talmud, with some defending all as proper and others rejecting those proselytes lacking in sincerity (*Yebamoth* f. 25b).

Obviously, judgment was difficult with regard to the motives of a proselyte when conditions were uncertain in terms of their effect on the motives of the convert. The man who became a proselyte "for the sake of a royal board or for the sake of joining Solomon's servants" was, of course, suspect (*Yebamoth* 5.24b). On the other hand, proselytes who joined the Jewish faith during times of hardship for the Jews were considered much more acceptable since the proselyte was not motivated by fear or material gain.

Inner processes of change   Among the four approaches to changing people, those of therapy and realization appear the least congruent with the usual view of the late ancient world, yet there is evidence that both of these approaches may have found application. The therapeutic approach is based on the directive that personal change can occur if the genuine urge to become healthy is given full reign and pursued along the lines presented by a given agency of change. The attraction of the Essenees may have approximated the therapeutic approach and was apparently effective as a means of maintaining the group's vigor. The Essenees are described as either being celibate or limiting family interaction to various degrees. Recruiting of new members from the outside community was necessary and must have been an active process (Graetz, 1956, vol 2, p 220). As portrayed by Philo, Josephus, and Pliny, the way of life of the Essenees attracted great throngs of newcomers. It is noteworthy that the branch of the Essenees in Egypt described by Philo were called the Therapeutae, perhaps meaning "healers." By their appearance and example, the Essenees could promise through their practices and resulting personal condition a life that was tranquil and healthy. The Essenees were blessed with powers of prophesy and so enhanced by the purity of their lives that they often lived to nearly a hundred years old, according to the descriptions of the various writers.

Self-realization is the most elusive of the approaches to human change and the most evanescent as a goal of a change agency. The message of realization, in Lifton's words is "You can change . . . if you are willing to confront yourself with ideas and approaches which challenge your present ways of knowing and acting" (Lifton, 1969, p 440). Lifton notes that while any change agency (educational, psychological, religious, or political) may espouse the approach of realization, the approach is notoriously vulnerable and is readily violated by the other demands of the change agency placed upon the individual. Indeed, realization as an approach to change brings into focus the inherent conflict of all change agencies. The willful participation and allegiance of the individual is being sought by an agency which hopes to impose its will on the yet unchanged individual. At a distance of two millenia it is likely that no firm conclusions will be reached on the use of realization among the political and religious factions of Palestine. In the writings of Josephus the workings of realization are posed by the author in his own educational career. He recounts his choice of Pharisee Judaism as resulting from a deliberate exploration of the three sects of Judaism. He describes himself as "determined to gain personal experience of the several sects" so that "after a thorough investigation, I should be in a position to select the best" (*Life* 10). He pursued an arduous course and at age 19 became an adherent of the Pharisees.

The Choice of Faith

From our present-day vantage point the ethnic, racial, and religious divisions of the ancient world appear to be very intense and well-defined ones. It is natural to assume that the distinctions between groups were firm ones and that the social groupings were often of significance in a vital, even life-supporting fashion. We know that the threat of excommunication or ejection from the community might leave an individual destitute, unable to attain a livelihood, and lacking entirely in support services. For example, in describing the group supports of the Essenee community, Josephus reports that when an individual member of the sect is excluded because of misconduct from their company, the individual may die of starvation, being unable to obtain food on his own (*J.W.* 2.143). In quite a different context, when Titus wished to punish a Roman soldier for duplicity and cowardice, he simply deprived the soldier of his status in the Roman army, a fate worse than death (*J.W.* 6.362).

On the other hand, there is evidence that there was considerable movement and choice in religious practice and belief. There are many references to Romans drifting into Jewish practices and conversions of both a passive as well as active form. It is relevant that Josephus describes his own youthful search in relation to religion in a manner to suggest that he had considerable active choice in defining his form of Judaism. He states that at age 16 he systematically examined the philosophies of the Pharisees, Sadducees, and Essenees and eventually decided upon the Pharisees as most congenial to his life course and style (*Life* 10–12). While Josephus may be anxious to impress us with his precocious ability, it is evident that the possibility of choice within the Jewish religion was readily available.

The spread of the three philosophies may be envisioned as based on efforts from within and without the group. The times were troubled and significant spiritual and emotional needs existed for the individual citizens who saw their culture and society in disarray and threatened by physical and cultural annihilation. The citizen under such stressful conditions turned to whatever sources of solace he might find in the world. The quest for personal salvation became uppermost in the minds of men at that time (Radin, 1915, p 149). The citizen uncertain of his future might be drawn toward the religion which seemed to offer a sense of comfort in terms of the future. Themes of immortality, resurrection, and the meaning of life beyond preoccupied many in the face of an uncertain future and catastrophic war with the mightiest temporal power of the time.

The theological views of the Essenees, in which the soul was viewed as immortal and imperishable, provided an irresistible attraction for "all who have once tasted their philosophy" (*J.W.* 2.158). The philosophy of the Essenees and their demonstration of absolute faith was to writers such as Josephus and Pliny (5.73) a strong attraction to new entrants into their sect. Josephus, however, after sampling the philosophy of the Essenees in his youth did not choose to continue as an Essene.

In contrast to the Jewish religion, the pagan religions of the time emphasized an initiation rite which was the central feature of the religious practice. The initiation into the Jewish religion involved the rather simple features of a declaration of commitment and baptism and, for the men, circumcision. The mysterious and often extravagantly expensive initiations of the pagan religions did not exist for the Jewish religion. Women in prominent positions are often mentioned as proselytes or observers of Jewish customs. Helena, queen of Adiabene, in northern Mesopotamia, was converted to Judaism (*Ant.* 20.17). The case of Fulvia has been mentioned. The wife of the Emperor Nero, Poppaea, who interceded for the Jews in 64 AD, is described as a "worshipper of God" suggesting that she carried out some Jewish practices (*Ant.* 20.195). The factor of circumcision probably explains why conversion to Judaism was much more common among Gentile women then men (Klausner, 1961, p 38).

The Jews of first-century Palestine lived in a milieu of strong religious pulls. Well-developed techniques by religious sects for influencing outsiders and indoctrinating followers were energetically applied. Outside of Palestine, Diaspora Jews exercised similar approaches and many Gentiles were drawn to Jewish practices or actual conversion.

Commitments were strong and the need for faith was unquestioned. However, the attachment to one of the Jewish sects might be shifted; for some the need for faith was mingled with a need to explore a variety of belief systems. The method of the talmudic sages bears ample witness to the ability of Jews of that era to consider every conceivable facet of a question. The willingness to shift from one sect to another, the interest in exploring new beliefs, and the openness to questioning provided the intellectual climate in which religious innovation was able to take root and grow. Christianity was one of the religious innovations of the first century. For the Jews confronting Roman tyranny in Palestine, the innovation of a religiopolitical philosophy of resistance was the critical development which made war inevitable. We shall now consider this development.

REBELS AND RIVALS

The promulgation of doctrine or religious innovation by the zealous efforts of a dedicated few appears to be a critical element in the religious history of the first century. The generation of novel ideas by itself does not account for religious movements. It is the existence of factors that facilitate the spread of ideas that is critical to their success. The first century seemed characterized by individuals who needed to spread their ideas and eagerly devoted their lives to the cause. These individuals were encouraged in their leadership roles by a populace which readily formed a following. The message of Jesus, as transmitted through his apostles, was seized upon by the lower classes with avidity. The Gospels depict Christ as directing his apostles to become "fishers of men," and the message is particularly targeted at the disadvantaged classes. Jaspers (1962, p 104) has discussed the impact of the great paradigmatic individuals of the ancient world: Buddha, Confucius, Socrates, and Jesus. Of the four, only Jesus addressed all strata of the population, requiring no sophistication in his listeners. The people, Jew and Gentile, of first-century Palestine were responsive to Jesus and other leaders who offered radical social or spiritual change.* The Fourth Philosophy of Judah of Galilee evoked a dedicated following among the restless population of the time; he and other radical Jewish leaders were encouraged to continue their efforts by the continued replenishment of the ranks of their followers from the general population.

Our inquiry into the radical and rebellious factions of first-century Palestine will consider their historical and political character, the psychology of their rank-and-file members, their patterns of leadership, and, finally, their role in the disaster of 70 AD.

Zealots and Zealotry

In the era preceding the war with the Romans, the three established philosophies in Judaism stood in contrast to many lesser schools and factions which had taken form. The latter included various messianic movements, the Samaritans, the Damascus sect who broke with the Pharisees over temple practices (Baron 1952, vol 2, pp 52, 348), and the Judeo-Christians who appeared after the death of Jesus. The three philosophies presented neither an absolute authority nor an established hierarchy but rather served as themes of theological commitment and loose subdivisions within the Jewish people. It will be recalled that Josephus himself studied all three of the philosophies before making the Pharisees his choice. It is evident that the divisions between Pharisees, Sadducees, and Essenees were clear ones but strong common bonds could predominate over differences, and all were drawn into events of the war to a degree. For example, the Essenees, the most pacific and retreatist of the philosophies, contributed a

---

*Leaders and leadership will be discussed below. Jesus, during his lifetime, did not attract a very large following or much attention, as evidenced by the lack of contemporary accounts. Furthermore, even after the crucifixion at about 30 AD, with the emergence of the aggressive Judeo-Christian leadership and the beginning formation of the church, the main arena for missionary activity moved quickly to beyond Palestine. The history of early Christianity is too complex and too significant to be dealt with here in terms of a few generalizations. For our purposes, suffice it to say, by the end of the first century, missionary efforts were to be found largely outside of Palestine and concentrated among the Gentiles (Baron, 1952, vol 2, pp 56–88).

general, John, during the war (*J.W.* 2.567) and were the object of Roman military action.

In the events leading to the war with the Romans and particularly in the siege of Jerusalem, several different fighter groups took the brunt of Roman might, forming a loosely related zealot movement committed to armed struggle. This zealot resistance movement stood in contrast to a considerable group who hoped for peace with the Romans and foresaw catastrophe in the rebellion. Those following peace apparently did not coalesce into a active peace party or antiwar movement, despite the fact that they represented a majority opinion. Most Pharisees favored peace (Heller, 1968). During the 70 AD siege of Jerusalem, the major Pharisee rabbi, Johanon ben Zakkai, used a ruse to escape and negotiate with the Romans for a peaceful settlement for a portion of the country. According to the talmudic account, the escape was arranged by having Johanon reported to have died and carried out of the city walls in a coffin by his students (*Gittin* f.56a; Goldin, 1955, p 35). About two years before the siege, as the war was closing in on Jerusalem, the small Judeo-Christian community quietly slipped out of the city to find haven on the other side of the Jordan in the heathen city of Pella (Schurer, 1961, p 260).

Among the active fighters, at least five different groups can be identified. Josephus names the Sicarii first in his listing of the rebel groups (*J.W.* 7.253–274). The Sicarii were those who traced their roots to the Galilean insurgents, Hezekiah and his son Judah. The followers of John of Gischala formed another resisting faction during the war. The small army of Simon bar Giora identified their leader with a messianic tradition. The Zealots, as specifically designated by Josephus, formed a separate faction (Baumbach, 1969). Another group with its own identity in the struggle were the Idumaeans, the Jewish descendents of the forced converts.

The factional struggle among the Jews during the war with the Romans reached a remarkable degree of enmity. At the very time in which the army of Titus was investing Jerusalem for the final siege and destruction, three separate rebel parties of Jews occupied their own sections of Jerusalem and warred with each other. The 6000-man army of John of Gischala occupied the Temple Mount; the forces of Simon bar Giora, 15,000 men, occupied the upper city and part of the lower city; Eleazar ben Simeon with 2400 Zealots occupied the inner court of the temple (*J.W.* 5.248–251). All three factions fought each other and even destroyed the supplies of food within the city in order to gain an advantage over the other (Schurer, 1961, p 264). In describing this ludicrous and destructive internal strife in the very face of external disaster, Josephus must have had in mind the repetition of history which he recorded during the siege of Jerusalem by Pompey in 63 BC.* At that time the defending forces of the Jews broke out into a rivalrous struggle, the brothers Hyrcanus and Aristobulus fighting each other (*J.W.* 1.141). Aristobulus and Hyrcanus were sons of Salome Alexandra and Alexander Jannaeus. Alexander Jannaeus had died in 78 BC and been succeeded by his widow, who reigned until 69 BC. At her final illness and death, her sons had become rivals for the throne. When the city finally fell to Pompey, most of the deaths among the Jews were due to the fighting between factions (*J.W.* 1.151).

---

*When Jerusalem was besieged by the Romans and the outcome appeared hopeless for the Jews, Josephus, in the service of his Roman captors, acted as a herald calling to the defenders on the city wall. Among the arguments which he used in urging them to surrender was the fate of Aristobulus and Hyrcanus in their resistance to Pompey (*J.W.* 5.396).

In the events which led to the war and the emergence of the several factions, the interplay of social, religious, and political factors is striking. The religious movements are inseparable from the social and political forces at work. Of particular significance is the religious development termed the Fourth Philosophy by Josephus which had its roots in events a hundred years before the fall of Jerusalem (Stern, 1973). It is labeled the Fourth Philosophy by Josephus to distinguish it from the established sects of Pharisees, Sadducees, and Essenees. In the years following the fall of Jerusalem to Pompey in 63 BC, resistance to Roman domination smoldered. A leading role was taken by Galilean provincials against the domination of Herod the Great and his Roman supporters. Herod rose swiftly to power and gained Roman favor by actively suppressing Jewish insurgents. Josephus regularly refers to them as bandits and robbers, a reflection of his pro-Roman bias which ignored their role as patriots resisting Roman and secular domination (Zeitlin, 1962, vol 1, p 405).† Among the resistors was their leader Hezekiah, executed summarily by Herod in 47 BC. For this arbitrary act, Herod was summoned to the court of the Sanhedrin but escaped punishment (*Ant.* 14.165-180). The son of Hezekiah, Judah of Galilee, continued the resistance movement and is specifically cited as the leader of the Fourth Philosophy (*Ant.* 18.23).

The insurgency was particularly spurred by the taxation efforts of the Romans. Judah of Galilee organized resistance in response to the census of Quirinius in 6 AD, with its threat of increased taxation and other burdens (*J.W.* 7.253). Judah enlisted the aid of a Pharisee, Saddok, in a broad appeal to national independence (*Ant.* 18.4-10). At that time the followers of Judah banded together and threatened and attacked any who were willing to consent to the Romans, demonstrating the willingness of the Fourth Philosphy to engender extremist forms. The New Testament describes the death of Judah of Galilee following the uprising "in the days of the registration" (*Acts* 5.37), presumably not long after 6 AD (*Encyclopedia Judaica,* 1972, vol 16, p 948). In tracing developments up to the war with the Romans, Josephus describes these earlier resistors as Sicarii (*J.W.* 7.254). The next generation of the family persisted and suffered for its insurgency as well. The sons of Judah, James and Simon, were tried and crucified around 47 AD by the Roman procurator Tiberius Alexander (*Ant.* 20.102).

The Fourth Philosophy adherents agreed in most ways with the traditions of the Pharisees except for a fanatic dedication to liberty and a willingness to die for their cause. God alone was their master and the acceptance of secular rule, ie, Roman, was equated with idolatry. The Pharisees believed in the immortality of the soul and the resurrection of the dead, and the Fourth Philosophy was an extension into everyday life of this belief. This willingness to die was coupled with an equal willingness to take vengeance on their fellows who accepted any form of submission (*Ant.* 18.23-25). The movement begun and extended by Hezekiah and Judah was continued into the war with the Romans, Menahem, the

†Josephus clearly refers to the illegal behavior of the bandits but is objective and detailed in his account and has allowed the full presentation of a picture which clearly distinguishes many of the insurgents from common criminals. A pattern of social banditry is evident in many of the examples from the account of Josephus. Social banditry is characterized by an emerging protest group responding to oppressive social conditions. The social bandits find support in the local village or general population, act to correct injustices, and share in the values of the local population. Horsley (1979) has traced the peaks of Jewish social banditry as occurring in the time before the consolidation of Herod's power, during the middle of the first century AD, and during the decade leading to the war with the Romans. The support of the local population for the social bandit and the interaction of a mutually beneficial nature between bandit and population is particularly illustrated in the case of Eleazar ben Dinai who was called on by the people to avenge a murder of a Galilean by the Samaritans.

son or grandson of Judah, becoming their main leader early in the revolt.

During the procuratorship of Felix (52–60 AD) when the Roman government took aggressive action against the insurgents, the Sicarii resorted to more terroristic methods. The name Sicarii is derived from their use of the sica, a short curved knife, to murder their rivals. The Sicarii used their daggers with shocking ease. They would mingle with the crowds during the festivals, dispose of their targets quickly, and then disappear in the crowd (J.W. 2.255). In acting as assassins against other Jews, the Sicarii aimed to eliminate those who favored adjustment or compromise with the Romans. They took hostages and are described as unbound by any conventions in their willingness to achieve their ends. The name Sicarii occurs in Roman law and was used by Josephus as an equivalent for the term assassins (Applebaum, 1971). In the Talmud they are referred to as *biryonim,* perhaps meaning guards of the *biryah* or palace (*Gittin* f.56a).

Masada, which contained an armory from the days of Herod the Great, was captured by the Sicarii and used by them as a base of operations (J.W. 2.433–434). In 66 AD, Menahem, the descendant of Hezekiah, left Jerusalem for Masada and returned with an armed bodyguard and, in royal robes, attempted to gain control of the city (J.W. 2.434, 444). The resulting battle saw the high priest killed by the Sicarii and, in turn, they were masacred along with Menahem (J.W. 2.446). A remnant of the Sicarii escaped to Masada led by Eleazar ben Yair, a relative of Menahem (J.W. 2.447). In addition to the account by Josephus, a Midrashic text mentions Menahem departing from Jerusalem accompanied by 800 elegantly dressed students. This may refer to his trip to Masada, to obtain arms, or the retreat of Eleazar ben Yair (Feldman, 1975, pp 218–248; Lieberman, 1942, p 181).

In its course as a radical group the Sicarii were ready to die or experience the worst torture and stress in the pursuit of their faith and freedom. The suicide of the 960 defenders of Masada in 74 AD is consistent with other acts of the Sicarii. In the account of the self-destruction of the Masada Sicarii, Josephus puts in the mouth of Eleazar ben Yair a lengthy speech in which he urges the Masadans to accept suicide (J.W. 7.323–336, 341–388). In this speech (which was not heard by Josephus) Eleazar states that "it is death which gives liberty to the soul and permits it to depart to its own pure abode . . . the soul . . . free from the weight that drags it down to earth and clings about it. . . . is restored to its proper sphere" (J.W. 7.344–346).

Even following the calamity of Masada, other groups of Sicarii continued to be involved in dramatic and catastrophic acts. In Egypt a group of them "again embarked on revolutionary schemes" and were tortured and killed by the Romans (J.W. 7.410–419). In the Libyan city of Cyrene under the influence of their leader Jonathan, a group of Sicarii were led into the desert with promises of a "display of signs and apparitions" (J.W. 7.438). The followers of Jonathan were pursued and destroyed by the Romans, and Jonathan was tortured and burned alive (J.W. 7.450).

It is relevant that the insurgent family dynasty which fostered the Fourth Philosophy was Galilean. The Galilee was the main population center of the am ha-aretz; and the burden of Roman taxation often fell most heavily on this peasant farmer (Baron, 1952, vol 1, pp 278–280). A Roman tax of one fourth of the farm crop together with a religious obligation of 12% of the remainder often drove the farmer to the point of starvation. When the burden on the Galilean am ha-aretz became intolerable he may have made his own choice of which levy to omit. Roman administration left little choice. The possibility that the Galilean farmer did not scrupulously observe the tithe and therefore made his produce unacceptable was one of the concerns that led the Pharisees to disparage the am ha-aretz. This situation, coupled with the distance from the capitol, made the Galilee a natural site for the development of a national liberation movement.

Early in the war, the group labeled Zealots (Hebrew, kannaim) by Josephus were prominent in the 66 AD Jewish victory at Beth-horon against a powerful Roman force led by Cestius Gallus, the Roman governor of Syria (*J.W.* 2.555). In the victory over the forces of Cestius, a Zealot leader, Eleazar ben Simeon, attained distinction and remained as the military leader of the Zealots who defended Jerusalem in the final siege by Titus. As the resistance to Rome progressed, scattered bands coalesced and entered Jerusalem to take the lead in the fight (*J.W.* 4.135, 146, 161).

In terms of allegiance the Zealots, from among all the zealot war movement groups, were associated with the temple priests. The Zealots drew heavily from among Jerusalemites, although others from around the country also made up their number. The Zealots were commited to armed resistance in contrast to other Pharisees in Jerusalem and occupied the temple as their base of operations against the Romans. Their military leadership included priests, and the Zealots may have had ideological roots traceable to a priest, Zadok the Pharisee, who, with Judah of Galilee, founded the Fourth Philosophy. The Zealots formed their own fighting forces and leadership separate from the Sicarii who were the main representation of the Fourth Philosophy (Stern, 1973). In contrast to the Sicarii, who were loyal to the Galilean dynasty of Judah ben Hezekiah, the Zealots had a collective leadership drawn heavily from the priesthood (Stern, 1973). The use of the term Zealot has led to a good deal of confusion but it is clear that this was not the group that perished at Masada (Stern, 1973; Hoenig, 1970).

A decisive religious and political role in the course of the revolt is assigned the Zealots by Josephus. It was the Zealot priests in the temple in 66 AD who rejected a customary daily temple offering on behalf of Rome and the emperor (*J.W.* 2.409). Josephus specifically cites Eleazar, the assistant to and son of the high priest Ananius (Hananiah), as the headstrong author of this decision. This act placed the temple outside the pale of the Roman Empire, making the breach irreconcilable and "laid the foundation of the war with the Romans" (*J.W.* 2.409). The Babylonian Talmud describes this turn of events in different detail but with an equally dramatic portent. According to the Talmud, the Roman authorities were informed of the rebellious attitude of the Jews and told to test them with an offering in the temple. The calf offered by the Romans was found to have a very minor blemish which caused it to be rejected, an insult to the Roman government. The Talmud concludes, "Through the scrupulousness of Rabbi Zechariah ben Abkulas our House has been destroyed, our Temple burnt and we ourselves exiled from our land" (*Gittin* f.56a).

Followers and Motives

Followers were in evidence for every new cause and trend. Religious splinter groups proliferated in first-century Palestine, and the war effort was dominated by factional rivalries. What can we conclude regarding the ease with which the men of this time and place joined in new movements, often with fatal consequences? Did Josephus perceive common characteristics for the rank and file of the many disparate movements and groups that his histories touched on?

In our own era, a range of explanations has been developed for the wave of religious interest and innovation. In particular, the seeming widespread youth involvement in new religious experience has been a focus of interest. Do the movements of today have their social or psychological equivalents in the developments of first-century Palestine?

Explanations for youthful conversions turn on such matters as the contemporary social and cultural crisis with the ostensible loss of attachments to society and past values, the need for security under the threat of a nuclear holocaust, the quest for altered states of consciousness in an era of substance abuse and sensate exploration, and loss of pressure for conventional marriage and weakened family ties and supports (Cox, 1977; Galanter et al, 1979; Gordon, 1977; Nicholi, 1974). It is theorized that the congeries of needs and threats propel the youthful seeker into the arms of an accepting group, the religious sect, which serves as a contemporary alternative to family ties.

The prominence of alienated or anomic young adults in the contemporary rise of religious sects does not have a counterpart in the events of the first century AD. The followers of the various groups were not alienated youth or a well-defined stratum. Sometimes the following within an individual sect was of a family or small group nature. The Maccabees may perhaps be the family prototype of the zealot group or innovative religious sect of the era. In the case of the Maccabees, a father and his sons formed the nucleus of a pointed drive against the offensive pressure of the encroaching empire. As discussed, the Fourth Philosophy was largely framed by Judah, son of the insurgent Hezekiah, and transmitted through three or more generations of independence fighters. Thus, family cohesiveness and not family dissolution served to facilitate sect or faction development and might even have been a necessary feature for the development of a new group under the conditions of the time.

The present-day involvement of youth with religious discovery is apt to be associated with a need for friendship and human warmth as well as meaningful human values. This also represents a significant difference from the motives for entry into a zealot faction in first-century AD Palestine. A need for friendship was not an apparent prevailing theme among the sects participating in the rebellion against Rome.

There is no sense that family or personal values were disintegrating or in any particular sense threatened by the events immediately preceding the war. However, in the second and first centuries BC the threat to the Jewish community had taken the form of Hellenization and the invitation to share in the world culture of the Greek and Roman empires. As the later Roman procurators applied various despotic threats to religious freedom, the issue became very clear and the battle was joined. While such late threats to security may explain the nature of the uprising and resistance, they do not explain the specifics of religious innovation among the Jews of the time. The major development, the Fourth Philosophy, had its beginnings over a century before the war with the Romans. It evolved as a reaction to secular government encroachments and represented an extension of Pharisee religious principles rather than an actual religious innovation. It did not involve the development of new religious ritual or practices. It did, however, put its followers on a course of progressively more extreme expressions of their commitment to resistance. They had no hesitation in assassinating Jews who were willing to accommodate to the Romans. Suicide was entirely acceptable to them in the course of their religious war for independence.

The economic condition of first-century Palestine contributed significantly to a general state of unrest (Baron, 1952, vol 1, pp 262–276, 412). The burden of taxation was extreme. Herod the Great had exploited every means to subsidize his international building program (Baron, 1952, vol 1, pp 236–237); and the Roman officials who succeeded him made personal fortunes through taxation. There was considerable poverty and unemployment among the people. The hope for economic relief was widespread.

The rebellious spirit Josephus depicts the assembled masses as easily aroused and swayed by the promises of a glib spokesman. While the crowd might be influenced by oratory and pamphlets, Josephus offers other insights into the forces influencing the group. He notes that "on festive occasions sedition is most apt to break out" (*J.W.* 1.89). As an example, in 4 BC a huge crowd from all the provinces assembled at the temple on the holiday of Pentecost. Part of the stimulus for such a huge gathering, however, was indignation at a planned confiscation of temple treasures by a Roman official (*J.W.* 2.42; *Ant.* 17.254). A bloody insurrection followed.

The festive occasions which Josephus alludes to were times when the Jews from surrounding areas and even from the Diaspora converged on Jerusalem. The pilgrimage was an act of faith, and the worshipers were in a state of devotion. Victor Turner (1969, 1974) has characterized the emotional state of the religious pilgrimage as one of *communitas*. At such times the individual shares with the group a sense of transition to a new state of existence, a temporary destructuring of ordinary attachments, and a peculiar openness to new experiences and ideas. It is perhaps not surprising that the festive religious pilgrimage to Jerusalem was the starting point for protest movements. It is interesting that the astuteness of Josephus has given us this observation and his generalization regarding it.

In the mind of Josephus it was human nature for some peoples to enjoy riot and disorder, ready to participate in anarchy and to welcome the downfall of the existing order. In a campaign around 38 BC by Herod, most of the Jews who followed him were motivated by a "blind love of change rather than hatred of the enemy" (*J.W.* 1.334). Are we dealing with the antiauthoritarianism of the first century and the subordinate's enjoyment of the downfall of the established or privileged classes? The Idumaeans, converted to Judaism under the sword, were a disorderly, turbulent people, "ever on the alert for commotion and delighting in revolutionary changes." They "only needed a little flattery from their suitors to seize their arms and rush into battle as to a feast" (*J.W.* 4.231). The Idumaeans who lived in the province to the south of Judea may have occupied a subordinate or second-class status. Their taint of forced conversion together with the fact of the Herodian dynasty which had ruled the nation for nearly a century were sources of tension in their relations with other Jews. A number of violent outbreaks are described.

Josephus was impressed with the factor of "contagion" in the revolution and the spiraling effect of intense emotions within a group (*J.W.* 3.4). The aroused public now became doubly susceptible to deliberate influences. In emphasizing group spirit in the rebellion, Josephus parallels the vivid description by Thucydides (*J.W.* 3.81–84) of the rage and abuse of an inflamed population. The Greek of Thucydides was often a model for Josephus (Thackeray, 1929, p 100) and probably represented a common fund of contemporary concepts as well as a source of literary excellence. The military leader John of Gischala was a master at instigating people to war through his demagogic powers (*J.W.* 4.126). In particular, youth were readily "seduced" by John's "harangues" into the war party whereas older men were less easily swayed (*J.W.* 4.129). Earlier, in the events surrounding the 6 AD uprising, the leaders Judah of Galilee and Saddok the Pharisee were most effective in inspiring "the younger element" with zeal for their Fourth Philosophy (*Ant.* 18.10).

Emotions which ran so high could change dramatically. Josephus was the object of great admiration and intense hatred within a short interval. Jotapata in the Galilee fell while under his command, and it was assumed that he had fallen as well. The report "filled Jerusalem with the profoundest grief." The city was in mourning, flute players were hired to accompany the funeral dirges, and the lamentations for Josephus were extended for 30 days (*J.W.* 3.435–437). This is a degree of mourning beyond the usual seven days and is reserved for the most outstanding leaders. When it was learned thereafter that Josephus was still alive and even well treated by the Romans, the people's mourning was replaced with wrath, and he was abused as a traitor and coward (*J.W.* 3.438).

Josephus described with regularity the massing of the people, often on festive occasions, and the ensuing public disorder. From his descriptions it would appear that the spontaneous assemblies often were the link to violent behavior. Crowd behavior has been analyzed in terms of collective processes (Lang and Lang, 1968). Different kinds of crowds may be discerned. In some crowds, individuals play an important role in triggering licentious or abandoned forms of self-indulgence. In the crowd manifesting hysterical or somatized symptoms, a primitive expression of anxiety is shared by a crowd after its initial expression by a few members within the group. These key individuals function as a catalyst for the spread of the hysterical behavior. In contrast to the licentious crowd and the hysterical crowd, the acting crowd is one which responds to grievances and provides a channel of expression and correction for its perceived wrong. The acting crowd reacts with violence and destructiveness against established authority, particularly when institutional channels for the correcting of their grievances appears absent, and authority is usurped by the acting crowd. In behaving this way, the acting crowd may represent "a method of social control" (Lang and Lang, 1968, p 583). Lang and Lang add some other important points which correspond to the crowd behavior described by Josephus. The acting crowd is pointed and specific in its selection of objects for its vengeance. Its destructiveness is not random or entirely irrational. However, they note that a crowd episode may pass through a series of mutations and pass on to phases removed from its initial instigation. Furthermore, a crowd unites diverse elements which are apt to produce diverse offshoots and new developments. All of these features are evident in the crowd behavior described by Josephus. The mobs were initiated in response to Roman oppression. Once initiated, however, the crowds indulged in widespread violence and other social action goals were drawn into the mob activities. New leaders arose with their own particular ambitions; an initial protest against a religious offense by the Romans might end up with an attack on the records of indebtedness. Slaves might join in crowd behavior with the obvious goal of obtaining freedom.

Leaders

The various factions and splinter groups had no dearth of leadership. In the progress of the resistance, leadership was often critical in shaping events, and the leader's personality and ability to urge on his group was often the balancing factor in the development of a particular event or movement. From Josephus and other sources there is sufficient detail to discern a variety of leadership forms and styles.

A significant feature of the Fourth Philosophy and the Sicarii who emerged as the philosophy's major faction was the existence of a dynastic leadership. Hezekiah, Judah, Menahem, and Eleazar ben Yair are a single direct family line (Kolitz, 1971). The cohesiveness given to the Sicarii is ironically in evidence in the fact that Hezekiah is the earliest named casualty among the resistors to Rome, early forties BC, and the Masadans under Eleazar were the last significant deaths in Palestine in the great war, falling in 74 AD (Kolitz, 1971). The Fourth Philosophy was evident through nearly 120 years of resistance to the Romans. When Masada fell, seven made good their escape, five children and two women. One of the women, presumably the leader of the tiny band since the other woman is noted to be old, is described as "a relative of Eleazar, superior in sagacity and training to most of her sex" (*J.W.* 7.399). Thus, in their last living act, the Sicarii of Masada are led by a member of this same zealous dynasty of Hezekiah.

In the final siege of Jerusalem, John of Gischala headed one of the three defending forces. Gischala or Gush Halav was a Galilee town in which John son of Levi was a central figure and successful businessman. He was a moderate and initially had urged restraint and loyalty to Roman rule among his townspeople (*Life* 43; Stern, 1973). The attack by non-Jews on Gischala led him to a more aggressive role, and he was inexorably drawn into the revolt against Rome. He fought the Romans well, was the last of the resistance in the Galilee, and, most importantly, led a devoted army in an escape from the Galilee to Jerusalem. His arrival in Jerusalem was greeted with great enthusiasm (*J.W.* 4.122), although Josephus regarded John as an opportunist and scoundrel (*J.W.* 4.84, 211) and refers to his forces as brigands (*J.W.* 4.121). There was considerable personal rivalry between the two men, both of whom confronted the Romans in the Galilee. While Josephus saw his forces annihilated at Jotapata, John escaped with his men to a position of leadership in Jerusalem.

In Jerusalem John of Gischala apparently was able to relate to both the popular peace party and the war-bound Zealots (*J.W.* 4.208–210). He may have come to share in the sentiments of the Zealots in his drive for leadership in Jerusalem and joined forces with them.

When the city's walls gave way, the forces of the Jews retreated to the protection of the temple. Then Titus directed Josephus to urge the Jews to spare their sanctuary desecration (*J.W.* 6.93–95). In one of the most ironic scenes of the war, Josephus, in his own words, urges John "to repent of misdeeds" and surrender before destruction is brought down on the city (*J.W.* 6.96–110). John greeted the collaborator's overture with "many invectives and imprecations upon Josephus" and we are left to imagine John's actual words. It is likely they were not genteel. John concluded that he "could never fear capture, since the city was God's" (*J.W.* 6.98). John was convinced of the operation of divine intercession in the war, although he was not an adherent of the Fourth Philosophy (Stern, 1973).

Among the leaders resisting the siege, Simon bar Giora is clearly the most charismatic (Stern, 1973). His name indicates that he was the son of a proselyte (Hebrew, ger), although it is not clear if this was a proper name (Roth, 1960; Stern, 1973). Since he came from Gerasa, a Hellenistic city in Transjordan, it is possible that he was the son of a convert in that city (*J.W.* 4.503; Roth, 1960). Bar Giora, taken prisoner after the fall of Jerusalem, was led in the triumphal procession in Rome in where he was executed, his being the only execution of this triumph (*J.W.* 7.154; Dio Cassius, *Epitome,* 65.7.1). In singling him out the Romans acknowledged the central role of bar Giora in the Jewish leadership.

Simon bar Giora first achieved attention in the victory over Cestius at Bethhoron in 66 AD (*J.W.* 2.521). He thereafter developed an armed force from among the lower classes of the villages of Judea, Idumaea, and Transjordan (Stern, 1973). As the strength and discipline (Michel, 1967-1968) of his forces grew, Simon prepared to enter Jerusalem (*J.W.* 4.513). The other factions resisted him, but he was eventually invited into the city to the acclaim of the population. He was hailed as the city's "savior and protector." He became master of Jerusalem in the spring of 69 AD (*J.W.* 4.577).

Simon bar Giora was distinguished in a number of ways as a resistance leader. He clearly hailed from the lower socioeconomic strata and had a special affinity for the disadvantaged classes. He is credited with freeing slaves and advocating correctives of social discrimination and oppression. His followers apparently associated messianic hopes with him and obeyed him like a king. The freeing of slaves by Simon suggests regal power since a historical precedent by King Zedekiah existed on this score (*Jeremiah* 34.8-10).

In defeat he did not consider suicide as did the Sicarii and other adherents of the Fourth Philosophy. Following the fall of Jerusalem and the temple, bar Giora went underground and hid in the passageways of the smoldering city. After a few days he chose to present himself unarmed and wearing white to the Roman soldiers (*J.W.* 7.27-28). He was taken prisoner and returned to Rome. His death, as might have been anticipated, was not inconsistent with messianic prophecies which included various advance signs of the messiah's advent. Such predecessors of the messiah might be expected to meet with an awful fate as a means of ushering in the messianic age.

Josephus refers to the appearance of Simon in white robes as a ruse in an attempt to impersonate a god to the Romans. Michel (1967-1968) has pointed out that Simon was surrendering himself in the temple as a sacrifice which might bring relief to his people or the furtherance of apocalyptic events. Dio Cassius in his description of the carnage as the temple burns describes how the Jews "met death willingly. . . . And it seemed to everybody, and especially to them, that so far from being destruction, it was victory and salvation and happiness to them that they perished along with the Temple" (*Epitome* 65.6.3). In a similar vein of self-sacrifice is the surrender of Jesus to the Romans (*John* 18.5-9). The proselyte origins of bar Giora may have meshed with the messianic theme as well since King David, the source of the future messiah, was himself descended from a righteous convert, Naomi (*Ruth* 4.22).

Simon was not the only Jewish leader in the war associated with messianic and royal themes. The descendant of Judah of Galilee, Menahem, who was killed during the fight for leadership at the beginning of the war, had similar associations. Menahem, however, was a northerner of an established Jewish family and came from a tradition of activism. Simon's appeal was probably more rooted in his humble origins and promises of social reform. Some resemblance to Simon's career may be found in uprisings following the death of Herod the Great. Around 3 AD a slave of Herod crowned himself and with his company burning the palace at Jericho went on a looting rampage until cut down (*J.W.* 2.57-59). In the same period, the shepherd Athrongaeus set himself up as king and his four brothers as the royal family. They engaged widely in plundering Judea until captured by the Romans (*J.W.* 2.60-65). Both the slave of Herod and Athrongaeus were distinguished by their good looks and physical vigor, qualities which they shared with Simon in addition to humble origins.

Before the war, other leaders labeled by Josephus as "deceivers and imposters" presented claims of divine inspiration and readily persuaded masses to follow them in the belief that they were indestructible (*J.W.* 2.260). When Cuspius Fadus was procurator of Judea (44–46 AD), a colorful impostor, Theudas, persuaded a large following that he was a prophet and would command the River Jordan to open to allow them passage across (*Ant.* 20.97–100). Fadus dispatched a squadron of cavalry to slaughter the followers and behead Theudas. In the New Testament account, following the death of Theudas and 400 followers, Rabbi Gamaliel arose in the Sanhedrin to warn of the consequences of such acts (*Acts* 5.33–36). An Egyptian false prophet, who arose around 58 AD, provoked an encounter with the Roman garrison, and he with his 30,000 followers were nearly totally annihilated (*J.W.* 2.261–263). The episode of the Egyptian false prophet was of considerable impact, and the search for the impostor was apparently widespread by the Romans. Among the suspects was Paul of Tarsus who was arrested and interrogated as the possible Egyptian false prophet (*Acts* 21.38).

As the siege of Jerusalem approached its grisly outcome, numerous prophets directed the people of the city to await God's help. On the very last day of the destruction, as the Roman soldiers pillaged the burning temple, one remaining portico was found to shelter 6000 women and children. They had taken refuge there at the claim of still another self-proclaimed prophet that God would send them the tokens of deliverance. The soldiers set fire to the portico and "not a soul escaped" (*J.W.* 6.283–288).

How does the military career of Josephus fit into our catalog of rebel leadership types? Josephus makes no claim to being an initiator or spur to the rebellion and by his many critical comments sets himself apart from the firebrands and innovators of the time. He even claims to have prophesied the eventual calamity of the military uprising. Josephus was given the military command in the Galilee following the Jewish victory over Cestus at Beth-horon in November 66 AD (*J.W.* 2.563). In his full account of the war, he describes a skillful and active role for himself in preparing the Jewish military operation in the Galilee (*J.W.* 2.569–584). He was about 29 when given this considerable responsibility, and he apparently acquitted himself well. In his autobiography, written perhaps a score of years after he wrote the *Jewish War*, he tones down his military responsibility and states only that after Beth-horon "the leading men in Jerusalem" dispatched him and "two other priests" to establish order in the Galilee and prevent the revolutionaries from attacking others (*Life* 28–30). In any case, the arrival of the Roman army plunged him into the conflict and within half a year, around July 67 AD, he was taken prisoner by the Romans and his military career was ended. In his descriptions of his preparations for war and the conduct of the defense of Jotapata, he describes acts by himself of bravery, skill, and cunning. These qualities and his youth are his only resemblance to the zealot movement leaders.

The Ingredients of Disaster

For a full century before the war, the Jews of Palestine contested among themselves the alternatives of accommodation and resistance to a Roman government. The leadership of the country came to be divided into war and peace factions. What influences led to the eventual ascendance of the war party? "Religious innovation," ie, the Fourth Philosophy, in the opinion of Josephus, was a major source of the disaster. The work of the Fourth Philosophy served to raise the concept of armed resistance to the level of religious obligation. Its followers had no conflict with existing religious practices and introduced no changes in ritual or observance. As an articulate doctrine, the Fourth Philosophy declared collaborators as equal to idolators and justified the destruction of the opposition party. Lifton's (1969) description of ideological totalism, which catalogs the techniques of thought reform, is relevant to the methods of the Fourth Philosophy. The contemporary thought reformist, as in Lifton's example of Communist China, places doctrinal considerations above all else, demands purity of thought among the reformees, and passes judgment on the existence of nonbelievers. The Fourth Philosophy followers were absolute in their view of God as leader and master and unhesitating in sacrificing even "kinsmen and friends" who did not share in their zeal for independence from Rome (*Ant.* 18.23). They acted as self-appointed judges and executioners in matters of loyalty to the faith.

The quality of leadership was significant in the outcome. Within the war movement a profusion of energetic and ambitious leaders emerged and organized their followers and fought among themselves. The murderous rivalry of the leadership accounted for many assassinations of both pro- and antiwar leaders. The Talmud refers to "hatred without cause" as leading to the destruction of the Second Temple (*Yoma* f.9b); and the spiteful nature of the competition is illustrated in the enormous stores of food destroyed by the rivals in the besieged city (*Gittin* f.56a).

While ambitious leaders were plentiful and their zeal uninhibited, the involvement of much of the public may have been passive. The masses of people were probably drawn into events entirely beyond their doing. In the final siege, for example, when the city was packed with over a million people, the troops gathered by Simon bar Giora, John of Gischala, and the Zealots amounted to less than 25,000. It is likely that most Pharisees, Sadducees, Essenees, and the priestly classes opposed the war. As a political phenomenon, the war movement may have been sparked and maintained by a small group of determined activists. The continuing provocations of the Roman procurators and the occasional success of insurgency kept the war movement alive until a full conflagration burst forth.

Astonishingly, the war effort did not end with the destruction of Jerusalem. The Sicarii held out at Masada for four lonely years, and elsewhere small bands continued the resistance until all were wiped out. The rebels' commitment to a world ruled by God was an absolute one, and their continued resistance did not depend on sustaining victories. When the Romans completed their mopping up operations, the resistance movement was all but annihilated physically. It now remained for those remnants of the Jewish people to face the future in a world changed by the loss of their capitol and central religious institution, the temple. Josephus had already chosen accommodation and survival in the milieu of Rome. The Judaeo-Christians had made their choice of a separate path before the final siege began. The Pharisees of the peace party, led by Johanon Ben Zakkai, undertook the renewal of Judaism out of the ashes of destruction (Neusner, 1970, 1973).

BIBLIOGRAPHY

Aharoni Y, Avi-Yonah M: *The Macmillan Bible Atlas.* New York, Macmillan, 1968.
Baron SW: *A Social and Religious History of the Jews,* vols 1 and 2. New York, Columbia University Press, 1952.

Baumbach G: The significance of the Zealots. *Theol Digest* Autumn 1969;17(3):241–246.

Breasted JH: *Development of Religion and Thought in Ancient Egypt.* New York, Harper, 1959.

Cox H: Eastern cults and western culture: Why young Americans are buying oriental religions. *Psychol Today* 1977;11(2):36–40, 42.

Diringer D: A millenium of early Hebrew culture as based on biblical archaeology and epigraphy, in Zimmels HJ, Rabbinowitz J, Finestein I (eds): *Essays Presented to Chief Rabbi Israel Brodie on the Occasion of his Seventieth Birthday.* London, Soncino Press, 1967, pp 67–80.

Doty, WG: *Letters in Primitive Christianity.* Philadelphia, Fortress Press, 1973.

Dubnov S: *History of the Jews,* 16 vols, New York, Thomas Yoseloff, 1967. *Encyclopaedia Judaica:* Jersalem, Keter Publishing House, 1972.

Feldman LH: Masada: A critique of recent scholarship in Neusner J (ed): *Christianity, Judaism and Other Greco-Roman Cults—Part 3, Judaism Before 70.* Leyden, EJ Brill, 1975, pp 218–248.

Festinger L: *A Theory of Cognitive Dissonance.* Stanford, CA, Stanford University Press, 1957.

Finkelstein L: *The Pharisees: The Sociological Background of Their Faith,* 2 vols, ed 3. Philadelphia, Jewish Publication Society of America, 1962.

Galanter M, Rabkin P, Rabkin J, et al: The "Moonies": A psychological study of conversion and membership in a contemporary religious cult. *Am J Psychiatry* 1979;136(2):165–170.

Gibbon E: *The History of the Decline and Fall of the Roman Empire,* 6 vols. Philadelphia, Porter and Coates, 1845.

Gittin (tractate): Babylonian Talmud.

Goldin J (translator): *The Fathers According to Rabbi Nathan.* New Haven, Yale University Press, 1955.

Gordon JS: Religious cults and today's young adults. *Children Today* 1977;6(4):24–27, 36.

Graetz H: *History of the Jews,* 6 vols. Philadelphia, Jewish Publication Society of America, 1956.

Hall CM: *Nicolaus of Damascus' Life of Augustus* (Smith College Classical Studies). Northampton, MA, Collegiate Press, 1923.

Hankoff LD: The psychology of totalism: A case study. *Hillside J Clin Psychiatry* 1979;1(2):207–230.

Heller B: Masada and the Talmud. *Tradition* Winter 1968;10(2):31–34.

Heschel AJ: *The Earth is the Lord's* and *The Sabbath.* New York, Harper and Row, 1966.

Hoenig SB: The Sicarii in Masada—Glory or infamy? *Tradition* Spring 1970;11(1):5–30.

Horsley RA: Josephus and the bandits. *J Study Judaism Persian, Helenistic Roman Period* July 1979;10(1):37–63.

Jaspers K: *The Great Philosophers: The Foundations.* New York, Harcourt, Brace & World, 1962.

Klausner J: *From Jesus to Paul.* Boston, Beacon, 1961.

Kolitz Z: Masada—Suicide or murder? *Tradition* Summer 1971;12(1):5–26.

Lang K, Lang GE: Collective behavior, in *International Encyclopedia of the Social Sciences.* New York, Macmillan, 1968, pp 556–565.

Lifton RJ: *Thought Reform and the Psychology of Totalism: A Study of Brainwashing in China.* New York, WW Norton, 1969.

Michel O: Studien zu Josephus: Simon bar Giora. *New Testament Studies* 1967–1968;14:402–408.

Moehring HR: The "Acta pro Judaeis" in the "Antiquities" of Flavius Josephus: A study in hellenistic and modern apologetic historiography, in Neusner J (ed): *Christianity, Judaism and Other Greco-Roman Cults (Studies for Morton Smith at Sixty),* Part Three, *Judaism Before 70.* Leiden, EJ Brill, 1975, pp 124–158.

Moore GF: *Judaism in the First Centuries of the Christian Era: The Age of the Tannaim,* 3 vols. Cambridge, MA, Harvard University Press, 1966.

Neusner J: *A Life of Yohanan Ben Zakkai.* Leiden, EJ Brill, 1970.

Neusner J: *From Politics to Piety: The Emergence of Pharisaic Judaism*. Englewood Cliffs, NJ, Prentice-Hall, 1973.

Nicholi AM: A new dimension of the youth culture. *AM J Psychiatry* April 1974;131(4): 396–401.

Patai R: *The Messiah Texts*. New York, Avon Books, 1979.

Pines S: *An Arabic Version of the Testimonium Flavianum and Its Implications*. Jerusalem, Israeli Academy of Sciences and Humanities, 1971.

Pritchard JB (ed): *Ancient Near Eastern Texts Relating to the Old Testament*. Princeton University Press, Princton, NJ, 1969.

Radin M: *The Jews Among the Greeks and Romans*. Philadelphia, Jewish Publication Society of America, 1915.

Roman History: (Horace White, translation) Appian, Claudius, Epitome, Flavius Josephus, Pliny, Suetonius, Tacitus. Cambridge, MA, Harvard University Press (Loeb Classical Library), 1968.

Roth C: Simon bar Giora, ancient Jewish hero. *Commentary* 1960;29:52–58.

Schurer E: *A History of the Jewish People in the Time of Jesus*. New York, Schocken, 1961.

Shutt RJH: *Studies in Josephus*. London, S.P.C.K., 1961.

Stern M: Zealots, *Encyclopedia Judaica Year Book 1973*. Jerusalem, Keter, 1973, pp 135–152.

Thackeray H StJ: *Josephus: The Man and the Historian*. New York, Jewish Institute of Religion Press, 1929.

Turner VW: *Dramas, Fields, and Metaphors: Symbolic Action in Human Society*. Ithaca, NY, Cornell University Press, 1974.

Turner VW: *The Ritual Process: Structure and Anti-Structure*. London, Routledge & Kegan Paul, 1969.

Waxman M: *A History of Jewish Literature*, 5 vols. London, Thomas Yoseloff, 1960.

Zeitlin S: The Essenees and messianic expectations. *Jewish Q Rev* 1954;45:83–119.

Zeitlin S: A survey of Jewish historiography: From the biblical books to the "Sefer Ha-Kabbalah" with special emphasis on Josephus. *Jewish Q Rev* 1969;69(3):171–214.

Zeitlin S: *The Rise and Fall of the Judaean State*, vol 1, 332–337 BCE, Philadelphia, Jewish Publication Society of America, 1962.

Modern Cults and Gnosticism:
Some Observations on Religious and Totalitarian Movements

V A N E S S A   W E B E R

M odern cults and Gnosticism are possibly two complementary religious
movements, which are the subjects of increasing attention and controversy.
Recently, several scholars have noted similarities between some of the cults and
Gnosticism. Most of these comparisons have been made on theological grounds
alone, but the issues go beyond questions of theology. In his book *The Gnostic
Religion,* Hans Jonas compares his interest in the work of Heidegger and
Gnosticism and notes

> . . . I was increasingly struck by the familiarity of the seemingly utterly strange.
> In retrospect, I am inclined to believe that it was the thrill of this dimly felt
> affinity which had lured me into the gnostic labyrinth in the first place. Then,
> after long sojourn in those distant lands returning to my own, the contemporary
> philosophic scene, I found that what I had learnt out there made me better
> understand the shore from which I had set out (Jonas, 1963, p 320).

A comparison of Gnostic theology with that of modern cults may provide some
clues about cognitive content and the psychology of cult affiliation.

Gnosticism has been attacked as heretical for almost 2000 years by orthodox
religions. Many modern cults claim they are being attacked for their deviance
from orthodoxy in a manner comparable to the earlier attacks on the Gnostics.
They claim that attacks on them are generated by their adherence to a belief
system with a view of God and reality that does not comply with that of their
critics. Critics of these cults maintain they are not attacking them primarily as
modern heresies, but mainly for their use of mind-control techniques. The question of whether mind-control or brainwashing techniques exist in cults stands independently of critiques of their theology as being heretical. This chapter takes a
new approach. It will examine some similarities between theologies of earlier

31

Gnostic systems and modern cults. It will attempt to examine whether or not the development of a totalist system may not be a readily predictable consequence of the adoption of Gnostic ideology and will examine the patterns of influence justified by such a system and its effect on the actions of its adherents.

At first glance it may appear that these movements have only their opponents in common. However, the early Gnostics were noted for their often elaborate theologies and secret writings, a trait many modern cults share. In his book *Religious and Spiritual Groups in Modern America,* Robert Ellwood, Jr, suggests the following working definition of the modern cult:

> A cult is a group derived from the experience of one or a few individuals who are able to enter (or are fascinated by the possibility of entering) a superior, ecstatic state of consciousness in which contact and rapport with all reaches of a nonhistorical and impersonal universe are possible with the help of in-termediaries (human and/or supernatural). In a cult an outer circle of members experience the presence of the sacred in these individuals, and seek to participate in their experience (Ellwood, 1973, p 19).

Thus, according to Ellwood, "all cults, virtually by definition, contain a strong element of [Gnosticism]" (Ellwood, 1973, p 116).

GNOSTICISM AND NEO-GNOSTICISM DEFINED

Gnosticism is a term that is usually applied to a heterogeneous group of sects that were most active in late antiquity and the early part of the Middle Ages. Gnostic manuscripts found in Nag Hammadi, Egypt, in 1945 have been dated to the third century AD and are copies of even older manuscripts (Pagels, 1979, p xvi). However, modern Gnostic groups exist today such as the Brotherhood of the Pleroma, the Pre-Nicene Catholic Church, the Church of the Gnosis, and others (Ellwood, 1973, p 118).

Gnosticism is more than a matter of theological beliefs. It is a whole nexus of intellectual dispositions, expectations, and attitudes toward man and his place in the world and his relationship to a sometimes unusually defined supreme being. Gnosticism is syncretistic in nature.

> The Gnostic system compounded everything—oriental mythologies, astrological doctrines, Iranian theology, elements of Jewish tradition, whether biblical, rab-binical or occult, Christian salvation—eschatology, Platonic terms and concepts (Jonas, 1963, p 25).

This syncretistic tendency has made Gnosticism difficult to define (almost as difficult to define as modern cults).* Ultimately, various types of Gnosticism emerged; the more dualistic version was influenced by the Iranians and the more monistic was influenced by the Syrian and Alexandrian Gnostics.†

---

*In an article prepared for the *Comprehensive Textbook of Psychiatry III,* Margaret Thaler Singer describes ten different typologies of modern cults. These include: 1) neo-Christian religious cults; 2) Hindu and Eastern religious cults; 3) occult, witchcraft, and satanism cults; 4) spiritualist cults; 5) Zen and other Sino-Japanese philosophical–mystical cults; 6) race cults; 7) flying saucer and outer space cults; 8) psychological cults; 9) political cults; and 10) certain communal and self-help or self-improvement groups that, over time, become transformed into cults (West and Singer, 1980, p 9).
†Dualism: "1) A philosophical doctrine which holds that mind and matter are distinct, equally real and not essentially related . . . . 2) A metaphysical system which holds that good and evil are the outcome or product of separate and equally ultimate first causes" (Cross, 1978, p 428). Monism: "The metaphysical theory that there is but one fundamental reality of which all others are but attributes or modes if they can be said to be real at all" (Harvey, 1964, p 154). Some Gnostic groups believe that evil has evolved out of this first cause.

What then is Gnosticism? The word *Gnosticism* is derived from the Greek word *gnosis,* which means "knowledge." This "knowledge" is not scientific, it is experiential. A Gnostic believes in an experiential knowledge necessary to gain salvation. Arthur Armstrong has suggested that Gnosticism is a belief system holding that there is

> divine saving truth . . . contained in an esoteric revelation only accessible to a chosen few to whom it has been transmitted in secret and mysterious ways, without saying anything about the content of that revelation (Armstrong, 1978, p 88).

These "elite" are chosen by virtue of their exposure to this revelation or by signs that indicate that they should be exposed to this revelation. These signs usually suggest that the individual has "divine" attributes. Those who are chosen are permitted to experience the "gnosis."

Central to Gnostic theology is the idea that man has fallen away from the true, good God who exists beyond this world or cosmos. The theology behind the Gnostic experience attempts to explain how this has occurred, why mankind is here, and how humanity can return to the God Beyond, the God of Light, the Source of the Universe.

The Gnostics believe that man is alien to this world and that this world is controlled by an evil and alien God. This alien God is often seen as the creator of the material realm, the God of the Old Testament. This God is also the God of orthodox Christianity, Judaism, and Islam. Since material creation is controlled by an evil God, matter itself is seen as intrinsically evil or controlled by forces of evil. The rulers and authority figures of this world are often considered the pawns of the alien God.

The purpose of the evil God is to prevent mankind from returning to the God beyond. This is done by keeping the soul from realizing that there *is* a God beyond. According to Gnostic theology, both matter and analytic reason contribute to keeping the soul distracted from this truth. In this sense, the world becomes a trap, ensnaring humanity into a state of perpetual "unconsciousness." Stephen Hoeller, a modern Gnostic and the leader of the Sophia Gnostic Center in Los Angeles, writes:

> Gnosticism may first of all be defined as *mystical religion* . . . . At the root-base of all consciousness there is a transcendental field, named Pleroma or fullness, from which emerge more limited fields of consciousness in series, each with properties revealing the original Principle. This fullness may perhaps be envisioned as identical with Collective Unconscious discovered by C.G. Jung, and the objective and purpose of the efforts of the Gnostic is to establish an effective, conscious contact with this ultimate Source of all Power and Life, which resides constantly at the very back of our consciousness, and is therefore always available. This unobstructed contact can be established only when the dominion of the rulers (demiurgoi, archons) is broken, that is, when man is no longer subject to the attachments and fascinations of the lower worlds of sense perceptions, emotions, and analytical reason, but having transcended the latter, has put on the "vesture of light" and thus accomplished what modern analytical psychology calls total integration, and the mystics of the first Christian centuries called "the divine Gnosis" (Ellwood, 1973, p 119).

For many Gnostics, the dominion of the rulers can be broken only by the transmission of this knowledge by divine messengers. These messengers are also alien to this world and often prepare the way for the ascent of the soul through the various levels of the Pleroma. In the "Hymn of the Pearl," an early Gnostic text in which the recovery of the "Pearl" represents the reuniting of the soul with its divine counterpart, the savior or divine messenger becomes trapped by the world below:

> I (he?) warned him (me?) against the Egyptians and the contact with the unclean ones. Yet I clothed myself in their garments, lest they suspect me as one coming from without to take the Pearl and arouse the serpent against me. But through some cause they marked that I was not their countryman, and they ingratiated themselves with me, and mixed me (drink) with their cunning, and gave me to taste of their meat; and I forgot that I was a king's son and served their king. I forgot the Pearl for which my parents had sent me. Through the heaviness of their nourishment I sank into deep slumber (Jonas, 1963, p 114).

If the savior is successful in his mission to impart the gnosis, the soul can rise through the spheres or levels and return to the God of Light:

> . . . denuded of the effects of the Harmony, (he) enters the nature of the Ogdoas (ie, the eighth sphere, that of the fixed stars), now in the possession of his own power, and with those already there . . . and having become like his companions . . . they rise up towards the Father and give themselves up to the Powers, and having become Powers themselves, enter the Godhead. This is the good end of those who have attained gnosis: to become God (Jonas, 1963, p 153).

Believing themselves to have attained perfection through gnosis, the Gnostics formed elitist groups which were either ascetic or libertine. Each system deals with the issues of perfection and morality differently. The ascetic Gnostics maintain that the world of matter, which is inherently evil, still represents a threat, and so they urge their members to separate from it entirely. This includes the abolition of sex, marriage, procreation, and certain foods. The libertine Gnostics believe that once they achieve perfect unity with God, the Cosmos, controlled by the evil demiurges and archons, can do nothing to them. In fact, libertine Gnostics believe that

> . . . all things are permitted, since the pneuma [spirit] is saved in its nature and can be neither sullied by actions nor frightened by the threat of archontic retribution . . . through the intentional violation of the demiurgical norms the pneumatic thwarts the design of the Archons and paradoxically contributes to the work of salvation (Jonas, 1963, p 46).

Gnostic groups may include elements of both asceticism and libertinism. The attitude upon which libertinism is based is not, as Hans Jonas points out, that far from ancient or modern nihilism.

Recently certain scholars have begun to use the term neo-Gnostic to describe a variety of cults. In *Update*, a periodical which critiques new religious movements, the terms Gnostic and neo-Gnostic are used to describe

> . . . a particular thought system which serves as the lowest common denominator of Hinduism, Buddhism, occultism and other esoteric traditions (*Update*, 1981, p 19).

Mark Albrecht, an editor of *Update,* has suggested that neo-Gnosticism has the following characteristics: "a monistic or pantheistic theology . . . The inference . . . that humanity is Divine. . . A salvation system in which the adept or devotee strives to become experientially one with the Divine [and] syncretism" (*Update,* 1981, p 23).

BRIEF HISTORICAL SURVEY

The history of Gnosticism is complex. By the third century AD, the Roman Empire was beginning to crumble. As it did, people thronged to the worship of new gods imported from the East, such as Mithra, the Persian sun and warrior god, and the Egyptian goddess Isis.*

The cults that formed around the worship of these gods, and had originated in the Hellenistic period, were mystery cults. They were distinct from earlier Greco-Roman cults, which had specific functions to perform within the society, such as healing. The mystery cults were different in that they promised salvation. In order to become "saved" in these cults, individuals would often undergo a purification ritual and then be expected to rise in a hierarchical fashion within the group.†

Several scholars of Gnosticism, including Elaine Pagels and E. Conze have suggested that Gnostic views have their roots in Hinduism and Buddhism (Pagels, 1979, p xxi). Pagels points out that the Buddhists were in touch with early Christians; that trade routes between the Far East and the Greco-Roman world were opening up during this period and that Roman Christians, such as Hippolytus, were aware of Brahmins who believed that God was "gnosis" (Pagels, 1979, p xxi).

With the rise of Oriental mysticism, attempts were made to unify these different belief systems into a cohesive whole. This was accomplished with varying degrees of success. Often, groups would form around one who had been the disciple of an earlier Gnostic teacher. At first, members might draw lots and, according to the lot drawn, would be designated a "priest," a "bishop," or a "prophet" (Pagels, 1979, p 41). At each meeting, the members would draw their lots anew. As Pagels points out, this procedure prevented some degree of envy among the membership (Pagels, 1979, p 43). However, it was not uncommon for the same individuals to regard their teacher as their divine messenger, a situation which later seems to have lent itself to increasingly hierarchical structures.

One of the earliest Gnostic teachers was Simon Magus.‡ According to orthodox tradition, he was regarded as the "father of all heresy" (Jonas, 1963, p 103). Magus (the word means magician) was considered to be "God," "the son of God," or a "divine Spirit" (Jonas, 1963, p 104). According to Simonian teaching, Jesus was the "precursory incarnation of Simon himself" (Jonas, 1963, p 103).

Simon Magus wandered around the Roman world as a self-proclaimed prophet and messiah, accompanied by Helena, a woman whom he claimed to have "saved" from a brothel in Tyre. Simon Magus believed that Helena was "the latest and

---

*The gods and goddesses of these cults should be distinguished from earlier variations of the deities. Isis, for instance, traditionally represented the wife of Osiris in Egyptian mythology. By this time, she was considered "queen of heaven and hell, of earth and sea, she was 'the past, the present and the future' . . . a pantheistic power that was everything in one" (Cumont, 1956, p 89).
†The followers of Mithra, for instance, could rise in successive order through the following ranks: Raven, Bride, Soldier, Lion, Persian, Courier of the Sun, and Father (Vermaseren, 1963, p 138).
‡Different traditions mention a Simon Magus. These include Acts 8:9–24. He may have been a native of Gitta in Samaria. Later writers claimed that he went to Rome during the rule of Claudius (41–54 AD), but he may have lived during the second century AD (Cross, 1978, p 1277).

lowliest incarnation of the fallen 'Thought' of God, redeemed by him and a means of redemption for all who believed in them both" (Jonas, 1963, p 104). Hans Jonas and others have suggested that Helena provides the model for Helen in the Faust legend. Others include stories about Simon Magus' death while attempting to fly to "God, whose power I am" (Jonas, 1963, p 111).

Later Gnostic groups included the Manichaeans. The Manichaeans were ascetic Gnostics who adopted various teachings. These included those of Mani, a Zoroastrian dualist, and Marcion, whose dualistic church later found itself the repository of many Gnostic ideas* (Runciman, 1961, p 8). The Manichaeans copied the organizational structure of Mani.

> The Manichaeans were divided into two classes, initiates and ordinary believers, monks and laity, or, as Mani called them, Elect and Hearers. . . . The Elect was the only true Manichaean, so receptive of the Light that the very food that he ate left by a process of metabolism its imprisoned Light in his body. The Hearers, who formed the bulk of the church, were strictly speaking only adherents or catechumens. . . . Above all they must see to every need of the Elect, devoting their alms to him, ensuring that he is properly fed and clothed—the giving of alms to the non-Manichaean was without merit and might indeed even be harmful, hindering the liberation of the Light (Runciman, 1961, p 16).

Although the Manichaeans were suppressed for the most part by the sixth century,† their teachings would reemerge in other groups from time to time.‡

Several authors have traced Gnosticism into the modern period. During the nineteenth and into the early part of the twentieth centuries, teachers such as George Ivanovitch Gurdjieff and Madame Petrovna Blavatsky attracted sizable followings. Gurdjieff, a Russian, believed that "he himself was a source of higher energy from which his disciples could draw" (Sklar, 1977, p 64). Blavatsky, an expatriate Russian, founded the Theosophical Society in New York in 1875. Theosophy combined aspects of Hinduism, Gnosticism, and pseudoscience (Sklar, 1977, p 11). The teachings of both were popular in Europe and the United States, and their schools still attract students. Another teacher during this period was Aleister Crowley. Crowley was well known as a "magician" and for his involvement with the world of the occult, such as the Ordo Templi Orientis (OTO). His title in the OTO was at one point *King of Ireland, Iona and all Britains within the Sanctuary of the Gnosis* (Kind, 1971, p 103). Much of Crowley's teachings have been incorporated into several of today's satanism cults.§

Robert Ellwood has suggested that there have been three groups of sects and cults in the United States since the early 1900s. The first group, which formed

---

*Marcion's theology did not include the notion that man had been separated from the God beyond and thus did not claim that man possessed a "Divine Spark." In this sense Marcion was not a true Gnostic. Early Marcionite dualism included the opposition, not of good and evil but justice and mercy, cruelty and love. By the third century, "the just God was becoming . . . the wicked God. The Kind Stranger was now ranged against, and Satan was the creator of the world" (Runciman, 1961, p 10).

†The Mandaeans (also known as the Nasoreans and Christians of St. John), are the closest and most directly related to the Manichaeans of any extant group. They originated in the first and second centuries east of the Jordan and can still be found south of Baghdad (Cross, 1978, p 863).

‡For further reading on Manichaean offshoots see: *The Medieval Manichee* by Steven Runciman, The Viking Press, New York, 1961.

§Scientology's founder, L. Ron Hubbard, has been said to have borrowed from Crowley's work although Scientology has denied this. It is clear however, that Hubbard knew Jack Parsons, one of Crowley's disciples. For discussions of this argument see: *The Road to Total Freedom,* by Roy Wallis, Columbia University Press, 1977, pp 111, 112, and *Update,* 1979, pp 65–66.

before the First World War, included Theosophy, New Thought, Spiritualism, and Vedanta and placed a "heavy emphasis on verbal communication" (Ellwood, 1973, p 82). The second group, which emerged between the wars, included syncretistic groups which were "usually centered on flamboyant, charismatic personalities (Ellwood, 1973, p 82). These included groups such as: "Self-Realization, the Krishnamurti enthusiasm in Theosophy, 'I Am,' (a possible forerunner of today's Church Universal and Triumphant, formerly known as The Summit Lighthouse) and the Meher Baba movement" (Ellwood, 1973, p 82). The third group emerged after the Second World War and became particularly prominent in the late sixties. According to Ellwood, this group seemed more interested in outwardly expressing alienation from society than conformity with it. In some ways, the more bizarre the group was, the more attractive it seemed at first.

Groups like The Process seem to exemplify the trend from the alienation of the sixties into the seeming conformity of the seventies and early eighties. The Process began in the mid-sixties as Compulsions Analysis, an offshoot of Scientology, in London. Its founders, Mary Anne and Robert de Grimstone were often referred to as "God" and the "Goddess" (Evans, 1973, p 119). The group soon became known as The Church of the Final Judgment. The Church worshipped Satan, Lucifer, and Jehovah, who represented lust, enjoyment, and duty, respectively. The members believed that Christ was a divine emissary and it was suggested that Robert was Christ. De Grimstone claimed that salvation was possible through the unity of Christ and Satan, both representing two opposite poles, the "white" and the "black." Anything that did not fit into one of these extreme categories was considered "grey" and prevented the unity of these opposites. Members of The Process originally wore impressive black uniforms, the Cross of Christ and the Goat of Satan on their chests (Bainbridge, 1978, p 125). This was tolerated by a curious public until the group was accused of having influenced Charles Manson.* Although this was disproved in court, it forced the church to change its outward appearance in order to recruit new members. Today, the group is known as The Foundation Faith of God, ostensibly a "Christian" group which promotes antivivisectionism. The group is currently led by Mary Anne, one of the few women cult leaders. Robert de Grimstone is no longer active as a cult leader.

"Destructive" Cults

By the early seventies, a new word was being used to describe some of the cults. The word was "destructive," and it was being used by a growing number of parents, mental health professionals, and ex-cult members to describe groups which seemed to produce a drastic and sudden personality change within their members. This change was characterized by the new recruit's often total and sudden denial of his past, his family, and his friends. The cult member frequently seemed evasive about what the group was or mumbled stock phrases such as "you'll have to experience it, it can't be explained." Many cult members turned over enormous amounts of money to the cult, spent all their time with the group, and often worked for it 20 hours a day with little or no remuneration. As a result

---

*This was not the first time The Process had met resistance, but it was the most damaging. There were some similarities between the theology of The Process and Manson's teachings. This is probably because both the de Grimstones and Manson had studied Scientology. For further information on The Process, see *Satan's Power, A Deviant Psychotherapy Cult,* by William Bainbridge, University of California Press, 1978.

of the dramatic shifts that accompanied the conversions of their usually intelligent, well-educated children, parents sought for explanations of how this could have happened. One conclusion was that their children had been "brainwashed" like the Korean prisoners of war.

A close look at the model most often used to define "brainwashing," ie, Robert J. Lifton's *Thought Reform ar.d The Psychology of Totalism, A Study of Brainwashing in China,* Chapter 22, reveals some striking similarities between the ideology that underlies these techniques and Gnostic theology. Lifton describes techniques of "brainwashing" under the headings of eight psychological themes. In each of these themes can be seen the glimmer of a Gnostic base.

The first theme is "milieu control." According to Lifton, since the leaders of the totalist environment believe that they have the "truth," they believe that they have the exclusive right to do anything to preserve this "truth." This includes the full control of both internal and external communication; all that the individual "sees and hears, reads and writes, experiences and expresses" (Lifton, 1963, p 420). When the individual tires of trying to sort out the ambiguities of this structured reality, he accepts the one he is in: that of his controllers.

The Gnostic believes that through the experience of "gnosis," he has been reunited with and is one with the God Beyond. To the Gnostic, the "truth" is that he is an alien on this planet. All material and human elements, such as reason, sensation, and emotion, are under the control of the evil Creator God. The leader of a Gnostic group might well feel justified in doing anything to preserve this "truth" from the forces of evil. As mentioned earlier, the Manichaeans believed that even giving alms to the non-Manichaean might hinder the liberation of the Light. The prohibition against non-Manichaeans might be considered control of external communication.

Lifton's second theme is "mystical manipulation." By this he means those activities done in the name of a group whose members see themselves as the vanguard of "some imminent law of social development" (Lifton, 1963, p 422). The activities themselves, although planned by the leaders, seem spontaneous to the members and thus more "mystical." Each such experience is interpreted as "proof" of the group's possession of the "truth." Any questioning of this experience is considered to be "stimulated by a lower purpose, to be backward, selfish, and petty in the face of the great overriding mission (Lifton, 1963, p 422).

One technique which produces "mystical experiences" is the constant use of mind-altering techniques. These include hypnosis, chanting, praying, glossalalia (speaking in tongues), and other repetitive activities. These techniques prevent analytical thought, which, as Stephen Hoeller points out, must be broken in order for the Gnostic to experience "total integration." This is another term for "gnosis," the experience of being one with the God Beyond. In order to become part of the Gnostic elite, some teachers instructed their students in praying and chanting sacred words and vowels. Pagels, citing *The Discourse on the Eighth and Ninth,* a Gnostic text, mentions a teacher who, after chanting, goes into an ecsatic state. During this state he says, "I have found the beginning of the power that is above all powers, the one that has no beginning . . . I have said, O my son, that I am Mind. I have seen! Language is not able to reveal this" (Pagels, 1979, p 137). The student then responds, "Let not my soul be deprived of the great divine vision. For everything is possible for you as master of the universe" (Pagels, 1979, p 137).

The third theme is "the demand for purity." This demand dictates that the world be divided into the absolutely pure and the absolutely impure, good and evil. According to Lifton, this demand creates an atmosphere in which the inability to achieve utter perfection results in guilt and shame.

The Gnostics are dualists, caught between the good God of Light and the evil Creator God. Since to be human is to have feelings and since these sensations are governed by the Creator God, to have emotions is an indication of one's worldliness.

The "cult of confession," the fourth theme, is closely related to the third. By experiencing the guilt and shame produced by the group for not attaining "perfection," the individual may feel the need to confess to further failures as an indication of his "willingness" to purify himself. In doing so, the individual gives up the right to mental privacy; "private ownership of the mind and its products— of imagination or of memory—become highly immoral" (Lifton, 1963, p 426). This produces a sense of "oneness" with the others who confess that Lifton has described as "orgiastic" (Lifton, 1963, p 426).

At the base of the Gnostic experience is the concept that there is no mind distinct from the self. Those who have experienced "gnosis" are an elite core who see themselves as gods together, as is illustrated in the example of the savior earlier. The God of Light cannot keep any secrets from the God of Light, but must keep them from the god of this world, the Creator God, if the mission to impart the gnosis is to be successful. This is also illustrated earlier in the "Hymn of the Pearl." Thus to keep personal secrets or privacy within the group might have been considered evil by the Gnostics, although we do not have any direct evidence of this.

The fifth theme is the "sacred science." According to Lifton, "The totalist milieu maintains an aura of sacredness around its basic dogma, holding it out as an ultimate moral vision for the ordering of human existence" (Lifton, 1963, p 427).

Underlying this is the belief that

> . . . man's *ideas* can be God: that an absolute science of ideas (and implicitly, an absolute science of man) exists, or is at least very close to being attained; that this science can be combined with an equally absolute body of moral principles; and that the resulting doctrine is true for all men at all times (Lifton, 1963, p 428).

Underlying Gnostic ideology is the belief that mankind has fallen away from the God of Light and is "alien" to this world. This world appears to be governed by rules of science which, in the Gnostic mind, are actually laws created by the evil Creator God. The Creator God's henchmen, the archons or rulers of this world, wish to prevent the soul from reuniting with the God of Light. This is done by altering history and the "true" principles of science. Some Gnostics, such as the Cainites, believed that the "alien" Cain was really a "pneumatic symbol and an honored position in the line leading to Christ" (Jonas, 1963, p 95). By interpreting the Old Testament in such a fashion, the Cainites turned it "upside down," creating an historical and scientific view of the world which could not be countered by traditional arguments. These were considered further examples of the Creator God's attempts to control the understanding of history. The ultimate Gnostic moral vision was thus anything which reversed anything orthodox.

"Loading the language," the sixth theme, reflects the tendency to speak in which Lifton calls, "the thought terminating cliche" (Lifton, 1963, p 429). These terms tend to be "ultimate terms," either "god terms," representatives of ultimate good; or "devil terms," representative of ultimate evil (Lifton, 1963, p 429). To use other terms denies the identity of the group's common experience and mind. The individual exposed to this use of language will use it even more strongly to express his "conformity" with the group when challenged.

The Gnostic religion is filled with examples of ultimate terms and imagery. Much of it is dreamlike, and yet it has a quality about it that seems almost real. Like the savior's quest in the "Hymn of the Pearl," the individual is confronted with the ultimate search in opposition to the ultimate threat, to reach the pearl and bypass the serpent. As pointed out already, in some cases the Gnostics used imagery which was radically different from orthodoxy, thus to embrace the imagery of the non-Gnostic was in itself an act which polarized the good and the evil. The embracing of a Gnostic interpretation was thus seen as an acceptance of the "truth" which the Gnostic possessed.*

Lifton's final themes are "the doctrine over person," and "the dispensing of existence." The core of the "doctrine" is that the beliefs of the group overrule any experiences with which it conflicts. This includes records of historical events as well as personal testimony. Many Gnostics believe that since the "divine spark" was encased within the soul, hidden and suppressed by the evil forces of the cosmos, that the "cosmic man" was thus prevented from recognizing the truth. Any attitude or experience which differed from this was perceived as directed by evil forces, usually orthodox Christianity or Judaism. To the Gnostic, orthodox theology was not an expression of individual experience or understanding of the Bible, but imposed on the member by the archons, the leaders of the orthodox Church. The "dispensing of existence" revolves around the idea that those who exist outside the totalist milieu do not truly exist at all. Only within the milieu which contains the "truth" can individuals be acknowledged as beings.

To most Gnostics, material reality is either a threat or an illusion. The body, for instance, might be seen as that which prevents the soul from escaping to its true far-off home, the God of Light. Since material reality is governed by the Creator God, the Gnostic rejects that which is considered "material," and all the images that surround it. This may mean rejection of the body, both in the group and outside of the group.

Some Gnostic groups, including the Cathars, denied the needs of the material body as much as it was possible to do. The Cathars were divided into the Believers and the Perfects. In order to become a Perfect, the Believer would have to accept physical denial which rivals that of any orthodox tradition. The Perfects meanwhile might engage in the *Endura*, the committing of suicide by self-starvation in order to escape the evil world of the Creator: "The whole process was undertaken with the observance of a ritual, and the actual deathbed was the scene of rejoicing amongst the sectaries, the dying man or woman being regarded with deep reverential admiration" (Runciman, 1961, p 159). Although this was not common, the "suicide was performed by more rapid means, by poison or the opening of veins" (Runciman, 1961, p 159).

An increasing number of cults are being called "destructive." Most of these seem to have Gnostic elements in their theologies and practices. Virtually all of the so-

---

*If, in fact, praying and chanting were used in great amounts to produce the ecstatic visions mentioned earlier, it is possible that this produced an altered state of consciousness in which everything seemed real and ultimate. For further reading on this see *Snapping*, by Flo Conway and Jim Siegelman, the works of Milton Erikson on the subject of hypnosis and classic texts on brainwashing such as *Battle for the Mind*, by William Sargant.

called "destructive" cults are controlled by leaders who claim that they are divine. Although much of the Gnostic theology is not immediately apparent (in fact, destructive cults are often accused of hiding their true purpose, not surprising in view of the Gnostic attitude), various suggestions are given out to the recruit that the cult has a secret that is only accessible to him if he is "ready" for the experience. Playing on fears that we all have of not being "grown up," the cult appeals to our "patience" (as opposed to childish impatience) and persuades us to be led further and further into the Gnostic system. Once deeply entranced in the system, the recruit suddenly "sees" what is meant and interprets all his past confusion in light of this "revelation." The cultist is now thinking in totalitarian terms.

The Divine Light Mission is a cult which has received much criticism. Founded by Guru Maharaj Ji in 1972, when the Guru was 15 years old, the group promises "knowledge" to its members or "Premies." This "knowledge" consists of the "ultimate understanding of the Source of all life" (Who is Guru Maharaj Ji?, 1973, p xi). In order to attain this "knowledge," one is expected to experience the Divine Light, Music, Nectar, and the Word. The Divine Light is described as "sun which is within ourselves which is much brighter than the sun you see in the sky. When the sun comes out, it only dispels the darkness, but when this sun comes out, it dispels the darkness and ignorance both" (Who is Guru Maharaj Ji?, 1973, p 20).

The Music is described as "the sound of life moving through otherwise lifeless matter . . . analogous to the light in that it is an interior sound which is not perceived through the ears (physical sensation)" (Who is Guru Maharaj Ji?, 1973, pp 21, 22).

The Nectar is "purifying fluid from the brain, which flows to the throat" (Who is Guru Maharaj Ji?, 1973, p 22), and the Word is described as "the primordial vibration that underlies everything in existence. . . . It is not a word we can speak. . . . This one Word is the one reality, the illogical yet undeniable 'first cause' of the universe. The universe itself" (Who is Guru Maharaj Ji?, 1973, p 23).

Guru Maharaj Ji is considered God by his followers. Former members have claimed that the techniques mentioned above are actually subtle hypnotic devices which aid the Premie in his or her belief of the guru's divinity. Critics say that the Divine Light can be experienced by pushing the finger against the closed eyelid; the Music by putting fingers in the ears—producing an internal echo chamber; the Nectar, they claim is actually postnasal drip. The Word, it appears, is experienced during meditation when all outside stimuli are cut off from the working mechanisms of the brain.

Today, the Divine Light Mission, like so many groups, has gone "undergound." It no longer calls itself the Divine Light Mission but has given its centers names such as The Bay Area Community (personal communication, former member of the Divine Light Mission).

Another group, the Unification Church, has also received its share of bad publicity. Founded by Sun Myung Moon in Korea, the group claims that Moon is the messiah who has come to finish Jesus' mission on earth, to restore the physical aspects of the world to its rightful owner, God. According to Moon, Jesus was able to redeem mankind on the spiritual level but was unsuccessful on the physical level. Because mankind had not been redeemed physically, he was not in a position of being in "Direct Dominion." According to one former member:

Direct Dominion means that mankind has an unobstructed connection with God. It is a kind of mystical union although it also happens while a person has a body. This is after the person has grown fully to perfection and a step beyond that. That's where Moon is right now. . . . It means that God has direct dominion over your life. Whatever God wills is automatically absorbed by you in your will as a desire. There's a distinction. . . . Persons aren't absorbed into God like a drop into the ocean, nonetheless there's a certain dissolving of separateness that is somewhat ambiguous (Gary Scharff, personal communication, 1982).

Members of the Unification Church are told that Satan deceived Eve into having intercourse and thus caused the "Fall of Man" when she mated with Adam. This broke the process of attaining Direct Dominion with God. In order to restore this, the individual must grow to a state of perfection, at which point one marries and has perfect children. Until one reaches that level, one is considered the "dwelling place of Satan" (Divine Principle, 1977, p 102). In fact, citing John 12:31, the Unification Church calls Satan "the ruler of this world" (Divine Principle, 1977, p 103). Since evil in the world is explained as resulting from the cutting off of the direct relationship to God, ie, Direct Dominion, those who do not believe in God (ie, atheists and communists) are considered agents of Satan, as is anyone who goes against the movement.

Finally, there is Scientology. Founded in the late fifties, L. Ron Hubbard, the creator of Scientology claimed that one could become "clear" of all difficulties through a process he called Dianetic auditing. This "auditing" is done with an E-meter, a machine which is like a lie detector and which measures bodily changes in response to stress. The purpose of auditing is to clear oneself of all reactions to any questions which might indicate the presence of an "engram," roughly translated as any block which prevents the individual from achieving perfection.

Perfection, as Scientology understands it, is to be God. The purpose of auditing is to show the recruit why he is a God. The following is a description of Scientology's myth of the God-Game and the Thetans:

> For those interested, the real secret of the universe is as follows. In the beginning are the Thetans. These are omnipotent, indestructible beings who suffer from being immortal. The reason they suffer is because immortality, when one has nothing to do, becomes intolerably boring. There are, it is true, other Thetans about, but since they too do nothing it's just as boring as if there were only one. Now in order to help while away eternity they decided to play some games. These consist, in the first instance, of creating universes of one kind and another, and playing with them. The games could be of any kind . . . . After a while this too becomes boring, and the Thetans realize that their omnipotence and omniscience is the real trouble. . . with a master stroke. . . they decide voluntarily to handicap themselves, limiting their powers and cutting down on their range of knowledge. . . the game becomes more interesting. . . . The Thetans enter into it with greater enthusiasm. Then. . . something begins to happen.

> Slowly but surely. . . the lures of the universe they have created out of matter, energy, space and time (MEST) begin to snare them. They become more and more immersed in the game, less and less concerned about their true status as Thetans. Slowly. . . they become more hopelessly trapped in the material universe, reaching their present state. . . many millions of years ago. . . . Nowadays the Thetans have forgotten what they really are, and go around thinking they are bodies. They have even forgotten that they are playing a game at all! (Evans, 1973, pp 43–44).

The Divine Light Mission provides us with an example of how an Eastern cult experience incorporates the Gnostic. The Unification Church provides us with an example of Gnostic dualism, and Scientology, a therapy cult, offers us a sample of a Gnostic myth which defines man as God and explains the underlying purpose of the techniques used: to "clear" the individual of the blocks which prevent him from realizing this truth.

Gnosticism inherently denies the existence of human limits. This is an appealing idea, especially to those who are under stress and living in a society whose social support networks are breaking down. Gnosticism's message is that even if the individual feels alien, he is really God and limitless. Most critics claim that recruits are most vulnerable during transitional phases in their lives: from high school to college, after a death in the family, a break-up, a loss, a move, or a career change. It is during these times that people find themselves feeling "alien," and altogether human, however "normal" and intelligent they are. It is during these times that individuals want to put aside their critical abilities in favor of the reduction of stress. To unconsciously want to reduce stress is not the same as choosing to become enmeshed in a Gnostic or totalitarian system, a point that many people seem to have difficulty in seeing. As several ex-cult members have said: "I never made a decision to join, I just never made the decision to leave."

Although not all Gnostic groups become totalitarian, the history of these movements seems to suggest that groups with a Gnostic base lend themselves to becoming totalitarian movements. Dusty Sklar has nicely pointed out the Gnostic roots of the Nazis, for instance. Further, as Elaine Pagels notes, there is a tendency for the Gnostic to equate self-knowledge as the knowledge of God. For this reason, certain new therapeutic movements seem heavily influenced by Gnostic concepts; it is perhaps these that must be watched most closely in the future.

It is clear that we are only just beginning to understand the phenomenon of cults and cult involvement, but as Hans Jonas said about Gnostic nihilism:

> The extended discourse with ancient nihilism proved—to me at least—a help in discerning and placing the meaning of modern nihilism: just as the latter had initially equipped me for spotting its obscure cousin in the past (Jonas, 1963, p 320).

Or, as Jim Jones, quoting Santayana, used to say: "Those who cannot remember the past are condemned to repeat it."

BIBLIOGRAPHY

Armstrong AH: Gnosis and Greek Philosophy, in Aland B, et al (eds): *Gnosis: Festschrift fuer Hans Jonas*. Gottingen, Vandenhoch & Ruprecht, 1978, p 88.

Bainbridge WS: *Satan's Power: A Deviant Psychotherapy Cult*. Los Angeles, University of California Press, 1978.

Conway F, Siegelman J: *Snapping: America's Epidemic of Sudden Personality Change*. New York, Dell/Delta Books, 1979.

Cross FL (ed): *Oxford Dictionary of the Christian Church*. Oxford, Oxford University Press, 1978.

Cumont F: *Oriental Religions in Roman Paganism*. New York, Dover Publications, 1956.

Divine Principle. New York, The Holy Spirit Association for the Unification of World Christianity, 1977.

Ellwood RS Jr: *Religious and Spiritual Groups in Modern America*. Englewood Cliffs, NJ, Prentice-Hall, 1973.

Evans C: *Cults of Unreason*. New York, Dell, 1973.

Harvey VA: *A Handbook of Theological Terms*. New York, Macmillan, 1964.

Jonas H: *The Gnostic Religion*. Boston, Beacon Press, 1963.

King F: *Sexuality, Magic and Perversion*. Secaucus, NJ, The Citadel Press, 1971.

Lifton RJ: *Thought Reform and the Psychology of Totalism: A Study of 'Brainwashing' in China*. New York, WW Norton, 1963.

Pagels E: *The Gnostic Gospels*. New York, Random House, 1979.

Runciman S: *The Medieval Manichee: A Study of the Christian Dualist Heresy*. New York, Viking Press, 1961.

Sargant W: *Battle For the Mind; A Physiology of Conversion and Brain-washing*. New York, Doubleday, 1957.

Sklar D: *Gods and Beasts: The Nazis and the Occult*. New York, Thomas Y. Crowell, 1977.

Update: New Religious Movements (periodical). Published by Dialogue Center, Katrinebjergvej 52, DK-8200 Arhus N. Denmark. Johannes Aagaard, (ed), vol 3, issue 3/4, Dec 1979; vol 5, issue 3/4, Dec 1981.

Vermaseren MJ: *Mithras, The Secret God*. London, Chatto & Windus, 1963.

Wallis R: *The Road to Total Freedom: A Sociological Analysis of Scientology*. New York, Columbia University Press, 1977.

West LJ, Singer MT: Cults, quacks, and nonprofessional psychotherapies, in Kaplan H, Freedman AM, Sadock BJ (eds): *Comprehensive Textbook of Psychiatry*, vol 3. Baltimore, Williams & Wilkins, 1980.

Who is Guru Maharaj Ji? New York, Bantam Books, 1973.

3

The Albigensian Cathari

J. LEE SHNEIDMAN
CONALEE LEVINE-SHNEIDMAN

T he Albigensian Cathari perception could be summarized by the statement "Satan created the world and everything therein."

The attitudes of the Albigensians, who lived in southern France, were a defense against the anxieties of the changing world of their period. The faster the mutations, the greater the anxiety and the less able were they to perceive rational solutions to real problems. The inability to deal with reality forced an accelerated pathology which culminated in a complete denial and rejection of reality and, finally, in the physical destruction of the organized system known as Albigensian Catharism (Fine, 1975, p 54; Fried and Agassi, 1976, p 61).

An explanation of Albigensian Catharism requires a brief overview of political and theological developments within the area.

Southern France had maintained a vague continuity with the ancient Roman civilization until about 700 AD. During the following century, bands of Muslims and Franks sought mastery of the area. By 800 AD the Christian Franks had crossed the Pyrenees and advanced toward the Ebro River. For various reasons the Frankish ruler, Charlemagne, divided the land south of the Loire into three major sections: Aquitaine, Septimania, and the Spanish March.

Despite being a battle ground, the area between the Loire and the Pyrenees manifested some of its former Roman heritage. Conquered, but not absorbed by the Germanic Franks, the Aquitanians and their neighbors in Septimania and along the Mediterranean littoral remained closer to their Roman culture than to the conquerors from the north.

Charlemagne's empire began to collapse before he died. By 813 AD Frankland was being attacked by Vikings, while the Muslims forced the Franks to retreat from the Ebro (Shneidman, 1970, vol 1, pp 162, 170).

Religious developments within the area initially followed a standard Roman model. By 200 AD, Roman, Greek, and Celtic paganism, Jewish and Christian monotheism, and Eastern Zoroastrian dualism flourished. Gallic troops, returning from the constant wars with the Persian Empire, carried west a version of Zoroastrianism called Manicheanism, named after the priest Mani, executed by Shah Sapor II in 276 (Daniel-Rops, 1963, vol 2, p 258). During the fifth century, the Germanic Visigoths entered the region, first as invaders and then as Roman allies. The Visigoths, as had many of the Germanic tribes, had been converted to Christianity by the followers of the Alexandrian bishop Arias, who denied the coequality of God and Christ.

Roman Imperial authority was but the specter that legitimatized the actions of the petty Germanic tribal kings. The Arian Visigoths ruled Iberia and Gaul south of the Loire; the Arian Ostrogoths dominated Italy and Gaul east of the Rhone (Provence); the pagan Franks held power north of the Loire to the Rhine. By 500 AD, however, Trinitarian Christianity had triumphed among the indigenous Romanized population. Some Manicheans, who were condemned by the Iberian Council of Braga in 563 (Niel, 1970, p 45), Jews, pagans and other non-Christians remained, but the primary religious conflict was between the Roman Christian Trinitarians and the Germanic Arian Christians.

Clovis, king of the Franks, capitalized upon the Trinitarian majority by converting to Trinitarianism in order to utilize the local population as a "fifth column" against his Gothic Arian foes. In 507 the Franks defeated the Visigoths and seized all Gaul north of the Pyrenees. Theoderic, the Ostrogothic sovereign who became the protector of the Visigoths, forced the Franks to return Septimania to the Visigoths.

During the sixth and seventh centuries Trinitarian Christianity continued to progress. Ostrogothic Italy and southeastern Iberia were reconquered by Trinitarian Romans from Constantinople. Rekkred, the Visigothic king of Iberia, realizing that the only hope he had of establishing a stable state was to unite the Trinitarians and Arians, converted to Trinitarianism. While pockets of Judaism, Arianism, Manicheanism and, perhaps, paganism remained, Trinitarian Christianity dominated western continental Europe.

The triumph of Trinitarian Christian monotheism was not accomplished without internal conflicts. All monotheism must deal with the problem of evil (Niel, 1970, p 11). If the monotheistic deity were all powerful and good, which he must be, then how is one to account for the existence of evil? One solution requires postulating and then denying a sadistic deity: The deity created evil to tempt the free soul of humans so that the deity could punish the humans for transgression and thus convince them of the wisdom of following the edicts of the almighty. Humans accepted the just punishment without noticing the sadism. The punishment became legitimate without comprehending the etiology of the seduction.

The contradictory nature of the deity created confusion among some who accepted the principles of Christ. To explain the dichotomy, a dualistic theory was advanced by people called Gnostics. To them, Christ was the true deity, while the Jehovah of the Old Testament was an evil manifestation. Although the Gnostics were effectively defeated as an organized force by the Trinitarians, Gnostic thought remained and would feed into the residue of Manicheanism (Warner, 1967, vol 1, p 16).

The spread of Islam during the period 632–733, while presenting a third monotheistic alternative, did nothing to destroy the dualistic pockets. Along the Christian–Islamic frontier, Christianity had to deal with ideologies which questioned the nature of Christ: Adoptionism in the West, and Monophysitism in the East.

Christianity, unlike Judaism and Islam, had to rationalize a deity who took a specific human form. The competitors either denied the realty of that form (Jews), or relegated the form to the status of prophet (Islam). The Trinitarian Christians had to defend the unique nature of Christ against the charges leveled by Arians, Luciferians, Adoptionists, and Monophysites. Trinitarians defeated each of the extremist ideologies, but unorthodox concepts remained and each successive reinterpretation of Christ's nature borrowed from a previously rejected alternative.

Trinitarianism had another problem which distinguished it from its monotheistic competition. St. Paul, in bypassing Orthodox Jews, had opened Christianity to Greek Gentiles who brought to the religion the philosophical concepts of their world. For our purposes, the most significant portion of that addendum was Plato's postulation that reality was the incorporeal thought rather than the visible manifestation.

In the initial stages of Christianity there was the belief that the Second Coming of Christ was imminent. Life on earth was but a testing to determine the permanent residence of the soul. Death was not to be feared, but to be welcomed with joy once it was certain that the everlasting soul would enter heaven. The primacy of the soul over the body was fundamental to Christianity in all its manifestations. The delay in the Second Coming in no way reduced the preeminence of the soul. Abbot Odo of Cluny, a Trinitarian who died in 942, had joyfully announced the death of his infant nephew three days after baptism (Morris, 1973, p 30).

An ideology that attempted to accommodate various monotheistic and dualist theologies was a Christianized version of Manicheanism called Catharism. The word *cathar* is of uncertain origin. It may have originated from the Hebrew *kether*, meaning crown, which, when transliterated into Greek contained the letters "chi" and "rho," or *Xp*, which became the Greek and Latin shorthand symbol for Christ (d'Ares, 1972, p 2). The word may also have originated with the Greek word *katharos*, the pure (Warner, 1967, vol 1, p 16).

Zoroastrianism had postulated a struggle between two coequal gods: Ahura Mazda (good) and Ahriman (evil) (Lea, 1955, vol 1, p 91). Mani had accepted this formula but elaborated upon it by stressing Mithra, son of Mazda, to whom were appended Christ-like attributes. Some non-Trinitarian Christians reversed the process by Mithraicizing Christ. In some versions of the non-Trinitarian beliefs Jehovah became Ahura Mazda, while Satan was Ahriman. Gnostics, for example, viewed Satan as a coequal god and not as a fallen angel (Sumption, 1978, p 33). Under Mani's indirect influence, the Gnostics viewed the Old Testament as having been written by Satan, and, therefore, invalid. To them, the God of the Old Testament was a liar and a murderer (Warner, 1967, vol 1, p 51) because of his sadistic activities. Jehovah of the Old Testament became Satan, while Christ of the New Testament became the true Jehovah. It was Satan who had created the physical church, established rules, regulations, symbols, and saints. It was Satan who had invented tales of the virgin birth, infant baptism, crucifixion, and resurrection (Wakefield, 1974, p 28; Madaule, 1967, p 35). Satan had also developed the fantasy of Hell and Purgatory (Sumption, 1978, p 52). It was Satan who had created the clay body of man to imprison the soul (Strayer, 1971, p 28).

To the Cathars, as to Plato, the corporeal world was unreal. "In principio erat verbium," was taken literally to mean that the original world was first an incorporeal "word" or "idea" which was then sullied by an evil agency (Nelli, 1975, p 16). Only that which was incorporeal was valid. Christ, as the true Jehovah, therefore, never existed in flesh; he only appeared to do so (Daniel-Rops, 1963, vol 2, p 290). Both Christ and Mary were illusions who came to earth to tell the truth and free man from the material world created by Satan (Wakefield, 1974, p 34; Erickson, 1976, p 99). Because reality was incorporeal, the outward manifestations of Christianity such as baptism and the Mass were invalid. True baptism was the spiritual laying on of the hand and not immersion in water; the bread and wine of the Mass were symbols and could not be accepted as the reality (Strayer, 1971, p 175; Lea, 1955, vol 1, p 91).

The Cathari accepted the Platonic concept (Plato, *Dialogue of Meno*) of metempsychosis, which had been rejected by Trinitarians because it denied the individuality of the soul. This concept, translated into the religious principle of reincarnation by Buddhist theologians, was incorporated into Zoroastrianism by Mani (Lea, 1955, vol 1, pp 89–90). To the Cathari, as to Buddhists, the soul would move from "body" to "body"; the quality of the new "body" depended upon the goodness of the soul in the previous "body." Thus, an evil soul could enter the "body" of an animal or, in extreme cases, a plant (Daniel-Rops, 1963, vol 2, p 289; Oldenbourg, 1962, p 35). It is uncertain whether Albigensian Catharism elaborated upon a final nirvana.

While various elements of non-Trinitarian thought existed in southern France since Roman days, the development of the Albigensian form of Catharism was achieved by an amalgam of local residues of non-Trinitarian belief with new ideas coming from the East (Madaule, 1967, p 51).

Some Christians, who inhabited the lands of the southern Caucausus, "Christianized" Manicheanism by substituting Christian names for the dualistic gods. These Christians, sometimes called Paulicians after Paul of Samosata, or Armenians, after their supposed homeland, were permitted considerable freedom within the eastern Roman Empire. Around 975 a Paulician community was established in the Balkans where they began to proselytize the Slavicized Bulgars who had originally converted to the eastern Trinitarian form of Christianity. The Paulician Bulgars called themselves "Bogomils" (Niel, 1970, pp 42–44; Sumption, 1978, p 35; Durban, 1968, pp 82–84). The Bogomils, however, were not complete dualists since they maintained the unity of Jehovah as creator of all and viewed Satan as the elder son of God, while Christ was accepted as a younger son (Wakefield, 1974, pp 27–29).

By 1000 both Paulician and Bogomil preachers were found in Italy. Within a century they had spread to France and Germany where they were known as Bourges, Bulgares, Poplicains, Publicains, or Cathari. At a Trinitarian church council held at Orleans in 1022, a Cathari preacher appeared and denounced the falsehoods of the Old Testament (D'Ares, 1972, p 7; Niel, 1970, pp 47, 59; Wakefield, 1974, p 27).

Outlining the growth of a religious movement does not explain its acceptance. The ideology postulated by dualists is pessimistic: it stressed the corruption and chaos of the world (Sumption, 1978, p 48; Strayer, 1971, p 180; Niel, 1970, p 51). The task now is to detail those socioeconomic and political conditions which led to a general acceptance of such a depressive view.

The area south of the Loire was one of the richest and most civilized parts of the Christian West (Durban, 1968, p 175; Oldenbourg, 1962, p 24); one scholar has claimed that life was "too easy" in comparison with the rest of Europe (Daniel-Rops, 1963, vol 2, p 294). The region was in the forefront in developing an urban cash economy (Strayer, 1971, p 5). To feed the cities, agriculture was expanded and improved. The population decline, which had begun with the collapse of the western portion of the Roman Empire, was reversed and some of the excess population found employment as soldiers for the various petty Muslim emirs attempting to dominate the remains of Muslim Iberia. These warriors were paid in gold and silver and thus aided the general economic development. The constitutional structure also favored urban development. Although the area south of the Loire recognized the King of France as sovereign while Provence was a fief of the Holy Roman Emperor, neither titular authority was able to exercise authority (Shneidman and Levine-Shneidman, 1965, pp 313-315). While the feudal aristocracy was the area's dominant military power, walled communities such as Beziers, Narbonne, Montpellier, and Toulous were able to establish middle-class governments which effectively defied extramural authority (Oldenbourg, 1962, p 21; Sumption, 1978, pp 18-20, 23).

The area's wealth and proximity to the intellectual font in Muslim Iberia fostered the population's cosmpolitan interests (Niel, 1970, pp 61-62). Through Jewish translators, the works of Muslim theorists entered the general literature. Through the Muslims, Greek speculative thought developed to serve as a challenge to Trinitarian dogma (Durban, 1968, pp 100-101; Lea, 1955, vol 1, p 67; Wakefield, 1974, p 78). Literacy was extensive, and aristocrats and burghers willingly paid for translations of the Bible and other works. Gradually, the local dialects of langue d'oc and provençal became the languages of the translations (Warner, vol 1, p 22).

There were liabilities to the socioeconomic and political realities. The lack of central authority exposed the area to petty feudal wars: the dukes of Aquitaine and the counts of Barcelona and Toulouse each failed in attempts to establish hegemony. The conflicts increased insecurity. The growing bourgeois wealth also created anxiety by challenging traditional values.

The generalized literacy caused further anxiety. Alongside the theological, philosophical, and scientific works imported from Iberia came erotic poetry. *The Dove's Neck-Ring,* written at the beginning of the eleventh century by Abu Muhammed 'Ali ibn Hazm al-Andalusi, and translated by the end of the century, brought Ovidian love to southern France (Capellanus, 1969, pp 8-9). After 1100 there was a marked increase in the local writing of erotic poetry (Morris, 1973, p 110). The ability to produce poetry became the hallmark of the educated aristocracy (Shneidman and Levine-Shneidman, 1970, p 323). Nobles established centers of courtly love where the poetry was produced and practiced. Among the more significant leaders of this movement were Eleanor of Aquitaine and her daughters by Louis VII of France, Marie of Champaigne and Alix of Blois (Capellanus, 1969, p 13).

With the external world in flux, individuals sometimes turn to the spiritual world to save them from seductive dangers (Guntrip, 1961, p 383). But the religious leaders of Occitania, as southern France was beginning to be called, were more interested in politics than in ministering to the needs of their parishoners (Strayer, 1971, p 19). More often than not local ecclesiastics were the children of local lords. The chief requirement of the cleric was loyalty to temporal authority (Shneidman, 1970, vol 1, pp 244-246; Southern, 1965, pp 120-123; Griffe, 1968, pp 226-236; Wakefield, 1974, p 18; Strayer, 1971, p 18). Unable to receive needed solace from the established religious system, the Occitanians sought an alternative.

One of the problems in Occitania was that many of the individuals who supported the alternative religion were responsible for creating the need for the counterculture. The initial devotees of Albigensian Catharism were members of the upper strata of temporal and spiritual society. The counts of Foix, who held extensive lands on both sides of the Pyrenees (Shneidman, 1970, vol 1, pp 167–168), were a case in point. Count Ramon Roger, active in creating political instability on both sides of the mountains, was not a Cathari, but his wife Philippa and sister Escalarmonda became important leaders of the movement and were protected at the Foix court (Wakefield, 1974, pp 73–74).

Trinitarians were aware of the challenge. Cathari positions were condemned by Trinitarian Councils at Orleans (1022), Charroux (1028), Rheims (1049), Toulouse (1056) and the Lateran Council of 1059, but to no avail (Warner, 1967, vol 1, pp 34–36, Daniel-Rops, 1963, vol 2, p 277). The movement became stronger. In the mid-eleventh century the cleric Berengar of Tours, influenced by Aristotelian ideas coming from Muslim Iberia, challenged Trinitarian dogmas (Daniel-Rops, 1963, vol 2, p 277). Occitanian knights led the First Crusade (1094–1095). On their march east they encountered Paulicians in Dalmatia, Macedonia, Antioch, and Tripoli. When they returned home they brought with them Paulician concepts which reinforced the native Catharism (Lea, 1955, vol 1 p 107; Sumption, 1978, p 36). Cathari preachers such as Tanchelm in Zeeland and Pierre de Bruys in Occitania spread Cathari doctrine from one end of France to the other (Lea, 1955, vol 1, pp 64–68; Wakefield, 1974, p 23).

Along with the dualistic ideas, the returning warriors brought an appreciation of the wealth and sensuality of the East. Silks, perfumes, and other luxuries were demanded and were increasingly available. There was a noticeable change in clothing style. Replacing the loose post-Roman blouse was a tight-fitting more revealing, more provocative, more ostentatious jacket (Morris, 1973, p 45). As sexuality became more open both in dress and conversation, the Cathari retreated into denial. Many of the courtly poets had linked sexuality to tenderness, but in reality, sexuality had become lust. The Cathari could not abide that "degradation" and, rather than attempt a rational alternative, denied the validity of all sexuality (Lampl de Groot, 1946, pp 77–78; Guntrip, 1961, p 430; Fine, 1975, p 8; Kernberg, 1976, p 20). Tertulian, an early church father, had described the conflict between Chasity (Pudictia) and Lust (Libido) with the eventual triumph of Chastity (Male, 1958, p 99); by the twelfth century, Chastity had to defend herself with shield and sword (Rose Window, Notre Dame de Paris, Male, 1958, p 137).

The Cathari valued virginity (Oldenbourg, 1962, p 65), but they took that position to an extreme. Perpetual virginity was heralded. Intercourse, even between those married, was considered adultery (Strayer, 1971, p 179). The attack upon conjugal intercourse was also an attack upon Occitanian Jews, whose writings were being studied in Trinitarian monasteries such as that of St. Victor. The cosmopolitan atmosphere had led Trinitarian theologians to examine Hebrew manuscripts, especially the opinions of Rashi of Troyes (1040–1105), and the Babylonian Talmud, copies of which were available in France and Germany. In that rendition of Hebrew tradition, it was advised that the "conjugal act as a matter of duty" be performed "once a day" (Capellanus, 1969, p 103). As a reward for abstinence, Cathari men and "bonae Christianae" could become "Perfecti" (Oldenbourg, 1962, p 61; Strayer, 1971, pp 34–35). To hide their bodies, male and female Perfecti wore long black robes (Sumption, 1978, p 51).

The Trinitarian Church remained ineffective in combatting the spread of

Cathari influence. When Pope Calixtus II appeared at the Council of Toulouse in 1119, he could do no more than excommunicate the Cathari and beg the local nobility not to harbor them. He had no power to stop their teachings (Warner, 1967, vol 1, p 37; Lea, 1955, vol 1, p 117).

In 1145 St. Bernard of Clairvaux went on a preaching crusade to convert the Cathari. He failed (Wakefield, 1974, p 83; Strayer, 1971, p 40). "The Churches are without people, the people without priests. . . . The Churches are regarded as Synagogues," he complained (Lea, 1955, vol 1, p 70). The councils of Tours and Lyon in 1163, the latter headed by Pope Alexander III, were unable to stem either the spread of Catharism or the ideas of Pere Valdes, founder of an ascetic Trinitarian group called Waldensians (Warner, 1967, vol 1, pp 41–42; Daniel-Rops, 1963, vol 2, p 297; Strayer, 1971, p 36; Lea, 1955, vol 1, pp 76–88).

The Second Crusade (1147–1149), led by Louis VII, his wife Eleanor of Aquitaine, and Emperor Conrad, increased the contacts with eastern dualists. After the crusaders returned home, dualistic theories seemed ubiquitous (Sumption, 1978, p 38; Lea, 1955, vol 1, pp 89–91; Wakefield, 1974, p 24).

The established church failed to offer the personal religious experience the populace demanded (Wakefield, 1974, p 77). Confession in the established church had become pro forma: it had become meaningless because it was not felt. The fact was admitted by the Trinitarian Otloh of St. Emmeram, and condemned by the scholastic Peter Abelard (Morris, 1973, pp 71–73). To meet the need for confession, the Cathari would attend a meeting once a month, usually at the home of a Perfecti, and publicly confess (Sumption, 1978, p 52).

Political conditions in Occitania became unstable. As early as 1112 the Count of Barcelona began to extend his authority north of the Pyrenees (Rosell, 1945–1947, vol 2, pp 843–846). The count, however, was considered on Occitanian (Shneidman and Levine-Shneidman, 1965, p 315). The dynastic union of Barcelona and the clearly Iberian Kingdom of Aragon brought Iberian power into Occitania. Further, Eleanor of Aquitaine's divorce from Louis VII and subsequent marriage to the Anglo-Norman Henry II, brought Norman greed south. By 1158 both the King-Count of Aragon-Barcelona, and the King-Duke of England-Normandy-Aquitaine challenged the authority of the local Occitanian lords (Sumption, 1978, p 23).

In response to the increased anxiety created by external forces, the Cathari determined to establish a visible counter-institution (Fornari, 1975, p 194). First at Lombers in 1165 (Warner, 1967, vol 1, p 43; Wakefield, 1974, p 30) and two years later at St. Felix de-Caraman, plans for such an organization were prepared. At the latter convocation, Nicetas, the Paulician bishop of Constantinople appeared and helped organize a functioning counterchurch (Sumption, 1978, p 49; Madaule, 1967, p 39; Warner, 1967, vol 1, p 15).

The Trinitarian Church became frightened. Henri, Abbot of Clairvaux, demanded immediate action lest there be no one "left in the neighborhood familiar with the name Jesus Christ" (Daniel-Rops, 1963, vol 2, p 296). A counteroffensive was organized by the Trinitarians. It had limited success: in Toulouse the merchant Pierre Maurand recanted and accepted his punishment of public flogging, fine, and a pilgrimage to Jerusalem (Wakefield, 1974, p 84). Generally speaking, however, the Trinitarian moves were resisted. The Third Lateran Council in 1179 proposed military force to destroy the Cathari. Two years later a Trinitarian force seized the castle at Lavaur. The castle belonged to Roger Trencaval II, a leading Cathari. After the victory, the "crusaders" disbanded and the Cathari returned (Wakefield, 1974, p 85; Sumption, 1978, p 56; Daniel-Rops, 1963, vol 2, p 297).

The threat to the Cathari came from sources other than just the military. Everywhere Cathari turned, they faced offensive poetry and symbols. The increased sexuality, exemplified by Andreas Capellanus' *The Art of Courtly Love,* allegedly depicting life in Poitiers during the period 1170–1174 (Capellanus, 1969, p 21), had to be denied. In art, Christ began to appear more like a Greek Pan than a sufferer who came to demonstrate the truth and redeem. The crucifix became a symbol of triumph and not sacrifice. The new Gothic art decorated churches with statues of the Hebrew kings and prophets, and it became difficult to differentiate between the statues of Christ and those of the Hebrews (Morris, 1973, pp 23, 155–157; Male, 1958, p 138). To the Cathari, Christ was incorporeal and all physical representations were demeaning; casting Christ as a Jew increased the insult.

The Cathari responded to the external danger by creating an administration that aped that of the Trinitarians (Daniel-Rops, 1963, vol 2, pp 292–293). Cathari bishops were elected to organize local centers. The bishops sent out preachers both to convert unbelievers and sustain those who had been converted (Oldenbourg, 1962, p 33). St. Bernard had denigrated the Cathari as "rustics, ignorant and utterly despicable" (Warner, 1967, vol 1, p 40). The reverse seems to have been true: The Cathari were educated and knew both the Old and New Testaments; they were effectively able to dispute with Trinitarian representatives (Lea, 1955, vol 1, pp 563–567). Literacy appears to have been the enemy of the Trinitarian Church (Warner, 1967, vol 1 p 12; Erickson, 1976, p 101; Morris, 1973, p 57). The Cathari believed in education and established schools to which many of the nobility sent their children (Daniel-Rops, 1963, vol 2, p 295).

The Cathari were divided into three grades. The "Credentes" were the simple believers who lived normal lives and accepted Cathari beliefs without adopting all the practices. Sexual intercourse was normal among Credentes. The next level was the "Boni Homines": men and women who had accepted all the beliefs and practices, including chastity, but had not endorsed the full ascetic life. The final stage was the "Perfecti," who lived an ascetic life (Warner, 1967, vol 1, pp 51–52).

It was not easy to become a Perfect. A "good person" who wished to attain that station first became a novice assigned for a year to a Perfect so that he or she might experience the ascetic life (Sumption, 1978, p 50). The Perfect followed the dietary laws of Endura, ie, complete abstinence from meat, eggs, milk, and cheese. Fish was consumed, but shellfish was to be avoided save during illness. Three days a week the Perfect and the novice would fast on bread and water (Wakefield, 1974, p 39; Lea, 1955, vol 1, p 97; Davis, 1948, p 39; Oldenbourg, 1962, p 51; Madaule, 1967, p 34). Once the novice passed the test he received the *consolamentum,* the Baptism of the Spirit, which was a simple laying on of the hands by a Perfect. Many who could not follow the demands of the ascetic life waited until the deathbed to receive the *consolamentum* (Madaule, 1967, pp 37–38; Wakefield, 1974, p 37; Oldenbourg, 1962, p 47; D'Ares, 1972, p 16; Davis, 1948, pp 32, 129, 140, 173, 201). At the time of the laying on of hands the Lord's Prayer was recited (Wakefield, 1974 p 37; Warner, 1967, vol 1, p 39; Strayer, 1971, p 32).

The simplicity of Cathari services attracted many. There was neither symbolism, as such, nor sacraments. Baptism and the Mass were not needed. At the service there was a sermon, public confession, and the breaking of bread. There were no threats of hell-fire because hell did not exist. Salvation would come by leading the good life and receiving the *consolamentum* (Duboc, 1970; Oldenbourg, 1962, p 38; Madaule, 1967, p 42; Lea, 1955, vol 1, p 94; Dossat, 1968, p 79; Niel, 1970, p 54; Warner, 1967, vol 1, pp 30–32).

In contrast to the simple service was a complex metaphysical theology that required a knowledge of Aristotelianism to fathom the challenge to transsubstantiation, and of Platonism to comprehend the peregrination of the soul. To the philosophical superstructure were added Paulician and Bogomil tracts explaining and interpreting Trinitarian tradition in a dualist frame (Daniel-Rops, 1963, vol 2, p 280; Wakefield, 1974 p 35). How many of the Cathari fully understood the metaphysical structure is unknown, but there could not have been many.

There seems little doubt that Catharism was accepted as the true Christianity (Wakefield, 1974, pp 31, 77–78; D'Ares, 1972, p 15). Perfecti and Perfectae were accepted as model Christians who lived the life Christ wished. Whether the Perfect ministered to the needs of the community or did nothing but contemplate God mattered little. The Perfect were considered God's chosen (Wakefield, 1974, p 74; Sumption, 1978, pp 51–52; Lea, 1955, vol 1, p 92; Daniel-Rops, 1963, vol 2, p 291).

The amalgam of political–economic instability and overt sexuality created an atmosphere that was too anxiety-provoking for the Cathari. Rather than adjust to that external world, they attempted to create a society that negated the reality and promised an everlasting tranquility (Madaule, 1967, p 33). To the Cathari, happiness could be achieved only by altering the external reality (Wallerstein, 1973, p 24). But they could not alter the external world and that world remained as a threat. Denials and rejection multiplied: every aspect of the external reality had to be denied and shunned. If Occitania were the home of military heroes, then killing, even in self-defense, was held illicit (Strayer, 1971, p 179). If the hope of resurrection were offered by Trinitarians, then the reality of resurrection was denied (Dossat, 1968, p 80). If society praised the human body, then the body was reduced to being the foul prison that held the beautiful soul captive (Wakefield, 1974, p 33). If writers marveled at the progress of the contemporary world, then that world was rejected for the greatness of the noncorporeal future world (Nelli, 1975, p 21). If Trinitarian theologians stressed the continuity of the Old and New Testaments, then the Cathari insisted upon the falseness of the Old Testament (Daniel-Rops, 1963, vol 2, p 290). If Trinitarians turned to Mary, as the Mother of God, to intercede with God, then the Cathari claimed that neither Christ nor Mary had physical form and that neither had been born and, therefore, Mary could not have been Christ's mother (Lea, 1955, vol 1, p 91). The denials and rejection seemed total.

On another level, however, there was neither rejection nor denial. At all times the Cathari insisted that they were the true Christians and that it was the Trinitarians who had prostituted the true religion. Further, the Cathari reacted rather than originated. Even when seemingly on the offensive, the Cathari replied rather than initiated. Albigensian Catharism was a synthesis of various traditional Christianized dualistic theories without producing innovative concepts.

Frightened by a society they could no longer control, members of the Cathari had fled to a nonexisting new world. Flight, however, is, on one level, an acknowledgment of defeat and a loss of self-esteem. To counter the unconscious awareness of defeat, the members of the Cathar church adopted a masochistic syndrome. Only by denying terrestrial pleasures could the sense of failure be overcome (Stolorow and Lachman, 1980, p 30). The ego, unable to come to terms with the blatant sexuality and the political–economic instability, surrendered itself to an all-powerful superego: God (Jones, 1974, p 185). Because members of the Cathar church had placed their self-esteem on a rock of opposition to Trinitarianism, compromise was impossible. Compromise would have confirmed their weakness and failure (Deutsch, 1977, p 46).

The real world had made those who became Cathari anxious. The anxiety had to be reduced to a tolerable level (Sandler and Joffee, 1969, p 84). To reduce the anxiety, a defense system was employed. That structure was geared to obviate those aspects which had initiated the anxiety (Kernberg, 1976, p 40; Levy, 1955, pp 213, 225). By denying the corporeal world which had created the distress, the Cathari endeavored to return to a fantasy primitive existence which was anxiety free. That was impossible, but the Cathari insisted that through their system they would achieve in the future that which had been in the past before being despoiled by Satan. The idealized past—the world of "in principio erat verbium"— had become the idealized future. By fusing past and future, the pain of the present seemed to disappear (Mitscherlich, 1970, p 145; Furman, 1974, p 66; Balint, 1965, p 60).

The Cathari failed to secure their society because their individual egos had been overwhelmed by the all powerful superego to such an extent that the problem-solving function of the ego became impotent (Wälder, 1936, pp 48, 53; Winnicott, 1966, p 16; Khan, 1974, p 233).

In rejecting and denying the validity of the corporeal world in which they lived, the Cathari also denied the symbolism that had been established to explain and reinforce abstract theories. "This is My Body and This is My Blcod," said Christ. But he could not have said this, insisted the Cathari, because Christ had neither body nor blood. The Mass was rejected, and with it the cannibalistic pleasure of ingesting the godhead. The crucifix, symbol of God's suffering, was rejected because God, having no body, could suffer no pain. In rejecting that symbol, the identification with a suffering God who provided hope was lost. In eschewing symbols, the Cathari denied both the concrete representations of the symbols and the more primitive, frequently anxiety-provoking, but eventually gratifying, meanings (Ferenczi, 1956, pp 232, 236; Sarnoff, 1976, pp 27, 320; Klein, 1930, p 26; Piaget, 1962, p 172; Jones, 1950, pp 89–90, 97, 102, 128–129).

By 1200 the Cathari seemed to have triumphed in Occitania and Cathari ideas had spread to Paris where Amaury Bene, a professor of theology, denied the validity of the sacraments. In Occitania there were between 1000 and 1500 Perfecti who proselytized (Daniel-Rops, 1963, vol 2, p 278; Wakefield, 1974, p 70).

An unforseen variable entered the picture in the person of Pope Innocent III. Trained as a lawyer, the pope viewed the papacy as the dominant political and spiritual force in Europe. Having forced kings and emperors to bend to his will, he had no intention to allow the Cathari freedom.

Innocent initially misread the situation. "The chief cause of all this evil," he stated, is "the Archbishop of Narbonne, whose God is money, whose heart is in his treasure, who is concerned only with gold" (Strayer, 1971, p 19). The pope thought that the Cistercians, led by the Iberian, Dominic de Guzman, would soon restore the people to the True Christ (Morris, 1973, p 77; Strayer, 1971, p 41). When Dominic met with only limited success, the pope dispatched a legate, Pierre de Castelnau, with authority to institute mass preaching (Daniel-Rops, 1963, vol 2, p 298; Wakefield, 1974, pp 89–91). Again there was only limited success because the Cathari, protected by the local nobility, were able to publicly dispute, and refute, the Trinitarians. Throughout Occitania the aristocracy protected Cathari even though the lords may not have been members of the sect (Strayer, 1971, p 22). Frustrated in his mission, the legate attempted to coerce the Occitanian nobility by excommunicating Count Raymond VI of Toulouse, who was not an overt Cathari. Pierre blundered. Raymond was the most powerful independent Occitanian lord and the excommunication was viewed a papal interference in secular affairs. On January 14, 1208, the count's henchmen murdered the legate (Strayer, 1971, pp 50–51; Sumption, 1978, p 15).

The pope proclaimed a "crusade" against the heretics. Since the town of Albi was one of the centers of the Cathari belief, the attack became known as the "Albigensian Crusade."

Spurred on by the south's legendary wealth—Toulouse was larger than Paris (Durban, 1968, p 33)—knights from "Germany, Bavaria, Saxony, Frisia, Anjou, Normandy, Brittany, Lombardy," (Martin-Chabot, 1960–1961, vol 1, pp 132–134) and central France moved against "de Bolgaria" (Martin-Chabot, 1960–1961, vol 1, p 10). The crusaders struck at the wealthy walled town of Beziers. Viscount Raymond-Roger, realizing the hopelessness of the struggle, gathered his troops and Jewish allies and fled, leaving the citizenry, Cathari and Trinitarian alike, to be slaughtered. Three weeks later, August 15, 1209, the impressive walled fortress of Carcassonne fell to the invaders (Daniel-Rops, 1963, vol 2, 302; Sumption, 1978, p 90; Wakefield, 1974, pp 102–103).

The invasion became a threat to Occitanian civilization. Pedro II, King of Aragon and Count of Barcelona, who had banished all Cathari from his realm in 1197 (Martin-Chabot, 1960–1961, vol 1, p 71), and who had married Marie, heiress of Montpellier, in order to build an empire from the Ebro to the Alps (Shneidman, 1970, vol 2, p 298; Martin-Chabot, 1960–1961, vol 1, pp 12–13) felt obliged to intervene. Raymond VI of Toulouse was his kinsman by marriage, and many of the Occitanian lords had become his vassals. Further, many of the king-count's Catalan vassals held extensive lands north of the Pyrenees and, after the crusaders had slaughtered loyal Trinitarians in Beziers, the Catalans feared for their holdings. Pedro II, called The Catholic, gathered his Trinitarian allies and marched north to defend the Count of Toulouse and Occitanian independence. At Muret, near Toulouse, the Catalans met the crusaders. Pedro was killed and the Catalans defeated (Shneidman, 1970, vol 2, p 298; Martin-Chabot, 1960–1961, vol 2, p 18).

The Albigensian Crusade had become political (Shneidman, 1970, vol 1, pp 4–5; Martin-Chabot, 1960–1961, vol 2, p 63, vol 3, pp 45, 239). With the death of Simon de Montfort on June 25, 1218, the crusaders lost their best general and leader. Within six years the Occitanian lords reestablished their independence (Martin-Chabot, 1960–1961, vol 3, p 309; Strayer, 1971, pp 115–122).

The Occitanians, however, could not maintain their position. The kings of France, first Louis VIII and then Louis IX, wishing to establish royal authority throughout the kingdom, planned to use the crusade as a means to unify France. Raymond VII of Toulouse, realizing that it was impossible to unite the various Occitanian forces, agreed to the marriage of his daughter Jeanne to Louis IX's younger brother, Alphonse of Poitiers, with the stipulation that Jeanne would inherit Toulouse. Power in Occitania thus passed from Toulouse to Paris (Strayer, 1971, pp 136–137). Only the king of Aragon had the power to alter the declining fortunes of Occitania, but the Aragonese sovereign was engaged elsewhere (Shneidman and Levine-Shneidman, 1965, p 327).

The crusade initially did not seriously restrict Cathari in those areas free of invaders. The Cathari found means to hoodwink local inquisitors (Wakefield, 1974 p 36); they were also able to produce new philosophical tracts defending dualism (Nelli, 1975, p 74). Gradually, however, a change was noticed: without the protection of the nobility, the Cathari were less able to counter the influx of Trinitarian preachers such as St. Anthony of Padua who were equal, if not superior, to the Cathari (Lea, 1955, vol 1, p 197), nor were they able to publicly refute new Trinitarian tracts such as those produced by Durand of Huesca (Nelli, 1975, p 137). In 1231 and again in 1233 Pope Gregory IX authorized the Dominicans to hold inquests to root out the heresy (Wakefield, 1974, p 140; Strayer, 1971, pp 144-147). It became impossible to defend Catharism openly. Violence became the norm: the Cathari merchants and artisans of Narbonne unsuccessfully revolted in 1234; two inquisitors and nine clerics were murdered in 1242, and in 1243-1244 a last-ditch military resistance was attempted at Montségur (Wakefield, 1974; p 144; Coulton, 1959, p 171; Strayer, 1971, p 141; Oldenbourg, 1962, pp 340-360).

Without the protection of those who held the military power, the Cathari were driven underground (Wakefield, 1974, p 149). By 1250 there were less than 200 Perfecti left and the continuity of the organization could not be maintained (Strayer, 1971, pp 152-153, 158). Cathari would still be found in the fourteenth century, but usually only among the lower middle class (Madaule, 1967, p 137; Davis, 1948, pp 20-23). Catharism had become an anachronism.

Catharism proved to be a tragedy for Occitania. The people of southern France had evolved a civilization superior to that of the north. In a political struggle between Paris and Toulouse, the latter should have won, but Catharism gave Paris allies from outside France. Further, Catharism lessened the south's ability to view alternatives in combatting northern aggression because, to many, the commitment was to religious and not to political factors (Janis and Mann, 1977, p 284).

While the Cathari fought for their religious beliefs, most of their allies fought for their political and economic position. Some of the invaders fought for Trinitarianism, but most joined the crusade for booty and political power (Wakefield, 1974, pp 195-196). The "heresy" had become an excuse for plunder and aggrandizement. Those who fought for riches and power and those who defended their property and position could reach an accommodation. Once those who fought for booty were assuaged, and those who defended their property were convinced that part of the property would be respected, there was no need for armed conflict and the defenders abandoned the Cathari (Deutsch, 1977, p 5; Strayer, 1971, pp 156-157).

The result of the failure to accurately perceive both the motives of the Parisian monarch and alternative methods of defense was dramatic: Occitanian political independence was lost without seriously effecting the area's economic prosperity, but the Occitanian language, replaced by that of northern France, disappeared as a vehicle for literary expression. Those nobles, whose main holdings were south of the Pyrenees and were not encumbered by Catharism, were able to perceive reality and developed a national identity (Catalan) which was able to withstand the centralizing power of Paris (Shneidman and Levine-Shneidman, 1965, pp 332-333).

As for the Cathari, many rejoined the Trinitarian Church rather than remain ostracized (Mitscherlich, 1970, p 97), while others fled to isolated valleys in the Alps and Pyrenees, or pretended to recant in order to await a revival. Some of the

Cathari would join other movements that affected the area after the outbreak of bubonic plague. Portions of Cathari ideals would surface in various subsequent "heresies," but Catharism as an effective organized challenge to Trinitarianism was finished.

Catharism was a pessimistic rejection and denial of the world as it existed. It developed as a response to the anxieties germinated by the real world. By rejecting the validity of reality, the Cathari were unable to adjust to the socioeconomic and political shifts within that world. Unable and unwilling to accommodate reality, the Cathari were unable to perceive rational alternatives and failed to produce a positive challenge to Trinitarian monotheism.

BIBLIOGRAPHY

Balint M: *Primary Love and Psycho-Analytic Technique.* New York, Liveright Publishing, 1965.

Capellanus A, in Parry JJ (ed): *The Art of Courtly Love.* New York, WW Norton, 1969.

Coulton GG: *Inquisition and Liberty.* Boston, Beacon Press, 1959.

Daniel-Rops, H: *Cathedral and Crusade,* 2 vols. Garden City, Image Books, 1963.

D'Ares J: *Cathares et Albigeois: Hérésie ou Retour aux Sources?* Paris, Institut Herméneutique, 1972.

Davis GW: *The Inquisition at Albi, 1299–1300.* New York, Columbia University Press, 1948.

Deutsch M: *The Resolution of Conflict,* 2d printing. New Haven, Yale University Press, 1977.

Dossat Y: Les Cathares d'apres les documents de l'inquisition. *Cahiers de Fanjeaux* 1968;3: 71–104.

Düboc J-P: *Histoire du Christianisme Cathare du Ier au XXᵉ siècle.* Narbonne, Editions Croix de Vie, 1970.

Durban P: *Actualité du Catharisme.* Toulouse, P. Durban, 1968.

Erickson C: *The Medieval Vision.* New York, Oxford University Press, 1976.

Ferenczi S: *Sex in Psycho-Analysis.* New York, Dover Publications, 1956.

Fine R: *Psychoanalytic Psychology.* New York, Jason Aronson, 1975.

Fornari F: *The Psychoanalysis of War.* Bloomington, Indiana University Press, 1975.

Fried Y, Agassi J: *Paranoia: A Study in Diagnosis.* Dordrecht, D. Reidel, 1976.

Furman E: *A Child's Parent Dies.* New Haven, Yale University Press, 1974.

Geiwitz PJ: *Non-Freudian Personality Theories.* Belmont, Brooks/Cole Publishing, 1969.

Griffe E: Le Catharisme dans le diocese de Carcassonne. *Cahiers de Fanjeaux* 1968;3: 215–236.

Guntrip H: *Personality Structure and Human Interaction.* New York, International Universities Press, 1961.

Janis IL, Mann L: *Decision Making.* New York, Free Press, 1977.

Jones E: *Papers on Psycho-Analysis.* London, Bailliére, Tindall and Cox, 1950.

Jones E: *Psycho-Myth, Psycho-History.* New York, Hillstone, 1974.

Kernberg OF: *Object-Relations Theory and Clinical Psychoanalyses.* New York, Jason Aronson, 1976.

Khan MMR: *The Privacy of the Self.* New York, International Universities Press, 1974.

Klein M: The importance of symbol formation in the development of the ego. *Inter J Psycho-Anal* 1930;11:24–39.

Lampl de Groot J: The pre-oedipal phase in the development of the male child. *Psychoanal Study Child* 1946;2:75–88.

Lea HC: *A History of the Inquisition of the Middle Ages,* 3 vols. New York, Russell & Russell, 1955.

Levy DM: Oppositional syndromes and oppositional behavior, in Hoch PH, Zubin J (eds): *Psychopathology of Childhood.* New York, Grune and Stratton, 1955, pp 204 226.

Madaule J: *The Albigensian Crusade.* New York, Fordham University Press, 1967.

Male E: *The Gothic Image.* New York, Harper & Row, 1958.

Martin-Chabot E (ed): *La Chanson de la Croisade Albigeoise,* 3 vols. Paris, Société d'édition, 1960–1961.

Mitscherlich A: *Society Without the Father.* New York, Schocken Books, 1970.

Morris C: *The Discovery of the Individual, 1050–1200.* New York, Harper & Row, 1973.

Nelli R: *La Philosophie du Catharisme.* Paris, Payat, 1975.

Niel F: *Albigeois et Cathars.* Paris, Presses Universitaires de France, 1970.

Oldenbourg Z: *Massacre at Montségur.* New York, Pantheon Books, 1962.

Piaget J: *Play, Dreams and Imitation in Childhood.* New York, WW Norton, 1962.

Plato: Dialog of Meno. *Roman History* (Horace White, translation). Cambridge, MA, Harvard University Press (Loeb Classical Library), 1968.

Rosell FM (ed): *Liber Feudorum Maior.* Barcelona, Consejo Superior de Investigaciones Cientificas, 1945–1947.

Sandler J, Joffee W: Towards a basic psychoanalytic model. *Inter J Psycho-Anal* 1969;50: 79–90.

Sarnoff C: *Latency.* New York, Jason Aronson, 1976.

Shneidman JL: *The Rise of the Aragonese-Catalan Empire, 1200–1350,* 2 vols. New York, New York University Press, 1970.

Shneidman JL, Levine-Shneidman C: Factors in the emergence of Catalan nationalism during the thirteenth century. *The Historian.* 1965;27:311–333.

Southern RW: *The Making of the Middle Ages.* New Haven, Yale University Press, 1965.

Stolorow RD, Lachman FM: *Psychoanalysis of Developmental Arrests.* New York, International Universities Press, 1980.

Strayer J: *The Albigensian Crusade.* New York, The Dial Press, 1971.

Sumption J: *The Albigensian Crusade.* London, Faber & Faber, 1978.

Wakefield WL: *Heresy, Crusade and Inquisition in Southern France, 1100–1250.* Berkeley, University of California Press, 1974.

Wälder R: The principle of multiple function: Observations on over-determination. *Psychoanal Q* 1936;5:45–62.

Wallerstein RS: Psychoanalytic perspectives on the problem of reality. *J Am Psychoanal Assoc* 1973;21:5–33.

Warner HT: *The Albigensian Heresy,* 2 vols. New York, Russell & Russell, 1967.

Winnicott DW: *The Maturational Process and the Facilitating Environment.* New York, International Universities Press, 1966.

The Prophet from Palmyra:
Joseph Smith and the Rise of Mormonism

KEVIN GARVEY

The social concerns that have accompanied the growth of cults within the broader society derive from two aspects of cult practice and preference: 1) the actual content of the cult doctrine and the degree to which it contradicts the more commonly held views of "reality"; and 2) the effect of that doctrine on the behavior of the cult members.

The surrounding culture reserves its strongest reactions to what it regards as bizarre, dangerous, or evil. The judgment of the larger society is often not based upon exhaustive appraisals of a group's dogma but on the dogma's relation to subsequent behavior. Society does not demand that a new "religion" be guided solely by compassion. Rather, it expresses concern when behavior ostensibly guided by compassion appears to be self-destructive to the individual cult members or to the broader social unity.

A wide variety of religiously grounded plans for the moral improvement of mankind and for the creation of the "perfect society" have stirred the imagination. The debacle of the People's Temple under the leadership of Jim Jones has created a continuing concern over the manner and mode in which self-appointed messianic leaders and charlatans are able to capitalize on the universal longing for a better society. The People's Temple did not simply appeal to the pathologically dependent or the gullible. It attracted members at all levels of society and of widely differing degrees of sophistication. In part, its appeal was due to the inherent seductiveness of a final and totalistic explanation for the profound questions of human existence. A comparison with an earlier movement that sought to found a utopian state in an isolated location under the aegis of a charismatic and controversial leader may provide a greater understanding of the denouement in Guyana. Although this earlier movement still flourishes and thrives as the Church of Jesus Christ of Latter Day Saints (popularly known to nonmembers—Gentiles—as the Mormons and referred to by members as the LDS

Church), it presents certain attributes which bear an eerie similarity with the People's Temple. To be sure, the flourishing, almost aggressively, all-American movement based in Salt Lake City bears no resemblance to the quasi-Marxist compound created in the depths of the South American jungle. But, within the context of their contemporaneous societies, is this comparison so farfetched? Or, forebearing the certainty of a divine plan and divine intervention—need the outcomes have been so totally different? In short, why do some millenarian movements succeed so dramatically while others fail so tragically?

E.D. Howe, writing in 1834 against the spread of Mormonism, noted of The Book of Mormon:

> The marvelous always has something about it, to fascinate, however coarsely it may be clad; and fiction has its charms, and when combined and presented to mind in the mantle of inspiration, it is not singular that the credulous and unsuspecting should be captivated (Howe, 1834).

Joseph Smith was the leader and prophet of Mormonism. He presented himself as the recipient of a divine revelation—*The Book of Mormon*. The Book of Mormon included a plan for the expected millenium as well as a series of actions the individual was obligated to follow, in the more immediate present, in order to comply with God's will. Joseph Smith's story of his revelation defied both the commonly accepted norms for material "reality" as well as the theologically accepted norms for divine practice. But, for a movement to grow, it requires more than faith. It requires the presence of catalytic forces. Mormonism benefitted from several.

Mormonism did not emerge from a religious vacuum. Early nineteenth century America was a place in which religious controversy was aggravated by religious fervor. The established Protestant denominations were beset by doctrinal conflicts which produced important intellectual, spiritual, and psychological ramifications. These conflicts undermined the preexisting consensus and confidence in the certainties of belief. Established churches divided into separate denominations because of unresolvable doctrinal disputes. There was an increasing sense of fragmentation within individuals with the dissipation of their confidence. Thus, the Second Awakening, as this period of religious enthusiasm is called, was experienced by many as a nightmarish period of uncertainty.

Several alternative pathways presented themselves as a means of dealing with this crisis of belief. The path followed reflected to a large degree the individual's former ties and social background. The dominant factor was the individual's educational level which was much more closely tied, in that era, to the individual's social standing. The more educated were exposed to the heady ideas which were being imported from Europe and, thus, were inclined to embrace exotic theologies. The more mundane needs of the less educated were satisfied by less sophisticated palliatives.

Within the educated levels of New England society, the enthusiasms of Ralph Waldo Emerson and his associates in the Transcendental Club were to strike deep roots. Emerson had resigned his ministry in the Unitarian Church because of his inability to accept orthodox ideas. In 1832, he traveled to Europe where he absorbed the main tenets of Romantic Idealism. Upon returning, he published his first important book, *Nature* (1836). This work helped Emerson to assume an ascendent role within the Transcendental Club. Along with other young ministers and intellectuals, Emerson launched a challenge to the prevailing religious doctrines. The influence of German Romanticism led Emerson to reject the commonsensical empirical philosophy of John Locke. Locke's empiricism defended the reality of material things. It was a major influence on Colonial theologians. Thus, Emerson's challenge was a challenge to the accepted norms of what was the real, the true, and the sacred. Emerson and the Transcendentalists

> remained convinced of the Unitarian emphasis on the oneness of God and of his benevolent character, but stressed a radical doctrine of divine immanence, the intuitive perception of truth, a rejection of external authority, and a radical social ethic (Handy, 1977, p 200).

The Transcendentalists effectively called into question the role of the senses and the intellect in ascertaining truth. Their challenge not only questioned the prevailing certainties about the material world, but those about the nature of the spiritual world, as well. Emerson openly attacked the crux of Christian theology and philosophy—the idea of Christ as the focal point of revelation. In his widely publicized sermon, the *Divinity School Address* delivered at Harvard in 1838, Emerson propounded that a universal soul, through its will, governed what was real—that it was the only reality and that, moreover, "it knows no person. It invites every man to expand to the full circle of the universe, and will have no preferences but those of spontaneous love" (Handy, 1977, p 201).

Emerson's view effectively severed moral questions from criticism grounded either within the senses or the intellect. This view elevated religion to a plane no longer susceptible to rational inquiry. What one "felt" was not only true, it was The Truth. Emerson's attack on reason was so pervasive that it impelled Theodore Parker, a Unitarian minister, to defend Emerson by stating that Christianity was "absolute, pure morality; absolute, pure religion" which would last even if Christ and the gospels were demonstrated to be total fiction (Handy, 1977, p 202). This affirmation of faith stifled the criticisms of the traditionalists. It was to be echoed by the Mormons. And with Emerson's call for a "new teacher," it contributed to the atmosphere which loosened religious ties.

Horace Bushnell eloquently pursued the defense of traditional norms. A graduate of the Yale Divinity School, he had absorbed some of the Romantic philosophy. However, he also sensed the damage caused by continuing theological disputes and organizational rivalries and sought to synthesize the contending positions. He stressed the organic nature of family, church, and community. Bushnell injected a balancing influence into the realm of theological disputation through his sermons and a succession of books. His apologetics restate the traditional views of Christ's atonement filtered through the insights of Romantic idealism from the early 1830s on to the 1860s. In the process, Bushnell upheld the reality of the material world and the necessity of developing the intellect's awareness of it. He felt that without the intellect there could not be the cultivation of a mature ethical and spiritual personality. His insistence that the family was a critical necessity in the moral development of the child appealed to traditionalists. His reservations about the "spontaneous love" affirmed by Emerson upset the Transcendentalists. In his defense of a middle ground between the camps of extremists, Bushnell illuminated the critical positions of the disputants. But in the heightened religious atmosphere of the Second Awakening, most attempts to resolve these questions sought a more exotic form.

Many manifestations of religious enthusiasm during the Second Awakening could not be expressed within the existing denominations. Doctrinal rivalries produced an atmosphere of heightened concern for the "perfect" Christian life. This stimulated the multiplication of communal societies loosely based on the presumed early Christian pattern of life. The presence of these rivalries in a country enjoying religious freedom that possessed both an abundance of open land and a sparsely settled population provided the opportunity for communal experimentation. One well-known group, the Shakers, had founded a dozen communities before the beginning of the nineteenth century (Handy, 1977, p 221). By midcentury, there were some 6000 Shakers in 20 communities who "saw themselves as a people who regarded biblical and millenial teachings with complete earnestness, and who were overcoming the evils of individualism and secularism" (Hardy, 1977, p 222).

The roots of the Second Awakening extended back to medieval Europe. Emmanuel Swedenborg, whose ideas were an immediate source of "enthusiasms," echoed the doctrines of some of the medieval heresies. But, the medieval movements themselves were also direct sources of inspiration. Their ideas and practices were well known and did not require intermediaries. Their influence expressed itself within the Millenarian communities that sprang up during this period. And, it is within these Millenarian communities that one finds the antecedents and presence of the theology and practices associated with Mormons and Mormonism.

The Millenarian tradition embodies the idea that the final conflict between good and evil is imminent. This is known to the select few because they have received a divine revelation. Those who embrace the revelation, follow its implications, and accept the authority of the divinely designated leader, will be saved and flourish in the thousand-year reign of good following the defeat of evil (Harrison, 1979). Those who follow the revelation become "pure." They are called upon to do battle with the "impure." And to the degree that they are willing to follow the authority of the revelation—as interpreted by those to whom it has been granted—they will share in the blessings to come. Anything performed in the service of the Millenium becomes pure even if the acts themselves would normally be considered as immoral or even reprehensible. In sum, Millenarian thinking divides society into two camps—those following the revelation are in the service of the good and those opposing it are under the sway of Satan. Matter controlled by the followers of revelation becomes pure and that which is not governed by revelation is impure. This radical dualism sanctions a multitude of contradictions. It is integral to an understanding of the psychological aberrations found in many Millenarian sects. It is reflected in the history of Mormonism.

A brief precis of a Millenarian movement is instructive. In 1534, during the Reformation, an uprising occurred in Munster, Germany. A group of extreme Millenarians overthrew the civil government and imposed control over the city. This group, the Anabaptists, attempted to establish a totalistic control over the city. Anything not divinely dictated was proscribed. Statues, manuscripts, paintings of the Westphalian school, musical instruments, were all destroyed. The "godless," ie, those who refused to accept the Anabaptist prophets, were expelled. Their property was confiscated and a communal ownership of all property was imposed. The deacons, of course, were placed in charge of all property. This communal ownership included wives—after all this was sanctioned in the Old Testament. And, after the expulsion of the "godless," there were three times as many women as men in Munster—so polygamy became attractive. None of these practices were novel (Shafarevich, 1980). Indeed, there is a continuity of such practices dating back to the heretical groups of the early Christian era.

> Bullinger, who wrote about the Anabaptists in 1560 says: 'Many basic and grave errors of theirs they share with the ancient sects of Novatians, Cathars, with Auxentius and Pelagius.' Cardinal Hosius (1504-70) . . . wrote: 'Still more harmful is the sect of Anabaptists, of which kind were the Waldensian Brethren also . . . (this heresy) has existed since Augustine's time' (Shafarevich, 1980, pp 61-63).

The ideas to which Cardinal Hosius referred had widespread currency within the host of those caught up in the enthusiasm of the Second Awakening. Even in Europe there was an interest in these enthusiasms. It is not accidental that Halevy's popular opera of the period, Le Prophete, details the tumultous reign of the Anabaptists.

The group in the United States which most clearly reflects the influence of the Anabaptist tradition was known as the Oneida Community. John Humphrey Noyes (1811-1886) founded this community in 1846. Inspired by Noyes' adoption of the concept of "spiritual perfection," the members felt that after a true conversion they could live free from sin because impure matter no longer retained its corrupting power. Noyes combined his spiritual concepts with socialist views. Property was held in common. "Complex" marriage was instituted, ie, every male was the husband of every female. Propogation was allowed only by community consent. Noyes maintained his control over the community through "mutual criticism." Eventually, public resistance and the increased restlessness within the community dissipated its uniqueness. Complex marriage was dropped in 1879. Communal ownership of property ended soon thereafter (Handy, 1977, pp 222-223).

The Second Awakening provided the context in which Joseph Smith and his *Book of Mormon* appeared. Because of the Second Awakening, large numbers were seeking solutions to their problems outside of the traditional religions. Emerson was not alone in his search for a new teacher. But it must be noted that the "new teacher" for whom he was searching was, like himself, a man who had

> a wholly orphic confidence that he had a direct revelation. . . . As a perfectionist in everything relating to his country, he assumed that emancipation from mere church and creed would give a special energy to the century of "progress." A "race of titan" might yet develop. . . . Emerson, who knew his exceptionality all too well and fully espoused the romantic cult of genius, had democracy less at the center of his thought than "ye must be perfect even as your Father in Heaven is perfect." Emerson's belief in the individual as pure power, "man thinking," an "active soul," was so secure in "the moral law" that he called it a law of nature proved by "science" (Kazin, 1982).

Thus, even at its most sophisticated, the philosophy in a new Romantic key was seeking a leader with "the same, romantic, Promethean sense of power gained by emancipation from conventional religion" (Kazin, 1982). When one considers the influence of these Romantic aspirations and the Millenarianism of the Second Awakening with its promise of release from the "evils" of the profane life and from the more mundane precariousness of secular life, the ease with which Joseph Smith gained center stage is more readily appreciated, although Emerson, with his "coldness," would himself have denied any continuity of belief or kinship with the exuberant American Millenarianism that sought to found the new Zion.

Joseph Smith played a central role in the birth of Mormonism. "Any estimate of Joseph Smith is almost bound to be received differently by Mormons and non-Mormons" (Harrison, 1979). To some—his followers—he was a prophetic religious leader who resolved his difficulties with established religious organizations by founding a church. To others—his enemies—he was a total charlatan who created a movement which

> pandered to the popular craving for the "comforts of religion," by which was meant religious excitement, novelty, and "internal revelations, visions, raptures and ecstacies of all sorts," ascribed to the direct influence of the Holy Spirit. The people who became Mormons were those who "have never sought much else in religion but to get periodical happy feelings. . . (and) every Mormon knows that Smith's book is true because he sought in agonizing prayer and God, by his Spirit, revealed it to him" (Harrison, 1979, p 188).

The truth is probably a complex combination of the two. It is an amalgam of his followers' acceptance of Smith as prophet, seer, and apostle and Smith's increasing acceptance of the role of prophet and revelator. In this, as in other movements dominated by a charismatic leader, the eventual fate of the leader is a complex interaction of his own beliefs, his followers' aspirations (the role that they project onto him), and his willingness to set reasonable boundaries on these fantasies.

Smith grew up in upstate New York, in an atmosphere fraught with uncertainties, religious concern, and a sense of divine immanence and intervention in daily life. It was a place and time deeply troubled by the continuing rivalries among the traditional denominations. He turned from them and sought direct inspiration. His faith was rewarded by the revelation that he was chosen to lead God's people into the wilderness, convert the Indians, and, establish a new Jerusalem. In Smith's own words:

> . . . that the preparatory work for the second coming of the Messiah was speedily to commence; that the time was at hand, for the Gospel in all its fullness to be preached in power, unto all nations, that a people might be prepared for the millenial reign.

> I was informed that I was chosen to be an instrument in the hands of God, to bring about some of his purposes in this glorious dispensation. . . (Harrison, 1979, p 179).

This revelation was given to Smith by the Angel Moroni. Smith also received *The Book of Mormon,* written on golden plates in a strange hieroglyphic script which he was able to read because the angel provided special spectacles for this purpose. In 1830, Smith published a "translation" of the golden plates. And the plates were swept away by the angel after the successful translation (Handy, 1977, p 224).

The Book of Mormon describes the journeys of the good Nephites and their conflict with the evil Lamaanites. The Nephites were the lost tribes of Israel who had settled in America during the biblical era. The Lamaanites defeated the Nephites. The Nephite leader, Mormon, and his son, Moroni, buried the plates describing this history. Joseph Smith claimed that their disclosure was a sign that the Last Judgment was imminent.

Smith's other disclosures adroitly paralleled the ideas of Emerson and of the Millenarians. In his accepting the revelation that he was a prophet, he assumed the mantle of the "new teacher." In declaring that the age of revelation was not over, Smith concurred in the theory of divine immanence and concern over His creation. In accepting the concept of the eternality of matter, Smith echoed a central concept of the medieval Cathari and the Anabaptists (Handy, 1977, pp 225–226).

Smith published his *Doctrine and Covenants* in 1835. This record of continued revelation lent an authoritative tone to his emerging authoritarian style of control. When problems arose, Smith would produce new revelations and, based on these, would declare his solutions. Outsiders were often not impressed. His growing powers led to serious political conflicts. Non-Mormon fears led to persecution and attack. The Mormons were forced to move repeatedly. Their first move was from western New York to Kirtland, Ohio. There, Smith received an infusion of followers from the Millenarian group, the Campbellites. Fresh revelations led the group to exchange all their worldly goods for an early experiment in communalism known as the United Order of Enoch. Eventually, the Mormons moved to Missouri. Opposition drove them back to Nauvoo, Illinois. In 1840, they became chartered as a "state within a state" (Handy, 1977, p 226). The addition of 4000 converts from England led to Nauvoo's becoming the largest city in Illinois: The success of Mormon missionaries in England is a testimony to the universality and sustained appeal of the Millenarian propensity.

The physical transitions and hardships of industrialization and the social turmoil of urbanization led to the throng of conversions. It would be tempting to see the conversion in primarily economic terms, ie, as a response of the dispossessed. But the actual converts were seen as "respectable." Solutions to this question may lie in the persistence of the Millenarian tradition within England (it had played a significant role during the Revolution prior to Cromwell's ascension to total power) and to the disengagement of traditional denominations from the less favored. Ultimately, the Mormon message of concern met with ready acceptance in a population that was ignored and that retained a willingness to believe that immanent divine intervention could provide solutions to their problems in a context where secular authorities were distant and unconcerned.

While individual Mormons were accepted, Smith's preaching of novel concepts such as the plurality of gods, ie, the divine mother, baptism of the dead, and marriage for eternity created intense opposition (Woodward, 1980). The final crisis of his life was precipitated by his growing secular grandiosity and his announcing his candidacy for the president in 1844. In assessing this action, it is important to appreciate that at that time he was functioning on a virtually independent basis in a relatively isolated area and had raised a substantial armed legion under his personal control. The destruction of a printing press owned by dissident Mormons who objected to Smith's use of continuing revelations for political purposes led to a virtual civil war in and around Nauvoo. Martial law was impsed by the Illinois governor. Joseph Smith and his brother, Hyrum, were arrested on charges of treason. On the night of June 27, 1844, a mob, with the collusion of the militia guard, broke into the prison and murdered the two brothers (*Britannica*, 1911). Their death, in the acerbic appraisal of John Fraser of the University of Chicago, was assessed thus:

> This shooting was the most fortunate thing that had ever happened to the Mormon cause with the halo of martyrdom and effacing public recollection of his vices in the lustre of a glorious death. Of the confusion that followed Smith's "taking off" Brigham Young profitted by procuring his own election to the Presidency by the Council of the Twelve Apostles—a position for which his splendid executive abilities well fitted him (*Werner's Encyclopedia,* 1909, vol 16, p 853).

In the ensuing conflict, the Mormon hold over Nauvoo was broken. However, rather than pursue a policy of vengeance, the new prophet, Brigham Young, proceeded to organize an exodus to the basin of the Great Salt Lake where the construction of the new "Zion" would commence. In a march comparable to the Long March of this century, converts from England and Scandinavia gathered, drawn by the "emphasis on the gathering of the Saints in their Western Zion in anticipation of the Millenium (Handy, 1977, p 226). The zeal and organization of the saints produced a community which flourishes to this day. Because of its current acceptance within the American mainstream, it is difficult to realize that a half century of conflict—at times armed—existed between the isolated almost theocratic government of Deseret and the United States federal government. The tragedy at Mountain Meadow in 1859 is but one example of the persisting conflict between the Mormon-dominated community of the Utah Territory and the broader society (Wise, 1976). This conflict takes on a contemporary relevance when the attempt to regulate the practices of novel religions is under increasing public scrutiny and consideration.

Joseph Smith is clearly a most complex and contradictory figure. Despite his obvious charm and charisma, he was the subject of critical review in E.D. Howe's *Mormonism Unveiled.* While it is easy to dismiss this polemic as being a typical traditional Protestant critique of religious heterodoxy (as it has been facile to dismiss recent criticisms against contemporary cults as simply being an expression of religious orthodoxy), this polemic written in 1834 draws upon many first-hand accounts to give the unsuspecting some awareness of their "leader's" background as well as information about the group's practices and beliefs. In his work, Howe demonstrated how the Mormons reflect the multiplicity of religious strains of their day and most especially their borrowing from the ubiquitous Millenarian groups of the period.

In Howe's work and in the work of subsequent investigators, it appears that Joseph Smith and his family developed in a society which still believed in spirits, witches, fortune-telling, and in searching for hidden treasures in the earth. Harrison notes that in his mother's memoirs, all significant events within her family are related to the appearance of dreams and prophetic visions. Within this still primitive society, Joseph Smith Sr and Joseph Smith Jr (the founder of the Mormons) were considered experts in the use of the divining rod and convincing friends to dig for hidden gold (Wise, 1980). Characteristically, Joseph Smith Jr claimed he could see gold through what he called a "peep stone" he hid in his hat, but, when no gold materialized he would tell his diggers "that the treasure was removed by a spirit. . . or that it sunk down deeper into the earth (Howe, 1834, p 12).

Howe presents a deposition by one Peter Ingersoll who apparently knew Smith prior to his rise in notoriety. In the deposition, Ingersoll relates how Smith regaled him with a story about his naive family—whom he convinced that he possessed a legendary Golden Bible supposedly found in Canada. This "Golden Bible" was at the time the subject of much reverential talk. Ingersoll wrote that Smith said, " 'To my surprise they were credulous enough to believe what I said. . . . I have got the damned fools fixed and will carry out the fun' " (Howe, 1834, p 236). It was to his family that Smith made first mention of his miraculous visitation by an angel in 1825. However, he first mentioned this visitation to his family in 1827. A curious lapse in view of its personal and presumed millenial importance. In all events, "In the month of September 1827, Joseph got possession of the plates, after a considerable struggle with a spirit" (Howe, 1834, p 17). Smith's own family were the first converts to his story. He then preached "among the credulous, and lovers of the marvelous, to the belief that Joseph had found a record of the first settlers of America" (Howe, 1834, p 18). It must be noted that Howe propounded the theory that the "Golden Bible"—later, *The Book of Mormon*—which was presented as the product of divine revelation was actually plagiarized from a historical romance, *The Manuscript Found,* originally written by a deceased printer, Solomon Spaulding, around 1816. Howe and others have supported this theory with a plausible account of how the work wound up in Smith's hands (Howe, 1834, pp 226–227).

Whatever its origin—as the product of divine revelation or not—*The Book of Mormon* presented an exciting story grounded firmly in the American assumption that the New World was uniquely destined to provide mankind with a new start. The adoption within this century of works of fiction as being a presentation of a specific historical reality, ie, Sherlock Holmes and the fans known as the Baker Street Irregulars, some of whom maintain that A. Conan Doyle was simply Holmes' amenuensis (all in fun presumably—or is it?), is ample evidence of the propensity of people to adopt a fictional work as evidence of a concrete higher reality when it suits their other needs. The fanciful history (to the unbeliever) is comparable to the other pseudohistories of the period, ie, Blake and the theory of British Israelites. Above all, it presented those with Millenarian propensities with grounding—a theory—which provided support and a direction for their aspirations. *Editor's Note:* After all, did Smith's contemporary Karl Marx in his *Communist Manifesto* provide an economic program or a more "scientific" support for a Millenarian scenario with its eschatological end being the "withering away of the state"? In the creation of myth, the relationship of the field and the ground is most complex, contradictory, and sometimes beyond the conscious awareness of the most self-conscious of myth-makers (Bernstein, personal communication, 1982).

The history of Smith's translation of the plates varied to suit the needs of the audience. In some accounts, he translated them one word at a time by means of his "peep stone." In another account, he claimed that large spectacles found with the plates were used. In others, these were identified as identical to the *Urim and Thumim* mentioned in Exodus 28–30, and brought from Jerusalem by the heroes of the book "to enable Smith to translate the plates *without looking at them*" (Howe, 1834, p 18). Nor was the concern of the Lord limited to Smith's successful translation of this body of truth. In His wisdom, God also saw fit to grant him the copyright as well "the Prophet's labors shall not go unrewarded."

The contents of the "bible" received immediate criticism on their publication in 1830. The book's style is very similar to that of the King James Bible. As this was written in 1611, and *The Book of Mormon* was ostensibly written in the era of the Patriarchs, glaring discrepancies existed for those who wished to see them.

An example (cited by Howe, 1834, p 38) is that while *The Book of Mormon* includes two chapters of Isaiah in a contemporary word-for-word version, the rest of the book is written in the King James manner.

> It is a remarkable coincidence that the author of our book should be able to give us an exact copy of those two chapters, reading them in a stone placed in a hat! . . . (yet) he attributes the authorship of the whole book to the Lord.

Presumably, Howe drily noted that the Lord would be capable of stylistic consistency!

Other aspects of *The Book of Mormon* caught the critical attention of contemporary observers. It contained beliefs known to be Anabaptist in origin, names the Freemasons, and declares they originated with a band of highwaymen, adds "that Freemasonry will be very prevalent in the days that the *unlearned man* shall find the plates" (Howe, 1834, pp 40, 81, 89). Indeed, Freemasonry is, ironically, severely rebuked because the members:

> . . . bound themselves by secret oaths to protect each other in all things from the justice of the law. The Nephites are represented as being Anti-Masons and Christians, which carries with it some evidence that the writer foresaw the politics of New York in 1828–29, or that work was revised at or about that time (Howe, 1834, p 81).

Moreover, the book includes unusual interpretations of Christ's ministry which turn St. Paul into a liar and make Christ himself more truthful to the Nephites than he was to his own apostles.

An integral aspect of Smith's role as head of the Mormons was his use of revelations. In 1830, his brother, Hyrum, claimed that he also had had revelations. Joseph quickly saw this to be an undesirable ability. He allowed no rivals and dealt with them by declaring their revelations the work of Satan. He then declared that it was "revealed" that his wife and his scribe, Oliver Cowdery, were to be his chief aides. At this time, he abandoned the necessity for the spectacles and "peep stone." He merely closed his eyes and was given "revelation" (rather in the manner that the early Freud gave up the practice of touching his patient's forehead, *Ed.*). Observers noted that:

> In this manner he governs his followers, by asking the Lord, as he says, from day to day. Every difficult question is thus decided—from it there is no appeal. He has taught them that to doubt their divine authority, is to endanger their salvation (Howe, 1834, p 102).

While the potential for the use of "revelations" for the manipulation of followers and dissidents is obvious, his use of continuing revelations reflected a deep understanding of the needs of his followers. Smith appealed to their spiritual starvation by revealing a "call" from God (Howe, 1834, p 106). He revealed that the Mormons were to move to the Promised Land and build a New Jerusalem where they would be safe from the coming destruction of the world (Howe, 1834, p 110). *The Book of Mormon* would provide governance for the Millenium (Howe, 1834, p 111). Prospective converts were privately warned that New York State would sink into the sea if they did not convert (Howe, 1834, p 116).

Joseph Smith's need to ensure his preeminent role with the church drew opposition. One disillusioned Mormon, Ezra Booth wrote:

.... it is clearly and explicitly stated, that the right of delivering written commandment, and revelations, belongs exclusively to Smith, and no other person can interfere, without being guilty of sacrilege. . . unless he (Smith) falls through transgression; and in such a case, he himself is authorized to appoint his successor (Howe, 1834, p 214).

How to detect a transgression? Smith's guilt will be visible by his inability to give and receive revelations:

Thus even if Smith were to "commit adultery" or murder the husband of the woman, he can do so so long as he retain the use of his tongue, so as to be able to utter his jargon. . . and retain the spotless innocence of the holiest among mortals; and must be continued in the office of revelator, and head of the Church (Howe, 1834, p 214).

In other words, Smith felt himself elevated by his special position and grace to a level free from the influence of matter and flesh—because he is spiritually pure, all he does is pure!

In his attempts to control every aspect of a follower's life, Smith "revealed" that a follower's love should be expressed by giving an unbreakable deed turning all property over to the church. Such property was then to be administered by the elders in a communitarian fashion where all received back what they needed and the residue would go into a pool to be administered to the poor. (This legacy from the earliest period of Mormon history has provided an enviable history of community support and concern. It is still operative.) However, the "saints" financial wealth was also to be pooled for the buying of land for the New Jerusalem. And, if any followers balked at this, Smith admonished with another revelation: "And it should come to pass that he that sinneth and repenteth not, shall be cast out, and shall not receive again that which he has consecrated unto me" (Howe, 1834, p 129). In short, charity was a oneway street.

Smith's continuing revelations assumed an increasingly dictatorial tone. His prophecies were always couched in terms not immediately refutable. Predictions were always of far off events which by themselves were plausible. If he failed, there was an easy rationalization. If he guessed correctly, it was used as proof of his divine agency. For example, Smith predicted that cholera, which had ravaged New York in 1832, would return to destroy the population. This was a safe prediction because cholera appeared to follow a cyclical pattern of epidemics. The prediction failed (Howe, 1834, p 131). His followers were nonplussed. Yet, having embraced as an essential tenet of their church's doctrine that Joseph Smith Jr was a divinely chosen prophet and leader—the agent responsible for the coming millenium—they rationalized this defect in prophecy and continued to work as his aides. In other words, faith and behavior reinforced one another because they believed that the spirit worked through them, individually, as it worked through their leader, Joseph Smith.

Many of them actually carried their power of discerning spirits, and their enthusiasm, so far, that they frequently declared, that if Smith and all his witnesses were now to come forward and say that his pretensions were a wicked deception, they would not believe a word of it—because the *Spirit* had shown it was true. . . for the Spirit had so informed them (Howe, 1834, p 130).

Having accepted Smith's claims to divine inspiration, his dictates became the word of a "god." And, as a corollary, the acts of the righteous are divine acts and the acts of any external threat are perceived as acts of God's adversary—Satan.

The phenomenon of "speaking in tongues" made its appearance rapidly among the early Mormons. With the adhesion of converts from other Millenarian movements, this began spontaneously. But, as Smith was not responsible for this he declared this development to be the work of Satan. However, when a succession of failures shook the credibility of Mormon claims that they could heal the sick, see spirits, and cast out devils, speaking in tongues was tamed and adopted as a substitute. This phenomenon served to verify the presence of the spirit among the "saints" and provided them with an emotional and psychological experience which refuted criticism. After all, the individual who believes that the spirit has transformed his being and given him the ability to spout previously unknown "languages" finds it difficult and undesirable to believe otherwise. A belief in the spirit's visitations makes the phenomenon of "tongues" possible. The experience merely strengthens their convictions, especially when it serves as an intellectual and spiritual cleaver which effectively verifies a doctrine of extreme dualism.

Eventually, those who remained within the church had the experience. Those who refused to accept Smith's incessant revelations—the godless—did not. Ultimately, those who remained within the Church no longer needed to verify their experiences by comparisons with "profane" reality. To the believers, arguments presented according to the standards drawn from this profane reality were not even refuted—they were simply declared to have no applicability. Thus, the Mormon true believer could not be swayed by proofs drawn from a world which he believed was soon to be destroyed in the imminent millenium. But this intense conviction among the followers also imposed a price on their leader. It exacted from the spirit and its agent, Joseph Smith, the necessity for an unending display of spiritual power. After all, even believers need reinforcement, especially when the agents of the profane powers were allying against them. And it may be this is the price that was paid when the dissatisfied noted that, in 1844, Smith's behavior was marked by "bad temper, drunkenness and instability, was not that of a mature Christian" (Booth, quoted in Howe, p 203). Indeed, Smith's statements that his drunkenness was part of his attempt to prove to his followers that "he was not a God" takes on a particular poignancy in the context of his attempt to deal with their demands (Wise, 1976).

In 1834, the Mormons experienced trouble with the surrounding population in Missouri. Fears about the Mormons—their growing political power and ultimate intensions—precipitated additional violence and threats of violence against them. Smith then had a revelation which included the obligation to obey the law: ". . . for this purpose I have established the Constitution of this land, by the hands of wise men whom I raised unto this very purpose, and redeemed the land by the shedding of blood" (Howe, 1834, pp 148–154).

The revelation carried the Lord's command to seek redress from the elected government, but it also adroitly included a command "that God's strong men should dwell on the land He had granted." Mormons were commanded to gather at points of rendezvous and to contribute five dollars and a weapon. In this commandment was the formation of the Nauvoo Legion and the Danites—paramilitary organizations and an independent militia. The importance of these organizations was highlighted in the near-civil war which prevailed in Missouri (at Jackson County near Kansas City) which was in part, as Governor Daniel

Dunklin of Missouri noted, the product of religious bigotry and outrages against the Mormons and also the result of the Mormon assumption that they have the right to "levy war" in taking possession of their presumed rights. The continuing turmoil in Missouri led Smith to his final move back across the Mississippi to Nauvoo (near Carthage, Illinois) in 1840.

It was in Nauvoo that Smith's career reached its apotheosis and untimely end. The actual denouement occurred in the context of Smith's continuing use of revelations to meet all challenges to his authority. As one dissident noted:

> Have you not often proven to your satisfaction that he says he knows things to be so by the Spirit, when they are not so? You most certainly have. . . . (and that his revelations) emanate from his own weak mind (Booth in Howe, 1834, p 203).

Revelation multiplied into a series of confusing dictates each superceding the other in a bizarre attempt to preserve the prophet's pretensions to infallibility. It is in this context that Smith began to reveal to close associates the doctrine of plural marriage. It was publicly denied during his lifetime (indeed it was decried within *The Book of Mormon* and subsequently by Smith's widow). The origin of this curious doctrine is not clear, and an exploration of its antecedents would be beyond the scope of this chapter. Effectively, however, polygamy separated the Mormons (or the Latter Day Saints as they were soon called) from the surrounding population. It created a sense of cohesiveness in which all members saw themselves prey to the intrusions of the non-Mormon legal system (Wise, 1976). In a more profound sense, it may be viewed as an expression of pairing and bonding which intensifies in all groups as they prepare to act out their utopian and Millenarian fantasies (see Chapter 14). Certainly, it has been a characteristic of other Millenarian groups such as the Anabaptists and may be seen as having had a nonsexual expression in the Shakers. The tenacity with which the "saints" defended this institution is extraordinary. It was outlawed in the Morrell Act of 1862. In 1887, the government disbanded the church, confiscated its property, and imprisoned those practicing polygamy. This federal government interference continued despite the vote of Mormon women in defense of this institution (Mormon women had been granted suffrage in 1870). Indeed, this prompted the federal government to retract their suffrage "for failure to emancipate themselves" (de Riencourt, 1974, p 325). Finally, when faced with this threat to effectively undermine every material gain the church had accomplished—a new revelation came forth. It was now against the Lord's command to have more than one wife. This acquiescence to common standards cleared the path for Utah's admission as a state, in 1896. It has remained a practice among fringe groups despite its denunciation by the Mormon establishment.

Mormonism did not end with Joseph Smith Jr. Under Brigham Young it continued, alone, of all the Millenarian groups of the Second Awakening. Barring the direct intervention of a divine plan, why has this group flourished while other comparable groups have disappeared? The explanations for this survival may be sought on many levels. While the potential for faith is universal, it can reach expression only in myth which offers an avenue by which the individual can immerse himself in the forces that surround him and in so doing participate in their majesty. Myth provides the individual with an opportunity to escape from the unbearable tension of isolation and the anxiety of termination. It provides an opportunity to lose oneself in a larger reality of being and to affirm that one actually *is*. Myth operates in conferring value to the individual's exist-

72

ence—although this process may be labeled identification and fusion and its cognitive content may simply provide a rationale for immersing oneself in the oceanic mother. With Smith's death, Young was able to utilize the myth of the new Zion to provide a task orientation for the conflicting groups of saints. His characteristic approach was to see that the question of prophetic succession was handled within an institutional framework. Indeed, it may be that in the plethora of institutions and levels that Smith created, some of the clues to Mormon survival may be found because each level provided areas of responsibility and autonomy to the members. While Joseph Smith may have been the leader "who makes possible a new experience, the expression of forbidden impulses, secret wishes and fantasies" (Becker, 1973), he also provided a detailed mythology and highly structured organizational pattern which provided both status and some sense of continuity. While Mormonism is theologically an expression of one man's vision, Joseph Smith retained a sense of his fallibility within his grandiose preachings. Unlike the Rev. James Jones, he could never say "I am your Bible." As Becker has pointed out, the essence of charismatic leadership may lay in its ability to tame the terror:

> Realistically the universe contains overwhelming power. Beyond ourselves we sense chaos. We can't really do much about this unbelievable power, except for one thing: we can endow certain persons with it (Becker, 1973, p 145).

In his creation of the myth of a new People of Israel, Smith provided an environment in which the powerless were granted explanation of their helplessness, their alienation, but, above all, were granted an avenue of escape. It was out of this confluence of myth and necessity that Brigham Young was able to forge a people whose active participation in creating their future enabled them to survive their martyred leader's death. In Brigham Young's organization of an exodus to the beyond may have been a recognition that Smith's time had passed and that prophets may not be destined to be the masons of the temples they prophesy. While prophets may confidently proclaim "Credo, ergo sum" (I believe therefore I am), the beehive is an appropriately chosen symbol with which to build the new Jerusalem. One wonders if Joseph Smith Jr, who doted on elaborate uniforms, had in mind the slightly dour religion which focuses on an eternity of domesticity.

BIBLIOGRAPHY

Becker E: *The Denial of Death.* New York, Free Press, 1973.
de Riencourt A: *Sex and Power in History.* New York, David McKay, 1974.
Handy R: *A History of the Churches in the United States and Canada.* New York, Oxford, 1977.
Harrison JFC: *The Second Coming: Popular Millenarianism.* New Brunswick, NJ, Rutgers University Press, 1979.
Howe ED: *Mormonism Unveiled.* Published by the author in 1834. Available from Modern Microfilm Co, Salt Lake City.
Kazin A: The father of us all. *New York Review of Books* 1982;28(21):2-6.
Shafarevich I: *The Socialist Phenomenon.* New York, Harper & Row, 1980.
Werner's Encyclopedia: Akron, OH, Werner's Publishing Co, 1909.
Wise W: *Massacre at Mountain Meadows.* New York, Crowell, 1976.
Woodward K: What Mormons believe. *Newsweek* January 1980;68-71.

The Messengers of the 1890 Ghost Dance

KATHERINE P. EWING

T he Ghost Dance of 1890 was a North American Indian religious movement which developed out of the teachings of the prophet Wovoka, a Northern Paiute of western Nevada. It was one of several religious movements to arise among the North American Indian tribes during the eighteenth and nineteenth centuries and one of the most widespread to be focused on the teachings of a central prophet.* Wovoka and his followers reported that he had been taken up to heaven on several occasions. He became the messenger of God and was given a dance which he was instructed to teach to his people. He taught that by performing this dance, the Indians would hasten the coming of the renewed earth, where the living would be reunited with the dead, game would be plentiful, and the white man would no longer be dominant over the Indian. In the early days of the Ghost Dance, Wovoka himself was believed to be Jesus Christ, who had been sent by God to announce the coming of the resurrection. The doctrine was clearly a synthesis of traditional and Christian ideas.

The movement spread rapidly across the Plains between 1889 and 1891, creating a millenarian excitement among many tribes. At the height of the dance, thousands of people from formerly hostile tribes would gather at the dance grounds, dancing together for days or even weeks at a time. White settlers and government agents found this activity extremely threatening, and in many areas the government made intensive efforts to suppress the Ghost Dance. Government agents tried to break up gatherings of Indians who danced and interfered with the movements of messengers who were spreading the doctrine. In most cases, these efforts at repression were not directly successful; as this chapter will show, the dance's popularity waxed and waned independently of government

---

*It is also one of the best documented, thanks to the researches of James Mooney, a journalist, who in 1891 was sent by the US Bureau of Ethnology to learn first-hand about the Ghost Dance. Not only did Mooney spend time among several Plains tribes, he personally made the pilgrimage to the prophet Wovoka, an act which gave him access to communications which would otherwise have been unavailable. Much of this paper is based on Mooney's reports (Mooney, 1896).

efforts to control it. But pressure from the whites, as well as the failure of the predicted resurrection to occur, did force changes in doctrine and practice. In an effort at accommodation with the missionaries, for instance, the identification of Wovoka with Jesus Christ was dropped. The relationships among whites and Indians are of central importance in explaining the development and evolution of the Ghost Dance.

AN EXPLANATION FOR THE EMERGENCE OF THE GHOST DANCE

Some explanations of the emergence of the Ghost Dance focus on economic forces affecting the Indians in the late nineteenth century and on psychological stress which is assumed to accompany material hardship. Lesser (1933, p 109), for instance, attributes the Ghost Dance to "feelings of desolation caused by the loss of economic stability and security." Aberle (1959) focuses on the perception of deprivation—the awareness of the worsening of material conditions of the tribe and/or exposure to new wants that cannot be satisfied. Carroll (1975) claims to measure psychological stress by the "objective" factor of the disappearance of the buffalo.

It is true that economic distress was acute and cultural loss extensive among the Plains tribes in the 1880s. There is, however, an issue more fundamental for the interpretation of a millenarian movement such as the Ghost Dance. Between economic conditions and "response" is the crucial intermediate step of the meaning of this distress to those who experienced it. Many societies have faced extreme hardship without resorting to millenarian movements. Loss of specific items of a culture is not significant in isolation: there are many instances of peoples who have readily given up much of their natal culture in order to embrace another. Even domination per se cannot explain despair or predict a reaction such as millenarianism (cf, Moore, 1978, pp 68–74, concerning cultural variation in reactions to a Nazi concentration camp).

Such instances suggest that the crucial issue is not economic or even political, but whether cultural patterns are available for securing cultural and individual self-esteem in such a situation of deprivation and/or domination. A variety of reactions is possible, and not all individuals will respond in the same way. They may draw upon or modify available patterns, "revitalizing" the society (Wallace, 1956); they may turn to sources of self-esteem provided by the new culture; or they may be frustrated in all their efforts. As Burridge (1969, p 117) puts it, at issue is the possibility for "the ennoblement of man."

In many encounters between whites and Indians, the latter were not treated as human beings to be engaged in meaningful dialogue. In addition, Indian cultures lacked devices by which such situations of domination could be made meaningful and allow the dominated a position in which self-esteem could be maintained. Plains cultures did not have, for instance, the South Asian model of passive action epitomized by the Buddha and, later, by Gandhi; these were cultures that placed particular stress on honor and status derived from bravery in warfare. But, as Spier et al (1959, p 87) argue, many North American Indian cultures did have a tradition of cult activity which might have originated from purely native preoccupations such as world renewal: "An older form was turned to nativistic and revivalistic account when acculturation conditions became intolerable."

The economic issue cannot be understood in isolation from the prestige system, and it is the prestige system that defines self-esteem in both cultural and individual (psychological) terms. Prestige was an extremely important basis for self-esteem in these cultures. For younger men, prestige derived largely from one's success as a warrior. Among the Sioux, for example, bravery was valued as one of the four fundamental virtues, along with fortitude, generosity, and wisdom. Wisdom as a source of prestige and authority came only with advancing age and was usually attributed to men who had also been great warriors (Hassrick, 1964, p 14). Contact with whites created a series of social interactions for which old categories and rules were inapplicable. The warrior societies had collapsed in several Plains societies. New sources of prestige and authority were problematic; for example, the Indian police acquired their authority from the white government, and their relationships with the traditional chiefs were confused and ambivalent.

As the criteria for prestige became loose and ill-defined, the criteria for personal integrity also come into doubt (Burridge, 1969, p 75). The painful consequences of this confusion are vividly protrayed in an account of the killing of Sitting Bull told by John Loneman, one of the Indian police involved. After the killing, he asked his family to prepare a sweat bath so that he could "cleanse himself for participating in a bloody fight with his fellow men." He recorded his reaction to the army's praise for the brave way in which he carried out his part in the fight with the Ghost Dancers: "I was not very brave right at that moment. His comment nearly set me a crying" (Vestal, 1934, pp 54, 55).

The whites were not the first to defeat any of the Plains societies and drive them off their land. The Sioux nation was a powerful society that had rapidly spread and come to dominate some Plains tribes during the 200 years before the influx of whites:

> The Sioux had such faith in their national destiny that they haughtily dominated the heartland of the Northern Plains for nearly a century. . . . They were hated by many and feared by most, and they boasted of this reputation. They were proud of their superiority and were vigilant in defending it (Hassrick, 1964, p 57).

Although the Sioux dominated other tribes militarily and economically, they did not try to change the rules of the game once they had won. The game was warfare, and the warring societies shared this idiom, this kind of communication. Their prestige systems were, in part, based on such warfare. The whites used warfare to demonstrate their power as well, but then in contrast to previous conquerors, they attempted to impose "peace" through total conquest. They invaded all spheres of activity. Not only did they take the land of others—nothing new on the Plains—they tried to wipe out Indian cultures. They denounced old sources of prestige and put the Indians at the bottom of the alien social hierarchy, imposing upon them new, humiliating criteria for self-definition.

Even in its most nativistic and hostile manifestations, the Ghost Dance was an effort to define a social world which not only accounted for whites but reestablished acceptable categories for defining self and other in a world which included them. The dance also provided rules for communication in the new social situations which the whites' presence had created. As they increasingly manifested their power—by killing off the buffalo, moving the Indians to reservations, putting their children in schools, placing missionaries on the reservations, etc—more and more of the Indians' daily activities and situations were structured or influenced by whites. Thus it became increasingly difficult to ignore this foreign presence, even when no outsiders were actually visible. To put the phenomenon in the language of dialogue, the white man became an omnipresent interlocuter, the "other" whose judgment cannot be ignored in the social presence of the self. Similarly, although many Ghost Dance activities occurred with no whites present, their impact was certainly felt.

Contact with whites undermined all communication, not simply that between whites and Indians but also within the Indian community itself. Old sources of authority, categories of leadership, and systems of prestige were no longer supported by consensus. The undermining of the prestige system also weakened culturally established categories for defining relationships between self and other.

Dialogue defines and redefines individuals relative to each other. Even in fairly stable societies, social interaction is an arena for affirming (or testing) self-esteem and for making public and affirming the relationships between self and other. In some contexts, the categories and rules are highly specific; self–other relations are clear or at least not overwhelmingly problematic. In others, for instance when individuals are jockeying for leadership positions or litigating disputes, the categories and rules may be clear but outcomes are not predictable. In such settings, however, both parties can at least walk away with a sense of what happened in the interaction. They are able to specify who lost face and who did not and to describe changes in the "power" relationship. They can define self and other in the interaction.

Religious movements such as the Ghost Dance involve the reorganization of cultural rules and categories so that new experiences and situations which cannot be accounted for by the old system can be explained. Cosmology is reorganized; new elements are fitted in. The Ghost Dance doctrine takes into account the white man as other, locates him with respect to the Indian, and locates both with respect to the total world. This idenficiation and location of self and other made by adherents of the doctrine often also involved a resistance to the white man's definition of contact situations, a rejection of the legitimacy of the authority which the whites claimed with respect to the Indian.

Formulations such as the Ghost Dance doctrine look forward and backward simultaneously. They provide an ideology which organizes goals and specifies a course of action to be followed to realize them. At the same time, these formulations reorganize the past, redefining all prior situations and relationships, and attempt to eliminate the ambiguity seen in current situations.

The Ghost Dance doctrine was not simply established once and for all. Every instance of transmission was a new formulation. Most of these formulations were not recorded, but thanks to Mooney's recording of many details, we know at least something of the context in which many were grounded. One may consider these versions as texts intended for specific audiences. In analyzing the doctrine as it appears in these specific manifestations, the intentions of the person providing the account must be considered.* Only in this way can one understand how a religious system or world view is created or modified (ie, how a cultural tradition is shaped) and the role of individuals seeking to explain the situations they have lived through, to put into words the relationships of self and other which they are struggling to establish.

---

*Most Ghost Dance activities occurred when whites were not present, yet most accounts of the dance and formulations of doctrine which were recorded were made to whites, or at least in their presence, often under duress.

TRANSMISSION OF THE DANCE

The transmission of the Ghost Dance to the Plains tribes with which Mooney had direct contact can be clearly documented. The pattern is quite consistent: when a tribe heard of the dance from a visiting outsider or from letters sent by relatives (often school children), the tribe would send its own delegation to the messiah in order to confirm the report with an eyewitness account. Upon the return of the messenger, a council would be held in which he would narrate his account of his journey to the messiah. If the report was favorable (and in some instances it was not), the messenger initiated the dance or, if the dance had already been initiated, he became a new leader and instructed the dancers in the messiah's updated specifications of ritual and doctrine. Such a pattern reveals the importance of the authority of the messenger and hence of the legitimacy of the message. Wovoka's doctrine and manner of receiving visitors changed as circumstances changed during the years of peak Ghost Dance activity, and so did the goals of the messengers who visited the prophet. There appear to be two key turning points in the direction of the movement: the massacre at Wounded Knee in December of 1890 and the passing of the spring of 1891. The first event was most immediately traumatic for the Sioux, but it demonstrated to all the Plains tribes the absolute power of the American government. Even the spiritual power drawn upon in the Ghost Dance was nothing in the face of this military force. Physical resistance would result in brutal annihilation.

Coupled with this realization was the coming of spring, and with it the passing of the date set for millenial redemption. The Ghost Dance continued, but it was clear that accommodation to the presence of the whites must be made and that a new world view must be able to account for and provide guidance in a social world which included whites.

After a total breakdown in communication, efforts were made on the part of both whites and Indians to move toward a dialogue. It must be kept in mind, of course, that this dialogue occurred in a situation of almost absolute domination. Old routes to prestige and authority had been thrown into question because of this domination. The following examination of the actions of leaders of the Ghost Dance movement (in recorded situations) should reveal the difficult choices and adjustments that these people made in the effort to reestablish a viable prestige system—and sources of self-esteem—that could not be undermined by the gaze of the white man.

One of the most significant delegations for the spread of the doctrine among the Plains tribes met with the prophet Wovoka in the winter of 1889–1890. This was a mixed group composed mostly of Sioux, with several Cheyennes and Arapahos. Several members of this delegation became powerful and influential leaders of the Ghost Dance. Among them were Porcupine, a northern Cheyenne whose detailed account of his journey was one of the first to reach the American government; Sitting Bull, a southern Arapaho who systematically spread the doctrine to many southern Plains tribes; and Short Bull, one of the Sioux leaders who played an important role in the agitation which ultimately led to the Wounded Knee massacre.

The political element was the most important part of the Ghost Dance doctrine as formulated by these messengers. Their primary concern was the actions that their listeners would or would not take as as result of their words, going beyond the performance of the dance to the millenial expectation that the world itself would be transformed. Despite its apocalyptic orientation, however, the focus in the formulations of all these messengers was on the relationship of Indians to whites.

The Sioux

According to Mooney (1896), the Sioux first heard rumors of the Ghost Dance in 1889, through students who had returned from government schools, letters from other tribes, and contact with Araphahos and Shoshones living to the west of them. In the fall of 1889, a council of Sioux chiefs appointed a delegation to travel west in order to learn about the new messiah. When the delegates returned to Pine Ridge Agency in the spring of 1890, another council was called but was not held because the postmaster at Pine Ridge, an educated Sioux, informed the government agent, who arrested at least one of the delegates. He was held in confinement for two days, refusing to talk when questioned. Upon the return of Kicking Bear, another of the delegates, the council was finally held and the Ghost Dance formally inaugurated, with the delegates acting as leaders of the ceremony.

The Sioux outbreak and the massacre at Wounded Knee occurred in December of 1890, after a summer and fall in which performances of the Ghost Dance intensified, to the alarm of the government agents and white settlers. Mooney (1896, p 828) stressed that the Ghost Dance "was only a symptom and expression of the real causes of dissatisfaction." He assigned as the real causes "1) unrest of the conservative element under the decay of the old life, 2) repeated neglect of promises made by the government, and 3) hunger" (Mooney 1896, p 824). But Mooney felt the precipitating factor was the appointment of an incompetent agent shortly before the massacre, which prevented any systematic unfolding of a consistent policy toward the Sioux.

Accounts of the massacre made it clear that the "battle" was not a premediated attack on either side. Both reacted in panic, not only in this climactic situation but also in the days and weeks preceding the event. The breakdown in communication was gradual but complete. Ultimately, most of the Sioux and whites came to regard each other as totally unpredictable, even inhuman or subhuman. Social interaction was no longer based on shared rules or common understandings.

Most writers focus on the material causes of the Sioux outbreak, and it is true that the Sioux were pushed to the point of desperation. But evidence from available accounts suggests that neither the threat of starvation nor even the loss of cultural traditions per se was the central issue. The Sioux were struggling with the problem of accounting for a world which included both whites and Indians and providing consistent rules for communication between them. It was imperative that such an accounting give the Sioux a self-image of dignity, power, and authority vis-a-vis the whites and themselves.

McGillycuddy, who was agent at Pine Ridge from 1879 to 1886, blamed the breakdown in communication that occurred under his successors to the incompentence of these agents. He attributed his own success to having placed "confidence" in the Indians:

> We established local courts, presided over by the Indians, with Indian juries; in fact we believed in having the Indians assist in working out their own salvation. We courted and secured the friendship and support of the progressive and orderly element, as against the mob element. . . . When my Democratic successor took charge in 1886,. . . all white men, half-breeds, or Indians who had

sustained the agent under the former administration were classified as Republicans and had to go. The progressive chiefs. . . were ignored, and the backing of the element of order and progress was alienated from the agent and government, and in the place of this strong backing that had maintained order for seven years was substituted Red Cloud and other nonprogressive chiefs, sustained by the ancient tribal system (Mooney, 1896, p 832).

When a new Republican agent "ignorant of Indians and their peculiarities," took over in October of 1890, he could not rely on the progressive leaders, who had been alienated by the former agent. These "progressive" leaders said "We, after incurring the enmity of the bad element among our people by sustaining the government, have been ignored and ill-treated by that government, hence this is not our affair." The agent "took the mob for a declaration of war, abandoned his agency, returned with troops—and you see the result" (quotes from Mooney, 1896, p 833).

In November 1890, less than a month before Wounded Knee, American Horse, a spokesman for the progressive Sioux who did not joint the Ghost Dance, charged the government commissioners to the Sioux with responsibility for starting the trouble. His statement is a list of broken promises: "The Great Father says if we do what he directs it will be to our benefit; but instead of this they are every year cutting down our rations. . ." (Mooney, 1896, p 840).

McGillycuddy's strategy as Sioux agent was to encourage an alternative source of power and guidance—the progressives and Indian police. He polarized the tribal leadership, with the progressives (on the side of order) vs the "mob." The Ghost Dance, in effect, gave the "mob" (ie, the traditional chiefs) a renewed source of power and a doctrine which accounted for the presence of whites. This, coupled with the undermining of the power and authority of the progressives, led to confrontation. The polarization was itself a part of the struggle to define the social world, stemming from white identification and definition of Indians and their culture. It explains in part why the Sioux formulations of Ghost Dance doctrine were so violently anti-white: Sioux culture and traditional sources of authority had already been defined as utterly incompatible with white civilization.

The Ghost Dance was not simply a rejection of the whites and an effort to return to a precontact world. It was, rather, a doctrine which simultaneously redefined the relationship of Indians and whites and attempted to appropriate the sources of power and authority which the whites drew upon. It also denied the legitimacy of white authority:

All the delegates agreed that there was a man near the base of the Sierras who said that he was the son of God, who had once been killed by the whites, and who bore on his body the scars of the crucifixion. He had now returned to punish the whites for their wickedness, especially for their injustice toward the Indians. With the coming of the next spring, (1891) he would wipe the whites from the face of the earth, and would then resurrect all the dead Indians, bring back the buffalo and other game, and restore the supremacy of the aboriginal race. He had before come to the whites, but they had rejected him. He was now the God of the Indians, and they must pray to him and call him "father," and prepare for his awful coming (Mooney, 1896, p 820).

The intense struggle over the definition of legitimate authority, and the overt power struggle associated with it, was exacerbated by the unwillingness of many whites to communicate in anything other than white (European) cultural categories and assumptions. There was no effort to make contact with the Sioux world view or establish common rules of discourse from there. McGillycuddy perpetuated the polarization of progressives and traditionalists in every situation and caused it to penetrate every aspect of Sioux community life. The initial polarization occurred after the signing of a bill presented by the government. As American Horse stated:

> I was speaker for the whole tribe. In a general council I signed the bill . . . and 580 signed with me. The other members of my band drew out and it divided us, and ever since these two parties have been divided. The nonprogressives started the ghost dance to draw from us (Mooney, 1896, pp 839–840).

The Indian community itself had been split, and no social situation could now be free of a relationship to white culture and power.

The perpetuation of that polarization and the struggle over defining legitimate sources of power and authority is clearly revealed in missionary Mary Collins's account of her dealings with Sitting Bull, the Sioux leader who had been a central figure in the 1876 battle against Custer and was a chief agitator in the events leading up to Wounded Knee. She regarded the teachings about Christ in the Ghost Dance as a direct challenge to her work, having been a missionary among the Sioux for five years when the Ghost Dance swept through the community. Her brief autobiography is organized around her relationship with Sitting Bull.

Collins's opening paragraph is a direct statement of her self-image relative to the other, the Indian. After discussing her extensive family history of missionaries to the Indians, she describes her peculiar capacity to understand their language. Even when she did not understand what they spoke, she "intuitively knew what they meant" (Vestal, 1934, p 61). In other words, she felt she was the all-comprehending authority figure, analogous to the parent of a 2-year-old who can understand him even when others cannot. Like the parent, she attributes her ability to some kind of genealogical tie: ". . . I decided that there must be something in my ancestry which accounted for my liking for and ease in comprehending them." Her characterization of their culture reveals a similar image of the unsocialized child: "I went to Standing Rock in 1885 when Sitting Bull's people were not civilized; they did not appear in the dress of later days but were wild and crude in all their ways" (Vestal, 1934, p 61).

Her struggle with Sitting Bull for authority over the tribe is expressed not only in the content of their encounters, but also in their etiquette, which she described in some detail. This struggle over the rules of social interaction reveals a marked shift in their relationship over time. Basically, Collins did not change her attitude or compromise. The Indians were to accept her view of reality or be punished for misbehavior. Sitting Bull's more complicated sequence of positions is revealed against the background of this inflexible other who refused to accept his authority in any sphere or even to grant him dignity in the interaction:

> He. . . tried to have me agree that I would not have the Indians leave their old ways of living but that I should teach them to read and to care for them when they are ill; he urged most strongly however that they must not be persuaded to abandon their dances. This of course I wouldn't consent to (Vestal, 1934, p 62).

Collins demonstrated the inflexibility of her position in the etiquette of their next encounter. Sitting Bull rode up to her home and called to her:

I heard him but did not answer. . . . Again he called me and still I did not answer. Then he swung off his horse and came to my door. Again he called me and then came in. I saw him and spoke to him. He was a little bit angry and said, 'Wenonah, I called and called you, did you not hear me?' 'Yes, Sitting Bull, I heard you.' 'Why then, didn't you answer me or come out to see what I wanted?' and I answered, 'Sitting Bull, ladies never go out to the fence to speak to gentlemen, gentlemen always come in to speak to ladies.' He looked down and replied, 'Oh, I didn't know that' (Vestal, 1934, p 63).

In this encounter, two different culturally patterned forms of etiquette collided, with nonverbal interaction made explicit. Sitting Bull was not only told what proper behavior is among whites; he was deliberately humiliated. She demonstrated her authority over him by trying to force him into a moment of bewilderment, created by her silence.

We cannot know in detail the significance of Sitting Bull's reaction. The reaction of casting down the eyes is far more pervasive among the Sioux than it is in our own culture; it is used in a wide range of situations. He may have felt bewildered, humiliated, or even furiously angry, but by lowering his eyes, he expressed the Sioux virtue of fortitude (see Hassrick, 1964, p 36). This gesture was undoubtedly misinterpreted by Collins.

Sitting Bull showed a continuing willingness to compromise. On his next visit, with 12 chiefs accompanying him, she further asserted the priority of her own customs when Sitting Bull took out his peace pipe and offered it to the others:

'Brother Sitting Bull,' I said, (for he always called me sister), 'I never have any smoking in my house so you will have to wait until after our conversation is over before you smoke that you may do so outside,' and he put away his peace pipe (Vestal, 1934, p 63).

The pipe was one of the most important ritual objects of the Sioux. Her statement was one that might have been made to an impolite young man in her parlor back east; it totally ignored the ritual significance of the pipe to the assembled chiefs. But her reference to it as a "peace pipe" suggests that her misinterpretation was deliberate and was intended to undermine Sioux culture and thus the authority and dignity of the chiefs. He continued to tolerate her, undoubtedly because she "told them the straight facts" concerning their relations with the government, unlike others who "left disagreeable things out" (Vestal, 1934, p 64). She was an important source of knowledge and, hence, of power for Sitting Bull.

During the peak of the Ghost Dance excitement, Collins conducted Sunday services in competition with a Ghost Dance which was occurring within earshot. Afterward, she had an encounter with Sitting Bull which was marked by a pattern of interaction that bore a remarkably parallel but inverted relationship to the structure of their earlier interactions.

After our services I went to the Holy Tent of Sitting Bull, and asked admittance. He sent out word that he could not see me at that time. I replied that I wished most earnestly to talk with him and after a while he sent out a message that he would speak with me. He directed that I must pass to the left and not step on certain places. I went in and sat down as he told me and he continued performing other ceremonies (Vestal, 1934, p 68).

This time, she went to him and was obliged to conform to the rules of his system.

She was, in effect, left calling with no response. Sitting Bull was no doubt exacting his vengeance for her previous behavior.

Yet her assumptions about their relationship did not change. She continued to treat him like a foolish child. She interrupted his ceremonies to say, "Sitting Bull, you know you do not believe these things you are telling your people, you know that the Indians have not risen from the dead. . . . The law orders you to go to Ft. Yates and you must obey" (Vestal, 1934, p 69). She then described how his people would be shot if he did not discontinue the dance. Although she does not describe his reaction—a striking gap in her account—it would probably be safe to speculate that he did not respond. His silence would parallel the silence she had forced him to live through in their early encounter.

Their assumptions about the world at this point were so totally at odds that there were no grounds for communication. To engage her in conversation would have meant once again accepting her assumptions, which would have undermined Sitting Bull's power and authority in the situation. As it was, he used nonverbal tactics that they had shared. His success is revealed in a passage earlier in her account: "He had some very indefinable power which could not be resisted by his own people or even others who came into contact with him" (Vestal, 1934, p 64). This statement is at least partly based on her experience of their final encounter. Sitting Bull had revealed the power to make her feel like a nonperson; he had overwhelmed her in their battle for power and recognition.

Collins's tactic of direct confrontation in a ritual context was more successful with other, less-powerful individuals. She simply refused to accept the legitimacy of the Ghost Dance experience at all:

> One man whom I knew well fell upon the ground affecting that he was unconscious. I went up to him and said, "Louis, get up, you are not unconscious, you are not ill; get up and help me to send these people home." Louis rose and looked around him. All the people saw him obey me and of course lost their faith in the dance (Vestal, 1934, p 69).

She had again been able to demonstrate her power relative to Sitting Bull, not in direct encounter, but in her ability to manipulate others. Her main strategy was humiliation and control, undermining the power of the ritual. Collins instructed her helpers in the same techniques in order to break up other Ghost Dance meetings.

Missionaries such as Collins saw the Ghost Dance doctrine primarily as being in direct competition with their own preaching and authority. She felt that Sitting Bull and other leaders were exploiting and perverting the "progress" she had made in converting and enlightening these people.

> Sitting Bull was endeavoring to make the people believe that he was a Christian and believed in the Christ as they did; consequently that a resurrection would come, not in the future for the Indians, but NOW. . . . He told them that the Christ had come for the Indians and not for the white people. . . (Vestal, 1934, pp 65-66).

It was in this atmosphere that the Sioux delegates worked to spread the Ghost Dance doctrine.

Short Bull   Short Bull was a member of the official Sioux delegation which met with the prophet Wovoka in the winter of 1889–1890. His formulation of Wovoka's message is recorded in the form of an impassioned speech which he made to a gathering of Sioux. It makes no effort to appease the white community and is in striking contrast to a formulation by the Cheyenne delegate Porcupine, which will be discussed below. In his address, Short Bull represented himself as a direct channel of communication between "our Father in heaven" and the people. He has become a new type of leader, even taking it upon himself to change the date of the predicted destruction of the old earth.

Short Bull's main focus was on pitting the power of the Ghost Dance directly against the power of the whites. Whites had been stripped of their spiritual sources of power, which came originally from Jesus Christ, so that they lost any ability to take effective action in the world. Not even their bullets would have any effect. He depicted a scene in which ghost dancers would be attacked by soldiers. The dancers would be protected by "holy shirts," and the soldiers would begin to drop dead because of the power of the song. The rest would sink into the earth, their guns powerless. There is no dialogue.

Another aspect of Short Bull's formulation is his depiction of a cosmic order that goes beyond the Sioux. He said, "We, the tribe of Indians, are those who are living a sacred life" (Mooney, 1896, p 789). He explicitly included other tribes in his sacred map of the world: "Our father in heaven has placed a mark at each point of the four winds." The clay pipe, according to Mooney the most sacred thing in Sioux mythology, lies at the setting of the sun. Similar objects representing the Cheyenne, Arapaho, and Crow lie in the north, east, and south. This formulation would seem to support Worsley's (1968) contention that millenarian movements serve to unite segmented societies in the face of colonial power. More directly, however, Short Bull's statements reveal a perception of all Indians as a part of the same moral community, as humans with legitimate spaces in the world, in contrast to the whites. He does not make the transition to the concept of a political confederation.

Short Bull's address, like Collins's account, reveals a deterioration of communication between whites and Sioux to the point of severence: "Whatever white men may tell you, do not listen to them, my relations" (Mooney, 1896, p 789). With the Ghost Dance the Sioux had a doctrine which could account for the presence of the whites in their world without acknowledging their legitimacy. Not only did the Sioux reject their power and authority, they denied the right of the whites to space on the earth. The doctrine did this by taking the central story of Christian teaching and turning it to their own purposes, but also by linking it to elements of their own world view, particularly to symbols expressing vehicles of spiritual power (a process common to all millenarian movements).

A revealing example of this process is the description of Satan provided by Kicking Bear, another member of the same delegation (Miller, 1959). Kicking Bear and the other delegates had been guided by Wovoka on a visit to the spirit land. There he saw the Great Spirit (Wakantanka) and "a tall man with large joints and short hair all over his body and face. This hairy man was a powerful evil spirit known to the whites as 'Devil.' He demanded half of the people inhabiting the world. At last Wakantanka said, 'The Indians are my chosen people. I will not give them up. But you may have the white man' " (Miller, 1959, p 51). This description of the Devil corresponds to a description which Straus gives of a Cheyenne spiritual being:

> The "hairy people" are human-like, live in caves, and cause sickness and death to those who encounter them. . . . Perhaps these bear-like "hairy people" are the unemerged, the ones who did not make it to the surface of the earth. . . . These

hairy ancestors are the unenlightened, the unlawful—still killing and consuming their own kind, animal in character and animal-like in the hairy cover of their bodies (Straus, 1976, p 103).

Straus was discussing Cheyenne beliefs about bears and human ancestors, but her account could also be a less than charitable description of Cheyenne perceptions of the white man. Grinnell makes the link between hairy ancestors and the Ghost Dance doctrine explicit: "The surface of the earth will become a mire in which the whites will sink, while the Indians will remain on the surface. . . . more than one tribe believes that the giants who used to inhabit the earth, before the creation of the Indians of today, were destroyed by the Deity in just this way" (Grinnell, 1891, p 67). These hairy creatures never emerged onto the surface of the earth.

Kicking Bear also describes the earth as rotten in many places. According to him, the great spirit promised to cover it "with new soil to a depth of five times the height of a man. Under this new land will be buried all the white men. . ." (Miller, 1959, p 52). This version suggests that the boundary between the surface of the earth and the prehuman land below had weakened. Whites were associated with subhuman hairy giants who have always threatened to snatch the Indians back below the surface of the earth, to take their knowledge and power away from them. The old threat was now realized. At that moment, Indians and whites were sinking into a rotten earth together. Contact with the spirit world had almost been lost. The old bridges, such as the warriors's vision quest, had been lost. But now a messenger from the spirit world had returned to reestablish the bond, to build a bridge linking the earth and the spirit land, and finally, to raise the surface of the earth, bringing it closer to the spirit land.

Whites were thus defined as nonhuman, as evil spirits with whom communication was impossible. Short Bull said, "Some of my relations have no ears, so I will have them blown away" (Mooney, 1896, p 788). As Straus points out, the Cheyenne, who also associate failure to listen with having no ears, believe that the ability to listen is a distinctively human characteristics (Straus, 1976, p 160). Listening is the source of knowledge. Whites will lose their knowledge. They too have no ears. They are not a part of the social world.

The Cheyenne and Arapaho Delegates

Members of the Arapaho and Cheyenne tribes accompanied the Sioux delegation of 1889–1890 and returned to their own communities to inaugurate the Ghost Dance. Most prominent among these were Porcupine, a Northern Cheyenne from the Tongue River Agency in Montana, and Sitting Bull, a Southern Arapaho (not to be confused with the Sioux chief of the same name), who systematically inaugurated the dance among several southern tribes.

Porcupine and Sitting Bull are revealing cases to examine from the perspective of efforts to define new criteria for leadership and that of their relationship to the formulation of a doctrine that explains the existence of the whites and provides rules for reconstructing a social world in which whites are present. Both received the teachings of Wovoka at the same time and in the same setting that the Sioux did. Hence, any differences in doctrine and activity cannot be explained in terms of changes in Wovoka's version of the doctrine or in his activities. Such changes, as we shall see, are significant for later messengers from the Arapaho, who encountered Wovoka after the crucial turning points of Wounded Knee and the passing of the spring of 1891, when marked changes in doctrine occurred.

Both Porcupine and Sitting Bull preached the coming of the Resurrection, the Millenium. The basic elements of the doctrine as they formulated it corresponded to Sioux accounts: Wovoka was Christ, who had returned to earth to tell of the coming of the Resurrection. Wovoka showed them scars from the crucifixion and guided those present on a spiritual journey to heaven, where they met dead relatives who would rejoin the living in the spring. The world would be renewed. Like the Sioux delegates, each became a leader of the dance upon his return. For each, we can examine the sources of authority from which he drew and his approach to the problem of the white invasion of his social world.

Porcupine   When Porcupine returned to the Northern Cheyenne reservation, he began preaching the Ghost Dance doctrine and organizing dances. Following some trouble between the Cheyennes and whites, the government agent called Porcupine in and forced him to give an account of these activities. In this situation of overt dominance of white over Indian, it is not surprising that Porcupine's formulation of doctrine was appeasing to the whites. One is tempted to say that Porcupine distorted the story to save his own life. His intention was perhaps the very immediate one of avoiding arrest.

The elements stressing white and Indian brotherhood are not simply tacked onto the beginning and end of Porcupine's story to appease the agent, however. They are built into the structure of the narrative itself. Porcupine begins the account in the everyday world, with a long description of his trip to the land of the messiah. Every aspect of the trip involved both whites and Indians. He traveled by railroad and talked with a government agent at each place he stopped. As he drew closer to Paiute territory, more and more people were involved in the Ghost Dance. The people encountered took on a mythical quality. He stressed that the people were all good people, unlike those at home: "I thought it strange that the people there should have been so good, so different from those here." He stressed that both whites and Indians danced the Ghost Dance: "I and my people have been in ignorance until I went and found out the truth. All the whites and Indians are brothers, I was told there. I never knew this before" (Mooney, 1896, p 794).

A close examination of the text of Porcupine's statement (which was recorded by the agent) reveals a set of intentions that can be read on least two levels. On one, many of his statements are oriented toward minimizing his own active role in the affair, or at least emphasizing that he did not disobey white laws. On another level, the narration of the journey has the structure of a vision quest, which traditionally confers power on the warrior or shaman. Finally, there is a strong stress on the noncontroversial nature of his teaching: he emphasizes that whites and Indians are brothers.

His emphasis on the "badness" of all his people explains the suffering they have gone through thus far; they have been punished for their sins. This is an element that also occurs in the Sioux version. He said that those who would not listen to the new teaching would be wiped off the earth. One could take this farther (as he probably did in a more congenial setting): if whites rejected the doctrine, they would be wiped out. Porcupine did not make this explicit to the agent. The changes made for the benefit of the agent do not appear to be fundamental alterations of the story, but rather shifts in emphasis.

The effort to link whites and Indians in the same system of meaning is especially revealed in Porcupine's description of Wovoka. The messiah was a conjunction, not only of the spirit and the world, but also of white and Indian. On the first encounter with the prophet, most of his dress was a white man's, except for his moccasins. Porcupine described his first reaction: "I had always thought that the Great Father was a white man, but this man looked like an Indian. (Mooney, 1896, p 795). On the second day, however, he modified his judgment. "He was not so dark as an Indian, nor so light as a white man."

Porcupine stressed that he did not choose to visit the messiah. His contention that he did not know of the Ghost Dance when he left the reservation is perhaps questionable, but it serves two purposes in the narrative. For the white audience, it minimized his role as a troublemaker. For his Indian audience it affirmed his leadership role, his "chosen" status. He drew upon a white source of power, assigning himself a place in the myth of the return of Jesus Christ; he was one of the 12 apostles who came from a far land.

Since the account simultaneously has the structure of a traditional journey to the spirit world (eg, a warrior quest), he managed to draw also upon the power traditionally acquired by the warrier and shaman. In addition, Porcupine emphasized that as a result of his journey he now had the power to return to the spirit world himself whenever he wished. Such an ability implied the continuous renewal of his power and authority. The Millenium did not arrive, however, and after a year of activity and expectation the Ghost Dance virtually collapsed as a religious movement among the Cheyenne.

Ten years after his first meeting with the messiah, Porcupine reappeared in the historical record because of his efforts to revive the Ghost Dance among the Northern Cheyenne. This time the emphasis of his doctrine was very different from that of ten years earlier. It was, in fact, close to the old Sioux version in its militant anti-white stance. Particularly reminiscent of the Sioux version was a "bulletproof" blanket, which Porcupine's disciple Crook wore. Incorporation of traditional elements is suggested by Crook's report that "Porcupine was teaching him to be a 'medicine man' " (US Office of Indian Affairs, 1902, p 163). This included cutting pieces of skin from the wrist and forearm, a traditional method for bringing one into contact with the spirit world. Porcupine was able to amass about 40 militant followers, who actively resisted when the police tried to bring Crook into the agency.

Porcupine prophesied that the resurrection would surely come in the summer, and in June he set out with a few followers to visit the "great messiah," a repeat of his trip of ten years earlier. Government agents were genuinely threatened by his actions and prevented him from reaching the prophet. He was arrested among the Bannocks in Idaho and brought back "without ever seeing the 'great messiah' or even securing the 'medicine arrows' he promised to bring back to use on the whites" (US Office of Indian Affairs, 1902, pp 164–165). Meanwhile other Cheyennes had held a council in which they condemned Porcupine's disrespectful language toward the government inspector and complained that he had been trying to make trouble for years. They and the government agreed that the safest course would be removal of Porcupine from the reservation. After five months in prison, Procupine promised that in the future he would cause no more trouble. Clearly his Ghost Dance power was no match for that of the United States Government.*

---

*Porcupine retained his status in the tribe as a famous medicine man. In the Medicine Lodge ritual which Grinnell witnessed in 1911, Porcupine participated as an elder. He gave a speech and bestowed honors upon a young member of a warrior society (Grinnel, 1923, vol 2, pp 249–250).

Sitting Bull   The vision quest aspect of the journey is even more explicit in those accounts of delegates which were intended for Indian audiences. Sitting Bull, the Arapaho, became the most influential proselytizer of the Ghost Dance among the southern Plains tribes. Grinnell, a journalist, talked with Sitting Bull in the autumn of 1890 and reported that he claimed to be the chief prophet of the new religion. Grinnell's account is rather confused but revealing, since it was written at the height of the Ghost Dance activity and lacks the standardization which hindsight often yields. Grinnell's earlier impression, presumably formed in conversations with Indians who had seen Sitting Bull, was that Sitting Bull had seen Christ in vision. Like Porcupine's account, the telling of an actual journey took on a mythical quality and followed the pattern of a vision journey, right down to the detail that on the return trip he ate buffalo meat and awoke near his own camp, far from where the meeting with Christ had occurred. Hearing the account secondhand, Grinnell did not realize that Sitting Bull's journey had occurred in the "real" world; there was no gap between the physical and spiritual realms. The trances which were experienced by the messengers in the presence of Wovoka were, in effect, continuations of the journey that had begun when they left home.

The continuity of Sitting Bull's formulation with traditional sources of power is evident in his use of eagle feathers. Birds, and eagles, in particular, were traditionally regarded as capable of leaving the surface of the earth and hence of approaching the realm of the sacred (Straus, 1976, p 132). Sitting Bull preached that the new earth, bearing the resurrected dead and game, would come from the west and slide over the old earth. This new earth would be preceded by a wall of fire that would drive the whites back across the ocean to their original and proper country. The Indians would be able to surmount the flames and reach the promised land by means of sacred feathers.

To accompany his doctrine, Sitting Bull inaugurated a formal ritual through which he initiated each tribe he visited into the secrets of the Ghost Dance. After establishing his reputation as a messenger by organizing a large Ghost Dance in the fall of 1890, Sitting Bull went from tribe to tribe, bearing feathers and paint which he had brought with him from the messiah. In a ritual which he consistently held in each tribe, he initiated seven men and women to be priests or leaders of the dance. In many cases, it was only with his visit that the trances which were characteristic of the dance began. He himself was the source of power and authority for the dance and was able to transmit it, at least for a short time.

The personal importance to Sitting Bull of the leadership role derived from his contact with Wovoka, and its consequent source of political power, is revealed in subsequent events. Another delegation, which included the Arapaho Black Coyote, visited Wovoka in the summer of 1891. Black Coyote returned with new instructions on how the Ghost Dance should be performed. The Millenium had not arrived as predicted in the Spring of 1891, and the dance was routinized. It was now to be held for four days every six weeks. Although the orders had come directly from Wovoka, Sitting Bull rejected the innovations. Black Coyote and other delegates soon became leaders of equal standing with Sitting Bull. As Mooney reports, Sitting Bull soon lost much of his interest in the dance (Mooney, 1896, p 901). He remained sufficiently concerned, however, to make a second journey, along with his wife and others, in 1892. When he returned his report was not enthusiastic.

During this period, Sitting Bull's formulation of the doctrine had undergone some changes of its own. In the summer of 1891, after the Millenium failed to arrive, the turning point of the Ghost Dance, Sitting Bull defended his version of the dance before a large council. The council had been called by the government agent presiding over the Kiowa tribe upon the return of their delegate to the messiah in the summer of 1891. Apiatan, the Kiowa delegate, had been totally disillusioned as a result of his meeting with Wovoka. He pointed out, for instance, the Wovoka did not appear to have scars remaining from the crucifixion.

In a report of a conversation with Sitting Bull which occurred after Apiatan's negative report had been received, Captain Scott, whose job it was to learn more about the Ghost Dance, attempted to clarify Sitting Bull's position. Sitting Bull did not believe that he had actually seen Jesus in the north, but rather a man who Jesus had helped or inspired. Sitting Bull had stressed to the captain that the dance would cause sickness and death to disappear but avoided questions about the coming of the buffalo and the like. One could say that, like Porcupine, he stressed only certain aspects of the doctrine when talking to a government representative, but he was also generalizing and adapting the doctrine for changing times. The point about Wovoka being the Christ was absolutely unacceptable to a white audience, especially the missionaries. The claim prevented dialogue between Indian and white man. Wovoka himself was modifying the doctrine in the same direction, giving up the claim to be Jesus Christ, and stressing instead the spiritual powers which his visions had bestowed upon him. Wovoka was moving in the direction of the traditional shaman.

DISSEMINATION OF DOCTRINE AFTER WOUNDED KNEE

Apiatan When news of the Ghost Dance first reached the Kiowa in the summer of 1890, they sent a delegation to the Cheyenne and Arapaho agency to learn more about it. The leader of this delegation inaugurated the dance and assumed direction of the ceremony (Mooney, 1896, p 908). The chiefs of the Kiowa decided to send a delegate to visit the messiah himself, and funds were collected to send Apiatan. Shortly after Apiatan's departure, Sitting Bull visited the Kiowa. He followed his established pattern and "consecrated seven men and women as leaders of the dance and teachers of the doctrine by giving to each a sacred feather. . ." (Mooney, 1896, p 909). Apiatan, in the meantime, was passing through the territories of the Sioux and Northern Arapaho and heard stories of the messiah. Mooney describes the moment of Apiatan's meeting with the messiah:

> The result was a complete disappointment. A single interview convinced him of the utter falsity of the pretensions of the new messiah and the deceptive character of the hopes he held out to believers.

> Saddened and disgusted, Apiatan made no stay, but started at once on his return home. On his way back he stopped at Bannock Agency at Fort Hall, Idaho, and from there sent a letter to his people, stating briefly that he had seen the messiah and that the messiah was a fraud (Mooney, 1896, p 911).

Mooney was present when the letter was received and read it to the assembled Indians.

> The result was a division of opinion. Some of the Indians, feeling that the ground had been taken from under them, at once gave up all hope and accepted the inevitable (sic) of despair. Others were disposed to doubt the genuineness of the

letter, as it had come through the medium of a white man, and decided to withhold their decision until they could hear directly from the delegate himself (Mooney, 1896, pp 911–912).

As mentioned, the agent assembled the Indians in a large council to hear Apiatan's report. He also arranged to have Sitting Bull present at the same time, so that the Indians could hear both sides. "For his services in reporting against the dance, Apiatan received a medal from President Harrison" (Mooney, 1896, p 914).

It was in this situation that Apiatan formulated his version of the Ghost Dance doctrine. Three key "scenes" or communication situations define Apiatan's position as leader, however temporary his position proved to be (we know no more of his personal history from Mooney's account). First, his departure was marked by an assembly of the whole tribe. The chiefs gave him their blessing. He was to be an official representative of the tribe.

His encounter with Wovoka, the second situation, was narrated in a third setting organized by whites. The extent to which this context may have influenced his account is impossible to determine. But the setting did affect the reaction of those to whom he addressed his story. Not all believed his discouraging report. It had no impact on any tribe outside his own, a fact which indicates the importance of the relationship of the messenger to the people receiving the message. Even the Kiowa had resumed the Ghost Dance, spurred on by the former leaders, by the time Mooney's report went to press, which suggests that Apiatan's report was regarded as suspect.

Expectations—based largely on culturally patterned categories and rules—are crucial to the structure of a communication situation. Apiatan expected to meet Jesus Christ. His image of Christ, formed in conversations with Indians he met on his journey, was that of an omniscient Messiah who could read his thoughts and speak all languages (Porcupine had reported that Wovoka could understand all the languages of those who came to visit him). Finally, he looked for the crucifixion scars that the Messiah was said to bear. Apiatan did not meet Wovoka in a ritual context, during a ghost dance, as did the 1889–1890 delegation, but in his home. Wovoka was a man, engaged in a personal, human dialogue. He did not fulfill the criteria for a spiritual being. He could not even read Apiatan's thoughts.

Equally important to consider are Wovoka's intentions in the situation. In the summer of 1890, he appeared to delegates in a cloud of smoke, employed other stage tricks, and used hypnotism. He was inspired by his message and assumed a leadership role to convey it. Apiatan met Wovoka shortly after the Wounded Knee massacre. He found Wovoka lying down, singing to himself, his face covered with a blanket. When Apiatan told him that he wanted to see his dead relatives, Wovoka replied that there were no spirits to be seen there, that others, especially the Sioux, had twisted his message around, and that Apiatan should tell his people to quit the whole business (Mooney, 1896, p 913).

Whether or not Apiatan told his story as he did because of manipulation by the government, he clearly was not overwhelmed or transformed by his experience. Wovoka did not act the part of the prophet. Although we cannot know Wovoka's motives directly, he may have been horrified at the outcome of his preaching, as Bailey portrays him in his fictionalized recreation (Bailey, 1957). He may have been threatened by the military. Whatever the reasons, there was a lack of power at the heart of the whole encounter with Apiatan.

The massacre at Wounded Knee was a vivid demonstration that no matter how fervently the Indians danced, the power of the American government would not be swayed. Wovoka or Apiatan or both had accepted the superior power of the whites. From this point on, most leaders, whether advocates of the Ghost Dance or its opponents, stressed accommodation to rather than competition with the whites, even within the doctrine itself. In many cases, potential leaders searched for additional sources of power, such as education and government jobs. As the scheduled date of the Millenium passed, strategies of accommodation to the whites often involved efforts to minimize the polarization of Indian progressives and traditionalists.

Black Coyote   After Sitting Bull, Black Coyote was the principal leader of the Ghost Dance among the Southern Arapaho. He was one of Mooney's principal informants. Mooney gives us a portrait of an innovative leader who sought out and created new paths of leadership in a rapidly changing society.

In sharp contrast to dance leaders among the Sioux, who were in opposition to the whites, or Sioux progressives, who were in opposition to the Ghost Dance and opposed tribesmen who were active in its spread, Black Coyote managed to combine these two types of leadership. He was tribal delegate to Washington, captain of the Indian police, and deputy sheriff of his county. At the same time, it was "the dream of his life to be a great priest and a medicine-man. . . . his priestly ambition led him to make the journey to the north, in which he brought back the first songs of the ghost dance (shortly before Sitting Bull arrived), and thus became a leader, and a year later he headed a delegation from Oklahoma to the Messiah of Walker Lake" (Mooney, 1896, pp 897–898). His was the delegation that returned with new instructions from Wovoka indicating how frequently the dance should be performed, and his leadership of the Ghost Dance subsequently rivaled that of Sitting Bull.

Black Coyote had also demonstrated his power according to traditional criteria. His body was covered with scars which he had made in obedience to a vision, as a sacrifice to save the lives of his children. He emphasized that he had not flinched during the procedure.

He also tried to synthesize leadership roles in the Indian and white communities, for example by asking Mooney to get for him a permanent license from the government to enable him to visit the various reservations at will as a general evangel of Indian medicine and ceremony (Mooney, 1896, p 898). He was trying to have those Indians in power recognize his authority as a traditional leader; but he was also trying to convince the government of the legitimacy of this traditional power without their considering it a threat.

One can compare Black Coyote's desire for a licence to Wovoka's letter to President Harrison, in which he asked Harrison to acknowledge his authority in the western half of the United States (he and Harrison would preside over America together). As in Black Coyote's case, an Indian leader was acknowledging not only the military power but also the spiritual authority (or at least legitimacy) of the American government, embodied in the president. By asking for an acknowledgment of his own spiritual authority, each was not only seeking to ensure his own personal power and leadership, but also to locate his power and authority within the context of the white system. Each was acknowledging the spiritual legitimacy of the American government and wanted a reciprocal acknowledgment of his own.

The significance of Washington to these people is further revealed in another event. A written statement recording Wovoka's doctrine—forbidden to be shown to white men—was given to Mooney by a member of Black Coyote's delegation. He requested that Mooney take it to Washington, because "the Cheyenne and Arapaho were now convinced that I (Mooney) would tell the truth about their religion. . ." (Mooney, 1896, p 780).

The Final Adaptation

By the time of the above delegation, the promised date of the Resurrection had passed, and the doctrine was beginning to lose its millenial orientation:

> . . . the doctrine gradually assumed its present form—that some time in the unknown future the Indian will be united with his friends who have gone before, to be forever supremely happy, and that this happiness may be anticipated in dreams, if not actually hastened in reality, by earnest and frequent attendance on the sacred dance (Mooney, 1896, p 778).

In his letter to the Cheyenne and Arapaho, Wovoka was still predicting that the dead would return soon, but he left the date unspecified. He also distinguished himself from Christ, a clear shift from the days when he showed delegates his scars. Accommodation to whites was stressed: "Do not refuse to work for the whites and do not make any trouble for them until you leave them" (Wovoka, in Mooney, 1896, p 781). They were also enjoined from fighting.

Mooney himself played an important role in the communication process between whites and Indians. Unlike the missionary Collins, who insisted on her superiority and on a conceptual system that had no room for the leaders with whom she interacted, Mooney did not compete with those he met. He listened. More importantly, he made the arduous journey to the messiah himself. This act was a striking contrast to one government agent's response to the Sioux Sitting Bull, who refused to even consider Sitting Bull's suggestion that the two of them go together to see for themselves whether the messiah was genuine. When Mooney returned to the Arapaho and Cheyenne, bearing sacred paint and pine nuts given to him by the prophet, he was himself treated as a source of spiritual power:

> . . . one chief even (held) out his hand toward me with short exclamations of hu! hu! hu! as is sometimes done by the devotees about a priest in the ghost dance, in the hope, as he himself explained, that he might thus be enabled to go into a trance then and there (Mooney, 1896, p 778).

Mooney undoubtedly facilitated the kind of communication that enabled men like Black Coyote to synthesize white and traditional sources of authority and thus to create a sense of community between whites and Indians. He came to respect the religion as preached in this version of the doctrine: "The moral code inculcated is as pure and comprehensive in its simplicity as anything found in religious systems from the days of Gautama Buddha to the time of Jesus Christ (Mooney, 1896, p 782).

I would like to thank William H. Reid, at whose initial suggestion this paper was written. He followed the entire progress of its preparation and provided extensive editorial comments and suggestions. I would also like to thank Regina Clifford, Thomas DiPrete, and Christine Gray for their comments on earlier drafts of this paper.

BIBLIOGRAPHY

Aberle DF: The prophet dance and reactions to white contact. *Southwest J Anthropol* 1959;15(1):74–83.

Bailey P: *Wovoka: The Indian Messiah.* Los Angeles, Westernlore Press, 1957.

Burridge K: *New Heaven, New Earth: A Study of Millenarian Activities.* New York, Schocken Books, 1969.

Carroll MP: Revitalization movements and social structure: Some quantitative tests. *Am Sociol Rev* 1975;40(3):389–401.

Grinnell GB: Account of the Northern Cheyennes concerning the messiah superstition. *J Am Folklore* 1891;4:61–69.

Grinnell GB: *The Cheyenne Indians,* 2 vols. New Haven, Yale University Press, 1923.

Hassrick RB: *The Sioux: Life and Customs of a Warrior Society.* Norman, OK, University of Oklahoma Press, 1964.

Lesser A: Cultural significance of the Ghost Dance. *Am Anthropol* 1933;35:108–115.

Miller DH: *Ghost Dance.* New York, Duell, Sloan, and Pearce, 1959.

Mooney J: *The Ghost-Dance Religion and the Sioux Outbreak of 1890.* 14th Annual Report of the Bureau of Ethnology, Part 2, 1892–93. Washington, DC, Government Printing Office, 1896.

Moore B: *Injustice: The Social Bases of Obedience and Revolt.* White Plains, NY, ME Sharpe, 1978.

Spier L, Suttles W, Herskovits MJ: Comment on Aberle's thesis of deprivation. *Southwest J Anthropol* 1959;15(1):84–88.

Straus AS: Being human in the Cheyenne way. PhD dissertation, University of Chicago, 1976.

US Office of Indian Affairs: Report of the Commissioner. 70th Annual Report of the Department of Interior, Part 1. Washington, DC, Government Printing Office, 1902.

Vestal S: *New Sources of Indian History 1850–1891* Norman, OK, University of Oklahoma Press, 1934.

Wallace A: Revitalization movements. *Am Anthropol* 1956; 58:264–281.

Worsley P: *The Trumpet Shall Sound: A Study of "Cargo" Cults in Melanesia.* London, MacGibbon and Kee, 1968.

The Native American Church

ROBERT J. PRESTON
CARL A. HAMMERSCHLAG

More than 100 years ago, the distinguished anthropologist, Weston LaBarre, wrote "the most widely prevalent religion among American Indians today is the peyote religion or Native American Church. Since its formal inception in the late nineteenth century it has assumed the proportion of the great intertribal religion."[1] Today, three decades later, it is still the single most significant pan-Indian religion.[2,3] In addition to an accumulation of traditional tribal beliefs, some ceremonies now include Christian symbolism. The Native American Church believes in the unity of God, in charity, and in brotherhood. It advocates abstinence from alcohol.

Meetings are held frequently whenever the need or desire arises. It may be a need for prayer to cure a sick person. It may be to pray for the well-being of a child who will go away to school, or a soldier going off to war. It is called at times of thanksgiving, thanks for healing or for a safe return. Ceremonies may be held on special Christian or National holidays, like Christmas or Easter, Thanksgiving or Armed Forces Day.

The Church was formally established in Oklahoma in 1918 as the Native American Church. In 1944, it was changed to the Native American Church of the United States; and, in 1955, it was named the Native American Church of North America to also include its Canadian breathren. But the Church is not new. This way is as old as creation. The Navajo believe that the gift of the sacrament peyote came with the emergence of humankind. Before the appearance of people, human beings existed only in a spiritual form. The Creator established woman as the first embodied person. At the time of her creation she existed in body but could not speak or move. The Creator caused a light beam to shine directly on the holy plant and that is how peyote was given to her. When she ate of it she became whole and could speak and walk.

It was prophesied that the Navajo were not yet ready for this gift. Only when they could demonstrate their belief through observance and faith in this way would the sacrament become available to all of them. The medicine was therefore given to the people of the South who became the keepers of the sacrament. There are Navajo traditionalists who do not partake of the sacrament not because they do not believe in its power but because they do not yet feel it is the time, that there does not yet exist demonstrable evidence of shared belief.

It has only been since 1978, with the passage of the Native American Religious Freedoms Act, not with the Founding fathers and the First Amendment, that peyotists have been given the right to openly use this sacrament of their Church in the practice of their traditional religion. Only in the last several years has it been legal for peyotists to stand up, be named, and make public their beliefs. Even so, few Peyote Chiefs have been willing to say very much. There is great reluctance, understandably so, feeling this last vestige of their uniqueness will also be invaded, studied, and taken over by the white man.

In what has thus far been written about Native American Church ceremonies, it has been concluded that the particular ceremony the author attended was somehow descriptive of all peyote ceremonies. The ceremony has many variations. Indeed each priest called Roadman, Roadchief, or simply Chief, is encouraged to find his own special way within the context of the prescribed ritual. The Native American Church has been particularly hospitable to many tribal variations which appear in the songs and ritual. Some meetings have considerable Christian symbolism and its services are conducted in the Crossfire Way. In more traditional meetings Christian symbolism is rarely included in the performance of the ritual, and these are carried out in the Halfmoon Way. The adaptability of the church and its unique Indianness has been the key to its spread and vitality among all Indian tribes. The place of peyote, which is simply called "medicine" is central in the religion. It is believed that the Great Spirit gave this special gift to Indian people so they might speak more directly with him.

Peyote comes from a small, spineless, carrot-shaped, mostly undergound cactus which has a small pincushion-like top protruding above the ground. The cactus is cut off at ground level and dried. One need not pick one's own peyote, or even be familiar with the cactus, to participate in ceremonies. The buttons that come from this cactus head are cork hard and initially bitter to the taste. The cacti grow from the Rio Grande into Northern Mexico. Most of the peyote used in ceremonials today comes from Texas wholesalers licensed to sell to authorized individuals.

The potency of natural peyote varies from season to season, from soil to soil, and from clump to clump. It is known botanically as Lomphophora Williamsii. Pharmacologic studies reveal that the average peyote button weighs 3 g and contains 45 mg of mescaline. It has been guessed that participants consume at least five and up to 25 buttons during the entire night-long service.[4,5] One eats the medicine all night long either as a whole or sliced button, crushed as fine powder, mixed with warm water as a paste or cereal, or boiled in tea.

Peyote does not produce any single characteristic physiologic response. The first-time users may experience initial nausea. Experienced participants rarely get nauseous. There can be a sense of exhilaration, serenity, or fearfulness. The most important contributor to how the medicine is experienced is the mind-set of the user. Peyote is not addictive. The peyote experience is shared by at least 40,000 church members from six times yearly to weekly.

The peyote experience for Native American Church members has not been marked by negative consequences. As a matter of fact, it has been shown to be remarkably safe. There are no long-lasting side effects. Chromosomal tests on Huichol Indians, each of whom had a life-long individual history of its use and whose tribe has a 1600-year tradition of its ingestion, revealed that multigenerational ingestion of peyote was not associated with any chromosomal abnormalities.[6,7] When used in Native American Church ceremonies it is remarkably safe.

PEYOTE: THE SPECIAL GIFT

Peyote, from the Aztec word "Peyotl," has been used sacramentally by tribal groups since pre-Columbian times. A peyote button found in a Mayan mortuary complex is one of the oldest materials ever submitted for chemical analysis and dates to 375 AD. Peyote offerings were made to the gods. In North and Central America, peyote was ritually consumed by priests from the Aztecs to the present-day Tarahumara, Yaquis, Otomi and Huicholes of the Northern Sonoran desert, and from them to the Indian tribes of the American Southwest.

There are many legends as to how the medicine came to man, but all agree it came through woman. One version says a pregnant girl became separated from her band. Alone and wandering, she lay down to give birth to her child. Following the birth, alone and exhausted, she was unable to attend to the newborn's needs. The flesh-eating birds circled overhead. A voice spoke to her that commanded her to eat the plant growing beside her. It told her that it was life, a blessing for her and for all of her people. She pulled up a small cactus, as it was the only plant in sight, and ate its head. Her strength returned. She lifted the child to her breast and fed it. Both replenished, she began to gather as many cacti as she could, and then became reunited with her people. She told them of this blessing and it was given to all the people as a gift from God. Whatever the tribal variety of the creation legend, it is always woman who brings the medicine to mankind. The medicine, when it is eaten, is seen as female, although the cactus head itself is seen as male. The importance of maleness and femaleness is central in the beliefs and ceremonials of the Native American Church. Fire is both male and female because wood is female, but air is male. Without both there cannot be combustion. Sky is father, earth and all its yieldings are from earth mother. The tipi in which the ceremony is held is female, enclosing the earth children in her womb. But the Road Chief is male. The evening, until midnight, is male. From midnight to dawn is female because it is that part of night that gives birth to the new day. Whether plants, animals, or man, all of life, say peyotists, comes from a combination of maleness and femaleness because male and female are what give life.

THE MODERN PSYCHOHISTORY OF PEYOTE

In the United States, the modern history of peyotism in tribal religions is intertwined with the history of Quanah Parker, the half-blood Comanche Indian leader, who, it is said, brought it with him to what is now western Oklahoma. Its history is also inextricably intertwined with the mood and history of the late 1800s. Remember that by the 1870s, the life of American Plains tribes was falling apart. These hunters, nomads and warriors were defeated by an expanding, Westward marching civilization, and relegated by force to living on reservations. Such an acute psychohistorical disconnection makes it difficult to trust and believe in the purpose and meaning of the old life-style.[8] The buffalo were disappearing, and defeat was imminent. Then came the missionaries and their churches; then the government administrators, all of whom would sow the seeds of cultural dissolution. From the psychohistorical perspective, when a previously sustaining way of life is abruptly ended, it has a powerful psychological impact on its survivors. Survivors are no longer able to believe that the old ways are sustaining, so they identify with the new. Yet the new ways are also ineffective in providing a better belief system—one that holds any greater promise for salvation.

In the late 1800s, the anger and hope were still alive. In 1870, the Kiowa held a ceremony to bring back the buffalo who were being wiped out by trail-driven cattle and hide hunters. The ceremony proved to no avail, and by 1872 the buffalo had already disappeared from the Southern plains. 1872 was also the year that a Paiute, named Wovoka, brought out his brand of religion. The boy raised by a white family was familiar with the fundamentalist Christian charismatic religions.[9,10] Wovoka decided that a self-induced trance state that was wrapped up in a religious framework might also work for Indians. So, he combined circle-dancing, the shaking of rattles, and ecstatic revelation into a ceremony that became known as the Ghost Dance. The expressed purpose of the Ghost Dance religion was to do away with whites and to bring back the life of the old days.

The Plains tribes could no longer practice the Sundance. Because of its self-''torturing'' elements, it had already been banned by missionaries and government administrators. The Plains tribes adapted to this revivalistic movement with enthusiasm and added their own tribal rituals. Unfortunately, the Ghost Dance was doomed from the beginning because the participants believed that by wearing a white-fringed cotton shirt or dress, on which were painted ceremonial designs, they would be rendered bulletproof. By 1891, after the Sioux uprisings, the Ghost Dance movement dissipated. It was into this atmosphere of despair, powerlessness, and acute psychohistorical discontinuity, that Quanah Parker brought peyote to his warrior–hunter–nomads, the Comanche.

Quanah was apparently a man of great personal power. His mother, Cynthia Parker, was the white daughter of a Texas rancher who was captured by a Comanche raiding party when she was only four or five years old. She eventually married a Comanche chieftain who was Quanah's father. The Parker family said that Quanah was brought back to Texas after his father died in a cavalry skirmish.[11] His mother, ultimately relocated by the Parker family, was encouraged to bring the children, their only survivors, back to Texas after her husband's death. So he, with his mother and sister, went to Texas. His mother and sister subsequently both died, from what was probably an infectious disease. Quanah was also taken seriously ill. He demanded to be treated in a traditional way when he seemed to be growing weaker. The only Indian healer his white grandmother could find was a Curandera, probably a Tarahumara Indian, who cured him with a bitter tea. Following his recovery, she instructed him as to its use. She cautioned him that the medicine should never be eaten for its own sake, for the feeling of well-being that it could bring. It must only be used for healing or in a religious service. It is Quanah who brings peyote and the ceremony to Oklahoma.

The Kiowa and Comanche had peyote by the 1870s. When Quanah returned to Oklahoma, the Plains peyotists say, he went to the Medicine Mountain near Cache, Oklahoma, to seek his own vision and guardian spirit, who would protect him and this new power. He prayed for healing strength, for courage, and prophecy in whatever form was becoming to a Comanche man. Quanah accepted this vision and made use of this spiritual energy to give this new gift to his people.

Quanah's revelations came at a singularly propitious time. The traditional Comanche way to life had been rendered inoperative. The tribe was now dependent on a counterfeit-nurturing neocolonial government. Into this atmosphere came the revelation, based on a traditional life-style handed down especially for Indians. For Indians, it became the alternative to the missionaries of the Christian churches. With its rapid acceptance and spread, the churches became alarmed and railed against what they saw as night-long sexual orgies that were the work of the devil. The campaign was quite effective and the Indians themselves turned against each other. If a meeting site became known, it was torn down by missionaries, Christian tribesmen, or government agents. This turmoil precipitated a tremendous amount of intrafamilial and intertribal strife—feelings that have been intensified over generations and some of which still exist.

By 1887, Public Law 33 of the Congress of the United States, pertaining to Indians living on reservation land, specifically prohibited "any person who shall sell, give away, dispose of, exchange, or barter any more spiritous or vinous liquor of any kind whatsoever or any extract, bitter, preparation, compound, or any article whatsoever under any name, label or brand which produces intoxication to any Indian." Peyote was included on the grounds that the plant was an intoxicant.

Still, by 1900, peyotists were thriving and rapidly spreading. Each tribe added its own songs and intonations so that the specific form of the ceremony changed from tribe to tribe and from one Roadman to another. The peyote worship ceremony spread from the Comanche to the neighboring Kiowa and Arapaho. Then it spread northward to the Sioux, Crow, and Cheyenne, and eastward even to the Cherokee in North Carolina; then, to the Pueblo, Navajo and Apache in the southwest, all the way to Washington state. The great unifying force of the religion passed on through songs or prayers, and the sacrament peyote.

Whether the ritual is conducted in the Kiowa way, the Comanche way, or the Navajo way, it is clearly not the syllables which make the difference. It is the feeling and the meaning of the cermony that is present for everyone. Peyote is the vehicle for intensifying its meaning. The "Father Peyote" cactus head is the focal center of the entire ritual. The ceremonial button rests on top of a crescent-shaped altar. The Roadman, or Chief, has complete authority over the conduct of the ceremony. He tells his meeting to watch the Father Peyote, for it is in his power that they themselves may receive a vision that will be useful for their enlightenment, growth, and health.

THE PEYOTE RITUAL

I am Robert Preston, a Navajo of the Bitter Water and Split Rock clans. Both my grandfathers were well-known medicinemen among our people. I learned from them the stories of how we became The People; how we came into this world of the "Bila Ash Dlaii," the five-fingered people. From other Roadchiefs, from the time I began my apprenticeship at 16, to the time I was ordained at 30, I learned why I am here. I want to give this to my children and to their generations. As a young man I came to these ceremonies and I felt so close to the feelings that my grandfathers inspired in me. I had, for a long time, wanted to rededicate my life to something that made me feel as good as I had as a child. Now I want to bring this awareness to my people. I have studied for many years to be NahaƚLahee, a spiritual leader. This is my way.

In the morning I put up my tipi, its poles I especially chose. They are important

98

to me. I cut them in a National forest in Southern Colorado after making prayers and sacrifices. When the ranger stopped me, I told him the poles were for a ceremonial tipi that I would use in an Indian prayer meeting. He let me go.

I lay out my poles before daybreak, like spokes from a center mark. I watch the rising sun and make a mark at the exact spot where the first rays of the sun shine. That is where the door will be. My family and friends help me put up the poles, as they are quite heavy. I cover the tipi poles with canvas, and build an altar. At the center mark, I place the fire. The sticks are shaped like a V, with their points at the exact center. In front of it I build an altar, a half-moon shaped earth mound. Its open ends face the door. Tonight I will sit at its center on its outer side. I put sage on the floor.

At sunset everyone lines in front of the tipi. I blow an eagle bone whistle four times, to each of the directions. I tell the people we are having this meeting to pray and sing for the sponsors who put up this meeting and also for ourselves who come together for fellowship and to ask the Creator, the Peyote Spirit, to be with us. We walk clockwise around the tipi and enter. I go to my place at the West, the sponsors sit at my left. Everyone finds a seat.

The Drumman sits next to me, for without him I cannot sing. It is not me who sings. The water drum helps me sing. I have made it by tying hide over an iron kettle, into which I have placed some coals and water. The coals and water symbolize fire, the heart of life, and water, the basic food. They are among the basic elements of all living things: Fire, water, animals, vegetation, and the air. These are the basic elements. The drum is the heartbeat of our mother, the Earth.

One man is Fireman, and will place wood on the fire and move the coals. I will put down my own cedar to make smoke, but some Naha⧸ahee use a Cedar Chief, in the way of the Cheyenne. When we are all seated, I take out from my bundle my Father Peyote, the Peyote Chief. This is the spiritual medium of my way, the Peyote Road. You follow life's road until you meet peyote and peyote changes your life, and you continue in its way. I place my Father Peyote carefully, respectfully, at the center of my altar on the peyote half-moon. Next to me are my bead-handled staff, my gourd, my eagle bone whistle, and my peyote fans. I greet the people and tell them why we have come to meet and who requested this meeting. I want them to know we are here to pray and to sing, that I made that moon here on the Earth Mother, in the open, below the Sky Father, and not in a cathedral because this is our way—this is the Indian way.

I put cedar on the coals and with the smoke I bless the cornhusks that we will use to roll our smokes. I roll a smoke, passing the cornhusks and tobacco clockwise around the tipi. The people roll their own smokes. I ask the sponsors to express themselves as to what spiritual guidance they want from this meeting, all the reasons they wanted this meeting, what they want from the Father Peyote spirit, and to inform the people who came here to be in fellowship with them. They speak, and I light my smoke with a firestick and pass it around clockwise. Then everyone lights their smokes. I tell the sponsors that we are having this meeting for them, as they put it up. We are going to pray for them so they will have the understanding they want and feel good again, and we will feel good for sharing this experience with them, thus helping ourselves. We put our smokes out and put them on the altar's outer edge. I take out my peyote and put cedar down. I bless my peyote with the smoke; we will eat the peyote to help us. Sometimes I mix it with warm water. This way of fellowship, in which we take our sacrament, makes me feel I want to put forth every effort, spiritually, physically, and mentally, to help everyone's wishes, here at the meeting, be granted. I know, too, that I do not have the power; only the Father, the Spirit, the Peyote, have the power. I am only an instrument. The peyote helps me to bring joy to the Creator. It helps me bring forth that effort in my songs and my prayers, and all night we will sing. First, the Opening Songs, then the Midnight Songs, then the Morning Songs. Everyone will sing. Each will pray and speak as the staff and gourd are passed to them. All night we will smoke, and we will put down cedar and eat medicine.

With the Midnight Water Song, we will drink and I will bless the people on behalf of the gift of water. I will tell them about those teachings I have learned. The Creator is the power and peyote his gift. I say that I feel that the air is filled with His presence, and that it is outside and inside of you—that you are filled with His power, and with it we can overcome anything that might be brought before us tonight to be resolved. We will overcome it with His spirit. In this way, the Creator, through peyote, brings insight to the problems of life. Always I feel its power and mystery. The more I experience it, the more I learn and understand from it. Each time I call upon it with sincerity and love, the peyote helps me.

After midnight we take a break. First the people on the south side go out, then the North side. We return and light up the main smoke. This is the focus of our meeting. The sponsors light up the main smoke and express themselves, their hopes, their wishes, their problems, and their fears. It does not matter if it's alcohol, family break-ups or sickness, or hopes. We talk to the peyote and it always enlightens us.

Sometimes I am called upon to heal. The coals speak to me, saying, "Take me. I can help cure." I pick up a burning coal with my hand and place it in my mouth, blowing the hot air and sparks onto the affected part. My hands and mouth are never burned. I don't know why.

In the morning, I greet the new day with my whistle, then the woman will bring in water. Later, she will bring corn, fruit and meat. The woman will bless the water with her smoke and express herself in words and prayer. The Drumman picks up the smoke from her and brings it to me. I smoke and give it to the Drumman and then to the Fireman. The, we all drink water brought by woman, the Earth Mother who brings everything that grows and sustains life. The buckskin covered drum is uncovered and the water spills out. The coals from within are put back into the fire. The Fireman takes out my instrument bundle, then takes the sage on which the Father Peyote rested, and gives it to the sponsors. After the morning songs and partaking of water and food, some express their appreciation for the meeting and share whatever they wish about the night's experience. Now, with the new day, the Fireman leads us out. We bless ourselves with the rays of the first morning's light, and feel appreciative for this opportunity to talk to the Creator. Each time I feel the warmth of this fellowship in my Indian way.

THE PEYOTE EXPERIENCE

The expectation of all church members who participate in this ritual and the taking of peyote believe it will be helpful. This expectation mirrors the expectations of psychotherapy, which emphasizes that belief in the practice, as well as in the practitioner, is of crucial importance in the outcome of treatment. Indeed many features of modern psychotherapy are shared by other healing rituals.[12,13,14]

There is the initial distress of the patient, the arousing of hope through dependence upon a socially sanctioned healer, a repetitive ritualistic relationship with the healer, and a socially shared set of assumptions about what makes people well and sick. Psychotherapists and healers mobilize guilt, heighten self-esteem, review a patient's past life, and socially reinforce new attitudes and behavior.

In the Native American Church, the healer–therapist is the Roadman. Someone with a knowledge of Indian culture, he is a figure of stability—someone who demonstrates a working knowledge of the ritual and the medicine. He is leader by example, but he also makes clear that he is a member of the group. He, too, seeks to find the way. Throughout the meeting the Roadman openly discusses his own feelings, reassures and makes suggestions, and, by example, encourages those present to also assume this mood of confession and humility. Confessions may be whispered to the Roadman, rather than publicly presenting them to the group. If whispered, he will speak only to the individual, not to the group. The atmosphere is permissive and safe. The Roadman sings, prays, talks and takes the medicine with his fellow participants. He offers a continual presence that centers the participant, during the ritual experience, to undertake his task which is self-awareness and enlightenment. The skilled Roadman guides the individual away from distractions that distort one's perception of one's real self (alcohol, neuroses) and refocuses consciousness toward an acceptance of one's "true self." The Roadman may say to a participant, "Stay behind it," meaning the experience needs to be felt rather than thought about. The feeling is that one may know more than another, but that knowing more does not mean you can use that knowledge any better to understand yourself and your relation to the universe. The beating drum, the trance-like state, the melodies and chants, all tend to allow the feeling, intuitive part to emerge unrestrained by the usually controlling, rational, thinking parts of the mind.

The Psychology of the Experience

Peyote's properties have a profound psychological impact. The structure and ritual provide for the expression of deeply held feelings, and for confessions that are an integral part of all group processes. When the effect of peyote is at its height, ego functions are at their lowest. One enters a realm of altered consciousness that can open one to new attitudes not normally received during the conscious state. Participants in the ceremonial are protected against its being harmfully experienced, because they expect that this religious, guided experience will have a positive outcome. The expectation is that the experience will be helpful. All Indian religious beliefs emphasize harmony and wholeness, and believers are rewarded by productivity and success.

The peyote experience is uniquely Indian, and its efficacy allows a closeness with a unique prideful, positive sense about one's Indianness—a feeling not easily aroused after a century's disenfranchisement.

There is a safety in the meeting's highly structured rhythm. Everything is done in a ritualized way and at its special time. One observes the rules. For example, you don't walk behind the Fireman as he tends the fire. You ask permission to leave, and preferably walk in a prescribed clockwise pattern, never between a smoker and the fire. The structure always helps its coming out the right way.

At times during the night, one may withdraw—feel isolated. Everyone is encouraged to follow their own path. If a participant wishes to speak, he may. If the Roadman senses that he wishes to speak to someone, he will, or he may fan him or sprinkle water on him. The exploration is focused through the self, but the experience is shared by the group. Everyone is together on the road.

The presence of maleness and femaleness everywhere in the ritual and belief serves as a powerful reminder of those aspects of all mankind. Men are not only strong, powerful and in control; nor are women always submissive and meek. The expectation is to be oneself, which is both. It is to be in touch with all one's qualities without judgment or condemnation.

The Native American Church has provided one of the most efficacious programs in dealing with the problem of Indian alcoholism.[15-17] Its success may not only be attributable to these psychodynamic formulations. Recent research has speculated that there may be a biochemical rationale. The formation of the addictive alkaloid derivatives of liquor comes from the interaction between biogenic amines and the ethanol metabolite, acetaldehyde. It has been posited that the effect of peyote in the treatment of alcoholism could, in part, be due to the replacement properties of the alkaloids in peyote for those in alcohol. Whatever the dynamics, participation in the Native American Church yields a noticeable improvement in alcohol-seeking behavior—more effective than most individual psychotherapy or tribal alcohol programs.

I (Carl A. Hammerschlag), once saw a 26-year-old American Indian Viet Nam war veteran who had previously been diagnosed as an undifferentiated chronic schizophrenic. For this illness he had received a medical discharge accompanied by disability payments. He was seen because he was regularly beating his wife bloody. These episodes occurred when intoxicated, a condition that occurred with frequency. For years he had been a resident of flop-houses, alcohol halfway-houses, and was chronically unemployed. His acute psychotic-like illness was triggered in the midst of a battle. During an assault on a Vietnamese village, he saw a child run out of her house. She was on fire. He rushed out to her to try to extinguish the flames, but the child dropped in front of him and was dead by the time he reached her. Turning away, he dropped his weapon and radio pack, and walked away mumbling incoherently. Years later, he spoke with me about his guilt, anger, and self-inflicted punishments. Yet, periodically he would start drinking and abusing his wife, or he would take out his rifle at night and stalk road signs. His wife was terrified that she might be shot. Now, eight years after the war, he was a casualty of the drug-conscious California 60s scene, of which he had been a part. He was not frightened by those visions. We discussed a peyote church ceremony, the religion of some family members, about both its risks and its potential efficacy. I encouraged him to try and seek a new vision. He visited a Roadman, who assured him that he thought it could be helpful. He said he would get out from inside what had destroyed him from the outside. The patient saw this as magical and without scientific base. But, he participated in the meeting that his family held in his honor. Later, he described to me how, at a point late in the evening, he again saw the burning child arise in the red hot coal. He wept and cried out to her. He tried to get up to climb into the flames, but was restrained by the Roadman and others. The Roadman sprinkled his face with water and made him focus on the burning child. He encouraged him to speak of her. So, he told of how he saw the girl as his sister, whom he had hurt as a child, and that he deserved to die. He then saw in the coals his own face and his future as an alcoholic, and he was horrified by the image. He told this, too, to the entire assembly that night.

The Roadman waved his eagle feather fan at the smoke, given color by cedar leaves, and he saw him brush the burning child, as well as his tormented image of himself, upward from the ashes through the smoke hole at the top of the tipi. The Roadman told him that through the gift of medicine, all around this circle were his brothers and sisters. All would stand with him on his road in life. He described a sense of a great weight being lifted from him, a euphoria. He continued as a church member, has been alcohol-free for two years, and is no longer in treatment. Such experiences are the rule, not the exception.[18,19]

The peyote experience can serve as a powerful focus for enlightenment in an atmosphere that reinforces cultural and religious values. Whether one calls the mechanism confessional, psychodynamic or hallucinatory, through the group, utilizing a skilled guide, and through identification with the awesome pharmacodynamic authority of the medicine, it is effective. In the Indian religious context, it is invariably therapeutic. This fact, however, has not quieted its psychologic detractors, who have argued that peyote only serves as a defense against the human fear of destruction and oblivion. The medicine is, therefore, seen by them as an anodyne, one which eases conflicts through rendering its users into narcotic repression, or some other altered state of consciousness. Such alterations, they say, are never constructive.[20] Peyotism, as a religious system, they argue, is a concrete dramatization of how power can be transferred to an object. That the object reduces the anxiety rather than changes in the individual, so that at one's core, the old conflicts remain. These are restatements of the Freudian principle that religion is the yearning of the unconscious for infantile dependence. From such a perspective, peyote, this inanimate object, becomes the potent transmitter of power, and the idealized projected salvation for one's feelings of weakness and dependency. Such wishes, it is argued, are always defensive. One must remove these rationalizations, projections, and evasions of real problems, if one wishes to be neurosis-free. These judgments are quite surprising when one considers that Freud and Breuer, the founders of psychoanalytic psychotherapy, made use of altered states of consciousness in their pioneering work, through their use of the hypnotic trance. In the analytic situation, Freud decreed, not only was the patient to use an altered state of consciousness, but the analyst, too, ought to be in a state of free-floating awareness. Both client and therapist are expected to change their normal state of consciousness while analyzing.

Alterations in consciousness are a prominent and dramatic component of many of the historical antecedents of contemporary psychodynamic psychotherapy. Whether through the use of trance states or the ingestion of hallucinogenic agents, such alterations remain prominent in the healing and worship in many cultures. Recent psychotherapeutic research indicates that a frank psychotherapeutic benefit may be obtained by regular self-induction of altered states.[21] Whether chemically or self-induced, altered states render such ego defense mechanisms as repression no longer functional, and may allow intrapsychic conflicts to emerge. The proper setting for its emergence can be office or tipi. Peyote, through its protective qualities, may provide its users with ways of handling aggressive feelings, fantasies, fears and anxieties. It does so in a ritualized way, a way without fear and retribution, a way in harmony with a special sense of one's Indianness, and in the company of others who "walk the same walk." This represents no essential difference from eating communion wafers or wearing prayer shawls. All may be signs of infantile dependence, but that truth does not mitigate against its utility. It is only through the utilization of all symbolic forms, perhaps especially altered states of consciousness, that we allow ourselves to let the unconscious forces emerge, an emergence that too long has been denied by our culture. It neuroses represent a bondage to a past that must be unlearned, then all roads which allow the patient to emerge into an unburdened presence are appropriate.

CONCLUSION

Peyote potentiates a heightened state of awareness that, once experienced in a Native American Church ritual, can become incorporated into the person's lifestyle. The tapping of such repressed affective material, whether by psychoanalytic technique or mind-altering medicine, is a startling, exciting experience of discovery. For peyotists, the individual's expectations, his state of mind, combined with the cultural context, results in an exchange between the masculine conscious, rational, problem-solving part of the mind, and the more mysterious, intuitive, feminine side. This interaction has yielded quite positive results.

In our culture, the experiencing of this intuitive, unencumbered, less controlled side of the mind has generally been repressed, an unfortunate consequence of the materialism of contemporary scientific (rational, reproducible, testable) attitudes, which reduce "being" to a world of singularly defined sensory experience. Such dogmatism in the way we speak of reality may not be helpful in opening ourselves up to multilevel states of being that may also teach us. For American Indians, the Native American Church has been a way of maintaining the connections between the rational and the intuitive aspects of being, with a past of harmony and health.

REFERENCES

1. LaBarre W: Primitive psychotherapy in Native American culture: Peyotism and Confession. *J Abnormal Soc Psychol* 1947;42:294–309.
2. LaBarre W: Peyotl and mescaline. *J Psychedelic Drugs* Jan–June 1979;2:1,2;34–39.
3. LaBarre W: *The Peyote Cult.* Hamden, CN, Shoe String Press, 1959.
4. Seevers MH: Summary of unpublished experiments on mescaline sulfate, ground peyote buttons and extracts of ether and chloroform soluble phenolic and non-phenolic fractions of peyote buttons in man, monkey and dog. University of Michigan, School of Medicine, Department of Pharmacology, Ann Arbor, MI, 1970.
5. Albaugh BJ, Anderson PO: Peyote in the treatment of alcoholism among American Indians. *Am J Psychiatry* November 1974;131:11.
6. Dorrance DL, Janiger O, Teplitz RL: Effect of peyote on human chromosomes. *JAMA* October 1975;234(3).
7. Bergman R: Navajo Peyote use: Its apparent safety. *Am J Psychiatry* December 1971; 123:6.
8. Beane S, Hammerschlag CA, Lewis J: Federal Indian policy: Old wine in new bottles. *White Cloud J* 1980;2(1).
9. Stewart OC: Origin of the peyote religion in the United States. *Plains Anthropologist* 1974;1:65, 211–223.
10. Stewart OC: The peyote religion and the ghost dance. *Indian Historian* 1972;4:27–30.
11. Marriott A, Rachlin CK: *Peyote.* New York, The New American Library, 1972.
12. Kiev A: *Magic, Faith and Healing.* New York, The Free Press, 1966.
13. Frank JO: *Persuasian and Healing.* Baltimore, MD, Johns Hopkins Press, 1961.
14. Torrey EF: *The Mind Game: Witchdoctors and Psychiatrists.* New York, J. Aronson, 1977.
15. Kunitz S: Navajo Drinking Patterns. Yale University, Department of Sociology, Unpublished doctoral dissertation, July 1970.

16. Pascarosa P, Futterman S, Halswerg M: Ethnopsychedelic therapy for alcoholics: Observations on the peyote ritual of the Native American Church. *J Psychedelic Drugs* 1976;8:3.
17. Blum K, Futterman SL, Pascarosa P: Peyote, a potential ethnopharmacologic agent for alcoholism and other drug dependence. *Clin Toxicology* 1977;11(4):459–479.
18. Slotkin JS: *The peyote religion: A study in Indian white relations.* Glencoe, IL, Free Press, 1956.
19. LaBarre W, in Kiev A (ed): *Magic, Faith and Healing,* op. cit.
20. Bromberg W, Tranter CL: Peyote intoxication: Some psychological aspects of the peyote rite. *J Nerv Ment Dis* 1943;97:409–420.
21. Glueck BC, Stroebel CF: Biofeedback and meditation in the treatment of psychiatric illness. *Comp Psych* 1975;16:303.

CHAPTER

7

Leonard Feeney:
The Priest who was more Catholic than the Pope

FRANCES M. SCAVULLO

During the 1930s and the 1940s Leonard J. Feeney, a Jesuit priest, was one of the best known Catholics in the United States. He was recognized as a poet, as the author of several books (*In Towns and Little Towns* [1927], *Fish on Friday* [1934], *Boundaries* [1936], *Riddle and Reverie* [1936] and five others) and as literary editor of the Jesuit weekly publication *America*. He had appeared regularly on the program "The Catholic Hour" and preached the 1937 Advent sermons at St. Patrick's Cathedral in New York City. He described himself as a man entranced with "the earthliness of heavenly things and the heavenliness of earthly things." He was successful in his chosen profession, had the respect of his peers, and was very much a part of the Catholic Church in the United States. By April 1949 he had been publicly censured by Archbishop Cushing of Boston and had been expelled from the Jesuit order and had formed a religious group known as "The Slaves of the Immaculate Heart of Mary." In 1953, he was excommunicated from the church by Pope Pius XII. At age 52, Feeney had changed his role from that of obedient son of the church to rebellious son and finally to that of a father who knew better than his own father or was in fact "more Catholic than the Pope."

In 1943 Feeney was assigned as chaplain to St. Benedict's Center, Cambridge, Massachusetts. St. Benedict's was a gathering place for Catholic students who attended college in the Boston area. Most of the students who went there attended Harvard, Radcliffe, and MIT. The center had originally been founded in 1940 by three Harvard Catholics including Avery Dulles, Margaret Knapp, and Catherine Goddard Clarke. Until Feeney was assigned there, Mrs. Clarke directed the center with the aid of various priests who served as guest lecturers. Feeney was at the height of his literary and lecture career when he became director. Under his guidance the center changed from a place where young Catholics could drop in for a cup of coffee to a full academic institution which taught Greek, philosophy, literature, church history, hagiography and, of course, Catholic theology. Avery

Dulles (1978), a Catholic convert, currently a Jesuit priest and theologian, son of John Foster Dulles, Secretary of State under Eisenhower, describes St. Benedict's as being lively and full of Apostolic zeal. He says Catherine Goddard Clarke was a charismatic, charming woman who had a contagious enthusiasm. Feeney is described as a man whose doctrine was solid and whose oratory was superb. He preached about the "integration of nature and grace," that is the earthly and the heavenly. He placed a high value on reason, as well as the senses and imagination. Feeney's style of preaching is described as being especially engaging. He would warm up his audience with anecdotes and poetry which showed his wonder of nature and reflected his sharp sense of humor. He would appear aware of each person in the room and look especially at those who seemed uninvolved in his lecture. "When at length he had the entire audience reacting as a unit, he would launch into the main body of his talk, leading from insight to insight, from emotion to emotion, until all were carried away, as if by an invisible force permeating the atmosphere" (Dulles, 1978, p 135). Feeney's audience grew until there was standing room only on Thursday nights when he lectured.

Feeney's effect was strong. Close to 100 members of St. Benedict's became priests or nuns and about 200 people converted to Catholicism through their association with St. Benedict's. Feeney's main attention, though, was given to a small group of people who made St. Benedict's the fulcrum of their lives. For these people, Feeney made himself available every day for personal and religious guidance. In the evening the group would dine together and have lively discussions and conversations with Feeney and Catherine Goddard Clarke.

From 1943 to 1949 Feeney's following grew, attracted to his keen biting wit, appreciation of reason, and poetic nature. In January 1949 Feeney was censured by Archbishop Cushing of Boston and formed a religious group called the "Slaves of the Immaculate Heart of Mary." The reason for the censure is unclear. It is known that Feeney had been reassigned to work at Holy Cross College, Worcester, Massachusetts, and had refused to go. This reassignment would have removed him from Boston and out of Cushing's jurisdiction. The censure was not made public until April 1949, when a series of incidents began which ended with Feeney directly opposing the Catholic Church.

Fahkri Maluf, Charles Ewaskio, and James Walsh were lay faculty at Boston College, a Catholic Jesuit-run school. Maluf and Ewaskio were converts, and all three were affiliated with the St. Benedict's Center. Maluf, in fact, led a weekly study group which discussed the "Summa Theologica" of St. Thomas Aquinas. At Boston College Maluf and Walsh taught philosophy and Ewaskio taught physics. In the December 1948 issue of *From the Housetops*, a quarterly journal published by St. Benedict's, Maluf wrote an article attacking the Jesuits for their liberalism. The three then wrote a letter to the president of the college, Father William L. Keleher, S.J., saying heretical doctrines were being taught at the college and that the faculty was too tolerant. A second letter stating the same thing was written to the pope. This letter was also signed by David Supple, a teacher of German at Boston College High School. President Keleher responded by asking the assistant professors to allow religion to be taught by those who had training (ie, the Jesuit priests) and to confine themselves to their areas of expertise. The professors then wrote a letter to the Provincial of the Eastern Province of the Society of Jesus (ie, the Jesuits) accusing Keleher of heresy and stating their consciences had been violated by Keleher requesting them not to speak on theological matters.

In dispute was the doctrine of "extra ecclessiam nulla salus" (outside the church, there is no salvation), a doctrine of the Catholic Church that dates back to the third century AD. The four men took the position that 1) there is no salvation outside the Catholic Church, 2) the Catholic Church is supreme among churches, and 3) a man must be submissive to the pope to be saved. The official position of the Catholic Church was clearly stated in the Baltimore Catechism. The catechism had undergone its first revision in 60 years. The new 1949 version stated "that those who remain outside the Roman Catholic Church, through no grave fault of their own, and do not know it is the true Church can be saved by making use of the graces which God gives them." The church holds that each man gets enough grace to achieve salvation. Only God knows how he chooses to use it.

When the four men refused to stop speaking on theological matters, President Keleher asked for their resignations saying that their views led to intolerance and bigotry. It was at this point that Feeney took his first public oppositional stance. Up until this time Feeney had not been publicly identified with "extra ecclessiam nulla salus." In fact his books reflected a certain tolerance of others, and this was noted by book reviewers of the era. A few days after the men were fired, Feeney was quoted in the Boston and New York papers as saying he did not understand why the four were forbidden to teach "the three basic premises of Catholic life—the very direction signs by which one finds it" (*New York Times*, April 18, 1949). The next day Archbishop Cushing forbad Catholics to go to St. Benedict's and deprived Feeney of his priestly functions; he was not allowed to say Mass or preach in the Boston archdiocese. Feeney responded by saying that the Archbishop's action came about "when I sought to protect four brave Catholic boys in a profession of faith similar to my own" (*New York Times*, April 20, 1949).

This statement of Feeney's gives some possible clues to the unconscious motivation for the radical change in his behavior. First, those "four brave Catholic boys" were in their thirties. Two of them were converts. It can be hypothesized that Feeney had a strong rescue fantasy towards them, that he had once rescued them from damnation through conversion to Catholicism and now needed to rescue them from the damnation of an overly punitive father, Archbishop Cushing. In addition, many of the people Feeney had converted had broken with their families and had given up substantial wealth and social status to become Catholics. This may have induced in him a distorted sense of his own power and responsibility for protecting his "children." Also, as the oldest of five children, four of whom had chosen a religious life, the role of protector and religious leader was most likely an old and familiar one to Feeney.

Feeney and his followers responded to the Archbishop in two ways. They rallied public support. Pickets appeared outside six Boston Churches carrying signs saying "No salvation outside the Church" and distributing the quarterly *From the Housetops.* They also escalated the argument to papal levels by asking for a rarely given "ex cathedra" statement from the pope on the dogma of "extra ecclessiam nulla salus." The Vatican responded by saying that local authorities had jurisdiction, thus implicitly supporting Cushing and somewhat curiously dodging the question of dogma.

Feeney closed St. Benedict's for one month, then reopened it as the St. Benedict's Center School, a title that in his mind sidestepped the archbishop's orders.

The Vatican did engage in the dispute in September 1949. A letter was sent from the Supreme Sacred Congregation of the Holy Office. The letter asked Feeney and the four teachers to drop charges of heresy and return to the church at the peril of their souls. It said it felt sure the dispute had grown from a lack of understanding and study of doctrine and had been made more difficult by a refusal to conform to church discipline. Feeney responded with a statement saying he still had received no answer to his doctrinal question of whether there was salvation for those outside the church. This statement was greeted with cheers by 50 members of St. Benedict's.

As the fight between Feeney and the church grew in intensity, the "Slaves of the Immaculate Heart of Mary" began to develop a strong group identity. The group had originally been formed January 17, 1949, by Feeney and Catherine Goddard Clarke. Its male and female members lived in separate dormitories near the St. Benedict's Center. "Outside the church there is no salvation" became the principle which unified the group and separated them from the outside world. The "Slaves" refused to relate to their Protestant and Jewish friends and family. Some also refused to speak or receive mail from their Catholic families as well. Several of them refused to graduate from Catholic colleges, feeling that the schools taught heresy and to accept a diploma would be to condone it. The men dressed in the black outfits of seminarians, the women wore black suits and black visored hats similar to nun novitiates. Around 1950 they began the practice of marching in Boston Common on Sunday. As their isolation from the outside grew, so did their fanaticism and radicalism. The procession would begin with hymns and Feeney and his followers (the Slaves) marching with a banner of the Virgin Mary and a statue of the child Jesus holding the world in his hands (the Infant of Prague). This would be followed by speeches in which one of the "Slaves" would make a statement such as "It is heresy to believe that there can be salvation for the Christ-hating and Mary-hating people. . . . Archbishop Cushing stuck his head out in heresy against us. . . . Our Lady, Scourge of Heretics, punish him" (*Time,* October 13, 1952). Feeney would then speak, making no secret of his hatred for Cushing and making statements such as "I come here to preach the love of the Blessed Virgin Mary, and I found nothing but filthy adulterous faces who attacked her. I preach hatred of those who hate Jesus. Am I a hate-priest when I want a man to be a child of Mary? Mother of God. I ask you to include those who hate me in your enemies" (*Time,* October 13, 1952). Feeney's anti-Semitism grew, as did his fear of communism and liberalism. His anti-Semitism evoked strong protests from Jewish organizations.

Jewish college students would go to Boston Common to protest Feeney, and the Anti-Defamation League expressed strong concern regarding his activities. His rhetoric was particularly powerful as the holocaust had recently ended, leaving Jews frightened and vulnerable. Israel was a new country with an unclear future and in strong need of American support. The Catholic Church most certainly must have felt public pressure to silence Feeney.

The "Slaves" supported themselves selling Feeney's books. They lived a semimonastic life of prayer, meditation, and preaching. They would visit various Catholic Colleges trying to convert others to their way of thinking. At Notre Dame College they were arrested for attempting to incite a riot. As they were being carried off the campus, one member shouted "The first sign of your approaching damnation is that Notre Dame has Protestants on its football team" (Deedy, 1978, p 117).

Feeney's rhetoric grew increasingly uncomfortable for the church. In 1953 he was ordered to go to Rome within a month to face charges or be excommunicated for "stubborn disobedience to an order legitimately enjoined upon him to appear in Rome before authorities of the Sacred Congregation" (*New York Times*, February 21, 1953). Feeney issued a statement saying he refused to go to Rome until charges against him had been stated as required by church law. He also said that any penalty without charges was void.

The church's formal steps against Feeney are curious. Each official banning was ascribed to his disobedience and not to his heretical statements. However, the church is hesitant to excommunicate priests. It is rarely done and not done for failure to follow orders to relocate. The excommunication was the church's way of saying Feeney spoke heresy.

Now completely outside the church, the "Slaves" continued. There were episodes of violence where they broke into Chicago Cardinal Stritch's office, demanding him to answer the question "Is Father Feeney a priest in the Catholic Church?" (*New York Times*, July 31, 1953). They also spread trash in the office of the editor of *The Pilot*, the Catholic paper in Boston. They sent letters to President Eisenhower and all members of Congress urging them to convert to Catholicism or be damned.

In 1958 after being harassed by building inspectors and neighbors, the "Slaves" moved to a farm in Still River, Massachusetts. There were about 86 members, 39 of them were children. Married couples were asked to take vows of celibacy and to live separately. All children were raised collectively, living separately from their parents. Father Feeney was solely responsible for their education. They did not know which members were their parents or siblings. No outsiders were allowed in the farm, nor were any radios, televisions or newspapers. The day began with a Latin Mass said by Feeney, followed by hard work on the farm's 146 acres. The day closed with Feeney leading religious reflections and recounting the news of the day. In 1964 Robert Colopy, a former member, sued for custody of his five children. When he had asked his wife, Loretta, to leave the community, she had refused. He then wrote a letter to the bishop asking for advice. When Loretta Colopy found the bishop's letter, she turned her husband into the community as a traitor. Colopy was then stripped naked and kept isolated for several days. He was then driven to Boston and the bishop helped him reconnect to current life. In his suit Colopy reported that St. Benedict's was as hard to get out of as to get in. He said that Feeney had grown more rigid, dogmatic, and suspicious of society. He said he was given to periods of rage and had slapped Colopy and broken his eyeglasses. Feeney frequently "denounced the Jews as responsible for communism, and Protestants for subverting Latin America from the Church" (*Time*, January 1, 1965). Dramatically Colopy testified that once one of his own sons had asked him "Mister, are you my father?" Colopy won custody of his children, but it was not easy. The children prayed for his death and at least two of them eventually returned to Still River.

With time, though, life in Still River relaxed to the point where the community would invite their Massachusetts neighbors to occasional parties at St. Benedict's. In 1972, through the intercession of the bishops of Boston and Worcester, Massachusetts, the ban of excommunication was lifted and Feeney and half the "Slaves" returned to the Catholic Church. There are no details describing under what conditions the excommunication was lifted. Feeney is quoted as saying he never recanted; however, without a confession of his sins the excommunication could not be lifted. It can be hypothesized that by 1972 Feeney was an old man approaching death, suffering from chronic heart disease and Parkinson's disease. The church may have felt compassion for his age, no longer seeing him as an active threat and also to have grown ecumenical enough to tolerate his conservative views. In 1977 the group, consisting of 26 men and 19 women, formed a new religious community known as the Pious Union of Benedictine Oblates of Still River. In 1978 at the age of 80, Father Feeney died.

The group continues today in the Benedictine tradition of prayer, meditation, and scholasticism. There is an elderly priest who comes daily from the town to say Mass in Latin. Fakhri Maluf heads the community. Men and women continue to live in separate buildings. There is a seminary, a convent, and a high school. Theology courses are offered to the public. The theological emphasis is a traditional, conservative, Catholic one. In many ways the original St. Benedict's Center of Cambridge, Massachusetts, has been re-created. One recent visitor reports a feeling of beauty, serenity, and peacefulness surrounds the community and its members.

What is most curious is what made Father Feeney, in mid-life, embark on such an eccentric trip. Not having known Feeney, one can only hypothesize. In his book *Fish on Friday*, Feeney says "I am given to superlatives. I overstate things. . . . I say most when I mean much! Without the words 'tremendous,' 'wonderful,' 'amazing,' and 'astounding,' my vocabulary would collapse. I couldn't talk. I couldn't think." This self-described character trait of exaggeration and enthusiasm certainly accounts for some of his extreme behavior. In addition it could be hypothesized that Feeney was acting out some unconscious oedipal conflicts by setting himself up as more "Catholic than the pope" and in direct competition with the archbishop and the pope. The name "Slaves of the Immaculate Heart of Mary" suggests a special and eternal relation with a mother who had not been sexually active with her husband and is both safe and available to her son. The community was strongly Mary-oriented. Their symbolic life consisted mainly of pictures of the Madonna and statues of the Infant Jesus. God the Father was strongly absent (and deposed).

Feeney's oedipal conflicts may have been reawakened at this time in his life due to his strong relationship with Catherine Goddard Clarke.

Mrs. Clarke was an attractive red-haired Irish woman of fanatical beliefs and independent wealth (power). One can safely hypothesize that her religious preoccupation and Irish background may have reminded Feeney of his own Irish mother, all but one of whose children followed a religious vocation. Together they made St. Benedict's Center in Boston a unique place for academic and religious discussion. Avery Dulles (1978, p 136), who knew both of them reports "In the company of Catherine Clarke and Leonard Feeney conversation was never known to lag." It was with Catherine Clarke that Father Feeney founded the "Slaves of the Immaculate Heart of Mary," and it was Catherine Clarke who wrote the only history of the events that led to Feeney's excommunication, *The Loyolas and the Cabots, The Story of the Boston Heresy Case* (Ravensgate, Boston, 1950).

Feeney's rigid rules of celibacy, even among married couples, and his preoccupation with the sins of adultery, may have been his way of coping with these sexual conflicts.

The "Slaves" were also a reactionary group response to a larger group, ie, a Catholic Church that was growing more ecumenical and liberal daily, culminating with Vatican Council II and the papacy of John XXIII. In addition, like many cults, it was a group that was superego ridden. This may have been their reaction to the aggression released with the 1945 bombing of Japan. The bombing seems to have aroused in them a preoccupation with salvation and death and fear that their aggressive drive could go "out of control."

The development of the "Slaves of the Immaculate Heart of Mary" was overly determined. It reflected the response of a group of people who felt lost and confused by the changes in an institution that they felt rarely changed, the Catholic Church. It was a response to the extreme destructiveness of World War II. It also grew out of the competitive instincts of one man, his desire for power, and his followers' admiration, inducing in him a strong sense of his power.

BIBLIOGRAPHY

Cogly J: Lonely Zealot. *Commonweal* 1953;57:570.

Deedy J: Update on Leonard Feeney. *Commonweal* 1977;104:5-7.

Deedy J: Leonard Feeney: The dragon turned reluctant, in *Seven American Catholics.* Chicago, The Thomas More Press, 1978, pp 97-123.

Dulles A: Leonard Feeney, In memoriam. *America* 1978;138:135-137.

Fenton J: Boston College ousts 4 teachers as intolerant: They charge heresy. *New York Times,* April 15, 1949, p 1.

Churches picketed over Boston ousters. *New York Times,* April 17, 1949, p 54.

Jesuit defends four in heresy case. *New York Times,* April 18, 1949, p 25.

Cushing upholds college ousters. *New York Times,* April 19, 1949, p 17.

Silenced priest calls act invalid. *New York Times,* April 20, 1949, p 13.

Papal rule asked on new catechism. *New York Times,* April 23, 1949, p 9.

Disobedience at St. Benedict's. *Time* 1949;53:67.

Heresy is charged to church leaders. *Life* 1949;26:53.

Girls quit college in new heresy row. *New York Times,* May 20, 1949, p 29.

Vatican reproves priest, teachers for charging "heresy' to college. *New York Times,* September 2, 1949, p 1.

Full "heresy" note is asked by priest. *New York Times,* September 3, 1949, p 15.

Feeney will appeal to vatican if banned. *New York Times,* September 4, 1949, p 26.

Clash in Boston. *Newsweek* 1949;34:75.

Absolved of heresy by pope, Feeney says. *New York Times,* August 23, 1950, p 13.

I preach hatred. *Time* 1952;60:78.

Feeney reported excommunicated. *New York Times,* February 20, 1953, p 13.

Priest to appeal to pope. *New York Times,* February 21, 1953, p 8.

Excommunication. *Time* 1953;61:54.

Father Feeney's excommunication. *Life* 1953;34:75.

Feeney followers held. *New York Times,* July 31, 1953, p 35.

Slaves of Leonard Feeney. *Time* 1965;85:45.

Feeney forgiven. *Time* 1974;104:81.

Leonard Feeney, Jesuit priest, 80; Ousted in dispute over salvation. *New York Times,* February 1, 1978, Section II, p 2.

CHAPTER

8

Psychiatric Perspectives on an Eastern-Style Cult

ALEXANDER DEUTSCH

Part I—Observations on a Sidewalk Ashram*

During the last few years, sects and cults based on Eastern religions have attracted growing numbers of Americans. The opportunity for observing such a group recently presented itself when, on a street corner bench adjoining Central Park in mid-Manhattan, a guru of American origin established himself and gradually collected a substantial following. The guru was called simply "Baba" and his followers had either chanced on him while passing by or learned of his presence from friends or the media. The devotees began referring to themselves as the "Family," while the outdoor assemblages were sometimes casually called the "ashram," meaning hermitage or school for yogis. In studying this group, I had in mind three general questions: What was happening in the assemblages? What kinds of people with what kinds of life experiences became followers of the guru? What sorts of yearnings or needs were being fulfilled by this experience?

BABA AND HIS ASHRAM

Baba, with a close follower at his feet, established himself near the park in September, 1972, and from then until the following January spent approximately 15 hours daily on his bench. His adherents would generally sit on the sidewalk in front of him. During a typical day perhaps 50 to 75 people would sit with the group for some period of time while Baba's closest followers would spend the bulk of their waking hours with him. Gifts of food and flowers were brought by followers throughout the day, which Baba passed on to the group, and in the evening a vegetarian Indian meal cooked in a nearby apartment was parceled out to those assembled. The outdoor assemblages held firm through the cold days and nights of December and early January but pressure mounted among some of the

*Part I of this chapter is reprinted in part with permission from the *Archives of General Psychiatry,* February 1975, Volume 32. Copyright 1975, American Medical Association.

devotees to go south with or without Baba. An old school bus was purchased and prepared for the journey and just prior to departure Baba dramatically indicated that he would go along. Approximately 30 disciples also made the journey south and this marked the end of the first phase of the Family's history.

Some details of Baba's life will be given in the second part of this chapter. He had recently returned from India where he spent time at the ashram of a well-known Hindu religious leader and miracle worker who will be referred to as "Swami." Baba himself had donned the garb and attained the appearance of a Hindu holy man. He had met Sid, a young seeker who was to become his closest disciple, and together they traveled through the country. Baba, with the help of Sid, devised a sign language and had given up speech entirely by the time the pair arrived in New York in September, 1972. Although this language was complex and continually being expanded by the guru, it was rapidly learned by several of Baba's closest followers in the sidewalk ashram.

The "Family" would greet members arriving for the day or curious passersby stopping to listen for a moment with a hearty "welcome home," which the guru would indicate by the gesture of opening his hands in front of his heart. Baba usually radiated acceptance and good humor and created an atmosphere of warmth that the Family basked in. Family members would often embrace each other joyously but generally all attention was focused on Baba. Members receiving Baba's attention in the form of an inquiry as to their well-being or an offer of a flower or a fruit would experience extreme gratification and, conversely, in the early weeks of the ashram, a few felt jealous and rejected and thought that the leader played favorites. These latter feelings tended to disappear as these individuals became convinced of Baba's evenhandedness and, moreover, attempted to follow his teachings concerning the "letting go" of all desire.

Baba's philosophy was expressed in the course of his comments on the dilemmas and personal problems about which his followers consulted him or as answers to abstract questions that were posed to him. The teachings are in the tradition of *bhakti,* a theistic, devotional form of Hinduism whose central scripture is the *Bhagavad Gita.*[1,2] In Baba's teachings, the quest for knowledge and love of God are central and, if pursued, these would supplant the self-centered and pain-producing strivings that people are prone to. Strivings or desires whether for wealth, power, or sex are "traps" in that fulfillment leads only to further need and eventual frustration. The road to spiritual contentment involves learning to let these desires "fall away." Desire is a manifestation of the "ego," the false sense of individuality that separates human beings from each other and from God. The God-realized person will see through the illusion to the manifestation of the godhead within each person and thus their basic sameness. With this awareness of reality, his love of others will tend to be unimpassioned and relatively impersonal, undemanding and "nonattached." If these ideals were fulfilled in his relationships, frustrations would not exist and pain on loss of the object would be minimized.

A person's behavior might bring him pain or contentment but is not to be judged by conventional moral standards that, along with the experience of guilt, belong to the world of illusion. This idea and the general absence of moral censure from the guru appeared to be very important for many of the devotees.

The doctrine of reincarnation and the related notion that man's ultimate aim is to break the cycle of rebirths and unite with the godhead underscored the futility of a life of desire and "attachment." Passivity as such was not advocated and the performance of one's work—provided one did not become attached in a prideful or avaricious way to the products of his labor—was seen as a valid spiritual path (karma yoga). Nonetheless, most of Baba's closest followers shunned work and school and appeared to draw support from his teachings to do so. The guru did not advocate asceticism or any severe discipline such as prolonged meditation. He declared that his "technique" in bringing people close to God was to "give food, share, give love, and welcome people home."

The Family spent considerable time in silent group meditation and in chanting. Early in the history of the assemblages, chants were improvised, reflecting both the leader's teachings ("start the day with love, spend the day with love, end the day with love, that's the way of God") and the blissful mood of the devotees that they analogized with psychedelic drug experiences ("gonna get high on God today").

Contributing to Baba's charisma and appeal were his clear-eyed good looks and his generally calm good humor in the fact of a variety of potentially unpleasant circumstances such as hostile questioning and freezing weather. He appeared to be successful in living what he preached—a life of contentment, reduced desire, and closeness to God. He was spoken of variously as a man without an ego, a man who was God-realized and someone through whom God spoke directly. A few attributed miraculous powers to him. Both his devotees and I were impressed by his empathic responses to those seeking counsel, but while some of them thought that he approached omniscience, I occasionally found him simplistic and overgeneralized. He was often firm and crisp-minded in challenging "word games" in his devotees' questions. Some of his followers saw him as a kind of therapist who helped them transcend their demanding self-centeredness and brought them closer to spiritual realities.

INTERVIEW PROCEDURES

I began sitting with Baba and his followers in late October and spent five to ten hours a week in the assemblages or interviewing individual devotees until the departure of the bus in January. After sitting with the group a few times I identified myself as a psychiatrist and, a bit later, described my interest in finding out the kinds of feelings and past experiences that may have led people to Baba and the sorts of benefits they were deriving from participation in the ashram.

Fourteen Family members (who will be referred to as the subjects) underwent semistructured interviews of two to five hours' duration (median four hours) in one to three sessions; material was also obtained from several others who were seen more briefly and informally. The subjects' accounts of the factors, both historical and emotional, that led them to Baba were ascertained as well as their explanations of the meaning of the current experience to them. Since psychedelic drug experiences appeared to be of significance, descriptions of some of their "trips" were elicited. In addition, the interviews were designed to obtain knowledge of the subjects' personality structures and dynamics and their family and personal histories to the end that the experience under investigation might be placed within a meaningful psychological context.

THE SUBJECTS
General Characteristics

The subjects, seven of whom were men and seven women, ranged in age from 19 to 35 years with a median age of 25. Eleven were Jewish by birth and three

Protestant, and all were white. Three of the subjects were married, but two of the marriages had broken up while the third was only questionably intact. One subject had not attended college, while seven had dropped out, and six had completed college. Three had some postgraduate education.

With one exception, the subjects all described themselves as having been basically unhappy for many years prior to their involvement with Eastern religion. It was generally difficult to date the onset of the dysphoria; with most it appeared to stretch indefinitely into their pasts, although with some, events such as starting school as a child, the birth of a sibling, puberty, the illness of a sibling, leaving for college, and the break-up of an affair seemed to be points of onset or distinct worsening. Chronic or recurrent feelings of depression, anxiety states, painful experiences of hurt pride and anger, shyness, low self-esteem, poor heterosexual relationships, the absence of goals and direction, and the feeling of being out of step with peers and with parental expectations were common symptoms. Sibling rivalries seemed unusually strong and unresolved, with the subjects, prior to their conversion, generally experiencing themselves as less favored, attended to, or competent than their sibs. Where older brothers or sisters were present, the subjects usually felt neglected or mistreated by them.

With the exception alluded to above, the subjects' relationships to at least one and usually both parents were experienced as unsatisfactory, with the parents themselves depicted as distant, domineering, or harshly critical. Aside from the more general complaints, significant psychiatric symptoms were spontaneously described in seven of the subjects' mothers. Six of the mothers (three each of male and female subjects) had either distinct episodes of depressive illness or chronic depressive complaints and one was phobic and hypochondriacal. Three (all of male subjects) required one or more hospitalizations and one of these committed suicide. The father of one of the female subjects had been hospitalized for manic-depressive disease. All but a few of the parental marriages were described as unhappy, with the most frequent pattern involving a domineering critical husband and a masochistic depressed wife. Aside from the suicide, one subject's father had died and there were three divorces; the other parental marriages were intact.

None of the subjects had a strongly religious upbringing but a few reported an upsurge of religious interest in early adolescence in the context of the idealization of a clergyman of their own faith. However, disinterest or disillusionment set in later in adolescence. In at least one case this religious interest already contained an expression of opposition to the parents. Eleven subjects had moderate to extensive experience with psychedelic drugs and most of these individuals believed that this experience had an important influence on the current direction of their lives. Marihuana usage appeared to have been universal. With few exceptions the devotees had contact with some form of yoga or Hinduism for several months up to a year or two prior to meeting Baba and making him their guru. Six of the women and four of the men had been in psychotherapy, and while the women generally regarded this experience as helpful but as not having gone far enough, the men tended to view their treatment less positively.

All the subjects experienced periods of euphoria or "bliss" after joining the Family and this contrasted with their unhappiness earlier in life. In explaining their improved mental states, they would frequently contrast Baba's attitudes and teachings and the atmosphere of their new "family" with the attitudes and conduct of their parents and other authority figures. A few of the subjects showed a good deal of mood fluctuation, shifting back and forth from depression, disgruntlement, or anxiety to a loving blissful acceptance of the guru and his teachings. (Baba compared the ups and downs of the novice yogi to a ride on a roller coaster.) I will attempt to define some of the factors in the devotees' new-found happiness and then I will describe and comment on some of the elements in their life-style. This will then be followed by observations on the influence of psychedelic drug usage.

Factors in the New Happiness

The search for acceptance   This was a theme common to the great majority of the devotees. Frequent concomitants were parents perceived as unloving, distant, or critical; strong inferiority feelings; and the subject experiencing himself as an unfavored sibling. It appeared that the guru and the new family provided the unconditional acceptance that these adherents craved along with a sense of security they often sorely lacked. For example, one devotee, Barbara, had felt ignored by her depressed mother, rejected by her attractive older sister and "torn down" by her critical father. A highly charismatic psychotherapist had, years earlier, bolstered her self-esteem and deeply influenced her, a process which seemed to be repeating itself with Baba. Another subject with a troubled family life had been told at age three that she was adopted. That seemed to set the stage for a life-long search for a perfect parent, loving, strong, and reliable, a quest that seemed satisfied in her relationship to Baba. It can be pointed out again that in these two cases, as in the majority of the subjects, both parents as seen by the devotees, seemed to be inadequate objects for loving attachments and identifications.

The relief of guilt   Baba's acceptance, lack of censure and deemphasis of conventional morality was important to a number of devotees, eg, one suffering guilt over a recent abortion, and another over masturbation. The powerful group leader, seen as carrying God's message, could be adopted as a superego replacement,[3] while his specific teachings seemed to relieve guilt feelings from a variety of sources.

Feeling free   Besides guilt over specific issues, a very frequent complaint of the devotees related to an ego-alien experience of inner restrictiveness that they usually saw as resulting from their parents' oppressive presence and general prohibitiveness, and that often seemed to be an important spur for their rebellion against their parents and their teachings. The relationship to the guru and the adoption of his values helped them attain a feeling of freedom.

Being good and loving   During periods of "bliss," the devotees experienced a flow of warm feeling toward people in the environment. In accounting for this feeling, some family members described themselves as somehow emulating Baba or as seeing the beloved guru in their objects. On his departure, a few spoke of having Baba within them. The emergence of loving feelings should be seen against the background of the chronic anger and disgruntlement and sometimes overt sadism that seemed to have been prevalent among the devotees.

The development of purpose   The inner sense of purposelessness that had marked the lives of almost all the devotees tended to cease with their involvement with Baba. Their path in life was now "spiritual" and their stated goal was to get close to God. For a few this path did not seem to involve any major commitment but most seemed quite dedicated to their spiritual goals. A few had parted with virtually all their possessions, including Western dress, and were preparing themselves for life in India. Evidence of imitation of Baba, particularly among the most devoted, abounded in dress, hair style, phraseology, and other habits. Several even were silent for days at a time, communicating only through the guru's sign language.

Elements of the Subjects' Life-styles

Sexuality   Some degree of renunciation of sexuality (*brahmacharya*) was undertaken by four of the male and four of the female subjects but tended to be more complete in the women. This was not advocated by the guru but was in line with his (and yogic) teachings that letting desires pass without gratification eventually leads to their diminution and permits the full development of spirituality.[4] The usual report from these subjects was that the sexual act "brought them down" from the "high" that they were experiencing. For the strongest adherents the "spiritual quest" was so consuming that there was no interest in any relationship other than that to Baba and God. With several of the devotees it was not difficult to see the defensive purposes that the attempt to renounce sexuality served.

Employment and ambition   In general, the subjects were not oriented toward careers, work, or earning money even at the time they met Baba. Only one held a full-time job on a professional level during the period of observation, and none was in school. The majority, who were living off minimal employment, savings, or parental handouts, had generally dropped out of the world of striving and competition including work and school some time earlier, some apparently aided in this process by their drug use and mystical leanings. Prior to their dropping out, most of the subjects had achieved, by conventional standards, at least moderate success in school or work. Typically, the attitude toward the future, even among those who professed some interest in a career, was that expressed by the guru, ie, one of not making plans and letting things happen. Although this was not his stated intention, it seemed that Baba helped influence the subjects toward a kind of passive unemployed spirituality much like his own. The experience of Barbara who had developed certain skills and interests under the influence of her therapist but who more or less relinquished them during her period with Baba to spend her time in spiritual pursuits, was not atypical.

In the case of another subject, Joe, longstanding conflicts around aggressive and competitive strivings led to a totally passive retreat under the influence of Baba. In this move any ambition or effort toward active mastery was squelched.

Food habits   Many of the subjects were strict vegetarians and all placed at least some restrictions on their food intake, eg, not eating meat, spicy foods, or nonorganically grown foods. The usual religiously tinged reasons were given for these practices, including the desirability of avoiding excessive sensual stimulation and food obtained by killing.[4] Of interest was the fact that in a substantial number of devotees food restriction preceded the adoption of Hinduism and thus appeared to have a dynamic of its own. Indeed, it frequently seemed to serve as an introduction to religious practices.

In the case of one subject who came from a working-class background, a childhood inhibition against eating meat led to a voluntary giving up of eating fish at age 12 and to a youthful identification with the image of a "bohemian intellectual" unlike anyone in his community. This subject saw the adoption of Hinduism as the ultimate fruition of a process that started with his deviant eating habits. In his case and in a few others where food restrictions were adopted while the individual lived in the parental home, the deviant eating habits upset the mother, caused conflict within the family, and made the subject the focus for special attention. One could not help but speculate that, aside from whatever special intrapsychic meanings the food deviance had in these devotees, on some fundamental level it was a representation of an opposition to "taking in" what their parents had to give and was relevant to their looking to a radically different source for nurturance and for the purpose of identification.

The Influence of Psychedelic Drugs

All but three of the subjects had made at least moderate use of LSD and other hallucinogens (5 to 50 "trips") prior to meeting Baba. These drug users saw their psychedelic experiences as influential or even essential in their embrace of Hinduism and Baba. The notion of this influence is commonplace among American followers of Eastern religions; Baba himself referred to the psychedelic experience as a "preview of coming attractions." The trips that the devotees believed had influenced their conversion typically had a "mystical" content such as experiences of unity with others or the cosmos, and revelations of universal love along with sensations of utter certainty and intense elation. At least two subjects had sensations of being God associated with their elation. (Joe explained that he subsequently realized that this was an "ego trip" and that God was actually in everyone.)

This kind of content is not atypical of psychedelic experience but what was striking was the lasting impression the trips seemed to have on the devotees. They believed that their psychedelic visions had given them an insight into "true reality." In extreme cases, LSD-induced illusions of seemingly trivial nature, such as experiencing a musical recording as being in direct communication with one's thoughts, appeared to have an ongoing importance and influence in the devotees' view of life. While "magical–mystical" beliefs have been found to be widespread among "acidheads,"[5] these subjects, some of whom had taken but a few trips, gave the impression that they had a special affinity for a primitive unified view of reality and perhaps a special vulnerability to the effects of the psychedelics.

In the typical case, the devotee would read one or more of the popular accounts of mystical religious conversion,[4,6] and excitedly note parallels between these accounts and his own psychedilic visions. The emphasis in Hinduism on ideas such as the presence of God within everyone and the desirability of achieving union with the godhead or some cosmic force seemed to provide a framework within which the yearnings that appeared to be awakened by the drugs could be fulfilled. In some instances the trips now took on a more specifically religious coloring and subjects would describe feelings of unity with God or seeing God. The stage was set for the devotees' further involvement with Hinduism and with a guru.

In the Family, the devotees embraced a variety of unusual beliefs without apparent inner resistance—from the idea of reincarnation to the notion that Baba's mentor, Swami, could materialize precious stones from thin air. While group pressure and the childlike transference to the guru probably affected the easy acceptance of these ideas, the influence of past psychedelic experiences was doubtless a factor in many cases. One of the least credulous devotees put it this way: "Baba says that he knows someone is coming if that person thinks of him on the way here. At one time that would have seemed ridiculous to me, but after all the unusual things I've experienced, under LSD I can believe it."

COMMENT

In attempting to understand the experiences of the devotees it is appropriate to review briefly some psychological and psychoanalytic concepts relating to conversion and mystical experience. "Conversion" has been defined by William James as "the process, gradual or sudden, by which a self hitherto divided, and consciously wrong, inferior and unhappy, becomes unified and consciously right, superior and happy, in consequence of its firmer hold upon religious realities.[7] Depending on the era and the population studied, conversion has been found to be a normative process, common in adolescence, or a relatively rare occurrence.[8] The term can be applied whether the religious affirmation involves the faith of one's parents or another faith; one would suppose, however, that the accompanying psychodynamics would differ in the two instances.

Sudden conversions such as that of Saint Paul, may be ushered in by a mystical experience[9] while the more gradual conversions are generally less related to mysticism.[10] The designation "mystical experience" generally refers to the direct apprehension of or union with the Divine or some absolute cosmic power, or to feelings of unity with the cosmos itself.[7,8,11] A lessening of the "demarcation between self and non-self" is involved. Characteristics of the mystical state as described by James include its ineffability, its noetic or revelatory quality, its transiency, and the mystic's experience of passivity.[7] The accompanying affect is that of ecstasy or bliss. Similarities between this state and the altered state of consciousness induced by hallucinogenic drugs have led to the consideration that the drug experiences are not essentially different in their religious significance or life-enhancing potential.[12,13]

While there are evident direct gratifications in the experience of union with a higher power or with the cosmos, the mystical state or conversion with mystical overtones has also been viewed in the psychiatric and psychoanalytic literature as a mode of conflict resolution.[14] In a case described by Freud,[15] it appeared that an episode causing a sudden upsurge of oedipal aggression in a man was resolved by a mystical conversion involving submission to the "father" in the form of God. An episode of "mystical illumination" that resulted in Bertrand Russell's conversion to pacifism[16] has been analyzed as being due to an awakening of childhood experiences involving rage at separation and abandonment. The dissociative state and the turn to pacifism were seen as defenses against aggression while the mystical feelings of union were simultaneously a compensation for the loss. Jacobson sees mystical states developing in adolescents and "evidently" nonpsychotic adults as a reaction to their being overpowered by homosexual or heterosexual desires.[17] In Salzman's disturbed patients who converted "away" from their religion of origin, the chief conflicts appeared to involve rage against authority.[10] The ability of certain schizophrenic patients to conjure up the mystical state has been seen as a "safeguard against overwhelming loneliness and resultant suicide."[18] It thus appears that conversion and mystical states can be employed to resolve a variety of conflicts involving both oedipal and preoedipal strivings, and sexual as well as aggressive urges.

In psychoanalytic formulations, the mystical state has been seen as a reflection of the infant's early experience of limitlessness of the self or of union with the mother before the boundaries of the self have been established.[14] Lewin related the ecstasies of mystics to those of elated patients and saw both as resulting from a fantasied merger with a more powerful object. The model in either case is the infant's calm sleep-producing acceptance of the oral relationship with the mother, which is perceived as a mutually incorporating fusion. Ecstasy can later be experienced in the fantasied merger with a paternal or superego figure or its internalized representative. The fusion with the object can be many layered, as in one of Lewin's patients who in her ecstatic merger with her lover "took in" the breast, the man, and his "superego ideals."[19] In Kohut's work, which also has pertinence to the understanding of religious ecstasy, a subgroup of patients with narcissistic personality disorders, namely those "fixated on the omnipotent object," is defined. It is believed that these patients, because of early traumatic disappointments in one or both parents, have not optimally internalized their idealized objects and hence suffer from structural defects in their personalities that they attempt to remedy by seeking out in adult life new idealized objects with which to merge and complete the self.[20]

While the devotees were immersed in mystical beliefs and strove for experiences of union through yogic practices, their nondrug-related ecstasies, for the most part, lacked the qualities of defined mystical experiences described by James. Their happiness seemed to result from their relationship with their all-wise and all-loving guru in all that he represented to his followers—parent, teacher, and representative of God. Based on the experiences of the devotees and the formulations above relating to sensations of ecstasy and bliss, one can speculate that fantasies of fusion with Baba were common in this group. The guru drew devotees who seemed to be seeking the perfect mother, as well as those seeking the perfect father, and we can speculate that by caring and feeding, by easing consciences and providing direction, he could, to some, represent both simultaneously (in a condensation similar to that of Lewin's patient). It can be noted that "baba," which in Indian languages means father, is Yiddish for grandmother.

The conflicts most pervasive among the devotees seemed to involve angry demandingness for love and attention. These conflicts were, in at least some cases, rekindled in the new family and then "resolved" in part in their relationship to the new parent figure. It would seem that what was involved in this "resolution" was not only the receipt of "unconditional positive regard" from Baba but, at least in some instances, the abolition of distance between the devotee and the omnipotent "parent" through an experience of merger.[21] The turning to the radically new parent often appeared also to contain an angry rejection of the original parents for their ostensible inadequacies.

The overriding feature of Baba's power and influence was his perceived closeness to God. This meant to the devotees that he shared in the Divine omnipotence and added to his charisma. As a man who had "found the way" himself, he became the perfect teacher and model. In identifying with him or in the more complete fusion experiences, the devotees took over Baba's philosophy of renunciation and emulated his "holiness." This aided the devotees in dealing with conflicts relating not only to childlike demandingness but also to sadism, sexuality, and competitive aggression. The relationship to Baba could serve in other ways too in aiding in the resolution of conflict. Thus, troublesome sexual feelings could be sublimated in the love for the "holy father" and painful competitive urges dealt with via a passive submission to the symbolic father.

We may speculate that in all the subjects latent wishes for union with a powerful object may have been particularly intense, and thus these individuals were especially open to the activation of these regressive wishes. The yearning for a bond with a powerful figure may conceivably have been stimulated by early traumatic frustrations or disappointments in parental figures in a manner similar to Kohut's narcissistic patients who are "fixated on the omnipotent object"[20] or Jacobson's cyclothymic patients.[22] The frequent complaints of the subjects relating to maternal disorder, unsatisfactory relations with both parents, and chronic dysphoria are not inconsistent with these conjectures concerning such early trauma. The psychoanalysis of a patient with "mystic pantheism" described by Carver in the early psychiatric literature[23] lends some backing to these broad speculations. In Carver's patient, the longing for mystical union was seen as a wish to return to a state of "primary identification" with the mother and appeared to be stimulated by the marked failure of his early "objective" relationship to her as well as to his father.

The question as to whether or not backgrounds similar to those of the subjects are found more generally among present-day converts to mystical creeds can only be answered by additional study. It would also be of interest to determine whether such converts are randomly distributed among different sects or if the different groupings—eg, the grandiose Divine Light Mission,[24] the Hare Krishna followers with their aggressive display, or the closed, guilt-inducing New Testament Missionary Fellowship[25]—each answer rather specific needs and attract devotees with recognizable differences in their personality patterns. In our group, for example, the ecumenism of the leader's teachings (manifested by his easy acceptance of holy men in other religion and sects) and his outdoor assemblages with an open welcome to passersby may have specifically satisfied deep needs of the devotees to feel in peaceful harmony with their surroundings.

Part II—A Guru's Psychosis

The preceding paper,[1] describes the formation of a cult in mid-Manhattan. In a subsequent work, "Tenacity of Affiliation to a Cult Leader,"[2] I traced the evolution of the "Family" as a rural commune and its ultimate fragmentation. The guru's increasing bizarreness and cruelty and its effect on the cult members were described. Family members who remained faithful to the guru dealt with the manifestations of his emotional deterioration through denial, rationalization and increased idealization.[2]

In this paper, I will attempt to provide insight into the cult leader's psychological dynamics before and during his emotional deterioration and subsequent religious conversion. I will suggest links between these dynamics and his teachings and behavior with the Family. The paper will also present a brief follow-up on developments in the Family after the guru abdicated leadership in 1976. As Baba has been called by his first name since that time, he will be referred to in this paper as "Jeff," a pseudonym. The data on Jeff to be presented was obtained from my encounters with him, my conversations with Family members, and particularly from some remarkable interviews with him recently published in a book about the Family.[3]

Jeff, now in his mid-40s, is of Jewish background. Little is known of his early life. He had an episode of mutism and paralysis at 18 which he regards as a mystical experience. A few years later, Jeff's father killed his wife (Jeff's mother) before comitting suicide. Jeff ultimately married, had two children and established himself in business, but in the late 1960s, he used psychedelics, left his family and embarked on his spiritual quest. He travelled through the country and he had one psychiatric hospitalization. Jeff describes his life at the time as empty and devoid of happiness.[3]

He hitched a ride one day with a devotee of a famous Indian holyman and miracle worker, "Swami," who was regarded by his followers as an incarnation of Divinity. He was introduced to a group of devotees and saw a film in which the holyman's powers were demonstrated. Upon going to sleep that night, Jeff had a vision of Swami's eyes which was both exulting and frightening. Following this experience, Jeff developed a powerful longing "to look into Swami's eyes" in order to "find release and freedom."[3]

Jeff travelled to Swami's ashram in India and begged him repeatedly for freedom from his inner torment. It was a frustrating experience. He states:

> Most of the time I didn't really listen to Swami because my mind was . . . busy with the big question. "Baba, can you give me freedom?" I finally had eye contact with Swami and something happened . . . there was a spiritual circuit of some kind, something that passed from his body to mine and . . . I received some occult powers in the exchange. After that, I was aware of future events to a certain extent. It satisfied a small part of me but still there was discontent.

One day, when Swami "materialized" sacred ash (the holyman's standard "miracle") and offered it to Jeff, Jeff said, "I don't want vibhuti (ash), I want freedom, Baba, can you give me freedom?" About this time Jeff began thinking of starting his own ashram, "a community devoted to God where people would serve each other . . . a place where anyone could get a hit of love."[3]

Jeff underwent extreme measures such as fasting and prolonged isolation to achieve "freedom and closeness to God." In spite of disturbing altered mental states, he remained dissatisfied. One day, he heard Swami reassure a sick woman who was afraid she would die. After the woman died two days later, Jeff accused Swami of a lack of truthfulness. Swami, stating that his intent was merely to comfort a frightened woman, became angry with Jeff and told him to leave the ashram.[3]

On an isolated beach where he spent the time meditating and chanting, Jeff "opened himself up to spiritual [occult] power." He became increasingly depressed "maybe entering into insanity." He decided to commit suicide, but before doing so he recited the mantra Swami had given him. Suddenly, two Westerners appeared and they engaged him in conversation. Jeff turned his head for a moment and his visitors disappeared but he no longer felt suicidal. He states that Swami subsequently indicated to him that it was he who had appeared to him on the beach.[3] (The holyman has the reputation of being able to transport himself in space and to assume different forms.)

When Jeff returned to the United States in 1971 after two years in India, his "body began to spin." This was due to a "spirit force within [him] which he gave himself up to." According to Jeff, it was this spirit that spun him to the Central Park bench where the Family got started.[3]

When I first saw Jeff on the bench in 1972, he seemed in reasonably good emotional balance. He was highly intelligent, responsive to his environment, and his communications via sign language were logical, coherent and pithy.[1] He manifested periodic facial grimaces which he attributed to the rising of the *Shakti* (spiritual energy). If one could accept certain unusual premises (relating to spirits, spinning and miracles) as his devotees were primed by their personal predilections, psychedelic experiences and countercultural worldview to do, one could see how he might attract a spirtual following.

Jeff's increasing bizarreness, sadism and general deterioration have been described in the "Tenacity" paper.[2] In addition to the fragmentation and incoherence of his communication, he often seemed in the throes of a paralyzing ambivalence which precluded sensible activity.

Jeff describes his inner experience during this period:

> Voices spoke to me. They'd tell me to go to California. I'd tell [a follower] to get the car ready and we'd . . . get as far as town and the voices would tell me to go back to the Hill. The voices told me if someone from far away was coming hours before they arrived. Sometimes the voices lied to me and no one came but usually the prophecy came true. . . .
>
> I had to walk backwards into temple. Otherwise I'd feel all the bad vibes which brought me down very low. I'd feel what everybody else was feeling. I'd take on his vibes, karma, his spirits. Others were helped to go into bliss when I held out my hand to them in a blessing, but I'd take on their bad experiences . . . I was the Family laundromat. They left [temple] feeling light and clean . . . I took on . . . dark spirits. Many times I'd take on the attributes of another person . . . I'd go back to my room and have hellish experiences. If a woman was afraid of mice, I'd take on her fear. The whole room would be crawling with mice, attacking me, climbing up my chair. I'd feel them clawing my skin, biting me. . . .
>
> I sat twenty hours a day stretched out in my chair, my torture rack. There were visions of sexual perversions which came straight from hell. I'd see visions of murders and horrible cruelty. And always the voices talking to me, telling me to do things . . . I wasn't even allowed to walk properly, the spirits controlled me completely, making me walk jerkily like a robot . . . Long ago I had to quit driving because several times when I was at the wheel of a car, . . . hands would steer my hands trying to wreck the car. They just took over the wheel and would have driven into other cars. . . .
>
> From the first time I started to spin, I was moved about by energies and spirits, not by my own will. I gave up my own desire and let the spirits move me where they would. Very often they would fling me into walls, bang me against buildings and cause me bodily hurt. I sincerely thought it was from God and that by surrendering more and more to it, I was getting closer to God.[3]

Towards the end of 1975, Jeff's voices and spirits were even more tormenting:

> One day as I shaved, the voices told me to put the blades in my mouth but I refused. The voices insisted and finally I put several razor blades in my mouth and I chewed them . . . They made me put my head close to the fire and set my hair afire . . . Shortly [after] I shaved my hair off . . . They controlled me completely . . . I did as they told me, at first because I wanted to get close to God and later because I was powerless.[3]

Jeff's reason for asking for a tape recorder[2] is as follows:

> The voices were talking, talking . . .I hadn't spoken for years and didn't know who was speaking, me or the voices. I decided if I had a tape recorder, I would speak and listen to my own voice. Then I would listen to the other voices. That way I could figure out who I was.[3]

He was brought a tape recorder/radio and gives this account of his conversion:

> I turned (the radio) on, rolled the dial and came to the Christian Broadcasting Network. The 700 Club was on . . . Men were telling fantastic things of God's

power . . . I listened to the 700 Club every time it was on . . . I heard Pat Robertson [a preacher] talk about the power of Jesus' name, about the power of the blood [of Christ]. . . . Shortly after . . . the demons were tormenting me badly. . . . I called out "Jesus help me" and the spirits left me in peace for a short while. . . . I wondered . . . could it be that Jesus was more powerful than Swami, more powerful than the spirits who controlled my body. . . .[3]

After Jeff exposed himself to Christian evangelical teachings his "spirits" were identified by him as "demons." His struggle with them went on for several more months. Learning about the events on the Hill, a local evangelist began making daily visits to teach the New Testament. Also, a merchant left a Christian tract along with his bill. This tract stated that not all spirits are from God, but only those that profess belief in Jesus. Jeff then had a vision of Jesus telling him he was following the wrong path. Jeff commanded the spirits who did not follow Christ to leave his body. He went around the Hill in a frenzied manner, saying "the spirit of truth has come," exorcizing the demons from his followers and demanding to be exorcized by them. He also travelled to exorcizers throughout the country. He demanded that all pictures and relics of Swami be burnt. His own house had to be removed from its foundations because pictures of Swami had been placed there when it was constructed; the house was replaced after the pictures were removed.[2,3]

Soon after, Jeff led his followers in Christian baptismal ceremonies and transformed the Hindu temple on the Hill into a church. He then told his followers that he no longer wanted to be their spiritual leader. One of his followers, who had control over the commune's land and who was not persuaded by the new "Christian trip" asked Jeff to leave the Hill and Jeff complied.[2,3]

It soon became clear that Christianity was just a phase for Jeff. Resuming his travels throughout the country, he adopted Hasidic Jewry as his religious profession and has sinced remained with it. When I last saw him, in 1980, he wore the Jewish ritual undergarment (the *talit katan*) with its fringes exposed as a Hasidic Jew would. While still somewhat bizarre in appearance, behavior and speech, he was in good humor and seemed content.

Like many Westerners, Jeff sought an answer to his problems in the wisdom of the East and from a grandiose figure who embodied this wisdom. We know very little in specific terms about what was bothering Jeff. We do know that he felt empty and tormented and that he sought "freedom" and closeness to God. From the start, there was clearly something extreme and unusual about his "spiritual quest." This is attested to both by the abandonment of his occupation and family and his immediate total transport by the image of Swami. His subsequent thoughts and actions leave little doubt that he was in a psychotic state. The initial wish to get close to the powerful good object may have stemmed from intolerable ambivalence conflicts and incipient loss of the object world ("torment" and "emptiness").[4] A central inference that I make in the brief analysis that follows is that Jeff dealt with Swami through magical incorporative fantasies. The work of Jacobson relating to self and object representations in highly regressed individuals provides a theoretical backdrop for this discussion.[4-7]

Jeff's interaction with Swami took a different form from that of the usual Western devotee and the Indian pilgrim. (I observed members of both these groups during a visit to Swami's ashram in the mid-1970s.) In the *bhakti* tradition which was followed at the ashram, the holyman is supreme, the devotees modest petitioners who bask in his radiance.[8] Psychological separateness between the devotee and the holyman rather than mystical merger is the rule. The holyman is approached with awe—not criticized, challenged or subjected to demands. Western devotees who felt angry towards Swami or doubtful about his powers or beneficence would deal with their ambivalence by using denial and rationalization and by further "surrendering" themselves to the holyman. (These are ways in which the Family later dealt with Jeff.[2])

In comparison to the mode, Jeff's interaction with Swami was grandiose and highly individualistic. He voiced demands from the holyman and criticized him for his "shortcomings." He was "transfused" with the holyman's occult powers and soon after thought of founding his own ashram. His suicidal feeling which followed Swami's rejection of him ended when the Divine leader miraculously rescued him; his ambivalence conflicts had thus, in a sense, taken on cosmic proportions.

From Jeff's account of his interaction with Swami, we can see the operation of his primitive incorporative and wish fulfillment fantasies. These fantasies seem to have been stimulated by his frustrations with the holyman.[4] It seems likely that becoming a guru was the result of Jeff's magical identification with the grandiose religious leader[6] and was a regressive substitute for a frustrating and ambivalent object relationship.

At about the time he left India, Jeff began a long-term relationship with his "spirits," forces which directed and ultimately controlled his actions. I would conjecture that the spirits represent part of the incorporated image of Swami positioned as a kind of primitive superego. In fact, it is of considerable interest that Jeff's relationship to his spirits mimic the relationship of other devotees to Swami (and ultimately the relationship of Jeff's own followers to their guru). In each of those cases the subordinate individuals dealt with frustration and ambivalence towards their particular "authority figure" by passive surrender with the belief that they are thereby surrendering to God's will.[2] It would seem that in a narcissistically regressed manner, Jeff employed the typical defenses of the devotee and continued his relationship to Swami through his spirits.

Surrender did not bring the desired state of bliss, however; instead Jeff feels progressively more tormented and the spirits are experienced as voices and demons who lie to him, torture him and wish to see him dead. One might see in this development Jeff's own hostility towards Swami as it becomes progressively stripped of any admixture of positive feeling, projected onto the spirits. To speculate further, homosexual anxieties stimulated by the attempt at spiritual surrender may account in part for the paranoidal shift. Alternatively, the spirit-demons, functioning as superego fragments,[6] might be meting out fantasied punishments to Jeff for his grandiose and exploitative behavior toward his followers.

In general, Jeff's relationship to his followers seemed to contribute to the progression of his psychosis. Their receptiveness to his bizarre leadership resulting from their emotional needs and curious ideas probably stimulated his megolamania and sadism rather than providing a reality corrective. In addition their interaction with him led to an increased loss of ego boundaries[5] on Jeff's part as he "took on their pain and suffering" (and towards the end believed them to be suffering his).

From another perspective, we may see Jeff using the Family as a vehicle for the acting out of psychotic conflicts[5] based on the postulated incorporation of Swami. In his beneficent "*Krishna* phase,"[2] he is Swami the bountiful, giving food and counsel—"hits of love"—to all assembled and probably vicariously enjoying those gifts. In his sadistic "*Shiva* phase,"[2] he identifies with the tormenting Swami, cruelly punishing all in his sphere and exhorting them to surrender to him just as he strives to surrender to Swami. Using projective identification in both instances, he attempts to gain mastery and control over his needs and conflicts by externalizing them onto the group in his thrall.[5]

Since the notions of letting go and surrender were so central to Jeff and his followers, we should say a few words about these ideas. Letting down barriers to sensation and inner experience along with the eschewal of struggle and ambition were hallmarks of the hippie culture that had influenced Jeff.[9] For many in this culture, the usefulness of going along with, rather than struggling against, inner sensation was demonstrated after being confronted with a bad LSD trip.[10] The Eastern philosophy adopted by members of the counterculture further encouraged giving oneself up to inner experience (in contrast, for example, to an uptight puritanical vigilance[11]) and lent the process a spiritual dimension. Indeed, it was felt that in opening oneself up through meditation, one can reach a level of consciousness that penetrates wordly illusion and enables one to see through the Godhead in all people.[10] Jeff seems to have developed these ideas in a most extreme way. In preaching about letting go in the early days of the Family, he told of his own sexual surrender to a man who had assaulted him. In this lesson, as in others, he advocated a passive, detached attitude not only towards inner experience but towards the outer world. An Eastern nondualism seemed to underlie these lessons—everything is Godly even if on the surface it appears otherwise. For Jeff and the Family, surrender to a force or situation became an act of faith in God. When the force was a Swami or guru, surrender was all the more compelling.

This philosophy did not succeed for Jeff as we have described; his attempts at surrender ultimately brought him increasing torment and bizarreness. At a critical point he was exposed to dualistic evangelical Christian teachings highlighting the dangers of sin and Satan.[11] He could then identify his spirits as demons and work towards banishing them rather than surrendering to them. The adherence to another God-figure, Jesus, gave him the strength, the philosophy and the direction to alter his deteriorating course. Conveivably, the request for the tape recorder that preceded his contact with evangelical Christianity may have reflected a self-curative impulse—to rediscover his own identity and thereby undo his fusion with Swami. The relationships to new (Christian) teachers doubtlessly helped in the undoing of his narcissistic regression and megalomania.

The effect on the Family of Jeff's conversion is of interest. They were all baptized, but with varying degrees of enthusiasm. However, the attempt to make the commune exclusively Christian and the concomitant banishment of Swami's influence met with resistance from a sizable segment of the Family.

When I visited the remnants of the commune about one year after Jeff had left, I learned that the Family had split into three groups: 1) "The Flower Children." They tended to be the youngest, most impressionable and dependent of the Family. Many of them had remained on the Hill after Jeff's departure, accepting the less exciting leadership in effect there. 2) "The Christians." The conversion

128

inspired by Jeff had "taken" in these people. Most of them had left the area and many were active in evangelical causes. 3) "The Yogis." They included some of the earliest and most strong-minded members of the Family. Many of them lived in the vicinity of the Hill, some working in countercultural-type jobs and some contemplating return to school. It was with this group that I had the most contact during my visit.

The yogis had established strong ties to each other and at the time that I saw them showed no great distress over the loss of Jeff's leadership. As always, they were highly interested in their own sensations and inner experiences, particularly if they bordered on the mystical or occult. They spent a good deal of time discussing Jeff, the Christians and the politics of the commune. They looked upon Jeff as an inspired teacher who had gone too far and who, in his madness, had abandoned precious wisdom. While tolerant of the evangelicals, they could not accept the notion of "the one true path"; to them both Jesus and Swami ranked as God-figures.

It appeared at that point that while they had been greatly influenced by Jeff, their fundamental inspiration was the counterculture from which both they and their guru had emerged. Their passive orientation, their absorption in internal experience, their religious eclectisism and their antirational sentiments were reflective of attitudes dominant in the psychedelic hippie culture[9] which had found resonance and reinforcement in certain teachings of Eastern religion.

REFERENCES

Part I

1. Berry T: *Religions of India: Hinduism, Yoga, Buddhism*. New York, Bruce Publishing Co, 1971.
2. Embree AT (ed): *The Hindu Tradition*. New York, Modern Library, 1966.
3. Freud S: Group psychology and the analysis of the ego, in Strachey J (trans): *Standard Edition of the Complete Psychological Works of Sigmund Freud*. London, Hogarth Press, vol 18, 1955.
4. Baba Ram Dass: *Remember, Be Here Now*. Albuquerque, NM, Lama Foundation, 1971.
5. Blacker KH, Jones RT, Stone GC, et al: Chronic users of LSD: The "acidheads." *Am J Psychiatry* 1968;125:341–351.
6. Yogananda P: *Autobiography of a Yogi*. Los Angeles, Self-Realization Fellowship, 1972.
7. James W: *The Varieties of Religious Experience*. New York, Modern Library, 1929.
8. Clark WH: *The Psychology of Religion*. New York, Macmillan Co, 1958.
9. Acts 9 (King James Version).
10. Salzman L: The psychology of religious and mystical conversion. *Psychiatry* 1953; 16:177–187.
11. Leuba JH: *The Psychology of Religious Mysticism*. Boston, Routledge and Kegan Paul, 1929, pp 1–7.
12. Huxley A: *The Doors of Perception*. New York, Harper & Row Publishers Inc, 1954.
13. Clark WH: *Chemical Ecstasy*. New York, Sheed and Ward, 1969.
14. Sterba R: Remarks on mystic states. *Am Imago* 1968;25:77–85.
15. Freud S: A religious experience, in Strachey J (trans): *Standard Edition of the Complete Psychological Works of Sigmund Freud*. London, Hogarth Press, vol 21, 1961.
16. Simon B, Simon N: The pacifist turn: An episode of mystic illumination in the autobiography of Bertrand Russell. *J Am Psychoanal Assoc* 1972;20:109–121.
17. Jacobson E: *The Self and the Object World*. New York, International Universities Press, 1964, p 191.

18. Horton PC: The mystical experience as a suicide preventive. *Am J Psychiatry* 1973; 130:294–296.
19. Lewin BD: *The Psychoanalysis of Elation.* New York, The Psychoanalytic Quarterly, 1961, pp 129–165.
20. Kohut H: *The Analysis of the Self.* New York, International Universities Press, 1971, pp 1–56.
21. Searles HF: Data concerning certain manifestations of incorporation. *Psychiatry* 1951; 14:397–413.
22. Jacobson E: The influence of infantile conflicts on recurring depressive states, in *Depression, Comparative Studies of Normal Neurotic, and Psychotic Conditions.* New York, International Universities Press, 1971, pp 204–227.
23. Carver E: Primary identification and mystical pantheism. *Br J Med Psychol* 1924;4: 102–113.
24. Gray FdP: Blissing out in Houston, in *The New York Review of Books.* 1973;20:36–43.
25. Roiphe A: Struggle over two sisters, in *The New York Times Magazine.* June 1973, pp 17–78.

Part II

1. Deutsch A: Observations on a sidewalk ashram. *Psychodynamic Perspectives on Religion, Sect and Cult.* Littleton, MA, John Wright • PSG Inc, 1983.
2. Deutsch A: Tenacity of affiliation to a cult leader—a psychiatric perspective. *Am J Psychiatry* 1980;137:1569–1573.
3. Pakkala L: *Yea God.* Trumansburg, NY, The Crossing Press, 1980.
4. Jacobson E: *The Self and the Object World.* New York, International Universities Press, 1964.
5. Jacobson E: *Psychotic Conflict and Reality.* New York, International Universities Press, 1967.
6. Jacobson E: Psychotic identifications, in *Depression, Comparative Studies of Normal, Neurotic and Psychotic Conditions.* New York, International Universities Press, 1971.
7. Jacobson E: Differences between schizophrenic and melancholic states of depression, in *Depression, Comparative Studies of Normal, Neurotic and Psychotic Conditions.* New York, International Universities Press, 1971.
8. Embree AT (ed): *The Hindu Tradition.* New York, Modern Library, 1966.
9. Roszak T: *The Making of a Counter Culture.* Garden City, NY, Anchor Books, 1969.
10. Ram Dass: *The Only Dance There Is.* Garden City, NY, Anchor Books, 1974.
11. Greven P: *The Protestant Temperament.* New York, Alfred A. Knopf, 1977.

S E C T I O N　　T W O

CONSIDERATIONS ON CULT AFFILIATION AND RELIGIOUS IDENTIFICATION

Anthropological Approaches to Religious Movements

JOHANNES FABIAN

The interested outsider who seeks illumination from anthropological writings on religious movements will be discouraged by confusing ethnographics and arcane controversies. What is this field of study about and where does it get us? I shall attempt to answer these questions, first by a brief review of past work and current concerns (Part One), then by venturing, as it were, to the frontiers of social scientific interpretation (Part Two).* The historical survey, apart from suggesting further readings, should demonstrate that anthropologists have progressed from "explaining" movements as transitory symptoms of a disturbed social order or of "culture contact" gone wrong, toward interpreting religious enthusiasm in its own terms. Sheer accumulation of more and better studies of particular movements has helped to appreciate as rational, culturally creative, and morally or esthetically innovative what once appeared the work of madmen and their misguided followers. But while a nonpathological view of religious movements now supersedes older positions, it may accomplish little more than moving, metaphorically speaking, religious enthusiasts from the asylum (and from colonial prisons) into the ghetto of cultural relativism in which "everything goes" as long as it can be kept at a distance. Religious movements are once again rendered harmless; their "objective" study may neutralize their pathos and eternalize their delusions. Therefore, I shall argue, objective study must include

*Longer versions of the two parts of this essay were previously published in Fabian J (ed): Beyond charisma: Religious movements as discourse. *Social Research* 1979;46:203. These papers were part of a project on the interpretation of Jamaa texts made possible by a grant from the Wenner-Gren Foundation for Anthropological Research, New York, whose support is gratefully acknowledged. Material for the Epilogue was gathered during fieldwork on work and communication sponsored by a grant from the National Endowment for the Humanities (RO-6150-72-149) and while serving at the National University of Zaire on a university aid program provided by the Rockefeller Foundation, New York.

critical confrontation. The minimal respect social scientists ought to pay prophets and charismatic leaders is to defy their claims if there are reasons to do so. Their madness may fire our desire for rational explanation, but our madness—the madness of "normal" social science doing the business of our "normal" societies—may make theirs rational.

This is not the position with which I started when I began research in an African country. Years of fieldwork (1966-1967, and occasional contacts during another project in 1972-1974) and many more years of struggling with texts and interpretations have kept me in constant confrontation with one particular religious movement known as Jamaa (a Swahili term which may be translated as family-group or community). Because I shall frequently refer to the Jamaa, I should briefly summarize its characteristics now.

The movement originated in the early fifties among African Catholics in Zaire, most of them workers in the mining towns of Shaba (the former Katanga). It is one of the few sizable (and durable) African religious movements to arise in a Catholic context (which was long considered to be immune to sectarian and separatist activities), and it has the almost unique distinction of having as its initiator a European missionary, Placide Tempels (1906-1977). Temples, a Flemish Franciscan, experienced a profound crisis as a missionary. The solution he eventually found to his own problems became the doctrinal core of a Bantu-Christian message which attracted, at the height of the movement's activities in the sixties, more than 200,000 followers.

Adepts of the Jamaa are, with rare exceptions, adult and married Catholics who gain full membership by progressive initiation into the movement. During most of its existence, the Jamaa remained ritually and organizationally linked to the mission church. It has been free, at least until recently, of sectarian and millennarian tendencies, emphasizing, instead, deep personal relationships among the members, a common search for the meaning of human existence, and simple, undramatic communal activities which required only rudiments of formal organization. The movement's identity is expressed most clearly in its teachings which in many cases preserve Tempels' original formulations although he left Zaire in 1962.

In its earlier stages, the Jamaa was a precarious but highly interesting phenomenon. More recently it has become quite complex, afflicted by internal schism and embattled by ecclesiastical and political authorities. Outright repression and what Weber called routinization of charisma are in part responsible for the fact that the Jamaa lost more and more of its unique characteristics. However, this late phase awaits study; no major research has been carried out since the early seventies.

PART ONE: FROM EXPLANATION TO INTERPRETATION
Whither the Study of Religious Movements?

The anthropological study of exotic religious[1] movements continues to attract attention and to mobilize considerable energies. Perhaps this is so because it created for itself an object which contains its own safeguards against "definitive" treatment. In a discipline which, by Kuhnian standards, generally lacks maturity, the study of movements in particular has managed to remain adolescent for a considerable time. Yet, by common consensus, the first "classic" monograph appeared three generations ago.[2] Even if, as is commonly done, we consider Linton's essay on nativistic movements[3] the landmark, a period of over 30 years, filled with monographs, surveys, typologies, and grand syntheses,[4] hardly justifies continued cultivation of a youthful image in this subdiscipline. Could it be that all these protestations of novelty and growth really mask a basic insecurity, a sense of failure and misspent efforts? And could this be symptomatic of anthropology as a whole? To make this connection may seem farfetched. After all, the study of movements—like its object—has long been considered somewhat marginal to the concerns of anthropology (why did Boas, Malinowski, Evans-Pritchard, and Lévi-Strauss never make substantial contributions?). But the argument that the discipline's ability, or inability, to deal with movements constitutes a crucial test was made convincingly more than a decade ago.[5]

More recently, several valiant attempts have been made to take stock, finally, and derive a unifying vision from the mass, and mess, of studies devoted to religious enthusiasm and its endless permutations. Notably Burridge, La Barre, and Lanternari—all of them legitimized as authors of now-classical monographs and syntheses—should be consulted by the reader who seeks a general introduction to the field.[6] Lanternari's "reconsideration" is the shortest and most concise statement of the three. It is written from a definite point of view, debated by others, namely, that colonial domination is the key causal factor in the rise of contemporary movements. But it concludes with a catalog of open questions, long enough to suggest that much, if not everything, remains to be done. What Lanternari recommends for further research is worth quoting here:

> 1) the identification of the socio-psychological aspects of protest, deprivation and frustration; 2) the singling out of those movements in tribal societies which do not result from acculturation or colonization; 3) the identification of a logical, sociological and chronological relationship between socio-religious protest, which is indirect, and direct socio-political protest, and consequently between religious movements and social unrest and revolution; 4) the relation between militancy and non-militancy; 5) that between activism and conservatism or passive escapism; and 6) that between the new religions and social economic, political and cultural development.[7]

No one offers a better appraisal of what has been done than La Barre in his awe-inspiring survey of the history of studies concerning "crisis cults," as he calls them; the almost 600 titles assembled in the bibliography are the best available introduction to material on a worldwide basis. Apart from being unusually well balanced and informative, the paper communicates a sense of urgency. Occasionally, it takes on a solemn, manifesto-like tone: "The day is past however. . . when students of crisis cults can be satisfied with detailed descriptions of single movements or treatments of limited areas. The time of all-embracing synoptic surveys is now upon us."[8]

And yet, after having scanned the globe and probed into historical depth, La Barre concludes that, ultimately, the problem posed by movements is not one of control of an enormous quantity of data; not empirical extensiveness but theoretical intensity is called for, because

> . . . in every age, sensitive, aberrant, creative individuals, in their personal anguish with life, and defrauded somehow of the comforts to be expected from old beliefs, come close to awareness of the dire contingency of all symbols. And then they imagine their own, which, in being nearer to contemporary need, may spread like an epidemic of the mind, while the old belief-world vanishes into myth. If any could understand this process, it should be we men of today, for we

have been living just such an epistemological crisis for some time. And if any could comprehend the situation it should be the anthropologists, whose very stock in trade is the cultural incommensurabilities of men.[9]

Here La Barre expresses a growing realization[10] that one reason why the study of movements has attracted anthropologists may be certain analogies (or homologies) between the phenomenon and the discipline that studies the phenomenon: both are communal endeavors to make sense of intellectual situations which can no longer be interpreted within the limits of narrow, established traditions.

Burridge faced that realization squarely.[11] His conclusions had to be disturbing to the many practitioners of anthropology who have grown accustomed to the comfort provided by cultural relativism. Its slippery dogma of irreducible "difference" permits one to study alien and disturbing behavior from a "scientific" distance, untouched by the challenges it poses to the analyst's own world view. But reality looks different:

> Every anthropologist has experienced "culture shock": a temporary inability, when moving from one culture to another. To grasp and act and think in terms of the assumptions upon which the newly entered culture is based. Not only is this shock experienced in fieldwork, while one learns the ways of a new culture, but it is experienced even more disconcertingly when one returns to one's own culture. Mind and emotions are confused; two different worlds have met in the same person. One alternative is insanity. Another is to comprehend one world in the terms of the other. In this restricted sense every anthropologist has some share in the experience of a prophet, and every prophet must have something of the anthropologist in him. Both must pare their experiences into what is communicable.[12]

Of course, there is no virtue in discomfort as such, unless it results in new, creative approaches and solution. These—and here are the limits of analogies between prophets and anthropologists—do not usually come to us in dreams and visions. Nor can they simply be communicated in prophetic messages and personal testimony. As the interpretation of culture, anthropology must elaborate its insights, belabor its principles and methods, in short, work on the production of knowledge.

It will be useful to describe very briefly the wider context of anthropological research on movements. Overclassifying and overconceptualizing have been detrimental to the understanding of religious enthusiasms. It will be shown that certain "cognitive interests" (in Habermas's sense of the term[13]) have been responsible for this. A different avenue to further investigations will be sketched: movements can be understood as providing historical conditions for the production of prophetic discourse. Through prophetic discourse movements become accessible to meaningful interpretation. In fact, it is their discursive nature which makes it possible to give accounts of them—discursive and critical narratives, not just causal or structural reductions.

Causes, Types, and Process

An explosive increase of writing on movements occurred after World War II. Undoubtedly this was related to an increased virulence of movement activities marking, for most African and many other Third World nations, a period of accession to political independence. But, as we know from other field of intellectual history, it is naive to assume that theoretical developments and methodological choices always follow the empirical incidence of a phenomenon.[14] In fact, as our historical horizon expands and as we realize that hardly any period, any corner of the world, has been without its movements, we begin to suspect that the rise of movement studies in the last 25-30 years really tells us more about developments in anthropology than about the phenomenon at which these investigations are aimed.[15]

Be that as it may, the bulk of these studies can be counted to fall into one or several of the following categories:

Causal explanations In extreme cases, these are single- or dominant-factor explanations; more frequently, though, they postulate a set of historical conditions and a series of triggering events. The most frequent and, perhaps, a most convincing claim is made for political and socioeconomic oppression as a root cause.[16] Most of this work leaves one with a yes-but attitude even if he does not hold the unreasonable view that causal explanation, to be at all valid, must explain every aspect of the phenomenon. At any rate, with the advantage of hindsight we can now point to a number of serious flaws in these approaches. For one thing, "cause" is not a neutral, innocent conceptualization of relationships between persons and events in history. It has been observed that the very beginning of anthropology as a field of study coincided with the development of a conception of history which was clearly not modeled on neutral "scientific" causation. As the French historian Duchet put it:

> The pair savage–civilized only determines the functioning of anthropological thought because the roles are distributed beforehand: ever since the discovery of Africa and America, since the beginning of the process of colonization, savage man is object, civilized man alone is subject; *he* civilizes, he carries civilization with him, he speaks it, thinks it, and because it is his mode of action, civilization becomes the subject (*référént*) of his discourse.[17]

Many studies of the religions-of-the-oppressed type are ennobled by their authors' political motives to reveal and denounce oppression. Similarly, much work on movements in terms of "acculturation" expressed moral concern with the effects of culture "contact." But paradoxically, to insist on colonization and acculturation as the causal core of movements implies an affirmation of the subject–object model of history. All too often these studies suggest, in the end, that charismatic leaders and their followers may think and say that they assemble to bring about the millennium, cargo, or universal brotherhood, while "in reality" they react to oppression and cultural contamination. What drives them, in other words, happens to them, behind their backs, so to speak. They are, studies of this type seem to claim, best understood as the objects of causation. Causation models of this kind are disturbing, not because of their moral implications (suggesting that religious movements are so many proofs of "civilized man's" guilt) but because of their epistemological consequences. As long as they remain, consciously or unconsciously, within the subject–object view of history, causation studies are forever condemned to produce a discourse which is about "civilization"—ourselves—and not about the "savage"—the others. Causal explanations in this vein necessarily "victimize" (make objects of) religious enthusiasts and are therefore incapable of understanding movements.[18]

Typologies and taxonomies If the rhetoric of causal accounts reflects the vision of history which gave rise to modern anthropology in the eighteenth century, typologizing in the study of religious movements recalls a roughly contemporary infatuation with classifying, an essential ingredient of what came to be called "natural history." (In fact, there remains much ambivalence in the discipline as to whether it should trace its origins back to "philosophical history" or to "natural history.") It does not appear that typologizers and classifiers of movements are disturbed by this connection and its implications.[19] Proponents of this approach are typically tentative, eager to refine their schemes, and quick to assert that their taxonomies are constructed above all to be useful (rather than explanatory or meaningful). Indeed, it would be difficult to do without some kind of classificatory procedure. (I am using one myself in this review of approaches.) Classifications are indispensable for the purpose of codification and retrieval of bibliographic resources. But the point is that typological syntheses of knowledge about religious movements aim at more than a static, archival system. They all contain implicit or explicit statements on a domain (intellectual, social, historical) to which movements belong and on sigificant dimensions (or properties, functions, variables) along which a given movement may be compared with any other and thus located in the domain.

If typologies serve as devices to organize interpretive discourse, they must affirm that any given movement be a "combination" of separable traits. In some extreme cases, the very methodology demands an "atomization" of the phenomenon, an extreme decontextualization of beliefs and activities, for the purpose of quantitative manipulation.[20] To be sure, most typologies are really causal explanations in disguise; hence they invite the same objections that can be leveled against the latter. But even those that profess to be "platonic" (according to Kopytoff's classification of classifications[21]), that is, idealizing and synthesizing, ultimately pronounce the verdict of "syncretism" on a great number of movements. Syncretism is a label, however, which apparently cannot be freed from connotations of illegitimate or ill-conceived "mixing" of "original" and "foreign" religious ideas. Thus typologizing surreptitiously fosters condescension, be it in the name of "high" traditions or of truly "primitive" religiosity. But the real danger lies in the epistemological consequences which are to prevent us from recognizing creative processes that go beyond the clever "syntheses" with which leaders and prophets are customarily credited.

Domestications It would seem that the science of religious movements finally found its proper, nonreductive, and dynamic concept in the notion of charisma. As someone who has held that view and who has experienced its interpretive value in his own empirical work, I find it hard to criticize "charisma" with the same detachment I applied to causal and classificatory approaches.

First of all, it must once more be pointed out that Weber's aim was not to do the impossible, that is, to formulate a sociological theory of charisma as a purely personal, "mystical" quality. His influential, if fragmentary, writings on charisma may at times encourage such a view, but he should not be held responsible for the kind of pop sociology the term charisma seems to inspire today. Weber's thought about charisma was embedded in two larger pursuits: 1) a general theory of types of authority which was developed on the basis of 2) an even wider search for the relationships between rational and irrational forces in society. The latter was epitomized by the problem of capitalism in Western society. As his critics and interpreters pointed out long ago,[22] Weber's theories shared basic structures with

Marxism. In fact he once defined his own intentions as a "positive critique of the materialist conception of history."[23] As far as the problems we are here examining are concerned, this had two important consequences: Weber's questions derived from, and were in a sense limited to, his own Western capitalist society. In choosing, the rationalizing power of economics as his basic referent, his comparative studies of great religious traditions were drawn into an interpretive scheme which, in its effects if not in method, was to resemble classical evolutionism. On the one hand, it allowed him to link these traditions to basic structures and concerns in Western society (by measuring them against economic rationalism). On the other hand, it kept non-Western traditions at bay, showing that they did not develop the kind of "ethic" that accounts for Western society.[24]

It is this double movement—drawing alien religious traditions into the sphere of rationality as we define it, and then "putting them into place" with the help of the very same criteria on which they were admitted—that I call "domestication." The "savage" (or the Oriental, as in Weber's case) is drawn into the intellectual economy of the West (and into its material economy, of course), but he is assigned a definite role. He exists, as it were, only inasmuch as he serves that economy. Nowhere is this clearer than in the theory of charisma proper. It has long been recognized that, logically speaking, charisma is a residual category[25]: it is the kind of authority that remains if one subtracts rational-bureaucratic or traditional legitimation. Or, conversely, it is the kind of authority which can be inferred as having existed prior to changes brought about by the emergence of other types. Furthermore, being structurally diffuse and amorphous, charisma seems to relate to bureaucracy and tradition like matter to form, passive to active.[26] Consider the following statement by Weber: "Routinization of charisma is essentially identical with adaptation to the conditions of economics as the everyday force which operates continuously. In *this* economics is leading, not led."[27] Undoubedly this was meant to apply within relatively self-contained societies. But given the realities of colonial imperialism—the context in which anthropology has studied manifestations of charisma—Weber's theory of routinization comes dangerously close to an ideological justification of Western "rational-economic" supremacy.

Thus, even though it rests on a theoretical basis which is much more complex and subtle than that of simple causation theories, Weber's conception of charisma ultimately harks back to the same subject–object model of history. The researcher who uncritically accepts Weber's theory of charisma plays with a deck of cards that is already stacked against charisma. When this aspect of Weber's theory is combined with a positivist-evolutionist view of religion in general (postulating that religion is intellectually, if not chronologically, passée) the results can be stultifying. Such a theoretical stance inevitably results in a disjointed, schizoid discourse; an account of the rational(izing) processes in Western society runs parallel to a counteraccount of charismatic irrationality and, despite all the talk of modernization, never the twain shall meet.[28]

Prophetic "Discourse" and the "Ethnographic Act"

What is it (to use an expression by Foucault) that permits religious, specifically prophet–charismatic, action and talk to pass over into another discourse, that of anthropology? To put the answer in the form of a thesis: If we look for legitimation of our interpretive discourse, we must come to grips with the nature of what I will call the ethnographic act. In most general terms, our discourse must be grounded in a praxis which, for the anthropologist, is typically one or the other form of concrete, actual, communicative interaction with his or her "subjects." But what does that mean specifically? Why call it praxis, and why insist that it needs to be considered theoretically since all that it seems to involve is fieldwork and data gathering? Rather than answering these questions directly with programmatic statements,[29] I should like to take them up in a roundabout fashion which, however, leads directly into some ethnography.

One of the most intriguing figures among the founders of prophetic–charismatic movements that have caught the attention of anthropologists is the Belgian Catholic missionary Placide Tempels. What makes him so interesting and unique (akin, perhaps, only to Jomo Kenyatta) is that his public personality oscillates between that of ethnographer–anthropologist and charismatic leader of an African movement. Whatever else can be said about him, he embodies dramatically what, in different degrees, has been a problem for many anthropologists: a loss of neat demarcations between the roles of observer and participant. Awareness of the precariousness of such boundaries is neither new nor unique to anthropology (in fact it was canonized in the notion of "participant observation"). Yet Tempels' case can help us to point out some of the not-so-obvious implications of this commonplace.

To be precise, Tempels was not trained as an anthropologist; he worked as a missionary–ethnographer. Judging from his early writings, he would have counted among the classic representatives of this group had he not decided to terminate his career with *Bantu Philosophy*.[30] Proclaiming the discovery of a genuinely African philosophy in contrast to what he felt was typically Western thought, Tempels had an important impact. His little book became a sort of manifesto in the struggle for African cultural independence. *Bantu Philosophy* was not a calm and detached synthesis of ethnographic findings; it was a colonizer's "general confession."[31] As we can now demonstrate, it contained a first formulation of the prophetic message later accepted by the Jamaa movement, which recognizes Tempels as its founder.[32] With certain reservations, which we need not specify here, Jamaa doctrine and ritual can be understood as the projection of crucial experiences made by Tempels, the missionary–ethnographer. One such projection is of special interest here: Tempels maintained that to understand, and to be able to report about, the "Bantu" presupposes a kind of active, total abandonment of one's own culture and past. In the ideology of the Jamaa this idea reappears, deepened and radicalized, in the notion of "encounter." On the one hand, encounter is the constituting event of the movement ("encounter" is what happens between initiating and initiands); it is the ground of the movement's social realization and the source of its "teachings," its discourse. On the other hand, encounter is surrounded by rules of secrecy and by an unswerving claim that it is unplannable, ineffable. In other words, the act or event that constitutes the movement as a social entity is (dogmatically) removed from the social sphere of planning and discussion—at least in theory.

Of course, what this mystification of encounter signals is not "ineffability"; as interaction between two or more members or candidates, encounter occurs in space and time and is, somehow, "speakable." But there is a censoring function inherent in the doctrine of encounter. By declaring the constitutive event uniquely personal, it protects it from—to use another expression of Foucault's —the "irruptive violence of time" and from that which comes with "time": reflection, regret, revision.

There is nothing unusual about such removal of a crucial religious act from the sphere of everyday talk and action. What makes this case interesting is the leader's double role as ethnographer and prophet. Tempels and the Jamaa invite comparison with anthropology. Quite similar strictures of silence and similar removal from ordinary rational discourse are often characteristic of attitudes toward the constituting acts of ethnography. Cover terms which signal their importance are easily available: "fieldwork," "participant observation," "empirical research," etc. And there are, to be sure, numerous elaborations of "field methods" which would seem to invalidate our comparison. But upon closer inspection, "field methods" typically consist of catalogs of procedures (input) and catalogs of expected data (output). The core of the ethnographic act—personal, concrete, historically situated interaction—remains hidden in the behaviorist's black box, a device protecting us not only from being bothered with what goes on "in the head of the native" but also from radical reflection on the nature of ethnography. The epistemological structure of the ethnographic act is seldom discussed; its psychological aspects are relegated to occasional statements that are clearly marked as autobiographical. Could it be that in anthropology, as in many religious movements, there is a censoring-out of its constitutive acts, expressing conscious or unconscious efforts to protect the discipline from realizing that, after all, it rests on a historically situated praxis, a mode of producing knowledge in which personal mediation is essential and must be "accounted for" instead of being simply presumed in such fuzzy axioms as "anthropology should be based on fieldwork"?[33]

To insist on concrete, personal mediations as being essential to the ethnographic act is but a first step. Next, one would have to ask what makes such mediation possible. Geertz is among the few anthropologists who offer an answer which responds to concerns voiced in this essay.

> ... the aim of anthropology is the enlargement of the universe of human discourse ... an aim to which a semiotic concept of culture is peculiarly well adapted. As interworked systems of construable signs (what, ignoring provincial usages, I would call symbols), culture is not a power, something to which social events, behaviors, institutions, or processes can be causally attributed; it is a context, something within which they can be intelligibly—that is, thickly—described.[34]

I suspect, however, that religious movements pose extraordinary challenges to semiotic theories of cultural description. To concentrate on "symbols" as that which make possible the interpretive work of anthropology somehow evokes a visual model of social reality. It suggests a view of culture as "things symbolic," a conception of ethnography as observation and of anthropology as description. Such a view is germane to the study of established cultures which offer highly visible and colorful mediations.[35] Many religious movements approach this image, but many do not. After all, if there remains any validity to Weber's theory, movements are by definition not "established," not, one is tempted to say, iconic. They do not usually offer great symbolic vistas; they do not hold still as synchronic objects for observation. Rather, they exist in the dimension of fleeting, elusive time whose structures and shapes are marked by sounds, the words and music of preaching, prayer, and instruction. Therefore, movements may be approached in terms of auditory and verbal rather than visual models, stressing the crucial importance of language and linguistic interaction. This could result in a notion of ethnography as listening and speaking (rather than observing) and an ideal of anthropology as interpretive discourse.

I hurry to emphasize that I am pointing out differentiation, subtleties in the conception of the ethnographic act, not opposing views. The point is worth making, however, because it helps to clarify the reasons for introducing the idea of discourse. As the concept is used here, it is not only aimed at the perpetual controversy over the relative importance of "words and deeds" (should movements be approached via ritual action or through ideas expressed in myth?). Rather, it raises a question that is currently more urgent: can prophetic messages be adequately interpreted as "systems of signs" (according to the semiological, structuralist project)? In my view, it is not enough to elaborate timeless codes of prophetic thought. We must retrace events and give accounts of the inevitable "temporal" articulations of prophetic messages. These efforts are served better by the notion of "discourse" than by catchwords of common currency such as "system of orientation," "symbol system," "semantic domain," and others. "Discourse" expresses, above all, an epistemological intent: to search for a theoretical and descriptive framework that is open, geared to understanding specific formulations of prophetic–charismatic messages, and based on a communicative view of ethnography. Perhaps the most that can be said by way of summarizing is that "discourse" serves to signal two related intentions: First, the idea of an anthropology which approaches the social reality of movements through language and communication but tries to avoid the traps of language–culture equations. This is how Foucault expresses the underlying issue:

> The question posed by language analysis of *some discursive fact or other* is always according to what rules has a particular statement been made, and consequently according to what rules could other similar statements be made? The description of *the events of discourse* poses a quite different question: how is it that one particular statement appeared rather than another.[36]

In other words, "discourse" points to a social praxis located, so to speak, between the levels of dumb (ie, speechless) "behavior" and abstract, disembodied language (or "grammar").

Second, "discourse" carries connotations of activity in space and time, of unfolding in a process of internal differentiation, and of openness to response and argument from an audience. All of these help to emphasize an interpretive approach to movements as historical phenomena, one, however, that does not reduce them to causes and forces which always would have to "predate" (logically if not chronologically) prophetic vision.[37]

PART TWO: TEXT AS TERROR—
SECOND THOUGHTS ABOUT CHARISMA

> Les idées n'existent que par les hommes; mais, c'est bien la le pathétique; elles vivent aux dépens d'eux.
>
> André Gide, *Les Faux-Monnayeurs*

Social realities and social theories are, or ought to be, mediated by a social praxis. Convention calls it fieldwork (perhaps I should say "one convention"; revolution also mediates between theories and realities). For anthropologists who study religious movements, fieldwork often means direct and total involvement, especially when, as is the case with new religious movements, known research "instruments" and other distancing devices (surveys, censuses, archives, and experiments) have little chance to produce original results. Empathy with the research "object" helps but is not enough. As a rule, the anthropologist must have communicative competences, which are acquired only through intensive and prolonged interaction with charismatic leaders and their followers. Almost inevitably, such engagement affects the choice of theoretical positions. After all, if we usually accept that science is not culture-free, why should we think that enculturation occurring during fieldwork should have no consequences? Furthermore, the very climate of religious enthusiasm seems to foster intellectual "conversations"—fairly radical changes in theoretical position analogous to dissent from, and protest against, established churches and religions. Of course, that is not a necessary outcome; many researchers remain untouched because they feel secure in their convictions, religious or scientific.

Fieldwork, with the involvement it demands (especially first fieldwork), is but one phase in the arduous task of interpretations. Theoretical perspectives and personal attitudes may change (again) through critical reflection, or simply through developments in a scholar's intellectual career. It may then become a problem to extricate oneself from the immediacy of experience, to seek dégagement. In itself, of course, the well-known need to finally drop a subject and proceed to another would be of little interest and theoretical value, unless it arises through confrontation with the same phenomenon that called for engagement. Up to this point, most of my writing on the Jamaa movement has emphasized the "way in." I will now concentrate on a "way out." It should be understood, though, that both "ways in" and "ways out" are aspects ("movements," in dialectical language) of critical understanding. I will offer some reasons for this turn of Jamaa material and comment on aspects which tend to get overlooked when one presents charisma unequivocally as a source of creative change.[38]

Recapturing the Negative

More than ten years ago, I found my theoretical (and professional) point of departure when I became convinced that the then leading Parsonian model of social reality could not conceive of sociocultural processes, let along innovation, except as "change," and not of change except as some kind of imbalance and disturbance. From what I had read on the ethnography of religious movements, and what I had come to accept from Max Weber's notion of charisma, I knew that there must be a way of dealing with process in positive terms. So many movements were manifestly not deviant, or marginal, or just "disturbing," but creative, constructive, and universally appealing; I did not realize then, or through most of the period during which I got my descriptions and analyses of the Jamaa together, that some day I would face the Parsonian dilemma once more, albeit in a different form: not only did this model force us to conceive of change in negative terms, it also generated a propensity to describe and analyze negative developments as (nothing but) "change," as elements of a story that always ends well. The rise of fascism may then be described as a process of ideological and political "change," although social scientists may check their neutralizing pathos with the help of their moral convictions. But these convictions played hardly any role until recently, when the violent technocapitalist expansion of the Western world produced libraries full of "acculturation" and "modernization" studies.

Weber appeared to offer a solution for the first dilemma. Charisma could be viewed as a creative revolutionary force. Yet he, too, cherished the idea that charismatic leaders and ideologies had a chance only if they contributed to the "well-being" of the followers.[39] What if "change" (and charisma) leads to, and, perhaps, thrives on, impoverishment, intransigence, righteousness, suffering, or plain boredom? Without paying much attention to it, I had seen all this in the field among convinced followers of the Jamaa (the founder being no exception). Obviously, these were not the only manifestations. In fact, they were easily over-shadowed by the dynamic and enthusiastic climate reigning at that time. But they existed, and sociological analysis would be self-defeating—defeating the purpose of liberation from the immediacy of social constraints—should its theories and concepts make it impossible to take them into account.

The main obstacle is, I believe, a failure to recognize that all human action is intrinsically constituted by positive and negative moments: it is affirmation and negation, acceptance and rejection, belief and doubt. Of course, no sensible social scientist would deny this—privately. But in the public exercise of social science, there has been a tendency to deny or neutralize this dialectic by placing the negative on the safe side of some kind of boundary, historical, developmental, or systematic. The negative then belongs to earlier periods (savagery), to extraor-dinary phases (anomie), or to external forces (ecological catastrophes being the current example).[40]

The studies of religious movements developed a language in which the negative was expressed as "rejection" of established religion, as "protest" against some of its forms, as "separation" from existing institutions, etc—negation always being directed toward something outside. Internally, movements were thought to be kept together by enthusiastic belief in a prophetic message, by renewal of faith after periods of doubt and anomie. Their essence was thought to be "search for security"; they were remedial institutions providing for their members a "place to feel at home."

But there are alternatives. Why not consider that anomie is not only a cause for movements of redress and reorientation but an occasion for overcontrolled humans to abandon themselves to the paradoxial forces of existence—to be nor-mal and crazy at the same time; to continue rational action for survival without banishing the risks of strong emotions; to sacrifice everyday security in the search for dreams? The positive force of charisma may be this (temporary) suspension which provides moments of truth revealing, to the follower as well as to the observer, the falseness of all merely positive rationalizations, be they ex-istential or scientific. Its (inevitably?) negative side lies in the reification of that truth, replacing suspended beliefs with new convictions. In fact, all empirical charisma, the one that manifests itself in movements, probably is to a large extent negative. Does this throw us back to Parson's horror mutationum? No, because the negative is now predicated on the existing reality (not on outside or future threats). Theoretically and methodologically, it means that the negative must be shown in the very processes that establish charismatic movements, it must not be projected into deviant and pathological developments. It is another question whether social science is practically ready to carry out such a program against the powerful myths of positivity it inherited from its positivitist ancestors. Mean-while we can make attempts.[41]

One problem poses itself immediately. The "negative" I invoked in the face of charisma—thoughtless submission, doubts, righteousness, boredom—all are reactions and attitudes of individuals. What, if any, are their social manifestations? The remainder of this paper will seek answers to that question. These answers are offered in a context of interpretation. Much effort has been spent on demonstrating the inner unity, distinctiveness, and ingenuity of *mawazo* (literally, ideas) by which the Jamaa designates the sum total of its thought as well as almost any of its particular manifestations. Inevitably, many of the views established during that period will be carried over into the present enterprise. Revisions will be piecemeal, but they must be done once their necessity is recognized, even if they mean a loss of consistency.

Text as Terror

There were numerous occasions when Placide Tempels, the founder of the Jamaa, and many of his followers would speak of what I should like to call, perhaps a bit too dramatically, the terror of mawazo.[42] In statements expressing acute self-criticism (often, I must admit, totally unexpected in view of my ideas of an enthusiastic religious movement) fhey showed their awareness of being caught, even dominated, by their own teachings. Jamaa leaders commented on the error of habit and ritualistic pedantry, and on the temptation that befalls the speaker of *mafundisho* (instructions) to exercise or acquire power by outteaching his opponents.[43]

The founder himself often expressed aversion for written "manuals" (by which he meant anything between a school catechism and a theological treatise). On the whole he gave to his movement a remarkable resistance against formalizing mawazo in any kind of organization based on explicit, written charts, membership rolls, or rules of procedure. More than once I heard members from the rank and file reject and ridicule intrusions of the mission bureaucracy as the work of *buku na crayon* (notebook and pencil).

Nevertheless, Tempels's prophetic message did become fixed and codified in (mostly oral) texts, and this created a situation which is inherently ambiguous: One may marvel at these texts since they open avenues toward understanding; one may also be frightened or at least limited by their rhetoric power and its constricting demands. There is evidence that members of the Jamaa are conscious of the textual realization of mawazo and apparently also of its ambivalent possibilities.

An illustration for this is the term *mukanda* and its use in Jamaa teaching. Its dominant connotation in Shaba Swahili is that of a written document. It may be used synonymously for *barua*, the letter, but more often it signifies all kinds of identity cards, written permits, references, travel documents, citations, in short the kinds of "texts" that colonial (and postcolonial) administration and enterprises produce to ensure their control over the population or labor force.

If one has witnessed the terror which forms and documents exercise over simple, often illiterate, people, one cannot help but be surprised at the positive interpretation which mukanda sometimes receives as a metaphor in Jamaa teaching. The *kitabu* of Musonoi,[44] for instance, contains the following passage:

> Fathers and mothers, God gave these three *mawazo* to this thought-man (the first Jamaa). . . . Then he told him: these *mawazo* I am giving to you, go with them into the world. Guard them also in the body, If you lose them you will never return to me because my *mawazo* are your *mukanda*, which makes it possible for you to return to me, your father.

This and similar statements show that very soon, before Weber's forces of routinization could have had an effect, mawazo was not only taught as a conception to be realized; it became a possession assuring safe passage back to a heavenly homeland. As a possession, mawazo is a means of discrimination. Some have it, other do not. Sociologically speaking, in order to have a visible social impact, the founder's prophetic vision had to be transformed into a charter; spontaneity had to become recursiveness; internal experience became objectified in testimony and instruction; the spiritual became documentary. Once the process of organizing the movement took its course, it was almost inevitable that mawazo should be conceived as mukanda. As has happened with monotonous regularity and predictability in the history of religious movements which had an innovative, revolutionary potential, ideas of liberation imperceptibly turn into schemes of domination or, at least, of administrative pedantry. In the case of the Jamaa, the discovery of unity between man and his creator and between man his fellow man may thus be reinterpreted as an insurance for the individual believer and as a defense of this personal salvation against the demands of those who, in his view, are not saved.

At the time when my fieldwork was conducted, there was ample evidence for this, but I also found numerous members and leaders who maintained a critical and self-critical view. It lies in the nature of critical statements that they are not easy to document; often they are made in oblique ways or appear as asides in other contexts.

Even if it were possible to draw an adequate textual documentation from these sources, it would still be difficult to discover a continuity and direction underneath the highly localized and personal expressions of doubt. However, statements of criticism and self-criticism may appear in Jamaa storytelling. The following fable will illustrate this point. The text was recorded in January 1967 in a situation of profound insecurity, following the nationalization of the copper mines (January 1, 1967). Hysterical outbreaks swept through the workshops and settlements, and Europeans and Africans alike feared that the violence and destruction they had withstood only a few years ago were about to resume. The speaker is baba K, leader of the group at Musonoi, and the story was part of a longer conversation about death. I remember quite vividly the exceptional, "liminal" situation in which we exchanged our views. Both of us were in a mood in which our everyday pursuits and certainties—baba K's involvement in the Jamaa, my anthropological fieldwork—appeared to dwindle in the face of imminent chaos. In a small way, it was a movement of truth that made him tell

The Story of the Letter (mukanda) from God

Once there was a man. This man used to laugh at other people whenever he saw that someone died. He began to laugh saying: Those big people, they do not know how to come to an understanding with God. Why does he die like a little child? I have come to an understanding with God. When my day to die comes, God will send me a letter to announce it: Your day to die is near. Get ready.

Some other time the maternal uncle of this man died. Again he laughed a lot saying: So, even the uncle, they are putting him through the same thing. Why did he stay here without coming to an understanding with God? God would have sent him a letter (to announce) the day when he was going to die. I won't be dying like this, I have come to an understanding with God.

Some other time his own father (or father's brother) died. He looked at it the same way, and laughed a lot. He told his father's relatives that they didn't know a thing. Only I know how to come to an understanding with God.

Some other day his child died too.

But see, one day this baba fell ill. When the illness had taken hold of him he heard God saying to him: Today is your day to die. You must return to me. He said to God: God, but I had an understanding with you. I told you when the day comes for me to die I shall not die like all the other children. You are going to send me a letter warning me: On this day you are going to die. And I am going to get my things ready. Why are you telling me today this is your day? So there was a disagreement between God and this man.

God told him: I sent you many, many letters. Why do you say now: You haven't sent me a letter? Haven't you seen my letter? He said: I did not see your letter.

Now God told him: Think of the time when your maternal uncle died. That is a long letter which I sent you so that you should know: so I am not from this world either. I am going to follow where the uncle went. Think also of the day when that big man died in your place. At that time I thought this is a letter which I sent to you. And the day when your father died, and the day when your child died; how many letters did I send you? But then you didn't think yourself: Truly where this fellow man goes I am going to go too. You were just looking for a letter to be sent to you: what kind of a letter? How were you going to get ready? If you wanted to get ready you should have done it when you saw how all these people died, because this is the letter from me, God.

When the man heard this he had to give up and he said: Truly I have lost this argument because when all these people died I saw them but I thought You are going to send me a letter through the mail saying: Read this letter. Prepare yourself and be ready to arrange all your things.

On the surface, the moral of the story seems to be derived from the familiar motif of a match of wits. Its conclusion is expressed as the resolution of an argument by the defeat of one party: Man had tied down God by an arrangement. He thought he would control the power of divinity, who sends death whenever it pleases. In the end, however, man failed because he misunderstood the very terms of his "arrangement."

As a document of formulated Jamaa thought the mukanda fable contains more than yet another exemplification of a familiar (and probably traditional) "folkloric" motif. If we want to do justice to the richness of its message, we must seek to understand the implications of the concrete terms, images, and relations it contains.

To begin with, the story is addressed to a problem: death, not in its abstract significance, but as the concrete existential anticipation of the termination of individual life. It is not the meaning of death in terms of its effects (afterlife in condemnation, salvation, or oblivion) which commands attention, but its precise moment. Insecurity is to be reduced by the possibility of controlling the event (the day of death) through preparation.

Another element of concreteness is added when the problem is placed, not in an abstract realm of reflection, but in the context of relationships between actors. The protagonists are "one man" and God. It is essential to the development of the narrative, though, that "one man" appears in the company of other people, all of whom are linked to him by relations of power (the "big ones" in the sense of elders and/or persons of authority), or of kinship (mother's brother, father, child).

Man sets himself apart from these relationships, that is, from the given context of life and death, by a special arrangement with God. The medium of that arrangement (or the object of transaction, as the symbol of the relationship) is mukanda, a document containing information about the moment of death. The goal of man's arrangement with God must not be confused with its presumed effect. The latter is a sense of security expressed in the main actor's laughing contempt for his fellow man. The goal is some kind of transcendence of a larger significance. It is not the pleasure derived from each case of surviving but a sense of total control of one's own destiny. It is the nature of the goal that eventually determines the significance of the outcome, man's failure. When, in the end, he shares the fate of those he once ridiculed, his scheme relapses into immanence. He is defeated by his own terms. In this sense, defeat is not depicted as a "sin" (ie, a failure to conform to a divine commandment or to a moral norm); it is a failure to understand, which is in turn based on a failure to interpret, experienced as mukanda.

Thus the paradox which generates the tension and the rhetorical appeal of the story can be formulated as follows: Man, in order to transcend his fate, relies on the availability of a text, a message which enables him to control events on the basis of information it contains. Possession of such information is to give him exclusiveness and security. Yet his scheme is doomed to fail precisely because exclusiveness and trust in the literal availability of information cut him off from the total context of which mukanda could have been one among many documents. Rather than searching for meaning through the labors of interpretation, man relies on a literal, immediately given sense. The more he concentrates and counts on the literal sense, the more likely he is to miss the mark of his desire for transcendence.

The story about the letter from God is a document for an emerging self-critical awareness among thinkers of mawazo. It contains several text-immanent features which clearly link it to the overall process of the formulation of Jamaa doctrine. Some of these are semantic, such as (apart from the term mukanda itself) the notion of *kusikilizana,* to have a mutual understanding. In the Jamaa clasifications of doctrinal terms, this concept is one of the "three rules" (the others are: *masaidiano,* mutual help, and *mapendo,* mutual love). In the practice of everyday interaction, kusikilizana has a crucial role. Mutual understanding is the first step toward "encounter," the event that is said to constitute Jamaa. It also is the basis of "arrangements" between a Jamaa group and the representative of the church hierarchy. The mukanda story suggests that in all these situations, the Jamaa constantly risks a self-defeating understanding of kusikilizana. There is always the possibility that mutual understanding may be at the expense of others who do not belong to the group who "guard mawazo."

Another connection between this particular story and the Jamaa is provided by the way in which the situation of the principal human actor is depicted. His special arrangement with God evokes the frequent self-categorization of the Jamaa as *bantu ya Mungu,* people of God. Like the protagonist, most members of the movement find themselves in situations in which they must test their convictions and defend their beliefs vis-á-vis those who hold the strongest claims on them—their uncommitted relatives and the representatives of traditional power and religion.

Finally, there is the fact that the story was narrated in the context of a testimony talk, one of the recognized, genres of oral communication in the movement.[45] That, however, does not make its interpretation any easier, since the gist of baba k's talk was precisely an affirmation of the security the Jamaa gives its members in facing death. In that context, the mukanda story does not appear as an expression of systematic doubt and self-critique, but rather as a piece of whimsical irony.

Irony certainly is a sign of life; where there is irony there cannot be total identification with a doctrine, and where there is no total identity between believer and belief, there is room for struggle with the dialectic of affirmation and negation. On the other hand, irony often is resignation, a tamed and muted expression of protest against the terror of doctrinal affirmations. And this, on the whole, is typical of Jamaa self-criticism.

Fatal Logic

What I called the "terror" of texts was to show that enthusiastic followers of a charismatic message may experience negativity not only in the form of doctrinal constraints but also as (misconceived) security. The very act of accepting the message contains in itself the risk of placing a wrong bet, so to speak, or of missing the point, as happened to the protagonist in the mukanda story. All this concerns relations between a system of beliefs, as the Parsonians would say, and the actors it motivates and orients. These relations quite clearly are not simple ones, nor are they simply positive, even in the pristine form of emerging belief–action systems such as charismatic movements. I shall now take these reflections one step further and consider to what extent negativity could be predicated on a given system of beliefs, irrespective of its motivational and orientational "effects" on individual actors. In other words, is it possible to diagnose negativity in the very "autonomy" (*Eigengesetzichkeit*) of belief systems invoked by Weber (and Parsons)?

It is commonly held that a system of thought may have to be altered, adapted, or abandoned if its adherents cannot cope with the challenges of time and continuity, and of organization and identity. This has occupied Max Weber in this theory of charisma and routinization. But social scientists tend to overlook that religious movements may successfully meet these challenges and still be doomed to sterility and eventual exhaustion or dispersion due to the specific, internal integration of their doctrinal tenets. It is in this sense that I tentatively speak of a fatal logic. The Jamaa may well be a case in point.

The Jamaa doctrine of *umuntu* (literally, "what it means to be human") is a total humanism. It owes its origin and acceptance to experiences with a world perceived as fragmented and inhuman. Tempels's writings and the teaching of his followers make it abundantly clear that, in order to restore human dignity, the Jamaa must surmount the barriers that separate people in the world in which the movement originated: barriers between colonizers and colonized, between white and black, between Western religion and African tradition, between missionaries and missionized, between members of one tribe and members of another.

Three devices (or inventions) permitted Tempels and his co-inventors to translate their malaise, vague desires, and visions into the kind of praxis we know as "Jamaa."

First, the idea of "encounter" as the event that is to constitute Jamaa presupposes a personalization of the various forms of fragmentation experienced in the colonial and postcolonial world. The divisiveness which the outside observer would attribute to relationships of political domination, economic exploitation, racism, religious fanaticism (or perhaps simply to the destructiveness of rapid urbanization–industrialization) is perceived by the Jamaa as personal failure: failure to love, to accept, and to understand a fellow human being is at the bottom of all that is wrong in this world. Undoubtedly, this idea gained power and attractiveness because it granted no exemptions. Failure was diagnosed in the official church as well as in the tradition among the colonizers as well as among the colonized. In this respect, Jamaa ideology clearly made an exception among similar movements.

Probably even more unusual was the second crucial device which led to the emergence of the movement: the specific definition the Jamaa gave to the nature of evil and to the means of transcending it. Jamaa founded its humanism not on a basis of universal guilt (ie, moral failure) but on a notion of ignorance or, perhaps, thoughtlessness. Consequently, it was mawazo—knowledge and thought—which was to conquer evil. In this sense of knowledge as salvation, Jamaa doctrine appears as a gnosis.[46] As in other gnostic systems, this entails a mythical conception of man and a pronounced concern with the origin and fate of mawazo in a history which encompasses man and God. Ultimately, innerworldly humanism and otherworldly religion, anthropology and theology, merge into one grand vision.

Thus, firmly grounded in mawazo, the Jamaa can turn to the task at hand which is to overcome the divisions and fragmentation initially diagnosed as personal failure. The social scientist, especially if he is of a utilitarian persuasion, would expect shared knowledge to result in concrete projects of action.[46] Protest, rejection, separation, and search for independence, revitalization, healing, or at least the expectation of a future Golden Age have therefore commanded attention in the analysis of religious movements. The case of the Jamaa shows that a movement may choose yet another course of action. Subject to further qualification, I shall refer to it as a ritualization of charisma, the third of Tempels's crucial inventions. All available evidence indicates that, from the first beginnings, the founder insisted on the practical realization of mawazo in the process of gradual initiation, so much so that becoming Jamaa and being Jamaa, means and ends, became indistinguishable.

When I say that charismatic action was "ritualized," I do not aim at the rather sterile observation that has hampered so much of sociological analysis, namely, that "myth" must somehow be paralleled by "ritual." This is demonstrably false, if meant as a universal rule. It is trivial, if it is to describe belief–action correspondences in an empirical case. Nor do I imply the time-worn distinction between instrumental vs expressive behavior. It is not a difference between kinds of projects I wish to demonstrate,[47] rather I envisage a tendency to neutralize altogether the discussion of "outer-directed" projects. Realization of mawazo calls for constant concentration on the crucial ideas themselves, on life, fecundity, and love in unity. Long and complicated courses of mafundisho are geared toward the gradual experience of each of them, culminating in a ritual event which, significantly, receives its external proof in a dream experience. Not as a project for concrete action, but as a redeeming substance, is mawazo incorporated in the believer.

Knowledgeable observers—among them the founder himself—realized that at this point the Jamaa notion of mawazo shades into the Luba conception of bwanga, usually translated as "magic." But there remains a decisive difference.

Concern for bwanga in traditional society was embedded in a wider conception of reality and directed toward a host of concrete projects (healing, protection, hunting, agriculture, etc). Being geared to particular projects, it allowed for distinctions, revisions, and even experimentation. For the people of the Jamaa to whom traditional magic is forbidden and who live in a world of modern labor and reduced family relations, mawazo has become a total outlook, claiming the meaning of every action. All and everything may now be transformed into "thought." Yet it cannot be said that the quasi-magic monopoly of mawazo in the Jamaa is simply an escape into a world of fantasies. No one who had experienced the calm, practical, thoroughly matter-of-fact attitude of most of the members would entertain such an idea. If anything, Jamaa doctrine is not escapist but "embracist," tout comprendre is the ultimate aim. To the nonmember, it is a smothering kind of comprehension, often accompanied by an irritating curiosity for matters he would like to keep private.

These tentative generalizations should not be misunderstood. It is not my intention to substitute critique with moralizing shortcuts. We can do better than that by focusing on the specific logic of mawazo which appears to determine the course of this personalized, mythical, and ritual vision of reality.

Consider the "three great thoughts" which are the foundation of Jamaa humanism and command so much attention in teaching and initiation. Man, Tempels and his followers tell us, seeks "only" life, fecundity, and love—a trinity of desires which flows from the divine Trinity (Father, Son, Spirit or Mother) into a trinity of rules (mutual understanding, mutual help, mutual love). In the system of teaching, these are derived, compared, and exemplified in innumerable permutations and applications. One is impressed by the skill, the subtlety, and the artistry with which the three mawazo are elaborated by speakers of the doctrine. Still, after prolonged exposure to Jamaa discourse, one begins to have second thoughts. Not only do repetition and redundancy become irritating, one also begins to suspect that all propositions based on these concepts are tautological.[48] Many Jamaa teachers are masters of equivocation; with great ease they manage to show that life is nothing but love, love nothing but fecundity, fecundity nothing but life. In Jamaa reasoning, innumerable tensions and conflicts which may arise between a desire for life force and the demands of love, between the search for fecundity and the limitations of strength, between unity in love and the pursuit of fecundity are often glossed over by facile and gratuitous argumentation.

On the whole, the edifice of mawazo appears to develop toward a system of equivalences, a kind of conceptual entropy which threatens it with internal collapse. One indicator confirming this observation may be the relative scarcity of metaphorical extension and innovation in Jamaa discourse which could be revealed by further and more thorough analyses. To be sure, the invention (or adoption) of mythical actors and situations, of certain cosmological notions, frequent insertion of concrete examples and applications, and finally creative symbolization in dreams and storytelling provide Jamaa thought with the possibility of expanding its concepts toward, and filling them with, new experiences. But if one considers the paramount importance of standardized mafundisho in the processes of communication that produce the movement, and within mafundisho the importance of doctrinal concepts, one is led to expect that Jamaa thought will indeed have to confront the threat of internal exhaustion.

At the level at which it can most easily be observed, the "fatal logic" is an intellectual problem. But undoubtedly it reflects and shapes the social praxis of the movement. In its social manifestations, the circularity of mawazo gives to groups of the movement the character of ultimate communitas (to borrow a concept introduced into anthropology by Victor Turner). Again one is led to suspect a self-defeating development. Let me explain this briefly. Asked about the kind of visible, behavioral changes which were brought about by the Jamaa and which characterize members in contrast to outsiders, many observers, including myself, usually named three as the most conspicuous ones.[49]

First, there is the value placed by the Jamaa on absolute equality and deep emotional unity among the spouses. Jamaa people themselves are eager to point out that in traditional society the wife was a slave; in the movement she is a human being. While there are reasons to doubt whether in traditional society the woman was in fact and always a "slave," one cannot dispute that spouses in the Jamaa often radically change their relations. This affects quite concrete issues and situations: common meals, shared housework and care for the children, common family budget, a great amount of time spent together in exchanging views, experiences, and news, common participation in movement activities. All this is done very self-consciously; in the course of initiation it is again and again discussed, reflected upon and always bound up with the ultimate goal: to become Jamaa by realizing mawazo. But the point is that realization of love, mutual understanding, respect, and equality are constantly bent back upon the couple and the community of the Jamaa group itself. The Jamaa does not address itself to the equality of the sexes as such, irrespective of their being involved in realizing mawazo. Much less does it face, as a rule, the objective cultural and economic conditions which continue to produce inequality, such as unequal access to education, unequal employment opportunities, exclusion from information, leisure and recreation activities, and a host of subtle barriers keeping African women "in their place." Equality among spouses in theory and practice of the Jamaa may indeed be an impressive achievement, but on a societal level it remains largely without consequence. It thrives in the protective intimacy of a small religious group and contributes little to the emancipatory processes in the postcolonial development of Zaire.

A second kind of change attributed to the Jamaa regards the relationship between African Christians and (until recently) the largely European hierarchy of the mission church. Jamaa teaching is replete with keen observations on the many cultural, economic, and psychological barriers which prevent "mutual understanding" between a group and the missionary. On the whole, the movement has insisted on, and in many cases achieved, unity, mutual respect, or at least tolerance. But one wonders how much this has in fact contributed toward "bridging" the gap. As far as integration into church ritual and organization is concerned, the Jamaa was able to maintain the precarious existence of a charismatic group within a theobureaucratic organization. It has done this for large numbers of people (ie, a considerable percentage of practicing Christians in Shaba and Kasai) and for quite a long period. Its versatility and lack of separatist fanaticism have often been praised as an example of a "true Africanization" of Western religion.

In concrete, local situations, however, the picture may look quite different. On the one hand, all Jamaa groups I have known expected and insisted that the missionary or local pastor "encounter" his group, that is, that he undergo formal instruction and initiation. Even with those members of the clergy who had seen the origin of the Jamaa and assumed leading positions, the groups tended to be relentless in asking for total loyalty and their terms. Some eventually left the movement; others lived in uneasy coexistence with it; others still were driven by the conflicting demands of their position in the movement and their offices in the church to physical and psychological breakdown. In fact, there have always been violent confrontations between Jamaa and mission church, accusations and counteraccusations, and finally mass excommunications. The point is that the movement probably never had a chance to achieve the kind of African synthesis of Christianity for which it was taken by many observers. The obvious intransigence of the mission church was matched by the subtle intransigence of the "guardians of mawazo." Both were of the same kind, since both defined encounter as conversion.

Thus the relationship between the movement and the church hierarchy offers a spectacle for which sociological analysis has as yet to find a frame of interpretation. It was a struggle that did not, on the whole, result in a centrifugal proliferation of sects or separatist replicas of the established church. The handy notion of a "revival" which has been invoked by observers of a similar phenomenon in East African missions with an Anglican background[50] helps little to grasp a process which proceeds by intensification of intransigence, not because it pursues ulterior goals of separation and independence but because it enacts the logic of mawazo. Little is gained if the emergence of the Jamaa is metaphorically understood as a booster to the "vitality" of the church. (In any case, such a view is the privilege of unconditionally committed believers; the anthropological interpreter's task is to discern the literal, historical meaning of actual processes of articulation and communication.) Our investigation, to return to the initial question, gives little support to the view that credits the Jamaa with a dramatic redefinition of the relationships between African Christians and the hierarchically constituted church.

A third type of change often attributed to the influence of Jamaa regards the predicament of most of its male members in the mining region of Shaba. Both De Craemer[51] and I were interested in learning whether being a member of the movement made any difference in the way an African worker views himself and is viewed by his fellow workers and his employers. The evidence was inconclusive, to say the least. Objective indicators are hard to find. In the labor force of South Shaba, social mobility was comparatively low. The range of opportunities for professional improvement was, despite elaborate systems of classification, quite narrow.[52] Whatever criteria one might select to measure economic success, they would have to be applied to a small range of variation. What I was able to ascertain showed that evaluations of Jamaa members reflected the distribution of the general worker population with, perhaps, a slight tendency to perform above average. Even if this could be determined more reliably, one would still have to ask what company evaluations mean. I got a glimpse of that when (in 1966–1967) I questioned several Europeans in supervisory positions. Somewhat noncommittally they would characterize Jamaa people as quiet, conscientious workers, remarkably helpful to fellow workers. Perhaps most important to them was that Jamaa people "never make any trouble." With one or two exceptions, members of the movement did not consider serious involvement with unions.

The picture becomes more differentiated when we turn to evaluations of labor and of the workers' predicament in the teaching of Jamaa. The results of a study devoted to that problem reveal on the one hand a great lexical importance of the concept of work *(kazi)* in mafundisho. On the other hand they demonstrate that the world of labor, as experience as well as project, is thoroughly integrated into the intellectual and ritual enactment of mawazo. Labor relations are personalized, their meaning is interpreted in terms of mythical models, and their praxis is understood as realization of the thoughts of life and love, but significantly not of fecundity. If anything, the Jamaa lives in an inconsequential symbiosis with the industrial world of South Shaba. Encapsulated in the logic of mawazo, the Jamaa worker is protected from the harshness, if not of economic, then of intellectual and moral exploitation. He is unlikely to be an agent for change toward better objective conditions for the African worker.[53]

Escapes

It should be clear that this view of the "fatal logic" is based on two kinds of supposition. One regards the specific conceptual makeup of the system of mawazo. It reveals the "circularity" or equivocality inherent in Jamaa teaching. It is not merely a "logical" conclusion, though. As a process of communication, Jamaa teaching is eminently practical as well as theoretical–conceptual. Although Lévi-Strauss and his followers may deny it, logical analyses in anthropology are in effect also historical verdicts. The "critique of cultural reason," if I may give that definition to the enterprise of an anthropology of the mind, cannot be carried out but through practical communicative interaction with the subjects of our study; nor can its results be kept from having, in turn, practical effects on the community to which they are reported (which may well include the people who were studied).

Yet historical verdicts should not be confused with moral condemnation. The latter is ruled out by a second kind of supposition guiding my view of the logic of mawazo. As far as their validity for individual members and actual occurrences is concerned, assertions of conceptual entropy, of a resorbent, resilient nature of mawazo, must be read with a conditional "if" in mind. I am not saying that a follower of the movement is condemned to intellectual sterility, circularity, and intransigence. What I try to demonstrate is a trend, a development inherent in the logic of the first premises rather than caused only by "deviation" or the operation of some socioeconomic law.

In this respect I have every reason to believe that my interpretation stands on firm ground. Many individual members attest to this; some show a surprising ability to verbalize their experiences with the "fatal logic." More importantly, many members have taken practical consequences in different forms of escape from the embrace of mawazo.

In the following I will briefly sketch categories of "defectors," well aware of the empirical and theoretical limitations on such an enterprise. Charismatic movements present great difficulties to sociological description in general. These difficulties become almost insurmountable in attempting to understand patterns of defection and dissolution. One problem is that defection as such has little theoretical significance except as a quantitative measure of membership turnover. To be of interest to the present concern, I must draw on cases in which defectors continue, in one way or the other, to define their positions with reference to the Jamaa. They must meet the seemingly paradoxical criterion of being Jamaa and not being Jamaa. During fieldwork, I struggled with establishing the identity of the movement; obviously, I could pay only marginal attention to the defectors. Nevertheless, enough information was gathered to propose the following typology with reasonable confidence.

Among persons to whom involvement in the Jamaa had remained important enough to come up as a topic in chance encounters and discussions one can distinguish five forms of escape from mawazo:

1. There are those who had been members for a certain time, especially during the virulent phase of the movement in the late fifties and early sixties. But after a period of involvement they returned to everyday life without showing any pronounced religious commitments. Faithful members would speculate on the reasons for these defections and generally agree that the moral and ritual demands became too heavy for these people: the burden of instruction, frequent participation in activities, and, above all, the idea of an intimate indissoluble union between the spouses. Naturally, defectors in this category would be reluctant to admit to personal failure and rather insist on a "loss of interest" in the affairs of the movement and of Christianity in general.

2. Another category of former members tended to deny ever having left the movement. They insisted—quite in accordance with certain Jamaa formulas —that "Jamaa" is nothing but the church. They would point out that they continued to practice the Catholic faith and regularly to receive the sacraments and that, in order to be Jamaa, they need not participate in the external activities of the group. Often, this kind of defection seemed to be linked to physical distance from Jamaa groups (and from the network of spiritual kinship established in initiation). In a few cases, it was due to social distance from former fellow members. One may assume, then, that these persons had never come to total identification with mawazo in its doctrinal and ritual dimensions. Otherwise they would not have given up these links. It is also likely that, because they remained in the ambience of mission Christianity, some of them would occasionally or permanently reactivate their memberships.

3. A third escape from the "fatal logic" puts the notion of defection to a hard test. Still, I feel that these persons must be included in the typology since they meet the basic paradoxical criterion formulated above. There is quite probably a small number of members who remain active in the movement and, more likely then not, continue to occupy positions of leadership. Nevertheless they have come to a point where they openly dismiss as unimportant or even dangerous what for the average member constitutes a major preoccupation: formal, standardized instruction and ritual initiation. I have met some who replaced fixation on mawazo with active, progressive intellectualizations. Those were leaders with plans for the spread of the Jamaa among "intellectuals" and into concrete social and political projects. Others had found an alternative in a highly personalized mysticism; they had become seekers of experiences and visions without, however, claiming for them a general, prophetic validity (ie, without actually introducing a visionary, spiritualist trend into the movement). A pietistic kind of personal devotion had become their main concern.

4. In the fourth category are defectors regarded by the mainstream Jamaa as "deviants." In many respects this phenomenon is one of the most interesting as well as most knotty problems. First, the number of these defectors is quite large in some places, presumably outnumbering those who are considered faithful. Second, defection of this kind occurred through, or at least resulted in, the formation of actual groups. These groups are known throughout the area by a specific name, *katete*. In most cases their leaders had once occupied prominent positions

in the movement. Nevertheless it is quite difficult to know whether a given member identifying himself as Jamaa is or is not a member of katete. Finally, despite a high degree of secretiveness surrounding the activities of these groups, we do not have the slightest evidence for important doctrinal deviation, or innovation, as it may be. I attempted an anlysis of this form of defection in my monograph and cannot add anything to those findings.[54] What interests me in the present context is whether and in what sense katete can be understood as a form of escape from mawazo.

If my information is accurate, katete groups have made a selection among the premises of Jamaa doctrine and carried them to their logical and existential extremes. Basic seems to be the reinterpretation of mawazo exclusively in terms of a life-giving force, to be maximized by an unbounded demonstration of love and fecundity. The emphasis on maximization and achievement, to the detriment of a principle of balance which the orthodox Jamaa has in the network of spiritual kinship, made it necessary continuously to extend the ritual gradations beyond the three degrees of initiation and consequently to invent new symbolic markers for each of them. It appears that these were derived, by and large, from variations and intensifications of sexual demonstrations of unity among participating couples.

It is easy to say that katete is nothing but a pretext for promiscuity. That explains neither its specific social manifestation nor its continued connection with the orthodox movement. Furthermore, sexual demonstrations of the enactment of mawazo are definitely part of the orthodox ritual. Should there be only a difference in degree? If so, why would "deviations" take such a well-defined social form as we see it in katete groups? At present we simply do not know enough about the development of katete, we do not have enough specific detail; nor can we draw on observations over extended periods. Nonetheless, it is tempting to speculate on a possibility. Ritualized, intensified sexual communion, far from being just an expected—because historically well-known—exuberance accompanying religious enthusiasm, may in fact signal an advanced stage of what I described as the fatal logic. This would especially be true if it could be shown that katete promiscuity occurs as a steady, continuous practice rather than in the form of occasional orgiastic rituals. But, how "promiscuous" can one get? It would seem reasonable to assume that in this situation of a nonseparated separatism, the system of mawazo continues to provide minimal but powerful boundaries. Perhaps we must conclude that if the logic of mawazo is fatal at all, death is very slow. Of course, this would be no exception in the history of religions.

5. Finally, there is another category of defectors which must be mentioned, although during fieldwork I found too little evidence to make a strong case. Individual members and perhaps entire groups of the heterodox type may become followers of one of the many independent churches and religious movements operating in the same area and in the same social context. For lack of precise information it is, of course, impossible to assess in what way a person would accept, let us say, Bapostolo doctrine and ritual as an escape from, or an alternative to, mawazo.

All in all, this brief review of de facto escapes from mawazo should be sufficient to underscore the initial contention. Whatever autonomy can be attributed to this system of meaning, it must be interpreted in the context of a communicative praxis. Such praxis, seen as the individual and communal synthesis of insights, knowledge, and experiences, is possible, factually as well as theoretically, only on the basis of an irreducible "difference." This is not just a by-and-large trivial difference between ideas and action, but the difference between producers and products. Mawazo is articulation, product of communication, not only a system of rules or norms governing communication. Products of human activity may assume an autonomous and indeed parasitic existence. Therein lies the possibility, if not necessity, of carrying anthropological interpretation beyond relativist accounts of "culture" toward historical critique. It is a difficult project because the social sciences are still dominated by the scientist notion of a difference in kind between living a culture and understanding a culture. Yet both occur in communicative contexts and processes. It follows, then, that the native, no less than the anthropologist, can confront, criticize, and transcend his culture through the labors of interpretation. It is at this point that his enterprise and the anthropologist's work may merge in the common task of interpretation as liberation. As yet, we are still groping with the fundamentals and very first realizations of such an approach.

Epilogue: Castrated Charisma

In the long run, Max Weber tells us, continued action of expert organizations wins against charismatic enthusiasm. Often, in fact, the leaders of opposing factions and interests may band together and assure "castration of charisma."[55]

His remark is tucked away in a small-print divagation on the intricacies of American elections. But it suggests a possibility that most of us have not seriously considered. I, at least, only envisaged these alternatives: Charismatic movements may simply run their course and disappear; they may become "routinized," either as otherworldly groups preserving charisma as a style if no longer as a force, or by becoming organized, economically viable sects or churches. In some cases they may change their character and turn into political (but not necessarily revolutionary) groups. In all this, I failed to give proper recognition to the role and power of oppression, not the kind of oppression that creates martyrs and may give new life to a movement, nor the kind that annihilates, but the one that "castrates," manipulates, and mutilates movements for its own gains and purposes.

A draft of the preceding essay was written before my return to Shaba in 1972. During the three years that followed I revisited many groups and met with most of the Jamaa members who had been my key "informants" in 1966-1967. Although our relations were now more cordial and free from the pressures of "fieldwork," I could not help but observe that the "terror of texts" and the "fatal logic" continued to claim their victims. Yet this account would not be fair without at least a brief summary of recent events whose "negativity" consisted, by and large, of outright oppression.

The Jamaa began in a world ruled by a trinity of powers: government, missions, and the copper company. In 1970, ten years after independence from Belgium, the line-up was the same, even though some of the players had begun to change. With an eye on the consequences for the Jamaa, I will briefly examine each of them.[56]

The mission   With the continued departure of old-timers who had witnessed the emergence of the movement and with the rise to power of second-rate holdovers and of an as yet insecure African clergy, sensitive to all challenges from independent-minded Christians, the Jamaa necessarily became a prime target of concern and increased supervision. In fact, by 1970, all movement activities except for inconsequential ones had been prohibited or "suspended" in the Kolwezi and Lubumbashi areas. There had always been local tensions and occasional open struggle between Jamaa groups and missionaries. Since about 1967 the mission hierarchy had been cranking up to reach a final solution. As it turned out, they underestimated unanimity and flexibility among the Jamaa and in some cases became so incensed that they operated on the borderlines of civil and canonic legality.

There are trustworthy reports of harassment and of threats to fire Jamaa members employed in church-run institutions. There were denunciations and accusations before the authorities. Jamaa members were, apparently without a formal decree of excommunication, excluded from church activities and denied church weddings and funerals. The peak was reached when expatriate pastors in the Kolwezi area asked for, and got, military help to clear churches of Jamaa members, who were beaten and roughed up. In the end, the Belgian bishop of Kolwezi even had three Belgian nuns, who were known as supporters of the movement and were working in a government hospital, expelled from his diocese and removed from their church-owned housing in the African town.

Accuracy demands to state that several members of the clergy, among them Zaireans, disagreed with the policy of ruthless repression and advocated talks and a peaceful settlement. But they were immobilized by the fact that the mission continued to receive its financial support through the Belgian Franciscans. Only in 1974, when the situation had become untenable, did the church appoint a Zairean bishop for Kolwezi.

The government The current regime has repeatedly sought ideological confrontation with the Catholic Church as a form of continued foreign influence. The ensuing struggle has been complicated and is far from being resolved. However, with regard to charismatic activities, the government pursued policies similar to those of the colonial regime.[57] Any small and "free" religious group is suspicious and undesirable. A new law regulating religious associations demands that a sum of 100,000 Zaire ($200,000) be deposited by any group seeking incorporation. This has been met only by the united Protestant churches, by the Catholic Church, and by the Kimbanguists. All other groups have been leading a more-or-less tolerated underground existence. From the perspective of local officials, they remain potential troublemakers to be dealt with when the occasion arises. However, despite attempts by the Catholic mission to denounce the Jamaa as an illegal sect, government officials usually sent the case back to the church to be dealt with as an internal matter because accused Jamaa members constantly denied—true to Jamaa doctrine—being anything but Catholic. It was not until mid-1974 that local authorities in Kolwezi accepted the mission's claims and formally prohibited the Jamaa as a "sect."

An article in the weekly *Mwanga* (September 28–October 5, 1974) reports on the arrest of 39 Jamaa members of Kolwezi and cites "Decision No. 010/74 of June 5, 1974" and "letter No. 201/0174 of the Division Règionale de la Justice as the legal basis against this sect of 'satanic inspiration, using barbaric and subversive methods'." The reporter implies that this movement is of recent origin and is "developing rapidly" (although it had existed in that area for more than 20 years). He also ignored that the "Jamaa" leader and followers who were arrested and jailed belonged to the katete, a heterodox branch of the movement that had been separated from the Jamaa for at least 10 years.[58]

In this context, I may mention that the Lumbumbashi press occasionally attacked the Jamaa as being counterrevolutionary and opposed to the party (MPR).

However, since Jamaa members did cooperate whenever called upon—many are members of the party—these attacks remained without consequence. In fact, at the peak of the confrontation with the mission, a prominent Jamaa leader in Lubumbashi was approached by the party's youth branch (JMPR) and asked to separate from the mission and found an "authentic" Zairean church.

The mining company (Gécamines) During colonial times, the company (then Union Miniére du Haut Katanga) had employed the services of missionaries in its workers' settlements, where the Jamaa first appeared. In the early seventies, relationships between the Gécamines and the mission were cooling off (for economic rather than idealogical reasons) and the exclusion of missionaries from company payrolls and their departure from company-provided installations seemed imminent. Nevertheless, presumptions of cooperation were strong enough in 1973 to result in an (unsuccessful) attempt by the church hierarchy to persuade top-level Zairean management to fire Jamaa members among the workers in cumulo. On the other hand, the company offered no resistance when government officials began to enforce measures. A few days after the 39 "Jamaa" members were arrested, I had a conversation with the Zairean chief of personnel at Kolwezi. I pointed out that some of the arrested persons were his workers and asked him whether he had any complaints against them. No, he replied, to his knowledge they all had excellent records, but they deserved to be punished for their religious *bêtises*.

In the face of such mounting and concerted rejection, the Jamaa remained, on the whole, firm without violence and united without total closure. It did respond with rudiments of formal organization (since 1967 in Lubumbashi and since about 1970 in Kolwezi). Governing committees were formed and mutual aid and defense funds were raised. Leaders in the Kolwezi area, after unsuccessful appeals to Cardinal Malula in Kinshasa, considered for a while to work for legal incorporation (implying legal separation from the mission church) but abandoned the idea because, as one of them put it, Father Tempels had not given up his priesthood either. Inevitably, though, the movement became politized and more aware of the objective forces of oppression which it saw mainly in the expatriate clergy. Many prominent leaders and members who had spent their adult lives searching for "unity" with the mission and had acted as defenders of the European clergy (after all, their founder was one of them) have now given up. They found little comfort among their African successors, some of whom became the most active opponents of the Jamaa. An important factor in these recent developments has been a growing hostility between the Jamaa and other church groups, especially the Legio Mariae. Members of the latter often acted as spies and denunciators and seem now to have the total confidence of the clergy.

In all this, the Jamaa pays a high price for continued adherence to mawazo as a utopian dream. There is a good chance that oppression will succeed in adding the movement to the long list of sectarian groups which vegetate as interesting but largely inconsequential byproducts of colonization and decolonization.

FOOTNOTES

[1]These two attributes are meant to indicate that the studies to be commented on aim 1) primarily at non-Western movements and 2) at phenomena that are customarily thought of as "religious." Neither qualification can be defined in a strict way, nor are such definitions necessary prerequisites for the study of movements. See Fabian, 1971, 163 ff, and especially the thoughtful discussion of these problems in R. Nicholas, 1973, pp 63–84.

158

[2]Mooney J: *The Ghost-Dance Religion and the Sioux Outbreak of 1890,* 1965. This book was originally published in 1896.

[3]Linton R: Nativistic movements. *Am Anthropol* 1943;45:230–240.

[4]Perhaps no one has a better command of the sheer bibliographic bulk than Harold W. Turner. With Robert C. Mitchell he compiled *A Bibliography of Modern African Religious Movements* (1966), which he has kept up to date in the *Journal of Religion in Africa.* At the University of Aberdeen, he directs a project devoted to the documentation of movement activities on a worldwide basis. See also the latest survey by James W. Fernandez, 1978.

[5]Ian C. Jarvie, 1964.

[6]Kenelm Burridge, 1969; Weston La Barre, 1971; Vittorio Lanternari, 1974.

[7]Lanternari, 1974, p 497.

[8]La Barre, 1971, p 8.

[9]La Barre, 1971, p 27.

[10]See also Munro S. Edmonson, 1960, and Fabian, 1971, p 3.

[11]Burridge, 1969, pp 153–164.

[12]Burridge, 1969, pp 159–160.

[13]Jurgen Habermas, 1973.

[14]This has been the case even in the history of the natural sciences, as has been pointed out most forcefully by Paul Feyerabend, 1975, especially pp 72–73.

[15]See Fabian, 1981; Manyoni, 1977.

[16]See, for example, Peter Worsley, 1968.

[17]Michele Duchet, 1971, p 17; my translation; and Vittorio Lanternari, 1963.

[18]On the history and significance of causation models for understanding "alien belief systems," see J.D.Y. Peel, 1969, pp 69–84. It would also be interesting to pursue the notion of movement itself—a key metaphor of social science derived from celestial mechanisms. Nicholas, 1973, p 67, has some perceptive observations on this. I suspect that the attractiveness of this metaphor lies in the fact that it allows us to think of some social processes as "pure" movement. Like Newtonian movement, these processes can be described and predicted in terms of equations between certain variables, but they need not—and, indeed, cannot—be "understood" as meaningful. In that respect they are opposed to the established social order.

[19]See Anthony F.C. Wallace, 1956, pp 264–281.

[20]The best example is still David B. Barrett, 1968. But even if qualitative rather than quantitative statements are intended, the result may be a combinatory trait list; see, for example, Willy De Craemer, Jan Vansina, and Renée Fox, 1976, pp 467–468. Notice that the authors of that paper explicitly reject "existing classifications of movements" (p 459), which suggests that an approach may be classificatory even if it does not propose explicit typologies. "Classificatoriness" is an epistemological stance, as we will try to show presently.

[21]Igor Kopytoff, 1964.

[22]For example, Siegfried Landshut, 1969, p 64 ff. This was originally published in 1929.

[23]Landshut, 1969, p 54.

[24] For example, Max Weber, 1958, p 4, 336 ff.

[25]It was Parsons who prepared the way for a logical assessment of charisma when he stated: "Every system, including both its theoretical propositions and its main relevant empirical insights, may be visualized as an illuminated spot enveloped by darkness. The logical name for the darkness is, in general, 'residual categories' " (Talcott Parsons, 1949, p 17). In the same context he noted that those "observable facts" which do not "fit into sharply, positively defined categories. . . tend to be given one or more blanket names which refer to categories negatively defined. . . " (Parsons, 1949, p 17). Such was clearly the case with Weber's groping definition of charisma as the "noneveryday" power (ausseralltäglish; see Max Weber, 1964, p 182). However, to be accurate, Parsons did not follow through this realization, except obliquely (see Parsons, 1949, p 663), probably because he wanted to prove the virtual identity of Weber's charisma and Durkheim's sacred, both being positive sources of "moral authority" (Parsons, 1949, pp 662, 669–670).

[26]See Talcott Parsons, 1951, p 502.

[27]Weber, 1964, p 188; my translation.

[28]See, for example, Bryan Wilson, 1975.

[29]I have done this in Fabrian, 1971b.

[30]Placide Tempels, 1969; originally published in 1945.

[31]Tempels, 1969, p 28.

[32]See Johannes Fabian, 1970.

[33]One notoriously overlooked exception is George Devereux, 1967. Its focus on the psychological aspects of research, however, makes it only indirectly relevant to the problem discussed here. A more recent appraisal is John J. Honigman, 1976.

[34]Clifford Geertz, 1973, p 14.

[35]This was recently observed, and exemplified, by James Boon in his *The Anthropological Romance of Bali*, 1977. He writes, for instance, about "pictorial emblems" in the history of Bali ethnography: "A major interest in the art of ethnology is to convey a sense of the whole society, to typify it in some vivid, compelling manner. Like any essential metaphorical procedure, ethnology thus resembles the arts of visual illusion, if one realizes there is no such thing as simple 'realism" and no possible one-to-one correspondance between that which is 'illusioned to' and the perceptual or conceptual apparatus by which the illusion is perpetrated" (p 18).

[36]Michel Foucault, 1976, p 27; my emphasis.

[37]In many ways, my view of the project common to these essays converges with the theory of discourse developed by Foucault in *The Archaeology of Knowledge*. Foucault also begins with the "negative work" (1976, p 21) of rejecting "ready-made syntheses" (p 22) of the kind represented here by causation theories, typologies, and "charisma." And he introduces "discource" as a means to lay the foundation of a "new history." It remains to be seen to what extent anthropologists will go along with specific tenets of his proposal. A crucial question will be whether or not Foucault's theory can cover the "ethnographic act" as the constitutive event of anthropology.

[38]On the history and enthnography of the Jamaa movement was Willy De Craemer, 1965, 1958, 1977; Willy De Craemer et al, 1976; Johannes Fabian, 1971, 1974.

[39]Max Weber, 1964, p 179, 835.

[40]It is only fair to note that anthropologists, most notably Victor Turner with his notion of "antistructure" (cf. 1974) have kept in touch, so to speak, with negativity rather than exorcizing it as mere deviance.

[41]Among the critics of Parsons, it was Alvin Gouldner who protested against his positive "platonism" and noted a "fatal confusion between the sociable and the social" (1970, p 428). But he and the other Marxist critics of the reigning paradigm are more concerned with vindicating common sense than with formulating badly needed philosophical foundations for a "negative dialectic." The latter was envisaged by the late Theodor Adorno, who postulated that "thinking. . . is negating, resistance against that which imposes itself; thinking inherited this from its model *(Urbild)*, the relationship between labor and its material. Nowadays, more than ever, ideology encourages thought to be positive. It does this based on the clever realization that positivity is contrary to thought and that thought needs friendly encouragement from social authority to get used to positivity" (1966, p 28; my translation). Adorno's attempt remained fragmentary; social science continues to be fundamentally positive. After completing this essay, I came upon Ulrich Sonnemann, *Negative Anthropologie: Vorstudien zur Sabotage des Schicksals* (1969), a book that is profound and exciting but also forbiddingly difficult.

[42]R. Sennett (1975), in an essay on Savonarola, spoke of the "terrifying quality" of charismatic action, suggesting that "terror" is inherent in what he calls the "experience of social relations beyond the rule of law." Paradoxically, it is the role of the charismatic leader to give assurance in the face of the terror he helps to create. While this is not exactly the sense in which I speak of the terror of mawazo, it is an unusually perceptive account of the "negative" in charismatic processes.

[43]Fabian, 1971, pp 98–99, 181–182.

[44]*Kitabu* is a written catechism of Jamaa teaching in the Kolwezi area. See Fabian, 1971a, p 126 ff.

[45]On genres of Jamaa oral communication, see Fabian, 1974.

[46]This is worked out in some detail in Fabian, 1969.

[47]This could be shown for the Jamaa as much as for other religious movements. Thus most meetings of local groups take place simply to give expression to Jamaa teachings; but some may be called for a specific project, for example, to settle a dispute or to take a collection for needy members.

[48]I was reminded by Thomas Chordas that this observation resembles Kenneth Burke's "tautological cycle of terms of order" (1970, pp 183-196). It does, up to a certain point. Burke, with his usual incisiveness, states the logical (or, in his terms, "logological") problem but is not immediately concerned with its practical consequences. These may be inferred, perhaps, from what he has to say about "dominion" and "mortification." He hints at the problematics of this essay when he suggests that there is a possibility to break out of "circularity in rectilinear (narrative, temporal) terms of a dramatic unfolding" (p 253).

[49]See also De Craemer, 1968.

[50]See M. Warren, 1954, and L.A. Fallers' preface to Fabian, 1971a.

[51]De Craemer, 1968.

[52]More information is given in Fabian, 1971, Appendix I. In 1972-1974, when I revisited the labor settlement of Musonoi, the principal site of my fieldwork in 1966-1967, I noticed hardly any changes in the membership of the Jamaa, except for some defections and departures due to retirement.

[53]Cf Fabian, 1973.

[54]Cf Fabian, 1971a, pp 190-195.

[55]Weber, 1964, p 851.

[56]I should emphasize that these observations are limited to two key locations in the Shaba region. Developments in other areas await further research.

[57]For background information on church-state relations in Zaire, see K.L. Adelman, 1975; on government policy toward cult movements in Katanga, see Edouard Bustin, 1975. During a brief visit to Zaire in December 1978, I found that the situation had changed very little.

[58]On katete see text and Fabian, 1971a, pp 190-195.

BIBLIOGRAPHY

Adelman KL: The church-state conflict in Zaire 1969-1974. *Afr Stud Rev* 1975;18: 102-116.

Adorno ThW: *Negative Dialektik*. Frankfurt, Suhrkamp, 1966.

Barrett DB: *Schism and Renewal in Africa: An Analysis of Six Thousand Contemporary Movements*. Nairobi, Oxford University Press, 1968.

Boon J: *The Anthropological Romance of Bali*. New York, Cambridge University Press, 1977.

Burke K: *The Rhetoric of Religion. Studies in Logology*. Berkeley, University of California Press, 1970.

Burridge K: *New Heaven New Earth*. Oxford, Basil Blackwell, 1969.

Bustin E: Government policy toward African cult movements: The case of Katanga, in Karp M (ed): *African Dimensions: Essays in Honor of William O. Brown*. Brookline, MA, African Studies Center, Boston University, 1975.

De Craemer W: *Analyse Sociologique de la Jamaa*. Léopoldville, Centre de Recherches Sociologiques, 1965.

De Craemer W: The Jamaa movement in the Katanga and Kasai regions of the Congo. *Rev Relig Res* 1968;10:11-23.

De Craemer W: *The Jamaa and the Church: A Bantu Catholic Movement in Zaire*. Oxford, Clarendon Press, 1977.

De Craemer W, Vansina J, Fox R: Religious movements in Central Africa: A theoretical study. *Comp Stud Soc His* 1976;18:458–475.

Devereux G: *From Anxiety to Method*. The Hague, Mouton, 1967.

Duchet M: *Anthropologie et Histoire au Siécle des Lumieres*. Paris, Francois Maspero. (Fabian's translation), 1971.

Edmonson MS: Nativism, syncretism and anthropological science, in *Nativism and Syncretism*. Middle American Research Institute Publications, New Orleans, Tulane University, 1960.

Fabian J: An African gnosis—for a reconsideration of an authoritative definition. *Hist Relig* 1969;9:42–58.

Fabian J: *Philosophie Bantoue: Placide Tempels et son Oeuvre vus dans une Perspective Historique*. Brussels, Etudes Africaines du CRISP, 1970.

Fabian J: *Jamaa, A Charismatic Movement in Katanga*. Evanston, Northwestern University Press, 1971a.

Fabian J: Language, history and anthropology. *Phil Soc Sci* 1971b;1:19–47.

Fabian J: Kazi, conceptualizations of labor in a charismatic movement among Swahili-speaking workers. *Cah d'Etud Afr* 1973;13:293–325.

Fabian J: Genres in an emerging tradition: An anthropological approach to religious communication, in Eister AW (ed): *Changing Perspectives in the Scientific Study of Religion*. New York, Wiley-Interscience, 1974, pp 249–272.

Fabian J: Six theses regarding the anthropology of African religious movements. *Religion* 1981;11:109–126.

Fernandez J: The mission of metaphor in expressive culture. *Curr Anthropol* 1978;15: 119–145.

Feyerabend P: *Against Method*. Atlantic Highlands, Humanities Press, 1975.

Foucault M: *The Archeology of Knowledge*. New York, Harper & Row, 1976.

Geertz C: *The Interpretation of Cultures*. New York, Basic Books, 1973.

Gouldner AW: *The Coming Crisis of Western Sociology*. New York, Basic Books, 1970.

Habermas J: *Knowledge and Human Interests*. Boston, Beacon Press, 1972.

Honigman JJ: The personal approach in cultural anthropological research. *Curr Anthropol* 1976;17:243–261.

Jarvie IC: *The Revolution in Anthropology*. New York, Humanities Press, 1964.

Kopytoff I: Classifications of religious movements: Analytical and synthetic, in Helm J (ed): *Symposium on New Approaches to the Study of Religion*. Seattle, University Press, 1964, pp 77–90.

La Barre W: Materials for a history of studies of crisis cults: A bibliographic essay. *Curr Anthropol* 1971;12:3–44.

Landshut S: *Kritik der Soziologie und andere Schriften zur Politik*. Neuwied, Luchterhand, 1969.

Lanternari V: *The Religions of the Oppressed: A Study of Modern Messianic Cults*. New York, Mentor, 1963. Originally published in 1929.

Lanternari V: Nativistic and socio-religious movements: A reconsideration. *Comp Stud Hist Soc* 1974;16:483–503.

Linton R: Nativistic movements. *Am Anthropol* 1943;45:230–240.

Manyoni JR: Anthropology and the study of schism in Africa. A re-examination of some anthropological theories. *Cah d'Etud Afr* 1977;68:599–631.

Mitchell RC, Turner HW: *A Bibliography of Modern African Religious Movements*. Evanston, Northwestern University Press, 1966.

Mooney J: *The Ghost-Dance Religion and the Sioux Outbreak of 1890*. Chicago, Phoenix Books, 1965. Originally published in 1896.

Nicholas RW: Social and political movements, in Siegel BJ (ed): *Annual Review of Anthropology*. Palo Alto, Annual Reviews Inc, 1973, pp 63–84.

Parsons T: *The Structure of Social Action*. Glencoe, Free Press, 1949.

Parsons T: *The Social System*. Glencoe, Free Press, 1951.

Peel JDY: Understanding alien belief systems. *Br J Sociol* 1969;20:69–84.

162

Sennett R: Charismatic de-legitimation: A case study. *Theory Soc* 1975;2:171–181.

Sonnemann U: *Negative Anthropologie. Vorstudien zur Sabotage du Schicksals.* Hamburg, Rowolt, 1969.

Tempels P: *Bantu Philosophy.* Paris, Présence Africaine, 1969.

Turner VW: Metphors of anti-structure in religious culture, in Eister AW (ed): *Changing Perspectives in the Scientific Study of Religion.* New York, Wiley-Interscience, 1974, pp 63–84.

Wallace AFC: Revitalization movements. *Am Anthropol* 1956;58:264–281.

Warren M: *Revival: An Enquiry.* London, SCM Press, 1954.

Weber M: *The Religion of India.* New York, Free Press, 1958.

Weber M: *Wirtschaft und Gesellschaft.* Cologne, Kiepenheuer & Witsch, 1964.

Wilson B: *The Noble Savages: The Primitive Origins of Charisma.* London, Oxford University Press, 1975.

10

Courage and Fanaticism:
The Charismatic Leader and Modern Religious Cults

CARL GOLDBERG

C ults command our attention. It has been reported that there are 2500 quasi-religious groups in the United States (Cushman and Moses, 1980), with a membership that is widely estimated between two and ten million followers. These cults are regarded as the fastest growing spiritual movements in the world. Each of these groups have been reputed to use various psychological means to rather effectively control their followers' thoughts, feelings, and actions (Cushman and Moses, 1980). We cannot avoid daily encountering these cult followers. They are found ubiquitiously in the portals of public life—begging at airports, on street corners, and in the interiors of restaurants. Many of these groups generate large revenue. One cult, the Unification Church, claims to raise about $20 million a year in the United States alone (Castelli, 1980). This income enables cults to retain the services of the best legal, political, and business professionals in promoting their mission.

Where have these cults sprung from? They have arisen from the dissatisfactions of adolescents and young adults who have experienced limited options in American society for pursuing what they consider to be meaningful lives. Symptomatic of the tenuous values in our turbulent society, the struggle for a livelihood has been replaced by the struggle to discover one's self (Sennett, 1980). We live in conflictual and distrustful times. The ordered society of yesterday has dissipated, leaving behind eroded structures and clouds of cynicism and discontentment. We feel immobilized by complex social problems that appear insoluble. We yearn for the warm regard and assurance of others. We wish to touch others deeply and caringly, but instead draw back in fear of our own malevolence, no less than that of our neighbors. We impute that we are not responsible for the destructive actions we have accorded others. We have tried to act as best we can to survive and to survive with our integrity intact. Toward these efforts Alexander Solzhenitsyn, the defiant defender of human rights, has bitterly depicted the Western world as plagued by a loss of courage and a destructive and irresponsible freedom which has been granted without limitation. In a word, we live in an era in which men find it onerous to accept responsibility for their own actions and for the embittered and hollow course their existence has taken. Man's guidelines for living stand broken, disjointed, and in disarray. No longer do men have clear reasons for living and for endeavoring. To whatever modern man attends, he discovers evidence that his presence is unnecessary. The magnitude and comprehensiveness of modern technology are such that a relatively few scientists and technicians can serve the physical requirements of the entire population. Modern man has been informed that God is dead; indeed, in man's ignorance and in his despair, he may have slain him. Nonetheless, he need not fear a dead God. Man finds that he is no longer held responsible for the children he has produced, nor the spouse to whom he was once committed. Modern man's existence may be freely egocentric and asocial to a degree not tolerated but a short while past. He is not actually required, other than in terms of an antiquated moral sense, to maintain a trade and life-style forged on supporting immediate and extended family. In the past, a man's destiny had always been his family. They were the root and essence of his existence. This is no longer true (Goldberg, 1980).

YOUTH'S SEARCH FOR A BETTER WORLD

Modern religious cults concentrate on recruiting the adolescent and young adult offspring of middle-class families, manipulating the vulnerabilities of this accessible generation. According to a study by Galanter and his associates (1979), members of the Unification Church group tend to be young (a mean age of 24.7), white (89%), and unmarried (91%). In another study Galanter and Buckley (1978) found that 76% of the Divine Light Mission sect had attended college, as had 71% of one or both of their parents. Reports of other cults tend to confirm these figures for cult followers in general.

The nature of youth in modern society renders them an especially cogent population for recruitment by religious cults. Each of the cult sects has put together a marketing program in terms of its own brand of mission that appeals to the youth's unique combination of idealism and optimism, no less than to his or her particular narcissistic striving (Stoner and Parke, 1979).

The primary responsibility of young adulthood is the creation of a viable value structure which will give the youth substance, support, and meaning as a person in the adult world. In a period of transition from adolescence to adulthood, he or she is struggling to shape for his/herself those values which separate the adult from adolescence: financial independence, enlightened citizenship, and parenthood. In a society that is itself changing at a galloping pace, the youth is caught between what his elders regard as the excessive idealism of adolescence and what his peers view as the overly conservative pragmatism of his parents' generation. His status in several overlapping social worlds is marginal because these various social systems are philosophically at variance with one another, deliquescing his identity as a person and subjecting his self-concept to abrupt shifts. He is continually frustrated by the variability between his own aspirations and that which is afforded and expected of him by the present social order. He gravitates toward peers in order to establish a viable purpose and the creation of a personal identity in the image of his own times from among what he perceives to be the pressing social priorities he has inherited from his parents' generation. Youth's immersion in and conversion to a peer group which is at variance with his parents' generation, as William James (1952) long ago observed, "is in its essence a normal adolescent phenomenon incidental to the passage from the child's small universe to the wider intellectual and spiritual life of maturity" (p 196). It is, however, the often insidious nature and implication of this conversion that concerns us in this chapter.

I am concerned in this chapter with examining the concepts of religious conviction, courage, and fanaticism in terms of religious cults.

The cult phenomenon is an especially complex one. It defies simple explanation and definition. The argument I will develop in this chapter runs counter to what I have read to date about cult groups. My thesis is that the cult leader, guru, or whatever he (rarely she*) is referred to, is not a Svengali figure who forces his followers to act contrary to their own wishes. Indeed, although each of the charismatic leaders varies greatly in wisdom, articulateness, persuasiveness, and authoritarian appeal, the common attribute of each is that he appears as some absurd figure, a melodramatic character cast from a Joseph Conrad novel. I will argue that despite the money and marketing tactics of Rev. Moon, the political skills of Jim Jones, the recall to fundamental religious doctrine of David Berg, these leaders could not attract a large following if they were not encountering youth who were actively seeking lapses from reality, who were constantly reindoctrinating their gurus to the prophet's own professed bizarre doctrines. Conway and Siegelman (1979) point to the crude, if not primitive, manipulative tactics of Jim Jones toward his followers in the People's Temple. The following is a statement that is found consistently throughout the accounts of both observers and ex-members of the People's Temple: "I cannot understand how so many bright, college educated people could have been taken in by a thing like this."

Each of the cult's followers, unwittingly, but no less pervasively, is seeking out a leader and a movement in which he or she can be involved in extreme behavior, even if this endeavor is simply not to be responsible for having to make decisions for his/herself. The accentuated passivity of the cult members appears to be a defense against uncontrollable rage, concomitant with the fear that one's dependent needs can never be met. It is then understandable that the use of a rattlesnake to attempt to kill an attorney investigating Synanon was condoned by the Synanon members, or the blatant use of blackmail, physical threats, and actual brutal beatings and torture of former and current cult members were tolerated by members of the People's Temple.

There is not space in this chapter to describe the entire proliferating cult phenomenon. The discussion will be confined to the best known cult—by virtue of the bizarre and tragic event that marked its termination—the People's Temple group. I will explore the development of this extraordinary cult in terms of the social and existential conditions which led to its emergence. I further will attempt to explain its continuance and its tragic end by examining the role of the charismatic leader in directing his followers toward a fanatical rather than a more open direction of their own personal intentionality and concerns.

THE ROLE OF COURAGE IN THE MODERN WORLD

To understand what happened at Jonestown and to appreciate the rapid proliferation of modern religious cults, we need to examine the role of courage in the

*To my knowledge an examination of female cult leadership has not been made by social scientists to date.

modern world. We will explore in this chapter the courage necessary for modern man to search for his own identity and to come to terms with his own malevolent, as well as his tender longings. Unfortunately, discussions of risk and courage have been long neglected in the social sciences. To the behavioral scientist, no doubt, courage is a term best left with athletes, soldiers, and true believers. Courage is an attribute which cannot be readily accounted for in scientific parlance—that is to say, deterministic terms. To the behavioral scientist ascribing courage to human actions smacks of endowing enviable characteristics to behaviors which would have inevitably occurred without the imposition of the hypothesized emotion which we call "courage." The imputation of the concept of courage is not actually necessary for accounting for human action. Nonetheless, courage has been held in highest regard by all known societies. It is vital that we acquaint ourselves with the implications of human courage. Without the attribution of courage, human dignity and passion become quickly dismantled. Our technological society has devoted itself to making life so soft that modern man has lost his human dignity, together with the other remnants of human purpose and intention, in facing up to the difficult issues of human existence (Goldberg, 1980). The resounding question is "Where have all the inspired leaders and heroes, who present us with exemplary models, gone?"

Without the presence of courage, modern man will continue to avert the deeper concerns of human existence. The demonstration of courage is vital for dealing with the personal and social concerns with which modern man is faced in everyday life, no less than in the trying and desperate existential concerns of exceptional circumstances and events. Courage is necessary because the human condition is by its very nature uncertain and conflictual. Courage is required that the individual ensure that his worth as a person is respected and that his existence not be subjected to the yoke of false prophets.

Rollo May (1978) has argued that each act of courage raises the moral conscience and the social consciousness of the society in which it is exhibited. The act of courage proclaims that the denial of certain values and ways of being are intolerable—that life without them, like the unexamined life, is not worth living. In the act of courage, the self suspends, postpones, and is even willing to relinquish, any claim to reciprocal benefit. The self proclaims by means of its act(s) an implicit trust that by its courageous conduct the self has created a bond with humanity to raise its consciousness, to accenuate its awareness, and to challenge its stolidness. In committing itself to a courageous act the self also makes the claim that these acts do make a difference in the world. The self, by its acts of courage, states its willingness to stand out and be accountable. The self's implicit trust is that humanity will be confronted and shaken by the self's act and, as a result, will also be more accountable.

The classic expression of the courageous act to which I am alluding is found in A Tale of Two Cities. Charles Dicken's protagonist, Sidney Carton, exclaims in the last moment prior to his taking the place at the guillotine for the lover of the woman for whom he experiences unrequited love, "It is a far, far better thing that I do than I have ever done before." With these words, Carton is expressing his long-suppressed sorrow and guilt that he had denied himself his own human dignity. He is exclaiming his moral indignation that he has permitted society to cast him off as worthless riffraff. In surrendering his life, Carton claims to have regained his humanity. He has also made a commitment to the values of love, compassion, and self-sacrifice in an age in which these sentiments and deeds were denied or in disrepute. Later in the chapter, in the context of the extreme behavior exhibited in the People's Temple, we will attempt to examine whether Carton's gesture was fanatic or an act of courage.

LIMITATIONS OF PSYCHOHISTORY

It is intellectually tempting to try to reconstitute the metamorphosis of Jim Jones' personality decompensation from a "crusading idealist to messianic monster" (*Newsweek*, April 21, 1980), who was responsible for "one of the most bizarre and awful massacres of our time" (Krause, 1978). To do so I must psychologically examine a person I have never met or, indeed, had never heard of prior to the tragic "White Night." Moreover, concerned with a social movement that has ceased to be, we are like the historian or the philosopher who is limited to the examination of events and circumstances beyond our ability to study directly or from within. Parenthetically, due to the difficulty of confronting rather complex problems, no more than a handful of field studies have attempted to study the dynamics of a turbulent social movement like the People's Temple from within (Goldberg, no date, unpublished manuscript).

Fortunately, there are several reports and a book (Mills, 1979) by former People's Temple followers. Mills' book included what she claims are letters and telephone transcripts of Jim Jones. There is also an abundance of eyewitness books by investigative journalists of the massacre and the events which led up to it.* As we have greater access to information about Jones' interactions with his followers, we can speak with more conviction about what he manifested in his behavior toward them than what prompted Jones to behave as he did.

CULTS AS PSEUDORELIGIOUS MOVEMENTS

If cultism has become, as claimed by the mass media, the new religion of the 1970s, it is necessary to examine the cult's religiosity—its purported intent and the effectiveness of its actual achievements—to understand why cults have proliferated with such vigor in recent years.

Religiosity is the ostensible purpose of the cult group. Sixty-seven percent of the followers of a cult group studied by Galanter and his associates (1979) regarded themselves as at least moderately committed to their family's religion prior to age 15. At sometime thereafter, 34% became at least moderately committed to one of the Eastern religious sects, while 19% identified with fundamental Christian movements. Moreover, 90% reported some prior confluence with fundamentalist sects. In fact, however, despite the initial attraction of religious doctrine of the new cults, these groups are pseudoreligious, political, and paramilitary movements. These organizations claim to be religious sects largely for the respectibility and legal and financial protection and benefits which accrue to religious organizations. I will be arguing later in this chapter that it is a particular type of politics and militancy in which religious cults specialize.

Numerous eyewitnesses confirm that Jim Jones was not only an extraordinarily gifted political manipulator but, in fact, frequently disclaimed his religious role, ridiculing and condemning religious believers. In September 1977, Jim Jones' wife, Marceline Jones, stated in an interview with the *New York Times*

> that Jones was a Marxist who held that religion's trappings were useful only for social and economic uplift. 'Jim has used religion to try to get some people out of

---

*The reader is referred to F. Conway and J. Siegelman: *Snapping*, New York, Dell, 1979, for a vivid description of what happened at Jonestown.

the opiate of religion', she said. Once in his wife's presence, Jones slammed down a Bible with the exclamation, 'Marcie, I've got to destroy this paper idol' (Krause, 1978, p 33).

The United States is a fertile climate for the emergence of pseudoreligious cults like People's Temple. These cults seem to have considerably more difficulty surviving outside of the United States. Organizations involved in exploitative manipulation of their followers have realized the facility with which they can avoid paying taxes on their revenue and escape official probes of their account books and activities by declaring themselves to be religious organizations. An article in the *New York Times* by Robert Lindsey (1980) indicated that, as defined by various rulings of the United States Court,

> a religion legally is any sincere, meaningful belief that occupies 'a place in the life of its possessor, parallel to that held by orthodox belief in God.' As a practical matter, virtually anyone can establish a religion and get the legal advantages that go with it.

To effectively operate from a loosely defined religious structure, Jones employed an impressive array of lawyers, business advisors, publicists, tipsters, spies, and strong-arm guards to intimidate anyone who threatened or, Jones feared, might attack his mission. Furthermore, as the head of a religious organization Jones was not only virtually immune from governmental probing but, no less importantly, he could ask more of his followers than as a political leader. Jones' talents as a politician, however, were only matched by the laxity of the various California, United States, and Guyanan governmental agencies within whose aegis the People's Temple operated. Jones' temple flourished in a laissez-faire climate. It seems abundantly evident that he had a quid pro quo relationship with local California politicians. In the face of rumors and reports of brutal and bizarre activities at the People's Temple, local politicians continued to write him complimentary letters, made speeches in his behalf, and selected him for community positions where Jones had considerable financial and political clout. In return Jones demonstrated a remarkable ability to bring in votes for his favorite candidates (*Newsweek,* April 21, 1980). He also had considerable flair in defaming and blackmailing people who would not cooperate with him (Mills, 1979). It is reasonable to argue that these political sanctions served to reinforce Jones' delusional system. He came to believe he could get away virtually with murder.

On the other hand, Congressman Ryan's visit to Jonestown and his confrontation of the conditions there undoubtedly triggered the "White Night" massacre. It was a startling attack on Jones' narcissism. Ryan's visit appears to have been one of the few, certainly the only substantial, face-to-face confrontations of Jones. The absence of cooperation among the various governmental agencies concerned with Jonestown gave Jones a virtual free hand for his tyrannical and bizarre activities. In the end, those temple members who stood up to Jones in trying to defend themselves or to monitor his brutality received no support from fellow temple members (Mills, 1979) or from governmental agencies (Nugent, 1979; Krause, 1978). They either backed down and gave into Jones' cruelty or left the church.

To understand the modern charismatic leader's appeal we need to appreciate that paradoxically he operates in a climate of both cynicism and hope.

CYNICISM

Present-day youth have become rather cynical about how other generations have responded to the problems and social ills which their world faces. Cynicism is a reaction to societal permissiveness, lack of firm values, and lack of commitment to anyone or anything except the pursuit of dilettante aims. Jones' ability to get away with his bizarre activities, in no small part, may be attributed to his realization that cynical people are drawn to self-indulgent leaders. Jones' personal refrigerator was stocked with the best quality fruits and meats; he did not labor at all. His rank-and-file followers, on the other hand, gave up all their savings and valuables to the People's Temple, then toiled laboriously, 16 hours or more, under a tropical sky, while subsisting on a nutritionally poor diet. Jones also smoked, drank, and boasted openly about both his hetero- and homosexual affairs. These were all activities strictly forbidden to all but his most trusted lieutenants. In fact, violations of these rules prompted severe and brutal punishment for Jones' followers. Accounts suggest that Jones learned some of his cynicism from the legendary black cult leader, Father Divine. Divine advised him that it was his "religious obligation to take possession of his flock and to satisfy the sexual cravings of the female members" (*Newsweek*, April 21, 1980).

In a true spirit of cynicism Jones could forbid his followers from engaging in sexual relations with their spouses while forcing a female lover to watch while he seduced her husband (*Newsweek*, April 21, 1980).

HOPE—THE RECONSTITUTED FAMILY

An inspirational source for the emergence of cults is a renewed interest in psychic phenomenon. Through the widespread experimentation with drugs in the 1960s many young people realized varieties of experience not readily accessible to ordinary consciousness. Together with a desire to foster a new world of brotherhood and understanding, these experiences of altered consciousness rendered these youth more susceptible to external influence than were their peers. This is especially cogent when these influences are predicated in messages contrary to common sense and reason—the hallmarks of a secular world these youth have come to distrust and have sought to reject (Swartz, 1980).

One cannot fail to notice that the concept of "family" plays a crucial role in each of the cult groups. For many youths attracted to cults (the communards), the requirement that the sect followers live in communes is the fulfillment of the hope for brotherhood and understanding. In these settings ex-members have reported that they felt an intimacy with their fellow members unrivaled by their experience in the world outside (Conway and Siegelman, 1979). Ungerleider and Wellisch (1979) have indicated that the cult members they examined

> revealed clinically an intellectual and philosophical bent that resembles what Lifton has termed 'strong ideological hunger,' regardless of their status in relation to the cult. These cults appear to provide, at least for a time nourishment for these ideological hungers as well as relief from the internal turmoil of ambivalence.

In reaction to the dissolution of the modern family, youth are in search of a more formed, sustaining, and caring surrogate family. Parents and societal authorities no longer provide meaningful value orientations and guidelines for living. According to figures published in *U.S. News and World Report*, 40% of the U.S. marriages since 1970 have ended in divorce. Youth today are desperately searching for someone who will stand strong and lead them out of their bottomless existential anomie and exhaustion. They erect a person or a group to do this for them and attribute strengths and virtues to their leaders, whether or not the leaders actually possess them, which will give their lives some purpose. But we must also realize that cults have flourished in our day because they teach in rather clear dictates to their followers "how to live": what is important in life and what the followers should do with their time and their energies.

RELIGIOUS SOCIAL MOVEMENTS

Sigmund Freud has said that religion is born of the need to make tolerable the helplessness of man (Stoner and Parke, 1979). In his journey through history men have erected, dedicated themselves to, and subsequently discarded countless images and conceptions of the forces that men have reputed to govern their destiny. In each era some men have found themselves footloose and unable to identify with and, therefore, to make firm commitment with the dominant values and ethos of their society. These persons have been regarded as marginal by those who made a commitment to the dominant societal values.

The marginal individual in experiencing himself as unfulfilled and dissatisfied with the course his life has taken is prone to anxiety, frustration, confusion, and seeks redress (Cantril, 1941; Maier, 1942; Edwards, 1944; King, 1956). Alone no man or woman can transform society or create a separate, improved world. Desperate persons have sought others who harbor similar strivings and possess the information and means of securing a better society.

Herbert Blumer, regarded as the authoritative interpreter of collective movements, indicated (1951) that social movements "have their inception in a condition of unrest, and derive their motive power on the one hand from dissatisfactions with the current form of life, and on the other hand, from wishes and hopes for a new scheme or system of living." Accordingly, a religious social movement is perceived as a consequence of social ferment attributed to the failure of the mainline religious sects and the various social orders to meet adequately the existential exigencies of a segment of the population (Elridge, 1950).

Once the stage is set for a social movement, the appearance of a charismatic leader is indispensable to the life of the movement. Unless an inspired leader comes to the fore, the movement will temporarily or permanently come to a halt. Throughout history there have been men and, occasionally, women who have been regarded as especially inspired and who have held out the promise of a better world to others. Many of these persons were deluded and poorly socialized. Still others were men of enlightenment like Socrates, Buddha, Jesus, Mohammed, and Confucius. These were men who, centuries after they lived, still profoundly influence the lives of others.

In admitting the new religious cults as social movements, we have to closely examine the particular form these movements have taken. Stoner and Parke (1979) have defined a religious cult as "a minority religious group regarded as spurious or unorthodox [in which there is] great or excessive devotion or dedication to some person, idea, or thing" (p 28).

According to Stoner and Parke (1979), these groups have a doctrine based upon a living leader's revelations, which usually supplants rather than supplements or accentuates traditional religious scripture and doctrine. The cult leader is always the sole judge of a follower's dedication to the cult and the leader enjoys absolute authority over the life of the group. He lives in rich splendor while his followers toil in abject poverty. The doctrines of the cult, unlike traditional religion, offer not only to revitalize the being of the cult followers, but promise a system in which a believer may work to save all of humanity. Ungerleider and Wellisch (1979) found that the cult members they interviewed had higher mean average scores on the performance tests of the WAIS (116) than on the verbal tests (mean 111). Although this difference was not statistically significant, it tends to suggest that many cult members better demonstrate their intelligence in performing tasks rather than critically thinking out problems and concerns. Many ex-cult members have come to realize that despite the grandiose promises of their leaders, cults actually sponsor no community-improvement programs. Cult religions are exclusive social clubs, promising that their followers will achieve salvation and happiness. Consequently, cult members are indoctrinated to believe that they are superior to everyone else, that they alone possess the truth. Programs of ego-restoration and psychological monitoring of members are integral to the regimentation of cult life, membership recruiting, and indoctrination. To ensure obedience to cult doctrine, critical thinking by its members is strongly discouraged by practices which dictate the suppression of negative thoughts about the cult, and in its place is fostered an emotional dependency on the cult authority which arrests the natural maturation into adulthood of its members.

THE PSYCHOLOGICAL CLIMATE OF CULTS

A study by Pattison and his associates (1973) on faith healing indicated that the conversion process to a cult doctrine is not congruent with improved psychological functioning. The investigators found through the employment of psychological inventories that

> A typical constellation of personality traits was found, including the use of denial, repression, projection, and disregard of reality. Faith healing does not result in alternative symptom formation, nor does it produce significant changes in life style. The primary function of faith healing is not to reduce symptoms, but to reinforce a magical belief system that is consonant with the subculture of these subjects.

This is advantageous for the cult leader. Cult leaders seem to be highly adroit in the induction of altered states of consciousness of their followers. Modern brain research seems to indicate that each of the brain's hemispheres has separate neurological functions. Moreover, each side of the brain is seen as having distinctly different ways of apprehending reality. Eastern thought has long insisted that there are separate realities. If this is valid, then it would appear that each hemisphere participates in a reality different from the other. The left hemisphere is rational and analytic. The right speaks the language of movement, imagery, and metaphor. By utilizing such tactics as "loading the language" as Lifton (1963) calls it, the cult authorities may begin to block out the critical faculties of the left hemisphere. By speaking in metaphoric phrases and cliches that relate to the usually unsophisticated and undeveloped right hemisphere of most individuals, they gradually take over the thought processes of their flock. According to Lifton (1963):

> The language of the totalist environment is characterized by the thought-terminating cliche. The most far-reaching and complex of human problems are

compressed into brief, highly reductive, definitive sounding phrases easily memorized and easily expressed. These become the start and finish of any ideological analysis. . . . For an individual person, the effect of the language of ideological totalism can be summed up in one word: constriction. He is, so to speak, linguistically deprived; and since language is so central to all human experience, his capacities for thinking and feeling are immensely narrowed. . . [his] uneasiness may result in a retreat into a rigid orthodoxy in which an individual shouts the ideological jargon all the louder in order to demonstrate his conformity, hide his own dilemma and his despair, and protect himself from the fear and guilt he would feel should he attempt to use words and phrases other than the correct ones" (pp 429–430).

Moreover, cult rituals and practices are frequently psychologically deleterious and physically dangerous. According to one ex-People's Temple member, Grace Stoen, Jones was able to get away with so much because the oppressiveness of his demands were increased very gradually over time (Conway and Siegelman, 1979). According to Mills (1979), Jones was a "genius" at stripping the defenses of his parishioners at all-night "catharsis" sessions.* During these evenings members would be accused of offenses, humiliated and beaten. The accusations and punishment began gradually and then increased. Anyone who expressed displeasure would also be called forth for punishment. Other cult practices involved the use of psychedelic and mood-altering drugs, deficient diets, and sensory and sleep deprivation. Taken together, these practices draw the cult follower into an induced, dependent, fugue state.

In short, the use of tactics such as "loading the language," skillfully phrased metaphors, and physical and emotional deprivation renders the follower highly accessible to suggestion and command. This comes about as a cult member is caught up in a series of existential paradoxes imposed by the interface of both overstimulation (eg, repetition of ritual and doctrine in sessions and church services which are experienced as unending) and understimulation (eg, intellectual and physical deprivation). In this paradoxical climate the follower is susceptible to interhemispheric brain conflict. One hemisphere inhibits the other in an attempt to repress a contradictory perception. It is as if the follower is not able to ascertain whether he is rejoicing in paradise or suffering in hell.

Nevertheless, for the closed-minded, poorly integrated person Jones was an attractive figure. He could present himself without doubt or trepidation. His followers required a leader like Jones to give them some semblance of reality—as tenuous as that reality might have been. It is small wonder that under such conditions the followers of the People's Temple accepted such typical absurdities of Jim Jones as: "I resent the implication that you make that I am unfair. If you really believed in the cause you would accept my decisions about these things and not expect me to explain them" (Mills, 1979, p 158).

Mills' book (1979) clearly documents that Jones' followers had sufficient evidence of his hyposcrisy, cowardice, duplicity, instability, and malevolence. But they apparently went to considerable efforts to deny what they saw and what they thought. Fear, punishment, contradiction, poverty, and continual labor

---

*The adroit use of psychological techniques is confirmed by Hill (1968), a psychiatrist who has indicated aspects of group psychotherapy and psychodrama used by a religious cult he investigated.
†A recent study by Deutsch (1980) indicates that profound submission of cult members can occur even in the absence of enforced isolation from outside influences, elaborate strategies of persuasion, and threats against those who wish to leave.

were the backbone of Jim Jones' utopia.† It was a paradoxical world in which Jones enticed his parishioners with his virtuous ideology and compassionate charisma and then humiliated and reduced them to a state of abject religious serf-dom (Krause, 1978). Lifton (1963) indicates that what has been referred to as "brain control" becomes possible when a leader has complete control of communication in an environment. Support for the hegemony of the cult over its followers comes from the study of Ungerleider and Wellisch (1979) which indicates that forcible removal of followers of a cult is extremely difficult if they have belonged to the group for more than a year. In a talk before a committee of the Vermont legislature, John Clark, a psychiatrist who has treated several ex-members of cults, documented the cognitive deterioration he had found in these young people: "Formerly, bright, fluent and creative individuals are rendered incapable of the use of irony or of metaphor and they speak with a smaller carefully constructed vocabulary filled with cliches and stereotyped ideas" (Stoner and Parke, 1979, p 328).

THE PARANOID LEADER

Throughout the reports of those who knew Jones over time there is a consistent and insidious theme. Jones was typically involved in duplicity, coercion, and rank denigration of others. He lied to people upon meeting them. He lied to and manipulated them after having favorably impressed them. He continued to lie to, manipulate, and humiliate people once they became his followers and questioned the contradictions in his practices. But more importantly, Jones even lied to and humiliated those who did his bidding devotedly and without question. What seems central was Jones' extraordinary need for control. He had the personal charm, cleverness, and seductiveness to impress others favorably and to get his way. But this was not enough! What Jones was trying to control was, then, internal—although in his accentuated need to conceal his vulnerabilities, perhaps to even himself, he directed it at external objects and circumstances. Jones, throughout his leadership of the People's Temple, seems to have been in the process of going out of control. He tried to flee his gradual decompensation. He left Indianapolis because he claimed having a vision of nuclear holocaust. He moved to Ukiah, California. He purported having divine revelation that northern California would be safe from a bomb blast and nuclear fallout. He then left Ukiah for San Francisco because he felt insufficiently appreciated. San Francisco, he said, is more politically relevant. Then he fled the United States for Guyana upon hearing rumors that *New West* magazine intended to publish an investigative story about the People's Temple. But Jones was grandiose enough to believe that he could flee without surrendering possessions, power, or control. These endeavors required considerable manic energy. What strikes us in Jones' endeavors is the liability of his moods and the wide fluctuations of his demeanor. At moments he appeared as kind and sensitive. At others he was shown to be brutal and demanding complete obedience. These behaviors cannot be attributed simply to the amphetamines and heroin he is reported to have used regularly. The progression of Jones' decompensation is obvious. As the final days at Jonestown drew nearer, Jones' moods seemed to shift increasingly more abruptly, going from one extreme to another in a moment. Whatever Jones was trying to control seemed to have overpowered him. I am not trying to develop a demoniac theory to explain the events at Jonestown. The duplicity, coercion, and humiliation Jones inflicted upon others were his own internal processes at war. We may speculate that they were shaped by unrealistic demands of him from his early object relationships to save them from the ills and offenses of the world. We are told that his father was an unemployed member of the Ku Klux Klan, who had been gassed in World War I. His mother was a fanciful dreamer. Nugent (1979) reports:

> Even when she was a factory worker she had time to spin fantasies during the monotonous bus rides each day to her job twenty miles away. In one of her daydreams she was a young anthropologist working with primitive tribes in Africa, trying to decide between career and marriage. Then from the far side of a river, her dead mother called to her and told her that she was to bear a son who would right the wrongs of the world. She soon accepted a marriage proposal, bore a son, and was convinced that James Warren Jones was the Messiah. That dream, told often by Jones in solemn tones with his mother in the audience, is best understood when one understands that Lynetta Jones also believed herself to be the reincarnation of Mark Twain (p 8).

The ironic and tragic observation is that Jim Jones' early object relationships led him to pursue that course of action where others would also come to regard Jones as a messiah who could cure them of the ills and the offenses of the world. Neither his early object relationships nor his later followers may have been able to tolerate an ordinary human as their guide. In the CBS docu-drama about Jonestown, a reformed prostitute is heard to say about Jim Jones: "Everything that Dad does is all right as long as he keeps on being a saint" (*Newsweek*, April 21, 1980).

Paranoid leaders operate from a matrix in which they and their followers are simultaneously in the process of active indoctrination of the other. While we are given sufficient evidence of Jones' manipulations and "bewitching" persuasiveness, we also see that his followers are people who have rather denigrative views of themselves. They appear extraordinarily eager to be Jones' subjects, if not his victims. Many of them were, undoubtedly, persons with strongly repressed rage, who were seeking a figure to give them permission to enact consciously disavowed aspects of their character without their having to acknowledge their motives. In short, Jim Jones served the disavowed purposes of his followers, no less than they served his.

Tragically, Jim Jones could look into the hearts of others but could not see into his own heart. In a sense, what led to the tragedy at Guyana was that Jones served a cruel internal master whom he could never actually locate in order to silence or appease. He bore this dilemma tragically. He viewed anyone who defected from or criticized the People's Temple as part of a conspiracy aimed at destroying him and his mission. According to Krause (1978), Jones exclaimed at such times: "Threat, threat, threat of extinction. I wish I wasn't born at times. I understand hate; love and hate are very close. They can have me" (p 48).

SUFFERING AND FANATICISM

One striking characteristic which markedly contrasted the People's Temple with other modern religious cults was that the temple was comprised of a wide cross-section of socioeconomic and age groups. Unlike the other cults, the People's Temple had a large population of elderly members and married couples with children. How do we account for this? Jim Jones' ability to look into the hearts of others, wedded to his unctuous rhetorical skills, enabled him to offer a most perverse yet profoundly attractive appeal to many different kinds of followers. Jones reproached his parishioners for their materialism. He espoused the notion that suffering is a sign of human courage. His appeal had reverent resonance with Judeo-Christian ethics. The martyrologies are replete with descriptions of how early Christians waited for their tortures, longed for their suffering, and "how they joyously sang hymns to their last breath" (Reik, 1949, p 355). Jones manipulated the fears and guilt of his followers to assume that a person is not morally respectable unless he or she is suffering. His poor and minority parishioners, already apprenticed in toil, frustration, and limitation, could be conferred with respectability with Jones' pontifications on suffering. On the other hand, his middle-class and professional followers were continually forced to go in search of hurt in order to justify their entitlement to legitimacy in their being a "have" rather than an "have not." This endeavor can gradually take over the intentionality of the person, as Sennett (1980) has recently indicated in a probing analysis of authority: "[T]he need to legitimize one's beliefs in terms of an injury or suffering to which one has been subjected attaches people more and more to the injuries themselves. [As a result], they conspire at their own suffering."

By typically sowing mistrust and fear, Jones turned his followers against one another. It was to Jones they came for redress. Jones also manipulated the delusional system of his parishioners about the forces surrounding the People's Temple. The identity of the conspirators changed from day to day for Jones in accord with his erratic world view. Not only do delusional people tend to prophesy to fulfill their claims but also we cannot fail to be aware that for the first time in history mankind has the means to totally annihilate the world. To the authoritarian mind anyone is a likely suspect—certainly organizations like the CIA and FBI which may be involved in carrying out clandestine activities. Jones induced in his parishioners the fear that through their identification with him they had become targets of the conspirators. It is understandable that under these conditions Jones would be at least half believed and his frightened parishioners would turn to him for divine revelation and deliverance when he reported that he had a dark vision that: "all black people in America are going into concentration camps or be hung—except for those who stay with me. I will protect you when the time comes" (Mills, 1979, p 98).

Slowly, but irreversibly, the People's Temple had become a fanatic cult in which the individuals who comprised the temple lost touch with what they intended for themselves as purposive beings.

The acts of fanaticism are evoked from profound despair. They come from a desire to achieve deeds not possible by ordinary effort in the normal course of events. The fanatic is an individual whose consciousness has been accentuated or manipulated so that he comes to identify with a group whose ideology and values and, frequently, political causes and physical actions are in imagined or actual conflict with other groups. Therefore, membership in these groups integrally involves risk and jeopardy to the fanatic's way of being, if not to his life, as well.

The natural question is whether fanaticism involves courage or a flight to avoid profound inner turmoil. For example, on April 15, 73 CE, nearly 1000 Jewish zealots, defenders of the fortress Masada, took their own lives rather than be taken prisoner and submit themselves to the yoke of the besieging Roman legions. Were they courageous or simply fanatic? It seems to me that there is a clear difference between fanaticism and courage. Whereas the source of courage is experienced as the accentuated sense of self, fanatic identification contributes to a loss of sense of self. There was nothing heroic about Jones' followers. They were timid, devoid of passion and purpose. They came alive only when Jones gave them permission. Fanatic acts occur in climates in which the self as an intentional being is forced to be denied because the self is experienced as evil and worthless. The positive and desirable aspects of the self are split off through projective identification onto an ego ideal in the person of a charismatic leader, a cause, or an ideology. The denigrative self phenomenologically experiences its own "bad" self as having to be sacrificed or destroyed in order that the "good" self—now psychically disowned from the "bad" self—can survive and reign. The courage to break away from this de-egoitation process is usually lacking in individuals who find their way into religious cults. The harsh superego introjects of the phenomenological self caught up in fanaticism claim that if the self cannot be all powerful and all knowing, then the self should not survive. Only the omniscient and omnipotent leader is worthy of survival. Thus, what the self cannot achieve in reality it magically aspires to realize in its identification with a cause.

For many youth, the cult experience is the last defense before psychological dissolution or even suicide. Horton (1973) reports cases where the ability of the subject to conjure up mystical states similar to the presence Jones attempted to elicit in his parishioners, appeared to lessen, if not altogether assuage suicidal ideation. Many came to the People's Temple out of extreme states of desperation and loneliness. Jones understood this well. He continually espoused themes of suffering, forced obligation, and vengeance. Jones became the repository of the projective identifications of his followers. As such he reflected the suffering and stunted ambitions inchoate in his followers.

THE CHARISMATIC LEADER AND HIS FOLLOWERS

The seductive danger of viewing events of massive human exploitation is to attempt to explain them by means of demoniac causation. Just as we would prefer to learn that human disasters were caused by natural phenomena, so we create inhuman monsters to distance ourselves from our own feared malevolent and destructive proclivities. In the mind of the primitive any attempt to understand the natural universe is a violation against the powers of the universe. In the primitive mind it is more efficacious and proper to barter for the protection of the unknown through homage and sacrifice than to seek to understand and master these forces. In a similar way, modern man tries to master his fate through denial. In creating a monster of Jim Jones and other erratic, charismatic figures, we have returned to a primitive mentality in which we pay homage to forces we do not comprehend. Jim Jones was not worth such adoration! Unless we recognize Jones as the frail being that he was, we cannot recognize that the disturbance demonstrated by Jones is native to us all. If we cannot recognize ourselves, we cannot come to terms with our disturbed motives. In short, it is both erroneous and dangerous to view the followers of a charismatic leader as passive victims. They need to be seen as actively and continually reindoctrinating themselves to wishes that conflict with common sense. The monster created of Jim Jones was the repository of the collective denied wishes of his followers. Eric Hoffer (1951) in his classical study of the true believer said:

> No matter how vital we think the role of leader in the rise of a mass movement, there is no doubt that the leader cannot create the conditions which make the rise of a movement possible. He cannot conjure a movement out of the void.

There had to be an eagerness to follow and obey, and an intense dissatisfaction with things as they are, before the movement and leader can make their appearance" (p 103).

To enable us to understand the complex chemistry between the charismatic leader and his followers, we can do no better than heed Weston LaBarre, an anthropologist who has intensively investigated religious consciousness. LaBarre (1980) writes:

Charisma, which seems to be a "supernatural *rightness*" stemming from the charismatic individual, is merely the emotional welcomeness of his message, *deja vu* in the prepotent unconscious wishes of each communicant. . . (p 29). . . . a large component of every religion is wishful belief. . . (p 49). . . . The *mysterium tremendum et fascinosum* in religion is therefore human, not divine. . . . Every religion is the dramatization on a cosmic scale of the fears, loves, and longings the child felt in his experience of his parents in the nuclear family (p 50). . . . "charisma," that supernatural animal magnetism that seems to steam compellingly from the sacred vatic personage or religious innovator, is really a quite secular circumstance psychologically. The compelling force comes not from the great man as he voices new supernatural truth: he speaks only to the powerful anticommonsensical fantasy already present in the unconscious wish of each communicant. . . . The voice of the vatic has an "uncanny" consistency with each one's private wish; . . . the charismatic leader is the liberator who unlocks the hidden wish; hence some psychopathic leaders can release psychopathic behavior in mobs that is usually repressed in the individuals composing the mob. When individuals emotionally abdicate the ego functions of reality testing in favor of wishful belief, they sometimes also abandon the superego repressions in their behavior. The leader of the mob and the mob itself mutually sanction each one's mob behavior. The psychological voltage of the leader's charisma is the exact measure of his emotional appeal (p 52).

The leader is as much a creature of his followers as they are of him. We can see then that a leader, regardless of his charisma, or more properly, because of it, can only evoke behavior already present in his followers. Indeed, his followers will go to considerable labor, as Festinger and his associates (1956) have documented in their investigation of prophecy-seeking cults, to believe in their leaders and their dogma, despite the failure of the leaders' predictions. The leader in a cult serves the purposes of those who fear to live courageously. Mills (1979) reports that there were perhaps hundreds of persons inside and outside of the People's Temple who knew directly or indirectly of Jones' sadism and cruelty. "[B]ut not one of them would speak out publicly. Each person had, in some way, been silenced by his threat or by his money" (p 51).

People believe what they find convenient to believe. A close examination of Jones' life shows that, rather than being the social reformer he claimed to be, he was for most of his life a consummate racist (Krause, 1978). To understand his appeal it is necessary to see how he wove together with impressive showmanship appeals to the yearnings and the vanities of those whose cooperation he wished to have: "To the religious, Jones offered religion; to the ideological, he offered politics; to the ignorant and gullible, he offered miracles (Krause, 1978, p 34).

Above all, Jones provided for his followers a meaning of life. Mills (1979) reports that from time to time she and her husband would ask themselves what had they done with their lives before they had met Jim Jones. Their answer was that their lives had had no meaning until Jones had instilled "a sense of purpose" in them. He had given them a reason to exist, and they dedicated their financial and emotional resources to please him. Mills (1979) states: "We believed that he loved us. We were certain that as long as we stayed in his group our lives would continue to be blissful (p 131).

Was Jim Jones' fatherly love powerful enough to sustain all of the bright, articulate, well-educated professionals that flocked to the People's Temple? Probably not, but Jones held other attractions for them. Nugent (1979) reports:

> By 1968 Jones' movement had attracted almost a hundred and fifty new members, mostly white and young and with specialties and skills that the Temple needed. There were accountants, writers, printers, social workers, lab technicians, executive secretaries, teachers, and street organizers. They also knew how to handle hustling, ghetto riots, peace marches, draft dodging, and even jail. . . . They understood politicians, and had studied Nietzsche, Freud, Marx, and Engels. Some held Phi Beta Kappa keys; some had done graduate work abroad; others were classical musicians, journalists, and students working on doctorates. . . . These were the talents Jones could master to move into every important structure in the city of San Francisco (p 26).

Without the recruitment of these bright, talented young people the People's Temple might have not survived to reach Guyana. It was from this crop of eager, young talent that Jones selected his most loyal and able lieutenants. Hoffer (1951) indicates that:

> The uncanny powers of a leader manifest themselves not so much in the hold he or she has on the masses as in his ability to dominate and almost bewitch a small group of able men. These men must be fearless, proud, intelligent and capable of organizing and running large-scale undertakings and yet they must submit wholly to the will of the leader, draw their inspiration and driving force from him, and glory in their submission (p 106).

It was not the religious appeal which attracted these talented lieutenants. It was the cult's purported commitment to action under the banner of social justice. Nugent (1979) tells us that:

> For the young new members, it was a time of tremendous excitement. They were being given two things sorely missing in their lives: challenge and responsibility. It was like working on a political campaign with a charismatic leader who drew rousing hysterical cheers from the crowd. Jones satisfied their egos; cheers for him in an audience confirmed his lieutenants' ability to make things happen. . . . They were in a twenty-four hour strategy room making monumental decisions for their world. To them, their world was *the* world (p 17).

If their world had become *the* world, it is then understandable how Jones' delusional system could have become socially contagious to all those who needed Jim Jones to express their fears and their ambitions. In Congressman Ryan's confrontation with the People's Temple, Jones appeared to act out his followers' helplessness and rage. Jones' behavior seemed to be exclaiming: "By calling me bad *you* make me bad. Therefore, I will hurt myself and others and it will be *your* fault."

While the violent, deluded behaviors Jones acted out for his followers are potential in all of us, some personalities are, undoubledly, more susceptible to their expression than are others. LaBarre (1980) indicates that:

>True believers are authoritarian personalities because they are infantile dependents on the divine authority of the Shaman, not mature assessors of their own judgments. Fundamentalists abjectly depend on part tribal culture, not on their own contemporary common sense. Every fundamentalism is an intellectual lobotomy (p 52).

Authoritarian personalities are cognitively closed-minded and defensive. Their personal strategies are largely inflexible and are generally isolated from one another; that is, authoritarian people often hold beliefs that are logically inconsistent with one another. They seem incapable or unwilling to withstand high degrees of anxiety or cognitive disorganization, which are inherent in situations that are cognitively complex, ambiguous, or involve considerable uncertainty of outcome. Because anxiety is easily aroused in such situations, they seek situations where quick, easy, and absolutely "correct" behavior can be readily anticipated (Goldberg, 1980). These personalities are ripe for charismatic leaders who appear to hold, like Jim Jones, unswaying conviction in their belief system.

This view is supported by the few empirical studies conducted on members of religious cults. Galanter and his associates (1979) employed psychiatric interviews and psychological tests to examine 20 members of the Unification Church. They found that their subjects had experienced a fair amount of psychological difficulty before joining the church. Thirty-nine percent felt that they had had serious emotional problems in the past. This had led 30% of professional help and 6% had been hospitalized. Moreover, 23% reported serious drug problems in the past. In a second study, Galanter and Buckley (1978) found that 38% of the Divine Light Mission had sought professional help for psychiatric disturbances before joining the mission, 9% had been hospitalized for emotional problems, while 27% had been arrested at some time prior to joining the cult.

In a study by Ungerleider and Wellisch (1979), consisting of psychiatric interviews and psychological testing, the investigators found that 50 members and former members of a variety of religious cults, who had contacted the investigators about the issue of deprograming, indicated difficulty with impulse control in several areas and attendant superego deficits. According to the investigators, the cults appear to serve as externalized superego substitutes. These difficulties were particularly important in terms of managing hostility. The trend toward concern over impulses and dependent use of alcohol and other drugs might be viewed as a reflection of frustrated oral dependency needs. Test results indicate that these impulses were dealt with by overconventionalism, repression, denial, and lack of insight. All of these can easily be seen to be incorporated in a cult life-style. The life-style in the People's Temple was forged from Jim Jones' situational morality.

THE NEW MORALITY AND SEXUAL POLITICS

Mills (1979) tells us that Jim Jones had taught his followers a new set of ethics: " 'The end justifies the means.' He also called it 'situational ethics.' The way it was translated to the church members was 'you do whatever Jim says because he knows what is needed for the cause' " (p 147).

The followers of the People's Temple professed to believe in social justice and human worth. Yet they permitted Jones and his cohorts to brutalize and humiliate them, their spouses, their children, friends, and neighbors. They gave in to Jones' relativistic morality. They lacked the courage to maintain their values and to insist that there are some things which are inherently right and others which are undeniably wrong. What was the payoff for the toil, suffering, humiliation, and dependency that these followers derived from their identification with Jones "new morality"? Mills (1979) reports that she and her husband were amazed at how little disagreement there was among the members of the People's Temple. Jones had virtually taken the existential difficulties out of their lives.

For most people securing meaningful and intimate relationships with others is a difficult endeavor. According to one investigative reporter, Nugent (1979), sexual liberation was the central dogma of Jim Jones' new morality. To understand the power that Jones held over his followers, the issue of sexual politics in messianic cults must be examined. Jones used sexual tactics and programs to dominate, blackmail, and humiliate his followers. Sexual politics, of course, is not singularly involved with physical intercourse. It includes all forms of power tactics, such as seduction, sadism, brutality, and humiliation to control the minds, bodies, and spirits of other people. Mills (1979) tells us that no follower was allowed to refuse a direct order from Jones. In Jones' doctrines there is considerable attention given not only to his parishioners' belief system but also how they feel, are reacted to, and treated in terms of their bodies and body images. Plato had indicated that the great error of his day was the treatment of the person in which the body was separated from the soul. Jones also recognized the tremendous power he could derive from his parishioners by manipulating their body images. Having done this, he was able to establish himself as the only legitimate object of sexual desire and activity in the cult. Jones had a secretary who arranged his sexual affairs. At the same time he would order brutal punishment for his parishioners for sexual activity they involved themselves in which Jones did not arrange.

Metaphorically, Jones demonstrated that he was the only person of worth in the sect. By utilizing unconventional and bizarre practices—whether by forbidding all sexual activities in the temple or by dictating precisely what kinds of sexual activities members of the temple were to have with persons he chose for them—Jones ensured that his temple followers were increasingly denied the integrity, autonomy, and ownership of their own bodies and how they were to function and interact with others. These prerogatives were taken over by Jones and those he appointed until the final scene in which he ordered his flock to commit mass suicide and dictated the manner and the sentiments which they were to experience in their demise. Reik (1949), as have other behavioral scientists, has revealed religious martyrdom as a manifestation of sexual masochism.

Sexual politics is most prevailing in societies in times of social unrest and uncertainty of values. For many individuals joining a cult is a means to avoid issues of intimacy and sexuality. In a study of the members of the Unification Church, Galanter and his associates (1979) report that 86% of the cult members studied felt that people who were not members of the Unification Church should "avoid thinking about sex" as they did. A leader of the Unification Church in an article in the Washington Star (Castelli, 1980) stated that: "Romantic love is a recent innovation and it's a failure."

Whether or not a particular cult encourages sexual promiscuity (as does the Church of God), discourages it (as does the Unification Church), or manipulates sexual relationships (as did the People's Temple), the lack of freedom in allowing their followers to function according to their own preferences is a manifestation of sexual politics. In sexual political regimes followers are relieved of the burden of choice and need not address their fears about their own capacities for caring and intimacy. In these regimes cult leaders become heir to sources of tremendous energy and power. However, to create a bond and an emotional valence with his followers, as LaBarre has indicated, a charismatic leader must have common ground with his followers. Both Jones and his followers seem to have been unable to acknowledge their fears of intimacy. A self-liberated leader may have freed them up to examine these fears. Tragically, despite Jim Jones' doctrine of sexual liberation, he apparently massively denied his own fears of imtimacy.

THE SEARCH FOR ONE'S DOUBLE

Many religious cults have come and gone but none in modern times have erupted into the tragedy of Jonestown. What was the tragic flaw in the Jonestown cult? Hoffer (1951) points to this flaw in the charismatic leader when he indicates the qualities of leadership which sustain a social movement:

> One of the striking traits of the successful mass movement leader is his readiness to imitate both friend and foe, both past and contemporary models. . . . This excessive capacity for imitation indicates that the hero is without a fully developed and realized self. There is much in him that is rudimentary and suppressed. His strength lies in his blind spots and in plugging all outlets but one (pp 107-108).

One of the earliest versions of the Narcissus legend comes from Plato. According to this myth, before the advent of the present race of man there was a far more noble group of beings. They seemed perfect in every way. They are frequently depicted as a symbol of science's four arms, four legs, two heads; indeed, they were two beings combined perfectly into one. Unlike ordinary beings who walk upright, this race conducted locomotion by performing cartwheels. The gods became infuriated by this race because of their self-aggrandizement. The gods initially were to destroy them. But because they were such a beautiful race of beings, they decided instead to cleave each being into two parts. These two distinct parts resemble what are now man and woman. Thus these beings have vanished from the earth. Their tormented souls however, are forever longing to find their other half—their soulmate, the companion of their anima or animus.

At its core, the myth of the double reveals struggles and conflicts of the most basic precursors of personal identity and selfhood. Interestingly, to my awareness, only one psychoanalytic investigator has pursued the theme of the double in his work. In 1925 Otto Rank published *The Double, A Psychoanalytic Study* (reprinted in 1971). In this work Rank examines myth and folk legend from the egregious Narcissus to the tormented writings of such authors as Dostoyevsky, Poe, Wilde, De Maupassant, and Hoffman. In his survey Rank sought the source of the deep fascination with a notion of a duplicate self. Rank regarded the double or imagined twin as a manifestation of and attempted resolution of puzzling contradictions and agonizing inner struggles between the fear of life and the fear of death, the paradoxic rapport and contradiction between love of self and love of others.

We cannot understand the nature of courage if we view the self as a solitary and complete entity. In the act of courage the self tries to transcend itself to reach out and rescue the disavowed and denied aspects of self. The notion of the double relates to this endeavor. I introduce this theme because I believe that what Jim Jones was trying to control and could not was his double—those aspects of his self he wished to come to terms with but could not. Because he apparently lacked the courage to examine these inner conflicts, he projected them onto his willing subjects. His futile struggle to define his own identity was manifested in the sexual politics Jones practiced in the People's Temple. While Jones sanctioned bizarre sexual experimentation, at the same time he discouraged the demonstration and expression of genuine caring and intimacy among members of the temple. Let us examine the essence of the sexual experience. At its core sexual endeavor contains a wish to merge with one's other (one's double)—the denied, unacceptable, unattainable parts of one's self. In the sexual act one may wish to truly discover and realize one's self through the stranger. This involves courage, for profound sexual exploration may evoke considerable anxiety and trepidation. Courage and intimacy are closely related. Acts of intimacy demonstrate a willingness to suspend certainty and allow the self to plunge into the unknown, to experience, in unison, that which the self cannot experience by itself. It prototypically leads to birth, hope, and possibility. Jim Jones, and other charismatic cult leaders, we suspect, cannot trust the other in such experiences. Thus, Jones must humiliate and denigrate those with whom he is intimate and sexual, lest they overwhelm him by asking what he cannot give them and, consequently, he be destroyed for his inadequacy.

Intimacy with another requires the capacity to be intimate with one's own self. Having a relationship with one's own depths allows the self to have a relationship with another self who is allowed to have his or her own mystery. Jones could not tolerate that his followers had thoughts and feelings of their own which he did not monitor or control. Caring is essential to intimacy. Courage is necessary in caring in order to permit the other to experience the self as the self "is." Courage is involved in the self's "letting go" to permit to emerge that which the self is experiencing at the present moment—in terms of values, desires, and vulnerability—as the self constitutes itself in the world. This process of "letting go" requires a caring for oneself without the defensive–protective stance of constraining other selves in relating to the self. Jones would not tolerate his parishioners regarding him as a mere human. He programed miracles, miracle cures, and other spectacular events to ensure a divine presence. As a leader who would not openly examine and address his human frailties, he offered an impossible role model for his followers as well as for himself. Mills (1979) tells us:

> To Jim Jones, life was a bore. His only source of pleasure was observing his followers' total devotion to him. At first, he was content just to observe us loving and respecting him. His need for pleasure became insatiable, and to derive enjoyment he wanted to watch us as we willingly suffered for him.

> The only true sexual stimulation he received was as a voyeur, and he eventually took delight in humiliating us as he made us undress and perform deviant sex acts with one another.

> Next his pleasure came from pitting us against one another, in wrestling and boxing matches, and even in flogging.

> Finally, his total pleasure came from watching his members drink poison to die for him. He had created his ultimate spectator sport (p 319).

Probably what saved the Mills' was their "closeness of mind and body." They had made a pact between them that they would never stop speaking with one another and never stop making love with one another (Mills, 1979). Perhaps their intimacy saved them.

THE TRUE PROPHET

It would be instructive to contrast the modern charismatic cult leader with such prophets of antiquity as Jesus, Socrates, Buddha, and Confucius. What is most impressive of the latter was the demonstration of deep concern for their disciples. Jaspers (1962) tells us that their basic masculine character was natural and striking. In contrast, we can never be sure who the mercurial and pretentious Jim Jones really was. Each of the prophets mentioned above presented himself as ordinary, not as a special being. Each was concerned with the development of selfhood. They guided their disciples in examining their lives but resisted leading them into social action. They appeared not to regard their mission as telling their followers how to live their lives. Instead, they patiently demonstrated by personal example and fostered a climate in which their disciples could question for themselves how they conducted their lives—permitting them to come to their own conclusions. Even as a believer in the paramount value of the life hereafter, Jesus never appeared to have asked his followers to sacrifice their mortal existence or to have minimized the importance of the present world. Above all, prophets like Socrates, Jesus, Buddha, and Confucius did not teach their disciples to hate or sanction flight from those who opposed them. Thus, we can see that Sidney Carton's act was a courageous one rather than a fanatic act. His motive was one of love rather than hate. In the end, it is this quality and motive which differentiates courage from fanaticism.

The fanatic is a follower who identifies with a charismatic leader who hates himself in other people, who rejects himself in others, who seeks to destroy himself through others. Because of his accentuated need to condone himself, he cannot forgive others. His need to deny his own self-hatred leads to the destruction of others. Jaspers (1962) indicates for all true prophets human love was unlimited and universal. Thus, although he may feel fear and doubt (as Jesus did on the cross) or resolute enlightenment (as Socrates did on choosing his existential death), he never pushes his people to validate his beliefs or to do what he, himself, will not. The true prophet does not need this dubious proof. By not presenting himself as all knowing and all powerful, the prophet gives the power of transformation to his flock. By permitting them to become transformed by their own chosen ordeal rather than those he requires of them, he permits them to become as powerful as he. In contrast, leaders like Jones require their flock to blindly follow their doctrines in order to validate their worth as gods, prophets, or men of worth. It is not surprising that we are told that Jim Jones rationalized and excused himself from token doses of ordeal and punishment that he demanded his parishioners, including children, bear in inordinate amounts without complaint.

In short, the true prophet asks his followers to courageously examine their lives. Courage, in this sense, is to know one's own limitations, to accept one's self as less than perfect, to live to the best of one's ability, and to come caringly together with others to heal the wounds of loneliness and dread of man's existence.

CONCLUSION

A unidimensional explanation of a social phenomenon—that a leader coerces his followers into bizarre and irrational behavior—is simplistic and erroneous. For the reader the most tragic consequence of examining the advent of the People's Temple is to come away believing that what happened at Jonestown was caused by Jim Jones' paranoid psychosis. There were similarities between Jonestown and the European holocaust. Adolph Hitler and Jim Jones, for somewhat different reasons, in different eras, and to different dimensions, were both used by and used their followers to commit atrocities. Leaders like Jones are erected by followers who are unwilling to examine their own duplicity and malevolent urges. The postulation of a demoniac theory, therefore, is a scapegoat ploy. In so doing we fail to understand that if men and women exist without the courage to live as they intend and do not restrain others from committing acts contrary to their conscience—Jonestown and the European holocaust will not be historical anomolies, but chapters in an unending book of atrocities.

BIBLIOGRAPHY

Blumer H: Collective behavior, in Lee AM (ed): *New Outline of the Principles of Sociology.* New York, Barnes and Noble, 1951.

Castelli J: Moonies still search for respectability. *Washington Star,* July 16, 1980.

Cantril H: *The Psychology of Social Movements.* New York, Wiley, 1941.

Conway F, Siegelman J: *Snapping.* New York, Dell, 1979.

Cushman P, Moses LS: Cults, religious needs and mind control. *The National Jewish Monthly,* May, 1980.

Deutsch A: Tenacity of attachment to a cult leader: A psychiatric perspective. *Am J Psychiatry* 1980;137(12):1569-1573.

Elridge S: *Fundamentals of Sociology.* New York, Crowell, 1950.

Edwards AL: The signs of incipient fascism. *J Abnorm Soc Psych* 1944;39:301-316.

Festinger L, Riecken HW, Schacter S: *When Prophecy Fails.* Minneapolis, University of Minnesota Press, 1956.

Galanter M, Buckley P: Evangelical religion and meditation: Psychotherapeutic effects. *J Nerv Ment Dis* 1978;166(10):685-691.

Galanter M, Rabkin R, Rabkin J, et al: The Moonies: A psychological study of conversion and membership in a contemporary religious sect. *Am J Psychiatry* 1979;136(2):165-170.

Goldberg C: *In Defense of Narcissism—The Creative Self in Search of Meaning.* New York, Gardner Press, 1980.

Goldberg C: A proposed field study of a social movement—An investigation of a student protest group. Unpublished manuscript.

Hill W: Some aspects of group psychotherapy and psychodrama used in a modern religious cult. *Group Psychotherapy* 1968;21(4):214-218.

Hoffer E: *The True Believer: Thoughts on the Nature of Mass Movements.* New York, New American Library, 1951.

Horton P: The mystical experience as a suicide preventive. *Am J Psychiatry* 1973;130(3): 294-296.

James W: *Varieties of Religious Experience.* New York, Modern Library, 1929.

Jaspers K: *Socrates, Buddha, Confucius, Jesus: The Paradigmatic Individuals.* New York, Harcourt, Brace and World, 1962.

King CW: *Social Movements in the United States.* New York, Random House, 1956.

Krause CA: *Guyana Massacre: The Eyewitness Account.* New York, Berkley, 1978.

LaBarre W: *Culture in Context.* Durham NC, Duke University Press, 1980.

Lifton RJ: *Thought Reform and the Psychology of Totalism.* New York, WW Norton, 1963.

Lindsey R: Can California control "sham" religious sects? And should it? *New York Times,* July 20, 1980.

Maier NR: The role of frustration in social movements. *Psychol Rev* 1942;49:586–599.

May R: *The Courage to Create.* New York, Bantam, 1978.

Mills J: *Six Years with God: Life Inside Rev. Jim Jones Peoples Temple.* New York, A and W Publishers, 1979.

Newsweek. CBS's Jonestown: Making of a "savior." April 21, 1980.

Nugent JP: *White Night: The Story of What Happened Before and Beyond Jonestown.* New York, Rawson, Wade, 1979.

Pattison EM, Lapins NA, Doerr HA: Faith healing: A study of personality and function. *J Nerv Ment Dis* 1973;156(6):397–409.

Rank O: *The Double—A Psychoanalytic Study.* New York, New American Library, 1971.

Reik T: *Masochism in Modern Man.* New York, Farrar, Straus and Co, 1949.

Sennett R: *Authority.* New York, Knopf, 1980.

Stoner C, Parke J: *All God's Children: The Cult Experience—Salvation or Slavery?* New York, Penguin Books, 1979.

Swartz J: Another sort of terrorism. *American Psychological Association Monitor* 1980;11(6):2.

Ungerleider JT, Wellisch DK: Coercive persuasion (brainwashing), religious cults, and deprogramming. *Am J Psychiatry* 1979;136(3):279–282.

CHAPTER

11

The Drug Rehabilitation Program:
Cults in Formation?

JAMES REBHAN

S ince the 1950s with the formation of Synanon, an addiction treatment community founded in California dedicated to the rehabilitation of drug addicts, many similar institutions have emerged. A sense of hope and optimism abounded with the initial success of Synanon-like programs. Much has been written both pro and con in regard to what many refer to as "therapeutic communities." One of the many criticisms that emerged from patients who prematurely leave these programs is a feeling of being "brainwashed" or "programed." Now some 20 years later we do in fact see some very interesting similarities between these types of programs and quasi-religious cults.

The purpose of this chapter is to explore the processes at work in these programs. In order to do a thorough job, a number of issues will be explored, including similarities and differences between the processes functioning in cults and drug programs, the notion of charisma, and the clinical predisposition of the leader/follower relationship. The elucidation of these issues helps to both clarify the therapeutic potential and identify and highlight the antitherapeutic dangers inherent in such a treatment modality.

Therapeutic communities can be seen on a continuum basis, with professionally staffed psychiatric hospitals on one end and paraprofessionally operated programs on the other. This article focuses specifically on the paraprofessional ex-addict-staffed drug program models that have emerged since the 1950s with the founding of Synanon. Some of the main characteristics in these types of programs include the use of a "second-chance family" or "communitas" treatment structure, the presence of a charismatic leader (who is usually an ex-addict), and the use of encounter or confrontation types of treatment modalities. The roles contained within these programs rely heavily upon the use of "charismatic experience" and a shared but highly structured milieu experience of members as the basis for the helping process. The role of charisma was examined in religious institutions by Max Weber. His analysis will be the starting point of our examination.

Religious interest is pursued through a series of religious ideas whose systematization is inhibited by traditionalism. When social crisis occurs (involving weakening of traditional values, emergence of group conflicts, and sharpening of class differences) the traditional order is challenged by the emergence of a "charismatic authority," the prophet who seeks to give a more coherent structure to religious ideas. The process of religious rationalization may take one or two ideal typical forms—ethical prophecy, in which the prophet is himself the embodiment of a divine will (eg, Mohamed, Jesus) or exemplary prophecy, in which the prophet provides a personal example guiding others to religious salvation. If the prophet is at all successful he helps create a charismatic order that employs either asceticism or mysticism as religious means [cf. Blaskoff, 1969].

As we examine these drug programs, particularly those staffed and administered by ex-addicts, and view them in some ways as the modern-day functional equivalent to religious structures of previous times, some interesting similarities emerge.

Anyone who has been involved in therapeutic communities (TCs) can speak of seeing or feeling the ascetism that exists throughout these structures. Historically, professional helpers were having little or no success in treating drug addiction with traditional practices. This "traditional order" (professional) was challenged in the late 1950s by an ex-alcoholic who formed Synanon, and can be seen as analogous to the "charismatic prophet." Synanon eventually emerged as the charismatic order to help drug addicts find some meaning to life in a time filled with a number of sharpening social crises. What we have seen since that time are a number of different "prophets" who have formed rehabilitation programs (charismatic orders), each having different, yet similar ideas about treatment.

The two ideal forms of prophecy mentioned above can also be seen operating in many of these programs. This charismatic authority either eventually embodies the divine will, or to a lesser degree acts as a guide for others to salvation. In all of these programs, "out there" (society) is seen as a dangerous place, and "in here" (TC) is stressed as a salvation. As we have seen in some cases, the charismatic leader has gone so far as to deify him/herself and the community begins to take on cult-like qualities. This process of programs taking on cult-like qualities raises many questions concerning the dynamic processes at work that foster transformation. The practitioner's dilemma that emerges is how to provide effective treatment without risking client indoctrination into an institution that becomes self-perpetuating by feeding off individual pathology.

One aspect of the transformation of these communities into cults is the previously mentioned, "in here–out there" duality. "Out there" for many addicts represents a life filled with pain, physical and psychological illness, crime, and fear. These people, for a number of reasons, were no longer able to cope with their lives and turned to these drug treatment programs for help. The manipulation of "fear" is used on a manifest level to induce anxiety and motivate change. On a latent level it adds power to the charismatic order and eventually leads back to the charismatic leader as a savior. Being "saved" or "reborn" are basic acknowledgments made by new members in many of these institutions. Alan Jensen examines the role of charisma:

Certain individuals who display an ability to deal with these forces and sway them for the group's benefit are said to be endowed with charisma and take on roles of religious leadership. Ostensibly this charisma is the ability to hypnotize (so to speak) collectives of humans. Over time the quasi-scientific magician is replaced by the prophet—an emissary from the greater force. The prophet establishes a religious community from those to whom his charisma is appealing. Later in a rational and business-like way a priest arises who has the role of executing the ritual and maintaining the everyday existence of the religion. Over time the ritual evolves into law.

Jensen then takes Weber's treatise one step further,

Charismatic authority is transformed into more stable types as a necessary practical consequence of ensuing the status of followers and disciples and some orderly process of succession—until another crisis stimulates new prophets [Jensen, 1971, pp 81-91].

It is at this point in the process of succession that cults form into more stable religions. In programs run by ex-addicts, the authority generally remains with the original leader or, holding to our analogy, "prophet." Andrew Greely states, "When charisma was routinized it lost its fire and vigor." It seems appropriate to examine the "fire and vigor" present in theapeutic communities in a more applicable, timely fashion.

Hummel has combined the work of Max Weber and Sigmund Freud and arrived at a psychosocial definition of charisma.

Charisma exists as the experience of a follower when there is:
1) a moment of distress/object loss;
2) complete personal devotion to a leader/love projection;
3) experiencing the leader's qualitites as extraordinary or supernatural/sense of the uncanny produced by the unconscious nature of the projection.

All three experiential elements must be present for a charismatic process to be at work.

This definition moves us to view charisma in a more timely, secular fashion. Hummel goes on to specify,

Charisma is an authority relationship initiated by at least one individual (potential follower) who suffers object loss, agonizes in mourning, and eventually melancholia and resolves his suffering and agony by subconsciously projecting his own love onto another person (potential leader) from whom he then perceives his own love returning in the form of an uncanny attraction (Hummel, 1975, pp 760-761).

Using this definition of charisma and the psychosocial processes contained within it, we are led to view the personality structures and predispositions of both leader and follower in drug programs.

Otto Fenichel classically defines the drug addict as having a need "to satisfy archaic oral longings, which is sexual longing, a need for security and a need for maintenance of self-esteem simultaneously." He goes on:

The pre-morbid personality, therefore is the decisive factor. Those persons become drug addicts for whom the effect of the drug has a special significance. For them it means the fulfillment, or at least the hope for fulfillment, of a deep and primitive desire, more urgently felt by them than are sexual or other instinctual longings for normal persons. This pleasure or the hope for it makes genital sexuality uninteresting for them. The genital organization breaks up and an extraordinary regression begins. The various points of fixation determine which fields of infantile sexuality—Oedipus complex, masturbation conflicts, and especially pre-genital impulses, come to the fore, and in the end the libido remains in form of an "amorphous erotic tension energy without differential characteristics or forms of organization." The previous study of impulse behavior makes it easy to understand what kind of pleasure addicts are seeking. Patients who are ready to give up all object libido are persons who never estimated object relationships very highly. They are fixated to a passive narcissistic aim and are interested solely in getting their gratification, never in satisfying their partners nor for that matter in the specific personalities of their partners. Erogenously, the leading zones are the oral zone and skin. Self-esteem, even existence are dependent on getting food and warmth.

Fenichel goes on to locate within the addict personality a dysfunction in the superego and problems in identification, as well as a deep depression resulting from the very primitive nature of the oral needs that are frustratingly insatiable.

> The behavior of persons with oral characteristics frequently shows signs of identification with the object by whom they want to be fed. Certain persons act as nursing mothers in all their object relationships. They are always generous and shower everybody with presents and help, under favorable libido-economic conditions in a genuine and altruistic way, under less favorable conditions in a very annoying manner. The attitude has the significance of a magical gesture: "As I shower you with love, I want to be showered" (Fenichel, 1945).

In summary, the addict shows low self-esteem, difficulties in identification processes, and is an object-hungry, depressed, oral character.

Dynamically addicts usually have weak egos; deficient, overly rigid superegos, due to inadequate identification with male father figures; an unrealistic future outlook; and a history of faulty interpersonal relationships, as well as a distrust of social institutions (Zax, 1972). The father figure is usually described as inadequate and family life is generally full of chaos and conflict. Mothers tend to be controlling people, usually bitter about relationships with men. In viewing the family dynamics of addicts one study conducted by John Schwarztman (1977) found

> . . . that a loss of control is a central concern and acted out by the inability of the addict's parents to set limits on him. The addict to orient himself within his families learns, internalizes and acts out the expectation that he is "out of control," which is validated by the lack of actual constraints on his behavior in the family.

The above article goes on to deal with how this process is carried to other social relationships and institutions. Clearly the dynamics at work in the addiction process are complex and stem from very primitive emotional needs that later affect ego development, the family, and all other social institutions the addict comes to deal with.

The clinical picture presented involves object loss, depression and projection, and "a hope for fulfillment." These are the same criteria earlier defined as essential for establishing an authoritative charismatic relationship. Along with the reliance on charismatic authority, another common characteristic of TCs is the use of a "family" structure. Other residents are defined as "brothers" or "sisters" and all are related to the leader as "children" of sorts. It would seem that a second-chance family run by a strong charismatic authority figure would be the ideal treatment modality for people who present addiction problems. In an attempt to understand why this modality falls short of providing therapeutic rehabilitation, an examination of some internal processes and techniques will be provided.

Freshly shaven bald heads, people wearing signs stating "I'm a baby, I can't control myself," or in some cases people wearing towels fashioned as diapers over their clothes, are the most striking visible aspects of the TC milieu. The shaving of heads is part and parcel of many programs. On a manifest level it functions as an image-breaking device. The shedding of the "street image" is the first major goal in these structures. The "image" reflects the internal psychosocial processes at work within the addict, and a great deal of time and energy is spent helping new "members" shed the street and take on a "family image." This is accomplished by utilizing various techniques that have grown out of the ex-addict-staffed drug-free movement. Constant confrontation by staff and peers is one such technique. "Brothers" and "sisters" give their other family members verbal "pull-ups" for various unaware aspects of their lives. Stress is also put on being totally aware of oneself from the waking moment until the moment of going to sleep. Rituals pervade every process. The feeling of a "family" way of doing things is presented at intake, and adherence to prescribed ritualized ways of functioning is stressed. "Pull-ups" are given for deviations from ritual or for simple unaware occurrences as small as dropping a pencil. "You dropped your pencil; you should be more aware of yourself," is an example. This would be followed by a "thank you" from the person who committed the indiscretion. The "pull-up" is then relayed to another person in the family with more authority and eventually reaches the staff. If the indiscretion is decided to be relevant by higher-ranking members, a verbal "haircut" is given. This is a two- to three-minute verbal spanking in which weaknesses and unaware aspects of the person's life are pointed out in very graphic terms. If the indiscretion continues or grows to larger proportions, a "learning experience" is applied. These take many forms, from wearing a sign or diaper to cleaning toilet bowls over and over again for days. Helping others to become aware of their smallest actions is believed to eventually help them become aware of who they are as people. On a less visible latent level, these processes help establish the authority and ensure the charismatic order. Not only are family members helping each other become "aware," they are also acknowledging the authority of the staff and its leaders and begin to define systematic dysfunctional reactions in each other.

The intensity that exists in these structures is incredible. People can be seen furiously working in virtually every corner for long, sometimes 12- to 14-hour, work days. Many of these structures are self-sufficient, each having its own division of labor (drawn from residents who work for free), usually based on physical plant priority (maintenance, etc), then by length of stay, and finally by sex. A definite hierarchy exists, having numerous strata and status positions. These stratifications generally lead up to the charismatic authority who can elevate, or "shoot down" any resident. The mobility, either up or down, is closely tied to building residents' self-esteem through positive milieu responses for upward mobility and vice versa for "shoot downs." The authority of the leader and his chosen staff is de facto. Hard work and cooperation are stressed on a manifest level to help the addict develop a "work" identity. These also are an indicator for reading how motivated and committed residents are to the "order." There are clear role expectations stated for each function in the environment. Each resident is committed to meeting these expectations for him/herself and more importantly for the "family."

The heterosexual makeup of these communities raises a particular problem considering the poor impulse control in the addict personality concerning sexual activity among "family" members. In many of these structures the problem is addressed through the pull-up system. Any "look" or conversation hinting at promiscuity is known as having "eyes" for another "family" member. Strong sanctions usually follow to eliminate the acting out potential and build impulse control. In some communities that have begun to take on cult-like qualities, it is not unusual for a resident to request sexual activity with another member of the community from the charismatic authority. In some cases the leader has been known to form couples without request from participating members.

"Pride" and belief in the community are ever present and stressed intensely. Each program contains its own unique belief system or "concept." The concept is relayed verbally, and generally begins with a notion of "blind faith" in the community, questioning of the "concept" is a serious violation and dealt with swiftly. The concept also stresses hard work, honesty, and various other traditional values. A new language or jargon usually exists to explain the rituals and concepts. The average work day consists of 12–14 hours in these programs. As the person becomes indoctrinated to the new lifestyle, he hopefully begins upward movement in the hierarchy. An outsider would see and hear, and possibly feel, what appears to be an intense devotion to the "family" and leader for saving them from jail or death on the "outside." This "saving" component exists in all rituals and processes as motivating force. If a person prematurely leaves the program, he becomes a "splitee," and all past evidences of his existence are eradicated from the environment. His name cannot be mentioned, he is in fact considered dead or in jail, or worse, on the street. Should he return, a very strict learning experience is applied and upward mobility is very slow. Public homage is usually required for allowing a second or third chance at survival. Encounter groups led by paraprofessionally trained ex-addicts are the chief therapeutic treatment modality.

The director/leader is visible, but on a very limited basis. The ideas and strategies developed by him are carried out by hand-chosen staff members. He usually has risen to a level such that cleaning his car or office is a privilege that one must earn. He is above "pull-ups" and is the link with the "outside." The more adequately he functions, the better the program is viewed. The commitment is made by individual family members to the leader, the family, and then the "self."

TCs are broken into program levels. Intake, treatment, and reentry are the approximate areas of demarcation. Each stage has requisite functioning expectations necessary for movement. These stages are connected to the higher valued roles and statuses. As the member advances, he earns more responsibility until he becomes responsible enough to deal with the "outside." All of the above processes are unfolding with little or no professional consultation. Movement and treatment are directed with little accountability due to the de facto nature of the authority structure. Professionals in many cases are frowned upon as being unable to relate to "family" members.

Upon viewing these processes on a manifest level, they seem to work well in attempting to help addicts change their lives. The addict, it is hoped, sheds his street image with the confrontational help given by "family" members and develops a more positive, "family" image that is part of an ex-addict identity. Self-esteem is enhanced by the successful completion of tasks that allow for upward mobility and new modes of relating to develop. The taking on of the ex-addict identity unfolds as a result of the milieu treatment directed in the final analysis by the charismatic authority. The question that must be raised is whether the development of a new social identity is enough to define rehabilitation and to what extent internal personality change is valued, as requisite for long-term abstinence from drugs.

In a paper entitled "Milieu Management in the Treatment of Drug Addiction, Hart (1972) states:

> In light of professional understanding of the concept of rehabilitation as a process committed to a speedy return of an inmate to a community, we must question whether Synanon program is pointed in that direction. . . . Sternberg doubts that rehabilitation is taking place; rather he feels that Synanon has created a "protective society." He further states that Synanon has done its job too well and that the addict has substituted for his drug dependency a new dependency on Synanon. This dependency upon the facility may not only be typical of Synanon, but may generally be true of drug facilities staffed and administered by paraprofessional ex-addicts. Also it has been suggested that Synanon may offer addicts membership in an ex-addict social system.

He further adds his observations of another ex-addict-run facility.

> The graduates generally never remove themselves directly from the extended drug subculture and never permanently place themselves in an entirely different situation where their interpersonal relationships are with those who have had little or no drug experience. The drug subculture "extends" from the street addict role to more acceptable roles, such as director and assistant directorships. The graduates are not being rehabilitated and returned to the community but appear to be being trained to staff new facilities. The program maintains itself through self-perpetuation (Hart, 1972, pp 65–69).

It appears that the development of a new social identity of ex-addict is not enough to define rehabilitation. In many cases the development and strengthening of such defenses as reaction-formation and identification with the aggressor are concomitant with the development of a new social identity within the "family" structure. A more detailed analysis of TCs is in order to further explore the differences between helping people to simply survive and helping people to grow and mature as unique individuals.

As mentioned, the addict presents a clinical picture filled with "the hope for fulfillment" from an object who is both strong and nurturing. The TC run by ex-addicts relies on a charismatic authority and a second-chance family structure as the main ingredients in the helping processes. We now turn to Freud (1938), who examined the leader/follower relationship in "Totem and Taboo." In recalling the sanction applied to a family member for having "eyes," we can see an interesting similarity between today's TC and more primitive cultures. "Almost everywhere where the totem prevails, there also exists a law that members of the same totem are not allowed to enter into sexual relations with each other."

The stress put on the "brother, sister" roles and what they mean on a more latent level of functioning are also strikingly similar.

> The kinship names which two Australians give each other do not necessarily point to a blood relationship between them, as they would have according to the custom of our language; they signify much more the social than the physical relations.

The importance of loyalty and belief in the family are also similar to more primitive customs: "The totem is the visible representation of the social religion of these races. It embodies the community which is the real object of their veneration." The "family" or "charismatic order" can be traced back as emanating from the authority figure. The "hope for fulfillment" in the addict's predisposition is met through the community (charismatic order, emanating from the prophet). In a sense the program and concept become the social religion of the program members. The use of the projective defense mechanism also sheds light and clarifies somewhat the nature of the addict's veneration: "As I shower you with love, I want to be showered." This holds true for both the leader and the community. In reference to the premature leaving of a resident, another similarity emerges. "Calling a dead person by name can also be traced back to contact with him, so that we can turn our attention to the more inclusive problem of why this contact is visited with such a severe taboo."

In TCs the link between outside and death serves to motivate, but also serves to add to the authority of the order in that "inside" is life which is directed by the charismatic leader.

Freud eventually traces the nature of authority of totem and taboo customs to the presence of ambivalence in taboo formulations. He then moves us to the role of the unconscious:

> Applied to the treatment of privileged persons this theory of an ambivalent feeling would reveal that their veneration, their very deification, is opposed in the unconscious by an intense hostile tendency, so that, as we had expected, the situation of an ambivalent feeling is here realized.

This is particularly relevant when considering the addict's clinical predisposition and the poor paternal relationships that are filled with preverbal rage. The other side of the intense love projection is an unconscious hostile emotion, directed and projected to the leader.

The presence of this unconscious hostility changes the way we view the charismatic relationship, due to the clinical predisposition of the addict personality. Freud analyzes the hostile tendency further, using his analysis of patients.

> The prototype which the paranoid reconstructs in the persecution mania is found in the relation of the child to its father. Such omnipotence is regularly attributed to the father in the imagination of the son, and distrust of the father has been shown to be intimately connected with the highest esteem for him.

In the case of the addict this distrust in many cases is reenforced in reality through the biological family structure and is then carried to all other social relationships and institutions. Thus the danger of relying so heavily on the charismatic order as a basis for rehabilitative treatment begins to emerge. In terms of the formation of a cult, though, the relationship between leader and follower in these programs is ripe. We find an object-hungry individual with low self-esteem who is very depressed at intake and who, through the use of projection and projective identification, begins to feel like a new person after a relatively brief period of time. The "wish for fulfillment" is filled by the charismatic leader and his followers; a new social identity is formed but only in relation to the "family" and its leader. Essentially the hope for fulfillment is moved from a dependence on drugs for a sense of self and self-esteem, to the charismatic relationship that is bound with a love projection and an unconscious hostility that is usually displaced on new members in the structure. It is true that the order does meet basic needs of food, clothing, and shelter and that some emotional needs are being met, but at what cost to the individuals involved?

The price that is levied is paid by both leader and followers in the charismatic relationship. The "fire and vigor" previously mentioned is certainly a powerful force for both parties. Let us turn now to the effect of this relationship on the charismatic leader. All too often these people are indicted for the failure of this type of modality. Let us examine the forces at work that shift these institutions from treatment programs to "cults," that thrive on a certain "social religion." The burden carried by the charismatic leader also is highlighted in Freud's writings.

> Another trait in the attitude of primitive races toward their rulers recalls a mechanism which is universally present in mental disturbances, and is openly revealed in the so-called delusions of persecution. Here the importance of a particular person is extraordinarily heightened and his omnipotence is raised to the improbable in order to make it easier to attribute to him the responsibility for everything painful which happens to the patient.

The leaders of cult-like organizations become, due to the reliance on the charismatic relationship, omnipotent figures. This type of relationship is especially dangerous with an object-hungry oral character structure whose needs for fulfillment and self-esteem are insatiable. This process of becoming a permanent parent has positive elements for the charismatic leader, too. "Parents are said to remain young with their children, and this is, in fact, one of the most valuable psychic benefits which parents derive from their children."

Seen in the context of the drug subculture, not only do charismatic ex-addict leaders reap psychic benefits but social benefits as well, as they are still part and parcel of their chosen subculture, only in more acceptable roles. In order to examine the ambivalence and unconscious hostility contained in the charismatic relationship, we again turn to Freud.

> Such hostility hidden in the unconscious behind tender love, exists in all cases of intense emotional allegiance to a particular person, indeed it represents the classic case, the prototype of the ambivalence of human emotions. There is always more or less of this ambivalence in everybody's disposition; normally it is not strong enough to give use to the obsessional reproaches we have described. But where there is abundant predisposition for it, it manifests itself in relation to those we love most, precisely where you would least expect it.

Clearly the premorbid predisposition of addicts gives rise to the aggressive, hostile allegiance to the leader couched in an exalting, venerating social commitment. The love and veneration as we begin to see are not an "adult" type of love, but are part and parcel of a preverbal projective process resulting from less than optimal early object relations. The hostility is further analyzed and takes on added significance upon examining it on the unconscious level.

> Thus also the taboo ceremonial of kings is nominally an expression of highest veneration and a means of guarding them; actually it is the punishment for their elevation, the revenge which their subject took upon them.

The preverbal rage of the addict personality is not only displaced onto incoming members, but also has an outlet in the manifest veneration of the charismatic leader.

What emerges is a self-perpetuating relationship that permeates the charismatic order based on the de facto authority of the leader and that feeds on the oral predispositions of the followers. The structure that ensues demands rigid role definitions for all persons involved. Systematically, programs of this sort begin to perpetuate themselves in order to ensure their survival. The structure begins to take on a life of its own. In an article entitled "Elements of the Perpetuation of Dependency in a Psychiatric Halfway House," the authors isolate three elements that perpetuate dependence on the structure. These are: role commitments, language, and mixed messages (Maines and Markowitz, 1979). Clearly in ex-addict-run facilities the language that is utilized uniquely for each program to explain "concept" is stressed as an integral piece of programing. The role commitments, due to the clinical predispositions of residents, are of central concern to everyone in the community. Mixed messages abound and filled with ambivalence as Freud has outlined, due to the nature of the leader/follower relationship. Addicts become "ex-addict" family members and in most cases never transcend their social identities to deal with who they are as individuals. This process moves closer to what we would define as the formation of a cult, rather than therapeutic rehabilitation. The leader is the object of unconscious projections based on the follower's insatiable need to be fed. This is coupled with the powerful preverbal rage and frustration in the addict that has an outlet in the charismatic order. As a basis for treatment of addiction, it is bound to fail; as a means of forming a cult, it is fertile soil. The leader, the structure, the premorbid personality structures of addictive personalities all lend themselves to the formation of a cult. This process has gone so far in some cases that the leaders see themselves as godlike, having special insights, ready to lead their followers, to a new and better world.

When TCs get locked into this process, they take on characteristics of millenarian movements. In an article "Millenarian Movements and Resocialization" (Lebra, 1972). The use of these types of movements is studied. The main difference between these cult-like movements and correctional or psychiatric facilities is discussed. Some differences include the presence of a belief in or for annihilation of the existing world, the absence of ecological barriers, like prison walls, and the sense of community rather than program. In these movements, three mechanisms are defined as necessary for resocialization: enlightenment, integration, and commitment. Integration, interestingly, is then defined as including such processes as dichotomization, reversal, and reenforcement of existing hierarchies and a sense of predestination. These are all found in force in TCs taking on cult-like qualities. Integration also refers to the "social engagement of the convert to the community." This process is then broken down to two aspects at work. One is solidarity, which is characterized by the lack of structural differentiation into roles and statuses, and entails acceptance of the person on one hand and submersion of individuals into a collectivity on the other.

The third aspect of millenarian cult-like movements is that of commitment, which involves abandonment of worldly possessions and a belief and involvement in the world to come. All of the aspects of these cult-like movements are present in many drug programs staffed and administered by ex-addicts. They are in a sense cult organizations built around a charismatic authority who espouses a social religion to the followers. The above article concludes, "The behavioral change of the convert, coupled with environmental change, may eventually place him in a more desirable position within secular society" (Lebra, 1972).

This is where the hope for the ex-addict having undergone treatment in an ex-addict-staffed program lies. It is contingent, however, on an environmental change. The goal of therapeutic treatment is termination. The structuring of this "environmental change" is faulty at best in ex-addict-run programs due to the reliance on the in/out dichotomy, stress put on social rather than psychological change, and the nature of the charismatic relationship. The treatment facility that does not return individuals to society in a manner that attempts to ensure their reintegration in a meaningful way must be questioned as to its merits. In essence we see a genuine "helping" community of ex-addicts perpetuating itself. Basic needs of food, clothing, and shelter are met. One must ask, though, is this enough? Therapy involves "healing" to ensure growth, not simply "helping" to ensure survival. There is not room in a therapeutic relationship for "saving." The reentry into society, with as many tools and skills necessary to ensure growth and development on some levels should be the goal of any therapeutic community. This is where in/out duality falls short as a therapeutic concept, and has a lot of strength as an indoctrinating tool for cults. "Out there" does not mean death, it means life and reality. That may be harsh, but that is the necessary component in any development process.

The "larger society" can also contribute to the rise of cult-like organizations. Cults emerge during crises in cultures.

> Culture crises are characterized by dislocations in communicational and orientational institutions of society, ie, those institutions that normally create and standardize symbols. Many of the ideological and organizational characteristics typically associated with cult movements can be interpreted as responses to culture crisis (Ester, 1972).

So we have psychosocial processes at work internally within both leader and follower fostering the transformation of programs into cults, since it is the nature of the complex and alienating society to have a constant state of culture crisis. Programs relying on the charismatic relationship, second-chance family structure in the 1960s and 1970s are institutions with the potential to evolve into self-perpetuating cults.

The challenge that we face as helpers is to somehow avoid throwing out the baby with the bathwater. The baby, TCs, certainly have the potential to act as healing institutions. They must, though, be held accountable for their processes, to their immediate community, to the funding sources, or to professional organizations. As every therapist knows, becoming a transferential object of a client is a complex process. One must be aware when the helper's needs are being met through the therapeutic relationship. This is accomplished through the therapeutic relationship, through personal introspection, some sort of supervision, and a grasp of theory and treatment that helps develop discipline in practice. Closed ex-addict-administered institutions founded to help must be introspective and be held accountable for their process, or, as we have seen, they can evolve into cults that become self-contained and perpetuating. This is borne out by the closing of many ex-addict-staffed facilities in recent years.

The challenge that the helping professions face is the eventual integration of the positive aspects of Synanon-type programs with professional techniques and practices involved in treatment. It is hoped this chapter can shed light on the complexities involved in the treatment and understanding of ex-cult members and spur future research in the processes involved in both drug-free programs and cults.

BIBLIOGRAPHY

Blaskoff A: *Theory in American Sociology: Major Sources and Applications.* New York, Crowell, 1969.

Bourne P: The therapeutic community phenomenon. *J Psychedelic Drugs* 1975;7(2): 203–207.

Fenichel O: *The Psychoanalytic Theory of Neurosis.* New York, WW Norton, 1945.

Ester A: An outline of a structural theory of cults. *J Scientific Study Religion* 1972;11(4):319–333.

Freud S: *Basic Writings.* New York, Random House, 1938.

Goldberg H, Scott D: The phenomenon of self-perpetuation in Synanon-type drug programs. *Hosp Commun Psychiatry* 1973;24(4):236–248.

Greely A: *The Denominational Society.* Scott Foreman, 1972.

Hummel R: The psychology of charismatic followers. *Psychological Reports* 1975;37: 759–770.

Jensen AF: *Sociology Concepts and Concerns.* Chicago, Rand McNally, 1971.

Lebra T: Millenarian movements and resocialization. *Am Behav Sci* 1972;16(2):195–217.

Maines DR, Markowitz M: Elements of the perpetuation of dependency in a psychiatric halfway house. *J Sociol Soc Welfare* 1979;6(1):53–69.

Mead D, Campbell S, Campbell E: Decision making and interaction by families with and without a drug abusing child. *Family Process* 1972;11:487–498.

Quarntelli E, Wenger D: A voice from the thirteenth century. *Urban Life Culture* 1973;1: 379–400.

Schwartzman J: Addict abstinence and the illusion of alternatives. *J Ethos* 1977;5:132–150.

Zax M, Cowen E: *Abnormal Psychology.* New York, Holt, Reinhart and Winston, 1972.

Cultist Phenomena in Psychoanalysis

ZVI LOTHANE

It might seem strange to include a chapter on cultist aspects of psychoanalysis in a volume dealing with the psychology and sociology of present-day cults. What is the relevance of a phenomenon like the Pied Piper of the People's Temple in Guyana, or any idol worship, to psychoanalysis, a science and itself a weapon against cults?

To answer this question, a few preliminary definitions are needed. Cult and culture derive from a common root meaning to till, to cultivate. The ideas of work and worship are thus connected in the broad meaning of "cult," ie, the attitudes and acts of belief and devotion. True religion embodies the positive concept of cult, or cultus, the worship of God and the collected religious practices and ceremonies. In the negative sense, cult means idolatry, the worship of false gods or idols. The Hebrews called it "avoda zara," literally strange work and figuratively strange worship of foreign or strange gods.

The narrow meaning of cult is worship of a person, thing, or idea. The worship of a person is related to being in love. In his famous monograph on group psychology, Freud (1921) extended the paradigm of being in love to the other varieties of personal attachment, or person worship: hypnosis, suggestion, and the leader–led relation. In all of these the person who loves loses himself in the person loved or, as Freud put it, "The object [the person loved] has, so to speak, consumed the ego," or the person who loves (Freud, 1921).

We shall not be concerned with person worship in this chapter. There has been a growing literature on the subject of person worship in the psychoanalytic movement. Freud himself has been the object of both extreme idol worship and idol smashing, while the psychoanalytic movement has been the stage for the vicissitudes of faith and heresy, devotion and betrayal, adoration and crucifixion. It is a recurrent phenomenon in any group, religious, secular, or pseudoreligious, between the leader and the led and among the led themselves.

Our concern is with the worship of ideas or ideologies. This calls for drawing a distinction between ideas and ideologies. An idea is either a percept, a concept, or a precept. Ideologies embrace concepts and precepts. One class of concepts are hypotheses about the causes of facts, to answer the question "why," as distinguished from the practical question "how." Etiologies are prone to become ideologies. Another class of opinions are precepts about the value of facts, things, and people, in answer to the question "to what end." Precepts also become ideologies. Both these classes of opinions, ideologies of cause and ideologies of purpose, are the stuff out of which culture is made. Ideologies are prone to become objects of cults, the culture's idols and fetishes.

Idols easily turn into false gods and ideologies may become breeding places of false opinions or fallacies. When Francis Bacon (1620) set out to define the new method for science in his *Novum Organum,* to correct the fallacies of Aristotle in his *Organon,* he depicted four "idols" (images), or false ideas, in the ways of looking at nature. He was describing four different types of opinion or ideology: due to human nature, to individual mental and physical differences, to the marketplace, and, lastly, to the dogmas and systems of philosophy. When the four "idols" were eliminated, the road lay open to replacing the word wisdom of the schoolmen with the practical scientific wisdom of observation and experimentation and for the sake of knowledge of nature and the power over nature. However, the old way was not entirely useless nor was the new way immune to being affected by new idols or errors, those created by science itself.

Bacon's ideas were the forerunners of the modern sciences of matter and measurement and of modern technology. Knowledge is power, and man did gain vast power over nature. But Bacon did not solve the ever-recurrent problem in the sciences between doing and theorizing, between method and doctrine, between work and worship. It is at this juncture that the problem of ideological cults finds its locus. In the sciences methods are about doings and lead to concepts which are operational, in Bridgman's sense, ie, derived from the doings themselves. At the same time, there is an unavoidable recourse to concepts which are nonoperational, not derived from doings, but of the nature of basic metaphysical postulates. There is a limit to radical operationism and to radical positivism. As practical, sciences remain operational in method and in application of method; as theoretical, they are either metaphysical, when they deal with causes of phenomena, or (at a further remove) theological when they are concerned with the ultimate cause and purpose of the universe. It is at the level of metaphysics and theology that ideologies and their transformations into cult are prone to make their entry.

Let us now consider some cultist phenomena in natural science and in the sciences of man, psychology, and psychoanalysis.

THE CULT OF MATTER IN NATURAL SCIENCE

Science deals with matter and measurement. Matter is a fact in reality. It is ubiquitous, and it is the substrate of life. Since both science and religion have their roots in primitive magic, the art of manipulating matter for the purposes of man, they have both retained a primordial reverence for matter as a touchstone of truth. But matter is not the only reality. Thought is also real. It is not an illusion, contrasted with the reality of matter and things. When reality is equated with substantiality, we have the ideology of materialism or the cult of matter. When thought is reduced to a thing, we have an ideology known as reification.

The cult of matter in the West reappears with Galileo in the seventeenth century with the revival of the theories of the Greek atomists. Galileo's was a twofold accomplishment. On the one hand, on the basis of ideas about acceleration of bodies, he founded the modern science of mechanics and thus paved the way for the spectacular achievements of modern technology. On the other hand, he also advanced a highly metaphysical anti-operational materialism. He regarded matter as the ultimate reality, as the cause of all causes, ie, God. This materialistic ideology had

> . . . the outspokenly religious character of its attitude towards the matter which is postulated as the only reality. It denied God, but only because it has transferred the attributes of God to matter, and being the offspring of a monotheistic tradition thinks one God quite enough (Collingwood, 1945).

This view became the basis for his fallacious doctrine of secondary qualities. It went as follows: Since matter is that which can be weighed and expressed in mathematical formulas, mass is the primary quality, the only object of certain, that is, objective, knowledge. Contrasted with matter, such qualities as colors, sounds, and smells are secondary. The latter are ephemeral, imponderable (literally, that which cannot be weighed), thus relative, subjective, not knowledge but mere illusion and opinion. The secondary qualities are the addition mind makes to matter, in Galileo's words, "nothing more than a name." We see how in the hands of Galileo a sound method was transformed into an unsound theory, as a result of which nature was split (or, as Whitehead said, bifurcated) into two incompatible realms.* This ideology had no effect on practical physics, but it did affect theoretical physics and the course of psychology from the seventeenth century on. It affected Descartes, Galileo's follower, and later Newton, from whom it passed to Hobbes, Locke, and the French sensationalists. With the development of knowledge about the reflex arc, begun by Descartes, and knowledge gained from the study of the effects of brain lesions, the picture was rounded out as follows: mind was due to motions of matter, specifically brain matter.

The main thrust of the foregoing discussion has been to bring out the difference between materialism as a fact of life, that matter and material phenomena exist, versus materialism as a metaphysical creed, a theology of causes. It is a historical fact that Western man has worshiped matter from the early Greek philosophers on. This tendency has even been manifest in the teachings of the Catholic Church (Dewey, 1929).

If substance has been such a magnet for religion, it has been no less of a fascination for the field that bridges theology and religion and science, namely philosophy and its branch called metaphysics. In the popular usage, "metaphysical" suggests something highly abstruse and unfounded, removed from the ordinary or the real. This vulgar image of metaphysics is the soul of the reform of metaphysics propounded by Auguste Comte around 1830 under the name of positivism. Positivists hounded metaphysics with the same fervor with which Voltaire had hounded religion and for a similar reason: for its use of concepts that go beyond the facts of observation. Again, the battle raged on the field of substantiality. Again, positivism suffered from the treatment it inflicted on others.

---

*"The really important world outside was a world hard, cold, colourless, silent and dead; a world of quantity, a world of mathematically computable motions in mechanical regularity. The world of qualities as immediately perceived by man became just a curious and quite minor effect of that infinite machine beyond it" (Burtt, 1924).

Comte's program was an important influence upon John Stuart Mill, Spencer, Wundt and academic psychology, upon Watson and behaviorism, all of which is also of relevance for the understanding of the history of psychology, Freud, and psychoanalysis.

According to Comte, mankind has passed through three successive stages in the development of thinking: the theological, the metaphysical, and the positive, all systems to explain the universe. In the theological stage, characterized by its anthropomorphism, man first regarded objects as animated (animism), passing then to a belief in invisible gods governing objects (polytheism), and finally to the conception of one God, creator and ruler of the world (monotheism). This stage was largely dominated by emotion.

In the metaphysical stage, phenomena are no longer explained by conscious wills but by abstractions considered as real beings. Nature is no longer governed by anthropomorphic divinities or God, but by forces and principles. The fictions earlier created by emotions are now replaced by fictions of reason. Ghosts of religion are replaced by souls and occult essences of metaphysics. Thus mythology and metaphysics, the twin daughters of illusion and ignorance, have kept mankind in shackles until the advent of science. Both sisters perish with the waning of the Middle Ages and with the emergence of the last and positive stage, the era of positive sciences, when facts, experiments, and immutable laws supersede mythological (theological) and metaphysical explanations.

Now each science, in the course of historical development, also had to pass through the three stages, theological, metaphysical, and positive, to become fully developed and mature. Thus chemistry was alchemy before becoming a positive science. By contrast, sociology, now named social physics, was still seen in Comte's day as struggling to free itself from the fetters of theology and metaphysics, but not altogether successfully. Positive philosophy is the true philosophy as positive science is true science: both are based on experience supplemented by induction and deduction. The paradigm of positive philosophy and positive science is to be found in the natural sciences. These are based on facts and investigations that are real, useful, certain, and positive, ie, not determined by negative criticism. Such criteria can only be met by facts that are physical and corporeal. From this Comte drew the following conclusion: there are no mental facts since one cannot be both the object and the subject of investigation. How is it possible to study one's own emotions when studying them requires the overcoming of those very emotions? Therefore, introspection is a chimera. This bias led him to a denial of psychology as a positive science altogether, a most characteristic aspect of the Comtian doctrine. There were two main offshoots of Comte's antipsychologism: on the one hand, the associationism of Mills and the introspectionism of Wundt became the foundation of academic psychology, the "psychology without a soul," culminating in the structuralism of a Titchener or a Boring. On the other hand, the most positive of them all, the studies of Pavlov and Watson became the animal psychology without consciousness and without introspection: a return to Descartes' living automatons and to La Mettrie's Homme-Machine.

But behaviorism is the best refutation of behaviorism, for, if true, its pronouncements would have no more validity than mere reflexes. For the same reason Comte's positivism was wrong about psychology. Self-reflexive awareness is possible and does exist: man is subject and object in one. Like the behaviorists, Comte was right in what he asserted but wrong in what he denied. Insofar as

Comte inveighed against the preoccupations of both theology and metaphysics with occult substances and causes, with divine stuff (God) and metaphysical stuff (the soul of idealism, the matter of materialism), to that extent positivism reaffirmed Occam's dictum that entities should not be multiplied without need. The only legitimate study for science was that of actual material objects and facts in the world, the proper objects of scientific observation and investigation. By contrast, the substances of theology and metaphysics were verbal inventions and illusions, fit only for the flame. Theology, metaphysics, and science have all made a claim to the solution of the problem of substance and cause. Science is clearly the only viable solution, science freed from unnecessary presuppositions about the nature, or essence, of substance. In this Comte performed an important service for the natural sciences. But Comte's error about psychology persisted, and all those who rallied to this slogan have compounded the confusion of the various psychological schools. However, he was inconsistent about psychology. Not only did he readmit psychology into his canon, under the guise of the reaffirmation of human reason and the need to believe; but he went on to proclaim a new positive religion of humanity inspired by the twin divinities, Progress and Order. In this religion God was dispensed with but mankind itself was deified and called *Le Grand Etre*, the Great Being. The believer in science became the fanatic of a new faith. His life story shows the perilous course between the Scylla of antimetaphysics and the Charybdis of antiscience.

The new religion, inspired by Catholicism but founded on positive science, had its holy days and its calendar of saints (among them Dante, Shakespeare and, strangely, two minor religious writers, Bonald and De Maistre, who earlier had been considered as arrested at the theological stage). The more it changes, the more it stays the same. His ardent follower, Pierre Lafitte, continued to promote the cult of mankind, read Comte like the Bible, held him to be the first high priest of mankind, and considered any disagreement with Comte as heresy. Comte's apostle in the United States was Henry Edger. In the 1870s the cult spread to Brazil where a positive church and an apostolate were established, headed by the apostle of mankind. The Great Temple of Mankind was built in Rio de Janeiro and the motto, Order and Progress, is still to be seen on the coat of arms of the Brazilian republic.

THE CULT OF ATOMS IN PSYCHOLOGY

Can psychology be scientific? It depends on our definition of scientific. If we define scientific as material, then we are back to the prejudices of materialism, reductionism, and reification. If we define scientific, in the manner of Collingwood, as an approach, as a systematic way of studying a subject matter, then we shall follow this principle: look for a method appropriate to the subject studied.

Prior to the seventeenth century, psychology, like the other sciences, was part of philosophy. To the extent that philosophy tried to impose philosophical methods, such as reason and analysis, upon the knowledge of substances, to that extent it hampered the progress of natural sciences. The sciences needed to emancipate themselves from their thralldom to theories about matter in order to develop their own methods for the study of material phenomena both in the state of nature and in the laboratory.

However, the emancipation of the natural sciences from philosophy was beneficial to the natural sciences. The war on philosophy in psychology has been a disaster, for the philosophical method is congenial to psychology, in fact, indispensable to it. At the material level man is subject to the laws of physics, biophysics, and biochemistry. The material level is transcended on passing to the biological level, or the organismic level (reproduction, maturation). The biological level is transcended on passing to the psychological level of self-reflection, spontaneous activity, creativity. It comes to this: at the most evolved level of human potentiality and activity, the philosophical method becomes a sine qua non for studying man, both in the choice of premises and orienting principles and in the gathering of the data of observation into lawlike propositions.

Psychology is different from the other natural sciences, and the difference is due to the nature of the subject matter, man. The subject matter and the method of studying man are not as readily agreed upon in the sciences of man as they are in the natural sciences. For here the definition of the subject matter and the methods are influenced by the ideology of the scientist, the way he lives as a man, and what he believes life should be all about. Thus, an atheist and a theist, a capitalist and a communist will readily agree on the subject of atomic physics even as they entertain different theories about subatomic particles. But on the subject of man they might be at odds with each other at best or fight each other to the death at worst, as is amply chronicled in the annals of history. There is also the temptation to treat a particular conception or theory with the fervor of a cult. A particular theory, worshiped as true revelation, becomes a rallying point for the cult followers no less magnetically than the personality of the theory's author himself. Another problem in psychology has been ideas as precepts. Ethics, or moral philosophy, is inseparable from the subject man. Once under the umbrella of religion and later banished by science, moral philosophy has had a way of sneaking in into the halls of science through the back door. The various schools of psychology have been covert ethical enterprises or cryptoethical systems. Like the repressed, ethics has been forever returning as a compromise formation, clothed in the garb of the reigning theory.

In its attempt to become scientific, psychology returned to the cult of matter, very much in the spirit of Galileo. In trying to recreate man in the image of the sciences of matter, it created a new idol, the cult of psychological atoms. This cult produced an idea of man as denatured (devoid of spontaneous psychological activity and of passions, including sexuality) and as dehumanized (devoid of moral conflicts).

This cult of psychological atoms was called structuralism by Titchener, the Englishmen who settled at Cornell. He continued the program of scientific psychology established by his master, Wundt, in Germany, in the third quarter of the nineteenth century (Murphy, 1949).

Structuralism was based on two assumptions. Firstly, on the analogy with the atoms of physics and chemistry, it posited the existence of psychic atoms, ie, alleged elements of consciousness, of which larger forms of experiencing, such as perceptions, were made up. Secondly, it claimed that these elements of consciousness were the so-called sensations, the ultimate or elementary forms of this experience, and that these were observed by means of introspection. Wundt also added a subsidiary thesis: There is a one-to-one correspondence between excitations in the cerebral cortex and the sensations. Structuralism claimed to provide a scientific psychology, superior to everyday observation and the "merely" descriptive classifications of faculty psychology, an old and venerable occupant of the intellectual house of Europe on which the structuralists declared holy war. Let us take a closer look at what it delivered.

In ordinary experience sensations refer to a direct awareness of touch, temperature, position, thirst, hunger. Such sensations are not irreducible elements of consciousness but knowledge of highly complex events in the organism. They are a form of knowledge; in fact, they are perceptions of bodily states. Other than our body, we directly perceive and know objects in the external world. But we do not have a sensation of a chair as distinct from a perception of a chair, nor are we aware of any event during which a stimulation of the receptors in the eye or brain turns into a perception of an object.

The sensations of the structuralists were not fact but inference: the hypothetical elementary forms of consciousness into which perceptions could be analyzed, or out of which they were synthesized. Since these alleged sensations cannot be differentiated in consciousness from simply perception, the claim that these elements were studied in the course of introspection was an outright hoax. Acts of memory and attention are indeed capable of being "introspected" (perish the word), but the alleged sensations are not, nor are any alleged interactions between them. These artificially created mental atoms may add up to a nice theory, but in no way are they the object which introspectionism was supposed to study. Not even the most skilled introspectionist was capable of noticing them and reporting them. Murphy mentions that some of them were found cheating, not unlike the grand hysterics of Charcot who were coached by the master's students to act their grand attacks. Not only were such psychic atoms nonexperimental, nonoperational items, the idea that they were similar to the atoms of chemistry was totally misleading. Once again, the emperor was stark naked. This idea of studying contents of consciousness was a methodological legacy of Descartes, embodied in his *cogito ergo sum*, "I think, therefore I am." In the hands of the structuralists, introspection became a distorted method. Interestingly, as noted above, introspection was not considered by Comte as meeting the criteria of positive science since introspection did neither measure nor quantify. This oversight may be easy to explain: the laboratory procedures and paraphernalia of the structuralists—after all, Wundt was the founder of experimental psychology—seemed to lend credibility to introspectionism. The point is not to dismiss introspection as totally unfounded, for it has its proper uses, but only to question the goods it purported to deliver according to the structuralist project. For the goods were those famed sensations, allegedly revealed by introspection.

Descartes has also been the precursor of the subsidiary thesis as the creator of the dualist myth of brain events and the "corresponding" mind events. The 1870s were a time when people got unusually excited about the parallelist story. It was in 1870, four years before the appearance of Wundt's *Physiological Psychology*, that Fritsch and Hitzig published their work on the responses of the cortex to electrical stimulation. After centuries of research in brain anatomy, the era of brain physiology had arrived. It was easy to assume that stimulation of the cortex by electricity was the model of stimulation of the cortex by the visible world to produce perception. But it is the same now as then: neurophysiological data and experiments exist, but psychological data and experiments exist also. However, the brain–mind interaction is not an operational datum, only a connection which may be used in the construction of various causal hypotheses about that interaction. Such causal hypotheses have been dubbed brain mythology (Lothane, 1982).

The structuralists thus engaged in the cult of materialism, reductionism, and reification. They converted the myth of psychic atoms, of those hypothetical sensations—ie, mechanics, of ideas and brain mythology—into a semblance of science. They twisted common experience out of shape. Science should add to common experience, enhance it by a dimension not available to everyday observation, as is achieved by scientific astronomy, biology, or physics. In psychology the result of this supposedly scientific program, conceived in the spirit of an indiscriminate aping of the natural sciences, created a myth.

The reaction to structuralism was not long in coming. It assumed two shapes: functionalism and Gestalt psychology. The basic position of functionalism was to study activities rather than contents of consciousness, actions rather than structures. "This was, in a sense, a return to faculty psychology. For faculty psychology is in essence a method of stating mental processes in a few main categories" (Murphy, 1949).

The functionalists (James, Dewey) rejected the structuralist claim that scientific psychology has no business studying activities. They focused precisely on activities and actions, on man as doer. In this they reverted to the commonsense and everyday, whole and unatomized psychological realities of man, to man in his natural habitat, as compared to the abstract, rarefied view of man reduced to elements of consciousness.

In light of the above, Freud, like William James, could be seen as a representative of the functionalist tradition. Both James and Freud subscribed to Pope's dictum that the proper study of mankind is man; both were Aristotelian in their conception of mental functions as activities and acts (both come under the influence of Brentano). They stood for a philosophy of life that acknowledges man as political and ethical, but as sons of their period they occasionally succumbed to the scientism of the day: brain mythology and atomistic structuralism.

In the thirty-fifth, the last of the *New Introductory Lectures,* Freud (1933) is concerned with the scientific status of psychoanalysis. Freud asserts that psychoanalysis as a science is free from ideology. His view is that "strictly speaking, there are only two sciences: psychology, pure and applied, and natural science." Natural science requires no further definition. "Sociology. . . dealing as it does with the behavior of people in society, cannot be anything but applied psychology." Psychoanalysis is defined as "specialist science, a branch of psychology—a depth psychology or psychology of the unconscious. . . ." The contribution psychology makes to natural science is "the investigation of the intellectual and emotional functions of man. . . ."

In the same lecture, Freud is critical of Marx as an author of an ideology which he compared to religion. He then proceeds to decry both Marx and religion as promoters of illusions and idol worship. But Marx, like Freud after him, was the one who maintained that religion is the opium of the people. Clearly, Freud failed to recognize a kindred spirit. He also remained blind to his ideological affinity— and rivalry—with Marx. Nor could he admit that other than being a science, psychoanalysis, next to Marxism, has been a most powerful ideology in Europe.

IDEOLOGIES IN FREUD

Freud echoed Newton's manifesto, *"Hypotheses non fingo"* (I do not invent fictitious entities),* with his own: "I am not at all partial to the fabrication of

---

*"Whatever is not deduced from the phenomena," argued Newton, "is to be called an hypothesis; and hypotheses, whether metaphysical or physical, whether of occult qualities or mechanical, have no place in experimental philosophy." Newton did not remain true to this professed radical positivist credo. Induction, the method he declared as valid for making generalizations, is itself a metaphysical assumption, not deduced from the phenomena themselves. So were his assumptions of absolute space and absolute time, since refuted by modern physics. As to his idea of ether, this was an hypostatized occult physical entity.

ideologies'' (Freud, 1931)† Freud defined ideology as ''. . . an intellectual construction which solves all the problems of our existence uniformly on the basis of one overriding hypothesis, which, accordingly, leaves no question unanswered and in which everything that interests us finds its place'' (1933). This comes close to what we often refer to as dogma, orthodoxy, or cultism in the realm of ideas.

Like Newton, Freud did not avoid fabricating theoretical fictions and ideologies: 1) he invented concepts to serve as explanatory doctrines not operationally supported by data of observation; and 2) he offered moral precepts under the pretense of science.

An example of the first kind are the twin concepts ''ego libido'' and ''object libido,'' invented to explain self-love, self-importance, and selfishness. These qualities came to be labeled as narcissism, a neologism not invented by Freud (Freud, 1914). These two varieties of libido ''were derived from the study of the intimate characteristics of neurotic and psychotic processes.'' The facts Freud sought to explain were the conflict between love and self-love in the neurotic and the psychotic. The neurotic, he said, is still capable of other-directed attachments, or transferences, while the psychotic withdraws his interest from the world and is only interested in himself. Thus hysteria was classed as a transference neurosis and schizophrenia as a narcissistic neurosis, ie, one in which no attachments are possible and, consequently, one which is not amenable to any influence, including psychoanalytic influence. The task of classification was thus followed by formulating an explanatory hypothesis.

The theory Freud advanced to explain the classification of transference and narcissistic neuroses fell back on a mechanistic, reductionist definition of behavior, as embodied in his old hydraulic metaphor depicting a flow of energies. The hydraulic model was pressed into the service of explaining the varieties of love behavior. ''The libido that has been withdrawn from the external world has been directed to the ego and thus gives rise to an *attitude* which may be called narcissism'' (italics added). We are back to the metaphysics of substance: a physical event (back-flow of energy) is hypothesized as causing an attitude, a character trait. A circular argument has been set up: narcissistic neurosis means absence of attachment; absence of attachment is due to a reflux of energy into the ego; damming up of energy within the ego creates self-love.

Since the hypostatized energies are not measurable nor quantifiable, the above amounts to a feat of reification and concretization of the energy metaphor. A literal application of such reifying has led others to treat these energies as if they were persons. A passage from Nunberg, a true follower, will serve as an example: ''The paranoiac, for instance, rejects the external world more or less completely. . . . From this behavior we may conclude that he chooses his own ego as the object of his libido. *The conduct of the libido of the schizophrenic* is thus similar to that of children'' (Nunberg, 1932; italics added). In this passage the feat of reification is complete. Libido has been personified and endowed with conduct.

Now libido, from the Roman poets on, has meant sexual desire or lust. Freud oscillates between the attitude of the novelist, writing of lust and love, and the natural scientist, who dispassionately describes forms of energy. Furthermore,

---

†In the original *Weltanschauungen,* from *Weltanschauung,* literally, world-view. The other German synonyms are *Weltansicht* (view of the world) and *Weltbild* (picture of the world). All imply a point of view, a philosophy of life. Freud thought the word was difficult to translate, while Strachey considered it untranslatable and used the German word in the English text throughout. Ideology, although not a literal translation, corresponds to the common understanding of the word and the way Freud understood it.

the phrase, "the object of his libido," is no more than a feat of renaming, of inventing a technical jargon for the ordinary expression, this person is the object of his or her desire, or, simply, that he or she loves this person. What is in a name? A pretense of being scientific, a possible object of cultism. The cult of libido had its heyday among psychoanalysts. It has since undergone an atrophy of disuse.

Freud was himself uneasy about these newly created occult energy entities, which exceeded empirical evidence and were fit for Occam's razor. "Would not the postulation of a single kind of psychical energy save us all the difficulties in differentiating energy of the ego-instincts from ego-libido and ego-libido from object-libido?" (Freud, 1914). We feel sympathy for Freud, for he admits to a measure of helplessness.

Neither the classifications nor the fanciful theories have stood the test of time. As I have argued elsewhere, his energetics were a scientific metaphor for his exegetics, or the pursuit of meaning (Lothane, 1980, 1981). However, he admitted this to be a weakness of his, whereas some of his followers, who multiplied such entities, did not follow the master's advice to hold such fictions expendable but, as is true of worshipers, held on to them with cultist tenacity. Freud's own verdict on such hypotheses was stated in his famous letter to Einstein: "It may perhaps seem to you as though our theories are a kind of mythology like this? Cannot the same be said to-day of your own physics?" (Freud, 1933).

Physics, the paragon of science, which psychoanalysis has so often sought to emulate, disparaged as mythomania? Surely, the "you, too" argument has been carried too far, an excuse for the psychoanalyst's own penchant for myth-making. Freud was right and wrong. For the main difference between it and psychoanalysis is in the subject studied. In the analytic situation, or in behavior called psychopathology, the personality does not split off in a manner similar to the splitting of the atom. He was wrong in equating the myths of physics with those of psychoanalysis. Atomic physics does deal operationally with experimenting in settings far removed from ordinary experiences. Its theoretical constructs are more often operationally validated.* Psychoanalysis deals with ordinary experiences. When psychoanalysts theorize like physicists, their theories tend to be more fictional and fanciful than the theories of physicists. Not that there is anything wrong with myth-making. It is an essential ingredient of culture, a fascinating pursuit. It is food for thought, it sates metaphysical hunger. It is a magnet that attracts adherents and cults. There is nothing wrong with it as long as one owns up to what one is doing, without falling into the fallacy of concreteness.

Let us now look at some of Freud's precepts. Freud's famous prescription for living was epitomized in two slogans: "Lieben und arbeiten" (love and work) and "Wo Es war soll Ich werden" ("where id was there shall ego be"). As with other moralists, from Hillel on, Freud was concerned with defining the canon of love and obedience to authority. The ground rules of the psychoanalytic situation and the psychoanalytic attitude already embodied the cardinal moral virtues of truth, honesty, and impartiality. In addition, the rule of abstinence, derived from the injunction not to use the patient for one's own needs, whether carnal or spiritual, was itself in the spirit of the Hippocratic oath.

---

*Not only has modern atomic physics come perilously close to metaphysics, but the investigative focus has also shifted. "For the science of nature, the subject matter of research is no longer nature in itself, but nature subjected to human questioning, and to this extent man, once again, meets only with himself" (Heisenberg, quoted in Huxley, 1963).

More than that, the scientific theories themselves are covert ideologies and prescriptions for living. In his seminal work, Philip Rieff (1959) noted that the *Three Essays on Sexuality* contained a powerful moral message of sexual liberation under the guise of scientific sexology.

For about two decades following the publication of the *Three Essays*, Freud continued to adhere to the idea that the neuroses have a sexual etiology and that personal attraction is reducible to sexual attraction, casting out Jung and Adler as heretics from the dogma of the sexual nature of the libido. As the movement of sexual hygiene and sex education gathered momentum in Europe in the twenties, the year 1927 marks an interesting fork in the road. That year saw the publication of Wilhelm Reich's first version of *Die Funktion des Orgasmus* (The Function of the Orgasm) and Heinz Hartmann's *Die Grundlagen der Psychoanalyse* (The Principles of Psychoanalysis). Both men were second-generation disciples of the master, but they could not have been ideologically further apart from each other.

Reich embraced the idea of sexuality and energy in the most concrete and literal sense, extending Freud's early idea of the *Aktualneurosen* (neuroses due to the damming up of undischarged libido) to a causal definition of all neuroses and to applications in sexology. Later Reich claimed to have found the same experimental proofs for the existence of orgone energy as the physicists have done for radioactive energy. This claim later led to his conviction on charges of federal fraud and his lonely death in the Lewisburg penitentiary. Thus he became a martyr of his own cult of energy (Rieff, 1966). Freud was cool to Reich's enthusiasm for sexuality. Ideologically the aging master was turning away from Reich's crusade for the sexual happiness of the masses and from sexuality in general to a more ascetic view of sexuality and to a new ideology: ego psychology. The slogan of "where id was there shall ego be" was the succinct expression of the new ideology, and his daughter Anna and Heinz Hartmann became its most eloquent spokesmen. Perhaps the most telling in the ponderous terminological armamentarium of the new orthodoxy was the metaphor of neutralization. The invention of this alleged fictional mechanism within the ego was the proper expression of the program of purging psychoanalysis of an unhealthy preoccupation with sexuality, of the undesirable reputation of a psychology profiting from a *succès de scandale*, thus making it "kosher" for the public as a "general psychology." The same attitude is implied in the recent schools that theorize about preoedipal love, ie, love for mother which is not yet sullied by oedipal (= lustful) desires. Thus the cult of eros was replaced by the cult of ego. Both Jung and Adler, whom Freud repudiated as apostates from true belief in sexuality, must have chuckled in their graves.

In 1923, the year ego psychology was born, under a heading "The Cornerstone of Psycho-Analytic Theory," Freud defined psychoanalytic orthodoxy as follows:

> The assumption that there are unconscious mental processes, the recognition of the theory of resistance and repression, the appreciation of the importance of sexuality and of the Oedipus complex—these constitute the principal subject matter of psycho-analysis and the foundation of its theory. *No one who cannot accept them all should count himself a psychoanalyst* [Freud, 1923; italics added].

This list is interesting in that it does not enumerate dream psychology, free association and transference, discussed in the same paper, as subjects on a par with the others. Two classes of theory are combined here: On the one hand, unconscious mental activity and defense, ie, dynamisms which belong to the psychoanalytic method and, on the other hand, the theory of sexuality and the Oedipus complex, which are in the category of causal theories or doctrines. But the very question of who is an orthodox analyst, when judged by the criteria of an adherence to a particular causal theory, is a religious, not a scientific question. There are no orthodox or heretical physicists or mathematicians. The psychoanalytic movement has been torn many times by ideological wars related to causal theories. By the criteria of orthodoxy spelled out in the above-quoted passage, not a few today would not be counted as psychoanalysts. Sexuality and the Oedipus complex have been on the wane as new shibboleths have appeared among the makers of theories.

KOHUT AND THE CULT OF THE SELF

Kohut is the founder of the most recent orthodoxy, the psychology of the self, which is considered as heresy by the believers in the preceding orthodoxy known as the structural theory. Like the master, Kohut addressed a very important area of the psychology of the individual and society, the problem of self-love. Like the master, he has not remained content with describing its manifestations and deriving inductive generalizations. He went out to formulate a new causal theory of self-love. Like the master, he invented an hypostasis, an entity, which he called the structure self. This fictional structure embodies an anatomical simile. The dynamic conflict model, another cornerstone of psychoanalysis, has been given up in favor of a quasi-neurological defect model. The deficit or defect in the structure can be corrected by an addition of a missing ingredient, love, which is renamed empathy. Thus the anatomical metaphor is the garment that drapes the essential Kohutian message: a sermon of love.

The word "self" in English is a reflexive pronoun or a prefix denoting transitive action (I wash myself = my own body; self-love = I love my own person). The noun form, the self meaning person, is a common usage in English. It is rare in German and does not exist in French, so that French analysts are reduced to the ignominy of speaking of "le self." The noun "self" is not in Freud. Thus, when Freud (1915) writes about a behavior (he called it an instinctual vicissitude) directed toward oneself, which he termed "Die Wendung gegen die eigene Person," literally "turning toward one's own person," we find Riviere translating it as "turning round upon the subject," whereas Strachey renders it "turning round upon the *subject's own self*" (italics added). Replacing "person" or "subject" by "self" paves the way for introducing reification and technical jargon. Heinz Hartmann (1950) contributed an important discussion of the concept self. He followed Freud's usage of the self as synonymous with one's own person.

Kohut (1971) defines the self in a new way:

> Ego, id and superego are the constituents of a specific high level, ie, experience-distant, abstraction in psychoanalysis: the psychic apparatus. The self, however, *emerges* in the psychoanalytic situation and is conceptualized in the mode of a comparatively low level, ie, comparatively experience-near, psychoanalytic abstraction, as *a content of the mental apparatus*. It is *a structure within the mind*. Being a psychic structure, the self has, furthermore, also a psychic location. To be more specific, various—and frequently inconsistent—self-representations are present not only within the id, the ego and the superego, but also *within a single agency* of the mind [italics added].

The above passage is filled with contradictions, inexactitudes, and obscurities: 1)

What does it mean that the self emerges in the psychoanalytic situation? What makes this emergence operational? The fact is that the concept self was found elsewhere as a ready-made occult entity and smuggled into the psychoanalytic situation. 2) An abstraction is an abstraction and only operations, or doings, are experience-near. In what sense is this newly defined self less abstract than the ego? This is a scholastic, not an empirical, evaluation. The experience-near terms are "person," also, "I," "me," "you," "he," "she." 3) It is also stated that this self is a content of the mental apparatus. This phraseology evokes Wundtian introspectionism. It is a jargon equivalent of: thoughts, feelings, etc. Thoughts are also here called representations, another relic of German academic psychology. Of course, the phrase mental apparatus was Freud's own jargon. Here two contradictory claims are made on behalf of this apparatus: it is experience-distant in the theories of Freud and others, but experience-near in Kohut. How was this change achieved? 4) This fictional self is further called a psychic structure, another high-level abstraction and metaphor, and it has a location within the mind. Is mind equivalent to psychic and mental apparatus? One wonders. If so, how is this structure different from id, ego, and superego, the items in the structural theory? If structure means patterns or habits of thought, then what is the benefit of calling them by a number of different names? 5) Lastly, this self, equated with self-representations, is not only within the id, ego, and superego but also within a single agency of the mind—but which agency is the last named?

Kohut's more recent definition of the concept self is nebulous and mystifying:

> The self, whether conceived in the framework of the psychology of the self in the narrow sense of the term, as a specific structure in the mental apparatus, or, within the framework of the self in the broad sense of the term, as the center of the individual's psychological universe, is, like all reality—physical reality (the data about the world perceived by the senses) or psychological reality (the data about the world perceived via introspection and empathy)—not knowable in its essence. We cannot, by introspection and empathy, penetrate the self per se; only its introspectively perceived manifestations are open to us (1977, pp 310–311).

In this ponderous passage Kohut misreads Kant and defines the "self" as an unknowable reality. But this is sheer cultist cant, which ends on solipsism. For such an unknowable self is a myth. The possible positive achievements of Kohut can stand without any such theoretical fabrications.

Kohut also made a fetish out of the word empathy, mentioned alongside introspection in the above passage. Empathy, made popular after 1912 as a result of its use by Theodor Lipps in his theories of esthetics, is a latter-day Greek translation of the native German word *Einfühlung* (= feeling into), the ability to share and enter into experiences and emotions outside ourselves. This ability has traditionally been called sympathy, or fellow feeling. More recently it has been called identification, which Alexander (1948) defined as a "way of putting oneself in another's situation," based on one's previous experiences. Alexander also called this introspection and differentiated as follows: Things are known by inspection, people are known through introspection. Such a looking into one's own mind to understand another person was, of course, different from the way Wundt saw it. This self-evident ability is not even specific to psychoanalysis. It is basic to every act of human communication.

In his 1959 paper, "Introspection, Empathy and Psychoanalysis," Kohut did not mention Alexander in connection with introspection. He championed the cause of empathy, calling it "vicarious introspection." He who adds takes away, says the Talmud. Since vicarious means by proxy, introspection cannot be vicarious. Furthermore, Kohut did not clarify how empathy and introspection were different, to justify the use of two names for one phenomenon. Calling empathy scientific is another example of making a fetish or cult out of science.

But there is a more important meaning Kohut gave to empathy: "the cluster of ill-defined meanings, calling forth associations of friendliness and emotional warmth" (Kohut, 1980). The word love is avoided. Made greasy through millennia of misuse, love has been scientifically laundered and renamed empathy.

The structure self and the ingredient empathy were combined into one theory. Through empathy, or empathic nurturing, obtained from a self-object, the self, stunted by defects due to a lack of such nurturing in early childhood, achieves a state of restoration: The self has "a need for a self-object to complete its development." In ordinary language this reads: a child needs a good mother to grow up healthy. In the older psychoanalese mother was called a love-object. Kohut has renamed her self-object. The cliché of the schizophrenogenic mother may not be as popular these days as it used to be, but the view that lovelessness is a source of all sorts of evil is still with us. As a matter of fact, lovelessness has become an endemic condition in the psychoanalytic movement itself and in psychoanalytic institutes. No doubt Kohut improves upon Freud and Hartmann, who found no place in their canon for any positive statements about love, leaving this lowly task to revisionists like Erich Fromm and Rollo May. Again, this important moral and humanistic message can stand by itself and requires no panache of a science, let alone a pseudoscience of self, to give it legitimacy.

Kohut makes an important contribution to the ways of loving the narcissistic personality in the clinical situation. From Freud to Kernberg and to the recent The Culture of Narcissism (Lasch, 1979), the person characterized as selfish, vain, shallow, empty, dependent, demanding, and angry, in short the narcissist, has been viewed rather negatively both in the psychological and sociological literature. By calling the narcissist the "tragic man," a social synonym of the structure self, Kohut has vindicated the preponderant pathological type of our time, as Freud had earlier rehabilitated the hysteric. In doing so, Kohut has defined the social and moral aspects of self-love, both pathological and healthy, and prescribed attitudes in the therapy of the narcissist: patience, love, friendliness, and the enhancement of his native ambitions, skills, and talents, helping him to "fulfill his creative, productive destiny."

As against this message of love and tolerance, Freud, Hartmann, and Kernberg have implied, each in his own style and in theories reflecting their moral intent, that conflict, hatred, and rage must be exorcised first, that love will be only given by default and only after the reductive work of analysis has been completed, leaving the work of synthesis, or the process of socialization through love, to the individual and society. Kohut spells out his art of loving in a positive and emphatic way. He insists that love, synthesis, and socialization should be part of the analytic setting.

Over and above the realm of the clinical, Kohut has offered an ideology as defined by Freud in the quote from the thirty-fifth lecture. He says so himself: self psychology is so encompassing in its scope that the "potentialities of self-psychology [in sociocultural and historical fields] are promising to surpass even its powerful leverage in the clinical setting." Here Kohut speaks with the voice of a social reformer.

LACAN'S CULT OF "THE UNCONSCIOUS"
AND "THE LITTLE LETTERS"

The process of an idea turning into ideology and an ideology becoming the rallying point of a sociopolitical cult is again seen in the story of the French psychoanalyst, Jacques Lacan, aptly nicknamed the "French Freud." Compared with Kohut, Lacan is a prominent and flamboyant cult figure mainly due to his revolutionary politics and his esoteric theories. These elements in Lacan parallel two sides of Freud: the theorist of the unconscious and the political conquistador. Once again, a creative idea of Freud is driven by Lacan to its limit, to the point of an ideology that pretends to be an ultimate science. In Lacan, "the" unconscious reified became the unconscious deified.

The story of the Lacanian revolution in the French psychoanalytic movement is skillfully told in Sherry Turkle's *Psychoanalytic Politics: Freud's French Revolution* (Turkle, 1978). After nearly 30 years of membership in the orthodox Paris Psychoanalytic Society, Lacan was excommunicated in 1963 and proceeded to establish his own Freudian school which he later dissolved. If the orthodox psychoanalytic movement were compared to the authoritarian Catholic Church, the orthodox theories to the theological canon, and the approved technique to the official liturgy, then Lacan could be compared to Luther. Lacan attacked the authority, the canon, and the practices of the orthodox Freudians, and it may not be easy to determine which hurt most: the economic competition, the ideological splitting of the movement, or the usurpation of the power to ordain. For example, Lacan abolished the routine of fixed length and frequency of analytic sessions, leaving such matters to the creativeness of the analyst or the mood of the moment. However, the same fees were charged for the shortened sessions. He also questioned the authority of the training institute to graduate students as analysts. Since analysis was a calling, an analyst became one when he felt he was ready to be one without waiting for the official stamp of approval by a self-proclaimed ordaining authority: "Only the analyst can authorize himself as analyst" (Turkle, 1978). This idea of self-appointment is in the spirit of the fundamental Protestant position that a man is the sole judge of his conscience and is capable of communicating with God without the mediation of theologians and confessors, especially since the morals of the latter were not always above suspicion. Like the religious schisms of the past, the moral stance and the theories were used to legitimize the drive for control, power, and the attracting of followers. Today's rebels are tomorrow's establishment. Before long, Lacan and his followers became enmeshed in their own power politics and wars of theories. This situation is endemic to the profession of psychoanalysis: a strong leader has often left his parent analytic society to establish a group of his own, purer and more puristic in the pursuit of its theories. With time and with the erosion of morale due to inexorable group processes, new splits and new leaders emerge and the cycle is repeated. *Plus que ça change, ça reste la même chose.*

In his ideas Lacan went through two phases. In the first phase Lacan championed a return to early Freud, to his concept unconscious as delineated in *The Interpretation of Dreams, The Psychopathology of Everyday Life,* and *Jokes and their Relationship to the Unconscious.* This early Freud has an affinity to language and literature, as compared with the later Freud, from 1911 on, who has an affinity to abstract metapsychology, biology, and biological theories. In general, the French psychoanalysts have maintained an allegiance to the earlier, literary concept of the unconscious, overtly opposing the Americans, who under the influence of

Anna Freud and Heinz Hartmann, advanced the biological conception of the unconscious and ego psychology.

When *The Interpretation of Dreams* was first translated into French it was titled *Science des Rêves (The Science of Dreams)*. Although science and dreaming might appear to be a contradiction in terms, the fact is that Freud was the first psychologist who discovered the laws governing representational thinking (imagery, dreams, and daydreams) and its relation to discursive thinking. He called this primary and secondary process thinking, respectively). In this context Hartmann's (1950) position that "Exact science, the highest form of thinking, attempts to exclude all images and qualities from the world of thought," in fact amounted to a revision of Freud's thought. Psychoanalysis is a science, but it is not physics. For whereas it is scientific enough to speak, with Hartmann, of the "biological meaning of thought processes" (Hartmann, 1950, p 307), in the context of the discourse about the adaptation of the organism to the environment, it is no less scientific to treat of the imaginary and the meaning of images. Hartmann's dictum above images amounts to disregarding an essential ingredient of human psychic reality and creating a scientist fiction, parallel to the fiction created by Galileo in his doctrine of secondary qualities and its latter-day offshoot, Wundtian academic psychology. Lacan continued Freud's researches of psychic reality which he described as the levels of the imaginary, the symbolic, and the real. He imitated the spirit and style of Freud's *The Interpretation of Dreams,* unifying subject matter and style. *The Interpretation of Dreams* is about dreams, and it reads like a dream: it has an appeal at multiple levels of meaning, it flows back and forth between discursive and representational thought and it reveals different facets of idea and mood with each new reading of the text. Lacan gave new expression to this unity of style and substance, as described in the following passage from a brilliant Yale monograph, "French Freud" (Mehlman, 1973).

> The unprepared reader may perhaps begin to find his bearings if we situate the *genre* into which our [Lacan's] text falls, somewhere in between intellectual prose poem and crossword puzzle. But this outrageousness, this insistence on mediating the ultimate (ly meaningful) through the nonsensical is part of an effort to revive that telling sense of impropriety which shocked the first readers of the *Traumdeutung* with the feeling that the book's "analyses" resembled nothing so much as a collection of (bad) jokes (p 26).

The difference between Freud and Lacan, however, is that Freud may be difficult to translate, but he was never unintelligible. Lacan often is. The French have notoriously glorified the word and Lacan is in the tradition of playing with the sensual sound of words, the multiple levels of punning, the multifaceted meanings of a phrase. He has, for example, described the father–son relationship as the *Nom-du-Père,* the father's name. This pithy aphorism condenses many levels of meaning: The parent, the oedipal father, the Lord, the symbolic lawgiver and law-enforcer, the name the child takes from the father. A pun on *Nom-du-Père* is *le non du père,* father's "no," his authority to forbid. A later pun, created by Lacan in 1973–1974, was *Les Non-Dupes Errent,* sounding the same as the two preceding phrases and meaning: those who are above being fooled (duped) are liable to make mistakes.

This playing with words, sounds, and meanings could be likened to a psychodrama of his leading theory in both content and form. This theory states:

the unconscious is structured like a language. This new structuralism is indeed in the spirit of Freud's determinism but was never stated by Freud. Freud's was also a reified conception of the system unconscious, or the reified id, but he conceived language as an instrument of expression of the forces of the id. The Lacanian innovation is in marrying linguistics, anthropology, and the Freudian unconscious to create a new idol, structural linguistics. He combined this structuralism with a peculiar style.

Freud, like Jesus, taught in parables. Lacan, like the Bible, writes in tropes (figures of speech), in allegories, and he speaks in puns, neologisms, and uses twisted syntax. He also plays with mathematical symbols.

The esoteric book of *Zohar* (1952) of the Jewish mystical tradition known as the Kabbalah views the Bible as follows (Book 111, 152a):

> Woe to the son of man who says the Torah contains common sayings and ordinary narratives. . . . No! Every word of the Law has a sublime sense and a heavenly mystery. . . . When it descended on earth, the Law had to put on earthly garments, in order to be understood by us, and the narratives are its garments. . . . Those who have understanding do not look at the garment but at the body [the esoteric meaning] beneath; while the wisest, the servants of the heavenly King, those who dwell in Mount Sinai, look at nothing but the soul.

We need a closer look at the truth Lacan is beholding and the garments in which it is clothed. Lacan has created a unique blend of Freud and two theorists, the Swiss linguist, Ferdinand de Saussure, and the French anthropologist, Claude Lévi-Strauss. More than simply assimilating the views of these theorists, Lacan has transformed them and transvaluated them, twisting original intentions and definitions.

At the beginning of the century Ferdinand de Saussure founded structural linguistics. He draw a distinction between universal and collective language *(langue)* and individual acts of speech *(parole)*. Language was seen as a system of relations between the word, ie, the sign or the signifier *(signifiant)* and the idea, ie, the signified *(signifié)*. Using language as a system of conventional signification and reference, each individual develops his own form and style of communicating, his own speech acts.

Saussure's definition of the signifier as pointing to the idea signified is useful as long as it is remembered, as taught by Cassirer (1944), that both ordinary language and the specialized language of mathematics are symbolic forms, ie, means of creating references to this or that aspect of the universe or of human life. Cassirer also made a careful distinction between communication by means of signs, or signals, and symbols, ie, between acts of signalizing and symbolizing. "Signals and symbols belong to different universes of discourse: a signal is part of a physical world of being; a symbol is part of the human world of meaning." People engage either in propositional acts of speech or in emotional acts of speech.

Freud (1900) compared dreams and symptoms to an encoded language or text: "Words, since they are the nodal points of numerous ideas, may be regarded as predestined to ambiguity; and the neuroses (eg, in framing obsessions and phobias), no less than dreams, make unashamed use of the advantages thus offered by words for purposes of condensation and disguise" (pp 340–341). In Freud's words, the dream and the symptom have reference not to material but to psychic reality. Thus, they may be fully compared to emotional speech acts.

The manifest dream content stands to the latent dream content in a relation of a sign to the signified, or a relation of reference. The dream language is not, like the Saussurean signifier, a universal language, but an individual language and what is more, a private code language. The encoding comes about as a result of the unconscious mental activity which Freud called the dream work. This dream work is a universal human capacity; like speaking a language and like language, it can be employed in shaping individual speech acts. Whereas linguistic texts can be read, dreams and symptoms can only be decoded.

Thus it can be seen that the Saussurean concept of speech is in keeping with the Freudian conception of dreams as acts of speech. Dreams are created through an innate human capability, the dream work, which is as innate as language. But as I have argued elsewhere (Lothane, 1981), reality is prior to the dream. Dreams are a response to reality and not just a result of a deterministic force or energy. They are caused by the person's experiences in reality and by his antecedent thoughts and feelings. Such a conception views man as having a capability for using unconscious mental activity rather than viewing the unconscious as lodged within man and directing his actions.

Lacan followed the French anthropologist, Claude Lévi-Strauss, reversing the natural order of reality as prior to the dream. Lévi-Strauss' dictum was that *"Le significant précède et détermine le signifié"* (the signifier precedes and determines the signified) (Mehlman, 1973). This is a succinct statement of linguistic structuralism or linguistic determinism. Language makes man, not man uses language to live his life. This linguistic structuralism is the French counterpart of the American biological structuralism. Like anatomical structures, linguistic structures are viewed as concrete morphological entities, not hypothetical or mythical ones. But causal theories, as we saw, can be turned into articles of faith and objects of cult. The difference between language and body parts is that linguistic structures are meaningful sounds and used to communicate meaning and intention. Laws of things, laws of thought and laws of speech do not overlap exactly. Reality and thought are larger than language. In positing language as a reality that determines all realities, language is viewed as something thing-like and god-like, rather than as man's tool for making meanings, intentions and purposes.

Lacan followed faithfully in Lévi-Strauss' footsteps: "Our program," states Lacan (1966) in the keynote paper of a selection of his works, "is from here on to know how a formal language determines the subject *[le sujet]*. For the basic reason that language with its structure preexists at the entrance that every person makes in it at a moment of his mental development."

To achieve this deterministic program he sets up a most ambiguous dialectic between the signifier as material cause and the signifier as determiner of meaning. He sets up two equations for the signifier. Language as signifier equals the Freudian id and it also equals the Other. This Other is not a Sartrian other, it is a new creation. Let us follow the way he shapes this new creation.

In considering Freud's famous dictum, *"Wo Es war soll Ich werden,"* Lacan affirms that it should not be translated, as is customary, "where the id was there shall ego be." The reason for this is that the id "is the true subject of the unconscious and the ego [is] constituted by a series of alienating identifications." In one clean stroke Lacan reverses Freud's later emphasis on the ego and repudiates all of ego psychology. His translation is: *"Là où c'etait il me faut advenir,"* ("I have a duty to come into being in the place of the id which is the place of being"). In addition, he plays on the homophony of the German Es (= id) with the first letter "s," of the word subject. With this simple linguistic trick he proves the equations id = subject, id = the other. It is in this sense that the id speaks before the conscious subject; it is in this sense that the signifier determines the signified, the structure determines the person, as he explains (Lacan, 1966).

> The effect of language, it is the cause introduced into the subject *[sujet]*. Because of this effect, he is not cause of himself, he carries within himself the worm of the cause that splits him. For his cause is the signifier without which there would be no subject in reality. But this subject is what the signifier represents, and he cannot represent anything but this for another signifier: to which, from here on, is reduced that subject that listens.

> Thus, one does not speak to a subject. It (the id) speaks from him, and this way he apprehends himself; and so much more so that prior to the single fact, ie, It (the id) addressing him and he disappearing as subject under the signifier which he becomes, he was absolutely nothing [p 835; author's translation].

Whereas in dream life and in the context of dream psychology communication is aimed at evocation, not information, it cannot be said that all human intercourse is reducible to dreaming. Equating dream psychology with the reified unconscious, Lacan maintains the "the efficacy of the unconscious does not stop with awakening." With this we agree, but such a radical extension should only complement, not negate, the power of conscious reason, as stated by the later Freud. This point was eloquently argued by Herbert Marcuse in *Eros and Civilization,* before Lacan. Curiously, Marcuse is not mentioned in Lacan's authors' index.

Lacan's return to the early conception of the unconscious is strongly reminiscent of the romantic German *Naturphilosophie*. The unconscious is the creative center of man and the repository of truth. The unconscious is God and Lacan is his prophet, speaking in the style of the Gospel:

> I, the truth, I speak. . . . It goes beyond allegory. It simply means all that can be said about truth, the only truth, namely that there is no metalanguage (an assertion meant to put in its place all logico-positivism), that no language is capable of saying the true about the true because truth is in what it speaks and that it has no other way to achieve it. And that is why the unconscious which says it, the true about the true, is structured like a language and that is why myself, when I teach this, I say the true about Freud, who knew how to let truth speak under the name of the unconscious [pp 867–868; author's translation].

In spite of this oracular attitude, Lacan, like Freud before him, takes pains to dissociate himself from any connection with established religion. However, in his attempt to define psychoanalysis as a "conjectural science," separate from all others, including biology and the humanities (Kohut also denied a connection to the humanities), we see the first cracks and non sequiturs in the logic of his discourse (Lacan, 1966).

> . . . the truth as cause in the sciences is known under the aspect of a formal cause. Psychoanalysis, on the other hand, emphasizes the aspect of the material cause. This is what marks its originality in science. This material cause is properly the form of occurrence of the signifier. In psychoanalysis the signifier is defined primarily as acting *separately from its* signification. It is here that we find the character of concreteness *[trait de caractère littéral]* which qualifies the *copulatory signifier*, the phallus, which emerges beyond the limits of the biological

> maturation of the person [subject]. . . . Thus, the subject of the signifier . . . carried [véhiculé] by the signifier, is to be sharply distinguished both from the biological individual and from any psychological evolution which may be subsumed under the category of the comprehending person. This, in minimal terms, is the function I accord to language in the theory. It seems to me compatible with historical materialism which has left a void there [p 875; author's translation italics added].

Is historical materialism the same as the dialectical materialism of Marx, toward whom Lévi-Strauss, Lacan, and his followers have professed a strange attraction? How does the concrete phallus fill the void left by materialism? What is meant by the phallus being concrete, but not biological? What is meant by the signifier separated from signification? This sounds like theory gone wild, not even euphonious, just plain erroneous. People have worshiped Lacan as a true cult hero. The oracle at Delphi may have been an object of as much worship as Lacan, but it certainly was more intelligible in its pronouncements about human nature.

One of the startling contradictions in Lacan is his use of the Cartesian *cogito ergo sum* (I think, therefore I am) in the context of his doctrine of the signifier. Nothing could be further removed from Freud than Descartes' idealism and the idealistic position that thinking is to be equated with conscious processes. Philosophers who followed the idealistic tradition were unanimous in rejecting the reality of unconscious mental activity, and Freud railed against them, and consequently, and erroneously, against all philosophy.

Lacan scales new heights in self-contradiction with his preoccupation with another Cartesian idea, that of a *mathesis universalis,* a universal mathematical language, based on mathematics and geometry, to be used as a criterion of all that is scientific discourse. To playing with word forms (puns, rebuses, crossword puzzles, metaphor and metonymy) Lacan has added playing with mathematical forms: algebraic equations (algorithms) and the branch of geometry called topology.

First there are in his texts assorted diagrams and schema reminiscent of Freud's *Project,* replete with upper- and lower-case letters, Greek characters, and German Gothic characters. Then there are the equations. His position is announced in the title of the paper: "The Instance of the Letter in the Unconscious." This is structuralism with a vengeance: the structures in the unconscious, or language, are no longer words but letters of the alphabet, literally so. Here structuralism has been pushed to an unprecedented degree of fragmentation and far removed from anything Lévi-Strauss even dreamt of. An example is taken from Appendix II, the Metaphor of the Subject. To explain what metaphor is about, he quotes an equation from the just-quoted paper on the letter in the unconscious, which is nowhere to be found there:

$$\frac{S}{s'_1} \quad \bullet \quad \frac{S'_2}{x} \quad \rightarrow \quad S\left(\frac{1}{s''}\right)$$

The equation contains big S for signifier and small s for signified. This equation is applied to the phrase "an ocean of false learning" (in English in the original) in the following manner:

$$\frac{\text{An ocean}}{\text{learning}} \text{ of } \frac{\text{false}}{\text{X}} \rightarrow \text{an ocean } \left(\frac{1}{?}\right).$$

Lacan explains: "Learning, teaching, indeed, are not science, and one can see much more clearly that this word has no more to do with the ocean than hair with soup." The same could be said of these equations and figures of speech.

Subsequent to the work which appears in the *Ecrits*, which do not go beyond 1966, Lacan pushed further the idea of the mathematization of psychoanalytic science. Already in the *Ecrits*, in a "Classified Index of Major Concepts," the devout Lacanian nonanalyst and philosopher, Jacques-Alain Miller (Lacan's son-in-law), employed such expressions as "the geometry of the ego," "the topology of the subject." Now, ten years later, Miller took literally Lacan's notion of the matheme, the equation made up of letters, to convert it into a scientific "psychoanalysis of little letters" (Turkle, 1978).

The culmination of such mathematical abracadabras can be seen in Lacan's use of topology, the special geometry of spheres, circles, and Borromean knots to define the imaginary, the real, the symbolic, and the symptom. The most mature fruit of this cultist quest for a true science is the marriage of mathematical psychology and psychoanalytic fictions.

Turkle (1978) describes Lacan's appearances in 1975 at MIT and Yale. At MIT he drew elaborate knots and circles and stated, "I call the knot with three circles the figure of psychic reality and Σ is the symptom. The symptom is the special mark of human dimension. Perhaps God has symptoms but his understanding is most probably paranoid. . . . What is illustrated best is paranoid knowledge." When asked about the relationship between interior and exterior, Lacan stated that "as an analyst, he was not at all certain that man even had an interior: The only thing that seems to me to testify to it is that which we produce as excrement. . . . Civilization means shit, *cloaca maxima.*"

At Yale, when asked about the relationship between psychoanalysis, linguistics, and hermeneutics (the science of interpretation), Lacan stated that, "Genuine science had to follow in the line of Galileo and Newton. . . . To explain ½ MV² [$\frac{1}{2}MV^2$], the relationship between mass and acceleration, by using language is a long detour. . . . Science is that which holds together in its relation to the real due to the usage of little letters."

With all forbearance, the above amounts to intellectual bankruptcy. Faced with this disaster, Turkle attempts to save appearances by pleading that in coming to America, like Freud before him, Lacan has "come to speak. In other words, he would not speak *of* psychoanalysis; the speech itself would *be* a psychoanalytic discourse, he himself characterized [it] at MIT as discourse close to delirium." But surely this goes too far. A science of the irrational need not itself be irrational. Like Oscar Wilde, Lacan liked the enchantment of the histrionic gesture. *Le style c'est l'homme.* Style does make the man, and the intellectual fetish as well.

Turkle, at home both in psychology and computer technology, an obvious but ambivalent admirer of Lacan, has viewed these efforts of the *Maître* as follows: "The mathematical modeler often sees his enterprise as scientific and precise, as opposed to literary or poetic. Lacan refuses this dichotomy. He cuts across a line between poetry and science that has become axiomatic in the philosophy if not the practice of Western science." She even ventures the hypothesis that "Perhaps in some important ways [the unconscious] is structured like mathematics as well; so that doing mathematics like dreaming can, if properly understood, give us access to what is normally hidden from us.''

This reasoning, as pious as it sounds, glosses over a serious confusion. Mathematical formulas, ''the dry fruits of the Pythagorean tree,'' as she so poetically puts it, were used by Galileo, Newton, and Einstein to express truths about the physical universe, not about man or human relations or the nature of love. Physics, mathematics, and music may be expressions of one great reality, but human reality, the reality of beauty, truth, joy and suffering, is still beyond equations and computers.

SOME CONCLUSIONS

The notion of cult of idols-as-gods has been applied to the cult of ideas-as-ideologies: to the worship of myths, prejudices and fallacies. A cult prominent in the West since the ancient Greeks is metaphysical materialism and its offshoots in psychology (and psychoanalysis): atomism, anatomism, structuralism, reification and reduction.

This materialism has resulted in a preoccupation with theorizing about mind, ie, what mind *is* and what *causes* mind, versus working with what mind *does*—love, work and ethical conduct. Such doings imply a doer, a person. Both the doings and the doer are in the realm of certain and operational ideas about mind. Theories about mind are doomed to remain in the realm of the probable.

Since Freud, psychoanalysts have oscillated between operational certainties and theoretical probabilities, confusing the certain and the probable, turning theory into dogma and worshiping dogma as an ideological panacea. However, as much as Freud himself set the example of working with mind and theorizing about mind, he never lost sight of the person at the center. Theorists after Freud have worshiped the idol of the depersonalized person: an abstraction spun out of their theories.

These new theories, no more than new names for old facts, have often been equated with progress in the science of psychoanalysis, on a par with break-throughs in technology. But advances in the sciences of matter have no counterpart in the sciences of man. Progress in the affairs of man is in the art of living: the manner in which men and women love and work and how ethically they act toward each other.

Psychoanalysis is both an art and a science. To paraphrase Freud, it is the impossible science. In the words of Alexis Carrel (1935) it realizes the impossible feat of being a science of the particular. It needs abstractions and generalizations, but at its center is the concrete individual who lives, loves, suffers and dies. Medicine, the other art and science of the particular, has been increasingly concerned with ethics. It is time for psychoanalysis to do likewise.

BIBLIOGRAPHY

Alexander F: *Fundamentals of Psychoanalysis.* New York, WW Norton, 1948.

Bacon F: *Novum Organum.* Quoted in the *Encyclopedia Britannica,* ed 11.

Burtt EA: *The Metaphysical Foundations of Modern Physical Science.* Garden City, NY, Doubleday, 1924.

Carrel A: *Man the Unknown.* New York, Harper & Brothers, 1935.

Cassirer F: *An Essay on Man.* Garden City, NY, Doubleday, 1944.

Collingwood RG: *The Idea of Nature.* London, Oxford University Press, 1945.

Dewey J: *The Quest of Certainty.* New York, GP Putnam's Sons, 1929.

Freud S: The interpretation of dreams. *Standard Edition.* London, Hogarth Press, 1900, vol 5.

Freud S: On narcissism: An introduction. *Standard Edition.* London, Hogarth Press, 1914.

Freud S: Instincts and their vicissitudes. *Standard Edition.* London, Hogarth Press, 1915, vol 14.

Freud S: Group psychology and the analysis of the ego. *Standard Edition.* London, Hogarth Press, 1921, vol 14.

Freud S: Two encyclopedia articles. *Standard Edition.* London, Hogarth Press, 1923, vol 18.

Freud S: Inhibitions, symptoms and anxiety. *Standard Edition.* London, Hogarth Press, 1926, vol 20.

Freud S: New introductory lectures. *Standard Edition.* London, Hogarth Press, 1933, vol 18.

Freud S: Why war? *Standard Edition.* London, Hogarth Press, 1933, vol 22.

Hartmann H: *Ego Psychology and the Problem of Adaptation.* New York, International Universities Press, 1950.

Huxley: *Literature and Science.* New York, Harper & Row, 1963.

Kohut H: Introspection, empathy and psychoanalysis. *J Am Psychoanal Assoc* 1959;7: 459–482.

Kohut H: in Goldberg A (ed): *The Analysis of the Self.* New York, International Universities Press, 1971.

Kohut H: in Goldberg A (ed): *The Restoration of the Self.* New York, International Universities Press, 1977.

Kohut H: Reflections, in Goldbert A (ed): *Advances in Self Psychology.* New York, International Universities Press, 1980.

Lacan J: *Ecrits.* Paris, Editions du Seuil, 1966.

Lasch C: *The Culture of Narcissism.* New York, Warner Books, 1979.

Lothane Z: The art of listening. *Psychoanal Rev* 1980;67:353–364.

Lothane Z: A perspective on Freud and psychoanalysis. *Psychoanal Rev* 1981;68:348–361.

Lothane Z: Listening with the third ear as an instrument in psychoanalysis. *Psychoanal Rev* 1981;68:487–504.

Lothane Z: The psychopathology of hallucinations—A methodological analysis. *Br J Med Psychology* 1982;55:335–348.

Lothane Z: Reality, trauma and dreams in the psychoanalytic-therapeutic situation. In press.

Mehlman J: *French Freud.* Yale French Studies. New Haven, Yale University Press, 1973.

Murphy G: *Historical Introduction to Modern Psychology.* New York, Harcourt, Brace & World, 1949.

Nunberg H: *Principles of Psychoanalysis.* New York, International Universities Press, 1932.

Rieff P: *Freud: The Mind of the Moralist.* New York, Doubleday, 1959.

Rieff P: *The Triumph of the Therapeutic.* New York, Harper & Row, 1966.

Turkle S: *Psychoanalytic Politics.* New York, Basic Books, 1978.

Zohar: Quoted in: G. de Purucker. *Fundamentals of the Esoteric Philosophy.* Philadelphia, David McKay, 1952, Book 111, 152A.

CHAPTER

13

Group Processes in Cult Affiliation and Recruitment*

DAVID A. HALPERIN

C ult affiliation and the apparent ease by which individuals transform their lives to follow unexpected and often strange gods is a matter of increasing concern. A wide variety of explanations have been offered for this profound and seemingly paradoxical transformation of open-minded, liberal, "laid back" late adolescents to constricted, inhibited religious zealots, which has both intrigued and puzzled mental health professionals and the cult members' unhappy families. Explanations of this process range from the absence of any strong internalized sense of religious or personal identity in an alienated adolescent, to the pathological need for strong, external structures to provide for separation in individuals who are symbiotically enmeshed in their families, to sophisticated formulations of coercive persuasion based on studies of brainwashing with the use of information restrictions, sleep deprivation and even protein restriction. Obviously, each of these explanations provides a partial understanding of a complex and multidimensional process.

The actual act of cult affiliation frequently occurs within a group setting. This aspect of the complex problem of affiliation and conversion is often dealt with under the rubric of "group pressures," without attempting to define or understand the dynamics that are operative within the group setting. This article explores the process of cult affiliation and the maintenance of cult membership from the vantage point of group dynamics. The recent additions to our understanding of group processes provided by object relations theory and the work of Bion (Kernberg, 1977) and Ezriel (1952) are particularly important as they reflect upon the inherent potential within all groups for cultlike transformation and on the regressive potential within individuals for loss of individually and autonomy.

There is considerable disagreement as to the actual mental status of the prospective cult member prior to cult affiliation. The preponderance of cult affiliates

*Reprinted with permission from the publisher, Bruner & Mazel, New York, *Group* 1982;6(2):13–24.

are late adolescents or young adults. They may be and often are afflicted with the sense of alienation and disengagement, the need to question adult authorities and the need to establish their own authority that is pervasive within this population (Eckstein, 1978). A substantial number (although this is open to widely divergent estimates) are severely dysfunctional prior to cult affiliation or come from families which are themselves conflict ridden. The prototypical cult affiliate is white, middle class and has had some post-high school education. Jews appear to be overrepresented as cult affiliates. Affiliation frequently occurs during a period of transition and is often associated with a severe loss or disappointment. Thus, the prospective cult affiliate is an individual who has just finished a period of schooling, who is without clear plans for the future, and who may have embarked on a *Wanderjahr* through the Golden West.

The recruitment procedures of different cult groups vary. During the course of psychiatric consultations at the Cult Hotline Project of the Jewish Board of Family and Children's Services and at the Cult Information Treatment Program of the Westchester Jewish Community Services, parents have given widely divergent histories of their children's cult recruitment and affiliation. Nonetheless, the very prominence of the Unification Church, both in numbers and as a source of parental concern, permit it to be considered as paradigmatic for both recruitment procedures and the manner in which these procedures reflect group processes and dynamics. Galper (1977) has succinctly described the recruitment program:

> Initial rapport is generally established on the street or the college campus. The potential recruit is invited to attend a dinner at one of the urban Unification residential centers. At the conclusion of the center dinner he is invited to participate in a weekend experience in an isolated rural setting. In California, the New Ideal City Ranch in Mendocino County and Camp Mozundar in the San Bernardino Mountains are the primary rural locations utilized. At the conclusion of the weekend experience recruits are invited to stay on at the camp for a week-long training session.

Personal accounts of cult affiliation, such as Christopher Edwards autobiography, *Crazy for God* (1979) or the moving account of Josh Freed, *Moonwebs* (1980), describe the protypical cult affiliate as arriving at one of the transportation terminals of a major Western city. Wearing his knapsack emblematically slung over his shoulder, he is accosted by a couple who greet him effusively as if he were a long-lost brother.

This encounter occurs prototypically in the context of a state—California—whose every name is a promise of limitless experience (Smelser, 1980). It may occur in a city—San Francisco—whose very existence is defined by its location at the boundary of the continent and whose harbor signifies a portal to the beyond rather than an entry into the nitty-gritty of human experience. For the white, middle-class, Eastern or Midwestern, late adolescent, California promises liberation from the confinements that other contexts impose in the name of ethnicity or religion. Its motto is *Plus Ultra*. It is a more inherently anonymous context despite the persistence of neighborhoods and towns—Telegraph Hill, Venice, or even Berkeley—which exist within the grid of freeways. Thus, it is hardly surprising that the newly arrived late adolescent, who has travelled West buoyed on the promise of liberation, experiences within it the threat of isolation and loneliness. When the friendly, seemingly disinterested, notably clean-cut couple invite the newcomer home for dinner with "congenial" friends, the newcomer may accept because the promise of a dinner with "friends" is intriguing as much for the sense of boundaries and home that it provides as for the meal it ensures.

The "house on Washington Street" of *Moonwebs* promises a place to eat. But, more importantly, it promises a context in which to relate. It provides a time and place for the individual who is literally at loose ends, at the end of the continent, to establish some human context in which to function. The need for boundaries—for human contexts in which to meet, eat and relate—is hardly pathological. Parenthetically, it may be that some of the nonchalance with which many Californians view unusual religious groupings derives from this recognition of the importance of ideological organizations in communities where the older ties based on ethnicity and mainstream religions no longer provide support. Indeed, the very rapidity by which Californians change their ideological or religious colors reflects an environment in which groups become more important for the boundaries they provide than for the ideology they purvey.

In the initial recruiting encounter, the prospective cult member is greeted with effusive and totally unjudgmental approval. His offhand comments are treated as revelations. This use of unqualified and total approval of the prospective cult member by the cult recruiter has been dubbed "love bombing." What role does it play in the process of cult affiliation? The very qualified nature of an interaction helps to preserve the autonomy and individuality of the participants. To give total approval without any type of qualification is to deny the existence of the observing ego on the part of either participant within a dialogue. Total approval can occur only within contexts which implicitly promote or explicitly celebrate merger and fusion. It is a staple of Romantic poetry and the literature of mysticism. But, in adult discourse, the presence of qualification is part and parcel of a maneuver to preserve ego boundaries and independence. Love bombing is, then, a very subtle but direct attack on the premises by which autonomy is preserved within a system of discourse. It promotes regression by promising a return to the very early symbiotic level of the mother's unqualified approval and love. The promotion of a symbiotic mode of interaction beyond this very early period threatens the individual's autonomy and potential for autonomous growth and development. Above all, it begs the question: How can anyone be repaid for the "total" sacrifice as in the fundamentalist slogan, "Christ died for your sins—what are you doing for him?" These implications of love bombing will be dealt with at a later point in this discussion.

The actual dinner at the recruiting center is followed by a survey of the world scene. This overview is a carefully rehearsed presentation in which the current scene is portrayed in apocalyptic terms. It is a presentation calculated to ally the cult recruiters with the adolescent's anger at the adult world for not living up to its pretensions of omnipotence and omniscience. Above all, it is calculated to heighten the prospective cult member's sense of estrangement from a world that is portrayed in menacing terms and heighten the desire to enter into a world/group that promises protection/survival. In individual terms, the recruiter allies himself with the primitive and punitive superego that is latent within this unformed group:

> Concretely, the temptation to identify with the early oedipal father perceived as the guardian of the law, the owner of all women, and the dangerous punisher for rebellion; the tendencies for authoritarian structuring of social reality, sexual repressiveness, and the idealization of autocractic leaders are there in all of us (Kernberg, 1977).

In a very basic sense, the cult recruiter's task is facilitated by the very isolation of the prospective recruitee which adds conviction to the assumption that, in some magical fashion, a group, any group, perhaps even this group will be able to help him solve the problem of anxiety and isolation. As Boris et al (1975) has noted:

> No one seems to challenge either the belief that there is such a thing as a group or the belief that the manifestation of things in common can possibly outmeasure the differences of every sort and variety that, in actuality, exist among the people present. . . . The energy and persistence they show in making a group suggests, moreover, that a group is a very valuable thing to have.

Moreover, the potential recruit is not aware of the fact that the group which he sees as loving and spontaneous has been carefully assembled to an end. Isolation and loneliness push the individual toward joining the group. The potential recruit sees in the recruiting group "the collective actualization of a shared fantasy" (Boris et al, 1975). In this context, love bombing serves to "augment the self by forcing an immediate alliance with the self against the differentiated parental introjects" (Boris et al, 1975).

The lecture at the recruiting center with its apocalyptic overtones may reflect the actual theological concerns of the parent group, but the presence of *Endtime* as a pervasive theme within groups as diverse as the Unification Church, the Jehovah's Witnesses, and the Seventh Day Adventists reflects other issues. It has a powerful appeal to the isolated and alienated adolescent who, finding himself at the end of the continent, is more than willing to consider the implications of the End of Days. Especially, when the group leader agrees with his strictures against a vain, self-involved, and absent adult world.

By his castigation of the outside world, the cult recruiter encourages the susceptible adolescent to join the group. The message is clear: Outside all is cold and unfeeling; huddle with us for protection and remake the world in your own image. Kernberg (1977) has noted:

> The Messianic temptations of small groups such as the search for "instant intimacy," or the breaking of ordinary sexual boundaries, illustrate the appeal of the various contemporary group movements that have exploited these processes in more or less sensationalist ways.

With his focus on Armageddon, the apocalyptic battle at the End, the cult recruiter encourages the prospective recruit to consider himself as a member of an organization that assumes many of the characteristics of a basic assumptions group. Bion has noted that all groups have the potential to regress to three basic assumptions when there is faulty group leadership or when the group is given tasks that are obviously so overwhelming that they cannot realistically be attained (Kernberg, 1977). The three basic assumptions are the "fight–flight" assumption, the "dependency" assumption, and the "pairing" assumption. Clearly, averting or surviving the apocalypse is a task of such a nature that any task orientation becomes ill-defined and both individual and group feel ill-equipped to cope with their "responsibility." Thus, the group members are encouraged to huddle around the group leader in defense against the impending end:

The "fight–flight" group is united against vaguely perceived external enemies, and expects the leader to direct the fight against such enemies, as well as to protect the group against any in-fighting. . . . The group's tendency to forcefully control the leader or to experience itself forcefully controlled by him to experience "closeness" in a shared denial of intergroup hostility, and to project aggression onto an outgroup, all are prevalent (Kernberg, 1977).

The world continues to be both depicted and derided in terms that reinforce this basic assumption among those who have already affiliated with the group or who contemplate entering under its "sheltering wings."

The ostensible purpose of the invitation to the recruiting session is to share a meal with "like-minded" people. The food supplied to the prospective cult members at this session and thereafter has often been described as a relatively textureless vegetarian stew. In a sense, this stew may presage the group's ultimate intentions toward the recruit—to reduce the individual to a cipher without the textures or taste that characterize individuality. The use of a monotonous and limited diet with its possible protein deprivation has been discussed elsewhere as an aspect of "brainwashing." But, as Levi-Strauss and others who have explored the profound meaning of eating rituals have demonstrated, this may be simplistic. In a very profound sense, groups that place a great emphasis on denigrating individuality must inevitably create a food which denies individual taste. Likewise, the vegetarian focus of many cults may not simply be a denial of "cruelty to animals" but rather reflects their need to denigrate assertion within the group and their need to externalize any aggression. Intriguingly, it has been noted retrospectively by family members that the first indicator of protocultic involvement was the refusal to eat meat and/or the use of dietary restrictions to separate the individual from his or her family. Certainly, as the individual progresses into a cult, the restrictions on the intake of meat and other dietary practices become symbolic of communion with the group and the masochistic denial of pleasure becomes a means of reaffirming group involvement.

During the course of this introductory dinner, the prospective recruit is urged to join the group for a weekend "seminar." The seminar is portrayed as a camp outing. The trip to it occurs at night. The "seminar" is conducted at an isolated rural retreat. The sense of a camp outing is reemphasized by the use of camplike and "campy" songs. Somerset Maugham is reputed to have once wittily observed that it is really striking how enjoyable cheap, popular music is. He referred to the individual's need to regress to periods in which the individual was able to enjoy experiences that lack complexity. Thus, the group sponsors a regression to childhood experiences of trust and protection when decision making was placed in others' hands.

On arrival at the recruiting compound, the prospective recruit is placed in a camplike atmosphere. Mattresses are everywhere. Members are encouraged to use their sleeping bags. The very absence of furniture deprives the members of adult objects that might provide sanctuary and boundaries that might limit the potential for regression. Even private access to bathrooms, etc, is infringed upon—the recruit is always accompanied by an assigned group member—and regression further encouraged since this parallels the individual's experience when, as a very young child, access to the bathroom was strictly monitored. Moreover, the group refers to itself as "The Family" and the individual monitors assume the role of "True Parents." Above all, recruits are strongly discouraged from exchanging ideas or information about their experience with other recruits. Contact is allowed only with established cult members whose controlling presence is ubiquitous and parental. Thus despite the presence of other recruits, the individual recruit is reduced to a condition of isolation, dependent solely on the established cult members for support, and in a condition of moral and intellectual impotence comparable to that described by Freud in *Group Psychology and the Analysis of the Ego* (1921).

The individual's sense of moral and intellectual impotence is heightened by the use of quasitherapeutic techniques. Recruits are asked to share personal experiences with members of a group (many of whom are already cult members). These group experiences are very carefully structured with a leader who is clearly vested with authority. Since many of the other members of the group are cult members, it is not surprising that they are comfortable both in sharing individual experiences of the precult life and in accepting the leader's authority. Thus, the unwary recruit is placed in a group which encourages the lowering of barriers to intimacy in a setting where the leader's authority is clearly enhanced and where the recruit expects some significant experience to occur. As Silverman (1979) has noted, this constellation may permit

> the activation [of a fantasy] which also may play a role in some of the noninsight agents of change under consideration here, one involving an internalization of the "oedipal father's" strength and power, and on a deeper level his penis. This fantasy . . . is activated in many real-life situations, perhaps most particularly in religious experiences in which God is unconsciously equated with father . . . [This fantasy] may be the primary agent of change in nonanalytic therapies, particularly treatment such as EST.

When one considers the authority vested in a group leader during the course of a psychotherapeutically oriented group experience, one can begin to appreciate the potential impact of this experience and how powerfully this can favor regression and change.

In this context, let us examine the crucial differences between a therapeutic group and a recruiting group. In a therapeutic group, all members are equal; in a recruiting group, many of the members are aware that the group is part of a carefully prearranged program. In a therapeutic group, members are encouraged to share experiences in an atmosphere which permits them to question the leader's authority; in a recruiting group, the individual is encouraged to share intimacies without the support and protection to his or her autonomy that would otherwise be available. Indeed, other group members are effectively in collusion with the group leader to subvert the individual's autonomy. Peer support is available only to the individual who is pliant and willing to acquiesce in the group leader's demands for greater and greater self-disclosure. Not surprisingly, any questions about the leader's authority are deflected in a manner which only superficially acknowledges the individual's concerns—"You'll understand better later on"—and never engages the questions themselves.

Other maneuvers are used to encourage regression in the recruit. Constant use is made of team sports, community sing-alongs and cheering to sponsor a sense of unity and to increase the affective level of the experience. Experiences like team sports are experiences in which the individual is expected to submerge his "selfish" individuality for the greater good. By using these activities as an extrapolation of earlier experiences, the recruiting camp presents itself as a parallel to earlier activities in which the individual was expected to accept direction without critical scrutiny.

As Peter Blos (1979) has perceptively said:

> The group permits identification as role tryouts without demanding any permanent commitments. It also allows for interactional experimentation as a severance action from childhood dependencies, prohibitions, and loyalties. [However,] whenever peer relationship simply replaces childhood dependencies, then the group has miscarried its function. In such cases, the adolescent process has been short-circuited with the result that unresolved emotional dependencies become permanent personality attributes. Under these circumstances life within the new generation unfolds strangely like a shadow play of the individual's past: What was to be avoided most repeats itself with fateful accuracy (p 160).

He later notes the danger of

> premature permanency, by molding in a definitive fashion the ego's relation to the outside world, thus bringing the adolescent process to a premature standstill rather than to a normative termination (p 168).

Thus in discussng adolescents and cultic involvement, the college fraternities with their rituals and quasi-religious ceremonials need to be considered as prototypical organizations, whose parallel evolution is a response to the same needs.

As Galper (1977) has noted:

> The content of their verbal communication tends to evoke mental associations of familial secure memories in the potential recruit. Subliminal evocation of imagery linked to childhood trust-laden experiences tends to relax the vigilance customarily experienced in unfamiliar social settings . . . The overall impression created is of a recreational camp populated by an extraordinarily affectionate, loving, and cohesive group of adults.

Moreover, the use of cheers and team sports allows violent feelings and regressive behavior to be expressed with an abandon that would cause the ordinarily more mature individual to withdraw. But no withdrawal is permitted and no time for private consideration of these activities is allowed. Thus, the recruiting camp exploits group experiences to promote regression in the individual by subtly altering earlier activities to create groups in which the basic assumptions of "dependency" and "fight–flight" replace individual expression and personal autonomy. In the team sports, rules are both altered eccentrically and subject to constant change. These alterations enhance the team leader's authority by depriving the individual participant of the support that consistency would provide. Likewise, the absence within the games of any goals or the possibility of an appeal to an impartial arbiter reinforces the merging of the individual within a "horde" or "mob" whose leader can then use his/her authority to undermine the individual's autonomy.

These activities are all conducted in an environment in which the individual is deprived of sleep and privacy. Thus deprived, the individual becomes more susceptible to the suspension of critical faculties. It is within this context that the actual indoctrination sessions must be regarded. In a series of "lectures," ideas of notable vagueness which consist of strings of abstractions with an absence of specific informational content are propounded with authority. The lecturer's control is reinforced by the emphastic approval of a claque at all sessions. As previously mentioned, any questions are evaded with the disclaimer that the individual will appreciate the importance of the specific ideas and lectures at a later point. The constant focus is on encouraging the individual to question both the validity of his or her doubts and the right to even raise the question of validity. The very vagueness of the ideas propounded creates an Ericksonian trance state, and the constant delegation of authority provides the lecturer with the ability to control the relationship. This simulates a hypnotic trance (Erickson et al, 1977). Thus, as the weekend proceeds, the recruit is less and less able to wonder why he is unable to see the King's New Clothes.

The location of the recruiting camps in relatively isolated areas increases the individual's dependence on the camp authorities for support. The camps are located in areas where individuals can provide neither food nor access for themselves. The remoteness sponsors the formation of basic assumptions groups in which both the fight–flight and dependency assumptions become prominent. It is in this context that the group's theology may assume importance because it allows the expression of the third basic assumption—the pairing assumption. Gibbard and Hartman (1973) have noted the formation of utopian fantasies within groups as they progress beyond the fight–flight and dependency assumptions:

> The fantasy that the group is, or could become, a utopia reflects the emergence, at both an individual and a collective level, of a variety of oedipal and pre-oedipal themes. More specifically, our experience suggests that utopian hopes engendered by these and other groups center on the largely unconscious fantasy that the group-as-a-whole is a maternal entity, or some facet of a maternal entity. Acting on this fantasy, the group members seek to establish and maintain contact with certain "good" (nurturant and protective) aspects of the group and to suppress or deny the existence of certain "bad" (abandoning and destructive) aspects of the group. The establishment of such a fantasied relationship appears to promise many positive gratifications. In addition, the fantasy offers some assurance that the more frightening, enveloping or destructive aspects of the group-as-mother will be held in check and that a host of oedipal feelings, libidinal and aggressive, will not become fully conscious and gain direct expression in the group. The essence of the utopian fantasy is that the good can be split off from the bad and that this separation can be maintained.

The development of the utopian fantasy as an expression of the pairing assumption is fostered by the entire recruiting process. Much of the initial indoctrination consists of attacks upon established authorities and, by inference, the adult world for not having lived up to their protestations of nurture and concern. The prospective recruits are often idealistic. They are fearful of the expression of anger toward parents whom they experience as having deserted them (by consenting to their *Wanderjahr*, etc) and have a great need to deny their need for anger (hence the name Unification Church and its stress on the concept of "unity"—Deutsch, 1979). Therefore, the utopian fantasy of the group as a source of nurture provides an intensely attractive *deus ex machina*. As Galper (1977) has noted:

> The camp training staff repetitively reinforces the Unification concept of unity. The illusion that total gratification of affectional and security needs is available

at the reality level within the confines of the "farm" environment is fostered. Depth interview data in this study reveal that emphasis on the "unity" theme evoked and intensified archaic desires for interpersonal merger or fusion in the patient group studied.

In a very real sense, the recruit's acceptance of the group as the expression of a utopian fantasy mirrors the process within any intense group whose task orientation is either unclear or overwhelming and in which the development of a basic assumptions group has been sponsored because of the psychopathology of the group leader. Thus, the formation of idealistic sounding quasifront organizations ("Collegiate Association for the Research of Principle") becomes both part and parcel of the recruiting process as well as an expression of the group's basic assumptions. The frequent promise of larger group support for individually significant activities certainly plays a part in the individual's initial affiliation with the group. And the threat of withdrawal of this support certainly helps to maintain the individual within this new "family."

Cults are defined in terms of the group's relationship to a controlling and charismatic leader. The actual cult leaders themselves are often unrepresentative of their group's membership. The question has been frequently asked: What do these leaders offer to the members—given both their unrepresentative character and the great disparity in lifestyles between the indulged and pampered leaders and their often impoverished members? Moreover, to what extent do the leaders believe the frequently extravagant claims that are made for them? These issues can be explored within the framework of the relationship of the leader to the basic assumptions group especially when the role of the utopian fantasy and the pairing assumption are considered.

Freud (1912) stressed the role of the group leader in preventing the members of the primeval horde from destroying one another. The leader's assumption of authority was sanctified in order to prevent the mutual destruction of the members of the extended tribe. While this conceptualization of the role of the group leader certainly reflects some of the experience of mankind, it partakes too much of a Hobbesian view of the experience of man in groups and does little to advance our understanding of the relationship of the cult leader to the cult. As Yalom (1974) notes, Freud's later views in *Group Psychology and the Analysis of the Ego* emphasize:

> the identification that exists between member and leader . . . Freud introduces the concept of the ego-ideal, a part of the ego which is the internalized standard to which each individual believes he must rise. It is what he expects and, unfortunately, demands that he become (the ego-ideal is an adumbration of the superego . . .) Members of the group, Freud suggests, tend to overvalue the leader, to experience him as their ego-ideal, and then put him in the place of their ego-ideal, introjecting him in the process.

While this explains much of the relationship between cult member and cult leader, it hardly seems to do justice to the tenancity and immediacy of cult affiliation. Rather, Bion (Kernberg, 1977), by directing our attention to the pairing assumption within basic assumptions groups provides a more dynamic understanding of the cult leader's hold over the cult member and the rapidity with which this hold is established. The pairing assumption is that the group will labor and create a new and more perfect group—that group members will attempt to avoid the experience of termination through the conception of another group whose birth will extend the life of the existing group. By focusing the group's attention on the apocalypse, the cult leader creates a setting in which his authority and his authority alone will save the group from termination. He alone possesses the magic that will avert the catastrophe of group termination. And, in time, his authority is buttressed by the formation of a hierarchy whose members defer to his "supreme authority." Their deference becomes, in itself, a powerful force for awakening and maintaining the group's ostensible, if overwhelming task. In a sense, because of the group members' identification with the leader and their introjection of him as the ego-ideal, his authority permits him to mobilize the more "positive" aspects of the individual's personality. It is the continuously reinforced involvement in these new tasks which replace the self-doubt and confusion which so often play a part in cult recruitment.

Cults form as part of a collective effort to survive apocalypse. But groups which exist as part of a "plan" to avoid termination are constantly challenged when "endtime" does not occur or when it does not happen according to schedule. However, the resourceful cult leader can preserve or even enhance his authority by simply postponing the apocalypse or by declaring that the cult's activity postponed the inevitable. The first approach is demonstrated in groups such as the Seventh Day Adventists, who declared their initial calculation of the Day of Armageddon as suggestive but not definitive. The second approach, which may involve a more immediate break in reality testing, is better represented in the recurrent prayer vigils of some fundamentalist Christian groups (prayer averted a collision between the comet Kohutek and the Earth) or within Transcendental Meditation (where members are dispatched all over the world for meditation vigils whose purpose is either to avert catastrophe or better yet to usher in the New Age). The anticipation of apocalypse can also be used to the leader's advantage, as in the repetitious "White Nights" of the People's Temple.

The pairing assumption finds its most direct expression in the theology of the Unification Church. The role of the "Lord of the Second Advent," Rev. Sun Myung Moon, is to father a new race of man who will be perfect and redeemed from the sin of Adam's Fall (Chapter 2). Not surprisingly, in expression of this *assumption,* an honorific title within the Unification Church is Eve, given the Rev. Moon's role as the new Adam. (The wife of the current head of the Uniflciation Church has assumed this title.) Thus, the goal of the Unification Church is an institutional expression of the pairing assumption! Within other groups these aspirations may be expressed less concretely and with a greater regard for the individual:

> That at this period of your history, mankind is ready for the individual autonomy that can form groups and for the group consciousness that becomes an entity in itself. Those who obstruct it, distort group consciousness into mass consciousness and individual consciousness into separatism. Those who follow it will create the new world, the life of the new age . . . It is important that you will be well aware of this principle and this possibility that is speedily ripening into a reality on your earth plane (Pierrakos, 1974).

To be sure, within all religious organizations a certain metaphorical, allegorical or even oracular style is common. But, the emphasis by cults on the imminence of creation has a millenarian style which is quite distinctive.

Viewing cults within the persepctive of the basic assumptions group, it seems perhaps less surprising that the cult leaders are more pushed toward a polygamous sexual expression. Jim Jones was apocryphally advised by Father Divine (the name is obviously suggestive) to *help* his followers by meeting *their* sexual needs. As Kernberg (1978) has said in another context:

> Creating a replication of the pathological internal world of object relations induced by borderline and severely psychotic patients in the group processes involving staff and these patients . . . serious psychopathology in the leader is, indeed, responsible for the problems of morale, of breakdown of task groups, and the development of regressive group processes. The problem, then, is to differentiate the symptomatic activation of emotional regression in the leader, reflecting problems in the institution, from the deterioration of organizational functioning reflecting psychopathology in the leader.

The development of intense erotic transferences towards the group leader may be seen less an expression of individual needs and more an expression of group needs and group regression. The disparity in lifestyle or even in the identity of the cult leader seems less surprising since the leader exists less as an expression of an ego-ideal than as the simple vehicle for the expression of group needs. From this perspective, the polygamy within groups as diverse as the Anabaptists of Munster, in 1535, and the Church of the Latter Day Saints may reflect the expression of the pairing assumption within isolated and beseiged groups rather than an antinomian theology, revelation or demography.

CONCLUSION

The individual's affiliation in a cult may be the expression of individual psychopathology and vulnerability or evidence of familial dysfunction. But it may also be a reflection of group processes occurring within emotionally charged environments where regression is encouraged and the formation of basic assumptions groups is sponsored. Within the destructive cult, the leader's need for self-aggrandizement creates a setting that covertly sponsors regression and overtly creates an ideology that justifies the institutionalization of regression. Many individuals enter cults at times when the continuities in their lives are placed in question. Cults exaggerate their concerns and provide an institutional framework in which these needs are met.

As therapists working with the current cult member or with the ex-cult member, it is our responsibility to help our patients become aware that these needs for continuity may be met without resorting to groups which inhibit their growth as individuals and demand the sacrifice of their autonomy.

BIBLIOGRAPHY

Blos P: The second individuation process, in *The Adolescent Passage.* New York, International Universities Press, 1979.

Boris HN, Zinberg NE, Boris M: Fantasies in group situations. *Contemporary Psychoanalysis* 1975;11(1):15–45.

Deutsch A, Miller MJ: Conflict, character and conversion to a new religion. *Adolescent Psychiatry* 1979;7.

Eckstein, R: The search and yearning for and the rebellion against the father—a group dilemma. *Int J Group Psychotherapy* 1978;28:435–442.

Edwards C: *Crazy for God.* Englewood, NJ, Prentice-Hall, 1979.

Erickson MH, Rossi EL, Rossi SI: *Hypnotic Realities: The Induction of Clinical Hypnosis and Forms of Indirect Suggestion.* New York, John Wiley, 1977.

Ezriel H: Notes on psychoanalytic psychotherapy. II. Interpretation and research. *Psychiatry* 1952;15:119–126.

Freed J: *Moonwebs.* Toronto, Dorset, 1980.

Freud S: Totem and taboo. *Standard Edition* 1912;13:1–164.

Freud S: Group psychology and the analysis of the ego. *Standard Edition* 1921;18:67–145.

Galper MF: Indoctrination methods of the Unification Church. Paper presented at the Annual Meeting of the California State Psychological Association, Los Angeles, March 13, 1977.

Gibbard G, Hartman J: The significance of utopian fantasies in small groups. *Int J Group Psychotherapy* 1973;23:125–147.

Kernberg O: Large group processes: Psychoanalytic understanding and applications. Paper presented at the American Psychoanalytic Association meeting, December 18, 1977.

Kernberg O: Leadership and organizational functioning: Organizational regression. *Int J Group Psychotherapy* 1978;28(1):3–27.

Pierrakos E: Lecture 225. Center for the Living Force, November 24, 1974.

Silverman LH: The unconscious fantasy as therapeutic agent in psychoanalytic treatment. *J Am Acad Psychoanal* 1979;7(2):189–218.

Smelser N: Collective myths and fantasies. Paper presented to the american Psychoanalytic Assocation meeting, May 1980.

Yalom I: Book review of S. Freud's "Group Psychology and the Analysis of the Ego." *Int J Group Psychotherapy* 1974;24:67–82.

Adolescent Involvement with the Supernatural and Cults:
Or New Bottles for Old Wine*

PETER A. OLSSON

Supernatural Self

Emptiness torments our searching.
The modern self, alone.
No turning back,
To easy comforts of sacredness
We seek meaning and excitement,
With a cold uneasy gut.
The dawn a familiar haunting.
Departed cocoon-company of sleep.
New day's novel ghosts,
The warmth of self deception.
We read, believe and view too glibly.
Hold on to favorite truths projected.
The night self-silence returns,
And old familiar God again.

Peter A. Olsson, MD

The modern adolescent adds heightened preoccupation with cults and the supernatural to the already established psychodelism of the 1960s. He or she is potentially overstimulated by the sophisticated communication media. The adolescent is rapidly presented with widely polarized and highly charged social, cultural, philosophical, religious and political ambiguities and uncertainties. His parents, teachers and other adult leaders are fellow strangers in this communally created strange modern land.

---

*First presented as the 1979 Judith Baskin offer lecture, October 2, 1979, at Michael Reese Hospital, Chicago, Illinois. Reprinted with permission from *Ann Psychoanalysis* 1980;8.

Many young people are obsessed, preoccupied, fused, amused or apparently just entertained with a geometrically expanding variety of supernatural topics. The popular literature and films over the last ten years are permeated with supernatural subjects. These creations vary enormously as to literary or cinematic merit. Their style, form, content and affect-producing power are often impressive. The adolescent can view or read about haunted or possessed airliners, ships, houses, trucks, bulldozers, animals, fish or fellow humans. Children or adolescents themselves are often portrayed in such modern media as possessed, haunted or abused by the possessed. Just a few examples are *The Excorcist, The Omen, The Manitou, Suffer the Children, Hostage to the Devil, The Sentinel* and *Rosemary's Baby*. These cleverly presented media exploit, exhalt, and entertain with a spectrum of supernatural and uncanny devices.

Cults are burgeoning to go hand in hand with the supernatural and adolescents. To cite just a few led by the ghastly climax in Guyana: The People's Temple, Sun Myung Moon's Unification Church, Divine Light Mission, Scientology, Synanon, Hare Krishna, "The Family," Children of God and Satanism. These cults all hold out 1) easy answers to the meaning of life, 2) instant comradeship and a quick sense of communally derived self worth, and 3) a typical, overly emotional type of persuasion to attract new members. So-called "Love Bombardment" is "the practice of verbally surrounding a person with "love," until he or she joins the group, and then removing that attention and demanding he or she give it to other members."[1] Cults and cult leaders manipulate and exploit powerful group processes in vulnerable recruits.

These preoccupations with the supernatural and cults are by no means new in history (Greek Dionysians are referred to by Plato), but are marked by the intensity of recent adolescent interest and media coverage. They seem to fall on a wide spectrum of supernatural preoccupation that might be described as 1) the traditionally religious supernatural, 2) the non-traditional religious supernatural, 3) the mediative-mystical-philosophic ("Eastern") supernatural, 4) occult-secular supernatural, and 5) the anti-religious or areligious (purely uncanny) supernatural. They all touch on the political–economic domains at times, and at the extremes blend into the frankly sociopathic, delinquent or criminal behaviors (ie, the Manson family).

At a socio-historical level of conceptualization, the ascendency of cults and the supernatural seem related to the decline of authoritative forms of traditional religion, urbanization, rapid shifts in the forms of family life, "feminine liberation," geographic mobility, mass media, political assassination and ever-present, but warded-off, reality-based fears of nuclear holocaust.

Many adolescents react to these supernatural currents with normal curiosity and sublimated aggressive or sexual excitement without perverse acting out. This chapter will focus on the others who are so often seen by therapists. They seem to entwine the supernatural with neurotic, borderline, narcissistic, prepsychotic or frankly psychotic symptomatology and processes. In many of the forms of supernatural adolescent preoccupation we see expression of what greatly resembles a perversion or addiction.

My approach will be to present three adolescent case histories whose psychopathology blended inextricably with their supernatural beliefs and preoccupations. I believe they will provide clinical data to support the thesis that the adolescent uses the supernatural and uncanny to grapple with the expression of old and familiar adolescent issues at an intrapsychic level. Then I will use theoretical perspectives of psychoanalysts to try to lend some order to our thinking about adolescents who seek the new and novel from the old and familiar realms of the supernatural.

A final section will discuss group process and group leadership in cults.

CLINICAL CASE PRESENTATIONS
Anita

Anita appeared at her college psychiatry health service when she was 19 years old. She expressed vague complaints about periodic depression, low self-esteem and poor self-confidence. After a recent rejection for a position as dorm counsellor, she cut both her wrist and arm so deeply as to be admitted through the emergency room.

The same fear of feeling rejected had begun early in high school and she had turned to a deep involvement with Satanism for "a focus of commitment." Her interest had begun with palmistry and moved in a tough progression through Ouija board, Tarot cards, and witchcraft readings to a culmination in Satanism. She remarked, "It sets you up to be your own god."

Early in her involvement with the supernatural she had taken Valium (her mother's prescription), dexedrine, mescaline and, most heavily, marijuana. These chemicals in no way measured up to the excitement of Satanism, so they were discontinued spontaneously.

The patient had experienced intense premonitions prior to her hospitalization. She felt that someone among her family or close friends would be hurt or hospitalized. She felt nauseated and told her friends "something is happening and it is really strange." The next week she learned a friend's brother had almost drowned, her father entered the hospital for surgery and then she was hospitalized as mentioned above.

The patient has been raised in a very "fervent," Protestant, fundamentalist church. She attended church regularly and extra sabbath activities such as church suppers and prayer meetings during the week. She was "baptized" at 10 years of age. Suddenly, in her last year of grade school, her parents quit going to church. They said, "You are old enough to make up your own mind about church." At the same time (sequence blurred), she had her first sexual experience with a boy. She was very aware of guilt about this but also noted "my values going wrong." She regarded all the people at her church as hypocrites and began to mock them in her thoughts and words. She began to be very promiscuous sexually and studied the "Satanic Bible" fervently. (She recognizes now after 35 psychotherapy sessions and carefully adjusted antipsychotic medications, that she was projecting "all the inner turmoil and my feelings onto the church.") At the time, she would chant Satanic, mocking, anti-Christian chants daily. She would make up anti-Christian prayers and was excited by the way the Satanic Bible made fun of Christ at the crucifixion with his "wormed cross and funny lewd expression." She would not tell her parents, but she had sweeping doubts and ruminations such as: "What is the reason to live for a future if there is no eternity?" "Satan says to make up your own rules." "Be independent!" "It's not what you do, it's how it affects you." "You're not past doing anything!" "You are powerful!"

One night late in high school, she found herself in her parent's bedroom in a "kind of trance" with a butcher knife poised above her father's head. She suddenly stopped herself and returned quietly to her room. She noted a gradual personality change from passively aggressive to overt, clear feelings of hostility and anger towards "everyone."

Anita described a polarity of paradox in her life. "I have always been very dependent on authority and always craved a lot of attention. "Yet," she went on, "Satanism stresses independency and tells you to make up your own rules." Her self-styled Satanism and witchcraft progressed slowly and relentlessly with its basis in her personal reading of the Satanic Bible and other books. Anita "just knew by the inner senses what Satan wanted me to do." Late in high school she made several suicidal gestures but the attempts were noticed by no one. Upon arrival in college she began to attend religious meetings and loved to sit at the back of the meetings and utter curse words and "mocking comments." A group of Christian girls took an interest in her and she underwent a religious "reconversion" her freshman year. She became roommates with one of these young women during her sophomore year. Unfortunately, her new roommate attempted to become a controlling, dominating "mother-figure." When she criticized the patient for descriptions of attraction to boys, the patient felt considerable ambivalence about her rediscovered religion and "heard the distance voices of Satan." She changed her major from music to math. She was then hospitalized after the episode of hypomania and hallucinations of Satan demanding she cut her arms.

Psychological testing revealed an IQ of 120 and documented "thought disorder," and a psychotic diagnosis.

The Kuder Preference Test revealed an interesting polarity. She had a very high interest in scientific and computational activities (paternal introject) plus high interest in musical and social services activities (maternal introject).

Anita is the eldest of four children with sisters aged 18 and 17 and one brother aged 13. Her father is a year younger than her mother and described as "a perfectionist and extremely work-oriented person." The patient said she and her father were alike in looks and personality. He was rigid and authoritative, and moves necessitated by his business both within the United States and abroad necessitated the patient's attending six different public school systems. One of Antia's roles in the family was to stand up to her father in order to divert his attention when he would be angry at another family member. He had a bad temper and because of this family members would tend to find gratification in individual rather than family group activities. Her father excelled in math and science and his constant obsession with work caused constant conflict with her mother. The patient also described chronic conflict between she and her father.

She described her mother as "real compassionate and caring." Her mother would constantly try to hold down dissention. The patient had been extremely close to her mother in her younger years but experienced her as "smothering" and "really weak." It is of note that her mother was a registered nurse but had not used her training professionally since Antia's birth. Anita really did not "feel feminine" and did not get much pleasure with sex. She enjoyed "the attention."

Anita has always made good grades, had several close friends and was never in conflict with teachers whom she frequently idealized. Her best grades were in math and science (like her father) and she successfully played flute and clarinet in the school band. She was selected drum major in her senior year of high school. When permission was asked for use of disguised material from her life history for this paper, she grew interested and excited but her therapist recalled how such "special attention" so often evoked "the return of feeling Satan's presence" and compulsions toward self-mutilation. Anita spotted this herself saying, "I always needed a lot of attention when I was committed to Satanism but that has broken down—maybe I'll start a foster home for abused children some day." Anita's treatment continues to progress nicely thus far.

Candy

Candy was 17 years old when seen for consultation. Soon after transfer from public school to a strict Catholic high school for her senior year she began to have behavior problems. She had a "poor attitude in class" and disrupted it with vague comments. She passed notes in class and would giggle inappropriately to herself. She expressed constant envy of other girls and enjoyed running off during the evening to smoke marijuana or drink beer with older young men who were out of high school and working.

Both Candy and her mother have had periodic, severe asthma attacks since they were 3 years old. Candy had seen a child psychiatrist at age 8 for breath-holding spells and enuresis. Psychotherapy was recommended but the family felt they could not afford this. Two other psychiatrists were consulted briefly for family therapy when Candy was 10 and 12 years old. At each occasion her father stopped treatment because he did not like the therapists. Though cooperative on the surface, he seemed angry and severely critical towards psychiatry. Candy's parents described her as always "emotional and creative" (she began writing poems at age 9). She had always had trouble sleeping at night and until the time of consultation would very frequently be found sleeping on the floor near her parents' bed or require one of them to be beside her until she fell asleep. They seemed to subtly encourage this.

At the first interview Candy described "thinking too much" and "speeded up thoughts." She would vacillate between writing love poems and "thinking lofty thoughts," to feeling rebellious and "supernatural." She felt she was possessed by some spirit of a poetess from "the past." She read about excorcism and felt that a slow process of demon-possession prevented her from sleeping, made objects change in size, speeded up her thoughts and made her feel in love with older men. She obsessed about her middle name really being *Zelda*. Actually, her middle name was Alice. She felt boys would not really love her if they knew her real middle name. If she married a man and he ever found out that her middle name was Zelda, he would divorce her on the spot. Later the therapist learned that a paternal cousin carried the name Zelda and had been "put in an institution" many years ago. This woman remained chronically psychotic despite psychiatric care and an attempt at excorcism. Her parents alleged that Candy had never been told of Zelda, because she looked so much like her. Candy's father said, "I adored Zelda and couldn't bear to tell Candy the sad story."

In a brief English class essay she shared with the therapist, Candy wrote:

I feel I have some special power or something or someone inside of me. Nature is the only thing we have left to grow on. Why do I feel so bored and alone? I am seeing but I don't like what I see. I am looking at the world through a microscope and not a telescope. I see the people but then again I don't. I cannot identify with them—are they unidentified specimens not yet ready to be studied? I hear the voices of the people and they are telling me to go back to my own little world and watch the world go by. . . . So here I am . . . I am behind a glass window and I see the people but they do not see me.

Candy further explained that she felt possessed by some person from the past. "This spirit is both beautiful and sunny but also haunted by dark clouds." Candy's poems speak for themselves:

Loneliness

I am haunted by loneliness, tortured by
What might have happened. I am alone
Now, no one cares or can they care?
Can they understand I want to be
Something? I wanted to be noticed by
Large crowds of people and admired
By both men and women. And of
Course I want to be loved.

Why are people always living in the past?
Instead of counting your
Mistakes, try counting your blessings.

Death?

Death—that's a word many people are frightened of—
But why should we be?
Sure death is mysterious, it's
Sinister; some say it's wicked.
To me death must be a certain
Trip, an adventure, a wonderful
Peaceful feeling with God and the
Universe . . . Death, to me must
Be like falling down a huge cliff
And never touching the bottom . . .
Maybe death is like being so free and
So peaceful and so filled with tranquility.
Death—it's what you make your
Destiny is where you choose.

Freedom

My soul is actually moving and I
Can feel the vibrations. I can
Actually "feel" the stereo music—I
Feel as if I am the music. I feel
Like that other person (Zelda?), that
Has been locked up inside of me
For so long, has finally broken the lock.

Other poems refer constantly to her middle name, a man she almost obtains and of being trapped behind a glass window "looking out at the world" (perhaps from some distance mental hospital). Her parents could not remember if Candy had gone to see Zelda at the mental hospital when she was young.

Candy's mother almost died of asthma when Candy was 12 years old. Her mother speaks of this often. Candy describes her mother as "nervous, thoughtful, edgy, easily upset, afraid of everything, sort of disturbed and on tranquilizers all the time." "She hovers over me and seems afraid that I can't make it." Candy has a married sister, four years her senior. Candy describes her father as intelligent, understanding, strong and moody (she describes herself as moody, also). She feels close to her father, talks to him easily and he often talks soothingly to her late into the night when she cannot sleep. At separate sessions her father expressed fear that Candy would be like his first cousin Zelda, who wrote poetry, was intelligent and "went insane." He wept as he spoke of this cousin who had been like a sister to him.

After the fifth psychotherapy session, Candy quadrupled her dose of Prolixin and had an acute oculogyric crisis with severe torticollis while talking between classes. Her eyes rolled up into her head so "only the whites were showing" and her neck twisted on itself. The other teenagers at the Catholic school felt she was possessed. The movie, *The Exorcist*, had been very popular at that time and "everybody had seen it and me." Candy was hallucinating visually and heard "demons cursing me." Later in the hospital she described a feeling that she was behind a glass window feeling both frightened but excited by all the attention during the extrapyramidal drug reaction.

After a brief hospital stay she made slow but steady progress despite overprotective stances by her parents who fought over "how to discipline her" on passes from the hospital. Her father insisted that her mother was "too fearful within herself to help Candy." Candy's mother admitted that she was overprotective, cautious and "afraid of life."

Despite confrontation, repeatedly and gently the parents refused therapy for themselves and abruptly terminated Candy's treatment after 30 sessions, when Candy became outspoken and demanded more freedom. They alleged financial problems but turned down referral to the medical school psychiatry clinic saying, "That was the beginning of the end for Zelda!"

At five-year follow-up via a colleague, I learned that a similar cycle of treatment had occurred with three subsequent psychiatrists. The bonds of symbiotic "love?" persist within the family triangle. From A to Z we see Candy, Father, Mother—all possessed by the old and familiar mystery of Zelda.

Lara

Eighteen-year-old Lara was admitted to the acute unit of a psychiatric hospital near the end of her summer vacation from college.

Lara is from a Jewish family but had been on a religious retreat conducted by "The Family," a devout Protestant religious sect that believes in the imminent coming to earth of Jesus Christ. Lara grew progressively excited, talkative and would talk to anyone day or night. Adults at the retreat grew concerned when she did not sleep for two nights and took her to a small general hospital. Sedation was only partially successful and very unfortunately her roommate in the hospital leaped from a hospital window to her death. The patient was convinced she had caused "that poor woman with *breast cancer* to leap to her death." Lara escaped from the general hospital "trying to get back to those kind, loving, caring people in The Family." Her father found her and brought her to the psychiatric hospital. Both her parents and her 16-year-old brother were greatly upset by her new-found religion. Her father felt her psychosis was related to upsets with her boyfriend and a close cousin who recently had to be hospitalized with a serious mental illness. Lara was described as always being too dependent and clinging but optimistic, exuberant, and outgoing.

Lara's father was an articulate, brilliant and benevolently controlling psychiatrist. Numerous family members had had severe psychiatric problems. The maternal great-grandfather died in a psychiatric hospital. A maternal aunt died by suicide. Her serious mental problems had begun at the patient's age of 18. This aunt had been in and out of hospitals but was unable to marry and actually took care of Lara for the first year of her life. When severe marital problems occurred, this aunt killed herself. The patient's parents had had a recent recurrence of marital problems. Lara had been promiscuous but enjoyed no pleasure at sex. "I just like to be held."

At first, Lara's mother seemed very passive, distant and completely subordinate to Lara's father who articulately described intricate history and dynamics of the family. Only after several meetings did the therapist learn that six months after Lara's mother became pregnant with Lara she was discovered to have bilateral breast cancer. Her mother waited until Lara's birth before having bilateral mastectomies. Lara's mother then became profoundly depressed for six or seven months. The deceased aunt (who she is named after) and her father acted as mother surrogates. Her father was studying child development at the time and would often stay up most of the night "to feed her at any sign of oral frustration or discomfort." Her father seemed to become mother–aunt–father in the face of her mother's depression and lengthy subsequent psychoanalysis. Lara had rebelled against her father through dating Protestant boys in grade school and hoped her father "would back off and let me live my own life." Lara revealed that in her moments of discouragement her mother had said she would commit suicide if she ever had a recurrence of her breast cancer.

Lara had always been very overweight, but beginning in the hospital she initiated a diet and has stayed trim since. Intensive family and individual therapy have helped father to see how over-involved he had been with Lara. When given freedom, Lara briefly rejoined "The Family," but with a tolerant attitude by the therapist she gradually got involved with her college work. She dropped her major in psychology and did well in fine arts.

After several years in intensive analytic therapy she had worked through "my panicky, manicky guilts about me, my mother and cancer." When her own family began to shift toward equilibrium, she slowly lost interest in "The Family" but still makes occasional friendly visits to their meetings, "mainly to see some of my friends there—we respectfully disagree about religion."

PSYCHOANALYTIC VIEWS ABOUT THE SUPERNATURAL, ADOLESCENTS AND "YOUTH CULTURES" OR CULTS
Sigmund Freud on the Supernatural and The Uncanny

The supernatural, the uncanny, parapsychology, the occult, telepathy and related subjects were always of great interest to Sigmund Freud and one senses that he had both personal and professional fascination for these unusual topics.

In his "Psychopathology of Everyday Life" (1901) Freud compares himself with the superstitious person:

> I believe in external (real) chance, it is true, but not in internal (psychical) accidental events. With the superstitious person it is the other way round. He knows nothing of the motivation of his chance actions and parapraxes, and believes in psychical accidental events. He has a tendency to ascribe to external chance happenings a meaning which will become manifest in real events, and to regard such chance happenings as a means of expressing something that is hidden from him in the external world. The differences between myself and the superstitious per-

son are two: first, he projects outwards a motivation which I look for within; secondly, he interprets chance as due to an event, while I trace it back to an unconscious thought.[2]

Freud concludes that in this regard two world views or belief systems emerge in responses to experiences of superstition or the supernatural. He calls one of these "the mythological view of the world" and the other "our modern scientific but as yet by no means perfect Weltanschaung."[3] Freud here connects the mythological Weltanschaung in an applied anthropologic formulation to the mentality of "pre-scientific peoples." Thus, Freud seems to equate the mentality of a person who frequently thinks superstitiously with the mental state of primitive people of past and present cultures. He subtly includes much past and present religious thinking in this formulation as he says,

> In point of fact I believe that a large part of the mythological view of the world, which extends a long way into the most modern religions, is nothing but psychology projected into the external world. The obscure recognition (the endopsychic perception) of psychical factors and relations in the unconscious is mirrored in the construction of a supernatural reality, which is destined to be changed back once more by science into the psychology of the unconscious. One could venture to explain in this way the myths of paradise and the fall of man, of God, of good and evil, of immortality, and so on, and to transform metaphysics into metapsychology.[4]

Freud in this his first published usage of the word metapsychology, draws the battle lines between scientific psychology and superstitious–anamistic conceptions of the world.

It is interesting how often the popular literature of the supernatural pits a rational and/or scientific hero against the irrational or demonic spirit from another culture or earlier, more animistically oriented culture. In The Exorcist, the humanitarian priest, Merrin, and the priest–psychiatrist, Damien Karras, stand in pitched battle with the demon, Pazuzu (personification of the southwest wind), who from earlier ages invades the psyche of preadolescent, 12-year-old Regan MacNeil in sophisticated contemporary American society.[5]

Many adolescents today seem to rebel against what seems to be their perception (perhaps true) that adults worship, animate or "religify" science or psychology itself. The modern literature of the supernatural and adolescent joining of anti-intellectual cults is often a rebellion against the pseudocertainty of science without humility.

In our cases of Anita, Candy and Lara we find fathers who were intellectually dominant, preoccupied with "hard science approaches" and sources of overstimulating conflict to their daughters. Each young woman seemed to use the supernatural in efforts to anger, defy or create a buffer between herself and a father or parental figure. The results were paradoxical for each. It is fascinating to imagine a lively adolescent in animated dialogue with Freud after just having presented his supernatural convictions or experiences.

Freud responds:

> Whether there are definitely no such things as true presentiments, prophetic dreams, telepathic experiences, manifestations of supernatural forces and the like. I am far from meaning to pass too sweeping a condemnation of these

phenomena, of which so many detailed observations have been made even by men of outstanding intellect, and which it would be best to make the subject of further investigation.[6]

The adolescent challenges, "Haven't you ever had one special supernatural experience?" Freud states with a glint of subtle humor in his eye:

> To my regret I must confess that I am one of those unworthy people in whose presence spirits suspend their activity and the supernatural vanishes away, so that I have never been in a position to experience anything myself which might arouse a belief in the miraculous. Like every human being, I have had presentiments and experienced trouble, but the two failed to coincide with one another, so that nothing followed the presentiments, and the trouble came upon me unannounced.[7]

Freud goes on after these qualifications to link superstition and the supernatural experience with paranoia, obsessional neurosis, and with the origins of religion. He says,

> Superstition derives from suppressed hostile and cruel impulses. Superstition is in part the expectation of trouble; and a person who had harbored frequent evil wishes against others, but has been brought up to be good and has therefore repressed such wishes into the unconscious will be especially ready to expect punishment for his unconscious wickedness in the form of trouble threatening him from without.[8]

Thus, the mental mechanism of projection comes into play as a central linking concept. The kernel of truth or validity as found in the paranoid who senses his inner aggressive or erotic strivings, but transforms these affects into delusions of external persecution is clearly described in the Schreber case.[9]

In each of our cases early symptoms of psychosis seemed to be rationalized or intellectualized in terms of supernatural phenomenology or process. Trances, dazes, feelings of unreality, visual–perceptual distortions, blocking, lability of mood, increasing emergence of primary process, early disturbances in ego function, such as attention, motility, drive regulation, impulse control, and later frank delusions or hallucinations, can all be ruminated about in supernatural terms. In each of our cases these progressive losses in contact with reality were so described and with a sense of mild elation at first.

In his famous case, "The Rat Man," Freud stresses the peculiarities of obsessional neurotics in their attitudes toward reality, superstition and death. Of the obsessive's need for doubt and uncertainty, Freud says:

> The predilection felt by obsessional neurotics for uncertainty and doubt leads them to turn their thoughts by preference to those subjects upon which all mankind are uncertain and upon which our knowledge and judgments must necessarily remain open to doubt. The chief subjects of this kind are paternity, length of life, life after death and memory.[10]

It is interesting that Freud himself frequently ruminated about the length of his life and the immortality of his work. These same ruminations present themselves in obsessional adolescent patients' inner thoughts and often drive them toward the supernatural for answers.

I hypothesize that one problem in the child rearing of modern adolescents has stemmed from a tragic misinterpretation of Freud's theories over several generations of parents. It has led to a pseudoscientific notion of child rearing in which free reign of impulse and all whims of the child seem to be valued, encouraged and vicariously enjoyed by parents. The superego defects and weaknesses fostered by such misconceptions and failures of empathy are widespread among many adolescents today. "Do your own thing" is so encouraged that many parents abdicate their role of authority. The weird, satanic or occult are used to provoke adult authority and also to subtly replace authority abdicated too completely by parents.

Regarding the uncanny, Freud's basic thesis is that "the uncanny is that class of the frightening which leads back to what is known of old and long familiar."[11]

To arrive at this conclusion Freud embarks on a fascinating examination of linguistic usage. The English word, "uncanny," means not only "cozy" but also "endowed with occult or magical powers." Freud then goes into exhaustive detail about the German words, "Heimlich" (homely, familiar, agreeable) and "Unheimlich" (the "apparent" opposite—everything that ought to have remained secret and hidden but has come to light). "Heimlich" however undergoes a subtle transition of meaning from the idea of "homelike," "belonging to the house" to something withdrawn from the eyes of strangers, something concealed, secret and this development in the direction of ambivalence leads to an identity with its opposite "Unheimlich." In summary, the uncanny is viewed in the same model as the return of the repressed in neurosis.

> The uncanny is in reality nothing new or alien, but something which is familiar and old—established in the mind which has become alienated from it only through the process of repression. Reference to repression enables us to understand Schelling's definition of the uncanny as something that ought to have remained hidden but has come to light.[12]

Freud then launches into an in-depth discussion of the things, persons, impressions, events, and situations which arouse feelings of the uncanny. He agrees with Jentsch's example of "doubts whether an apparently animate being is really alive; or conversely, whether a lifeless object might not in fact animate." Thus, wax work figures, ingeniously constructed dolls, automata, the uncanny effects of epilepsy and psychotic behavior or analogous techniques are often seen in literary craftsmanship.

As an illustration of a unique literary figure who is the master of these techniques Jentsch and Freud discuss E.T.A. Hoffman's work and his story of "The Sandman" in particular. The recurrent theme is of the Sandman who tears out children's eyes. The key character, a late adolescent student, Nathaniel, despite his present happiness, cannot banish the childhood memories associated with the mysterious and terrifying death of his beloved father. On certain evenings his mother used to send the children to bed early, warning them that "the Sandman was coming." Later Nathaniel hides to try to see the Sandman. His father barely saves Nathaniel from the Sandman's attack on his eyes. At another visit of the Sandman his father is killed by an explosion. The Sandman is a disturber of love who separates Nathaniel from his betrothed and from her brother, his best friend. He destroys the narcissistic object of his second love, Olympia, a lonely life-like doll. Then "the Sandman" drives Nathaniel to suicide at the moment he has won back his betrothed and is about to be happily united to her. Hoffman, the author, was the child of an unhappy marriage. When he was 3 years old, his father left and never returned.

Freud discussed the uncanny fear of losing or damaging one's eye. Expressions such as "apple of our eye" and eyeballs, etc, related to the study of myths and dreams where the fear of going blind is often a substitute for the dread of being castrated. The Sandman story also seems to me to be a means by which parents try to scare their children into staying in bed so that they can be alone for sex together. Thus, the wish to see and the fear of seeing "the primal scene" seems to be involved as well. Many of the incestuous, sexual and lewd scenes in the modern, popular literature of the supernatural seem to be permeated with this deeply unconscious theme. A striking example is the scene of the conception of *Rosemary's Baby* as the product of a grotesque intercourse of a demon and a lovely woman.

In many cults appealing to adolescents there is value in "seeing the light" or a visual encounter with the leader–hero of the cult. The supernatural eyes of Charles Manson or the Rev. Jim Jones have been described with surrendering awe by their followers. At her oculogyric crisis at school Candy's classmates kept saying, "Look at her eyes! Look at her eyes!"

Freud discussed in detail the notion of projected envy involved in the "dread of the evil eye." To support my idea about an unconscious repetition compulsion in children and adults to view the uncanny primal scene, Freud discussed Otto Rank's volume, *The Incest Complex,* in Freud's "Preface to Reik's Ritual." Here Rank emphasizes that the dramatist and writer work over the oedipal theme in a great variety of modifications, distortions and disguises. This reflects an attempt to master the emotional attitudes toward one's mother and father (ie, family).

Freud discusses the extraordinary strong feelings of something uncanny that pervades the conception of "the double." Here there are telepathic experiences so that the one possesses knowledge, feelings, and experience in common with the other. This has been a powerful theme in great literature. "In other words, there is a doubling, dividing and interchanging of the self."[13] Freud also says:

> The theme of the "double" has been very thoroughly treated by Otto Rank. He has gone into the connections the "double" has with reflections in mirrors, with shadows, with guardian spirits, with the belief in the soul and with the fear of death . . . For the "double" was originally an insurance against the destruction of the ego, an energetic denial of the power of death. Rank says, "and probably the immortal soul was the first 'double' of the body."[14]

As well as the uncanny aspect, as Freud goes on to relate the notion of the "double" to the idea of primary narcissism and "conscience" we see anticipation and conceptual premonitions of Kohut's *Psychology of the Self* (50 years later). It would be tempting to speculate that the vast popularity of literature about twins stems from the uncanny aspect of the relationship between twins. Freud would say, twins are really an old and familiar idea (to us all) of the "double" belonging to hopefully surmounted narcissism of our earliest developmental times. Only much later (1971) would Kohut describe in more detail the twinship transferences seen in narcissistic personality disorders and help in our understanding of some adolescent patients' preoccupations with the supernatural.

Freud reviews in his paper on "The Uncanny" a whole section from *Totem and*

Taboo, which offers us a penetrating tool to understand the supernatural in cults and adolescent strivings.

> Our analysis of instances of the uncanny has led us back to the old, animistic conception of the universe. This was characterized by the idea that the world was peopled by the spirits of human beings; by the subject's narcissistic over-valuation of his own mental processes; by the belief in the omnipotence of thoughts and the technique of magic based on that belief; by the attribution to various outside persons and things of carefully graded magical powers, or mana; as well as by all the other creations with the help of which man, in the unrestricted narcissism of the stage of development, strove to fend off the manifest prohibitions of reality. It seems as if each one of us has been through a phase of individual development corresponding to this animistic stage in primitive man, and none of us has passed through it without preserving certain residues and traces of it which are still capable of manifesting themselves, and that everything which strikes us as "uncanny" fulfills the condition of touching those residues of animistic mental activity within us and bringing them to ex-pression.[15]

James Hamilton in his fascinating paper, "The Excorcist: Some Psycodynamic Considerations," reminds us of Freud's unique paper in 1923, "A Seventeenth Century Demonological Neurosis." Hamilton's reference to Freud's paper is aptly chosen. Freud carefully analyzes the record of the possession of Christoph Haizmann, a painter, who grew depressed, work-inhibited and suffered "frightful convulsions" after his father's death. The subsequent nine-year pact with the devil is seen by Freud as a neurotic solution to the loss of father via ob-taining the devil as a father substitute. Freud stresses how God and the devil in Christian mythology are really a psychodynamic unity. The son's affectionate-submissive longing for the father is ambivalently fused with the son's fear of father with its feeling companions of hostility and defiance toward him. This dynamic of young adolescent followers in cults is common. The supernatural father figures found in Satanism and devil worship often reflect adolescents' search for recapitulation of a physically or psychologically absent father of their childhoods. Hamilton also notes the significance of object loss and the use of primitive defense mechanisms of introjection, incorporation, projection, denial and splitting associated with the failure to mourn in the genesis of so-called demon possession.[17]

We see these same vivid dynamics in Candy and Anita. Lara, who joined a cult, discovered a new "Family" as a replacement for the old family of ambivalent feelings. She had fled, but never mourned or separated from intrapsychically. In our three cases, however, the surface power struggles and separation–individu-ation conflicts of these adolescent girls with their fathers, raises questions of earlier more profound difficulties with their maternal objects. All three girls were very protective of their mothers when they spoke of them. All three admitted they were closer to their fathers emotionally or in regard to intensity of affects of love/hate. The maternal objects emerging from between the lines were weak, phobic, narcissistically vulnerable or potentially enveloping. The fathers then became relatively more stable objects of attachment, attack, distant longing or rebellion. The supernatural metaphors of preoccupation (Anita and Candy) or the cult (Lara) became compromise arenas to unconsciously portray their difficulties. Pre-oedipal conflicts seem to have been more prominent in our three cases.

In summary of Freud: I believe he would see the supernatural preoccupations and uncanny experiences of our patients in terms of the return of repressed affects, preverbal experiences, conflicts and vague traumas from their personal pasts (really old and familiar to the unconscious).

Waelder (1951) refines this notion (return of the repressed—of Tausk), when he describes his notion of isomorphism. Waelder says, "If the defense mechanism had the form of denial, the return must have the form of an assertion"[18] ("The Devil made me do it."[19]) This principle of isomorphism in regard to the relationship to inner drive, conflict and symptom, symptomatic behavior and defense, is heuristically helpful when more primitive mechanisms are present. In all three of our patients and I think in adolescents with severe problems expressed in terms of the supernatural, we find preponderance of denial, projection, projective identification, paranoid–persecutory ideation and pervasive splitting mechanisms. Anita said, "I heard the distant voices of Satan again. They told me to cut my arms, and I did." The isomorphism idea might be extended to acting out behaviors as reflection of the return of old and familiar abusive behavior by parents toward their children (child abuse and incest being ever more in our attention). Though Lara did not act self-destructively, she felt she had caused her hospital roommate's suicide (possible maternal object surrogate). Anita and Candy had strong self-destructive and acting-out difficulties. When acting out involves promiscuity, lewd profanity or self-destructive ritual then we often see adolescents involved with supernatural or uncanny cults as channels for acting out expression.

Satanism, Perversion and the Supernatural

Anita was involved in intense intrapsychic rumination and study of Satanism, and I discuss it in further detail because some adolescents today go far beyond where Anita's treatment fortunately intervened. These ritualized, truly perverse behaviors reach profound extremes in the "mass murders" (Houston, Chicago, and many other locations) of the recent decade. These activities at the extreme find young adolescents sexually stimulated, tortured in ritualized ways and then usually murdered. What intrapsychic forces could be at work to even have a young person near such potential situations? Some perspectives come from some further exploration of the concepts of Satanism and perversion.

Satanism began in the third or fourth century. A pattern of "Satanist" belief and behavior has built up over the centuries. Its essential two ingredients are 1) worship of the devil and 2) reversal of Christian values.

> A Satanist has renounced Christ and his church (parent and family intraphychically), and blasphemously maltreated its sacred objects, symbols and ceremonies; he adores the Devil in the form of a man (parental surrogate) or animal; he sings and dances in the Devil's honor and obscenely kisses and fondles his person (pre-oedipal-oral issues) and he revelled in child slaughter and cannibalism, indescriminate sexual orgies, perversion, homosexuality and every species of crime and abomination. This same pattern is described for witches and objects of the irreligious or a religious supernatural. (There is a vivid, illustrative, account of the "Black Mass" in J.K. Huysman's novel La'-Bas, probably drawn from real life.)[20]

Satanism's content seems to peculiarly fit the rebellious externalizations or projective identifications of adolescent intraphychic struggles; really recapitulations of pre-oedipal and oedipal themes and their distortions.

Robert Stoller writes:

> Sexual excitement depends on a scenario the person to be aroused has been writing since childhood. The story is an adventure, an autobiography disguised as fiction, in mysteries, screen memories of actual traumatic events and the resolution of these into a happy ending, best celebrated by orgasm. The function of the fantasy is to take these painful experiences and convert them to pleasure-triumph. In order to sharpen excitement—the vibration between the fear of original traumas repeating and the hope of a pleasurable conclusion this time—one introduces into the story elements of risk (approximations of trauma) meant to prevent boredom.[21]

Anita described sexual excitement as she obeyed the Satanic command to cut herself. Candy felt exhibitionistic excitement as her classmates watched her apparent demon-possession. For the most part all three young women described severe dissociation of tenderness, orgasm and deeply felt sexual excitement. None gave much detail about sex. Very late in her therapy Lara was able to get somewhat beyond her intense pre-oedipal and oedipal conflicts. As her parents resolved their marital conflicts and Lara individuated, she met and really got to know a young man. Tenderness began to combine with sexual excitement for the first time.

In the fully developed Satan cults one finds the full-blown symbolism of perversion. Stoller writes in his aptly titled book, *Perversion: The Erotic Form of Hatred:*

> In men, perversion may be at bottom a gender disorder constructed out of a *triad of hostility:* rage at giving up one's earliest bliss and identification with mother, fear of not escaping out of her orbit, and a need for revenge for putting one in this predicament.[22]

Stoller also says

> A phallus is dangerous but not mysterious; the womb's danger comes from silence, secrecy, and growth in darkness—which is mystery.[23]

The bizarre extremes of Satanism that require detached female submission and mocking male cruelty, concretize and act out old and familiar mysteries of male/female dilemmas. In the cases of Candy and Anita, Satan as father/God substitute propounded by Freud, seems to have relevance and fortunately neither girl had found a bizarre group cult to act out the destructive extremes. Such cases I am sure could be documented. Full discussion of delinquent and criminal groups and behaviors that have implications for study of adolescents in this "supernatural vein" is beyond the scope of this chapter, but has clear relevance and importance.

Adolescence, Separation–Individuation and the Supernatural

Peter Blos says:

> Adolescence (as a phase and process) must accomplish the renunciation of the primary love objects, the parents, as sexual objects; siblings and parent substitutes have to be included in this process of renunciation. This phase, then, is concerned essentially with object relinquishment and object finding, and these

processes reverberate in the ego to produce cathectic shifts which influence both the existing object representations and self-representation. Consequently, the sense of self or sense of identity acquires a heretofore unknown lability.

During adolescence the drive turns toward *genitality* (combination in experience of tenderness, maturity, intimacy, generativity and sexual excitement.[24]), the libidinous objects change from the preoedipal and oedipal to the nonincestuous, heterosexual object. The ego safeguards its integrity through defensive operations; some of these are ego restricting and require counter-cathectic energy for their maintenance, while others prove to be adaptive, and to allow aim-inhibited (sublimatory) drive discharge; these become the permanent regulators of self esteem.[25]

In all three cases we can identify severe problems in the reenunciation–new object-finding process described by Blos. The supernatural preoccupations seemed to form or give mental representation to abortive symbolic efforts to effect such shifts away from the paternal objects. The pre-oedipally problematic mothers were all variously weak and narcissistic and thus poor models for identification or full unambivalent renunciation. The incestuous struggles then become in this context uncanny and mysterious for Antia, Candy and Lara. They are all still in various ways struggling with these issues of identity.

A discussion of Margaret S. Mahler's work in regard to the case histories and implications for a study of the supernatural and uncanny could be voluminous; so I will present some of her comments about the third subphase of separation-individuation she calls *rapprochement*. She says:

> The rapprochement struggle has its origin in the species specific human dilemma that arises out of the fact that on the one hand, the toddler is obliged, by the rapid maturation of his ego, to recognize his separateness, while on the other hand, he is as yet unable to stand alone.[26]

She goes on:

> In some children, the rapprochement leads to great ambivalence and even to splitting of the object world into "good" and "bad," the consequences of which may later become organized into neurotic symptoms of the narcissistic variety. In still other children, islands of developmental failures lead to borderline symptomatology in latency and adolescence. Fixation at the level of rapprochement may be seen every so often in the widening range of child and adult patients who nowadays seek our help. Their most pervasive anxiety is separation anxiety. Their affects may be dominated by narcissistic rage with temper trantrums, which may subside and give way to altruistic surrender (A. Freud, 1936). Their basic conflict is to be sought and found, we believe, in the primitive narcissistic struggle that was acted out in the rapprochement crisis, but that may have become a central internal conflict pertaining mainly to their uncertain sense of identity.[27]

It seems to me that the polarized supernatural metaphors of God/Satan, white/black, saint/sinner, angel/demon, good/evil, heaven/hell, found/lost have a natural fit with the splitting mechanisms and their origin, as Mahler described them, or, as Freud would suggest, reminiscent of old and familiar preverbal, primitive, affective cognitive, magical omnipotent states like that of the infant or primitive tribes. The primitive group processes in some cults seem to blend as natural old and familiar interpersonal context for these dilemmas for borderline, narcissistic or very neurotic adolescents.

Mahler, above, referred to Anna Freud's delineation of the term coined by Edward Bibring, *altruistic surrender*. Anna Freud, after her lucid descriptions of "identification with the aggressor," reversal (primarily love/hate) and their relationship to projection in its negative interpersonal connotations then goes on to say:

> But it [projection] may work in another way as well, enabling us to form valuable positive attachments and so to consolidate our relations with one another. This normal and less conspicuous form of projection might be described as "alturistic surrender" of our own instinctual impulses in favor of other people.[28]

She points out that "this defensive process has its origin in the infantile conflict with parental authority about some form of instinctual gratification of others via projection and unconscious identification. I propose that in some troubled adolescents we see another variation of this process that might be termed "malevolent surrender."[29] Here the unresolved, primitive islands of sadistic, masochistic, and phallic narcissistic strivings find sustained, untamed existence via malignant forms of supernatural preoccupations, obsessions, ruminations and perverse behaviors in adolescents. The supernatural in these areas provides a perfect haven for the preservation of the immature, infantile and the destructive.

Views from the Therapeutic Dyad Back Out to the Social Field

Heinz Kohut offers some helpful perspectives on our topic. I want to avoid the theoretical and semantic quarrels associated with Kohut's formulations but rather will assume the reader has such knowledge or refer him to the primary sources or four fine, critical and concise reviews.[30-32]

Kohut's sensitive delineation of the spectrum of so-called "self-object transferences" or "transference-like states" is very enlightening in regard to expanding on Freud's discussion of the uncanny aspects of "the double" and a theoretical perspective on the supernatural as experienced by adolescents. Kohut describes various "mirror transferences" (alter ego or twinship, archaic merger and mirror transference in the narrower sense). The early traumatic disappointments in the maternal object, later disappointments with the fathers and intense separation–individuation problems of our three cases could be viewed in terms of tremendous problems in the narcissistic sector of their personalities. The implications of the psychology of the self for understanding the inherent grandiosity and uncanny power of supernatural preoccupations in the lives of narcissistically vulnerable adolescents are many.[33] For Anita, Satan became a kind of twin, double, alter-ego of grandiose power and sustenance. The idealizing transference established quickly with the therapist became crucial to sustain the therapeutic work as she examined the self-object qualities of her relationship to the therapist and his medication. To even interpret the oral, anal, oedipal or other traditionally viewed conflict areas, before extensive work with the narcissistic (perhaps pre-oedipal), self-object aspects of her case, would lead to precarious situations.

The supernatural, uncanny and some cults' primitive belief systems and metaphors have a unique phenomenological fit with inner narcissistic and borderline dynamics and problems of psychic structure. The supernatural metaphors seem to act as foci for "transmuting externalizations" as compromise formations in these troubled adolescents. It is clear how delicate technique of therapy must be as the therapist approaches these areas during sessions. It is not unlike the great sensitivity one must use in approaching creative literary–artistic productions of adolescents.[34] The adolescent can indeed be and feel very creative and vulnerable in his use of the supernatural metaphors. Empathic mirroring of the degree of self-cohesion provided by the supernatural must take place if such malignant transmuting externalizations are to be eventually contained and worked through as transmuting internalizations of a well-conducted therapy. The supernatural involvements may be used by the patient as a buffer or desperate defense against overwhelming merger anxiety toward the therapist as the power-ful mind reader. Kohut's "bipolar self" notion was very helpful in attempting to understand Candy as she exclaimed, "I vacillate between seeing myself as think-ing lofty thoughts and being a famous poetess; and then feeling haunted, bored, rebellious and depressed."

One final area I wish to explore is nicely put into persepctive by Kohut:

> But now I shall turn to a field that lies beyond the bounds of the basic rule: the field where the scrutiny of psychological factors and the scrutiny of social factors converge.

> I shall go directly to the heart of the matter by making the claim that the psycho-logical danger that puts the psychological survival of modern Western man into the greatest jeopardy is changing. Until comparatively recent times the dominant threat to the individual was unsolvable inner conflict. And the correlated domi-nant interpersonal constellations to which the western civilization was exposed were the emotional overcloseness between parents and children and intense emotional relationships between the parents—perhaps to be looked upon as the unwholesome obverse of such corresponding wholesome social factors as firm-ness of the family unit, a social life concentrated on the home and its immediate vicinity, and a clear-cut definition of the roles of father and mother.

> Today's child has fewer and fewer opportunities to observe its parents at work or at least to participate emotionally, via concrete, understandable imagery, in the parents' competence and in their pride in the work situation where their selves are most profoundly engaged. Today's child can at best observe the parents' ac-tivities during their leisure hours.[35]

Kohut acknowledges that leisure time together has positive aspects but that the child's forming "nuclear self" does not get the same nutriment as the emotional participation in the activities of real life day to day. Kohut particularly feels that the progressive, limited, optimal, nontraumatic parental failures that can provide the fuel for transmuting internalizations is not available. Kohut further refines this:

> The environment which used to be experienced as threateningly close, is now experienced more and more as threateningly distant: where children were formerly overstimulated by the emotional (including the erotic) life of their parents, they are now often understimulated; where formerly the child's eroticism aimed at pleasure gain and led to internal conflict because of parental prohibitions and the rivalries of the oedipal constellation, many children now seek the effect of erotic stimulation in order to relieve loneliness, in order to fill an emotional void.[36]

This sort of applied analysis is always risky but I think Kohut frames for us where the troubled adolescent's intense preoccupations with the supernatural, uncanny and cults seem to fit psychosocially. He states:

> In the narcissistic-defense sphere, it is clear that children (and adolescents) often undertake both solitary sexual activities and group activities of a sexual, near-sexual, or sexualized nature in the attempt to relieve the lethargy and depression resulting from the unavailability of a mirroring and of an idealizing self object.[37]

Kohut lends some perspective here on the narcissistic, masturbatory-like and perverse intensity of some adolescents' preoccupations with the stimulation of supernatural and uncanny cults. In the acted-out extremes, Stoller's words, "the erotic form of hatred" sums it up nicely. Perhaps the children-rearing ethos described by Kohut leads to a relative increase in borderline and narcissistic pathologies in a society and such a society with mass media available has an increased preoccupation with overstimulating supernaturalism.

Otto Kernberg, in a paper very germane to our discussion, "Cultural Impact and Intrapsychic Change," cautions us against too hasty conclusions. He points out:

> I do not think that changes in contemporary morality have effects on the sense of self in the direction of fortering identity diffusion or loss of the sense of self. I think the syndrome of identity diffusion always reflects serious psychopathology related to borderline personality organization which stems from vicissitudes of very early development; the underlying intrapsychic structures which reflect such psychopathology are probably crystalized within the first five years of life. . . I do not think that changes in contemporary morality (or perhaps super-natural preoccupations) have effects on patterns of object relationships if we define object relationships not simply in terms of actual interactions between a person and others but in terms of the intrapsychic structures which govern such interactions, and in terms of the internal capacity to relate in depth with others. Many authors have talked about what has been called this "age of alienation," and it has been implied that social and cultural alienation may foster disintegration of the capacity of involvement in depth with others. I think that clinically speaking this does not hold true.
>
> Keniston's work (1960, 1968) comparing youth in protest with alienated youth has provided important sociological evidence indicating that generalized withdrawal from relationships with others and incapacities to establish deep, lasting relationships are not a direct reflection of youth culture, but stem from very early childhood conflicts and family pathology. By the same token, I do not think that changes in contemporary morality have changed the need and the capacity for intimacy in various forms. This does not mean to say that such changes in the patterns of intimacy could not occur over a period of several generations if and when changes in cultural patterns affect family structure to such an extent that earliest development in childhood would be affected.[38]

Several paragraphs later Kernberg continues:

> All this does not mean that the deciding factor of where an adolescent stands in the cultural struggle is determined exclusively by the degree and type of his or her personal psychopathology. I feel very critical about the tendency to explain away cultural identities in terms of a purely individual psychology or psychopathology. . . . However, certain cultures select or highlight certain types of

psychopathologies because they fit into it better, and thus convey—erroneously —the impression that a certain culture has brought about a certain type of individual psychopathology.

Kernberg then nicely and concisely summarizes Jacobson's "Levels of Superego Development" (1964) and concludes:

> What needs to be stressed is that the main reorganization in adolescence of superego identification relates to those of the oedipal period, in connection with a definite growing out of the oedipal conflicts of childhood. Jacobson points out that it is only in patients with severe borderline or narcissistic character structures that reprojection of more primitive superego nuclei takes place, which indicates that the superego was poorly consolidated and integrated in the first place. In this case, we find a combination of primitive idealizations which reflect the tendency toward narcissistic self-aggrandizement, general devaluation of value systems and external objects, a chaotic shift in group identifications, and lack of capacity to empathize in depth with other persons. Patients with these borderline and/or narcissistic features may emerge as temporary leaders or predominant exponents of protesting, alienated, or bizarrely oppositional groups, rapidly adapting to the unusual or far out, rationalizing their socially drifting quality and lack of consistency in terms of a chaotic social structure.[39]

In summary, Blos, Mahler, Stoller, Kohut and Kernberg help us toward an awareness of the adolescent at risk for "malevolent surrender" to perverse, supernatural cults. This hypothetical young person has intense "pre-oedipal" unresolved conflicts. He or she would have 1) major separation–individuation conflicts, 2) gender-role confusion, 3) incestuous attachments, 4) conflicted internalized object relations, 5) defensive structures typical of narcissistic or borderline personality, and 6) a vulnerability to powerful, perverse supernatural overstimulation because of parental understimulation via lack of empathic, collaborative parental contact.

Very careful observation is required to sift out what is really going on with each individual adolescent. This must take into account 1) the cultural milieu, often over several generations, 2) the intrapsychic structure or lack of it as it related to supernatural preoccupations, and 3) the self-object aspects of our therapeutic relationship with an adolescent so preoccupied.

NARCISSISTIC VULNERABILITY
AND GROUP LEADERSHIP IN CULTS

Daniel H. Kriegman, in an unpublished masters thesis "A Psychosocial Study of Religious Cults: An Exploration of the Relationship of Narcissistic Vulnerability to the Susceptability of Cultism" (1979), makes several observations that concur with my own. He states:

> Our contention is that the organizational structure of the cult group functions in such a way as to appeal to, absorb, channel and sustain narcissistic personality configurations as described by Kohut.

He goes on:

> The special relationship between follower and guru (narcissistic cult leader), resembles above all else that particular relationship which arises between certain narcissistic patients and their therapist.

He refers to the various forms of idealizing and mirror transferences. What appears to be the lifework of the cult, says Kriegman, "is to actively encourage the development of an (unresolved!) idealizing transference," which freezes or locks the individual in that position. It would also follow that for a cult member to leave the cult, might result in a fragmented sense of self and a pervasive feeling of emptiness. This indeed seems to be the case, as evidenced by the intense experiences of "deprogramming" and or supportive family therapy that such a passage often requires. The spectrum of narcissistic personality disorders and narcissistic psychopathologies do seem to lend themselves to particular influence by the messianic or charismatic leader and his cult. Kriegman is pursuing questionnaire and other empirical data to support these hypotheses.

SUMMARY

In recent years there appears to be a heightened adolescent interest in the supernatural and variously related or associated cults. The spectrum of supernatural preoccupations can be arbitrarily divided along a spectrum: 1) the traditionally religious supernatural, 2) the non-traditionally religious supernatural, 3) the meditative ("Eastern') supernatural, 4) the secular (occult) supernatural, and 5) the anti-religious or areligious supernatural.

The adolescent's responses to potentially overstimulating media and peer barrage with the supernatural varies from normal curiosity and sublimated entertaining excitement, devout interest via sudden "conversion" and/or an entwining of these supernatural preoccupations with major neurotic, characterologic, narcissistic, borderline, prepsychotic or frankly psychotic psychopathology.

Three cases were presented to illustrate how adolescents weave supernatural involvements into their major psychopathology. These cases were used to focus perspectives from prominent psychoanalytic thinkers upon adolescents and the supernatural. The cases presented typify the predominant "pre-oedipal," borderline and highly narcissistic trends that the supernatural metaphors uniquely fit into phenomenologically. These images of good/bad, white/black, God/Satan, saint/sinner, angel/demon, etc, of the supernatural belief systems, relate like friendly bedfellows to primitive intrapsychic defenses such as denial, projection, "malevolent surrender," splitting and projective identification.

The general conclusion is that adolescent preoccupation with cults and the supernatural is really reflective of old and familier adolescent psychodynamic, psychoeconomic and psychogenetic issues. Great care must be taken so as not to glibly assume that sudden surface shifts in varieties of "youth culture" or cults easily affect intrapsychic structure or functioning. On the other hand, over several evolving generations, sociocultural phenomena can lead to significant changes in child-rearing and thus intrapsychic pathology may be effected.

Valuable observations can be made on "youth culture" issues from within the psychoanalytic psychotherapy dyad, to combine with careful sociocultural–historical observation, towards contributing to in-depth perspectives on such phenomenon as adolescent preoccupation with cults and the supernatural.

The potentially perverse and/or violent extremes of recent supernatural preoccupations and cults is a clear indication for teachers, leaders and therapists of adolescents to be knowledgeable about such phenomena, especially in regard to issues of narcissistic vulnerability as appealing to the defective sense of self found in narcissistic personality disorders.

REFERENCES AND NOTES

1. *The Houston Post,* December 13, 1978.
2. Freud S: The psychopathology of everyday life. *Standard Edition* 1955;6:257-258.
3. Freud S: 6:258.
4. Freud S: 6:259.
5. Blatty WP: *The Exorcist.* New York, Harper & Row, 1971.
6. Freud S: 6:261.
7. Freud S: 6:261.
8. Freud S: 6:260.
9. Freud S: A case of Dementia paranoides. *Standard Edition* 1955;12:66.
10. Freud S: Notes upon a case of obsessional neurosis (1909)—ratman. *Standard Edition* 1955;10:232-233.
11. Freud S: The uncanny. *Standard Edition* 1955;17:219.
12. Freud S: 17:220.
13. Freud S: 17:234.
14. Freud S: 17:234-235.
15. Freud S: 17:240-241. See also: Freud, *Totem and Taboo,* Essay III, "Animism, Magic and the Omnipotence of Thoughts," *Standard Edition* 1955;13.
16. Hamilton J: The exorcist: Some psychodynamic considerations. *J Philadelphia Assoc Psychoanal* 1976;3(1,2):38.
17. Hamilton J: p. 45.
18. Waelder R: The structure of paranoid ideas. *Int J Psychoanal* 1951;32:176.
19. Wilson, Flip: (Popular American comedian).
20. *The Occult and the Supernatural.* New York, Crescent Books of Crown Publishers, Inc, 1975.
21. Stoller R: Sexual excitement. *Arch Gen Psychiatry* 1976;33:899.
22. Stoller R: *Perversion: The Erotic Form of Hatred.* New York, Pantheon Books, Random House, 1975, p 99.
23. Stoller R: p 98.
24. Parenthesis added by this author.
25. Blos P: *On Adolescence: A Psychoanalytic Interpretation.* Illinois, The Free Press of Glencoe, 1962, p 75.
26. Mahler MS, Pine F, Bergman A: *The Psychological Birth of the Human Infant.* New York, Basic Books, Inc, 1975, p 229.
27. Mahler M, et al: pp 229-230.
28. Freud A: The ego and the mechanisms of defense, in *The Writings of Anna Freud,* vol 2. New York, International University Press, Inc, 1936 (1966), p 123.
29. Freud A: p 130.
30. Spruiell V: Three strands of narcissism. *The Psychoanalytic Quarterly* 1975;44(4):577-596.
31. Loewald H: The restoration of the self—book review. *The Psychoanalytic Quarterly* 1975;47:441-451.
32. Schwartz L: The restoration of the self—book review. *The Psychoanalytic Quarterly* 1975;47:436-443.
33. Schwartz, reference 32; and Loewald, reference 31.
34. Skolnikoff A: The creative process and borderline patients. Paper presented at the Annual Meeting of the American Psychiatric Association, Miami, May 1976.
35. Kohut H: *The Restoration of the Self.* New York, International University Press, Inc.
36. Kohut H: p 271.
37. Kohut H: p 272.
38. Kernberg O: Cultural impact and intrapsychic change, in Feinstein, Giovacchini (eds): *Adolescent Psychiatry,* vol 4. New York, Jason Aronson, Inc, 1975, pp 39-40.
39. Kernberg O: pp 41-42.

Gnosticism in High Tech:
Science Fiction and Cult Formation

DAVID A. HALPERIN

A pocalypse. Armageddon. The Last Judgment. These are the majestic visions of the ends to human existence. They are the stuff of oracular prophecy, eschatological concern, and science fiction. The recent prominence of fictional scenarios of the apocalypse often accompanied by a secular messianism, and the increasing visibility of cults is neither fortuitous nor accidental. This chapter discusses the relationship between two superficially dissimilar approaches to human dilemmas—the "mystical" and/or cultic, and the hypertechnological modern literary genre in which "Endtime" finds both its most persistent creative expression—science fiction—and its most avid consumer—the older adolescent and young adult. Both are responses to and attempts to master the inner turmoil of the adolescent. Science fiction plays a role for the older adolescent comparable to that of the fairy tale for the younger child. It provides the adolescent with the opportunity:

> . . . to master the psychological problems of growing up—overcoming nar-
> cissistic disappointments, oedipal dilemmas, sibling rivalries; becoming able to
> relinquish childhood dependencies; gaining a feeling of selfhood and of self-
> worth, and a sense of moral obligation (Bettelheim, 1977).

In exploring the manner in which the "scientific imagination is profoundly touched by the atheistic mysticism" (Thompson, 1972), it will enable us to appreciate more fully the concerns that may lead to cult affiliation and which find parallel literary expression in both the theology of cults and science fiction. Moreover, there are surprising interfaces between science fiction and religiosity, so that by understanding one we will increase our appreciation of the other.

One historical root of science fiction is in the romance of displacement such as Plato's *Timaeus,* More's *Utopia* and Swift's *Gulliver's Travels.* These works reflect their author's attempt to comment on his contemporary world by displacing the scene of his comments. An intriguing example of the interface of religion and science fiction is the role of a pre-Columbian, pseudohistorical romance of displacement by one Solomon Spaulding as a possible precursor of *The Book of Mormon.*

As a self-conscious literary genre, science fiction is a product of the nineteenth century. It is a descendant of gothic romances such as Walpole's *Castle of Otranto. Frankenstein* by Mary Shelley may be the first consciously created science fiction novel. Science fiction developed in the hands of Jules Verne and H.G. Wells, whose works retain both their potency and popularity to this day particularly among adolescents. Within their oeuvre, Verne and Wells confronted the profound changes industralization imposed on the Western world in the late nineteenth century. It is not accidental that literary creations which are a response to transitions within society occurring under the aegis of technological "progress," find their most important audience in adolescents who are themselves in transition from their home to the fearful, frightening unknown outside world—whence they are treading under the banner of "progress" as well. Particularly, within the work of Verne, the individual confronts the unknown from a position of comfort and encapsulation. His protagonists confront the alien world outside the submarine of Capt. Nemo much as the adolescent confronts the alien world of adulthood. Indeed, Nemo's need for vengenance ostensibly springs from his rage against an adult and imperialistic world.

Science fiction's indebtedness to the gothic romance is most apparent in the work of H.P. Lovecraft. Lovecraft, a reclusive and talented writer, self-consciously modeled himself and his work on that of Edgar Alan Poe. His debt to Poe is most apparent in his convoluted prose and eccentricity. Lovecraft created an elaborate mythological cycle—the Cthulhu mythos—detailing the efforts of an "Elder Race" (the Ancient Ones) to return and dominate the Earth. The Cthulhu mythos is a transposition of the Gnostic battle between Good and Evil into a prototypical New England village, Arkham (ne Salem). The Elder Race is kept at bay by elaborate magic ritual (detailed in the *Necronomicron* written by the "mad Arab" Abdul Alhazared). Within this battle is the ritualized attempt to prevent the return of the repressed, Cthulhu and his throng seem very much to be the representation of fertility and elemental nature.

The appeal to the adolescent seeking magic means of controlling his impulses is obvious. The parallelism to Lovecraft whose brief marriage ended with his return to his mother's home is intriguing. Lovecraft's apparent inspiration for this "mythology" was the work of Mme. Blavatsky and Aleister Crowley, both figures of notoriety and cultic character (Derleth, 1946). Lovecraft mined the fields of theosophy and occultism to create his own world in which he battled the forces of chaos which he experienced as overwhelming. In a broader sense, the growth of occultism and theosophy in the latter part of the nineteenth century may be seen both as a tribute to Mme. Blavatsky's ability to sense that the Orient and its traditions are a source of endless intrigue for Occidentals and that:

> "Spiritualism" offered Americans a last frontier of sorts; a mystical wilderness to replace the now populated wilderness of American legend: The woodsman with his long rifle had become a city dweller with a talent for trance experience and hypnosis (Zweig, 1980).

In considering the interrelationship of new religions and science fiction, it is noteworthy that the movement founded by Mme. Blavatsky is still active.

The utopia and its contemporary representative, the dystopia, are among the most preeminent and persistent themes of science fiction. More's *Utopia* is, not surprisingly, an early exemplar. Edward Bellamy's *Looking Backward* is a more recent and influential example. However, within this century, the dystopia—the portrayal of the antiutopia—has become the pervasive mode. A prominent early example is H.G. Wells's *The Time Machine*, which provided Wells with an opportunity to extrapolate to its apocalyptic end the social and class divisions of Victorian England. Aldous Huxley's *Brave New World* is another powerful example of the dystopia in the service of satire. A variant dystopia is the alternate history novel; ie, what would have happened if?, such as Kingsley Amis's *Alteration* (portraying an Inquisition ridden England after the victory of the Spanish Armada), Henry Sobel's *For Want of a Nail* (North America after a British victory at Saratoga), or Len Deighton's *SS-GB* (a Nazi victory over England). These novels provide entertaining and perceptive opportunities to explore the meaning of events.

The most influential modern dystopian novel is George Orwell's *1984*. In *1984*, the author's vision, literary artistry and intensity have combined to create a compelling portrait of an authoritarian dystopia. The novel's title has become a byword for the totalitarian state with its techniques for mind control, subversion of the individual's autonomy, required celibacy and the cult of Big Brother. Of particular relevance, in Orwell's portrayal of *1984* is the profound contrast between the authoritarian Airstrip-One (once England) and Edwardian England. Orwell created both a vision of dystopia and an allegory of *Paradise Lost*. The implications are profound. For Orwell, as for many others, there is the profound sense of an explusion from the primeval Garden into a cold world of unreasoning authority. Orwell's idealization of anarchy prevents him from accepting any authority from being truly legitimate. It is in this wariness of authority that he speaks so powerfully to the adolescent. As Harry Levin (1980) has so eloquently noted:

> Looking backward across so many generations who looked forward with ever-changing hopes, we are apt to envisage the contemporary scene as a future which has arrived, but which fulfill's George Orwell's grim prediction for the Eighties. . . . If we try to imagine experiments in communal living today, our memories are fatefully overclouded with images of Auschwitz and Gulag, not forgetting Jonestown. . . . We should remember, too, that those rebellious students, there and everywhere, were the first generation to grow up in the shadow of a demonstrable millenium; the apocalyptic consciousness that the world's populace could be suddenly destroyed.

Levin reflects on the crisis of authority in a post-Hiroshima and post-Vietnam America as being comparable to that which impelled Orwell and is so magisterially explored in Paul Fussell's *The Great War and the Literary Imagination* (1976). It found reflection in the pessimism of Freud's later work, eg, *The Future of An Illusion*. This sense of a "world betrayed" and of "the expulsion from paradise" finds its most popular expression in the apocalyptic novel. It is a form in which the ideology of cult life imitates the reality of art.

The apocalyptic novel presents the world after The Fall—frequently after the technologically precipitated expulsion from Eden. A representative scenario is presented in Robert Merle's *Malevil*. An unspecified holocaust (presumably thermonuclear) apparently destroys all of France except for a group of men deep in a wine cellar (this *is* a French novel). Gradually, other survivors appear, including women, who intrude into this homosexual commune. Life resumes but as an archaic rustic idyll. Eventually, the group's leader dies, and by book's end, he is venerated as a cult figure by the survivors. In his vows of obedience, chastity (his sexual orientation is ambiguous), he exemplifies his status of cult icon. Charity is not a conspicuous virtue in the world of Malevil—much of its dramatic tension is generated by the acceptance of the rule of *tirage*—the viewpoint best expressed in the logic of the "boat is full."

In a novel with fewer literary pretensions, *Lucifer's Hammer* (the title is suggestive) by Larry Niven and Jerry Pourcelle, a comet collides with the earth. Civilization barely survives. Its remnants are led by a rigid, technocratic oligarchy whose major concern is to save a nuclear power plant—to preserve "the promise of nuclear technology" from the machinations of ecology oriented religious fanatics. Despite the superficially dissimilar ideologies which invest these novels (Merle looks backwards and Niven and Pourcelle express a touching faith in technology), both novels aspire to the creation of a redoubt where an elect will survive under the guidance of a benign, authoritarian leader. Groups outside the redoubt are suspect. Dissent is equated with betrayal. Sexuality is similarly suspect and/or circumscribed. These novels speak with nostalgia for an authoritarian, rigid world with clearly defined goals and sexual roles. Presumably, authoritarianism (temporal and/or spiritual) will have survival value after Armageddon. Is this very far from the Rev. Jim Jones and his hegira to Ukiah from Indianapolis to escape nuclear attack? Nor were/are Jones's concerns a unique product of his paranoia, as the following show:

Survival Havens in America

Doomsday? Havens from disaster—Let's discuss the unthinkable—because it *could* happen. Suppose for a moment: Russia launched a massive missile attack on this country . . . there were hundreds of megaton detonations . . . and then came the fallout, sweeping across the U.S. with the prevailing winds. Would anyone escape? . . . . The answer is *YES* (Center for Survival Research, 1981).

or,

Sect Moves into Shelters to Await Atom War Today

Leland Jensen and his small band of religious followers headed for their fallout shelters today to await the destruction of the world by nuclear war that they say will come tomorrow. . . . Other members of the religious group, called *Baha'i Under the Provisions of the Covenant* planned to go underground. . . . Mr. Jensen said he would not be concerned if his prophecy did not come true. There will be a nuclear holocaust some day, he said, "and by having a definite date established, we've accomplished tremendous things" (New York Times, April 28, 1981).

Thus, prophecy and science fiction meet in providing a justification for ostensibly "task" oriented group work under the control of a self-appointed leader.

Not all dystopias are the product of a sudden nuclear apocalypse. The concern over ecology has created within the individual a sense of nature betrayed. The film, *Soylent Green*, with its portrayal of America in the year 2020 as an over-populated, ecological catastrophe with institutionalized "cannibalism" is a dramatic example. In this context, the potential to exploit ecological concerns by cultic groups as a symbol of the apocalypse must be noted. It is not accidental that Squeaky Fromme, a member of the Manson family, described herself as being very concerned about the possible extermination of whales on the night prior to her attempt at assassinating President Ford. No doubt, cult affiliation may be in part a product of the same appeal to idealism that appropriately invests a concern with man's environment. But, as ecological concerns may often express a certain loosely pantheistic attitude towards nature, it is not surprising that these concerns may take a more formal religious tone.

A particularly intriguing demonstration of the potential ambivalence of ecological concerns is shown in D. Keith Mano's powerful dystopic novel, *The Bridge*. In The Bridge, humanity almost successfully commits suicide in atonement for its sins against nature. Mano ironically resolves this in the creation of a rigid, archaic world governed by a religion in which the ritual of communion is replaced by ritually circumscribed cannibalism. If, as Manuel has said there is a "utopian propensity" (Manuel and Manuel, 1979), then the dystopic propensity may be succinctly expressed in the following apocryphal dialog preserved by Gita Mehta as having occurred at the World Conference on the Future of Mankind:

> "Don't live in the shadow of death, young man," he warned.
>
> "Let us say there is a nuclear holocaust. What will it do? I shall tell you what it will do. It will cleanse the world!
>
> "Don't you understand? We are going forward toward a post-nuclear post-Armageddon *Golden Age!*"
>
> The American student nodded sagely and sat down, grasping the moral significance of nuclear war for the first time (Mehta, 1979).

The "cleansing" potential of apocalypse is expressed in Stephen King's popular novel, *The Stand*. The United States has been devastated through the accidental release of an artificial product developed at a bacteriological warfare laboratory. The survivors wander across America with surprising equanimity in a landscape in which hecatombs fester in the hot July sun. The novel is a veritable Robinsonade in which adolescents gather to recreate civilization under the aegis of a superannuated mystical black woman who leads them against the forces of demonic *Evil*.

Why should such grim and pessimistic prophecy be a literary staple among the older adolescent? Adolescence is a time for separation, individuation, and, a reconciliation with authority (Blos, 1976). The dystopian and apocalyptic novels express both the adolescent's inner turmoil and may even point toward a kind of solution which may be offered by cult affiliation. As McDermott and Lum (1980) have perceptively noted in their *Star Wars: The Modern Developmental Fairy Tale*:

> . . . perhaps suggesting a shift in elements central to present-day personality development. For the film seems to emphasize adolescent fantasy, separations from parents and childhood, and an overcoming of the destructive forces within oneself, prerequisites for moving on to maturity and sexuality.

The increased duration of adolescence has made the separation from home by modern adolescents a more traumatic experience. As the long period of peace preceding World War I intensified, the sense of apocalypse among the generation of 1914 (a generation that then sought solutions among secular cults), so the prolongation of adolescence has intensified a sense of loss engendered by the temporary deprivations of early adulthood. This has taken on a particular intensity because of a loss of confidence in the adult world to solve problems that are experienced (and may be) increasingly intractable. The "make it new" dictum which parallels the technological surge of the twenties and provided the cultural renaissance after the apocalypse of 1914–1918, no longer seems credible. *Looking Backward* cedes place of expectation to *Brave New World*. And, like Huxley himself, the modern adolescent seeks more magical, Oriental solutions to personal dilemmas. The "new age" after the fall, often expresses a nostalgia for the vanished world where parents imposed order, and aspires to the imposition of control under the aegis of parental surrogates. It is a time in which the adolescent magically becomes one of the elect and his skills are at a premium unrestrained by the irrelevant complexities of adult life. The primary virtues of the "new age" are adolescent virtues—group cohesiveness, sacrifice, and obedience. In a world dominated by "survival skills," sexuality is confined within rigidly imposed rules and the only vocation is survival. Thus, in a climate of opinion created by apocalyptic concerns, the literature of the apocalypse and the religion of Armageddon flourish side by side.

The relationship between science fiction and cult ideology is demonstrated in another, and perhaps most characteristic, theme of science fiction: the encounter with the wanderer from the stars or the apotheosis of the alien among us. *The Man Who Fell to Earth, Close Encounters of the Third Kind, Superman I* and *II*, and *E.T.: Extraterrestrial* are recent cinematic examples. These films describe the adventures and/or misadventures of an alien, superior being after his arrival on earth. In *The Man Who Fell to Earth,* David Bowie portrays, in an angelic, androgynous manner, a superior being who "falls" to earth in a vain effort to bring water back to his parched, desert-like home planet. The "man" is prevented from realizing his mission after he is tortured and condemned to remain on Earth by representatives of the adult world—the FBI and CIA. It is a parable of angelism undone by earthly corruption. The "man" finds solace if not redemption in the love of a naive, adolescent female of uncertain morality (she may be an agent of the adult corrupters).

The theme of the uncorrupted and uncorruptible superhuman alien battling against the forces of evil finds expression in *Superman I* and *II*. The change in emphasis since the character's creation is intriguing. In the original forties comic strip, Superman arrives on Earth via cosmic cradle from Krypton (The Hidden One, an allusive name for God frequently found in the literature of mysticism—also note Kryptonite—Superman's source of strength). The parallels to Moses and Jesus are obvious (Heldman, personal communication, 1981). However, his original role was as the secular, all-American counterfoil to the Nazi UeberMensch. In contrast, within the recent films, great emphasis is placed on his planet of origin and the supernal wisdom of his parents who live within pure Towers of Glass. Has a decline in confidence in a liberal, humane nationalism led to this change? In *Superman I,* he undergoes a "quasimonastic" initiation into his superhuman status, undergoing a return to his parents' realm of wisdom via pure, undefiled crystals which have recorded their culture. In both films, the major threat to his powers appears to be his feelings for and the sexual appetite of Lois Lane. In *Superman II,* he is confronted with fellow Kryptonians, who act as archetypal fallen angels. The leading fallen angel confirms his rascality by his sneering at Superman's "pure" Tower of Glass home as a "sentimental recreation of a lost world," and, parenthetically confirming his appreciation of this adult, earthly realm.

In *Close Encounters of the Third Kind,* the aliens are fragile, child-like, passive beings who visit the Earth via flying saucer for inscrutable reasons of their own. These aliens seem to be most comfortable with the marginal, the obsessed or with children rather than the mature inhabitants of Earth. Similarly, in *E.T.,* the good scientist assures Eliot that "it's best you found him first." This angelic character of aliens has prompted Rev. Andrew Greeley's witty observation that in *Close Encounters,* angels have returned in technological garb (New York Times, March, 1978). As Jung has observed:

> As one can see from all this, the observation and interpretation of Ufo's have already led to the formation of a regular legend. . . they have become a *living myth.* We have here a golden opportunity of seeing how a legend is formed, and how in a difficult and dark time for humanity and miraculous tale grows up of an attempted intervention by extra-terrestrial "heavenly" power (Jung, 1958, pp 16–17).

It is particularly relevant that in his epilog to *Flying Saucers: A Modern Myth of Things Seen in the Skies,* Jung describes a book, *The Secret of the Saucers* by Orfeo M. Angelucci in which Mr Angelucci describes his encounter with inhabitants of a flying saucer. Jung archly adds that "He makes his living now by preaching the gospel revealed to him by the Saucers." Nor was/is Mr Angelucci unique in his revelation as the presence of other similarly inspired groups demonstrates (West and Singer, 1980). In *Close Encounters,* a religious gloss pervades the entire film, climaxed by the obsessed hero's departure as a "pilgrim" to a higher realm—a departure preceded by an ecumenical service. The darker potentials of this theme were recently presented in a television film, *We* (a couple from a far galaxy), with a Jonestown-like apotheosis.

In these very popular films, a common theme emerges: An angelic being from a higher realm falls to Earth (literally and metaphorically) and attempts to return to his higher realm. Superficially, this attempt at return is presented in concrete terms but it is clear that it has a spiritual dimension. As Hans Jonas (1963, p 49) has noted, a pervasive theme in many varieties of Gnosticism is poetically expressed in this Mandaean composition:

> In the name of the great first alien life from the worlds of light, the sublime that stands above all works. . .

Jonas further notes:

> The alien is that which stems from elsewhere and does not belong here. To those who do belong here it is thus the strange, the unfamiliar and incomprehensible; but their world on its part is just as incomprehensible to the alien that comes to dwell here, and like a foreign land where it is far from home.

This is not simply a matter of metaphorical religious metalanguage concretized coincidentally with that of technological romance. Rather, it indicates a congruence of theme. Mark Rose, in his recent *Alien Encounters: An Anatomy of Science Fiction,* has observed:

Like science fiction, religion is concerned with the relationship between the human and the nonhuman or, more specifically, the relationship between the human and the divine (p 39).

and further that:

the human is like to be conceived as fallen and in need of salvation. In its crudest form this pattern appears in those narratives in which extraterrestrials arrive in flying saucers to save humanity from atomic self-destruction (p 41).

Rose finally notes:

I specified the content of science fiction as a displacement of religion. Now that content may be further specified as the sense of the infinite or rather as the sense of the finitude of the self, the conscious ego, in relation to the boundlessness of the cosmos that is not the self. This is indeed a religious theme, possibly the paramount religious theme (p 191).

This is very close indeed to Gnositicism and to modern existentialism who both share a sense:

. . . which Pascal was the first to face in its frightening implications to expound the full force of his eloquence: man's loneliness in the physical universe of modern cosmology. "Cast into the infinite immensity of spaces of which I am ignorant and which know me not, I am frightened" (Jonas, 1963, p 322).

Thus, science fiction, modern existentialism and Gnosticism share a common concern with man's relationship to an infinite, harsh and disinterested universe. It is a concern that takes on particular relevance as the adolescent attempts to achieve some relevance in his relations with the adult world. Hence, the transformation of Doris Lessing from the novelist chronicling adolescent alienation in colonial Africa to the writer of science fiction parables in the *Canopus in Argo* series. Her work reflects a common existential concern despite the distance of the arenas in which action occurs. Not surprisingly, her creative transformation may also reflect her interest in the work of Idris Shah, a Persian mystic. In this context, it becomes less surprising that the founder of the Church of Scientology, L. Ron Hubbard was a science fiction writer (*Dianetics* originally appeared in Astounding Science Fiction). Theologically, the Church of Scientology asserts that a superior race, The Thetans, were corrupted on their fall to Earth.

The needs that express themselves in the arrival of a transcendent alien race may also express themselves in fantasies of the creation of a transcendent religious order. In the film version of H.G. Wells's *The Shape of Things to Come*, an elite order of technocrats, "Wings Over the World," sustains civilization. In *A Canticle for Liebowitz*, a religious order preserves civilization after the holocaust. Even in its most self-consciously secular mode, science fiction offers the religious order as a solution to secular problems. Thus, the *Foundation* trilogy by Isaac Asimov (1951), a self-avowed secular humanist, uses Hari Seldom's "laws of psychohistory" which is defined: "to be that branch of mathematics which deals with the reactions of human conglomerates to fixed social and economic stimuli," as a secular gnosis to reconstruct society after the fall of the Galactic Empire. Not surprisingly, these novels of quasimonastic solutions share a common sexual reticence (which Asimov himself has noted) which may reflect the anxieties of their readers.

This secular "monasticism" with its elitism and sexual reticence is reflected with particular clarity in the recent films, *Star Wars* and its sequel, *The Empire Strikes Back*. In *Empire*, Luke Skywalker's Telemachus-like peregrinations lead him to Yoda, a nonhuman guru who delivers parables in sentences that end in verbs as a means of expressing their profundity. Yoda rather resembles a cross between Fritz Perls and Mahareshi. In an unself-conscious parody of both EST and Transcendental Meditation, the Force changes from "an energy and power that surrounds all of us, directs our actions, and is activated when one trusts his inner self" (McDermott and Lum, 1979) to the power of levitation and telekinesis. Although the structural language of the films remain reminiscent of the World War II films, it becomes increasingly apparent that the Force is magic to be wielded only by the elite Jedi Knights. Thus, this technological romance shares with all romance:

> Indeed, at the core of all romance forms appears to be a Manichaean vision of the universe as a struggle between good and bad magic. Science fiction has its own rationalized versions of the romance wizard (Rose, 1981, p 9).

This transformation from the modern "developmental fairy tale" to the cult initiation of the *Empire* reflects an increasing sense within the adolescent subculture of impotence and an acceptance of magical and/or supernatural solutions with all their implications and eccentricities. The Luke Skywalker of *Star Wars* can be comfortably understood within the dynamic framework of his search for his absent father and his conflict between the idealism of Kenobi and the cynicism of Han Solo in his creation of his identity. In *Empire*, the focus shifts dramatically in the direction of religious allegory. Darth Vader (Death Father) is the oedipally destructive father. But, Darth Vader is also the all-powerful earthly God that the Gnostics repudiated because he was the author of their earthly prison. Luke's search has changed from a search for his identity to a search for magic which will allow him to transcend his (and this) world. It is a transformation that is paralleled within the Gnostic tradition which regarded God, the Father, as a demiurge and elevated Jesus as a son who must transcend his earthly (and paternal) realm if he is to find his *true* identity (Jonas, 1963). The change from the search for a viable adult identity to a quest for realization through magical machinations as the member of a cultic order has ominous potential.

SUMMARY

Millenarian ideas become commonplace in any period of transition and dislocation. The tendency of cultures to express their mythology within technologically familiar contexts explains, to some extent, the common language of science fiction and cults or "new" religions (Jung, 1958, p 22). But, the continuing popularity of science fiction reflects its central concern—the attempt to confront and assimilate the unknowable. In a world that is seen as increasingly unpredictable, science fiction deals with the older adolescent's fear of separation from the familiar world of childhood and his confrontation with the unknown and alien world of adults. Moreover, in dramatizing these confrontations, it validates the adolescent's lack of experience and sense of alienation. In a comparable fashion, cults provide their members with magical solutions which allow them to confront the world of adulthood. Like science fiction, they often profess a nostalgia for lost innocence and provide means of reconstituting new worlds after the fall. And, in their deriding adult concerns and the knowledge of maturity, they validate the ignorance of the traveller to the strange world of adulthood.

BIBLIOGRAPHY

Asimov I: *Foundation*. New York, Avon (equinox), 1974.

Bettelheim B: *The Uses of Enchantment: The Meaning and Importance of Fairy Tales*. New York, Random House, 1977.

Blos P: *The generation gap, in: The Adolescent Passage*. New York, International Universities Press, 1976.

Derleth A: *HPL: A Memoir*. Milwaukee, Arkham, 1946.

Fussel P: *The Great War and the Literary Imagination*. New York, Oxford University Press, 1976.

Jonas H: *The Gnostic Religion*. Boston, Beacon, 1963.

Jung CG: *Flying Saucers: A Modern Myth of Things Seen in the Sky*. Princeton, Bollingen, 1958, vols 10, 18.

Levin H: The great good place, in: *New York Review of Books* March 6, 1980;27(8):47–50.

McDermott JF, Lum KY: Star Wars: The Modern Developmental Fairy Tale. *Bull Menninger Clin* 1980;44(4):381–390.

Mano DK: *The Bridge*. Garden City, Doubleday, 1973.

Manuel F, Manuel F: *Utopian Thought in the Western World*. Cambridge, MA, Harvard (Belknap), 1979.

Mehta G: *Karma Cola*. New York, Simon and Shuster, 1979.

Rose M: *Alien Encounters: An Anatomy of Science Fiction*. Cambridge, MA, Harvard, 1981.

Survival Havens in America. Mt. Vernon, NY, Survival Research.

Thompson WI: *At the Edge of History: Speculations on the Transformation of Culture*. New York, Harper, 1972.

West LJ, Singer MT: Cults, quacks and nonprofessional therapies, in Kaplan H, Freedman AM, Sadock BJ (eds): *Comprehensive Textbook of Psychiatry*. Baltimore, Williams and Wilkins, 1980, vol 3.

Zweig P: Talking to the Dead and Other Amusements in *New York Times Book Review*, October 5, 1980, p 11.

Alienated Jewish Youth and Religious Seminaries:
An Alternative to Cults?*

SAUL V. LEVINE

I n recent years a small but growing percentage of North American and other Western Jewish youth have left their families, life-styles, and their "charted courses" to enter Orthodox religious seminaries in Israel, called yeshivot. Since 1967 there have been about a half dozen yeshivot established in Jerusalem catering exclusively to Jewish youth of the Diaspora (United States, Canada, England, South Africa, Australia). This is particularly remarkable in that the vast majority of the young men and women who join these seminaries are from nonreligious, "progressive" secular, or "humanistic" homes, albeit retaining a flavor of cultural Judaism. They are called "chozrei b'tchuva," or returners (to faith) via redemption.

From the point of view of at least some of their parents, these young people have "strayed," are acting self-destructively, and are "losing" valuable time during which they could be pursuing higher education, careers, or other middle-class activities. From the perspective of still others, their offspring have done no better than to join cults, although this time the cult is somewhat less alien. It was these sentiments which prompted this particular study. It was felt that much more could be learned about religious cults and their members using a more "palatable" or acceptable option or model.

PROCEDURE

In a series of studies[1-6] of young people in fringe religious groups and other movements, the author looked at the backgrounds, personalities, and experiences of various members. It was decided to apply the same structured interview procedure to members (the chozrei b'tchuva) of these particular yeshivot in Jerusalem.

---

*This work was conducted while the author was in Israel 1979–1980 as Lady Davis Visiting Professor in Child Psychiatry, Hebrew University Medical School–Hadassah Medical Centre.

In a nine-month period, the author interviewed extensively a total of 110 young men mainly from the United States (77) and Canada (20) (the remainder were from England, South Africa, and Australia), who had joined yeshivot during the prior few years and months. To be included they had to have been a member of a yeshiva for a minimum of six months. (During that time 16 young women were also interviewed, but the very different data from that section will not be dealt with here.) The majority of the interviewees came from two large yeshivot in the Old City of Jerusalem (88), while the remainder came from three others in religious parts of the New City.

The yeshivot vary considerably from each other in their approach to Orthodoxy, the kinds of young men and women they attract (usually a strong reflection of their milieu or atmosphere), the degree of secular activities they encourage (eg, music, reading, athletics), and their goals and aspirations. But they all share an overriding faith in the Torah (Old Testament), a relatively rigid interpretation of the Halacha (Jewish laws) and, as in any other orthodoxies, relatively inflexible demands of their members' religious behavior—prayer, study, rituals, etc, and personal demeanor—no premarital sex, no masturbation, no drugs, no frivolous behavior. Each has a strong head rabbi (rosh yeshiva) who, if not deified, is treated with reverence, awe, and obedience, and a number of young rabbis who do the brunt of the teaching and programing. It is a tribute to the confidence and flexibility of the head rabbi, that he enabled the author to participate in programs and conduct interviews even though he was obviously not an Orthodox Jew. The author, after conferring with the rosh yeshivot, presented his proposal to the members after a religious service. The interviewees were all volunteers; nobody who refused to be interviewed or avoided the study was in any way pressured into participating. As it turned out, the young men overwhelmed the author with their enthusiasm about this study and their willingness to (each) spend a couple of hours being interviewed. Total confidentiality, access to the findings, feedback and mutual openness were promised—and delivered. Obviously, the sample utilized could not in any way be described as random, and its degree of representativeness can only be exactly ascertained or corroborated by other studies.

FINDINGS

While there were major differences between the various yeshivot, and between the members of each yeshiva, these will be highlighted in this chapter only when they are of particular significance. A further publication will deal with the differences in more depth. Otherwise, the results will be based on uniform data from all the yeshivot.

The members ranged in age from 18 to 29, with the median age 22.5 years. The vast majority (92 or 81%) were from upper-middle-class backgrounds. Almost none (4%) were from working-class or lower-class socioeconomic levels. At present, however, all were living in extremely modest circumstances: tiny apartments or rooms with bare subsistence levels of income. Communal food consisted of plain fare, clothing was functional, outside entertainment uncommon. Their lives were (are) entirely devoted to the study of the Torah and the demands of the yeshivot.

Of the 110 males interviewed, only 15 were married. Of these the majority came from one particular yeshiva which not only strongly encourages marriage, but has a female counterpart run by the wife of the chief rabbi (the "rebbetzen"), which provides most of the marital partners. Even among those who were not married, however, the goal of eventual marriage was espoused by virtually all of them.

Only 4 (3.5%) came from Orthodox backgrounds—that is, the vast majority discovered anew their roots in Jewish fundamentalism. This is tantamount to a conversion experience, although it has been termed an "indirect consolidation," referring to the "compatibility" of the new identity with the old. Most of the newcomers to Orthodoxy came from Jewish Conservative homes (25 or 22.5%). Reform or Progressive homes (54 or 50%), Reconstructionist (3 or 2.5%), or secular–humanistic (22 or 20%) backgrounds.

Most of the families of the interviewees were intact (84 or 76%); a minority (20 or 18%) had divorced parents, and fewer (7 or 6%) had been raised by a widowed parent. More than half (57 or 52%) rated their relationship with their parents prior to joining the yeshiva as "very good" or excellent; 29 (26%) rated this same relationship as "average," while 24 (21%) rated it as only "fair" or "poor." The majority of the members were first-born sons (64 or 49%) or second (54 or 37%), and most came from small families (median size 2.4 children).

As would be expected from a predominantly upper-middle-class group, the members were well-educated—only 8 (7%) did not complete high school. Given this statistic, and the relatively large number which attended college (92 or 84%), it is noteworthy that only 12 (11%) had graduated from university. This is particularly significant because their comparable peers would have been through university in relatively much greater numbers. There were no professionals or businessmen in this particular sample, although in a subsequent survey, a very small number (2%) were noted.

They were not, however, a group lacking in skills. Some of the young men had been social, student council, or group leaders prior to their involvement in the yeshiva. They were a bright group, and many had had varied and broad interests of the world around them. Many were accomplished musicians—as a matter of fact, one of the yeshivot had as many as four bands (religious rock and traditional music) performing as part of their proselytization program. Others were above average, or even exceptional athletes, and some of these still pursued some form of athletic exercise—jogging, weights, yoga. Still others had had brilliant academic careers, and some of these were still intellectually inclined, albeit towards a different area of study. But it is also fair to say that all of these pursuits became relegated to a low status level, way below the pursuit of religious knowledge and life-style. For many it meant a radical departure from heretofore aggressively pursued activities, accomplishments, and aspirations. It was both the suddenness of the shift and the direction of the change which upset most parents (see below).

There were other, less socially condoned behaviors, which also underwent sudden transformations, especially in the areas of socializing (dancing, parties, etc), drinking and drugs, and sex. Most (90 or 83%) admitted to varying degrees of social activities, including dates, parties, dancing, etc. Prior to joining the yeshiva, the majority (84 or 76%) had had either extensive (23 or 21%) or some (61 or 55%) sexual experience (heterosexual intercourse). (None reported homosexual experiences—but the moral injunction against homosexuality is powerful here.) Similarly, most interviewees (20 or 18%) had had either extensive or some (64 or 58%) alcohol–soft drug (marijuana, hashish) experience before becoming Orthodox. These behaviors ceased abruptly and absolutely upon joining the yeshiva. The rapid change, particularly in the area of sexuality, proved to

problem for many of the young men, especially in light of the strict moral
e (forbidding even masturbation) and lack of opportunity or encouragement
discuss their conflicted feelings and drives. Cognitive dissonance[7] and anxiety
ere not unusual, but the method of coping was via denial, suppression, and
sublimation in ritual and studying. There was often an obsessive quality to these
pursuits which concerned parents and old friends (and the author—see below).

It was in the area of mental health history that major discrepancies between the
yeshivot were seen. The reason for this situation is quite clear: virtually all the
popular yeshivot catering to Diaspora Jewry screen their applicants carefully and
try, as much as possible, to reject any individuals who present even a slight
psychiatric risk on the basis of history and interview. One yeshiva, however, has
made it a policy to take young men and women even if they have obvious
psychological problems. Hence a truly skewed sample evolves. In this latter
yeshiva, 51 men were interviewed. Of these, 25 (50%) had had some form of
psychotherapeutic assessment and/or treatment, and six (12%) had been
hospitalized. In addition, as in any other young adult population, there were
clinical manifestations of a wide range of mild to moderate disorders or symptoms—anxiety, depression, obsessive characteristics, disorganization, confusion
in some of the interviewees, and the inevitable ubiquitous issues of that
age—search for meaning, existential questions, angst, etc.

In the other four yeshivot (37 interviewed in one, 22 in three others), the mental health problems were less apparent. Again, this is in part because of the
screening procedures, but also because the milieu became known, and like applicants were directed to specific yeshivot. Of these 59 members, 10 (17%) had
had some contact with a mental health professional, and only one had been
hospitalized (<1%). In general, these latter members presented themselves as
more competent, better "copers," than the first group. But it is important to note
that 1) in general, the yeshiva, like other religious groups, does not attract a more
inherently disturbed population,[5] and 2) by its very nature and function, again as
with other groups, there are important therapeutic functions performed by the
yeshivot. The mental health aspects of yeshivot and other religious groups are
dealt with in another paper.[8]

In spite of the fact that these religious seminaries are Jewish, and along the
same cultural continuum that the parents of the youth find themselves (albeit far
along), many of the youths reported a deterioration in their relationships with
their parents (and siblings and friends too) since their commitment to the
yeshiva. Fully 61 (55%) stated that their parents had voiced strong negative feelings at least once about their sons' new direction in life, and 35 (32%) had expressed some degree of concern. These results are based on the reports of each of
the interviewees and interviews with 22 sets of parents of members of yeshivot.

What bothered the parents most were the degree, the suddenness, and the
direction of change in their sons. They were concerned about an open-ended
commitment to a "nonproductive" way of life, the interruption in their schooling, and what they saw as a blind rejection of mores and values with which they
had been brought up and inculcated. It was not the "year off' that bothered them,
as much as the questions "To what end?" and "When will it end?" Terms
familiar to the author in other settings[5,6,9] were brought up in interviews with
some of the parents of these young men—"cult," "brainwashing," "parasites,"
"programed," and others were used. As would be expected, this raised considerable conflict within these adults, many of whom had been raised in at-

mospheres not too dissimilar from that espoused by the yeshivot. Some parents were obviously pleased or at least accepting of their sons' decision or had come to terms with it after a period of agonizing, arguing, and working through. Some others (a small minority) were in fact relieved by their offsprings' involvement in Orthodoxy, seeing this as preferable to antisocial activities, non-Jewish cults, or as a haven for their "lost" or disturbed young sons.

The routes to the yeshivot were actually few and fairly consistent. Almost all of the young men came to Israel without any thought of even looking at a yeshiva. Some were well bankrolled by parents, others came on a shoestring. Some came to explore, some to tour, some to work on kibbutzim (collective farms), some to visit friends or family. But all had at least some degree of feeling or "belonging" in Israel. This, combined with a considerable dissatisfaction with themselves and their lives, made them open to emotional and spiritual experiences in that country.

And then came Jerusalem. This phenomenally beautiful, mystical city reactivated all their questions about their lives and their world. Many reported alternating euphoria and dysphoria; the majority talked about a paradoxical "high" which heightened their anxiety and sense of ambiguity. In this state they met a "recruiter" either at the Western Wall (a mystical experience in itself) or in the New City, who suggested a wonderful experience for them, no commitment necessary, at one of the yeshivot. There they found happy, dedicated, purposeful young men, who welcomed them warmly, and "sold" the yeshiva. Most who have this experience are moved and provoked in a positive sense, but the majority pass through after a very brief stay (not unlike the Moonies, where only 12% of those recruited actually stay for extended periods). If not actively recruited, other vehicles for their entry into the yeshiva are via friends, curiosity, seeing and hearing members at the Wall or elsewhere, and (very few) "sent" by parents, relatives, doctors, or rabbis back home.

In describing their emotional states prior to joining (ie, "where their heads were at"), most used terms like "searching," "alone," "confused," "unhappy," "unfulfilled," and made statements like, "There's got to be more to life than this!", in addition to the more traditional existential identity-related questions like "Where am I going?" and "Why?" They fit our previous definitions of alienation (normlessness, powerlessness, futility, leaderlessness, estrangement),[10,11] demoralization,[12] and low self esteem.[13] Again this is not to say that this is a particularly disturbed group of young people—many of our youth harbor these feelings.[14-17] No matter that many of these young men were accomplished, popular, achievement-oriented individuals—their self-perceptions did not square with their public persona or others' perception of them. The interviewees made it quite clear that there was also a spiritual and "meaning" void in their lives prior to joining, as well as an absence of a close group in which they felt totally and unequivocally accepted.

It became clear that they did not get excited by their initial encounter with the yeshivot for purely religious reasons—rather, it was a combination of those and psychological reasons. In fact, when asked at the end of a long interview, and after trust had been established, about the changes in their lives since having joined their yeshivot, the majority of the responses (64%) were along the latter (psychological) lines—happier, less anxiety, like themselves better, less hung up, a purpose in life, less pride or self-indulgence, less alone, less pressure, etc. The religious reasons (36%) were along the lines of "closer to God," "living a holy life," being a "real Jew," etc. This is entirely consistent with our findings in an earlier study of members of fringe religious groups in North America.[5] It is not the answer one gets, however, on brief or superficial questioning.

In our interviews with the members, aside from a small group of manifestly disturbed individuals, most came across as fulfilling criteria of relative mental health. At least there were no gross differences from the general peer population in this regard. And yet there was a quality of "packaged proselytization"—especially in interviews with heavily committed members, when the rationale for their belonging was discussed. Furthermore, as with our studies with other groups, the presentation of this rationale was virtually identical among members of the same yeshiva—the same catch words, phrases, logic. The author experienced uncomfortable feelings of "autoprograming"—volitional adoption of the language of the particular rabbis in their yeshiva. This is not unusual, nor is it restricted to yeshivot; its implictions, however, are complex (see below).

DISCUSSION—CULTS AND YESHIVAS

In the case of this study, the population is composed virtually entirely of those of Jewish background, but even in some so-called "cults," a disproportionate number of the members are Jewish.[5] We have then an entirely comparable population to that involved in fringe religious groups or cults—Western, middle class or higher, young, affluent, educated, most from intact homes and enhancing backgrounds, cared for, stimulated, with multiple options for their lives at their disposal.

Are we dealing with just another cult? If we adopt a rather loose definition of that admittedly pejorative term, it is a group of people who follow a dominant leader, often living; whose leader makes absolute claims about his being—that he is divine, God incarnate, God's emissary; he is omniscient and infallible, ie, perfect; in which membership is contingent on complete and literal acceptance of the leader's claims and acceptance of his doctrines and dogma; complete, unquestioning loyalty, allegiance, and obeisance to him; which promise personal salvation through achievement of special, perhaps secret, knowledge (Scientology); that ultimate salvation lies within the liberation of powers within the self (Scientology, Human Potential Movement); or by belonging to a sacred community (Hare Krishna, Divine Light Movement). To this we add a "different" way of viewing the world, of acting, dressing or thinking.[9],[18]

As with other definitions, exceptions at times exceed the rule. But using this model, there are some caveats we must interject a priori: First of all, cults need not be religious to satisfy this definition—they can be political or even therapeutic. Second, established or "respectable" religions were once seen as dangerous cults and persecuted. Third, all cults should not be seen as intrinsically evil or dangerous any more than they should be praised indiscriminately. Fourth, cults have been in existence in North America for at least a hundred years.[19],[20] During times of uncertainty, "cults of unreason" offering solutions or special salvation have been particularly attractive.

What do yeshivot share in common with other groups, popularly referred to as cults? All of the latter have rituals, mystical aspects, a theological tone, a fairly rigid hierarchy and set of rules, relative asceticism, and houses of worship; they all promise some degree of personal salvation through prayer or through development of the self. Chanting, dietary restrictions, rules regarding dress, etc, are common. Even somewhat similar recruitment techniques and the same susceptible appearances of eligible members (especially youth with knapsacks) are targeted. Finally, most of the cults are preoccuped with personal salvation and have little involvement with social issues or relevancies. And they all give relatively simple answers to the modern life—life is more secure, comfortable, and existential dilemmas are dramatically removed. In these regards yeshivot are not dissimilar.

But the yeshivot studied do not deify their head rabbis; they do not "demand" total obeisance to an individual, although group pressure in effect often accomplishes that end. The members of yeshivot tend not to be involved in direct fund-raising, although they often do proselytize, and they certainly are aware of the fund-raising activities of their leaders. There is no subterfuge, dishonesty, coercion, or threats (indeed these activities are highly variable in other cults). Finally there is no encouragement of estrangement from or hostility to parents; rather, rapprochement and support are actively pursued.

While not attracting a particularly disturbed group (the one exception noted notwithstanding), the yeshiva does provide therapeutic support to its needy members. By virtue of clear expectations, structure, group support, a strong father figure, unequivocal acceptance, reduction of choices, consensual sublimation, and magical expectations, symptoms of anxiety, depression, and confusion often diminish markedly. But even those who do not manifest any clinical signs—ie, the majority—are clearly strengthened in some ways. Certainly the feelings of alienation, demoralization, and low self-esteem alluded to earlier are markedly reduced or even removed. The yeshiva (as other groups) gives them two powerful mutually reinforcing impetuses: first, a strong belief system is engendered, a raison d'etre, a seemingly coherent system of ideas and values; and second, the rapid development of a sense of belonging, of communality, of being an integral part of a like-minded group with shared values, aspirations, and experiences. These two experiences, belief and belonging, in turn produce a third vital effect, the enhancement of the individual self-image (or increase in self-esteem).[10],[21] Most of the individual members report that they feel great, eat and sleep well, and are enthusiastic about their lives and optimistic. An individual with a strong sense of identity, good feelings about himself, and in a supportive group which shared his views is obviously very difficult to dissuade from his choice and course (in the yeshiva or elsewhere).[9],[22]

Why then are so many of these Jewish parents concerned about their sons' commitment to an Orthodox seminary? As was mentioned above, many of their concerns have to do with the suddenness of their sons' change and in a direction which they never would have predicted or considered. They worry about time lost from school, social relationships, lack of "future orientation," and the almost total rejection of their values. Parents who are largely achievement-, producitivity-, creativity-, and learning-oriented have difficulties with their sons' adoption of a way of life which they see as inimical to these interests. And they get no reassurance from discussions with their sons. The latter not only substantiate their parents' fears, but are often openly critical of their way of life, which they consider at best misguided, and at worst, sinful.

All of this is difficult for many mothers and fathers to "swallow," but in fact most of them do, with some initial soul-searching, confrontation, and agonizing. Rapprochment is effected in many instances, not in the sense of total support, but at least in terms of resigned tolerance. If the time off from school could be viewed as a "psychosocial moratorium,"[23] if they could feel somewhat optimistic that their sons would resume a "productive" (in a middle-class sense) life, even in an

Orthodox context, they would feel less lost and depressed about the whole phenomenon.

But there is another major dimension to the concerns of some parents of members of yeshivas (and other religious or dedicated movements) which is more difficult to define or even to assess in terms of the basis for those concerns. And it is shared by the author. To varying degrees, members are "true believers,"[24] with an intense, narrow, unwavering commitment to a "cause." There are questions about flexibility, openness to new or conflicting ideas, adaptability to change, and ability to cope with crisis once out of the closed group. There are doubts about the continuation of broad intellectual growth, emotional maturation, and social experiences and maturity. There is concern about the degree of genuine caring for others and the extent of members' tolerance for others' ideas and behavior (an irony, since these groups so often feel persecuted or maligned by others). The happiness and bliss exuded by many members of these (and other) groups is not "contagious," at least to many outsiders. There is a (again, an outsider's) feeling of affected, nonspontaneous, group-enhanced, and quite conscious joviality. Obviously this suffers from admitted subjectivity, but its appearance has been seen with uncomfortable regularity in all the groups studied.

Finally, the "programed" quality of explanation or rationale is of considerable concern. As mentioned above, it is not unusual for members of any close knit group to "parrot" the leader, using the common language prevalent in the milieu. When it is done in such a manner as to inhibit further intercourse of ideas, when it effects a closure to discussion, when it suggests a narrowing of field, a close-mindedness and a diminution in intellectual reasoning, it is particularly disconcerting. This was seen especially in one yeshiva, which uses a quasi-intellectual hyperlogical, and so-called scientific approach to the elucidation of both the meaning of the Torah and the underpinnings of human behavior. (This more extreme manifestation of "true believing" is commonly seen in the Divine Light Mission and among Moonies, for example.)[5,6,8]

CONCLUSION

It is no surprise to learn that a disproportionate number of the members of North American urban, avant-garde social, religious, or political movements over the past two decades have been Jewish youth. The free-speech movement, the antiwar movement, the drug scene, the counter culture, religious cults—to name but a few—have all documented a higher representation of Jewish older adolescents and young adults among their members than would be expected from pure demographic characteristics. And these are all groups which have little or nothing to do with Jewish cultural or religious traditions.

There are ample hypothetical analyses of the reasons for this phenomenon—traditions of intellectual curiosity, higher education, liberalism, questioning and dissatisfaction with the status quo, existential searching, ideological indulgence afforded by affluence, and alienation, as well as more intrapsychic and psychodynamic causes—rebellion, oedipal strivings against the father figure, fulfilling their parents' vicarious needs, affirming their self-worth through assertion, and reducing anxiety and existential angst via group involvement and outer-directed commitment.

In an earlier report, it was suggested that young people join cults because of personal dissatisfaction with their lot and the fact that the religious group makes itsef available at a psychological correlate of a "critical period" in their lives.[5] If not for that fortuitous happenstance, the young person might have gone an entirely different route, not necessarily religious in nature (political, therapeutic, etc, are just two other possibilities). Further research has corroborated this hypothesis.

However, in the case of Jewish young men and yeshivot, a major qualification is in order. The crucial difference in this circumstance is not the fact that these Jewish youth are specifically searching for their own religious orthodoxy or roots. Rather it is that the "critical period," the time when the openness and vulnerability of the individual is confronted by the seductiveness and ministrations of a religious recruiter or group, occurs in Jerusalem, or Israel. Obviously, the Moonies or Hare Krishna would have a much tougher time in the Old City, particularly at the Wall, in attracting members to their religious persuasions, but the author has no doubt that some would definitely be recruited. The fact, however, that these young men "find themselves" in Israel is not coincidental or fortuitous. They go to Israel because somewhere in their education, upbringing, or consciousness, they have learned that a part of them "belongs" in that country, although they might have difficulty expounding on this. In spite of this, the majority of interviewees came to Israel with no thought, at least consciously, of any activity other than touring and having a good time.

There are similarities between yeshivot dedicated to Jewish youth who have recently discovered Orthodoxy and what are popularly depicted as "cults." Some young people have always been susceptible to ideologies, belief systems, and mass movements.[25] Alienation, demoralization, and low self-esteem make individuals particularly vulnerable to groups offering salvation and answers to life's dilemmas.[10,21] These are overcome rapidly via the adoption of a strong belief system and intense communal support group. There are also clear differences between cults and yeshivot. The youth and parents go through much the same experience in wrestling with any conversion. This one, however, produces considerable internal conflict within the parents.

Jewish youth in North America and other Western countries gravitate to Israel because it is inculcated, even subtly, into their consciousness, sometimes in spite of the efforts of their parents. If alienated and in an existential quandry, even if nonreligious, the yeshivot provide a haven from angst and a rationale for their lives.

REFERENCES

1. Levine SV: Draft dodgers: Coping with stress, adapting to exile. *Am J Orthopsychiatry* 1972;42(3):431–446.
2. Levine SV, Lloyd D, Longdon W: The speed user: Social and psychological factors in amphetamine abuse. *Can Psychiatr Assoc J* 1972;17(3):229–241.
3. Levine SV, Carr R, Horenblas W: The urban commune: Fact or fancy, promise or pipe dream? *Am J Orthopsychiatry* 1973;43(1):149–163.
4. Levine SV, Salter N: Youth and contemporary religious movements: Psychosocial findings. *Can Psychiatr Assoc J* 1976;21(6):411–420.
5. Levine SV: Fringe religions: Data and dilemmas. *Ann Am Soc Adolescent Psychiatry* 1978;6:45–89.
6. Levine SV: Report on physical and mental health aspects of religious cults and mind expansion groups, in *Study of Mind Development Groups, Sects and Cults in Ontario.* Government of Ontario, Queen's Park, Ontario, 1980, pp 665–738.
7. Festinger L: *A Theory of Cognitive Dissonance.* Evanston, IL, Row, Peterson, 1957.
8. Levine SV: Cults, religious groups and mental health, 1982, in press.

9. Levine SV: The role of psychiatry in the phenomenon of cults. *Can Psychiatr Assoc J* 1979;24(7):593–603.
10. Levine SV: Alienation as an affect in adolescents, in *The Adolescent and Mood Disturbance.* New York, International Universal Press, 1982, chapter 5.
11. Seaman N: On the meaning of alienation. *Am Sociol Rev* 1959;24(6):783.
12. Frank J: The demoralized mind. *Psychol Today* April 1973, p 24.
13. Rosenberg M: The dissonant context and the adolescent self-concept, in Dragastin S, Elder G (eds): *Adolescence in the Life Cycle.* New York, John Wiley, 1976.
14. Keniston K: *The Uncommitted: Alienated Youth in America.* New York, Harcourt, Brace, World, 1965.
15. Leighton D: *The Character of Danger.* New York, Basic Books, 1963.
16. Offer D: *The Psychological World of the Teenager.* New York, Basic Books, 1969.
17. Pasamanick B: A survey of mental disease in an urban population, in *Epidemiology of Mental Disorder.* New York, American Association for the Advancement of Science, 1959.
18. Jewish Community Relations Council of Greater Philadelphia: *The Challenge of the Cults.* January 1978.
19. Needleman J, Bierman AK, Gould JA: *Religion for a New Generation.* New York, Macmillan, 1973.
20. Zaretsky I, Leone M: *Religious Movements in Contemporary America.* Princeton, NJ, Princeton University Press, 1974.
21. Levine SV: Adolescents, believing and belonging. *Ann Am Soc Adolescent Psychiatry* 1979;5:41–53.
22. Pattison EM: Religious Youth Cults: Alternative Healing Social Networks. Paper presented to 56th annual meeting of the American Orthopsychiatry Association, 1979.
23. Erikson E: *Identity: Youth and Crisis.* New York, Norton, 1968.
24. Hoffer E: *The True Believer.* New York, Harper and Row, 1951.
25. Braungart R: Youth and social movements, in Dragastin S, Elder G (eds): *Adolescence in the Life Cycle.* New York, John Wiley, 1976.

The Psychologic Determinants of Jewish Identity*

MORTIMER OSTOW

W e use the term "Jewish identity" to signify one's identity with special reference to one's Jewishness. The term "identity" itself deserves a little interest.
Literally it means sameness. Applied to one's personality, it denotes those
features which are characteristic, distinctive, and relatively enduring. It would
not be incorrect, therefore, to speak of one's identity in terms of those features of
one's personality visible to others. However, in common use, it is taken to signify
one's image of one's self, using the term image broadly, to include physical, intellectual, moral, psychologic, and social characteristics. The term "Jewish identity" therefore loosely denotes the Jewish components of one's self-image. When
we are concerned about a person's "Jewish identity," we are concerned with
how prominent a place Jewishness occupies in his view of himself.

A man of German-Jewish descent, who had been taught by his parents, and encouraged by his liberal and radical associates to disdain religion and all other
kinds of Jewishness, when he became depressed, found comfort in associating
with a moderately observant family and participating in their observance. He
developed an interest in Jewishness. When he recovered from his depression,
this interest subsided but remained consistently well above the level which had
prevailed before his illness.

A man whose parents had turned away from the Jewish religion which had been
practiced by their parents, and had brought up their children with little or no
concern for their Jewishness, associated with almost no Jews and gave little
thought to his Jewish roots and ties. When his wife died in 1939, he became
depressed. He left home and office, went to France, and there, using his own
resources and his friendships and connections, he occupied himself with bringing Jews out of the gathering Holocaust and to the United States. After the better

*This essay was published originally in *Israel Ann Psychiatry Related Disciplines*
1977;15(4):313–335 and was reprinted in Ostow M (ed): *Judaism and Psychoanalysis.* New
York, KTAW Publishing House Inc, 1982. It is reprinted here with permission.

part of a year in which he had rescued over 50 Jews, he returned to his home, resumed his profession and his indifference to the Jewish community.

A man who was contemptuous of the profession of his father, an Episcopalian clergyman, and contemptuous of religion, became depressed. As his illness became more intense, he described visions of the face of his dead mother, and alongside it the face of the baby Jesus. It was surprising to hear this expression of religious sentiment by a man so antipathetic to religion, but it is not uncommon to encounter a reversion (the proper technical term would be "regression") to childhood attitudes in the course of mental illness. What was more surprising was his desperate exclamation a few days later, as his decline continued (drug therapy of depression in many cases requires at least four weeks of treatment before improvement begins), "I feel like an old Jew at the Wailing Wall." His mother had been Jewish. When he recovered, any thought of his considering himself Jewish was inconceivable.

Similar cases are encountered quite frequently. They demonstrate that under the influence of mental illness, one's view of oneself changes. Usually there is a reversion to components of one's self-image that were conscious in childhood but which seemingly were discarded subsequently. We see here that they were not discarded, but repressed, that is, excluded from consciousness. As illness evolves, it facilitates the escape of these earlier aspects of the self-image from repression.

In general, close study of identity—and this is as true of its Jewish components as it is of others—reveals that over the course of the life cycle manifest identity changes. There are two types of change: There is the change that occurs gradually, as an aspect of the process of passing through the life cycle from birth to death. One sees oneself differently as one matures, acquires experience, and alters the nature and objects of one's affection. There is the change that occurs more abruptly from time to time as one's mental state responds to stress or its removal, especially when the response involves lapse into illness.

I believe we are justified in making the following generalization: Identity, as we ordinarily use the term, refers to the self-image of which one is conscious. However this manifest self-image changes in response to maturation and aging and in response to changes induced by stress. What is probably fairly fixed after childhood is an unconscious core self-image, individual components of which become conscious as one's position in life and in the community demand. Let us consider first the determinants of this unconscious core and then the determinants of the manifest expression of the individual components of this core.

One of the earliest tasks of the infant is to differentiate his image of himself from his image of his mother. While we can never know with certainty the contents and processes of the infant's mind, we can make some reasonable guesses based upon our observations. We infer that as the first conscious sensations and impressions appear in the infant's mind, he does not at first "know" of any distinction between his own body and his mother's. During his first and second years, he learns to make that distinction and at the same time to attempt to make himself more independent of his mother. He wants to see himself as separate and to act as if he were separate and independent.

Yet, despite this tendency to differentiate, the opposite tendency, to remain close to mother—and conceptually part of mother—becomes stronger, even as the need to separate grows. Separation and, as time goes on, ultimately emancipation and independence are driven by a biologic maturational thrust. However, complying with this thrust implies facing the danger of the unfamiliar and forgoing the comfort of the familiar. For the small child, his need to cling to mother—and later to father too—influences both his behavior and his view of himself. Psychologically, the regressive tendency to cling to parents finds expression in seeing oneself as similar to them. The child tends to maintain an identity, or at least a similarity, between his image of himself and his image of his parents. We say that he "identifies" with them. The identification becomes more and more subtle as the child becomes aware of the finer, more abstract, and more subtle features of his parents' identity.

While in the earliest years he does not identify with their Jewishness as distinguished from other aspects of their personality, nor between their Jewishness and the non-Jewishness of other parents, his identification does incorporate indiscriminately the Jewish components together with all others. It is only after the age of 5, when he begins to socialize with peers, that he begins to recognize both distinctions and similarities between his parents and other parents, and therefore between his image of himself and his image of his friends. These distinctions may include many of the ways in which a person is Jewish. In a sense, the child becomes Jewish before he knows that Jewishness exists. The earliest identifications arise out of the child's need to retain the gratification and protection of the earliest love relations, even as these relations must be permitted to weaken in order to make way for new love relations and for independence. However, it is also true that parents enjoy seeing their children identify with them and encourage identification. Therefore by identifying with the parent, the child earns the bonus of the parent's continuing love.

Identification is one method by which the young child copes with the need to separate from mother; continuity is another. At some point in his early years, the child becomes aware that some people are separated from their families, for a shorter or longer time, and some separations are permanent. He can use identification to prepare for such a loss and to defend himself against its impact when it does occur. He can also create the illusion of changelessness by making himself sensitive to the quality of continuity: continuity of the life of the individual and continuity of life across the generations. He becomes interested then in the concept of ancestors and forebears, and sees his grandparents as living demonstrations of generational continuity. Generational continuity is expressed in family and community tradition. Among Jews, Jewish tradition carries the feeling of continuity, and therefore it appeals to the child who is trying to protect himself against the feared separations and discontinuities of life. Grandparents are not only themselves the living representatives of the past, and therefore a guarantee of an unending future, but they also teach tradition. They are therefore as influential in making the child Jewish as the parents, and sometimes more so.

The child seeks continuity not only through the generational chain, but by relating to a wider circle of family members, the family then coming to replace the mother, as the exclusive relation with her is gradually relinquished. At each point in time, the child draws a circumferential line between the extending family which he finds familiar and strangers. No matter how large a group is encompassed within the area of familiarity, the child always feels more comfortable with them than with the strangers, towards whom he is always more or less defensive. To help him in drawing this line, he strives to discern those qualities which distinguish the familiar from the strange; to establish that he is a member of the familiar, he assumes these qualities as fully as he can. In a society in which the Jewish child comes into contact with non-Jewish children, to the extent that he learns from his parents that the distinction between Jewish and non-Jewish is significant, he becomes sensitive to the difference and includes it among the criteria that distinguish between the familiar and the strange.

Cohesive groups tend to reinforce their cohesion by elaborating on their common origin. These accounts, usually partly history and partly fiction, are, in the process of group repetition and transmission, given a form which serves the current needs of the group. As the needs of the group alter, the specific content of the myth changes accordingly. (I shall use the term "myth" here to designate stories, including history or fiction or both in any proportion, which achieve currency within a group and purport to be accounts of significant events in the life of the group.) Subscription to this myth establishes the individual's membership in the group. To be useful, the myth must serve the needs of both the group and the individual. It can do so because, in most instances, the history of the individual and the history of the group are congruent or can be made to seem so.

Among the most powerful of such myths are myths of origin and myths of crisis. In the former, the origin of the group is portrayed as a remarkable event which came to pass despite the hostility of the environment. In the latter, the existence of the group is threatened by an enemy or a natural event. An actual threat to a group impels its members to reinforce their commitment to each other for purposes of defense of the group; a recollected threat exerts a similar influence. The elaboration and propagation of the crisis myth is a group function which elicits maximal commitment from its members. Individuals subscribe to these myths for two reasons. They perceive and enjoy the cohesive influence of these myths, and the account of surviving attack and triumphing over enemies reminds the individual that he too can overcome danger and confers upon him a sense of potency and optimism. Both of these reasons appeal to children as much, or perhaps even more than, to adults. Children too enjoy hearing these myths and committing themselves to the group process which they engender.

The Jewish myths which contribute to the core identity of the Jewish child are offered to him in folk form by his parents, especially on the occasion of Jewish holidays and by instruction in the earliest grades of Jewish schools. He identifies with the Jews and their legendary victories and defeats and retains the identification and the values conveyed by the myths, at least unconsciously, even when, as a result of maturation and higher education, the myths are displaced by more realistic historical accounts. It is because the childhood experience of the major events of the Jewish calendar have made such a strong impression on the child that they continue to exert a major attraction to the adult as well.

What we learn of the earliest memories of awareness of Jewishness teaches us that it is conveyed by specific vehicles, usually conventions and rituals. One of the most potent cohesive influences in any group is the use of a specific language, distinctive for the group. The use of the language, realistically but not always accurately, distinguishes members of the group from nonmembers. In encountering strangers, it helps to ascertain whether the stranger is a member of the group. (The unthinking application of this test has at times led Jews into traps set by their enemies who have employed renegade Jews or even non-Jews speaking the prevailing Jewish language.) However, the language, because it binds the members of the group together, seems to possess a magical power, calling for and usually eliciting a sympathetic response from the hearer. The accents, intonations, and sounds of the language convey a message apart from its content. Mother's lullaby, when heard in later years, powerfully reevokes the feelings of love, closeness, and identity which it originally elicited. Even the language in which it is sung acquires some of the lullaby's magic. The children of Jewish immigrants to the United States have, for the most part, abandoned Yiddish, but they will still use it, or individual words or expressions, when an assertion of their Jewishness is appropriate. Their children were exposed in childhood to only these fragments and so they can scarcely utilize Yiddish for asserting Jewish identity. They will still respond to it, but they will not be able to convey it to their children. Encouraged by the revival of Hebrew in Israel, many self-conscious young Jews are becoming familiar with it and are using it as the language of Jewish identity. It is not likely, however, to become nearly as widespread in the United States as Yiddish was in the past.

A second "magical" identifying device is the name. In an alien environment, language is often given up, but names, signifying actual continuity with one's literal parents are abandoned less readily. Yet the tension between old and new, between the requirement for continuity and the desire for change, manifests itself in manipulation of names. The first change to be made is to abandon clearly Jewish given names. That is, babies are given names characteristic of the surrounding culture. These names reflect the desire of the parents to be accepted without minority and inferior status. Either or both of two concessions are generally made to continuity. A second name, in Hebrew or Yiddish, is given along with the first. The second name is a parallel name (not a middle name), to be used on religious occasions, but not to be employed in school, at work, or in social relations. The second name is usually that of a deceased relative whom the parents wish to honor, often a deceased grandparent, memorialized out of respect for a surviving parent. Frequently the initial letter of the ("English" as distinct from "Jewish") given name or names corresponds to the initial letter of the name of the ancestor who is being memorialized. A third possibility, utilized by Jews who do not wish to seem to be assimilating, and yet who feel that a specifically Jewish name might be a handicap in daily affairs, is the use of a name from the Jewish Bible, since the latter is used as a source of names by Christians as well. This practice often has significant consequences, for the child will not infrequently identify with his historical namesake and choose his career and shape his destiny accordingly.

Abandoning a characteristically Jewish family name of one's parents is a more difficult step. Often the name is shortened and made to appear less distinctively Jewish. Since the name is one of the principal components of core Jewish identity, the gradual abandonment of characteristic names does diminish the content of this core. In general, a child is likely to interpret his name as an assignment. If it is a characteristically Jewish name, the assignment is to take one's Jewishness seriously. If it is the name of one who is spoken of frequently by the parents and who perished in the Holocaust, the assignment is to become a living memorial to the victim. How he reacts to this assignment will depend upon how he reacts to his core identity.

Dress is commonly used to intensify group cohesiveness. On occasion when group cohesiveness is critically important, for example in war time, uniforms are used. Uniforms also help to distinguish members of a group from nonmembers. The uniform itself comes to signify the group, just as the flag does. Adolescents will assert their membership in their peer group by dressing alike, but differently from their parents.

Jews do not dress in any particularly Jewish way—at least not deliberately.

Chassidim dress to assert their adherence to Chassidic tradition. Orthodox Jews in the street in a hatless environment will be recognized by the fact that they are wearing hats while others are not. Orthodox Jewish women will generally dress more modestly than non-Orthodox or non-Jewish women. One element of dress which does label the male Jew is the skullcap. When a man wearing a skullcap is seen on television or in photographs in the newspaper, the entire Jewish community becomes alert to whether he will make a good or bad impression and thus reflect credit or discredit on the entire Jewish community. The tallith (prayer shawl) is the uniform of the synagogue; t'fillin (phylacteries) to a much lesser degree, since they are used when the congregation is smaller and therefore are seen so much less frequently. The young child's view of the synagogue includes these distinctive elements of dress, skullcap and tallith, and they become incorporated into his core view of Jewishness, so that his donning them, in his view, makes him a Jew.

Ritual is a device employed when individuals fear a tendency to fail to perform a necessary act or a tendency to perform a destructive act.

> An obsessive-compulsive man, who was torn between a desire to repudiate a demanding father and a feeling of guilt toward him, made a daily practice of kissing the tallith bag which his father had given to him. To him the act had religious significance. In terms of the religion it had none. He did not use the tallith or its container for any other purpose and neglected almost all other religious obligations. In caricaturing religious practice, he was degrading his father and his father's religious practices. Since the form of "worship" that he selected was kissing, we may infer that his conflict dealt with his affection for his father. The ritual therefore signified both rebellion and submission simultaneously.

To take an example from normal daily life, in the operating room or in the cockpit of an airliner, when it is necessary to prevent individual error, many maneuvers are reduced to ritual form. To the child, ritual signifies the continuity which he craves. Children love to hear the same story, read exactly the same way, any number of times. They must prepare for bed in exactly the same way every evening. Rituals are developed by children especially in the face of separation, for example at bed time, or when going to school. The child's ritual promises continuity in two ways. First, in form it represents sameness. Second, in content, it symbolically wards off or cancels separation and change. Children find religious ritual agreeable, and when introduced to it in childhood, will incorporate it into core Jewish identity, so that whether or not it is subsequently abandoned, it will always elicit an affective response.

One cannot speak of Jewish identity without considering circumcision, for millennia an integral part of the Jewishness of the male. While it is not at all distinctive in the Middle East or in the United States, in Europe, during the Holocaust, it was used to identify Jews for persecution. Circumcision does not easily fall into the category of core Jewishness, at least to the extent that the latter is created in childhood. Few Jewish children, before 8 or 9, are aware of circumcision. Being circumcised is never something relegated to the unconscious. After one has become aware of it, one always knows whether one is or is not. When we think of those aspects of our behavior or personality which demonstrate our Jewishness, we seldom think of circumcision. I suppose it should be considered "core" because of its centrality and great symbolic value. It is usually the last thing even the assimilating Jew gives up.

The act of circumcising is authorized by the parent. The father whose child is being circumcised feels that he is making the commitment to Judaism, accepting his own father's imperative. Circumcising one's child then should be considered an act of assertion of Jewish identity, although the circumcision itself probably does not play a central role in the young child's view of his being Jewish.

It occasionally happens during the course of life that we are confronted by mystical images that come to the surface or to which we find ourselves responding. While most sophisticated American Jews will disavow belief in an anthropomorphic god, the image that comes to mind during earnest prayer or during the intensity of the Kol Nidre or the Ni'ilah service of Yom Kippur, will usually tend to assume anthropomorphic characteristics. A painting, a song, a play will sometimes elicit an affective response, often powerful, often without specific content. Under psychoanalytic scrutiny, such moving experiences can usually be traced back to childhood memories. Among Jews the significant events of life, such as weddings and funerals, are usually experienced within a religious context. They too usually elicit powerful feelings, some concerning the principals of the events, some concerning the subject himself. Inevitably they tend to elicit memories of childhood, especially the earliest experiences of separation and of reunion. These experiences will usually reflect early childhood impressions of oneself, of the people one loves, and of the nature of the love. To the extent that one's early childhood is colored by Jewishness in the ways that we have discussed, the mystical images of adult life will tap one's Jewish identity.

It is difficult to select any small sample of Jewish myths without including instances of misfortune and sacrifice: flood, Akedah (Abraham sacrificing Isaac), Egyptian slavery, desert hardships, wars of conquest, exile, destruction of Temple and city, Maccabean wars, Roman persecution, Moslem and Christian persecution, Holocaust, defense of Israel. Although one would expect that such dismal events might discourage youngsters from identifying with a group which had encountered so many misfortunes, in fact, they do not. On the contrary, they seem to elicit sentiments of loyalty, as though the sacrifice of others were an obligation which demanded one's own loyalty.

I should like to suggest that the theme, not merely of danger, but of actual sacrifice exerts a powerful mobilizing influence. The principal theme of Christianity is that Christians were saved by the sacrifice of Jesus, and that they are thereby obligated to accept Him as their Savior and commit themselves to His community. The role of obligating martyr, which Jesus plays in Christianity, is played in Judaism by the long list of Jewish victims, including recent victims of anti-Semitic persecution. The Christian theologic doctrine that the victim is also the savior reflects what I take to be the psychic reality that individual salvation (read: reunion with lost parents) can be obtained by sacrifice, even by the sacrifice of another member of the group. In the Yom Kippur service, Jews invoke the merits of their forefathers (Z'chuth avoth) and especially the merit of Isaac who permitted himself to be bound for sacrifice, as a justification for their prayer for redemption. (In current, as distinguished from historical, practice the repetition of the Akedah story and the accompanying invocation of merit, form part of the daily morning service.) One can see circumcising one's child as an act of sacrifice to God and so community which creates the feeling of having acquired merit for both oneself and the child.

One of the most painful acknowledgments which the young child is forced to make is that he must share his parents with brothers and sisters and each parent with the other. Each child likes to see himself as special in some way so that he may make special claims upon each of his parents. The Jewish conception of election, although it offers the child no advantage with respect to his literal siblings, does offer the comfort of special divine protection. It reinforces the child's self-esteem and helps him to resist indications of impaired self-esteem among discontent parents or other members of the community. This concept of specialness may become significant subsequently whenever issues of self-esteem, especially communal self-esteem are raised.

Many adolescents and adults who acknowledge commitment to the Jewish community but feel that they must dissent from one or more aspects of Judaism like to distinguish among the various kinds of Judaism: religious, secular, Zionist, philanthropic, cultural, and ethnic. These distinctions are not made by children in their earliest experiences of initiation into the Jewish community, and they therefore probably do not exist in the core concepts of Jewish identification. In making these distinctions, the individual is actually distinguishing which of these features, with which he has already identified in childhood, he will consciously and deliberately accept and which he will reject as an adolescent or adult.

The influence of the experiences which we have discussed persists as a core identity, although not all of this core is readily accessible to consciousness during adolescence and adult life. Some components of this identity are consciously accepted; others are consciously rejected; some are ignored; some are not even retrievable by conscious thought. However, the whole of this core identity persists as a reservoir from which elements can be extracted and to which they can be returned as external circumstances and current psychic need require.

The process of adolescence is a complex and profound one which could certainly not be encompassed properly even by the whole of an essay of this size. It is the process by which the young person becomes transformed from a child who sees himself primarily under the protection of his parents, to an independent person oriented toward playing a role in society and undertaking the care of spouse and children of his own. The process is driven by the somatic and psychologic changes characteristic of this period. In a sense, these changes "demand" of the individual the revision of his attitudes toward himself and others. The dimensions of the adolescent transformation include sexual identity and behavior, attitude toward parents, attitude toward society, readiness to undertake responsibility for self and others, and the crystallization of a personality and character in which changes in all of these dimensions are integrated. These processes are never really completed even by the close of adolescence and continue throughout life as social expectations and physiologic state change.

Obviously some of these changes must affect the individual's view of himself as a Jew. For example, in his struggle to emancipate himself from the influence of his parents, he may reject aspects of his earlier identification with them. If his peer group is self-consciously Jewish, he may use his Jewishness as a means of identifying with them, this latter identification succeeding and building upon the basic identification with the parents and reinforcing it. If the peer group is non-Jewish, his eagerness to identify with them may involve consciously rejecting his core Jewishness. Note that such rejection does not imply that the Jewish identification is eradicated, merely that it is inactivated for the time being, while retaining the potential to be reactivated when and if the occasion should arise in the future.

In a sense the process of adolescence resembles the process whereby the young child separates from his parents in his second and third year. In early adolescence as in this childhood period, the separation, although driven by a maturational thrust, is nevertheless frightening. In early adolescence therefore, as in childhood, many young people will take defensive measures. One may be a reinforcement of childhood identification with the parents. In the case of Jewishness, the young person may reinforce his Jewish identity, less as a matter of commitment to Jewishness as such than for the purpose of pleasing his parents and securing their continuing affection. Another may be the effort to assert continuity within the family and across generations.

This need for the assertion of continuity, within the generation and across generations, may also be satisfied by seeing oneself as a member of the Jewish community. It is elicited primarily by confrontation with separation. The young adolescent does not often, in the course of the ordinary vicissitudes of life, face serious threats of separation. Being sent off to boarding school and, to a lesser degree, summer camp are generally the most upsetting of such experiences. Of course the separation and divorce of the parents or the death of a parent are far more serious but less frequent examples. However, separations recur throughout life, and they are usually met, at all ages, by reassertions of continuity. It is for this reason that people turn to their religious heritage on the occasions of life's milestones, marriage, illness, death, and the birth of children. For many Jews, the invoking of religious tradition on such occasions is their only association with the Jewish community.

One of the major issues for the adolescent is that of commitment to society. There is the inner need on the part of the adolescent himself to make such a commitment. It is an aspect of his maturation. Biologically it is the expression of his readiness to sacrifice himself for the defense and well-being of his family and community. It includes such things as the readiness of the young man to risk his life in battle and the readiness of the young woman to accept the discomfort, pain, and risk of pregnancy and parturition. Complementing this inner need is the expectation of society that it possesses the adolescent's loyalty and can call upon him and depend upon him for service and sacrifice. It is this readiness for commitment that finds expression in the sacrifice and martyr myths which we have discussed above.

The adolescent's readiness to make sacrifices for the group depends upon his courage, that is upon the advancement of his maturation. Some adolescents are eager for the opportunity to commit themselves; others are timid but will respond to clear and present danger; still others will avoid commitment under all circumstances. Since the Jewish community in many times and places requires the defensive efforts of its young people, and since being a committed Jew has often meant the incurring of hostility and danger, timid adolescents are often fearful of making a commitment to the Jewish community.

It has scarcely been possible to get even this far into the discussion of the determinants of the expression of Jewish identity without referring to the nature of the environment in which the Jew lives. In *galuth* (exile) the Jew is always a small distance away from non-Jewish and potentially hostile neighbors. In Israel, the individual Jewish family does not feel threatened by living in the midst of a non-Jewish community, but the knowledge of the hostility of closely neighboring nations is always immediate. Clearly the surrounding community, and the relation of the Jewish community with it, play a signal role in influencing the individual's Jewishness. The very visible relative advantages of being a non-Jew in a non-Jewish environment, with respect to physical safety, to opportunities for economic advancement, to achievement of prestige, has resulted in the past in the loss of large numbers of Jews by assimilation. A deliberate decision by a young person to "pass" as a non-Jew is merely a rejection of the childhood core identification. That the latter can be activated once more under adequate stress was illustrated by the cases cited at the beginning of this chapter.

Low-self-esteem is one of the frequent findings in mental illness, presenting, among the most prominent symptoms in melancholic depression, schizophrenia, and the common personality disorders. We do not understand its origin too well, but many of the manifestations of mental illness are devices designed to protect the individual against his self-condemnation. I should like to note parenthetically that I am not considering in this essay the influence of mental illness on Jewish identity, except when it can throw light on the normal. Problems of self-esteem occur widely among individuals who are not mentally ill, and they often play a significant role in determining what we ordinarily consider normal behavior.

The relevance to the subject of our concern is that the individual with problems of self-esteem may occasionally attribute the felt inferiority to his Jewishness. Some of the reasons are fairly obvious. Since the Jewish minor community is often viewed with condescension if not contempt by the host community, it requires a vigorous self-respect to resist this external influence. A second reason lies in the rabbinic renunciation of military resistance following the destruction of the Temple, and the subsequent policy of the Jews to purchase security by submission and self-effacement.

The Jewish community attempts to resist these influences. The emphasis on the doctrine of election, the frequent reference to the nobility of our ancestors, the pride in our way of life, all serve this resistance. I am reminded here of Goldin's protest in his introduction to the English version of Agnon's Yamim Noraim (Days of Awe) that the latter omitted the saying attributed to Rabbi Solomon of Karlin, "Der grester yezer horeh is az mi far-gest az mi is ein ben melekh." ("The worst of the impulses to evil is to forget one's royal descent.")

Given then an individual with problems of self-esteem arising from his own imperfect development, or his inability to meet current challenge, he tends to blame his felt inferiority on his Jewishness, and the real challenges to the Jew's self-respect lend verisimilitude to his fantasy.

> A man descended from a distinguished Jewish family failed at everything to which he turned his hand, although he was given many special advantages out of respect for his family and their position in the Jewish community. As the only failure in a brilliantly successful family, he entertained a low opinion of himself. But he blamed his failures on anti-Semitic prejudice.

Among the issues determining the adolescent's position with respect to his Jewish identity, we have discussed issues of identification with parents, influence of peers, threats to continuity, demands of the Jewish community for commitment and sacrifice, advantages of "passing" out of the Jewish community, and problems of self-esteem. These are probably the central determinants, but not the only ones. His attitude toward religion is often influenced by the adolescent's need, on the one hand, to control importunate sexual impulses, and on the other, by a temptation to retreat from social obligations to a self-indulgent sensuality. The attitude toward idealism and morality are influenced by a need to overcome persistent childhood selfishness. The attitude toward religious tradition and authority is influenced by the need to overcome—or at least to appear to overcome—dependence upon parents and a childlike need to submit to authority.

However, mental evolution does not cease with the passage from adolescence into adult life. Subsequent changes influence most aspects of the individual's personality, including those which determine his Jewishness. Freud called attention to the phenomenon which he named *deferred obedience*. The adolescent, out of his need to assert his independence from his father, rejects the latter's values, and pursues a very different modus vivendi. However, as he grows older, and the need to rebel and assert independence subsides, he may attempt to recapture his feeling of unity with his father by adopting his values and life-style. Such a delayed resumption of identity is especially apt to be precipitated by the death of the father and by the individual's becoming a parent. It is this principle which accounts for the familiar observation that young people who as adolescents had ignored the Jewish community, return to it when they become parents. One need not credit fully their claim that they are doing it only "for the children."

Often during the late teens and early twenties, there is a surge of courage which impels the young person to seek adventure and to favor militancy in defense of some group under attack. When the Jewish community is in need of defense, he may become militantly Jewish. When the Jewish community is at ease and others are apparently oppressed or in danger, he may turn militantly toward the latter and away from, or even against, the Jewish community. In either case, after 25, this aggressiveness subsides and the associated attitude toward the Jewish community relents.

As parents die, and as the individual himself begins to observe his powers and faculties waning, his search for continuity becomes more active. He may pursue it by strengthening his interest in religion. At all ages, individuals tend to respond to danger to the Jewish community by renewing their commitment to it; they tend to respond to situations of relaxation of danger by relative indifference.

The foregoing considerations apply to Jews living in the Jewish community of the Diaspora in general. Let us consider some of the details of our current situation in the United States, as they affect the Jewish identity of American Jews.

The early childhood of the children of the American Jewish community is, by and large, not nearly as saturated with Jewish experiences or folk ways as that of children growing up in the more homogeneously Jewish communities of say, the shtetl. In the United States the saturation of this early exposure does vary from community to community and from family to family. Obviously, the children less intensively exposed will be left with a weaker identity core than those more intensively exposed. Fortunately in his first few years, the child is impressed easily by experiences which are significant for his problems of closeness and distance, continuity and separation, similarities and differences. Such impressions, occurring infrequently or even once, appealing to his current anxieties or defenses, may remain within conscious memory throughout his life. In the instances of surprising recurrence of conscious Jewish identity, exhibited in the illustrative reports at the beginning of this chapter, the identity was, in each case, based upon brief exposure to grandparents and their ritual practices, or, in one case, merely the mention of them. To the extent that American Jewish families today are more dispersed than in the past, and that young children are less exposed to their grandparents, the Jewish identity core will be less vigorous. The decrement in outcome, however, will be considerably less than proportional to the decrement in exposure.

One of the reasons for our current concern with Jewish identity is the disturbing evidence of Jewish young people who seem to be turning their backs on the Jewish community. They include: the political radicals who oppose Israel's struggle for survival, those who marry out, and those who commit themselves to the many non-Jewish religions and quasi-religious sects. It is important to distinguish between the most shocking examples of this anti-Jewishness, usually adolescents whose struggle to resolve the conflicts of adolescence take a deviant form, and similar but usually more temperate instances among young people whom one could not consider deviant. True, it would be difficult to find instances of actual betrayal of one's own group which one would not consider pathologic. Similarly, adherence to sects which, from the point of view of one's origin in the middle-class American Jewish community, must be considered bizarre, cannot easily be labeled normal. The deviant young people, that is, those whose turn away from the Jewish community results primarily from inner struggle, need not necessarily be considered a great loss. If their illness had taken a different form, say depression or just helpless resignation, they would make no greater contribution to the Jewish community. They may be a source of real difficulty in two eventualities. If they have children, their children will probably be lost to the Jewish community. In times of social unrest, they may set an unwholesome example to contemporaries who are troubled and confused but not disabled by illness. Our interest in these young people, from the point of view of Jewish identity, is that the environmental influences and the dynamic mechanisms which determine the pathologic outcome in their case are often the same as those which are active in the normal as well, although the outcome is less extreme.

Perhaps the most troublesome issue with regard to Jewish identity today is the problem of intermarriage. I shall not discuss either marrying down, that is, marrying someone clearly inferior socially, economically, or educationally; or marrying up which is marrying someone above one in these respects. The first is a common neurotic attempt to deal with the problem of low self-esteem by choosing a partner whose evident low status makes one feel higher. The second, often encouraged by a non-Jewish environment which rewards assimilation, also attempts to deal with low self-esteem, in this instance by attaching oneself to a partner of higher station and acquiring his or her prestige by association. The troublesome issue today is *marrying across,* that is, marrying a partner, appropriate in every respect except in being non-Jewish. It is more common in the United States today than in recent years and seems to pose a threat to the strength of the Jewish community. It is interesting that in most instances, there is no effort to deny one's Jewishness, no change in name, no rejection of friends or family, and often an effort even to introduce a Jewish component into the marriage ceremony. In many instances, the partner is asked to convert to Judaism. Usually the children are expected to consider themselves Jewish.

It would be misleading to try to account for this phenomenon without considering many relevant influences which we have discussed above. One necessary but obviously not sufficient condition favoring intermarriage is that Jewish young people are now more easily accepted by their non-Jewish peers than previously. One might think that these young people are wandering away because they are not close to their parents. The fact is that many of them are close, and although they may understand that they are hurting their parents, they do not wish to be rejected. I believe that a fear of commitment is usually involved here.

One formula which seems applicable to many cases is the following: The adolescent retains too strong an attachment to his parents. To demonstrate his independence, he attempts to dissociate himself from them in symbolic ways, including his choice of the peer group to which he attaches himself. Fearfulness and timidity accompany excessively strong parental attachment and in turn make the individual hesitant about making a commitment to a person or group. The Jewish community, with its intense cohesiveness, with its demands and expectations, seems overwhelming to the timid young person. He feels less threatened by a non-Jewish community which is more easy going, less threatening, and less demanding.

However, as is the case with the resolution of all neurotic conflict, small differences in the relative strength of the contending forces may induce large differences in outcome. For example, the individual may be too timid even to make gestures of independence. He may look upon the Jewish community as an extension of his family and as a refuge and assert his Jewishness in order to obtain the protection of the community. On the other hand, the adolescent who is courageous may welcome the opportunity to undertake a serious commitment to defend the Jewish community. He will find in this commitment fulfillment of his maturational and social responsibilities. If we do not examine carefully what Jewish identity means to each of these two adolescents, we shall miss the significant difference. It matters not only whether one sees oneself as Jewish, but also how one sees oneself as Jewish. I suspect that in many instances of intermarriage, the timid young Jew attempts to deny his fear of anti-Semitism by assuring himself via marriage, that he is really loved by the Gentiles.

It follows from our discussion that when and if significant threat to the Jewish community materalizes, many of those who resisted making a full commitment to it previously will be motivated to respond with vigor and new-found courage, since the willingness to sacrifice, to a certain extent, is a function of the awareness of clear and present danger. The man in the second case history which I cited was responding not merely to his depression, but to the impending Holocaust. Such instances illustrate that, given an unconscious core of Jewish identity, the social and political climate which prevails during one's adolescence and adulthood will influence the degree of one's conscious Jewishness.

Our discussion also throws some light on the influence of Jewish education upon Jewish identity. It is evident from everyday observation, as well as from the argument which we have been considering, that Jewish education, although very helpful in the individual's cultivation of his Jewish identity, is neither sufficient nor even necessary for its inception and development. Core identity is established early in childhood by home influence, although the early years of education can contribute to it. The evolution of conscious identity is influenced by inner psychic disposition and by external demands and expectations.

Jewish education can play a significant environmental role in encouraging Jewish identification. Jewish education provides content to associate with Jewishness and to replace the content of childhood Jewish mythology. The realistic content can now carry the values and emotional commitment of the mythology. For example, the history of the Holocaust and of the creation of the State of Israel lend meaning to the ancient history of Egyptian slavery and redemption. Education in Jewish schools, camps, and social groups provides a peer community with which the young person can identify as he tries to emancipate himself from his parents. Jewish education provides instruction in how to be a Jew. If Jewish education is limited to a few years of elementary material, the young person is left with a child's eye view of Jewishness which favors his disparaging it and seeing it as detracting from his self-esteem. Higher Jewish education permits one to see Jewishness as admirable. But a respectful view toward Jewishness is probably necessary before the adolescent will accept higher Jewish education. While it will reinforce Jewishness as a source of self-respect, it cannot be counted on by itself to serve as an instrument for strengthening Jewish identity in the uncommitted.

It is obvious that the Holocaust has strongly influenced the Jewish identity of American Jews. But the nature of the influence is complex and composed of several factors. When one thinks of the Holocaust or reads about it, the first reaction is guilt. American Jews, influenced by the current mode of social activism, believe that they could have made more aggressive efforts to protect their brothers. It is a kind of "survivor guilt." The term "survivor guilt" implies that the survivor feels guilty toward the victim, as though he had contributed to the victim's death. I believe the explanation for guilt, when it occurs, may be slightly more complicated. It may be that the guilt applies not simply to surviving, but to having failed to offer oneself on the field of combat in defense of the common cause. It is not that the individual has personally victimized the one who perished; it is that he has not offered to make an equivalent sacrifice for the group. What I am suggesting is that the guilt that does recur at certain times among some survivors is a manifestation of the individual's tie to the group, rather than an interpersonal transaction.

A second reaction of Jews to the Holocaust is the feeling that utopian and universalist hopes which Jews had held in the first quarter of this century were disappointed. Therefore Jews are not only justified in closing ranks against the outside but are obligated to do so. We have already discussed the tendency of young Jews in the United States to intermarry, as an effort to escape the intensity of Jewish family ties, into the apparently more relaxed casualness of the surrounding non-Jewish world.

A second reason for the tendency to intermarry is a hopeful restatement of a belief that anti-Jewish hostility has indeed ended and that the era of universalism has finally come. This continued resurgence of hope for acceptance by non-Jews arises from the need to escape the emotional intensity, the possessiveness, the expectations, and demands of the Jewish community; the impairment of self-esteem implicit in being a second-class minority group within a first-class majority culture and community; and a need to deny both historically demonstrated recurrent dangers to the Jewish community and the obligation which Jewish destiny imposes on the individual. Therefore those young people whose personal disposition welcomes obligation and challenge respond to the Holocaust with militancy, while those whose disposition does not easily tolerate obligation and challenge will be impatient with recollection of the Hollocaust, will try to minimize it, and attempt to act as though anti-Semitism were eliminated forever. A test of the orientation of the young person with respect to this dimension, is his attitude toward the "sh'foch chamathcha*. . . " during the Passover Seder service. Identification with it indicates militant, self-assertive Jewishness, while a rejection of it betrays the universalist orientation designed to resist the hazards and obligations of Jewishness.

---

*A brief paragraph of prayer for the destruction of those pagan nations that have attempted to exterminate the Jewish people.

One sees these reactions more intensely displayed among the children of actual concentration camp survivors. These survivors, by virtue of their own experience, generally exhibit an aggressiveness in pursuit of self-interest, the interest of their children, of the community of survivors, and of the Jewish community as a whole. This aggressiveness and the possessive protectiveness toward their children are not easy for the children to accept. While some of the latter accept and identify with their parents' militance, many others attempt to escape and deny by embracing universalist attitudes and orienting themselves away from the Jewish community.

Since we are considering here the secondary encouraging and discouraging influences upon manifest Jewish identity, rather than its unconscious core, it follows that the attitudes we have been discussing may change as circumstances change and as the individual matures. A new round of dangerous anti-Semitism may compel the loyalty of the universalists. Or, as the individual leaves the early decades of life, he often becomes less militant and more accommodating and compromising. We should not overlook the fact that although most Holocaust survivors feel committed to aggressive defense of the Jewish community, a few others have responded with an assimilationist strategy, hoping thereby to protect their descendants from similar persecution in the future. Such assimilationist survivors often refuse to circumcise their children. Note that although the manifestation of this type of assimilationism resembles those of the universalist young, its psychologic basis is quite different, and so is its fate. In the face of renewed persecution, those who are attempting to escape Jewish destiny will be spurred to intensify their dissociation from the Jewish community, while those who are trying to escape only the psychic demands of the Jewish family and community are likely to assert their Jewishness more positively.

A third response to the Holocaust is a feeling that Jews have acquired a certain claim on the rest of the world for respect and protection. In oversimplified form, this claim is a claim for financial reparation. In practice it may take the form of expecting the rest of the world to acknowledge a moral obligation to protect the State of Israel. I believe that underlying both of these ideas is the conviction of having acquired merit and a feeling of being deserving by identifying with the victim of the Holocaust. A readiness to make a sacrifice for the community confers a sense of distinction, or merit, and a feeling of deserving special consideration and indulgence. It is interesting that the non-Jewish world understands this response of the Jews. Germany has acknowledged obligation and paid financial reparations. Other countries and many non-Jewish individuals acknowledge a moral obligation toward Jewry and the State of Israel. Still others whose self-interests seem to them to run counter to such sentiments deny that the Holocaust of Jews ever took place. They seem to acknowledge in this way that if it did, the obligation to Jews and to Israel would be valid. Therefore they attempt to disavow the obligation by denying the event.

It is obvious that the self-esteem of American Jews has been elevated by the heroism of Israel and Israelis. The hitherto passive, accommodating, acquiescent role of the Jew which has been traditional since the Roman destruction of the Temple has been replaced with military and aggressive self-defense that has been universally admired. In addition, American Jews see themselves and are seen by their neighbors as meritorious not merely by identification with the victims of the Holocaust, but also by identification with the Israelis who defend themselves and their country so courageously and effectively. American Jews attempt to give substance to this identification by making financial sacrifice and by visiting Israel. Also, the State of Israel, its Biblically named cities and regions, its embattled positions among many ferocious enemies, all recall Jewish myths and mythologized fragments of history, which have been recorded in the core of Jewish identity. It is as though this current reality lends verisimilitude and affective cogency to the positive experiences which formed the basis for the childhood unconscious nucleus of Jewish identity.

We have spoken of the Holocaust and Israel individually. However, there is a sense in which they belong together. Apocalypse is a fantasy which has long attracted adherents in the Western world. The classical fantasy is that there will be a final catastrophe in which very large numbers of people will be destroyed by forces of evil, but the latter will be conquered by forces of good. Out of the desolation, the world will be reborn and in the reborn world, good will prevail. That in the course of human history there have been catastrophes, and that many of them have been followed by reconstruction, seems to validate the apocalyptic idea of the succession of death by rebirth. The apocalyptic expectation that good will triumph over evil is often in the minds of those who initiate apocalyptic wars, although succeeding generations wonder how their predecessors could have been so naive. The construction of the State of Israel immediately upon the termination of the Holocaust again conforms to the scheme of apocalypse and seems to confer supernatural sanction to both the state and to surviving Jews. It seems to confirm the core concept of election.

Since its inception, the State of Israel seems to have been endowed with divine sanction, and yet to be threatened by mortal political, military, and economic forces. The concept of messianism is for many people a component of core Jewish identity. It has been widely observed that Zionism has functioned as a real political movement which has carried with it a messianic flavor. It is the latter and its appeal to unconscious Jewish identity which has served to make a movement which was politically so improbable actually such a success. The messianic role of Zionism confers, in the mind of the Jew, an additional quantum of supernatural sanction and vitality to the State of Israel.

SUMMARY

Jewish identity is based upon two components. One, the core, is established in the early years of childhood, and much of it may become and remain unconscious. The second, the manifest identity, may vary from time to time in response to external circumstances and the individual's current psychic state.

The unconscious core of Jewish identity is established by identification of the young child with the parent; his need for generational continuity; his sensitivity to the distinction between family and nonfamily; his acceptance of group myths; and his use of sensitivity to language, names, dress, and ritual as a means of establishing identification with family and community.

Manifest Jewish identity is determined by the operation of several influences upon core identity. These include: the vicissitudes of adolescent development, adolescent need for continuity, adolescent need for and fear of commitment, the pluralistic American social environment, the problems of regulation of self-esteem, as well as changes of outlook and social expectation after the first two decades of life.

On the current American scene, the core identity offered to Jewish children is attenuated in several respects but not critically so. While one is distressed by obvious problems in Jewish identity exhibited by many deviant young people, their problems should not be confused with the situation prevailing among more wholesome adolescents. One result of troubled Jewish identity is the increase in intermarriage. Jewish education, as we know it, may reinforce Jewish identity, but it is neither sufficient nor necessary for its establishment or manifestation. The Holocaust and the State of Israel, individually and together, influence manifestations of Jewish identity in a number of different ways which lead to a flavoring of the recognition of the problems of Jews in the real world with a feeling of supernatural election and protection.

SECTION THREE

THERAPEUTIC APPROACHES AND ISSUES

Individual Psychodynamic Intervention with the Cult Devotee:
Diagnostic and Treatment Procedure with a Dysautonomous Religious Personality*

MOSHE HALEVI SPERO

To date, the slowly growing literature and the professional conventions devoted to understanding and treating the cult devotee have been primarily descriptive rather than prescriptive (Clark, 1979; Conway and Siegelman, 1978; Cultism, 1979; Cultism and the young, 1976; Cults: Why so appealing? 1980; Deutsch, 1975; Etemad, 1979; Galanter and Buckley, 1978; Galanter et al, 1979; Goldberg and Goldberg, 1982; Jonestown: Special report, 1978; Levine, 1978; Levine and Slater, 1976; Lifton, 1961; Maleson, 1981; Pattison, 1980; Pruyser, 1979; Shapiro, 1977; Singer, 1979, 1981; Spero, 1977; Schwartz and Isser, 1979; Ungerleider and Wellisch, 1979a, b). On one hand, this reflects the somewhat habitual tendency of clinicians to adapt to novel clinical entities by assimilating them into standard theoretical and diagnostic categories, but often without making significant modifications in therapeutic technique which may be called for due to unique aspects of the novel clinical entity. Many professionals contemplating the same tendency would not hesitate to admit, I think, to simply having no particular technique for working with the cult devotee other than to lamely follow the behavior of the cult devotee during the course of psychotherapy, without having a clear sense of the direction of therapy (Maleson, 1981).

On the other hand, a few clinicians have claimed success in rehabilitating the cult devotee through the application of certain creative therapeutic innovations,

---

*A portion of this article previously appeared in the *J Nerv Mental Dis* 1982;170:6 and is reprinted with permission of Williams and Wilkins, Inc, Baltimore.

such as highly intense and directive, multisession "marathon" therapy (Etemad, 1979), reentry groups, and family therapy (Clark, 1979; Goldberg and Goldberg, 1982; Singer, 1979, 1981), without which, it is believed, the cult devotee is not likely to cooperate in a therapeutic alliance. At the same time, these therapeutic innovators have not yet provided adequate psychological test data, or pre- and posttherapeutic reports which clearly adumbrate the unique psychological characteristics they address in their work or which explain the therapeutic changes they have achieved.

The approach expressed in this chapter is based on my outpatient office practice of psychodynamically oriented psychotherapy* with 65 cult devotees, 51 of whom have been followed posttherapy at intervals of six months and one year. As I will describe below, I consider my data base more or less typical of the majority of cult devotees who present for psychotherapy, with the exception of frankly psychotic cult members, or the extremely irrational and decompensated patient needing hospitalization and possibly medication.

CULTIC RELIGIOSITY AS A LEGITIMATE THERAPEUTIC TARGET

An additional introductory comment is in order regarding clinical work with the cult devotee. Clinicians who work with the psychologically disordered patient who also has religious beliefs and commitments must formulate some practical hypotheses regarding the relationship between psychopathology and religiosity in the psychotherapeutic alliance (see Spero, 1976, 1980). This is not to be confused with an overall psychological theory of religion. The hypotheses I refer to serve to guide the clinician in differentiating psychopathological from mature religious belief, religious belief which has become coopted in service of dysautonomous or conflict-ridden ego functioning from autonomous or healthy religious belief. In short, such hypotheses enable the mental health professional to clarify that which is the rightful target of interventive techniques and that which is not.

Cultic religiosity can be considered pathological in two senses:

1. It represents commitment to regressive religious beliefs and doctrines, as defined by Saltzman (1953, 1954) and Pruyser (1979), and as demonstrated by a) the lack of achievement by the devotee of creative philosophical growth which can be shared with nonbelievers in a meaningful and noncompulsory way; b) the radical breaking of contact from former affiliations and personal relationships even in areas or aspects of relationships not related to religious belief; c) the failure among such devotees to achieve autonomous development beyond the primitive modes of thinking and feeling reinforced by cultic religiosity; and d) the apparent inability of these belief systems to secure adherants among persons who are not amenable to psychological and attitudinal manipulation, and who do not eventually indicate a), b), and c).

2. The quality of cultic religious commitment is pathological in itself in that it precipitates and then actively reinforces significantly regressive physical and psychosocial changes in the believer, as demonstrated in medical reports, comparison of pre- and postcommitment and posttherapeutic testimonies of former

---

*I use this term to indicate that, although my general orientation is more strictly psychoanalytic, these patients are not analyzed in the broad or narrow sense of the term, but rather are offered an intensive dynamic psychotherapeutic relationship which adheres to many of the procedures and assumptions of contemporary psychoanalytic, object-relational, and ego psychological psychotherapy.

cult devotees, clinical psychological data, and so forth. In other words, whether or not cultic religious beliefs are themselves "spurious" (Saltzman, 1954) or "seamy" (Pruyser, 1979), the cult devotee's psychological profile seems to be demonstrably dysautonomous from the ego psychological perspective.

Each of these regressive aspects of cultic commitment seems adequate to justify psychotherapeutic intervention with the devotee who, if adult, elects psychotherapy or, if a minor, is brought to psychotherapy by parents or guardians. No doubt, my assumptions ought to be subjected to further philosophical analysis, but I think they would survive close scrutiny. Moreover, these assumptions do not suggest that all religious belief is psychologically regressive nor do they reduce all transcendental experiences to regressive manifestations of disturbed egos. Rather, they pertain to a fairly narrow category of religious beliefs, the majority of whose adherents have either become or have been described as candidates for psychiatric treatment. To my knowledge, this final characteristic is unique to cultic religiosity.

In accord with this theoretical and clinical perspective, the clinician working with the regressive characteristics of pseudo-religious patients aims to liberate elements of authentic or potentially authentic religious belief from psychological conflict and to explore the dysautonomous aspects of the religious belief system. In this approach, the targets of intervention—and the interpretable matter of the patient's communications—are the conflict-ridden psychological needs, compromises, and pseudo-solutions which underwrite the patient's unhealthy religious beliefs and mannerisms, rather than the beliefs and mannerisms per se.

A second tenet which follows from the above perspective is that the aim of psychotherapy with the cult devotee is not just achieving an "exit" from the cult, but helping the devotee to deal with ego conflicts and object-relational needs which have partly encouraged the attraction to regressive phenomena like cults. To neglect this goal—to attribute cult involvement solely to the effectiveness of cultic indoctrination technique or former family life-style, etc—misses the primary "lesson" which can be derived from this contemporary religious phenomenon. Only by eventually exploring the devotee's unsatisfactory object-relations and other deficits in ego functioning can we effectively minimize the likelihood of the devotee's subsequent recidivism to cultic affiliation or to some other regressive life-style.

In the following sections I will describe: 1) the establishment of the therapeutic contract, 2) assessment procedures, including some of my diagnostic findings secured from psychological testing of cult devotees during various stages of religious commitment, 3) specific features of the psychotherapeutic process, and 4) possible rationale for the effectiveness of the approaches described. In a final section, I will discuss some broader theoretical perspectives on cult attractiveness.

CHARACTERISTICS OF THE CLINICAL POPULATION

Cult devotees have been described through a variety of precommitment characteristics, although these profiles have been collected largely from self-reports, parental assessment, and other subjective sources. Prior to cultic commitment, devotees are reported as being: unhappy (an unhappiness which seems to extend indefinitely into their past); egotistic; excessively "inward-looking"; having problems with impulse control (related to superego surfiets and deficits); suffering from chronic and recurrent feelings of depression, anxiety, or general tenseness; indecisive; shy; poor sense of self-esteem; lacking goals and direction;

feeling out of step with peers and parental expectations; unusually strong and unworked sibling rivalries; "ideologically hungry"; and often depicting their parents as domineering, distant, harsh, and critical.

The "symptoms" of cult involvement have been depicted as follows: deteriorated physical health or neglect of former health habits; wide-eyed, singleminded, and sometimes manic enthusiasm with cultic life-style; incapable of carrying on "normal" conversation uninterrupted by cultic jargon; hypercautious and even paranoid; phobic; constricted thought processes, with a marked tendency for black-and-white thinking; spontaneous emotional expression isolated behind polar and oftentimes autistic preoccupations; distanced from early identifications; devalued former self-image; defensive tendencies of denial, projection, and externalization; depersonalized; and oscillating in moods from insecurity and disgruntlement to a loving, blissful acceptance of religious teachings. Few cult devotees present all of these characteristics, but none present fewer than five or six of the most common, such as constricted cognitive and emotional responsivity, manic enthusiasm for cultic beliefs, blind obedience to cult leadership, hypercautious stance toward former identifications and others in the out-group, egotism, and so forth.

This clinical picture of regressive ego functioning represents an unquestionable challenge for the traditional psychotherapist. However, I have found that our basic diagnostic and therapeutic conventions are adequate for conceptualizing the phenomenology and "causes" of such regression. I have also found that psychodynamic psychotherapeutic technique does not need to be modified in any major way in order to achieve therapeutic success with such patients. The procedures to be outlined below have perhaps been reinterpreted so as to emphasize their conformity with the needs of such patients, or have been recast in terms which highlight the way in which certain essential characteristics of standard procedures can be utilized to great advantage with the cult devotee who elects psychotherapy.

My population ranged in age between 14 and 27 years old, 52 of whom were older than 18 years. Of the 65 patients, 51 successfully achieved therapeutic goals upon termination. Of the 14 unsuccessful cases (usually those who dropped out after four or five sessions), 10 subjects reentered cult life and four cannot be accounted for. As of my last follow-up of the 51 successful cases (2 years posttherapy), there has been no recidivism among this group. Eighteen members of this group have become affiliated with more conventional or "mature" religious communities, although some of these religionists bear in their personal manner of religious expression certain qualities significantly less pathological than but reminiscent of their earlier intense cultic religiosity (eg, tendency to idealize their religious leaders, black-and-white attitudes).

The duration of psychotherapy consisted on the average of 15 months of one (or occasionally two) hour sessions, three to four times per week. No individual from the group of 51 successful cases received less than nine months of psychotherapy.* Adjuncts to psychotherapy are discussed below (see Aspects of Psychotherapy, No. 10).

Forty-three of the subjects were youngest children, 11 were middle children,

---

*Cf Etemad (1979) who advocates treatment sessions in a psychiatric facility, with sessions of 1 to 2 hours, followed by a 10 to 15 minute break, and then resumption for at least 6 to 10 hours per day, followed daily for a total of 30 to 60 hours.

and six were only children. Among the parents of my subjects, 12 couples had manifest marital problems, three sets of parents were divorced, and six other parents had obvious personal psychiatric problems (three were alcoholics). In the case of 17 other families, patients eventually described serious conflict with the parenting style of one or other parents (eg, guilt-oriented or autocratic or distant). Restating the above data, 35 cult devotees were members of mildly to seriously disturbed families. Twenty subjects from this subgroup had personal histories of prior psychiatric or school psychological consultation, and 13 had actually attended psychotherapy for at least two months. Only one of these subjects attended psychotherapy prior to cult commitment for as long as 10 months.

The average duration of cult commitment for the subjects was 3.2 years, with none devoted for less than 13 months prior to the date of initial therapeutic contact. All of the subjects presented with at least six or seven of the common clinical characteristics of cultic commitment noted in the literature, including two cases of traumatic anxiety reaction due to painful disenchantment episodes, 24 cases manifesting frank borderline-type phenomena during testing and early months of treatment, and three cases which featured frequent depersonalization episodes alternating with mania throughout a significantly longer period of psychotherapy than their cohorts (ie, even during the 10th or 11th month of treatment).

All such data must be viewed idiographically given that 1) we are often unable to collect specific or complete information pertaining to the precommitment and intracommitment status of these patients, 2) lacking such data, we have little against which to more adequately gauge subsequent changes, 3) because we have so little adequate diagnostic data, and 4) because different cults may have slightly different effects upon personality. In this sense each cult devotee must be regarded as atypical. Nonetheless, the high degree of consensus, at least among descriptive reports, allows us to speak tentatively about trends in profile and process to which the following therapeutic procedures can be applied.

PRELIMINARIES TO THERAPEUTIC CONTACT

Following initial telephone or personal contact by significant others of the cult devotee, the psychotherapist begins to explore the possibility of establishing an initial contact with the informants so as to begin the assessment process (see Diagnostic Test Characteristics of Cult Committment) and to help them present the possibility of counseling or psychotherapy to the devotee.

1. In the case of adult subjects, the therapist must never recommend or participate in any illegal or covert activities intended to forcefully secure the devotee from his or her cult. In the case of minors, parents may have specific legal recourse which they are encouraged to discuss with a legal expert. In either situation, the therapist must make it clear that his professional activities begin from the time the subject appears in the doorway of his office.

2. The therapist may suggest to parents some of the following ways to present the possibility of psychotherapy to the devotee:

A. Do not nag the subject about current life-style or beliefs. Parents should attempt to establish a few sessions of open-ended conversation with the devotee during which time nonjudgmental and open inquiry may be made about the devotee's life-style, his feelings, his successes, and his daily routine. Parents should remain nonanxious about the devotee's monologues or diatribes against their own values and beliefs and should convey that they are making every attempt to appreciate the devotee's perspectives.

B. Parents are advised to suggest that it is they who may have failed to understand the devotee in the past and that they might be more successful if they could all meet with an interested third party who had become acquainted with many persons "like yourself." Alternatively, parents may directly offer the devotee the opportunity for a private meeting with the interested third party so that the devotee might give this professional insight into how best the parents might understand the devotee's life-style.

C. Parents are prepared for the possibility that the devotee has been taught to regard all mental health professionals as devious, satanic, evil, or otherwise noxious. They are advised to resist debating this point. Rather, parents should accept the devotee's views, saying that perhaps the subject could be discussed again at some later point. I have had several experiences where this maneuver has caught the devotee off guard, and where parents were subsequently rewarded for their patience on their third or fourth effort.

D. It is sometimes helpful for parents to initiate discussion during such meetings about some good or happy memory or event that occurred in the devotee's past. This may have a long-term effect of bringing the devotee face to face with some of the pleasant features of his former life-style. Usually, the devotee will challenge or attempt to avoid such discussion, but parents should remain undisturbed by this, rolling with the punch, as it were. By patiently and consistently accepting these rebuffs, one helps corrode the devotee's belief that his parents are disinterested in his welfare and will challenge his every newfound belief.

E. At each meeting, parents should offer to provide the therapist's telephone number so the devotee can initiate his own contact, and they must stress that such contact will be held in the strictest confidence from both themselves as well as from the cult. Parents are advised to repeat that this process is one that only the devotee can initiate.

3. The therapist empathizes with the parents' frustrations and their oftentimes hostile attitude to suggestions which they "have heard a million times before," or have "tried, but didn't work," and so forth. He may note that we are all experimenters in this particular line of work, but that patience and consistency still seem the most favorable variables effecting change.

4. Parents will frequently deny family or personal problems, especially when the therapist recommends approach 2-B and 2-C. The therapist must help parents understand that in the majority of cases the cult devotee has initially been motivated by some discontent with aspects of former life-style and that they must make every effort to come to terms with unrecognized tensions, conflicts, or other factors which may have contributed to the devotee's flight. If ambivalence about or lack of family religion appears to be an issue, parents should be urged to confront this so that they will be able to discuss such issues with the devotee. If parents can begin to show sincere interest in their own religious affiliation and beliefs and practices, this should be presented to the devotee for it often poses a major challenge to the cult's attractiveness to the subject.

5. Parents often inquire about the option of deprograming (see Maleson, 1981). I explain that deprograming is actually a generic term, including some rather harsh, covert, and dubiously effective attempts to "bust" the devotee out of a cult, and some authentic, professionally managed, and relatively effective "marathon" sessions in a psychiatric facility, and also traditional psychotherapy. I advise parents against utilizing the first form of deprograming, itemizing the

possible benefits as well as the real risks. At the same time, I assure them that I am prepared to offer traditional psychotherapy to the subject whether or not he or she has been deprogramed in any other sense of the term. It has been my experience that all deprogramed cultists still need psychotherapy, whether or not they are considered healthy following radical forms of deprograming or have had previous psychiatric problems. I have also found no tendency to relapse among nondeprogramed individuals who have had traditional psychotherapy. These findings are frankly shared with parents.

ESTABLISHING INITIAL CONTACT WITH THE DEVOTEE

The initial contact with the cult devotee is critical for the future of the psychotherapeutic process which largely depends upon the qualities of trust, empathy, stability, and respect the therapist can convey to the subject.

1. I have found it necessary and effective to maintain my typical professional posture when meeting such patients for the first time. I thank the devotee for having the courage to contact me and to actually carry through with our appointment. Rather than beginning with the customary "What brings you to therapy?" or "What's on your mind?" I initiate the conversation with something to the effect of, "What do you know about (me, counseling, therapy) and what are your expectations?" I have found this type of question useful in that it temporarily relieves the devotee of the obligation to present himself as a "problem" and allows me to begin to understand and explore some of the antitherapeutic beliefs the devotee has about psychotherapy.

2. At the appropriate time—often by way of addressing some of the devotee's animadversions about therapy—I make it quite clear that the devotee is not expected to modify his beliefs for either my sake or his parents' sake. He can use the time provided to understand the meaning and richness of cult life for him and perhaps to actually improve his understanding of religious life. (I am able to make this statement with no devious intentions due to the perspective outlined in Cultic Religiosity as a Legitimate Therapeutic Target.) I allow the devotee to absorb the sense that my office is a safe place for reflecting upon feelings, thoughts, family problems, and so forth. Finally, I frequently weave into the conversation that we would be entering a completely confidential relationship.

3. In stressing my singular commitment to the devotee, I add that our confidential relationship extends even following the termination of our meetings, whether this session becomes our last meeting or whether the relationship extends for a longer period of time. Such statements help bring the devotee in focus with realistic time frames as well as with the extent of my sincerity. I remark that although his parents or guardians are, of course, paying me for my time, I can still offer him such strict privacy since his parents are actually paying for that as well! I stress also that this confidentiality is a two-way commitment and that I would not advise him to discuss his therapeutic contacts with anyone else. I tell the devotee that if he feels the need to have his discussions monitored or subject them to cultic peer review, this will be taken by me as an indication that I have not made myself sufficiently trustworthy.

4. Sometime during the middle of the first hour, I attempt to discuss the topic of "commitment," exploring what the term means for him. The devotee usually picks up on this topic from the standpoint of religious commitment—and projects into it many of his intensely held beliefs. The devotee's monologue is not challenged. However, at some point, I ask whether he can make yet another sort

of commitment: can he commit himself to attending at least three or four additional sessions during which time I will make every effort to understand his way of life and belief. I add that if, at the end of these three or four sessions, he feels so misunderstood or uncomfortable that he can no longer tolerate further sessions, he is free to leave—as he is free to not make any commitment to additional sessions. My comments are concluded with the expression of my sincerest hope that the devotee has found the current session useful. Generally, I say nothing for the remainder of the hour.

5. If the devotee expresses positive interest in further work, I offer him hourly sessions at a rate of three to four times per week. I express that the time spent together will be intense but also that I have no wish to overwhelm him. I explain further that the schedule offered may seem a small amount of time, but that I have found it ample for our needs. I also note that it is important for the patient to come on time because our sessions will end on time and that there is no need for him to come earlier than scheduled.

I deliberate with the devotee over these matters because of my finding that cult victims suffer from a protracted, unlimited sense of time, reinforced by a life-style where the regular day–night/work–rest/private–public frames have been willfully disrupted and reorganized. While I am seeking to eventually supplant the cult and its leader as an object suitable for a narcissistic and subsequently more healthy transference alliance, my long-term goal is to establish with the devotee an essentially different and realistically distinct relationship. I work at all times with an awareness of the need to help the devotee become increasingly more cognitively and emotionally differentiated, on both an intrapsychic and interpersonal level. Therefore, I purposely maintain a certain distance while being empathic at the same time; I provide time to be shared only between ourselves, but which is of definite duration and frequency; I am vulnerable to the patient, but I allow myself and the patient time to separate from each other.

INITIAL ASSESSMENT INTERVIEWS

The assessment and diagnostic stages are obviously also crucial for effective psychotherapeutic work with the cult devotee. This stage is essential for obtaining adequate history of the subject's previous involvements with similar phenomena or other fads, his habits, disappointments, conflicts, peer and sibling relationships, and also to establish the specific degree of impairment of his ego functions. Finally, psychological diagnostic data provide a base against which qualitative therapeutic change can be objectively measured through subsequent testing.

There is a third value in good diagnostic testing of the cult devotee. My experience indicates that such testing can be a valuable therapeutic experience in its own right, giving the patient an initial glimpse, even through the barriers of his cultic defenses, of his intellectual performance, bringing into the range of his experiences thinking processes and emotional resources long dormant or severely constricted. With a personality such as the cult devotee's whose hypervigilant and often dedifferentiated state of mind might otherwise represent a considerable impediment to therapy, the experience of psychological testing serves a facilitating role in motivating ego resources necessary for change.

1. During the initial interviews with parents or guardians of the cult devotee (see Preliminaries to Therapeutic Contact), a complete history of the subject and his family is obtained following the customary anamnestic procedures. I have

found it helpful to construct for my personal use an itemized interview guide-sheet which ensures that I obtain information in the same areas from all interviewees and prevents a sloppy tendency to make assumptions where information is lacking.

2. Aside from gaining important data of the type previously described, such interviews allow an opportunity to appreciate parental and family dynamics, communication styles, and so forth.

3. The family's religious affiliations and levels of commitment and practice are explored. Synagogue, church, or any other communal memberships and activities are noted. Given that cult involvement for many devotees seems to partly satisfy a heretofore unmet need for the transitional and other potentially beneficial psychosocial qualities of religious belief, it is critical to have a sound understanding of the quality of religious atmosphere, or the lack of it, within which the devotee was raised. Parental biases against other forms of religious expression should be noted.

4. During the early interviews contracted with the devotee himself, diagnostic psychological testing is introduced as a way to understand the abilities and interests of the subject. It is stressed that such testing will help the therapist gain objective knowledge of the devotee based on his own behavior, unbiased by subjective input from other sources.

DIAGNOSTIC TEST CHARACTERISTICS OF CULT COMMITMENT

To date, only two studies have reported some type of psychological test data obtained from cult devotees. Since this aspect of therapeutic work with cult devotees represents a significant lacunum in the extant literature, it would be helpful to summarize here these two studies before presenting my own diagnostic findings.

Ungerleider and Wellisch (1979a, b) report intelligence scores obtained through the administration of the WAIS (short form) to one group of cult devotees. Ungerleider and Wellisch report slight differences between the verbal and performance subscales: IQ verbal range is 103 to 114 (overall mean, 111); IQ performance range is 114 to 120 (overall mean, 116); Full Scale IQ range is 115 to 119 (overall mean IQ, 117). It would, in fact, have been more useful to know the subscale scores of specific subjects so as to be able to gauge relative performance on the two subscales. The report of Ungerleider and Wellisch only tells us that the performance mean tended overall to be slightly higher than the verbal subscale mean. In my experience, however, the performance subscale (range, 102 to 110; overall mean, 105) tended to be significantly lower than the verbal subscale score (range, 106 to 120; overall mean, 118), as will be discussed below.

These authors also administered the MMPI to one group of devotees and report profiles which indicated neurotic characteristics, including the prominent use of the defenses of repression, denial, and lack of insight. While both the ex-member and in-group subjects tended to fall within the "grossly normal range," ex-members tended to have peaks on the Psychopathic-Deviance and Hysteria scales, while the in-group tended to peak on the Schizophrenia and Paranoia scales. "Subjects who were still cult members indicated difficulty with impulses in several areas and attendant superego deficits. . . . These difficulties were particularly strong in the area of management of hostility" (1979b, p 281).

Ungerleider and Wellisch also found that despite the self-description generally of satisfaction with cultic life, a strenuous effort had been made to present this "happier" side (evidenced by elevated K and L scales on the MMPI). This phenomenon is consistent with Pattison's observations from his studies of faith-healing communities (Pattison et al, 1973) that self-reports of cures and overall satisfaction with communal beliefs frequently occur despite the persistence of symptoms. This phenomenon emphasizes dramatically the powerful influence of group pressure on individual perception in successfully reducing cognitive dissonance. A similar process is typically seen during assessment and actual therapeutic work with the cult devotee, although such perception techniques are less effective in suppressing the evidence of dissonance and other indications of ego regression on projective tests. It is also of considerable interest that such phenomena are considered more likely to occur with field-dependent personalities or persons who have difficulties in the ability of psychological differentiation, as interpreted by Witkin (1965), Witkin and Goodenough (1981), and Witkin et al (1968). We will see that the perspective of psychological differentiation illuminates many of the phenomena observed on diagnostic projective testing and actual psychotherapeutic communication with the cult devotee.

Finally, Ungerleider and Wellisch report that the Draw-a-Person test was administered in their battery, but the undoubtedly instructive results are not reported in their study. Also, and consistent with earlier descriptive reports, the authors found significant psychological difficulties among their subjects prior to cult involvement and after exit from cults, including social and emotional alienation and mastery–competence problems.

In another study, Galanter et al (1979) reported test results obtained from 20 cult members ("Moonies"). Using a combined battery consisting of a Neurotic Distress Scale, Religiosity Scale, and a General Well-Being Schedule (GWBS), Galanter et al observed that a) members experienced a "fair amount" of psychological difficulty before joining the cult; b) current emotional well-being during membership, reflected on the GWBS, was lower than that for a matched comparison group even though these subjects reported a decline in neurotic distress over the course of membership; and c) some subjects who reported greater improvement of neurotic distress over the course of initial conversion tended to return to their previous levels of distress over the course of extended membership. Galanter et al also interpret the perception of "relief" or lessened neurotic distress in terms of attention and set theory (see also Galanter, 1978; Galanter and Buckley, 1978), similar to Pattison's cognitive interpretation noted above.

Absent from both studies, however, is data obtained from less structured and "obvious" or direct instruments, such as projective tests. Both sets of authors make mention of the possibility that their subjects may have consciously presented favorable perceptions of cultic life. Projective tests, on the other hand, would not "lead" subjects into the need to consciously present a favorable portrait of cultic life-style. Moreover, such tests would provide more focused information regarding changes in cognitive style,* defense tendencies, object relationships, ARISE functioning, and so forth. While I have made no attempt to statistically analyze my data, I present the following results from the diagnostic testing of cult devotees.

1. In my practice, I have routinely administered, in the following order, the

---

*The WAIS administered by Ungerleider and Wellisch could have been interpreted along these lines, but this was apparently not their approach.

WAIS, Bender-Gestalt, DAP test, Sentence-Completion, occasionally the Early Memory Inventory, TAT, and Rorschach. This battery covers a broad continuum of subject behaviors ranging from current intellectual performance, cognitive style, and psychomotor functioning, to the potential or adaptive regression, and including the quality of object-relations.

As noted earlier (Initial Assesment Interviews), the sequence and task-content of the various tests in this battery allow the devotee to display his most well-retained abilities on relatively unintrusive tests such as the WAIS and Bender-Gestalt, and to then settle less hesitantly into relatively more demanding tests, such as the Rorschach, which "pull" at deeper levels of personality. The test process itself seems to have considerable positive impact upon the cult devotee, evoking for the first time in a long while emotional responsivities, memories, and anxieties that have been repressed or constricted, or *dis*inhibited, during the cult indoctrination process and the subsequent maintainance of cultic commitment and antiparental, antisocial, and antiself posture.

2. The cult devotees in my population exhibited two general test patterns pointing, in the main, to several unintegrated qualities which seem to typify sudden and intense cultic commitment. The two basic profiles are a) significant constriction in cognitive processes with a clearly defined preference for stereotypy, or b) a manic denial of depressive trends, which also features deficiencies in optimum psychological differentiation, exceedingly quick response times, emotionally labile rather than constricted responses, featuring unrealistic and idealistic object-relational themes. I am not yet able to state whether the manic profile is merely another side of the constricted profile, but one does note that even "constricted" cult personalities undergo a manic phase during recovery as the subject attempts to deal with increasingly painful object-loss following deidealization of the cult leader, group identity, or the therapist.

3. There are certain characteristics common to both profiles: a) a highly other-oriented and dependent quality of interpersonal relationships, b) externalization and projection of negative, hateful self- and other-introjects, c) intensely ambivalent or unsatisfactory early oral experiences, d) narcissistic trends, e) a weakening of critical judgment and reasoning faculties, f) mildly to severely dedifferentiated reality frames (eg, inner/outer, past/present, self-boundaries, memory/dream), and g), in general, a strongly preoedipal rather than oedipal quality in defense structure, reality orientation, and object-relational needs. Also, while nonprojective test performance tends to be fairly well-retained immediately following cult exit, certain qualities such as cognitive slippage, dedifferentiation, paranoid tendencies, and so forth are evident (eg, typically lower weighted scores on Picture Arrangement and Object Assembly subtests of the WAIS with significantly higher weighted scores on Picture Completion, on which subjects frequently assert that "persons" seem to be missing from the incomplete pictures, but then correct themselves, noting the accurate response).

4. Overall, during subsequent postcommitment stages, and associated with increased differentiation and self-consciousness following psychotherapy, the diagnostic profile becomes richer in adaptive defense mechanisms, improved reality testing and judgment; more normative reaction times are noted; there is lessened rigidity and stereotypy; object-loss seems to have been adequately dealt with (eg, faster reaction times on Rorschach, with a healthier use of *FC* and improved $F+\%$ in the protocols of persons who previously responded to the cards with many F and $F-$ responses, little use of C—except an occasional C_{name} or

C_{arb}—and poor $F+\%$); and qualitatively improved object-relational themes in early memories and more empathic stories told on TAT. With therapeutic progress, one also notices that Sentence-Completion responses are less filled with ideologically tinged and vague statements, and fewer manifest self-references are denied.

5. Protocols obtained from some subjects following termination indicate far better functioning on many indices, but still suggest narcissistic trends (eg, 34% of the Rorschach responses collected from posttherapy subjects included observations regarding the symmetry of the blots—"Here's two men talking to each other, sort of face-to-face," "This is a little beaver climbing a tree . . . and there's another one on this side," "This looks like a mirror image of two identical trees' shadows on the water") and passive or dependent cognitive qualities (eg, questioning satisfactory responses on the WAIS with, "Is this what you wanted?"). These shifts suggest that for many subjects the deeper-rooted narcissistic object-relational needs have not been completely met during the purposely limited psychotherapeutic relationship offered them or, alternatively, that such subjects have not yet achieved an optimal level of psychological differentiation. Individuals who manifested these persistent characteristics were carefully monitored on these issues during posttherapeutic follow-up sessions. Although, as I indicated earlier, there was no recidivism among these subjects, many of them had adopted more conventional or mature religious affiliations but also showed certain subtle qualities in their personal form of religious belief and behavior reminiscent of earlier narcissistic problems and tendencies toward weak judgment.

6. I will now discuss some specific illustrations of the above generalizations.

During the immediate postcommitment stage, one finds some of the following examples of impairment in ego functioning (see Meyer and Caruth, 1970):

A. A tendency to dwell on outer events and closure to past and future, evidenced in inadequate responses to the TAT story in terms of "What has lead up to what you see here and what will happen in the end?".

B. A tendency to externalize by looking outside for clues or other accidental sources to explain what is happening in the self, evidenced by constant checking with the examiner about the accuracy of the subject's response, arbitrary explanations of percepts seen in Rorschach blots, and paranoid imputations on the WAIS (see G below).

C. Splitting of good and bad self- and other-images, evidenced by TAT stories featuring all-good "divinities" and healers (on card 12M), "disgusting" women and men (on cards 12F and 7BM), or unhappy persons who suddenly become happy, fulfilled, etc.

D. Radical denial of fantasy and repudiation of aggressive feelings, evidenced particularly on the Rorschach, through shading denial and shading evasion; minimal tendency toward M and C; poor $D\%$; high $W-\%$; an exceptional preference for $A\%$ and minimal $H\%$, or uses H naively ("Uh. . . a nice man waiting for something"). The manic profile consists of a different Rorschach picture, featuring high $W\%$, minimal $D\%$, great amounts of color shock, and a tendency for CF and a few C' references.

E. Object depletion, as evidenced by seeing "persons" as missing on Picture Completion, completing Sentence Completion blank, I am "lonely" or "hungry," seeing the boy with the violin on the TAT as "alone in the world, his friends have left him."

F. Passivity, as evidenced by vague stories with naive outcomes on the TAT, eg, "He'll be OK, someone will help him out of it," and by minimal $D\%$, no Ad or Hd on the Rorschach.

G. Paranoid imputations, evidenced by questioning the examiner about the purposes and intent of psychological tests; viewing the purpose of marriage licenses (WAIS Comprehension) as being for "surveillance purposes," "to catch adulterers," describing the king's helper (WAIS Picture Arrangement) as "the king's spy."*

H. Depression, indicated by a consistent pattern of lower scores on performance subtests than on verbal subtests. Among the performance subtests, tasks requiring optimal psychological differentiation and other perceptual-motor abilities (Picture Arrangement, Block Design, and Object Assembly) seem to be the most severely compromised.

I. The Bender-Gestalt is generally excecuted with no more than one or two minor errors, but is performed very deliberately, with constant comparing of the subject's own product to the test card during the second administration done with the cards present. Despite good results when drawn from memory, these subjects seem to find the card's presence during the second administration something of a challenge they fear they will not meet. Drawings are also executed with an excessive amount of hand pressure.

J. The human figures drawn on the DAP tended to be smaller than one third of the page, and were often qualitatively inadequate or developmentally inferior, eg, missing hands, torsos, eyes, imbalanced, grossly asymmetrical, and often shaded (54%). Twelve subjects drew group scenes rather than individuals, which is yet another dramatic indication of the intensity of the group process and the dedifferentiation of our subjects.

7. One notes that many of the types of responses of these subjects to projective test instruments are similar to the higher-level borderline patient's test responses (see Kwawer et al, 1980), with saving features such as no severe reality lapses, fabulized combinations on the Rorschach, or primitive imagery on Rorschach, TAT, and early memories. One problem in the more constricted subjects, however, was the marked lack of anxiety during initial testing about peculiar or impoverished responses or about grossly asymmetrical drawings on the DAP.

8. Following approximately 10 to 12 months of psychotherapy, dramatic changes are noted on the protocols of these patients. In the "constricted" group, there is a return of spontaneity, less stereotypy, and a reinvestment in healthier ideational activity, emotional responsivity, and judgment. TAT stories which at four months depicted less disguised themes of oral depletion, interpersonal loneliness, intrapersonal emptiness, and counterreactionary idealizing tendencies begin to transform into more healthy stories, depicting more realistic themes, including painful yet sensible accounts of individual and family struggle. For many subjects, the fear of being overwhelmed is only expressed after gaining some distance from cultic commitment ["It strikes me now that this man may really have sick plans in store for the boy" (to TAT 12M).] The omnipotent figures depicted in some TAT stories are transformed into more realistic images. The "manic" subgroup also initially shows a surfacing of a deeper depressive core,

---

*Singer (1981) states that the cult personality cannot be detected on the WAIS, but my experience has been quite to the contrary.

leveling out to more healthy object-relational themes and less labile emotional responsivity. In the case of these transformations—even the not entirely complete transformations—we are witnessing the ego move from a maladaptively dedifferentiated state toward more clearly differentiated internal and external perception.

9. There are thus many indications that the precommitment personalities of cult devotees probably consist of qualities that conduce toward intense searches for certain maladaptive solutions to internal needs and conflicts which are also offered by cultic life-style. This tentative conclusion is also supported by the persistence of some of the above-mentioned qualities even following otherwise successful psychotherapy, in addition to the evidence forwarded in the descriptive literature of previous psychological conflicts in the lives of cult devotees.

10. I stated earlier that the psychological test process itself can stimulate healthy ego processes and thus plays an important role in the psychotherapeutic process. Testing demands from cult devotees the creative use of psychological operations and abilities which have been held in check and also evokes rich material from the subject's experiences. If carefully reflected to the patient, this material and his performance in general can elicit a healthy sort of cognitive dissonance, challenging the patient with the task of confronting his own psychological processes, anxieties, and fears, and his self-perceptions.

For example, while testing the limits during the Rorschach testing of one subject who had just given a record of 28 responses with no use of color, I asked, "Some people see a red necktie on this card. Can you see it?" The subject's response was revealing. As if awakening from a stupor, the subject studied the card and said in a soft, almost awestruck voice, "Gosh- I didn't even *see* the red here. . . [motioning for the other cards on my lap] Hey! Many of these cards are colored and I didn't even take notice of it! I mean, would you believe me if I told you that I *really* saw them as just black and white?" The same point is illustrated in the case of another subject who was having great difficulty producing any responses to the TAT cards. I reached for an illustrated, young children's book I happened to have in my toy drawer which tells a simple story about a man who worried too much. I did not particularly select this book for its theme, but rather because it is colorfully illustrated and because it tells a simple story which has a beginning, a middle, and an end. I invited the subject to read the story aloud to me. This he did, adding that the story was "sweet." I then asked him to tell me about the story. I also asked him to tell me why he thought a book like this would appeal to young children. He interpreted its value as lying in the bright colors, the simple sentences, and the easy-to-follow story. I then asked him if he could develop some stories like the type he just described in response to the TAT illustrations. The subject said he would try and, in fact, was now able to give some very useful stories and even a few spontaneous memories.

11. It is important to repeat at the end of the testing sessions that all of the patient's material will be confidential. I then generally inquire how the patient found the testing experience, whether it was as he expected it would be, what were his hardest tasks, his easiest, least and most enjoyable, and so forth. This process, again, gives the devotee the opportunity to spontaneously respond to questions in terms of personal likes and dislikes and also orients the patient toward a broad range of positive and negative feelings.

I inform the patient that we will refer to the test material at different intervals during our relationship to see what he thinks or feels about his responses.

ASPECTS OF PSYCHOTHERAPY

1. In order to provide an adequate "holding environment" for the cult devotee, the therapist must practice nonjudgmentalness, patience, an unanxious willingness to tolerate rumination and often meaningless cultic jargon. The therapist must minimize his interuptions of the devotee's monologues, such as in the form of questions, interpretations, and debate. The therapist must also strictly respect the prearranged time schedule, resisting the benevolent temptation to offer unlimited time to the patient.

2. Silences of moderate duration should be tolerated rather than punctured by intrusive questioning aimed at getting at "cult material," and so forth. At appropriate intervals, the therapist should reflect to the patient that it is often hard to find what to talk about, but that if he will just attempt to share his feelings—even feelings about silence—useful material will flow. The therapist also must let the devotee know that the therapist is not anxious about silences and that the devotee need not feel embarrassed during silences. One conveys to the patient that the therapist is comfortable just being with the patient.

3. During the initial weeks of therapy, devotees tend to ruminate about cultic activities, their real or indoctrinated feelings of awe and love for cultic leadership, and their satisfaction and happiness with cult life. Alternatively, devotees may fill many hours hurling invectives at parents, noncult life-styles, amorphous "evils" in society at large, and the therapist himself. Much of this monologue is sprinkled with cultic jargon and hypnosis-inducing code words which serve as a final anchor to cultic life. The therapist will often feel himself hard pressed to restrain the desire to simply shut the patient up, to counter his naive and often childish beliefs, and to puncture his obviously inconsistent beliefs. Such restraint, however, is crucial. I have never found it productive to challenge the cultist's beliefs directly.

4. While debate of doctrine is contraindicated, it is important to consistently and ever-patiently reflect to the devotee the qualities of his communications, their shifts in intensity and length, their apparent lack of connection to other material, and the devotee's various moods when discussing different types of material. The therapist may also cautiously reflect to the patient the feelings the therapist experiences during their communication, exploring whether the devotee can empathize with such feelings. This procedure helps induce empathy in the patient and also helps him regain control over his thinking processes. This procedure also serves to model self-critical and introspective skills for the patient. After the patient has begun to acquire sufficient self-critical skills and a general lessening of cognitive constriction (usually around the third or fourth month of therapy), one can begin to label specific indoctrination techniques and ensnarement patterns which are evident in the devotee's behavior and which seem responsible for some of his difficulties.

5. As in any psychotherapeutic encounter, therapists who have their own conflicts regarding the conflicts and other dynamics which come to the fore during work with the cult devotee may unconsciously prevent the devotee from usefully exploring such areas, causing premature flight from critical conflict areas or closure of topics before they are adequately resolved and worked through. For this reason, I have strong doubts whether cult devotees can receive adequate treatment from "therapists" whose sole or primary professional claim is that they themselves are ex-cultists, unless these therapists have themselves had psychotherapy or have otherwise gained thorough self-understanding. I have not

found the ability to assert "I've been there!" necessary for effective change. "Having been a cult member" is only one, gross way to describe one's experience and is of limited value to therapist or patient unless such experience is exhaustively analyzed in terms of the ego qualities, dynamic and object-relational needs, cognitive and emotional responses, and so forth, which comprise the cult experience.

In the case of six patients who came to me following attempted therapy with "exit counselors" who were themselves ex-cultists (two of whom actually had a few months of group therapy with fellow ex-cultists), a consistent discontent was a sense that such counselors could not tolerate the subjects' needs to rehash prior experiences and had too much tendency to fill in gaps in conversation with personal accounts. On the other hand, the authentic willingness of the therapist who has never been a cult devotee to learn from the patient, to understand rather than to compare, to allow self-discovery and reflection rather than to confirm his own sanity and the security of his own anti-cult resolve are far more important qualities than merely being an ex-cultist.

We know that therapeutic work with religious patients in general can evoke significant countertransference reactions in the psychotherapist along the continuum of transitional and other psychodynamic qualities he himself finds uncomfortable or conflict-ridden. This finding has supported the call for serious and intensive self-exploration before work with such patients can be successful. The cult devotee's significantly more regressive and antisocial psychological qualities must evoke similar reactions in the religious, nonreligious, and certainly in the antireligious psychotherapist. Such reactions can only be monitored if the therapist understands his potential stimulus value for the devotee as well as the cult devotee's stimulus value for the therapist. This is not to say that previous cult affiliation is a therapeutic deficit. It is to suggest that such past experience is as potentially capable of evoking distortive countertransference as can any of the other unanalyzed neurotic conflicts of psychotherapists.

6. There are salient dynamic qualities which underwrite cult experience and the process of resolution of cult involvement to which the therapist must remain sensitive and perhaps wonder about should such qualities be conspicuously absent during therapeutic progress. Before listing some of these, I would add that it has proven invaluable in this regard to nurture the transference relationship and to interpret such transference in terms of these characteristics.

Some of these qualities are: inability to tolerate ambiguity and emotional ambivalence; separation–individuation issues; dependence–independence issues; shame-proneness; idealizing tendencies, such as the idealization and introjection of negative self-images and negative *ethnic* self-images (eg, the victimized Jew, the victimizing Jew); death anxiety; schizoid tendencies.

I noted that one frequently encounters idealizing trends in the cult patient during psychotherapy, manifested in idealization of the therapist, group worker, or even the image of "ex-cultist." This tendency is forcefully stimulated as the devotee begins to experience mourning reactions over the loss of self- and other-images which had been assimilated during cult membership—which he may attempt to deal with by supplanting his lost objects with the idealized image of the therapist or by a desire to return to the cult (see Diagnostic Test Characteristics of Cult Commitment, 2, 3). The idealizing tendency, reinforced by the cult-induced dedifferentiation of self-boundaries, is perhaps one of the most important characteristics of the cult devotee in therapy. Accordingly, it must be consistently and thoroughly analyzed so that the patient can a) gain insight into this proclivity from a benign authority (the therapist) who does not monopolize on this tendency, and b) grow from his idealization of the therapist's healthy self toward a reintegration and internalization of healthy aspects of his own self. Without this step, the idealizing need remains, waiting to absorb some new object which will replenish the intrapersonal vacuum within, and at the expense of new loss of self. As the patient becomes progressively more differentiated from the cultic "other" into which mass he had earlier identified, he becomes more and more able to experience the therapist as well as himself and others in a realistic and stable way (see also Witkin, 1965; Witkin et al, 1968). From this standpoint, psychotherapy with the cult devotee is a corrective object-relational experience.

7. Typically, the therapist is also constantly involved in the process of disinhibiting emotional and cognitive processes that have been drastically inhibited (eg, constriction in spontaneous judgment, adaptive processes) and relearning inhibitions, which in the healthy ego guard important ego functions that have been disinhibited during cultic indoctrination (eg, polarized guilts and anxieties, negative self-images and shaming introjects, psychological differentiation). The return of appropriate levels of inhibition can be observed during pre- and postcommitment and posttherapy psychological testing.

8. During early stages of psychotherapy, the therapist may sense that the cult devotee has become suddenly and radically distant from the current time-and-place orientation, perhaps staring blankly out of the window or gazing directly ahead in a glassy-eyed way. Apparently, as I and others have noted (Clark, 1979; Conway and Siegelman, 1978; Goldberg and Goldberg, 1982; Singer, 1979, 1981; Spero, 1977), this phenomenon can be the result of: a) a reappearance of a learned habit of "tuning out" via the use of self-hypnotic techniques when confronted with beliefs or emergent feelings that challenge cultic doctrine (cf Maleson, 1981, p 927), or b) an actually involuntary "flashback" or "slipping" into an altered state of consciousness, due either to the same dynamics as depersonalization and derealization or to the weakened inhibiting faculties of the devotee's ego. Important issues at the stage when such reactions are likely to occur are remnant or renewed grief reactions over object-loss, and the resurgence of strong impulses to return to the cult. The conflict between these impulses and current emotional progress in therapy may evoke such dissociation episodes as the patient struggles to cope with conflicting allegiances and feelings.

It is helpful during such episodes to remain nonanxious by realizing that such states are transient and are expected artifacts of psychotherapy with such patients. Second, the therapist should quietly inform the patient that he is comfortable being with the patient and is trying to understand what the patient is experiencing. He should then specify the behavior he is referring to, asking the patient if he can describe what he is experiencing in his own terms. If this fails to bring the patient out of the dissociated state, the therapist should comment that the patient seems to be experiencing a "foggy, far-away feeling" or being in a sort of "way out and beyond place" like he perhaps used to experience sometimes during his cult membership days. The therapist should calmly encourage the patient to continue to have his experience as long as he needs to, but that if the patient wishes to pull away from this feeling, he might try to recollect the things he was thinking about just prior to the onset of this state. If this is unsuccessful, one may calmly ask the patient about basic information, such as name, place, the therapist's name, the date, and so forth.

Following such episodes, the therapist should help the devotee focus on feelings during the depersonalized or derealized state, his feelings upon emerging from the state, how he used to experience such episodes and feelings during cult days, and so forth.

9. As one moves closer toward termination, one needs to deal more directly with certain trends characteristic of "postcommitment syndrome." I have not seen a postcommitment syndrome adequately described in the literature, but in the general experience of the professional community, ex-affiliates are initially depressed and irritable, followed by a brief period of isolation and anomie and a tendency to caution in resuming interpersonal relationships, followed by a period of expressed happiness to have "returned to normal." Typically, following this last stage, the ex-devotee may enter an extended period of active protest against cults, occupying most of his or her time with an anticult mission, or may enter an anomic vacuum of indecision and insecurity created by the absence of commitment to either cultic, precultic, or postcultic life-style. When the latter occurs, the ex-cult personality is at serious risk of reentering his old cult, a new cult, or becoming preoccupied with some new transitional cause or belief system.

Of course, there probably is no single postcommitment syndrome, but rather a group of different postcommitment adjustment reactions which are determined by: a) the nature of the devotee's precommitment psychological integrity and quality of object-relations; b) the extent and duration of actual commitment; c) the degree of antiestablishment, antiparental, and antiself identification demanded during cult commitment; d) the nature of the exit process; eg, deprograming, self-initiated, with or without supportive counseling and therapy; e) the quality of the devotee's ongoing postcommitment psychotherapy; f) various other postcommitment environmental factors eg, rejecting/supportive family, peer reaction, ability to continue education or occupation, the availability of alternative religious models, etc.

10. It is only following the successful resolution of these various aspects of psychotherapy that the ex-devotee is truly prepared to benefit from concurrent or subsequent group counseling with other ex-cultists or family. Such adjuncts may be initiated in order to deal with reabsorption into precult affiliations or, in many cases, for focused attention to modifying undesirable aspects of precult life-style and family or peer relationships (see Goldberg and Goldberg, 1982).

11. At the proper time, I announce my feeling that we appear to be moving toward termination, asking the devotee to reflect upon his own feelings and perceptions about this possibility. I make this announcement with the expressed anticipation of spending at least one to two months dealing with termination issues, allowing the patient to set the approximate termination week.

During the termination phase, I have almost always found that the patient experiences a recrudescence of conflicts regarding precisely those object-relational qualities which disposed the patient toward cultic involvement in the first place, eg, flight, separation–individuation conflict, indecision, appeals to authority. Each of these issues must be dealt with.

12. At termination, I schedule a single follow-up session for the ex-devotee six months posttherapy, conveying to the person that he or she is not on trial, but rather that such a session allows me the opportunity to share and learn from the ex-devotee's experiences during this interval. Of the 51 successful subjects, only five attempted to contact me during the six-month interval with concerns about specific dreams, the recurrence of "slipping" or "floating" episodes, or angry

feelings associated with having met (and effectively rebuffed) a former cult colleague. Additional sessions were then arranged for these subjects.

CONCLUSIONS FROM THERAPEUTIC EXPERIENCE

My work has not indicated the existence of an entirely novel psychiatric category, but has confirmed the consistent frequency of specific personality weaknesses in the pre-, intra-, and postcommitment profiles of devotees, such as object-hunger, helplessness, indecisiveness, separation–individuation conflicts, field-dependence, poorly internalized superego structure, and mastery–competence problems.

My experience with the diagnosis and treatment of 65 cult devotees also leads to the conclusion that while cult indoctrination techniques may be directly responsible for many of the psychological phenomena seen in our subjects, there are also several indications that candidacy for cult membership is most likely to occur among adolescents and young adults whose personalities characteristically include certain qualitative weaknesses in ego functioning and conflicted object-relational needs. Witkin and Goodenough (1981, pp 22, 50), for example, have recently noted that the field-dependent personality—featuring the type of cognitive style my preliminary diagnostic work with cultists reveals—is prone to search out the company of others who have only achieved (or regressed to) poor self-nonself segregation. This phenomenon is confirmed in the attraction to and the net quality of cultic commradship. These qualities may in turn create or exacerbate certain philosophical or existential anxieties or other developmentally normal conflicts inherent in contemporary life which represent the manifest motive for the discontent and searching which leads to cult involvement (see Spero, 1977).

These same needs may also motivate those who turn to authentic religiosity or mystical beliefs, but there is a crucial difference between these persons and the type of religious personality represented by the cult devotee. Specifically, the eventual result of cultic commitment is a dedifferentiated and impaired ego state which, unlike the so-called mature religious state, cannot be adaptively controlled by the subject and does not lead to creative self-discovery or any other significant form of psychological maturation (Glenn, 1970; Hood, 1976). In fact, any apparent psychological relief obtained during the initial period of cult membership seems to dissipate, with communards eventually experiencing a return to previous levels of distress.

The idea that the cult devotee is a completely normal person who has simply been duped into cultic life and has no significant intrapsychic problems seems to be a grand defense utilized by some ex-cultists to reduce stigma and hide their continuing fears and anxieties, by parents to preserve the image of their good parenting abilities, and even by some professionals in the effort to justify "wild" therapy or premature termination of therapeutic work with such patients. (See Maleson's discussion [1981, p 928] of the dangers of accepting the "brainwashing model" too literally, and ignoring the intrapsychic conflict model.)

One can also view the flight to cults from another "depth" perspective. Jules Masserman (1964) has spoken of three universal defenses utilized by humankind since earliest history through which to avoid direct confrontation with the full and oftentime unassimilable impact of everyday living. He listed, a) man's belief in his immortality and invincibility, supported by the institution of religion, b) man's belief in the omnipotence of his various authority figures, and c) man's confidence in the positive function of society and family and in man's ultimate concern for his fellows. According to this perspective, all persons have a deeply seated need to invest power in certain institutions as an indirect route to securing personal stability.

In contemporary times, however, man's ability to remain confident in his fellows' concern for him is constantly challenged by media revelations and through one's own experiences with the world. The post-Holocaust and post-Vietnam generation finds itself bereft of symbolic systems which can make sense of modern history and pacify the increasingly sharp anxiety of human mortality and evil. An exaggerated awareness of death permeates our society to such a degree that our defenses against archaic separation anxiety are constantly challenged. The once normal fears involved in growing up into an adult world (Maslow, 1954; Fromm, 1964) are merely heightened by an adult world which presents myriad choices and little guidance, ambiguous sexual models, and little hope for an end to alienation (Keniston, 1960; Conger, 1973). With the decline of personal religion, the search for a way to deal with human limitations and the need for meaning have become more difficult to satisfy.

Little wonder, then, that our era has been characterized variously as suffering from "historical dislocation" (Lifton, 1971) and "existential outcastness" (Keniston, 1960). There has been a break in the sense of connection humankind has long shared with universal history and experience as mediated by cultural traditions and through important religious symbols. Through mass media, we are flooded daily with imagery produced by the flow of modern cultural influence. As Lifton put it, each individual is touched by everything; overwhelmed by superficial messages, undigested elements of culture, and endless partial alternatives to all aspects of life. The cults have apparently provided many contemporary youths with alternative "symbols" and "social networks" (Pattison, 1980) through which to mediate these experiences, while at the same time reducing the individual's exposure to these stimuli to such a degree that the alternative symbols lose all meaning, save to reinforce cultic like-mindedness and behavioral uniformity.

SUMMARY

A great deal of clinically based data has been presented here in the effort to specify assessment, diagnostic, and therapeutic procedures particularly suited for work with the cult devotee. By way of general conclusion, we have found that:

1. Intensive psychotherapy is suitable if not mandatory for successful deregression from cultic commitment, for the return of adaptive cognitive and emotional functioning, and to dispose the ex-devotee to more healthy reintegration into normal living. This has proven to be so despite the significant clinical challenges represented by the cultic personality in its various presentations.

2. Diagnostic psychological testing objectively reveals significant forms of regression in numerous ego functions and cognitive processes as a consequence of cultic commitment and also reveals the dramatic reversal during and following psychotherapy of many of the indices of this regression. We have also found that test process itself to be an inherently positive adjunct to psychotherapy.

3. Some of the psychological qualities which tend to remain in admittedly healthier form even following psychotherapy suggest that certain personalities are more likely than others to become ensnared into cultic life and belief. This is due to the interaction of a disposition toward regressive solutions or compromises

to internal and external conflicts, the overwhelming difficulties encountered in adapting to modern life, and the indoctrination techniques of cults which are designed to manipulate such variables.

BIBLIOGRAPHY

Blos P: Prolonged adolescence: The formulation of a syndrome and its therapeutic implications. *Am J Orthopsychiatry* 1954;24:733-742.

Clark JG: Cults. *J Am Med Assoc* 1979;242(3):279-281.

Conger JJ: *Adolescence and Youth: Psychological Development in a Changing World.* New York, Harper & Row, 1973.

Conway F, Siegelman J: *Snapping: America's Epidemic of Sudden Personality Change.* New York, JB Lippincott, 1978.

Cultism. *Behavioral Medicine* 1979;6:41-43.

Cultism and the young. *Roche Reports* 1976;6:2-7.

Cults: Why so appealing? *Mind and Medicine* 1980;7:2-7.

Deutsch A: Observations on a sidewalk ashram. *Arch Gen Psychiatry* 1975;32:166-175.

Etemad B: Extrication from cultism, in Masserman J (ed): *Current Psychiatric Therapies.* New York, Grune & Stratton, 1979, vol 18.

Fromm E: *The Heart of Man.* New York, Harper & Row, 1964.

Galanter M: The "relief effect": A sociological model of neurotic distress and large-group therapy. *Am J Psychiatry* 1978;135:588-591.

Galanter M, Buckley P: Evangelical religion and meditation: Psychotherapeutic effects. *J Nerv Ment Dis* 1978;166:685-691.

Galanter M, Rabkin R, Rabkin J, et al: The "Moonies": A psychological study of conversion and membership in a contemporary religious sect. *Am J Psychiatry* 1979;136:165-170.

Glenn ML: Religious conversion and the mystical experience. *Psychiatric Quarterly* 1970; 44:636-651.

Goldberg L, Goldberg W: Group work with former cultists. *Social Work* 1982;27:165-170.

Hood RW: Conceptual reconsideration of regressive explanations of mysticism. *Rev Relig Res* 1976;17:179-188.

Jonestown: Special report. *Newsweek,* December 4, 1978, pp 39-78.

Keniston K: *The Uncommited: Alienated Youth in American Society.* New York, Dell, 1960.

Krohn A, Mayman M: Level of object relationships in dreams and projective tests. *Bull Menninger Clin* 1974;38:445-466.

Kwawer J, Lerner H, Lerner P, et al: *Borderline Phenomena and the Rorschach Test.* New York, International University Press, 1980.

Levine SV: Youth and religious cults: A societal and clinical dilemma. *Adolescent Psychiatry* 1978;6:75-89.

Levine SV, Slater N: Youth and contemporary religious movements: Psycho-social findings. *Can Psychiatr Assoc J* 1976;21:411-420.

Lifton RJ: *Thought Reform and the Psychology of Totalism.* New York, WW Norton, 1961.

Lifton RJ: *History and Human Survival.* New York, Vintage, 1971.

Maleson FG: Dilemmas in evaluation and management of religious cultists. *Am J Psychiatry* 1981;136:925-929.

Maslow A: *Toward a Psychology of Being.* Princeton, Van Nostrand, 1954.

Masserman J: The biodynamic approaches, in Arieti S (ed): *American Handbook of Psychiatry.* New York, Basic Books, 1964, vol 2.

Meyer M, Caruth E: Rorschach indices of ego processes, in Klopfer B, Meyer M, Brawer F (eds): *Developments in the Rorschach Technique: Aspects of Personality Structure.* New York, Harcourt, Brace & Jovanovich, 1970.

Pattison EM: Religious youth cults: Alternative healing social networks. *J Relig Health* 1980;19:275-286.

Pattison EM, Labins NA, Doerr HA: Faith healing: A study of personality and function. *J Nerv Ment Dis* 1973;157:397-409.

Pruyser P: The seamy side of current religious beliefs. *Bull Menninger Clin* 1979;41(4): 329-348.

Saltzman L: The psychology of religious and ideological conversion. *Psychiatry* 1953;16: 177-187.

Saltzman L: The psychology of regressive religious conversion. *J Pastoral Care* 1954;8: 61-75.

Shapiro E: Destructive cults. *Am Fam Phys* 1977;15(2):80-83.

Singer MT: Coming out of cults. *Psychology Today* 1979;12:79-81.

Singer MT: Psychological aspects of cults and cult devotees. Unpublished paper presented at Colloquium on the Jewish Family and Cult Involvement, New York, April 5-6, 1981.

Spero MH: Clinical aspects of religion as neurosis. *Am J Psychoanal* 1976;36:361-365.

Spero MH: Cults: Theoretical and practical perspectives. *J Jew Communal Serv* 1977;53: 330-339.

Spero MH: The contemporary penitent personality: Diagnostic, treatment, and ethical considerations with a particular type of religious personality. *J Psychol Jud* 1980;4:133-190.

Schwartz LL, Isser N: Psychohistorical perspective on involuntary conversion. *Adolescence* 1979;14(3):351-359.

Ungerleider J, Wellisch DK: Coercive persuasion (brainwashing), religious cults, and deprogramming. *Am J Psychiatry* 1979;136:279-282.

Ungerleider J, Wellisch DK: Cultism, thought control, and deprogramming: Observations on a phenomenon. *Psychiatr Opinion* 1979;16:10-15.

Witkin HA: Psychological differentiation and forms of pathology. *J Abnorm Psychol* 1975; 70:317-336.

Witkin HA, Goodenough DR: *Cognitive Styles: Essence and Origin.* New York, International Universities Press, 1981.

Witkin HA, Lewis HB, Weil E: Affective reactions and patient-therapist interaction among more differentiated and less differentiated patients in therapy. *J Nerv Ment Dis* 1968; 146:193-208.

CHAPTER

19

Psychiatric Consultation and Supervision in the Treatment of Cult Members

DAVID A. HALPERIN

The interface between obsessional ideation and religious commitment has always been obscure. Since Hippocrates, efforts have been made to demarcate the boundary between excessive, eccentric religious concern and merely nonconforming behavior. This obscurity is often reflected in the confusion experienced by the psychotherapist in attempting to work with a patient who has developed an intense religious commitment. This article discusses the problems and challenges of psychiatric consultation and supervision as part of the treatment process in the psychotherapy of cult members.

There is a tradition of distance and skepticism by psychodynamically oriented psychotherapists towards any intense religious commitment. Psychotherapists all share a high regard for the individual's autonomy. The mental health professional, whether he acts as a consultant, supervisor, or primary therapist, inevitably confronts Schafer's proposition that:

> To talk of responsibility for one's actions and choices, that is to talk of a right way of being, is to be concerned with issues and ethics; but it does not mean that one is therefore moralizing. . . . Psychoanalysis cannot be ethically neutral, in the sense of having no ethics (Lothane, 1978).

This issue consistently arises during the process of consultation and supervision of the treatment process of a cult member, as consultant and primary therapist attempt to assess whether or not their patient has, indeed, joined a group that promotes the surrender of the individual's autonomy. It arises as both consultant and therapist attempt to assess the cult member's preentry status and explore the possibility that membership in certain rigidly hierarchical organizations may be helpful to the seriously dysfunctional individual. It is present as both consultant and therapist consider the appropriateness of either their

318

attempting to support whatever fragile resolution of conflicts the patient has obtained by his new religious commitment, or the efforts of his family members to disturb this new source of "strength."

Moreover, while both the consultant and the primary therapist may be comfortable with Freud's sardonic dictum that "the goal of an analysis is to replace neurotic anxiety with everyday discontent," the patient under consideration need not accept this dour summation. In short, the goals of the therapeutic enterprise reflect the patient's right to choose a belief system that the mental health professional finds personally most distasteful and his assessment of the patient's status should exclude any sense of narcissistic injury because the patient has chosen an alternate, competing model towards security. Finally, the process of supervision and consultation must be conducted in an atmosphere of openness and respect for an honest difference in clinical judgment. The treatment of a cult member may evoke extraordinarily intense feelings within the patient's family, the primary therapist, the referring therapist, and the psychiatric consultant or supervisor. Only in a setting where the professionalism of each party is accepted can the therapeutic enterprise be conducted with integrity.

These issues are discussed in the context of three cases where preexisting psychopathology and cult affiliation interacted and presented complex problems to both psychiatric consultant and the primary/referring therapist.

THE CASE OF SEYMOUR T.

Seymour T. was placed in residential treatment at age 17 because of episodes of exhibitionism. The referral was in the context of his avoiding legal penalties for his behavior. At the time of entry into the residence, he was described as anxious, gawky, superficially amiable, and very dependent. Obviously intelligent, he superficially accepted the need for long-term residential treatment but was skeptical of its utility.

Seymour was the third of three sons born to a lower middle-class Jewish family. His father consistently attributed his failure to graduate from college to the financial pressures created by Seymour's birth. His early life was remarkable in that at the age of three, he was separated from his mother who had required hospitalization for a mastectomy. He was very concerned about her absence. Soon after her return, his tics began. His upper muscle girdle tics continued without real remission until, at age nine, he was diagnosed as having Gilles de la Tourette syndrome (coprolalia never formed a feature of his illness). Treated with haloperidol, he obtained a remission. Despite this, his illness became the focus of his parent's constant arguments. His father resented the alliance Seymour formed with his mother against him. And, the Gilles de la Tourette Society became the social focus of the family life.

During his early adolescence, Seymour's adjustment was marginal. He had few friends and no apparent sexual interests prior to the activities that precipitated his entry into long-term residential treatment. He began to show interest in the evangelical movement at age 18. Three factors appeared to be of paramount importance in his "conversion"; 1) his impending entry into college, 2) his therapist's vacation, and 3) his increasing contact with his older brother who had already undergone a conversion. Seymour's new religious affiliation expressed itself in his "witnessing" to all his fellow residents and the residence's staff. In "witnessing," Seymour attempted to engage one and all in intense and highly inappropriate theological discussions. Despite the pressure of his presentations, Seymour vigorously denied any feelings of anger. He was quite unaware of the provocative nature of activities.

Seymour's diagnoses were: 1) borderline personality disorder R/O schizophrenia, latent type, 2) Gilles de la Tourette syndrome (by history and in good remission).

Seymour's therapist sought psychiatric consultation because his treatment appeared to be at an impasse. Seymour viewed any psychotherapy primarily as an attempt to control him and change his religious orientation. On the other hand, his therapist began to view his contacts with his elusive patient as: "an almost masochistic submission to the patient's aggression, [with] disproportionate doubts in their own capacity and exaggerated fears of criticism by third parties" (Kernberg, 1975).

Thus, psychiatric consultation was required to support a psychotherapist who was attempting to treat an individual whose borderline pathology and evangelical commitment interacted to create an elusive, demanding style and who ultimately denied any real validity to his role as patient.

Seymour's conversion had increased his resistance to engagement in psychotherapy by providing him with an alternate belief system that supported his unwillingness to examine any aspect of his behavior as the product of unconscious processes. Not surprisingly, his therapist had responded to this by dismissing his religious concerns simply as a resistance to psychotherapy without attempting to examine either their content or the role they played in Seymour's life. Thus, a therapeutic standoff threatened. In this context, it was of primary importance for the psychiatric consultant to help the psychotherapist recognize that despite Seymour's overt denials of any interest in the treatment process and that despite his insistence on examining his behavior in theological terms, he was indeed participating in the therapeutic enterprise by attending sessions etc.

Seymour exemplified the borderline patient in whom:

> There is little basic trust. The borderline patient does not relate to the therapist as a real, whole, both positive and negative object but as a part-object that is either positive or negative (Masterson, 1978).

The psychiatric consultant appreciated the pressure imposed upon the psychotherapist by this absence of trust—an absence exacerbated and abetted by Seymour's peers within the evangelical group who sought to provide a theological underpinning to Seymour's reluctance to share with his therapist any details of the group's activities or beliefs. Moreover, Seymour would split objects by describing his religious activities in glowing terms and consistently denigrating all noncult activities as being petty, prosaic, or materialistic. In effect, the process of supervision and consultation was able to create a nonjudgmental atmosphere in which the primary therapist was able to appreciate the role that Seymour's conversion played and was playing within his life. By providing consistent support, the consultant helped the therapist to avoid accepting Seymour's view of him as the denying part-object preventing his reunion with the rewarding mother.

Seymour's conversion had been affected by his older brother. It was this brother who had scapegoated him throughout his adolescence. Seymour had dealt with his rage towards this tormenting brother by splitting. He embraced his brother's religious beliefs and projected onto the vacationing therapist his "feelings of abandonment, and with this projection continued in his denial of the possibility of any therapeutic benefit" (Masterson, 1978). Moreover, in his insistence of Seymour's attending college, the therapist had heightened Seymour's fears of separation. It was in this context that his religious conversion provided him with needed guarantees of present and future security. His conversion had enabled him to rationalize his social isolation ("the price one had to pay for doing God's work in the world") and had even provided him with an answer to why he had suffered from Gilles de la Tourette syndrome ("a stigmata like Job's boils showing he was destined to do God's work"). Likewise, in his act of "witnessing" he was reaching out to his comrades but in a manner which effectively precluded any contact. In an ultimate sense, Seymour's conversion provided him with both the simulacrum of closeness and a means of separation. He continued his close relationship with his mother but with the presence of an organizational barrier that made symbiosis impossible. He could continue to attend his sessions but his religious convictions enabled him to remain at arm's length and without any overt expression of therapeutic engagement.

Within the open and respectful atmosphere of supervision, the therapist was able to explore his countertransference feelings towards Seymour and the anger which Seymour's provocative behavior elicited (Halperin, 1978). It was then possible for the therapist to appreciate that despite his insistent disdain for therapy, Seymour was, indeed, using treatment as a means of avoiding total commitment to the cult. Thus, the therapist was able to focus profitably and consistently on Seymour's difficulties in the here and now. By providing a concerned and empathic atmosphere, the therapist was eventually able to provide Seymour with the means to obtain support within the secular world without the restrictions and sanctions that the cult sought to impose. He was eventually able to leave the residence as a self-supporting individual who still maintained some minimal contact with his fellowship. By helping the therapist to recognize the role religious conversion played in his patient's life, the consultant had allowed the therapist to disengage from an incipient power struggle with his patient and seize upon those aspects of the patient's personality that were seeking more autonomous expression.

THE CASE OF HELENA O.

Helena O. was an 18-year-old, attractive, tall Jewish female whose parents contacted a Jewish Social Service Agency because of her increasing interest in an Eastern religious group. She was contemplating leaving college to enter the group's ashram. Impatient at what they perceived was the dilatory pace of agency evaluation, they sought a private psychiatric consultation.

On psychiatric evaluation, Helena was an alert, articulate young lady who deemphasized her interest in entering an ashram. Rather, she readily discussed her profound disappointment at not being able to pursue a career as a modern dancer because of incipient orthopedic problems. She alluded to her religious interests only in passing and referred to them as a stage she had passed through because of a boyfriend's interest in them. During a family interview, it was obvious that Helena and her parents had a most conflictual relationship. Her difficulties had obviously predated her current religious concerns. Both Helena and her parents were confronted with the desirability of Helena's entering psychotherapy for treatment of her depression. Helena readily agreed. Subsequently, the family canceled her sessions and sought treatment with a "deprogramer." Her "deprograming" was conducted on a voluntary basis and concluded with her disavowing any interest in the cult group.

A comparison between the cases of Seymour T. and Helena O. is interesting. In both cases, the individuals were presented with the opportunity for psychotherapy while still involved in a cult. Seymour T. chose to use his cult involvement, in part, as a resistance to psychotherapy but he nonetheless continued in treatment. Helena O. and her family used the cult involvement as a means of resisting any therapeutic contact in which the focus of therapy would be Helena's depression. Rather, the family denied the existence of conflict and chose to regard Helena's problems as solely cultic in origin. The use of cult affiliation as a resistance to engagement in therapy has been noted by Maleson (1981).

In a sense, the creation of a cult world and the noncult world mirrors the splitting that occurs in borderline pathology. Both Seymour and Helena employed splitting as a resistance to treatment in their relegating the psychotherapist the role of the depriving mother and in their portrayal of the cult world as one in which their needs and wishes would be existentially gratified. Seymour utilized his therapy to create a viable distance between him and his cult. Helena was able to give up her cult involvement because the threat of cult affiliation rallied her parents to her—providing a rapprochement that had been signally lacking in their previous rejection of her. By promising to explore the unconscious processes, the psychiatrist threatened this impending rapprochement. In this context, the deprograming provided parents and child with an opportunity for reconciliation without an exploration of the familial dysfunction or the intrapsychic pathology that had led Helena to such a potentially destructive position. Other aspects of the psychiatric consultation in the treatment of a cult member are illustrated in the case of Jack D.

THE CASE OF JACK D.

Jack D. was initially referred for psychiatric evaluation because of his increasing disorganization and inability to work. He had been hospitalized briefly in 1974 and 1976 after the breakup of his marriage and the failure of his business. He had always been interested in metaphysics and the occult. In the year preceding psychiatric consultation he had become excessively interested in an Eastern religious group and had practiced meditation and yoga for hours on end. Finally, when his guru within the group informed him that his retaining a relationship with a former group member threatened his advancement towards "higher purity," he precipitously left the group. He was referred to a psychiatrist who promptly referred him elsewhere because the queston of cult involvement was raised.

On initial psychiatric evaluation, Jack was a short, disheveled, extremely anxious male, appearing his stated age of 37. His speech was pressured and contained numerous references to the cult metaphysical system. He was obsessed with the fear of being controlled by the leaders of the group and he referred to his fear of control using numerous, obscure metaphors.

The use of religious and cult metaphor and metaphysics in the service of schizophrenic speech has long been noted. Freud (1911) in his analysis of the case of Paul Schreiber discussed Schreiber's quasi-religious productions and related them to the general problem of the "paraphrenias." More recently, with the end of a consensus of liberal rationalism within our society, the mental health professional has tended to adopt a more relativistic approach to bizarre productions which have a religious cast especially if there is some group/consensual validation of these productions. Jack's productions reflected the Eastern group's theology. Yet his pressured description of the "force fields" that were controlling him and "the higher energy levels" that he sought to maintain seemed to be the product of a paranoid system. In this context, the psychiatrist dealt with his productions as symbolic and existential attempts to describe the reality of his cult affiliation. His teachers and the cult leader were attempting to order his life. His fear of control and his ambivalence about the isolation in which he found himself after leaving the cult reflected common postcult symptoms. By recognizing that Jack's productions were a reflection of the experiences that many people report on leaving a cult, the psychiatrist was able to establish a therapeutic alliance with Jack. When the question of medication was raised, Jack's immediate response was negative. At that point, the therapist expressed to Jack his appreciation that, having been affiliated with a cult group in which people he had trusted had attempted to control him, it was very difficult for Jack to accept the psychiatrist's bona fides and no medication would be prescribed until Jack could comfortably accept its use. He requested medication at the next session. Jack had a long-term history of severe psychopathology. By recognizing the role that the postcult syndrome was playing, it was possible to establish a constructive therapeutic alliance and to avoid what had appeared to be an inevitable hospitalization.

DISCUSSION

In the three cases that have been presented, there is both severe preexisting illness and present cult affiliation. In all three cases, the fact of cult affiliation presented a potential resistance to the formation of a therapeutic alliance. In the cases of Seymour T. and Jack D., the psychiatrist consultant recognized that the patient's extensive use of religious allusion and metaphor were an attempt to describe an existential situation of isolation, depression, and control. By recognizing this, while expressing his skepticism about the religious affiliation, but working with the needs that cult affiliation sought to meet, the psychiatrist consultant was able to establish a strong and constructive therapeutic alliance. Where the psychiatric consultant was seduced into viewing the patient primarily within the perspective of a neurotic illness, therapeutic engagement did not occur. In that context, by not recognizing the meaning to the family of the patient's cult involvement, splitting and a further psychiatric referral ensued.

SUMMARY

Three cases are presented in which individuals with preexisting psychiatric illness joined a cult. Some of the problems of establishing a therapeutic alliance and which may affect the course of psychiatric consultation and supervision are described. Particular reference is made to the approaches that the primary therapist and the psychiatric consultant must take vis-a-vis the use of cult affiliation to produce splitting and resistance to therapeutic engagement.

BIBLIOGRAPHY

Freud S: Psycho-analytic notes on an autobiographical account of a case of paranoia. *Standard Edition* 1911;12:3.

Halperin D: The psychiatrist and the paraprofessional: Consultation and supervision, in Nash K, Lifton N, Smith S (eds): *The Paraprofessional: Selected Readings.* New Haven, Advocate, 1978, pp 163–174.

Kernberg O: *Borderline Conditions and Pathological Narcissism.* New York, Jason Aronson, 1975.

Lothane Z: Reflections on Roy Schafer. *Colloquium* 1978;1:12–15.

Maleson F: Dilemmas in the evaluation and management of religious cultists. *Am J Psychiatry* 1981;138(7):925–930.

Masterson JF: The borderline adult: Therapeutic alliance and transference. *Am J Psychiatry* 1978;135:437–441.

CHAPTER

20

The Role of Family Therapy in the Treatment of Symptoms Associated with Cult Affiliation

Many mental health professionals have reported on the growing number of families and individuals who seek relief from problems and symptoms associated with cult involvement. Singer (1979) has reported on a specific cluster of symptoms manifested by the over 500 cult group members she studied, while others such as Clark (1977, 1979) have warned of the dangers of destructive cults upon their members. Common symptoms observed during withdrawal from a cult included disassociation (floating), flashbacks to episodes of cult life, indecisiveness, and loss of critical thinking. The literature produced by former cult members and their families is further evidence of the significant problems created by the recent wave of cults, missionary religious sects, and mass therapy groups, Edwards (1979), Freed (1980).

In 1972 Yalom and Lieberman published a study on the potential psychological damage on participants of various group therapy techniques. Their findings were a significant forewarning of the risks involved in participation in certain types of groups. Yalom and Lieberman (1972) reported that encounter group casualties seemed to be ". . . truly caused, not merely hastened or facilitated by leadership style." They described these leaders as "characterized by intrusive, aggressive stimulation, by high charisma, by high challenging and confrontation of each of the members and by authoritarian control." The groups led by these leaders accounted for a disportionately large percentage of the psychological casualties. Prospective members of some cults, missionary religious sects, and mass therapy groups should heed the warning contained in their concluding statement that "Individuals who are psychologically vulnerable and who over-invest their hopes in the magic of salvation of encounter groups are particularly vulnerable when they interact with leaders who believe that they can offer deliverance. Such an interaction is a potent synergistic force for destructive outcome" (Yalom and Lieberman, 1972, p 253). The leadership style and group practices of destructive cult groups, some missionary religious sects, and mass therapy groups are comparable to the confrontational charismatic groups that Yalom and Lieberman described as responsible for the large percentage of psychological casualties in their study.

Discussion of the treatment of individuals and families affected by cult involvement has focused on the use of individual or group psychotherapy and with the exception of Schwartz and Kaslow (1979), there has been very little written about the role of either family dynamics or family therapy in the treatment of this distressed population.

As director of the Cult Hotline and Clinic of the Jewish Board of Family and Children's Services of New York, I have worked with over 60 current or recent cult group members, and the parents of over 400 other cultists. The focus of this chapter is on the role of family therapy in the treatment of symptoms and problems associated with cult involvement.

Distressed parents come to the clinic with different clinical needs. Some couples, those who are supportive of each other, may be struggling with their ambivalence in taking a firm stand in relation to their child's cult involvement. These parents need to resolve their ambivalence to be effective in maintaining open communication with the cult member as well as taking further steps in retrieving their child.

For other couples, their child's cult involvement has tended to exacerbate previous dormant conflicts and divisions within the marital relationship. In these instances, the parents are so anxious, angry, and guilt-ridden that they easily turn against their spouses. If they have a critical or blaming style, they may blame the spouse for the child's cult involvement. These conflicts need to be addressed through conjoint counseling with the couple.

These issues can be seen in the context of the following case example:

CASE OF THE K FAMILY

Mr and Mrs K were referred to the Cult Clinic for help with concern over the plan of their 26-year-old son, Jon, to leave his job with a major corporation to live full time with a well-known "therapy" oriented cult group that he had recently joined. His increased isolation from the family, donation of over 40% of his earnings to the cult group, and "the strange, vacant look in his eyes and a change in his facial expressions" aroused Mr and Mrs K's fears for Jon's well-being. Until recently, Jon appeared to be doing well living in another city where he was employed.

At our initial consultation the parents displayed a great deal of knowledge about the cult group and wanted to develop a plan to deter Jon "from throwing his life away" by living and working with the cult group. This was Mr and Mrs K's only area of agreement.

Mrs K bitterly chastised her husband for being timid and unconcerned about the dangers of Jon's plan. Mr K, on the other hand, verbally attacked his wife for being hysterical and charged that "she would not be satisfied until she broke him," referring to Jon. Polarized and locked in an orbit of escalating accusations the Ks replayed a long-standing marital conflict. Mrs K felt devalued and unattended by her husband, while Mr K often felt angry over being burdened by a dependent, hysterical, and demanding wife.

Mrs K sought to align herself with the therapist by referring to her past successful experiences in psychotherapy and complaints about her husband's refusal to join her for marital therapy. Mrs K sought to use our sessions to prove that Mr K was in the wrong in taking a laid-back approach to evaluating Jon's situation and had hoped that I would alarm him further. They had been in contact with two deprogramers who had recommended forcible deprograming, something Mr K was not willing to do. In addition, the deprogramers had been induced into siding with Mrs K and confided to her that they felt Mr K did not fully appreciate the gravity of the situation. Mrs K was so distraught that she threatened to divorce her husband. Her son's cult affiliation was viewed as the result of an unhappy family life and precipitated Mrs K's guilt feelings and contempt for her husband for years of marital conflict. Conflicted marriages that gravitate toward some equilibrium are frequently unbalanced by the partners' devisiveness that is provoked by a child's cult involvement—a phenomenon demonstrated in this case vignette.

The clinical work with this couple involved crisis work to shore up the marriage so they could be mutually supportive of each other by reducing their anxiety and anger. The best approach was a strategic one which required that Mr K be given support for his position.

This strategy was followed despite the fact that Mrs K was more knowledgeable about the effectiveness of the cult's recruiting techniques while Mr K remained doubtful. In addition, Mrs K was viewed as the emotionally confirming parent and the one who dealt with Jon. However, I felt that if the Ks were to protect their marital relationship, reduce their individual stress, and to be successful in dealing with their son, Mr K needed to hold a more esteemed position. In this family system, Mr K had been emotionally excluded from the coalition between Jon and Mrs K.

Supporting Mr K proved to be quite successful. He developed a solid approach that involved the use of a voluntary exit counselor, ie, a person familiar with the cult group who would be able to point out the cult's deceptive technqiues and other aspects of cult practices. Mr K was thorough in finding ex-cult members from Jon's group, input from other cult experts, and in our sessions he was effective in dealing with Mrs K without threats or the angry outbursts that had characterized their relationship. His command of the situation and growing competence reduced Mrs K's anxiety and enabled her to withhold her criticisms. The unified position taken by Mr and Mrs K and the reduction of the devisiveness enabled them to deal with Jon directly and effectively. Jon agreed to talk to the exit counselor Mr K found and after several days he decided to part company with the cult group. It is noteworthy that Jon maintained his work schedule, was free to come and go, and at no time were threats or force employed to negotiate with him.

In the K case the mother–son alliance was apparent. In the following case example of the H family, the unconscious issues are more evident. Mrs H's identification with her daughter and the desire for her daughter to "like her" prevented Mrs H from expressing her objections to the cult life-style.

CASE OF THE H FAMILY

Mr and Mrs H came to the Cult Clinic for help with Mrs H's daughter from a previous marriage. Her daughter, Marion, is 32 years old, married, and the mother of a 3-year-old girl. Marion and her husband have been members of a California communal cult for 10 years but do not live as husband and wife, according to the cult leader's instructions. The cult members are under constant pressure to bring in money by selling courses on meditation, sexual fulfillment, and acupressure massages. Often new recruits are sexually seduced to bring them into the cult group.

The cult members themselves pay $100 per hour for "training sessions" and live in fear of the leader's disapproval and physical harm if they were to leave the group.

For many years Mrs H had denied that her daughter and son-in-law were involved in a cult group, but when they fled the group in fear following a falling out with a segment of the group, Mrs H became wary of these "nice people" with whom her daughter lived. When the trouble was settled and the young couple returned to the cult, Mrs H realized that the cult leader controlled them totally and she came to fear for her daughter and grandchild. Marion told her mother that she had become dissatisfied with the group, feared them, but had become too dependent on the group to leave.

The treatment with this family involved helping Mrs H come to grips with her fear of Marion's anger if she would suggest that Marion and her family should leave the group. Mrs H was also unable to take a firm stand in refusing various requests for financial assistance which amounted to a few thousand dollars. Mrs H came to the cult clinic feeling despair and hopelessness, feelings that resulted from her suppressed anger at Marion, the cult leader, and the other cult members. She was angry that her daughter allowed herself to the controlled and dependent on the cult and angry at the leader and the other members for ensnaring and victimizing her daughter. Furthermore, she was angry at the loss of receiving the pleasures she felt entitled to as a grandmother but instead lived in fear of her granddaughter's physical and emotional neglect in the cult's "nursery." Reports of sexual abuse of children in this cult had been received by Mrs H and were confirmed by sources I consulted in California.

Through the course of treatment with Mrs H, who also participated in a multifamily parent support group at the Cult Clinic, Mrs H faced the dilemma of risking her "open communication" with Marion by pressuring her daughter to leave the group. In addition, she prided herself on being open-minded about alternate life-styles and, in effect, condoned the cult involvement.

In this regard Mrs H sought to preserve her own self-esteem by protecting herself from her daughter's criticism that she did not understand Marion's desire to live a different life-stye. Mrs H has learned to tolerate her anxiety over confronting her daughter and has openly expressed objections to the cult and its leader. This has been done with an understanding of how the cult maintains control, and she has pointed this out to Marion. Marion eventually decided to live outside of the cult's commune but she still relies on the cult group for social contacts. Living away from the cult has been difficult for Marion, who was attacked and sexually molested in San Francisco. This left Mrs H feeling guilty and wondering if Marion had been better off living in the cult's commune. Once again, the element of unconscious collusion between Mrs H and her daughter emerged. Despite Mrs H's ambivalence and permissive tendencies she has held firm in her resolve to help Marion to give up her cult involvement. The opportunity to express herself has relieved Mrs H of her despair, obsessive ruminating about her daughter and grandchild's fate, and has relieved Mrs H's guilt for having failed her daughter in some way. Mrs H's ability to acknowledge her anger has helped to put some emotional distance between herself and Marion which in turn enabled her to express her feelings more effectively.

Using systems theory, I have conceptualized the families seen at the cult clinic as assimilative rather than accommodative family systems. While the assimilative family system has rather fixed expectations of how family members should think and behave, the accommodative family system is more flexible in that it accommodates to the individual's differences, talents, wants, and needs. Hence, the assimilative system has a rigid, enmeshed structure and adapts poorly to change, making developmental transitions most stressful for all family members. The transition to adult life for young family members becomes a most threatening developmental crisis for the entire family system. The cult members I have treated often report a failure to attain their own and their family's unrealistic expectations and goals. Their inability to deal with this blow to their self-esteem and tolerate this frustration have made them vulnerable to the sophisticated techniques of cult recruiters.

Among the assimilative families, some are dysfunctional while others are more severely pathological. In the less pathological family, we see the close-knit, enmeshed family where one or both parents depend upon their child's achievements to confirm them as successful parents and elevate the parents' self-esteem. Their dependence and their inability to tolerate separation from their child prevents them from taking a strong stand against the cult involvement, out of fear that the son or daughter will be angry and reject them. The role of treatment with this family type is to help them recognize their dependency and denied anger at the cult-involved child, to be able to take a firm stand, and to tolerate their child's anger.

The more pathological family presents clear evidence of symbiotic fusion between one parent and the cult member. The child in this family is necessary for the psychological survival of the fused parent—often in these cases the opposite sexed parent. The focus of treatment with these families is to mobilize the parent who is left out of the parent–child coalition to the degree that he or she can negotiate with the cult-involved child. The more fused parent is given a great deal of support so as not to sabotage these negotiations. Similar issues existed in the K family cited earlier. A clearer case than the H family is the A family.

CASE OF THE A FAMILY

Mrs A initially consulted the JBFCS Cult Clinic for information on the cult group her son belonged to and on how she could improve communication with him. Mrs A stated that although she tried to control herself whenever she talked to her son, Ethan, their infrequent telephone calls would end with Mrs A derogating the cult leader and the cult members. In addition, Ethan had not left Colorado since the group moved there three years earlier. Mr and Mrs A were having marital troubles and separated after Ethan joined the cult group.

Mrs A is an intelligent, insightful woman pursuing a doctorate degree in the social sciences. Her insights into her son's cult involvement were informative and revealing. She believed that "cult members came from homes where the father was a weak figure" and in her case, her son was, in effect, the man of the house and did the chores and supported her emotionally. "Unfortunately he threw away" a promising career in science after graduating from an Ivy League college and was accepted into medical school.

The treatment involved bringing Mrs and Mr A together and pointing out that they would need a joint policy to pursue their wish to deal with Ethan effectively.

Also, it was decided that the A's should not make any plans for exit counseling until their marital situation was resolved further either by reconciliation or a divorce because Ethan had been triangulated into their marital relationships. Mrs A continued to be seen and participated in a parent support group. These parent support groups provide an opportunity to exchange information and to share feelings and experiences with other parents in similar situations. It has been noted that the parent groups can provide support for families dealing with intense emotions such as shame, guilt, and a sense of failure and who are often isolated from others due to this heavy emotional burden.

Mr and Mrs A decided to try to have Ethan join them for a visit—his first in over two years. At this point, Mr A was encouraged to take charge of the negotiations with Ethan. This was a departure from the family's usual pattern. His intervention was required to break the symbiotic tie between Mrs A and Ethan which would then allow the covert father–son relationship to emerge. In a sense, Ethan's role as "the man in the house" had helped his father to hold the marriage together until Ethan's departure from the home. The oedipal aspects of this case are quite evident and may continue to play a role in Ethan's continued involvement in a cult whose activities are directed towards a search for repentance for "transgressions."

After great effort and with the therapist's support, Mrs A was able to control her criticism of her husband and tolerate setbacks. Mr A established a harmonious relationship with Ethan and was effective in getting his son home for a visit. Furthermore, Ethan agreed to speak with an exit counselor who was able to get Ethan to live outside of the cult group to reconsider his affiliation in exchange for Mr and Mrs A's agreement to accept Ethan's final choice of a life-style.

These negotiations helped to decrease the familial tensions and eliminated Mrs A's blaming her husband for a decision Ethan made. The family relationship improved, with Mr A maintaining his share of parental leadership. Mrs A felt gratified by her husband's responsiveness and his strength in dealing with Ethan—she decided to try for a marital reconciliation. Our work enabled Mr A to intervene in the mother–son coalition and to claim his appropriate role as father and husband.

An important aspect of family therapy with the family of the returned ex-cult member is to help the parents alter their unrealistic expectations of their child. The parent who describes his cult-involved son or daughter as "the child who had so much promise" must be reminded of the question "promise for whom?" In this context it must be noted that vulnerability to cult recruitment appears to be greatest at "low points" in the prospect's life. Therefore, a crucial predisposing factor is often a setback in the cult member's expectations and goals such as failing an important college course, inability to form gratifying intimate relationships, or career confusion. These internalized familial expectations often continue to play an active role. Parental expectations, which may be either unachievable or unrealistic, need to be addressed when the ex-cult member returns from his or her cult group.

Family treatment is used to free the ex-cultists from these disabling parental expectations, projective identifications, and his own introjected identifications. If possible, this focus of family therapy should be undertaken during the period of cult affiliation. These issues are exemplified by the T family.

CASE OF THE T FAMILY

Mrs T had initially contacted the Cult Clinic about her 28-year-old son, Jerry. He had been a member of the Eastern Meditation Group for several years. He did not live in an ashram, but he moved around the country to attend the many "festivals" the group held each year. Therefore, Jerry could only work on temporary assignments in his profession as a physical therapist. Furthermore, he was not licensed in several states and supported himself by working on menial jobs that included selling hot dogs to raise money for his cult group.

During one of his infrequent visits to New York, Jerry agreed to see me with his parents who used the session to present their objections to his cult affiliation. They objected to Jerry's lack of career development, his emotional isolation from the family, and to the group's pull on Jerry to leave Judaism. The last shocked Jerry who retorted that the family had barely observed the religion and that he was the family member closest to God. However, Jerry reluctantly agreed to stay in the New York area to continue the family sessions for a few weeks.

It is important to note that Jerry displayed clear signs of being in a state of mind control. This was manifested by his constricted affect, dilated pupils that constantly stared, and a controlled, evenly paced speech pattern. His initial presentation had a schizoid quality which diminished over the course of a few sessions.

A most significant point in the treatment occurred when Mrs T began to weep about missing Jerry, who lived far from the family. Although upset by this, Jerry was able to give his mother an explanation of his feeling burdened by her emotional needs. Furthermore, he was able to discuss his feeling afraid of the challenge of opening an office to practice physical therapy. Jerry did not share his parents' goal for him to be in private practice (his father is a physician). He had chosen to escape parental disapproval and his own sense of guilt for "abdicating responsibility" via life with the cult group where he thought he could reach a "higher state of consciousness" via meditation. Through the course of the three months of family treatment (with some individual sessions for Jerry), Mr and Mrs T were able to convey to Jerry their hope that he would resume a life-style with the potential for adult development—for his benefit. They accepted responsibility that their expectations were "very middle class." Somewhat freed of his parents' expectations for achievement, Jerry found a permanent position as a physical therapist in Boston, a city close enough to maintain family ties yet far enough for Jerry to be autonomous. His parents were able to tolerate Jerry's participation in the cult group which parenthetically decreased over the next few months.

Specific postcult issues need to be addressed in family therapy following a family member's departure from a cult group. Minuchin's (1978, p 98) description of the issues in the treatment of enmeshed families can be adopted here with special emphasis on problems of individuation, competence, and intrusiveness.

Parents who object to their children's cult membership need to examine whether their concerns and objections arise out of a desire for their child's continued growth and development rather than out of a need to control or manipulate them. If the family pattern was one of manipulation and control, the family therapy needs to address this issue quickly, with the therapist supporting individuation in order to break the pattern of parental manipulation.

Individuation   A close knit, enmeshed family can be quite supportive, but if it squelches autonomy and holds to rigid expectations, the family needs to change from an assimilative to an accommodative family.

One way to increase individuation is for the therapist to "deprogram" or debrief the entire family in family sessions. All the family members have just gone through a life crisis, and they will have a need to touch each other emotionally. Each family member should be encouraged to describe how he or she experienced the recent events around the departure from the cult. Most families will want to focus only on the ex-cultist's experiences while they present a monolithic view. This needs to be gently challenged to allow each person to describe individual experiences and feelings. Furthermore, no one can be allowed to speak for another person.

Competence Parents of recent ex-cult members are understandably fearful that their child will return to the cult group—a fear that is supported by past experience with other former ex-cultists. However, this can thwart autonomy and erode the returnee's sense of competence. Parents often view their child's cult involvement as proof of the child's incompetency. This notion needs to be changed if the ex-cultist is to readjust to the pressures and frustrations of daily life. Furthermore, life in cult groups has inordinate challenges that often require the discipline to master physically strenuous yoga exercises, fasting, going without sleep for several days, and working 18 hours a day. I accentuate these accomplishments and frame them as evidence of discipline that will be helpful in new endeavors. Parents are often upset to hear that there is anything positive in the cult experience but they can be helped to accept it.

Intrusiveness Depressive feelings are often experienced after leaving a cult group and will need to be ventilated. Parents are frequently frightened and some are quite anxious if their child should cry over their sense of loss. Sensitivity and support on the part of the family is important. But, to maintain individuation, it is often necessary to restrain parents from exploring the reasons for the tears and to block constant questions in the parents' attempt to be supportive. The message here is that each person has a right to privacy (a right which the cults conspicuously deny). By seeing these clients in individual sessions, the opportunity to ventilate feelings and to explore the content behind the depressive affect is provided. Resolution of these issues can be a crucial factor in the ex-cult member's readjustment as we will see in the following case example.

CASE OF SUSAN S

Susan S recently returned from the "Eastern" cult she joined seven years ago, at the age of 20. Her mother, a widow for five years, was overwhelmed with what appeared to be Susan's "nervous breakdown." When Susan was seen at the Cult Clinic she was suffering from the acute symptoms that often occur upon leaving a cult. These symptoms included spontaneous crying, disassociation, depression, alienation from family, and the intense fear that she is unable to survive outside of the cult because she had defied a divine desire that she serve God through life in the ashram. Flashbacks to life inside the ashram, and "hearing" the chants eroded Susan's confidence that she could "leave cold, and never go back." She had left the group because of the competition and tension that emerged after the leader's death in July 1981, three months earlier.

Susan's treatment at the Cult Clinic required crisis intervention with frequent individual and family sessions with her mother and sisters. Among the many issues explored in the family therapy sessions was the family's covert expectation that Susan would take over as her mother's caretaker. Furthermore, Mrs S pressured Susan to study accounting and work as a bookkeeper (a job Mrs S could teach Susan), and to live at "home" with her and relieve Mrs S's rather isolated life as a widow. Susan's desire to plan her own life and to explore a less austere mainstream religious life-style created intense arguments between mother and daughter. As Mrs S spoke of Susan's inability to think maturely and warned her daughter that she was making terrible mistakes, Susan fought for her right to make her own mistakes. Sessions with Susan and her sisters were successful in bringing together these three young women who had become estranged from each other. They were able to acknowledge that they shared the problem of their mother's intrusiveness but yet each was concerned with hurting their mother's feelings. Each sister seemed to know of their mother's complaints about the others but were unable to overcome many of their grievances with each other to become a supportive subsystem. Pointing out how the youngest sister had covertly been mother's protector helped her to give up this role and express her anger over shouldering the burden. With her sisters' support Susan was able to move into a small apartment with another young woman. She has returned to college to pursue her career goal to work with children and supports herself with a part-time job.

Susan has met other former cultists through the Cult Clinic. Meeting other young people who have "followed a spiritual path" has been helpful to this young woman.

SUMMARY

Family therapy plays an important role in the treatment of problems associated with cult involvement. There are three phases to this treatment:

Phase 1   Family therapy is employed to help parents and other family members develop and improve communication with the family's cult member. During this phase family members need to resolve their ambivalence or trepidation in approaching a family member. For the treatment of parental distress and more overt symptoms often presented by parents, family and multiple family therapy is the treatment of choice.

Phase 2   After the initial consultation in phase 1, the family is asked to bring in the cult member. Frequently, this cannot be done, but in many cases it is possible. The parents and the cult member work on their differences, disappointments and estrangement. A plan to meet with an exit counselor or former cult member is on a voluntary basis and is often worked out in these sessions. Exit counseling is a reeducation process and works best when supported by preparatory and concurrent family therapy.

In phases 1 and 2 it is essential to structurally assess the familial alliances and coalitions. Typically, a parent involved in a parent–child coalition is unable to deal effectively with the cult member. The nonconfirming parent needs to break the fusion of the coalition and negotiate with the cult member while the spouse is given support to not disrupt the negotiations.

Phase 3   Family therapy is essential following a cult member's departure from the group to allow the entire family to be deprogramed or defused, to address long-term patterns of dysfunction, and to help parents give up old expectations in exchange for more realistic expectations that accommodate to their child's overall needs. Family involvement is essential to facilitate successful readjustment of the ex-cultist to his family and the frustrations of everyday life.

332

BIBLIOGRAPHY

Clark J Jr: Investigating the effects of some religious cults on the health and welfare of their converts. Testimony given to the Special Investigating Committee of the Vermont Senate by John Clark, Jr, MD, 1979.

Clark J Jr: Cults. *J Am Med Assoc* 1979;242(3):279–281.

Edwards C: *Crazy for God*. Englewood Cliffs, NJ, Prentice Hall, 1979.

Freed J: *Moonwebs*. Toronto, Dorset Publishing Co, 1980.

Minuchin S, Rosman BL, Barber L: *Psychosomatic Families*. Cambridge, MA Harvard University Press, 1978.

Schwartz LL, Kaslow F: Religious cults, the individual and the family. *J Marital and Family Ther* April 1979;5-2:15–26.

Singer MT: Coming out of the cults. *Psychol Today* January 1979;12-1:72–82.

Yalom I, Lieberman MA: A study of encounter group casualties, in Sager C, Kaplan, Singer H (eds): *Progress in Group and Family Therapy*. New York, Bruner Mazel, 1972, pp 223–254.

CHAPTER

21

Self-Help Groups for Parents of Cult Members:
Agenda, Issues, and the Role of the Group Leader*

D.A V I D A. H A L P E R I N

A ffiliation with new and exotic religions is a matter of increasing recent concern. America has always been characterized by a multiplicity of religious
groups and quasi-religious organizations. Fundamentalist and evangelical groups
of various persuasions and persuasiveness have been part of the American scene
since the arrival of John Wesley in the 1740s and the Great Awakening of the last
century. The recent expansion of these groups beyond the traditional Bible Belt is
a new development. Likewise, the recent increase in affiliation to the new
religions by middle-class, well-educated, "intellectual" youth represents a new
phenomenon. Converts are no longer limited to the impoverished, educationally
deprived, socially isolated, racially victimized, or even the alienated. Indeed,
these new religious groups often seem to have focused their recruiting activities
towards the college-educated, middle-class, and ostensibly sophisticated adolescent who has experienced neither economic nor social deprivation. Moreover,
Jewish youth appear to be represented in numbers well out of proportion to the
general population.

Middle-class families must suddenly confront issues of religious identification
and a degree of religious commitment on their children's part which would have
been quite unthinkable in the rationalistic, humanistic climate that has been
prevalent in America. Idealistic youth and their often idealistic parents—parents
who prided themselves on their openness and their refusal to be either
authoritarian or judgmental—now find themselves separated by their feelings
and/or concern over their children's new religious commitments. Indeed, the
children may have joined groups which either by design or by practice effectively
limit their communiction with their families and the outside world.

---

*A version of this chapter was presented at the Annual Meeting of the American Association of
Psychiatric Services for Children, November 1981.

Parental concern has led to the formation of self-help and support groups for the parents of cult members under the auspices of more broadly based community organizations such as the Westchester Jewish Community Services and the Jewish Board of Family and Children's Services of New York City. These groups have been formed to provide "support" to the parents of the cult members and to explore what types of outreach might be useful to the cult members themselves. A secondary agenda, in itself of great importance, has been to develop an understanding within the family context of those factors which may have led to cult affiliation. This chapter reflects the author's activity as group leader of a self-help group formed under the sponsorship of the Westchester Jewish Community Services (WJCS) and as consulting psychiatrist to the Cult Hotline and Clinic of the Jewish Board of Family and Children's Services (JBFCS). This activity has meant working with people in great anguish whose deep human needs have just begun to be acknowledged by society.

The parents' self-help group of the WJCS was formed as part of a Family Life Education Program open to the general public. The initial task of the workshop as described in a brochure was to help parents and children live with the family member who has joined a cult—"The cult's impact on the family, who joins cults, how not to cut off communication will be discussed." The only requirement for attendance was the participants' willingness to identify themselves to ensure that those participating would act responsibly. Sessions were scheduled to last (and have lasted) for one and a half hours. After the initial series of three sessions which were held on consecutive weeks, group sessions have met every three to four weeks. The initial meetings drew 15 to 20 members (most of whom have remained with the group). The members supplement the group's formal meetings with a wide variety of informal contacts (attendance at meetings of the Citizen's Freedom Foundation [CFF] etc). However, their attendance at the sessions of the self-help group provides a framework (time and place) for the interactions that occur both beyond and before the formal meetings.

"Our cult" includes a wide diversity of religious and/or quasi-religious groups. The Unification Church (Rev Sun Myung Moon), Divine Light Mission, Church Universal and Triumphant, Transcendental Meditation, and a variety of fundamentalist or evangelical groups are represented. In striking contrast to this diversity was the uniformity with which parent after parent described having always regarded their child as being "fragile." In an early session, a mother talked about "how I always felt that I couldn't make her angry—that she couldn't take it." Even in the first session, parents focused on their sense of their child's being "damaged." Indeed, in one family, this sense of "damage" was so great that the parents had enrolled their child in a school sponsored by an Eastern religious qua self-improvement group because of its supposed "therapeutic" orientation. Other parents noted that their child had always seemed to fear competition, wondering if some of the cult's initial appeal lay in its providing a noncompetitive environment.

This contrast between the wide diversity of cults and an apparently uniform description by parents of the premorbid personality of the cult member raises intriguing questions. Among them are: 1) do cults attract members from an undifferentiated pool of vulnerable adolescents? and 2) does each group have an intrinsic appeal because of its message, theology, ritual, and structure which meets the needs of a specific population? These questions have no simple answers. Nonetheless, it was striking the way in which parents joined in regarding the future cult member as being both more dependent and less able to cope, as requiring significantly more support than his/her siblings. At times, it even appeared that there had been a parental consensus that to provide for the child's future some significant degree of additional structuring was necessary. The implication to draw from this is not that the family necessarily saw the future cult member as "sick" but rather that the future cult member appeared to have been more passive, less autonomous, and simply more in need of parental direction. The possibility that the parents had projected onto the future cult member their own sense of fragility and vulnerability is intriguing (Harwood, personal communication, 1982) and deserves consideration but not investigation within the framework of a self-help group.

Parental concerns over their child's fragility expressed themselves in their questioning the consequences of the child's leaving the cult—might the child not simply revert to his/her previously depressed state of anomie and aimlessness? Likewise, parental presumptions of fragility led to a limited recognition that cult affiliation may have met their child's needs to a limited degree. This acceptance of their child's need for direction might also express itself in the parents repeatedly questioning whether or not there was any legitimacy to their concerns, because their children were only exercising their rights under the First Amendment, and furthermore their children would tell them repeatedly about their newfound happiness. In this regard, the discussions within the early group meetings paralleled those within the broader society. The demands placed upon the group "leader" to facilitate the formation of a task-oriented group out of these conflicting expectations, realizations, and despair can be readily appreciated. They will be discussed at length later in this chapter.

An issue that was striking in its absence was the lack of strong parental response over the issue of religious affiliation per se. All the members of the group (with one exception) were Jewish. None of the group members discussed their child's new religious affiliation primarily within a religious frame of reference. None had ever considered responding to their child's apostasy in the traditional Jewish manner which is to sit in mourning. Their lack of response may reflect the nominal nature of their own religious commitments. Thus, their concerns were less with the fact of religious change than with the demands and constraints that this change imposed on their children. They expressed relatively little feeling about their children's absence during religious festival as being symbolic of religious change, but a great deal of anger at their children's having been summoned to participate in a meditation vigil on virtually a moment's notice halfway round the world (effectively removing them from their family).

Indeed, the primary religious commitment of the self-help group members appeared to lie in a liberal humanism. They expressed a deep skepticism about any belief system which convinced a son to give up his promising career in biochemistry or had so changed a daughter that she gave up her concerns about ecology to work in a fish canning factory. Given the intensity of feelings evoked in parents by their child's affiliation to a cult, it is not surprising that the mental health professional who is on the receiving end of parental confusion and anguish may readily label these parents as religious fanatics simply interfering with their child's freedom of religious expression or "as being as crazy as their children." The members of the self-help group did not conform to these stereotypes. Their concerns about their children were and are legitimate. Their confusion is understandable when the skepticism and sanctimoniousness with which their anxiety had been often greeted is considered. Their desire for support was and is appropriate (Levine, 1981).

When the topic of "deprograming" or "exit counseling" arose, the group members were far from being anticult fanatics. The parents who saw their children as "fragile" would wonder about their children's ability to function in the less structured world outside the cults. Parents frequently questioned if it was even in their children's interest to leave a cult after years of cult affiliation. Indeed, rather than expressing a primarily narcissistic concern over their "failure" as parents, the group members would discuss their children's successes within the less competitive cult world—wondering if it might not be in their children's interest to remain there and continue their "limited" lives. Almost unexpectedly, as group leader my role was one of helping people to explore their feelings and their reluctance to act or bite the "magic bullet" of deprograming, rather than to restrain people in the hotheaded pursuit of their children aided and abetted by "deprogramers." The group leader's role became one of facilitating the group members' exploration of their feelings and the problems that arose in relating to individuals who might remain in a cult setting for the foreseeable future. Not surprisingly, people who originally viewed their children as "damaged" required support to see their children as being capable of a higher, more autonomous level of functioning (and this skepticism often interfered with their actual ability to communicate with their children).

Despite superficial similarities, the various cult groups are quite diverse. This diversity reflects itself in the actual degree of communication and contact allowed between parents and children. The individual's actual position within a cult may also allow a degree of communication between parent and child that belies the stereotype of a "slave" selling flowers and abjectly subject to a group's/guru's authority. Parental response to a child's cult affiliation varied in relationship to the actual amount of contact allowed with their children. Parents in frequent contact with a child may not accept the child's new religious orientation but they hardly have the same sense of loss as do the parents whose child is effectively isolated. The preservation of communication between parent and child became a major focus of the group's activity.

Parental reluctance to consider any assertion or confrontation in an attempt to change their child's religious orientation reflected a pervasive fear of terminating whatever communication or contact existed. On receipt of a letter from a child expressing any positive feelings towards them, parents became almost euphoric. Their depression was profound on their learning that the letter might well have been, in effect, merely a form letter sent out at the direction of the cult leader ("establish and maintain contact with your parents"). Parents would discuss their feeling of being blackmailed by children who implicitly threatened to sever all communication with them if the parents were to confront them with any disapproval of their cult affiliation. Indeed. the self-help group was particularly helpful to its members in supporting their efforts to establish a meaningful dialogue with their children in which the parents were able to effectively discuss their feelings about their child's new religious orientation.

Parental difficulties in communicating with their children extended beyond the establishment of some measure of consistent contact. Communicating with children who are involved in bizarre activities, ie, "levitation" or the restoration of peace to Nicaragua through meditation, presents to the uninitiated problems comparable to those experienced by the mental health professional in dealing with the delusional productions of a psychotic patient. Here, there is the important exception that the production is not an individual's isolated creation but is part of a schema that is given consensual validation by a group which liberates itself from the confines of reality because of its religious auspices. The parent's difficulties are exacerbated by their child's production being delivered articulately and often without the overt signs of disorganization that are present in a psychosis. The flatness and detachment that often accompany any contact between parents and cult member, not surprisingly, intensify the parental concern. Thus, parents face a deep dilemma in dealing with loved ones who only superficially appear to be emotionally intact and who remain fixed and immobile in their "delusions" and incapable of recognizing the apparent "absurdity" of their views.

The potential for the disruption of communication between parent and child is immense. At times, parental anger may be exacerbated by their recognition that their child's new religious affiliation is an attempt to provide needed structure and to deal with a sense of fragility and aimlessness. In this context, the parent may interpret the child's new religious affiliation as a reflection of their own "failure" as parents. Not surprisingly, parents may seek refuge from this sense of failure by attributing their child's new religious affiliation entirely to coercive persuasion and become extremely reluctant to explore within the self-help group any previous difficulties they experienced in relationship to the cult member. Parents may respect the child's need for the structure a totalistic setting provides, but they are often hard pressed to respect this need and at the same time preserve their own sense of intellectual integrity by not acquiescing in inimical beliefs. Within the group, parents discussed their sense of constant challenge from the cult member's volubly expressed relief at having found "salvation" combined with their own awareness of the cult member's past depression and presumed fragility. In short, dare they disturb their child's fragile equilibrium?, especially if the result of their efforts at confrontation is to be relegated to the ranks of the "satanic" enemy.

As an individual remains in a cult, he may lose practical skills and the ability to discuss/deal with non-cult–related issues. The loss of time that he might have otherwise spent in conventional academic pursuits may create a feeling within parents that their child has no options other than to remain within the cult. If a child achieves a position of leadership within the cult, that position may assuage whatever narcissistic injury the parents may feel as a result of the child's failure to pursue a conventional career (and to fulfill their past expectations for the child). They may even interpret their child's success within the cult as evidence of his achieving sufficient maturity to leave the cult (an expectation that is occasionally realized). Above all, it is difficult for parents to share in the success their child has experienced in propogating the "enemy" camp. Thus, as their realms of discourse increasingly drift apart, it is not surprising that parents begin to limit their contacts with the cult member.

Parental withdrawal may also be in response to their child's intense dependency strivings (which may continue to be expressed despite continued cult involvement). The parent who has always felt uncomfortable in expressing anger towards a "fragile," dependent child may well withdraw rather than confront a child who continues to express bizarre ideas without regard to their impact on either his parents or his siblings. A parent discussed within the group her ambivalence at her relief at her not having her child still call in the early morning to seek her approval after trivial disappointments. The parent who has experienced a child's dependency needs as bottomless may not always strenuously object when the child has found a suprahuman agency to provide support. This withdrawal may be rationalized (with some realistic concern) as a desire to protect other "vulnerable" siblings from the cult member's influence. The self-help group was particularly helpful to members who expressed guilt over their withdrawal from their children by supporting their acceptance of the necessity and appropriateness of periods of disengagement and by pointing out that this did not constitute abandonment and might even promote the cult member's return.

The parents of the cult members had experienced them as "fragile." Of what did this "fragility" consist? What was its relationship, if any, to cult affiliation? Some members of the self-help group noted that the future cult member had required professional mental health consultation. None of the children of the self-help group members had required hospitalization. However, a wide range of dysfunction including periods of dysphoria, an inability to relate to authority figures cooperatively or constructively, an inability to accept realistic limitations, and/or grandiosity over their own potentials seemed to be present. However, it must be noted that these symptoms are characteristic of "normal" adolescent turmoil.

Parents described the actual period prior to cult affiliation in strikingly uniform terms. Their child had just completed a stage in the educational process. This termination was followed by travel—a *wanderjahr*—unencumbered by the structures of college or work. Adrift and accompanied by friends with whom the child has formed an overly idealized relationship (a relationship often terminated with intense disappointment), the future cult member meets a group of "interested" people who promise to provide a supportive network. The vulnerable adolescent accepts this support without questioning its motivation. The vulnerable adolescents' need for structure and support and their naivete and credulity gives full rein to the deceptive practices of the cult recruiter.

Not surprisingly, within the self-help group sessions, parents movingly described their having acquiesced into allowing their children to pursue a sabbatical from structure in which their children would "find" themselves because they had been "assured" that structure was outmoded. This parental confusion was exacerbated by the parents' own identification with their idealistic children and the children's anger towards adult superficiality and moral pretension. Thus, within the self-help group, parents dealt with their sense of failure at not having provided either the necessary support for realistic plans for the future or the necessary authority to help their children through a period of transition. Their chronic sense of failure was heightened because, in some cases, a severe or incapacitating illness had prevented them from providing this support. The question, of course, arises as to whether or not this threat to parental physical integrity may not have in itself precipitated the vulnerable adolescent's interest in finding a suprahuman source of support—a question that parents raised and used as a vehicle for self-criticism.

The members of the self-help group recognized that cults do "provide" a service to adolescents—vocational guidance. Within cults, intellectual demands are limited, and the work is often highly routinized with clearly defined goals in which competition is recognized only in terms of its providing support for a higher goal. Parents were often able to accept these strictures on a temporary basis. But as these limitations became permanent, parents were often driven into the paradoxical position of hoping that their children might be given a position of authority either within the cult or its subsidiary business enterprises, because their children might then gain management or executive skills which might then make them more receptive to exit counseling. A particularly striking aspect of the self-help group is the presence of this ambivalence among the members about the positive and negative aspects of the cult experience. It expressed and expresses itself in a continuing resolve to be in very close contact with their children despite a recognition that some separation might ultimately pave the way towards a reconciliation. It parallels the behavior of the cult member who, enraged at the adult world which he feels "deserted" him in his hour of need by not providing certainties and structure, proceeds to dramatize his separation from his parents by joining organizations which encourage regression and infantilization.

This parallelism between the behavior of the cult member and of the parents within the self-help group was highlighted in other ways as well. As parents described their child's departure from the "constricted" East Coast to the "golden" West, it was clear that parents and children alike had shared in the American myth of rebirth in California (Niederland, 1971). Likewise, the suddenness of the cult member's conversion is paralleled by the self-help group member's expectations of "deprograming." Deprograming was frequently discussed in almost magical terms. And much of the group's activity was devoted to an exploration of the risks of this procedure which has assumed heroic status for many. Indeed, the presence or potential for a magic solution to these complex problems served to diffuse some of the very real, intense self-exploration that occurred within the self-help group (a phenomenon noted in the individual context as well [Maleson, 1981]).

The use by cult groups of a wide variety of "front" organizations provided a particular focus for parental anger. In part, this may reflect an effort by parents to deal with their children's cult affiliation in less narcissistically damaging terms—"my children were taken away from me by deception." But their anguish cannot be simply dismissed with this observation. After all, when children make a profoundly limiting choice during an "ecologically oriented" weekend sponsored by an organization with an abstract, idealistic title without hint of a religious affiliation, parental anger is appropriate. It was most important for the group leader to see this intense parental concern as being much more than a response to a narcissistic injury. In this context, parents often presented deprograming as an appropriate solution to the problem of deceptive recruiting. In general, however, parents were appropriately cautious about undertaking any aggressive activity given their knowledge that they might be resisted by their child and that if it was unsuccessful it might end any contact between parent and child. The group leader was hard pressed as he helped parents to explore their feelings, options and to develop an awareness of the consequences of any activity.

Defining the role of the group leader/facilitator within the self-help group is difficult. In a very real sense, the task of the self-help group was defined primarily in terms of the member's relationship to someone else. The members of the self-help group were not patients. The attempt to relate to them within the traditional framework of therapist and patient would not be appropriate. Broadly speaking, the self-help group has gone through two phases. In the first session, the group members defined the group leader's task as giving them a magical formula which would enable them to extract their children from the cults. As has been noted, this demand for a magical solution may parallel their children's demand for a magical solution to the problems of life. It may reflect a part of the family process that provides an explanation to the cult member's initial vulnerability and his joining a cult. It may also reflect the basic assumptions operative in the early phases of any group. The group's initial task had been defined in terms of attempting to improve communication between parent and child and to share with one another the problems and feelings that cult membership engenders in the affected families. In order to refocus the group towards the exploration of the member's feelings and substitute exploration as a task in place of a magical solution for the problem of cult affiliation, the group leader defined the group's tasks into a threefold formulation: 1) our feelings about our children's entry into a cult, 2) our feelings about ourselves as the parents of cult members, and 3) problems that arise in communicating with a child still actively in a cult and in helping a child leave a cult.

By frustrating the group's demands for magical solutions, the leader provided a supportive framework in which members could deal with this extraordinarily traumatic event. In this context, all interpretations were cast into a group-as-a-whole mold, eg, "some parents seem to have always had a sense of their child's fragility" or "some parents appear to have withdrawn from constant conflict with their children over cult membership and have been able to reform their own lives without losing contact with their children." These interpretations refocused the group onto here-and-now issues, took cognizance of past familial dynamic issues, but did not attempt to explore intrapsychic issues. While these interpretations were/are not devoid of psychotherapeutic content or (hopefully) impact, they were consistently presented in a manner which expressed group concerns and fostered group cohesiveness. When members discussed matters of general political concern, the interpretive focus was always on bringing the discussion back to an exploration of problems in communication while only dealing with the group resistance in a nonjudgmental manner. Similarly, as the group leader is the keeper of the group's boundaries of time and place, the reluctance of certain members not to meet more frequently was discussed only in terms of group rather than individual resistances. Above all, when working with parents who have profound questions about their past effectiveness as parents, a group leader who exaggerates their doubts will ultimately be contratherapeutic by inhibiting their ability to exchange feelings in an open and relevant manner.

In working with a self-help group, the group leader must recognize that even though he is working with parents who have suffered a profound loss and disappointment, he is also working with parents who may be profoundly ambivalent about their future relationship with their children. While all parents ostensibly attended the group with the aim of finding the magic formula that would extract their child from a cult, it rapidly became clear that their actual agenda for attendance at the self-help group was to obtain support for their continued inaction. The self-help group thus provided a place in which they could contain their anxiety a la Winnicott (James 1982). Parents whose children were often dysfunctional prior to entry into a cult are/were, not surprisingly, skeptical as to how functional they would be after leaving a cult. Moreover, as cult affiliation appeared to be part of a pattern of hostile, dependent interaction between parent and child, the parents were not unreasonably concerned about whether their interaction might revert to its past status. By creating an atmosphere of openness, contradictory positions could be explored. By maintaining a stance of guarded optimism, the group members were allowed to voice their ambivalent feelings about their loss and their reluctance to pursue increased confrontations with their children in the future.

The role of the group leader–consultant–facilitator is complex. Neither the detachment of the psychoanalyst nor the hortatory stance of the religious leader is appropriate. The demands placed upon the group leader for support and compassion are great. A cotherapist may be useful simply to help the group leader(s) maintain a task orientation. Ultimately, the value of the self-help group is not determined by the number of children extracted from the cults but in the relief experienced by the group members. If parents can approach their children with a realistic awareness of their feelings and their children's limitations, then the groundwork is laid for other and more positive activity.

SUMMARY

Self-help groups have been created to help parents deal with the issue of their children's cult affiliation. This chapter discussed the issues raised by members during their attendance in a self-help group, the role of the group leader in facilitating the meetings of a self-help group, and the problems raised in the act of cult affiliation.

BIBLIOGRAPHY

James C: Bion's "containing" and Winnicott's holding in the context of the group matrix. Presented at the 1982 Conference of the AGPA, 1982.

Levine S: Cults and mental health: Clinical conclusions. *Can J Psychiatry* 1981;26:12.

Maleson FG: Dilemmas in the evaluation and management of religious cultists. *Am J Psych* 1981;138(7):925–930.

Niederland WG: The history and meaning of California: A psychoanalytic inquiry. *Psychoanal Q* 1971;40:485–490.

Networking:
A Service Delivery Approach
to the Treatment of Cult Members

PHILIP CUSHMAN

Too often within social service agencies, private practices, congregations, and schools those of us who work in the helping professions have been practicing the gentle art of the ostrich. We have been avoiding dealing with the noisy, sometimes messy lives of people caught in one of the most mystifying, complex, and ultimately significant issues of our time: coercive persuasion within a restrictive group. We are willing to talk about it, but we do not do much about it. Our offices continue to remain neat and pristine, relatively untouched by the struggle of forces we do not understand. One is moved to recall Andrew Marvell's (1962) famous stanza:

> The grave's a fine and private place,
> But none, I think, do there embrace.

We are the people paid to help. But in order to offer effective help, we must admit that we need to study, learn from regular people (often on the street), and perhaps most threatening of all, take an ethical stand. For many of us, this is unacceptable. In effect, we make ourselves "disappear" from the situation, and families seeking our help soon get the message. We can remove ourselves, but at what price to our society?

Fortunately, despite the seeming neglect of professionals, a widespread self-help network has grown up to help ex-cult members and families who have a member in a cult. This self-help network is one of the most remarkable, unofficial, and spontaneously generated organizations in the country today. For years now assistance for ex-cult members and families has depended almost entirely upon the dedication and knowledge of this small group of people. Those of us who work with young adults or who care about our younger generations owe this group of people an enormous debt of gratitude.

Yet, as remarkable as their efforts are, the self-help network presents certain problems. Everyone has limitations, even the most well-meaning and dedicated. The individuals who comprise this countercult movement are primarily parents of cultists or ex-cultists; they have specific limitations. For all their native talents, they are not trained as either therapists or community organizers. There are gaps in their skills and theoretical knowledge. Most lack degrees in related fields and therefore do not command the respect of the professional community. For the most part, they are not financially able to devote their full working hours to the field. They are vastly overworked and underpaid. For these reasons they are not able to organize their loose networks in a more structured, efficient manner.

Their greatest strength is also their most significant limitation: their enormous emotional investment. It is often overlaid with anger, guilt, fear, and ambivalence. Without the therapist's indispensible tool—the analysis of counter-transference—defense mechanisms such as projection, reaction formation, and denial often occur and greatly reduce the effectiveness of a counseling contact or the appropriateness of a referral. There also seems to be some tendency towards hero worship of some of the more charismatic "deprogramers," which further clouds the crucial judgments needed for an effective assessment/referral process.

A well-meaning endearing kind of chaos has developed. At times, the anticult network resembles a kind of psychologized cops-and-robbers "B" movie. The good guys and the bad guys are somewhat too distinct, and the excitement of the chase sometimes becomes more important than the resolution of the individual's problems. Lost in the thrill of rescue is the completion of essential but unglamorous tasks such as data collection about who, why, and when cult affiliation occurs.

In the absence of any administrative supervision, decisions are often made on an ad hoc basis. There is no ongoing clinical supervision with the enhancement of clinical skills among professionals or paraprofessionals vis-a-vis the whole nexus of questions that the act of cult affiliation raises. Clinical supervision is essential for those ex-cult members working as counselors because the distinction between personal issues and the professional task at hand often becomes blurred and the counseling itself directionless. Moreover, as the self-help network operates on a piecework model rather than on a sliding-scale agency model, the richer clients sometimes pay too much and the poorer clients get too little service, or none at all. The more difficult clinical decisions such as those involving rehabilitation, counseling, counselor assignments, or even the need for hospitalization are often inadequately made.

There is a continuing need for mental health professionals to learn from and cooperate with the anticult networks. Together, these two groups of workers, the professional (and paraprofessional) and the concerned laymen, could shape a coherent, unified delivery system that is based on a sound, sophisticated theoretical framework; one that is flexible yet with appropriate structure; one that is capable of accurate assessment/referral strategies; one that assures quality control through proper clinical supervision; and one that can properly outline and supervise the rehabilitation period after successful counseling has been achieved. This article discusses and outlines approaches in the formation of this vitally needed structure.

Even without major funding, a creative program can be formed by utilizing the resources already available in the established human care agencies, synagogues and churches, and schools. Expertise, office space, and public credibility are all indispensible to a smoothly run crisis-delivery system. Minor modifications of job descriptions and a willingness to be open to families in crisis is required.

Professionals should not attempt to take over the anticult network (they could not even if they wanted to). Rather, their role should be to provide consultation and supervision (when needed) and, above all, surround the "exit counseling" with a therapeutic plan for the entire family which can be guided to completion.

The field of restrictive cult groups and mass therapy organizations responsible for sudden personality change is enormously complex and varied. There are a number of distinctly different tasks to be done, each of which requires different skills, knowledge bases, and temperaments. No one can do them all, and no one needs to. The task is not to attempt to learn the whole field and to do everything within it. Rather, the task is simply to find a place within the system that feels comfortable and that is appropriate to one's training and interests.

The first step in the creation of any delivery system is a firm understanding of what is to be accomplished. This necessitates that every member of the delivery system have a personal overview of the field of restrictive group process, sudden personality change, coercive persuasion, and the developmental processes of late adolescence and young adulthood. Above all, the members of any delivery system must fully appreciate that the issue is not religion—it is not a disagreement over specific religious teachings—the issue is politics. It is a one of profound concern over the potential loss of personal autonomy and over the ability to make a free, informed choice (Stoner and Parke, 1977). Religious ideology is not an issue—countercult groups are not attacking religious liberty, they are advocating and fighting for it (Underwood and Underwood, 1979). They are deeply concerned that religious liberty is being taken away from our younger adults with increasing effectiveness and an alarming absence of public protest.

The countercult groups protest against the process by which a group recruits and indoctrinates new members. They protest against the use of coercive and fraudulent methods for recruitment that are unethical and possibly illegal. This recruitment process works to deny new members the free exercise of their rights and to force from them an ill-defined commitment that will restrict their lives and control their behavior for years to come. It is essential that members of any delivery system have a clear appreciation of these issues; without this understanding their own countertransference may lead them to dismiss the anguished, desperate people with whom they will be working (Halperin, 1982). Above all, they must have a full appreciation of what membership in a cult entails for the individual. Cult affiliation is not simply a shift in religious affiliation, but a political process which reforms the individual through a radical personality change that seems to bring on terrifying moments of disorientation, hallucinations, delusions, panic, guilt, shame, and paranoia (Singer, 1979). It can force a deep regressive, narcissistic-like dependency (see Kohut, 1977).

The members of a delivery team must appreciate that the cult member is often a young adult, albeit with the anxiety that is pandemic within the transition from adolescence to adulthood. Within our society a cacaphony of external answers are proposed by self-appointed gurus, messiahs, political leaders, advertisers, and (even) psychotherapists. With this welter of "information" and the absence of structures and ceremonies within the society to aid in this transition, it is not surprising that the young adult often feels confused, helpless, betrayed, and alone. These powerful existential moments appear because of or are coupled with an intensely personal experience of loneliness, confusion, or loss of meaning.

This combination creates a synergistic effect that multiplies and personalizes the impact of such a moment (Underwood and Underwood, 1979).

It is at such a moment that young adults are most vulnerable to the seductive lure of magical cures and the absolutist claims of spiritual technologies. The experienced cult recruiter has been trained to recognize this pivotal moment and to use it to the cult's advantage. The young adult's despair moves him to say yes to activities he would normally refuse. During intensive group experiences, the utilization of severe environmental and emotional manipulation forces the individual into a state of suggestibility and emotional dependence. The cult calls this a conversion; others call it information disease (Conway and Siegelman, 1978). It is similar to what Lifton (1961) has called thought reform and Meerloo (1956) has called menticide.

The cult forces a commitment to the group which allows them to exclude the least hint of ambiguity from their thoughts. In the tradition of American consumerism, this commitment functions as a magic detergent which washes the individual clean of the necessity for change, growth, and conflict resolution.

Above all, it must be understood that the cult member has undergone a process in which "unconditional" friendship has been used to subvert the member's ideas, opinions, family relationships, and perceptions of the past and present. The cult member has been seductively introduced into a system that required him to bend and twist his behavior and then his inner experience to conform to the requirements of the new reference group: the cult (Stoner and Parke, 1977). In this context the offer of support and assistance by a mental health professional may be seen as a threat to his entire existence and is usually met with skepticism, distance, and even rage.

Any professionally organized service delivery system for the families of cult members and for the ex-members must be based upon voluntary "exit" counseling. Voluntary exit counseling may be defined as an attempt to give the individual the opportunity to think for himself again (Rudin and Rudin, 1980). Exit counseling is not a coercive attempt to change an individual's religious convictions. Rather, it is an attempt to assist the individual in remembering his own convictions and reawakening his critical faculties in an atmosphere in which pertinent information is available. The individual is given the opportunity to explore in an open and noncoercive manner of the boundary that separates the beliefs of the group from those of the individual. It is a time to reown the self (Underwood and Underwood, 1979).

Several things may aid in the progress and process of exit counseling. The presence of parents, and when appropriate, siblings, other family members, or even close friends may greatly assist the cult member to recall his precult life. Their presence and love serve to undermine the cult's insistence that no one loves the individual as genuinely and purely as his new "family"—that all "outside" people are by definition bad, mean, unenlightened, satanic, demonic, etc. The fact of just being separated from the milieu of the cult aids in the process of liberation (as does a good night's sleep and a nutritious meal). Moreover, accurate information about the real behavior of the cult, its activities and those of its leader (financial, sexual, or drug-involved) may help the individual question the validity of the cult's claims to infallibility and perfection.

Within the exit counseling process, the cult member is helped to realize that his whole support system has become tied into the cult, that it has become coterminous with his life. This is a frightening realization. The individual may panic, become overtly angry, or even abusive upon realizing the extent of his dependency on the cult. Thus, it is essential that any exit counseling be conducted in a calm, gentle, and compassionate atmosphere. During the period of cult membership, the individual lives with the fantasy that he can achieve perfection and that the usual concerns and problems of "banal," uninitiated people are irrelevant, that he is somehow transcendent or superhuman. Exit counseling gives the individual the opportunity to regain his humanity—the pain as well as the joy. This may not be an altogether pleasing prospect; mortality takes getting used to. What is often so remarkable is the individual's striving for health and humanity and how often the individual chooses the rough, uneven path of fallible individuality to the desperate fantasy compounded out of magic.

A delivery system must offer more than voluntary exit counseling services to the cult member. It must also offer both services and appropriate referrals to the family prior to and after the initial exit counseling sessions.

A proposed system could be described as offering both horizontal and vertical services. Services should be offered to a number of different persons who have differing relationships to the cult member (vertical services), and these services should extend over an undetermined period of time (horizontal services). The more complete the variety of services offered, the more probable the successful outcome.

Given the above theoretical issues and behavioral goals, it is possible to discuss the actual shape of a proposed system. The following plans are adapted, in part, from the activities of the unofficial delivery system used by the countercult network in northern California.

Figure 22-1 is a pictorial representation of a proposed voluntary exit counseling system. The left side of the chart depicts the process to be followed if the group in question is known to the countercult network and information indicates that it is restrictive and controlling. The right side of the chart demonstrates how to proceed if the group is not well known to the network or if the group uses some form of coercion that is significantly less controlling than those used by the more widely known and/or destructive groups. There is some tendency for borderline groups to become increasingly restrictive. So it is possible that the left side of the chart will become increasingly significant in the years to come.

The key element to a successful exit counseling delivery system is knowing the strengths and limitations of its workers and having the power within the system to make and carry out those decisions that will best utilize those strengths. Therefore, it is crucial to have one person supervising the administrative process from beginning to end.

To facilitate a smooth decision-making process, the plethora of initial phone calls from distraught parents or friends can be best handled by channeling them through a central switchboard (Figure 22-1a). If this is impossible, referrals to that central phone should be made as soon as possible. In this way, only the person assigned to this task of intake needs to have a comprehensive picture of the entire system.

This intake person must have an understanding of the goals and abilities of the system, for he will be making crucial administrative decisions. Decisions such as when to act, where to assign the case, and whom to assign as counselor, if and/or when to change counselors, and what to establish as a fee are ultimately this person's responsibilities.

Unfortunately, in most informal networks, this position is either shared by

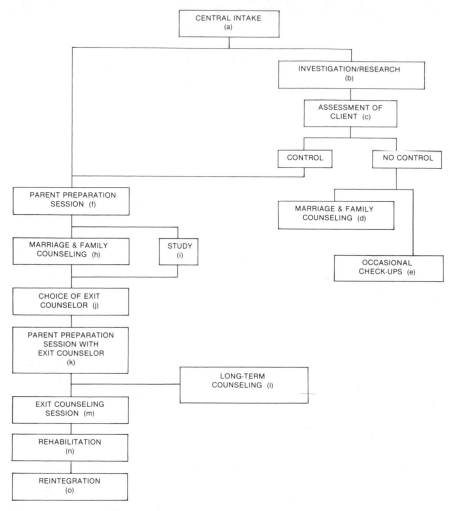

Figure 22-1

several people or people with the network act as if no one has either responsibility or authority. In any event, the client may suffer because of a duplication of effort, administrative confusion, and divergent styles or methods. Moreover, the very anguish of the family and their sense of immediacy may stir up the latent personality clashes within the network or foster disagreements over possible "incompetence" or strategic mistakes. The end result is an inconsistent process that hinders rather than enhances the feelings of trust and confidence between family members and the counselor. It is these feelings of trust and confidence that will make it easier for the cult member to engage in the process of listening and ultimately thinking for himself. The confusion that led to the act of cult affiliation should not be replicated in the exit counseling process. The less intrusive the administrative process, the more probably successful the outcome of the counseling process.

After the initial call is received and the intake information gathered, the intake person must make the first of many decisions. Usually, the initial call has been made by a parent or a friend of the new cult member. The intake person must assess if the information received from the caller is accurate and sufficiently complete. If the information is incomplete, the caller should be asked to gather more information and perhaps to read material relating to the field and call again.

If, after helping the caller to clarify and refine his information about the group and its relationship to the new group member, central intake may decide that the network's informational system simply does not know enough about the group to begin the process of exit counseling. At that time, the intake person will then place the case on the right side of the chart, and assign an investigator/researcher to learn more about the group, both from study and personal observation (Figure 22-1b). This action preserves the intellectual and ethical integrity of the network. A group (and there are perhaps 3000 groups classifiable as cults) should not be questioned simply because of its adherence to a certain set of eccentric beliefs, but only if, during research, the group is found to use deception and mind control as a means of recruitment and indoctrination or if its practices appear to put the individual in serious jeopardy.

Second, the central intake then should assign a counselor to assess the nature of the relationship between the group member and the group (Figure 22-1c). If possible, this should be done with the group member's knowledge and agreement. Past experience has shown that if the group does not appear to be heavily controlling, or if the control is more sophisticated (less overtly restrictive), the group member will usually agree to a meeting with a counselor without much hesitation. Even if the group member does not agree to meet and talk with a counselor, an informal assessment can be done through observation of the group's actions and its interaction with the group member. One important issue to clarify is whether or not the new group member can still distinguish between his own personal beliefs and the belief/value system of the group. A second important issue is the ability of the new group member to question/evaluate behavioral patterns within the group and their consequences or ideological statements of the group and their relationship to the group's overt belief system.

If, after the investigation and assessment steps, the counselors decide that the group does not appear to practice mind-control techniques or deception—that the member is not "controlled"—then the counselors may recommend family and/or individual therapy (Figure 22-1d). The counselor may also recommend that the member meet with him for periodic consultations (Figure 22-1e). If the central intake and counselors decide that the group might exercise unethical control over the group member then, after consultation with the investigators, the intake person should schedule a parent preparation session (Figure 22-1f). The procedure would then continue according to the left side of the chart. Obviously, these decisions can be made more rapidly when the group is well known to the network.

Timing is of the essence in scheduling a parent preparation session. It is determined by the individual cult member's personal crisis, the current living situation of the cult member, and the actual political and/or social climate within the cult. This counseling session is usually, but not always, conducted by the parent of an ex-cult member (preferably from the same group) and is an indispensable part of the process. It is here that parents, friends, or spouse learn first-hand what options are available, how successful they might be, and what is actually involved in arranging for voluntary exit counseling. In effect, a quick course in assertiveness training is given. The parents must also learn about the important part that hope and love will play in this process. If this session goes well and the important lessons are learned, then the ultimate success of the process is greatly enhanced. This first parent preparation session may last up to six hours. It often demonstrates the enormous value of the nonprofessional in the network. The entire process of exit counseling depends heavily upon this first session.

The person (professional or nonprofessional) who conducts this session should then meet with the central administrator. Together they should decide on how to proceed. It may become clear that the family members are experiencing so much family or marital strife at this time that they are unable to be of help to the cult member. Therefore, a recommendation may be made to become involved in family or marital therapy (Figure 22-1h). The process is then delayed until such time as they can act in a mutually supportive and united fashion. It may be determined that the family is too confused about the issues to be helpful; in that case the recommendation may be to wait until they clarify their positions. It may even be decided that for reasons outside the family's control, ie, conditions within the group or the emotional health of the cult member, the most effective strategy may be to do nothing except wait for a more propitious time.

If the family is prepared and ready, the time is right to proceed to the assignment of the exit counselor (Figure 22-1j). Often, due to the scarcity of skilled counselors, this crucial determination of timing is made without proper forethought or clinical input. Moreover, a proper match between counselor, family, and group member is an indispensable element in the process.

A meeting should be set up between the counselor, the family, and (if possible) the parent preparation counselor (Figure 22-1k). It is time to get to know one another, to give the counselor as much helpful information about the cult member and the cult as possible. It is also a time to plan strategy: 1) how to locate the group member (restrictive cults often attempt to hide members from their families), 2) how to contact the cult member, and 3) how to talk to the cult member in such a manner that he will voluntarily agree to meet with the counselor (hence the importance of assertiveness training). By the time the family leaves this session, they should have a well-thought out, rehearsed plan in which they feel confident and to which they feel commited. They should understand what options are available if events do not go according to plan, what their alternatives are, and what the future may be. They often leave feeling frightened, excited, sad, angry, anxious, and hopeful.

It may be determined that a single, marathon exit counseling session is not appropriate intervention for a particular individual or cult. Shorter sessions over a longer interval may be prescribed (Figure 22-1l). The factors to be considered are the age, marital status, emotional status of the cult member, and even the nature of the group itself. All of this must be fully explained by the professionals involved since mutual agreement by the family and the voluntary compliance of the cult member is, of course, necessary.

If the strategy chosen is a single marathon session, and the cult member voluntarily agrees to appear (and does, indeed, appear), then all concerned will be involved in one of the most emotionally and intellectually challenging experiences of their lives (Figure 22-1m). If the process proceeds to this point and the cult member is engaged in a caring, sincere dialogue with a trained exit counselor, an estimated 75% success rate has been obtained in northern California. Thus, the most difficult tasks involved preparing and setting up the counseling session(s).

During the counseling sessions, the goal is to help the cult member to reactivate his critical faculties: to listen, to evaluate, to think. If the cult member (now ex-member) decides to leave the cult, it is time to celebrate and to plan for the immediate future. Although the ex-cult member will feel moments of great relief and even exhilaration, he may also experience moments of confusion, anger at the group, fear of retaliation, panic at the sense of having fallen from grace, depersonalization, identity diffusion, and possibly paranoia (Singer, 1979). Weeks and months after leaving a cult, ex-members may be buffered by rage, guilt, sorrow, and fear for/from those still in the cult. A sense of isolation and distinctiveness may persist as well as the continued loss of intellectual function.

The ex-cult member is leaving behind all that has been precious and valuable to him for months or even years. Friends, beliefs, work—his entire world is effectively left behind. It is an extraordinarily painful decision to make. Thus, the rehabilitation period becomes crucial and must be planned with skill and care.

Rehabilitation should ideally last about four weeks and be a period in which the ex-member is able to think, talk to other ex-members, study, rest, and eat healthy food. Above all, it is a time to process the experiences of cult life and exit counseling. It should be a time to balance things out and to think about the future. It requires a protective environment because the ex-cult member is often in an extraordinarily vulnerable position as old problems resurface (problems which may have made him initially vulnerable to cult affiliation). After all, the real world which is always difficult to face becomes especially trying to those who have experienced a magic "escape." There are also times when the seductiveness of instant answers and the desire to create a perfect world with an immortal future become enticing even to the person who knows their price.

Without a thoughtful, professionally supervised rehabilitation plan, the ex-cult member is at risk of reaffiliation. Unfortunately, there are few adequate rehabilitation centers. They are expensive. Resources may not be available to the family. However, if the rehabilitation plan is treated as an important part of the entire process and there is continuing administrative and therapeutic involvement, recidivism can be reduced. Above all, the family must be helped to recognize that the ex-cult member needs to be involved in the rehabilitation process and that the simplistic answer of coercive persuasion does not necessarily explain the fact of cult affiliation.

The final step in rehabilitation is the reintegration of the ex-cult member into the outside world (Figure 22-1o). During this period, the problems that may have initially made the individual vulnerable to cult entrapment are faced. Issues that relate to the individual's spiritual quest, religious needs, family system, career decisions, and social and sexual relationships may require exploration. The appropriate referral to clergy, psychotherapist, guidance counselor, or group is necessary and should not be made on a whim.

Throughout this period of reintegration, the ex-cult member needs to work with a caretaking figure who respects his worth as an individual and who respects his ability to grow towards health. This includes a respect for the idealism that led to the act of cult affiliation and for whatever skills were gained during the period of cult affiliation. If the ex-cult member is not able to integrate this aspect of his past into his present, the ex-cult member may continue to live within a restrictive framework and may even be vulnerable to other forms of restrictive group experiences.

352

SUMMARY

This chapter presents a schema for the formation of a network employing professionals and nonprofessionals to assist individuals to leave restrictive groups and to help those families in which a member remains within a restrictive group. It reflects the experience in a particular place and time. It is not the final word. It is an attempt to conceptualize the needs of cult-members, their families, and the needs of those individuals who have fought to reown their autonomy.

BIBLIOGRAPHY

Conway F, Siegelman J: *Snapping: America's Epidemic of Sudden Personality Change.* Philadelphia, JB Lippincott, 1978.

Halperin D: *Issues in the Development of a Training Program for a Cult Treatment Program.* 1982, unpublished manuscript.

Kohut H: *The Restoration of the Self.* New York, International Universities Press, 1977.

Lifton RJ: Thought Reform and the Psychology of Totalism. New York, WW Norton, 1961.

Marvell A: To his coy mistress, in Abrams MH (ed): *The Norton Anthology of English Literature.* New York, WW Norton, 1962, vol 1.

Meerloo JAM: *The Rape of the Mind.* New York, Grosset & Dunlap, 1956.

Rudin AJ, Rudin MR: *Prison or Paradise: The New Religious Cults.* Philadelphia, Fortress Press, 1980.

Singer MT: Coming out of the cults. *Psychol Today* January 1979;12–1:72–82.

Stoner C, Parke JA: *All God's Children: The Cult Experience—Salvation or Slavery.* Radnor, PA, Chilton, 1977.

Underwood B, Underwood B: *Hostage to Heaven.* New York, Clarkson N. Potter, 1979.

The Atypical Dissociative Disorder:
Some Etiological, Diagnostic, and Treatment Issues*

MARVIN F. GALPER

I n 1980 the American Psychiatric Association published the third edition of its *Diagnostic and Statistical Manual of Mental Disorders* (DSM-III). The new diagnostic category of Atypical Dissociative Disorder (300.15) appears for the first time in this edition. The DMS-III provides the following description in terms of this previously unrecognized form of psychological disturbance:

> This is a residual category to be used for individuals who appear to have a Dissociative Disorder but do not satisfy the criteria for a specific Dissociative Disorder. Examples include trance-like states, derealization unaccompanied by depersonalization, and those more prolonged dissociative states that may occur in persons who have been subjected to periods of prolonged and intense coercive persuasion (brainwashing, thought reform, and indoctrination while the captive of terrorists or cultists).

The focus of this chapter is on the dissociative disorder induced by the extremist religious cult environment and is based on the writer's clinical experience in diagnosis and treatment of extremist religious cult members over the past ten years. A general consensus has existed among the mental health professionals for some time with regard to the existence of psychopathological altered states of consciousness. The mental state produced by excessive alcohol intake or other such forms of chemical imbalance in the body system can be mentioned as examples. There is also general agreement with regard to the existence of benign

---

*This report is an integration of the following papers presented at professional meetings: The Cult Indoctrinee: A New Clinical Syndrome, presented at the June 1976 meeting of the Tampa–St. Petersburg–Clearwater Psychiatric Society; Indoctrination Methods of the Unification Church, presented at the annual meeting of the California State Psychological Assocation, March 1977, in Los Angeles; and Extremist Religious Cults and Today's Youth, presented at the International Conference on the Effects on Physical and Mental Health of New Totalitarian Religions, November 1981, in Bonn, West Germany.

trance states such as the state of exaltation very likely experienced by mystics such as Moses, Theresa of Avila, or the state of artistic ferment of William Blake while immersed in the creation of his great literary productions. In the interest of maximum diagnostic clarity, therefore, it becomes important to indicate clearly that in this context the psychopathological consequences of cult indoctrination are the focus of attention.

ETIOLOGICAL CONSIDERATIONS

Both sociocultural and individual factors are of relevance in the emergence of this clinical syndrome. Placed in the broadest historical context, it is significant to note that proliferation of extremist cultist phenomena has been characteristic of periods of social upheaval throughout history. For many young Americans, the extremist cult milieu offered a ready made pseudo-identity which obviated the need for intense inner struggle which is part of the normal individuation and maturation process.

A cursory review of the gamut of dissociative disorders listed in DSM-III indicates that relatively consistent group environmental factors are a strikingly more significant causative factor with regard to the cult-induced dissociative disorder in comparison with the other categories. For this reason it would seem appropriate to include some description of the cult interactional pattern which induces the latter pathological mental state within the context of this paper. This writer's experience has indicated that clear-cut intercult variations exist in both the intensity of coercive persuasion techniques employed and the degree of separation effected between the cult member and his previously established matrix of social support systems. Based on patients' verbal reports, the indoctrination methods of the Unification Church clearly fall towards the high-intensity, high-separation end of the continuum. The following section reports the results of a series of individual interviews conducted with 65 patients in the 19 to 26 age range who are former Unification Church members.

The focus of interview inquiry was on the personal indoctrination experiences of these persons. Of relevance in this regard is the theoretical framework evolved by Schein (1961) to account for modifications in individual frame of reference which are effected within a relatively closed social system. In his study of Chinese Communist "brainwashing" techniques, Schein developed the concept of coercive persuasion. Schein sees many parallels to Chinese coercive persuasion methods in non-Communist institutional settings. Shor's concept (1959) of the generalized reality orientation is also of theoretical relevance. This concept is defined as "the usual state of consciousness characterized by the mobilization of a structured frame of reference in the background of attention which supports, interprets and gives meaning to all experiences." According to Shor, any state in which the generalized reality orientation has faded to relatively nonfunctional awareness may be termed a trance state.

Unification recruitment is carried out by established members who seek out and make contact with young adults in the community. The potential recruit is invited to attend a dinner at one of the urban Unification residential centers. After acceptance of the invitation and arrival at the center, the potential new member is met by cult recruiters who relate to the "target" individual in an extremely emotionally seductive fashion, showering the person with an extraordinary degree of attention and what is perceived as unparalleled warmth combined with total unconditional acceptance. The unusual emotional spontaneity of the cult recruiter frequently leads to the establishment of an emotional bond with the new recruit. Reports received from ex-Unification Church members with regard to their experiences as active recruiters during their period of group membership yields some interesting insights into this phenomenon. The apparent spontaneity to which the naive recruit responds is frequently, in actuality, a highly contrived and deliberate pseudo-spontaneity. Interviews with ex-members which focus on this issue indicate that the recruiter is acting out a highly stereotyped and time-worn manipulative pattern which is repeated in a relatively mechanical fashion over a long series of recruitment overtures.

At the conclusion of the center dinner he is invited to participate in a weekend experience in an isolated rural setting. At the conclusion of the weekend experience recruits are invited to stay on at the camp for a week-long training session. There are no hard statistical data currently available regarding the percentage of weekend attendants who remain for the additional week of indoctrination. However, study participants have provided informal estimates which average in the 80% to 95% range. This patient group also estimated that approximately 90% to 95% of those who remain for the week training session go on to become full-time Unification Church members. It should be noted, however, that there is some controversy in the research literature with regard to the effectiveness of Unification indoctrination methods.

Study participants experienced a radical alteration in ideological perspective and life-style subsequent to indoctrination. Rejection of previously cathected education and career goals was a consistently found feature. Social isolation from the mainstream of community involvement which was initiated in the rural camp later became institutionalized into a segregated existence in a series of urban Unification residential centers. Psychic and physical energies became exclusively invested in cult ideology and pursuits. Primary activities were the recruitment of new members and fund-raising in public settings, in marked contrast to the orientation of conventional established churches. In the interviewed group of cult members, an extraordinary narrowing and intensification in the phenomenological field of conscious attention was the most striking feature noted. Reduced cognitive flexibility was evidenced by varying degrees of difficulty in adapting to novel situations. Narrowing and blunting in the range of consciously experienced affect was also apparent.

Unification members appear to be governed by the internalized concept of "heavenly deception" in interaction with the general public. This concept is based on the view that the community at large is dominated by Satan and is, therefore, deceptive. Consequently, it is held, God must rely on deception in winning souls for his perfect family, which is seen as synonymous with the Unification Church. Study of social influence techniques utilized in congruence with the "heavenly deception" concept indicates that indoctrination takes place within a framework of massive psychological manipulation. Withholding of key reality data emerges as a major feature in this process. Unification members are committed to the goal of total conversion of potential recruits contacted. However, this goal remains a hidden agenda during interaction with recruits in initial street encounters, later at the urban cult center, and still later at the rural camp or farm. The target individual is presented with a paucity of straightforward reality input. He generally has no awareness that he is participating in training activities of an aggressive proselytizing religious organization until the conclusion of the weekend rural camp experience. He is not overtly presented with clear intellectual or behavioral options for conscious reflection and deliberation. This organizational strategy sharply reduces the recruit's ability to choose to withdraw from the cult environment.

The newcomer who accepts the invitation to dinner at the urban residential center finds himself in a large and rather pleasant home setting. There are no signs on the exterior building facade or on the interior walls which identify the center as property of the Unification Church. Unification members relate to the target individual in an extremely warm and interested manner and convey the misperception that their motivation is primarily social. The content of their verbal communication tends to evoke mental associations of familial secure memories in the potential recruit. Subliminal evocation of imagery linked to childhood trust-laden experiences tends to relax the vigilance customarily experienced in unfamiliar social settings. At the Washington Street Center in San Francisco, the newcomer group is presented with an after-dinner slide show of the rural training camp. This isolated setting is one of the major Unification indoctrination facilities. It is described to the guests as "our farm." Slides which are presented portray recreational activities such as group singing sessions or volleyball games in progress. The overall impression created is of a recreational camp populated by an extraordinarily affectionate, loving, and cohesive group of adults. At the conclusion of the urban center evening the potential recruit group is urged to spend the weekend at "the farm."

Study data indicate that, for this patient population, immersion in the intense rural camp resulted in a fading of the generalized reality orientation. In their investigations of indirect suggestion in clinical hypnosis, Erickson et al (1977) state that construction of the attentional field creates an unstable equilibrium in individual consciousness. They find that, in this psychic condition, usual conscious sets can be "depotentiated" and bypassed with relative ease. In his analysis of the hypnotic relationship, Haley (1958) maintains that trance behavior takes place when the hypnotist has control over the relationship and the relationship cannot be clearly defined by the subject. In descriptions of the camp environment provided by study participants, the above-mentioned interactional features emerge in central significance.

At the farm the recruit finds himself in a state of geographic and psychological encapsulation which appears to facilitate the development of an ongoing hypnotic trance state. The newcomer is immersed in a constant round of highly focused and emotion-laden group activities. He experiences a marked narrowing and intensification in the focus of conscious attention. A high level of affective arousal is generated and maintained. The highly structured program permits no leisure or private time to engage in personal reflection. Thus the newcomer has minimal opportunity to evaluate or integrate his experiences within the context of his previously established frame of reference. This difficulty is increased by geographical separation from his accustomed environment and matrix of relationships. A heightened level of suggestibility is developed which undergoes gradual intensification during the course of indoctrination.

The image of a harmonious and loving family which was introduced at the urban center is now powerfully reinforced at the verbal level and also via frequent displays of what would appear to be nondiscriminatory affection. Frequently scheduled group singing in unison fosters the development of an extraordinarily rapid and powerful emotional bonding between the recruit and his newly found "family." Development of the trance state and concomitant diminishment in personal judgment lead to greater vulnerability in primitive wishes in the psyche of the recruit group. At the same time, the camp training staff repetitively reinforces the Unification concept of "unity." The illusions that total gratification of affectional and security needs is available at the reality level within the confines of the "farm" environment is fostered. Depth interview data in this study reveal that emphasis on the "unity" theme evoked and intensified archaic desires for interpersonal merger or fusion in the patient group studied.

Patients interviewed report that a remarkable degree of ideological and behavioral conformity is achieved in the majority of the newcomer group by the conclusion of the weekend experience. It would appear that, on the preconscious level, recruit conformity motives were powerfully reinforced by the anxiety-laden perception that rejection by this new "family" would lead to loss of the earlier mention fantasized gratifications.

During the course of the weekend and subsequent week-long indoctrination experience, indirect suggestions were conveyed to the newcomer group. Suggestions are conveyed at interspersed intervals and are perceived by the indoctrinee at the threshold level of awareness. Internalized suggestions compound and coalesce within the recruit psyche with a cumulative reality restructuring effect. In the majority of cases, massive coercive persuasion influences resulted in the establishment of a radical new frame of reference within the brief time period of a weekend rural experience. One sees markedly altered perceptions of self, the external environment, and the individual's relation to the external environment.

At the conclusion of a week of indoctrination, patients treated were firmly entrenched in the view that Sun Myung Moon was the messiah, that their families and the community at large were dominated by Satan, and that spiritual growth was exclusively available to Unification Church members. These individuals abandoned previously held educational and career goals. They thereupon immersed themselves with extraordinary intensity in recruitment and fund-raising activities for the Unification Church.

DIAGNOSTIC ISSUES

In reviewing the overall pattern of symptomatology evidenced in the cult-induced dissociative disorder, identity loss emerges as a significant feature. One finds that coercive persuasion indoctrination methods, in both the religious and political context, deliberately mobilize an "identity crisis" in seeking to achieve as profound and rapid identification with the group ideology as possible. One finds interesting parallels between the just-described Unification Church indoctrination techniques and the coercion persuasion methods which were utilized in the North Korean prisoner of war camps in the attempt to effect "prisoner conversion" to Communist ideology. Both the prison camp captive and the cult indoctrinee are led to believe that their total previous life pattern had been totally wasted and misled, in that they had previously been completely unconscious of the truth that should embody their central mission in life. The truth, of course, is alternatively couched in terms of the enlightenment and salvation associated with Communist society on the one hand, and with spiritual salvation flowing from exclusive proximity to the Divine Being on the other hand. In the acute identity crisis which is precipitated, the indoctrinee rejects his previously established identity and then feels compelled to adopt the world view of his new mentors in order to escape the acutely painful experience of nothingness felt in the psychological vacuum thereby created.

Clinical experience has indicated that psychological regression is the most salient feature of the cult-induced altered state of consciousness. One sees a diminution in "secondary process" kinds of thinking accompanied by an intensification of "primary process" thought in persons suffering from this syndrome. Reduced capacities for effective rational thought, in part evidenced by diminution in independent decision-making skills, is frequently seen in active members of extremist religious cults. Independent judgment is also impaired in terms of reduced capacity to form realistic appraisals of persons and events. Limitations in cognitive flexibility emerge as well, as seen in varying degrees of difficulty in adaptation to novel situations.

Intensified and amplified infantile feelings of infantile fusion are another significant dimension of the overall regressive patterns. Former cult members have reported in the context of psychotherapeutic sessions that while immersed in the cultic milieu they had been involved in group prayer activities which involved hymn singing or mantra chanting characterized by a frequency and intensity far beyond what is generally experienced in established conventional religion. These patients report that they experienced a sustained sense of group intimacy and exaltation during such activities far beyond what they had known in their life prior to or subsequent to the period of active cult membership. The extraordinary sense of profound emotional gratification experienced at such times seems to stem from the evocation of powerful infantile feelings of fusion having their origins in the earliest preweaning phase of the mother–child relationship. Clinical evidence, therefore, strongly suggests that the regressive impact of the cult environment stems in part from the powerful and sustained gratification of needs which take their origin in the earliest period of life, when the infant's sense of bliss in union with its mother has not yet been diminished by a budding sense of developing individuality. Depth interviews with these persons reveal additional dimensions of intensified infantile thought process. Many of these patients experience an intensification of magical omnipotent thinking in terms of their perceptions of cult leaders and/or themselves, specifically in terms of tremendous "spiritual" powers.

Extraordinary narrowing and intensification in the phenomenological field of conscious attention is another significant feature of this disorder. Psychic energies are almost exclusively invested in cultic ideology and associated fantasies. The conscious experience of the individual is laden with "programed-in" cult affects. For this patient group, interactions become dominated by powerful needs to recruit others which vary in blatancy depending on the cult member's level of social sophistication. Narrowing and blunting in the range of consciously experienced affect was also apparent. Dramatic postindoctrination changes frequently occurred in the quality of relationships with family, previous friends, and the community at large. Concerned nuclear family members of these persons very frequently report that their spouse or child displayed a loss of previous capacities for compassion or tenderness following involvement in the cult environment.

It is of major significance that the social norms of the various cult groups studied consistently devalued the development of personal individuality and uniqueness. Cult members who comprise this patient population had, without exception, internalized these norms and consequently experienced both a loss of autonomy and delay in personal growth during their period of immersion in the cult subculture. At the same time, it is significant to note that for a few individuals who had been suffering an acute psychotic decompensation immediately prior to cult indoctrination, the cultic milieu had a reconstitutive effect in terms of resulting in a marked improvement in their capacity for reality testing. For these extremely disturbed individuals, the cult structured environment provided them with a group ego and obviated their need for autonomy and independent decision-making, substantially reducing the amount of experienced stress.

TREATMENT CONSIDERATIONS

Two phases can be delineated in the psychotherapeutic treatment of the active cult member who is suffering from a dissociative disorder. The goal of the first treatment phase is release of the person from the pathological trance state and facilitating restoration of the generalized reality orientation. In the second treatment phase the therapeutic goal is support of the person in achieving a successful readjustment to the community mainstream subsequent to his rejection of the prior cultic involvement.

In the first phase of treatment, clinical experience has shown that marathon treatment sessions tend to be considerably more effective in release from the dissociative state than the traditional once- or twice-a-week variety of office psychotherapy. The therapist treating this patient population finds resistance to involvement in therapy as a very characteristic pattern. Cult members tend to stereotype the clinician as a member of the "unenlightened" mainstream community.

In this context, it seems appropriate to mention some of the professional equipment which, in this writer's opinion, facilitates effectiveness for the therapist engaged in the treatment of active religious cult members. A thorough knowledge of the belief system, specialized jargon, and group interactional pattern of the specific cult will aid substantially in the establishment of therapist–patient rapport and in initiation of meaningful dialogue. Communicating with these patients in their own esoteric jargon tends to conflict with their own stereotyped expectations and results in greater receptivity to the mental health professional who seeks to provide treatment assistance. Belief in a higher power is a central feature in the overall psychological orientation of the cult member. For the psychotherapist who does entertain a personal conviction in the existence of a higher power, conveyance of that basic fact to the patient will also, I feel, tend to promote rapport. Needless to say, the code of ethics of the major mental health professions explicitly states that the therapist cannot tamper with the religious beliefs held by his patients. At the same time, successful treatment of the active cult member, in the great majority of cases, results in that person's voluntary departure from the cult. Therapeutic release from the dissociative disorder is almost invariably accompanied by a rejection of the cult belief system which the patient had previously internalized.

In the second phase of psychotherapy, it is important to note that many of the cult member's needs were met during his period of active conversion, albeit not in a fashion conducive to his or her personal growth and development towards maturity. These persons had experienced an ideological commitment and an intense sense of the community which they now have left behind them. As mentioned earlier, they had experienced powerfully gratifying group intimacy within the cult which was facilitated by a mass denial of individual differences combined with an extraordinary sameness in belief and action shared with their cultic peers. Some depressive feelings stemming from a sense of grief associated with loss of this intense involvement is consequently frequently found. Therapeutic assistance with this issue involves clarification of the distinction between regressive intimacy, which involves the gratification of infantile fusion fantasies, and mature intimacy which requires successful acceptance of and accommodation to separate individualities. Providing opportunities for the working through of grief feelings in the therapeutic sessions is an important part of this second phase.

The phenomenon of "floating" reported by ex-cult members during this readjustment phase is of extraordinary clinical interest, in that it appears to reflect transient returns to the cultic dissociative mental state. "Floating" episodes, which tend to occur primarily during the earlier phase of rehabilitation, are generally characterized by the reentry into consciousness of cult mantra or hymns in an automatized fashion and in a manner which is experienced as outside of the conscious volition of the patient. The sense of euphoria which had been connected to these activities during the time of cult membership is transiently reexperienced at such moments. The patient during this transitional period is struggling to reestablish mastery of "secondary process' thought modes within his psyche. Cognitive impairment continues to be an impediment for varying lengths of time for such individuals, in part dependent on their level of basic ego strength and the amount of support available to them in the community. Problems with attention and recall are frequently reported. Former cult members who resume their university education frequently find that their ability to function intellectually in the classroom is significantly reduced in comparison with their precultic learning capacities, particularly within the first six months or year subsequent to their exit from the cult.

Former cult members frequently need professional assistance in the establishment of long-range educational and career goals. In order to gain a sense of intellectual mastery with regard to the period of cult membership, such patients can profit from insight provided with regard to the process of coercive indoctrination, both in general terms and also in terms of their own personal experience. The former cult member is in acute need of a meaningful social support system as he struggles to readjust to the community. The immediate family is, of course, a powerful potential source of ongoing emotional support. Family counseling which seeks to maximize mature communication, combined with a sense of family solidarity, can be extremely beneficial during this transitional period. Participation in an ongoing group of former cult members which meets on a regular basis can also serve as a powerful source of empathic support for the former cult member.

SUMMARY

This chapter represents an initial exploratory attempt to delineate some etiological, diagnostic, and treatment issues related to the cult-induced variety of atypical dissociative disorder. Findings are relevant from the broad sociopsychological perspective of social conformity influences within a relatively closed social system. There is a need for further research into situational and intrapsychic variables which interact in evocation of the altered state of consciousness. Multidisciplinary social science investigations which incorporate clinical, sociological, and anthropological perspectives are likely to be particularly fruitful in the future study of such trance phenomena.

BIBLIOGRAPHY

Diagnostic and Statistical Manual of Mental Disorders, ed 3. American Psychiatric Association, 1980.

Erickson MH, Rossi EL, Rossi SI: *Hypnotic Realities: The Induction of Clinical Hypnosis and Forms of Indirect Suggestion.* New York, John Wiley, 1977.

Galper MF: The cult phenomenon: Behavioral service perspectives applied to therapy. *Marriage and Family Review* Fall/Winter 1981;4(314):141-149.

Haley J: An interactional explanation of hypnosis. *Am J Clin Hypno* 1958;1:41-57.

Schein EH: *Coercive Persuasion.* New York, WW Norton, 1961.

Shor RE: Hypnosis and the concept of the generalized reality orientation. *Am J Psychother* 1959;13:582-602.

On the Further Study of Destructive Cultism

JOHN G. CLARK, JR

C ults, both destructive and benign, have been with us in various guises since time immemorial. But cults in our time, especially the truly destructive ones, show a genuinely new aspect: the sophisticated application of recently developed or newly refined techniques of mass communication and psychological manipulation. So, what Dr. Margaret Singer rightly calls a "folk art" persists, but in new, contemporary forms. Now, as ever, cults afford a rich source of information about both the realtively unchanging aspects of human nature and the effects of culture on this nature.

Indeed, in the study of groups generally regarded as destructive—because of their emphasis on money, power, proselytizing, the dissolution of family ties, and often blatant outlawry—there is material aplenty for sociologists, historians, theologians, psychologists, legal scholars, and various branches of medicine. Each discipline has something to learn and each can usefully add its bit of new knowledge to the general enlightenment. Each can also contribute to ameliorating a very serious problem by communicating this knowledge to the public and helping professionals who are grappling with it daily.

Theologians, quite naturally, have been among the scholars most fascinated by the burgeoning "new religions"—destructive cults among them. And well might they be, because the rapid change in belief systems characteristic of cult conversions appears to mirror, in many ways, the conversion experiences reported by those involved in mainline religions. This raises questions about what constitutes a genuine conversion experience.

Religious thinkers also have the rare opportunity to observe cults trying to construct full-fledged religions by deliberate intent. The development of contemporary cults has unfolded so quickly that we get an idea of how religions may have grown up in the ill-documented past. But cults are also fascinating for what they suggest about the nature of man: if people can enter cults as skeptics and exit believing in demons and magic, this raises anew the question of how we come to know what we know.

Unfortunately, for all their interest in these issues, theologians and philosophers have, for the most part, avoided other questions which usually fall within their purview: ethical questions, for instance, like those highlighted by the calculated deceit and crass manipulation integral to many cults. Such concerns must necessarily remain largely unexplored when observers take a tenderly nurturant "hands-off" approach, much as anthropologists do who chance upon one among the dwindling number of truly isolated tribes in a "state of nature."

Social socientists, too, have scrutinized the cult phenomenon. They have provided us with some good structural views of many cultic groups, specified nicely the social backgrounds of the converts, pointed out how some individuals function better (or no worse) in than out of a cult, and they have illuminated for us the cultural forces which predispose people to seek out cults or to be susceptible to their lure. But these same observers, with notable exceptions, have disregarded the central psychological processes involved in conversion and the calculated techniques which have so effectively seduced even wary nonseekers.

Similarly, many psychologists and psychiatrists have become knowledgeable about destructive cults in the course of their work with patients affected by the problem. Yet scholars in these fields, as well as all too many clinicians, tend still to explain conversions, as well as the difficulties arising from them, as results of long-standing personality or familial problems, as expressions of normal developmental crises, or even as manifestations of formal mental disorders. These observers, however, like their colleagues in the social sciences and humanities, tend to ignore the necessary role played by the cult milieu in causing the radical personality changes and family schisms that have clearly affected so many previously normal people and reasonably well-integrated families.

I believe that these defects in the various scholarly approaches to the cult phenomenon stem partly from our understandable habit of fitting new information into already well-developed explanatory categories and of treating each aspect as one in a series of variations on familiar themes without stepping back to discern a qualitatively different and new whole. We are also reticent, as a culture, to criticize anything called "religion." Legal scholars are especially wary here, on behalf of their colleagues in other disciplines, and indeed on behalf of our best traditions, because our sense of justice would have to be revised if we were to agree that a cult's manipulation of an individual may render the notion of "informed consent" meaningless, or that certain practices should not escape scrutiny simply because they are said to be "religious."

The foregoing criticisms of various disciplines' attitudes toward destructive cults is not meant to condemn but to suggest that scholars have a moral responsibility to look more closely into the matter, even if this is unpleasant. If scholars want to sustain the culture that allows them to practice their trade, they must respond more fully to these destructive groups. If they do not, cults and cultish ways of thinking will destroy not only scholarship but also the culture that sustains it.

If we are to respond to this challenge, then we ought to be prepared to learn from one another, because the wall between disciplines certainly accounts in good part for our continuing inability to grasp the problem whole. In order to begin to do this, we ought first to review carefully what we know and then formulate an interdisciplinary plan to achieve a more comprehensive level of understanding. For me, such a review must be from the psychiatric viewpoint, although the perceptions of colleagues in other disciplines have clearly enriched and conditioned my own formulation of the direction I think we should take.

Like some other psychiatrists, I have observed the clinical situation, noting the harms and occasional benefits of the cult experience. This clinical view has illuminated some of the essential aspects of cults, including the activities leading to control of the mind and to drastic personality change. Such clinical impressions have provided data with which to construct hypotheses about destructive cult conversions. My own view is that:

1. Cult victims are characteristically experiencing stressful, often painful, life situations at the time of the cult recruiter makes an approach. However, along with Margaret Singer and Mark Galanter, I emphasize the fact that a majority of converts have no significant psychological or developmental problems in their personal histories. I agree with these authors that between 25% and 39% may have been troubled a priori. Moreover, I maintain that to search for the a priori weaknesses and personality traits of the victims, really a disguised attempt to blame the victims themselves, obscures more relevant information.

2. The interplay of the prospect and the proselytizer is one of rapid access by proffered friendship to a troubled and lonely person. The prospect's attention is carefully obtained by the simplest of interpersonal tactics: a deep show of interest and the offer of love and safety from understanding and loving people.

3. If the subject will agree to hear and see more, further manipulation within the larger group in a controlled atmosphere leads to a state of narrowed attention—a trance or state of dissociation.

4. Through careful and deliberate milieu and interpersonal control a state of altered consciousness is maintained for a significant time—several days or more.

5. In order to adapt to this chronic alteration of the mechanisms of the mind, the subject must either become psychotic or identify with the group and its doctrinal content.

6. For most of the converts, the maintenance of a second, factitious personality is achieved by careful group control including the use of glossolalia, meditation, dancing, praying, sleep deprivation, and the like.

7. This sequence may be interrupted by frequent reversions to the original personality as a result of cult failures, biological and unknown factors, and/or direct intervention by parents and deprogramers.

8. The postdeprograming syndrome lasts about a year, with subjects showing many debilitating symptoms such as depression, flashbacks or sensations of floating between cult and precult personalities, and other problems interfering seriously with normal functioning.

These observations and hypotheses make it clear that a comprehensive theory of conversion must take into account all personal, group, and biological experiences, as well as the notions: 1) that the mind, as a working, choosing, deciding entity, is controlled primarily by its identification with the surrounding culture; 2) that the mind, which is normally pliable, can be massively changed by many forces, especially those having to do with adaptation to the group, but also by physiological, mental, and other forces; and 3) that all of this involves a severing of the connections of the personality and remembered history through a process that can be described as dissociation.

The phenomenon of dissociation has been well illustrated in the literature on hypnosis. In addition, we have identified the use of induced dissociation and the maintenance of that state in the cult milieu. Further, we have defined many of the techniques of induced dissociation and have begun to characterize them by different psychological and physiological categories. We have also noted that many of the changes in behavior and thinking exhibited by cult converts may relate to physiological processes in the central nervous system. One way to explore these changes is to observe that brain functions can be changed by lesions or other biological forces, eg, temporal lobe epilepsy, sexual excitement, and many other conditions such as those we see in the formal mental diseases.

We have collected a great amount of evidence—in books, essays, memoirs, other investigations—which details the gross phenomenology of relevant processes. However, most of the inferences one can draw from this evidence cannot be substantiated scientifically, albeit much of the information is useful in constructing a fuller and more accurate perspective.

What is missing, especially, is a more stringent research plan which would include observation of the evidence at first hand, a sort of anthropological approach which would reveal both the techniques and results of coercive conversion. But we cannot go into the cults to do the kind of research that this implies. So it may be that we will continue to depend on literary and clinical observations by nonprofessionals for part of our argument. But a reasonable argument may nonetheless be constructed. We could, theoretically, go into the laboratory and play with the mind the way the cults do, and really put the process under a microscope. But for us, if not for the cults, this would be an impermissible experiment.

Despite this, we must still, whether we like it or not, deal with cults not only as an intellectual exercise but as a practical problem as well. Each discipline has something to contribute in the attempt to define adequately and deal in a unified way with the issue. The difficulty with the collaborative approach is that we fail, with our diverse viewpoints, to understand and relate to one another. We have become isolated in our different mind sets and different practical concerns, although sharing the common problem.

The collaborative approach, then, must begin by linking front-line workers, who provide much of the raw data, with scholars who can investigate and elaborate the implications of these data. By front-line workers, I mean those who have to deal with the daily torments of destructive cultism: the scientifically trained clinicians, the pastoral counselors, the lawyers, even the politicians. These people need to confirm their experiences with scholarly analyses as a prelude to dealing with cults in a more scientific manner, and as a means to better understand cult issues. Thus the clinician, in consultation with the scholar, may learn how to recognize the syndrome, report it in a systematic way, and best help the afflicted.

First, however, it is important for the scholars of the many relevant disciplines to listen to these clinicians, because it is the latter who have been steeped in the phenomenology of destructive cultism. I would emphasize here that among front-line workers to whom I have been referring as clinicians, the scientifically trained therapists are the natural translators of the core of the cult conversion process—its psychology—to the other sciences. We might think of this kind of clinician as a sort of fieldworker serving a consortium of disciplines with information.

I am not, however, suggesting that the clinician has no role in the logically subsequent theorizing on the matter. Indeed, the clinician's attempts to alleviate pain quite often result in practical hypotheses which scholars may use or not as they see fit. What is most crucial, then, is an effective interchange of knowledge between scholars and clinicians which will shed light on the relationship between culture and the individual within the destructive cult context.

In order to be successful at this task, the various disciplines must solve a fundamental language problem caused by the use of different jargons which tend to obscure important shared principles and make it virtually impossible to achieve mutual comprehension. For example, the concept of "dissociation" is used by Professor Jolyon West to describe "a psycho-physiological process whereby information—incoming, stored or outgoing—is actively deflected from integration with its usual or expected association." Yet most hypnotists use the word "trance" to describe this condition. But "trance" evokes an image of something different from what we suspect happens during many cult conversions. Moreover, the hypnotist tends to deny the phenomenon of trance in extraclinical circumstances, including cult conversion, except in cases of severe pathology or in special rituals.

Similarly, neurophysiologists, who may yet have a great deal to say about cult conversions, treat symptoms like dissociation and trance as if they were strictly biological/pathological phenomena. Neurophysiologists ought to help make the intellectual connection between temporal lobe epilepsy and other dissociated states if, as I think, both are related by basic physiological processes. They ought also to consider the evidence, provided by clinicians and others, that information introduced into the brain can indeed create symptoms of narrowed consciousness/dissociation.

Again, consider that the state of mind I have been referring to as "dissociation" is often described as "ecstacy" or "possession" in religious circles, and as "falling in love" in other contexts. These and the foregoing examples should make it clear that dissociation can stem from pressures of various kinds, either internally or externally generated, and in a variety of contexts; that the condition, and its induction, is a central feature of the management of information by the brain; and that dissociation often involves rapid change in personality or mental functioning.

These observations suggest that the various disciplines must together write a guide to a phenomenon which has many faces, all of which must be kept in mind simultaneously. We need to develop a shared, working vocabulary in order to define, encompass, and illuminate cult-related concepts and processes. By starting with the hypothesis that dissociative states are common to cults and also to the operation of the brain, we can allow for more elaborate descriptions of that phenomenon which will require new terminology and even new measurement systems.

Let me finally suggest how various professionals, and not only scholars, can begin collectively to comprehend the cult problem and subsequently implement collective action. Clinicians, first of all, as I suggested earlier, must learn to recognize the cult syndrome and get used to dealing with dissociated states. They must also report on their treatment strategies which, if such strategies work, will provide information about the process itself. Clinicians must also note aspects of the victims' personalities which may have predisposed them to conversion.

Social scientists, who already know a great deal about change and its agents, ought now to look more closely at cults in this regard, concentrating especially on the methods used to effect mind control through dissociation and radical personality change. To do this better, they ought to learn from clinicians about the psychology and even the physiology of the process. The resultant understanding is certain to help virtually everyone who needs sound theoretical formulations and authoritative factual information in order to respond constructively to the problem.

Legal scholars, for example, can become familiar with developing clinical and social science thought on the issue. Then, having reviewed the growing body of cult-related litigation, these scholars might suggest to their colleagues in the judicial and legislative systems that certain kinds of change—shifts of interpretation, the introduction of new statutes concerning such concepts as "free choice," "capacity," "informed consent"—may be both necessary and just. This sort of work, with care for the rights of all affected individuals and organizations, will in turn help courtroom lawyers whose representations will actually lead the way to defining or redefining such questions as what constitutes the kind of excessive psychological pressure which leads to peonage or how much information ought to be given by purveyors to the consumers of philosophies, theologies, and therapies.

Theologians, meanwhile, learning from other scholars and contributing their own perspectives to the debate, can begin to come to terms with the notion that bad religions exist as well as good ones and that to find serious fault with the one is not to condemn the other. Pastors, for their part, can use the cult phenomenon to examine their own personal and institutional methods for influencing their congregations. Importantly, everyone involved in religious matters can remind the rest of us of the Judeo-Christian proscription of magic, a proscription characteristically breached by cults which instead tend to proscribe rational thought.

Indeed, it is rational thought, based on attention to all of the facts of the cult phenomenon, and not just to some of them, that can lead to real understanding of the problem. But this understanding will be grossly inadequate until scholars begin to speak with and listen to those who have experienced the phenomenon at first hand and until they respect the truth of what these victims say.

CHAPTER

25

Legal Aspects of Dealing with the New Religions

ARTHUR N. FRAKT

The relationship between secular government and sectarian enterprises is uneasy, ambivalent, and complex. Professionals in the mental health field are unlikely to find much affirmative guidance from the law when they are confronted with a psychological or social problem in which religious beliefs and practices play a central role. Indeed, to the extent that legal guidelines are explicit, their effect on treatment has been largely but not exclusively negative.

This chapter will explore the law which may be relevant to the treatment of those who have come under the influence of religious cults and will also attempt to explain the apparent lack of support which legal institutions may afford to those attempting to counter the influence of the cults.

I must begin by stating the bias of my approach. It is assumed that the determination has been made that the involvement of an individual or group with a particular religion, sect, or cult has had a negative, antisocial effect with substantial mental health implications. The vast majority of adult Americans have had a distinctly adverse reaction to a number of the new religious groups and their leaders. Annoyance at being accosted and proselytized in air terminals is a widely shared sentiment. Shock at the outrage of Jonestown and frustration at the growing financial power of Sun Myung Moon are general throughout society.

The general responses to some of the new religions have a sharp personal counterpart in the anger, rage, and depression experienced by the parents, family, and friends of cult victims. The apparent capitulation of the mind, personality and, often, the property of a young adult to the seemingly inhumane and weirdly unearthly philosophy of a cult inevitably triggers insistent demands for governmental action.

Certainly, it is easy to sympathize with the view that there should be some legal means of controlling, if not eliminating, the excessive activities of the cults and their leaders. Nevertheless, the candid response to such a desire is that effective legal controls on these religiously based actions are not likely to be readily

369

available unless we are willing to alter our basic societal foundation in profound and probably dangerous ways.

With specific reference to the mental health profession, it is evident that to this point such legal tools as guardianships, conservatorships, involuntary commitments, and writs of habeas corpus have had limited practical value in creating and maintaining treatment opportunities for the young adults who are the principal victims of cult indoctrination. Furthermore, despite a generally sympathetic attitude of law enforcement officials, courts, and juries toward the families of cult members, such radical measures as physical seizures, forced therapy or "deprograming," involuntary private incarceration, and the related extreme tactics resorted to by Ted Patrick and a small number of lay therapists have not been tolerated by most courts. Although, until Patrick's recent conviction and sentencing for felonious kidnapping,[1] it appeared that penalities were often minimal, the hazards of extreme action have now been clearly acknowledged by the law. As Judge Ehrenfreund put it in passing sentence on Patrick in the San Diego Superior Court, "we must observe the law that makes it a crime to abduct another human being. . . . There must be no further deprograming as in the past."[2]

There has been some limited judicial sanction for "deprograming" under coercive conditions. In *Weiss v Patrick*,[3] a sympathetic court ruled that the efforts of Patrick on behalf of the dying mother of a 23-year-old "extremely troubled" "Moonie" did not amount to false imprisonment and arrest and would not subject the defendant to damages. The court found that the young woman had willingly gone along with her family on the occasion of a Thanksgiving dinner and had suffered no physical or psychic injuries during her brief period with Patrick. The court expressed great sympathy for "maternal solicitude" and stated that the "plaintiff's mother has the parental right to freely advocate a point of view to her daughter whether she be minor or adult." Patrick and his associate were given the benefit of this tolerance since they were aiding the mother. Nevertheless, the court indicated that its dismissal of the suit turned on the lack of protest on the part of the plaintiff, despite her dramatic escape through a window and her subsequent statements that she had been held against her will.

Most recently the Minnesota Supreme Court went substantially beyond the Weiss case and ruled that deprograming of defendant's adult daughter was a legally justifiable remedy for "psychological kidnapping."

In the landmark case of *Peterson v Sorlien*,[4] a divided court acknowledged that the First Amendment rights of religious freedom require "the least restrictive alternative" in fashioning a remedy for a religious cult's "coercive persuasion" or "mind control." Nevertheless, despite the threat to public order embodied in forced deprograming, the court held that if there is voluntary acquiescence at some point within the deprograming period, then despite the subject's initial resistance, and later reaffirmation of that resistance, a charge of false imprisonment will be rejected.

In the Peterson case, the plaintiff had joined a group known as "The Way" when she was a 21-year-old college senior. At her parents' instigation she was transported from her apartment to a basement bedroom of a Minneapolis home where she was kept by her father and four deprogramers for 16 days. There is some dispute about her willingness to accompany her father to the home where she was held, but she claimed that she was "kicking and screaming" in resistance. For the first three days she cried and was unresponsive, but then the court found she remained willingly and appeared cooperative for the next 13 days despite several opportunities to escape. Despite the fact that the plaintiff eventually bolted to join her fiance at the cult's headquarters, the court majority found it significant that her actions after the first three days were an "affirmation" of her acceptance of the original deprograming. Her consent was manifested by her conduct as a "function of time."

This extraordinary conclusion was justified by the court because of "the method of cult indoctrination" which impairs "the capacity for informed consent." "While we acknowledge that other social institutions may utilize a degree of coercion in promoting their objectives, none do so in the same extent or extend the same consequence [as the cults]." The court found that there was a compelling societal interest to prevent the impairment of the judgmental capacity of cult inductees which overrides "colorable religious auspices." Furthermore, parents may appropriately judge when their adult children have reached that state of impairment. Thus, the defendant parents were exonerated. The dissenting justices[5] found that the majority viewpoint violated the constitutional rights of the plaintiff to hold "unorthodox" religious views despite parental objections.

The United States Supreme Court declined to review the Peterson decision. It should be noted that although the decision stands, it is far from a complete license to forceably deprogram. Although Justice Sherin, writing for the majority, does not specify preferable alternates, he does note the potential availability of "temporary guardianship" which might put the cult member into a therapeutic setting. In any event, a psychiatrist, psychologist, or other mental health professional can hardly rely on this opinion to justify participation in forceable, nonlegally sanctioned deprograming. At best, the case only affords the possibility of avoiding liability if, at some time during the process, the patient manifests consent and if the court determines that the particular indoctrination program is so dangerous that a "compelling" state interest justifies the overriding of constitutional protections. At worst, the deprograming professional may be subject to the criminal as well as civil sanctions which have plagued Ted Patrick.

The Peterson decision may be too slim a reed on which to base any firm conclusions that abuses by religious cults of their constitutional protections will lead to a general judicial reevaluation of the extent of those protections; nevertheless Peterson is not the only indication of a growing legal awareness that the courts may be required to reassess their reluctance to venture upon the perilous zone where the temporal and spiritual collide.

In another recent development, a group of deprogramers who claimed that they were being harassed by the Unification Church brought a law suit in federal court in New York City alleging that the church had abused the legal process by encouraging and, in fact, funding law suits by church members charging the deprogramers with assault, battery, false imprisonment, and a variety of other tortious conduct. The deprogramers also alleged that they were being subjected to constant surveillance and harassment by agents of the Unification Church. Although the suit was dismissed by the district court, the prestigious Second Circuit Court of Appeals reinstituted the claims for abuse of process, malicious prosecution and, with regard to the extrajudicial harassment, intentional infliction of emotional harm.[6]

Whether or not the deprogramers are ultimately successful, the fact that the court recognized a claim for abuse of process is highly significant. Courts are extremely reluctant to seriously entertain charges that legal processes are being utilized for improper ends. Such actions run counter to the general principle that courts welcome litigants to submit their disputes to lawful resolution. Although it is not spelled out in the decision, the circuit court's action may be interpreted as a reflection of a growing judicial awareness of the questionable tactics and dangerous designs of some of the cult groups and as a corresponding increasing reluctance to permit the cults to manipulate both constitutional and common-law principles for societally destructive ends. Growing judicial tolerance for governmental inquiries into the financial affairs of religious groups also reflects contemporary judicial skepticism.[7]

Despite these straws in the wind, as noted earlier there has only been a very limited use of the law as an adjunct to the psychiatric treatment of cult adherents.[8] Before exploring this further, and as a key to understanding the problems that lie in the way of expanded use of the law as a major force in the struggle against cult indoctrination, a brief review of the major constitutional elements in the governmental–religious relationship is necessary. Perhaps more importantly, an understanding of the complexities and uncertainties of the legal experience with religion may afford an insight into the larger societal problems which are obscured by the dramatic immediacy of individual cases upon which mental health professionals naturally and inevitably focus.

CONSTITUTIONAL DIMENSIONS
OF THE NEW RELIGION ISSUE

The United States Constitution's expression of fundamental religious rights set forth in the First Amendment and applied to the states through the due-process clause of the Fourteenth Amendment is ambivalent if not actually contradictory. Whereas the abridgement of freedom of speech and of the press is unequivocally prohibited in simple language, there are two somewhat ambiguous religion clauses: the "establishment" clause ("Congress shall make no law respecting an establishment of religion. . . ") and the "free exercise" clause (. . . or prohibiting the free exercise thereof. . . . ").

It should be recalled that the establishment clause had its roots in the attitudes of free-thinkers and deists like Jefferson and Madison who opposed state sponsorship of official religions and assessments for religious purposes.[9] Others who advocated official religions within their particular states did not want a federal religion imposed upon them. In any event, long before the time it became universally recognized that the principal prohibitions and strictures of the Bill of Rights were equally applicable to state and local government, all of the state constitutions had followed the federal example and, by the middle of the nineteenth century, there were no longer any state religions. Nevertheless vestiges of state sponsorship of religion and antagonism to minority faiths and atheism have continued to the modern day. State requirements that office-holders assert a belief in God were not fully eliminated until the Supreme Court held them unconstitutional in a 1961 case involving a Maryland notary public who refused to take a religious oath,[10] and the elimination of state mandated school prayer whether out of a Christian Bible[11] or composed as a "nondenominational" exercise by a government body[12] is still an issue of smoldering concern to many Americans.

Most of the recent controversies concerning the "establishment" clause do not stem from direct government sponsorship of religion, but rather from government efforts to support the secular activities of religious organizations. Since it is obvious that aiding a religious group's secular activities frees funds for and generally enhances the pursuit of the religious mission, the Supreme Court has evolved a set of guidelines to aid in determining when governmental involvement becomes so pervasive that it is effectively an establishment of religion. Most of the cases have stemmed from issues concerning aid to religion-sponsored education.

"First, the statute [or ordinance or administrative regulation] must have a secular purpose; second its principal or primary effect must be one that neither advances nor inhibits religion. . . ; finally, the statute must not foster 'an excessive governmental entanglement with religion. . . .' "[13]

The use of this test has resulted in some delicate (some would say, arbitrary) line drawing. For example, federal aid for construction of libraries and language laboratories at religious colleges was upheld, while similar grants for parochial high schools are denied.[14] Loans of secular texts in high schools are approved while provision of instructional materials is rejected as being too likely to involve government directly in religious activities.[15] Diagnostic but not therapeutic counseling services are permitted within a parochial school. On the other hand, provision of auxiliary services including "therapeutic, guidance and remedial services" are upheld when provided by government employees in trailers located adjacent to, but not within, the schools because the "pressures of the [religious] environment" would not be so intrusive.[16]

Although most of these establishment clause cases do not directly relate to the concern with cult religions, there is one ironic case in which adherence to the strict establishment clause test eliminated a potentially threatening invasion of the public schools by a group which may arguably be classified as a cult or sect. In *Malnak v Yogi*,[17] a federal court of appeals held that the teaching of a course called "The Science of Creative Intelligence/Transcendental Meditation" in a New Jersey high school was an unconstitutional establishment of religion because of various spiritual–sectarian elements including a ceremony or a "puja" in which the students acquired a "mantra" and in which the ceremonially attired teacher participated in a ritual offering to a deified "Guru Dev." Furthermore, as the district court had determined earlier, SCI/TM's text revealed nondemonstrable truths from the pen of Maharishi Mahesh Yogi on the "pure creative intelligence" which, it is suggested, is the basis of life.

Whether or not one agrees that Transcendental Meditation is religious, the Malnak case illustrates two points: first, it is very difficult to draw the line between religion and philosophy, the spiritual and the scientific. Second, at least in the context of public education, the courts have taken a rather broad approach to the constitutional demands of the establishment clause.

Ironically, the very difficulties which have led the courts to take an expansive view of what is an "establishment" of religion by the state have also contributed to broad judicial protection for arguably religious activities under the "free exercise" clause. This is where the greatest legal difficulties for the treatment of cult adherents arise. Judicial reluctance to impinge upon free exercise of religion is understandable when viewed in the context of: 1) the difficulties of defining religion, 2) the constitutionally motivated necessity to avoid selecting a narrow range of widely held Judeo-Christian-Muslim beliefs as being the only ones which are truly religious in nature, and 3) the fact that the proselytizing and solicitation undertaken by many of the cults involves not only the free exercise clause but also the First Amendment's mandates protecting freedom of speech, assembly, and the press.

Up through the middle of this century, most of the "free exercise" cases which reached the appellate courts involved conflicts between general societal mores and values, reflected in the criminal law and in government regulations, on the one hand, and the desires of religious minorities and sects to actively engage in religiously mandated conduct, on the other. These cases demonstrate little judicial difficulty in distinguishing between the freedom of sect members to believe whatever they wished to, and the freedom of society to punish or prohibit unacceptable conduct, even if religiously inspired.

The last point is illustrated by a series of cases involving the former Mormon practice of polygamy. In the leading case, *Reynolds v United States,*[18] the Supreme Court upheld a polygamy conviction. "Congress was deprived of all legislative power over mere opinion, but was left free to reach actions which were in violation of social duties or subversive of good order." In later cases, the court went even further noting that to call the Mormons' advocacy of polygamy a tenet of religion "is to offend the common sense of mankind."[19] The court further distinguished religion as "one's views of his relation to his Creator" from 'cultus'. . . or the form of worship of a particular sect."

Compulsory vaccination,[20] Sunday closing laws,[21] prohibition of the public selling of religious literature by young children,[22] and prosecutions for engaging in such bizarre and dangerous religious activities as snake-handling[23] were all upheld by the courts against claims that these requirements or prohibitions seriously interfered with religious beliefs. On the other hand, when prohibition of religious activities had serious implications for other First Amendment rights, particularly in the free speech area, the courts were more sympathetic to claims of infringement of free exercise. Thus the Supreme Court upheld the right of adult Jehovah's Witnesses to distribute religious pamphlets and the refusal of their children to participate in flag-saluting ceremonies.[25]

In recent years these kinds of constitutional concerns have been manifested in a series of cases involving largely unsuccessful efforts by airport and other local officials to severely limit the proselytizing and solicitation activities of members of the Hare Krishna sect.

In a significant recent decision, the Supreme Court ruled that although Krishna devotees could not be stopped from speaking to and proselytizing patrons of the Minnesota state fair, they could be restricted to a booth for solicitation of funds and sales and distribution of pamphlets and books.

Although the case was decided on traditional "time, place, and manner" grounds, it is noteworthy that the court gave short shrift to the argument that since "sankirtan" was central to Krishna, the restrictions violated free exercise. The Court held that, at least insofar as solicitations were concerned:

> None of our cases suggest that the inclusion of peripatetic solicitation as part of a church ritual entitles church workers to solicitation rights in a public forum superior to those of members of other religious groups that raise money, but do not ritualize the process.[26]

Despite this potentially significant development, with the emergence of the Warren Court in the late 1950s and early 60s and continuing through the contemporary Burger court decisions, a philosophy of affording significantly increased judicial protection for the free exercise of religion has resulted in several decisions which have elevated individual religious activities to the point at which traditional governmental police power functions for the protection of health, safety, and welfare must often give way to the greater constitutional merits of the free exercise clause. This has been accomplished by judicial insistence that rather than government justifying its actions by showing a mere rational relationship between its regulation or statute and a legitimate governmental purpose, where free exercise is seriously impinged upon, government must have a "compelling" or (as more conservative court members prefer) "substantial" reason to infringe upon religious activities and officials must carry out their mandate by "the least intrusive or restrictive means."[27] These terms may seem like so much definitional rhetoric to nonlawyers, but the practical effect of such changes has been to put a very heavy burden on government restrictions and regulation of activity which has a colorable religious basis. For example in *Sherbert v Verner*,[28] South Carolina could not refuse unemployment benefits to a Seventh Day Adventist who, by reason of her religion, was not available for work on Saturday and, therefore, could not keep a job in the textile industry which operated on a six-day week.

The most significant case to date in which a minority sect was permitted to maintain a religious practice substantially at odds with widely accepted public policy was *Wisconsin v Yoder*,[29] a 1972 decision in which Chief Justice Burger held that the state could not compel members of the Amish church to send their children to school beyond the eighth grade despite a law requiring education until the age of 16.

The chief justice appeared to be influenced by the image of the Amish as simple, God-fearing productive citizens who wished only to preserve their admirable, if intellectually limited, way of life. Since the Amish children would still be exposed to the fundamentals of reading, writing, and arithmetic, the interests of the state in their health, safety, and welfare was not substantially threatened.

In partial dissent, Justice Douglas pointed out that it would be very difficult for Amish children who became dissatisfied with the limitations of their religiously dominated lives to overcome the handicaps imposed upon them by judicially sanctioned removal from school at the age of 13 or 14. There was also substantial psychological evidence that many Amish children would become discontented and frustrated. The court majority refused to consider this aspect of the controversy.

The Yoder decision not only illustrates the growing emphasis on freedom of religious exercise beyond the ceremonial sphere, it also illustrates the pitfalls that await the judiciary when they attempt to evaluate the merits of a particular cult or sect, either as a religion per se or as a vehicle for the inculcation of social attitudes and behavior which reflect the court's own value system.

What happens when the law becomes concerned with cults and sects whose distance from the mainstream of American religious belief is so great or whose activities appear so threatening to the public at large that adherence to the tenets of religious freedom are apt to be severely strained? The early Mormon polygamy decisions discussed above suggest that complete neutrality with regard to dogma has not always been easily maintained. Nevertheless, despite the resentment and fear that unorthodox religious beliefs may engender, at least insofar as the truthfulness of a belief, the position of the courts is one of rigid doctrinal neutrality. Logically this is an admirable, indeed a necessary, posture. Since it is no more or less scientifically demonstrable that Moses parted the waters of the Red Sea or Jesus rose from the tomb than that Sun Myung Moon is God incarnate (or whatever his murky theology claims him to be) or that the Maharishi can spirtually levitate, how are the courts to differentiate among truthful and fraudulent religions?

In the most significant case to reach the Supreme Court on the issue, *United States v Ballard*,[30] the defendants, Donald and Edna Ballard, held themselves out to be divine messengers of the "I am" movement with supernatural healing powers. After their indictment and conviction on charges of fraudulently collecting donations, the court ultimately ruled that both religion clauses prohibited inquiry into the truth or falsity of their religious claims. Such a hearing would be the modern equivalent of a heresy trial. On the other hand, the court indicated that there could be an inquiry into the sincerity of the professed beliefs. Thus an individual promoting a fraudulent charity on some sort of religious basis could be prosecuted if it could be proven that the religious aspects were a mere subterfuge.

Where groups and individuals claim a religious basis for activities which obviously appear to have a clear secular purpose, courts may give close scrutiny to the sincerity of their spiritual claims. Individuals with mail order ordinations who attempt to escape property taxes by claiming their homes are really churches may expect a searching inquiry.

The most dramatic examples of this judicial flexibility may be found in the area of the use of narcotic and hallucinogenic substances. The California Supreme Court held that the members of the Native American Church could not be convicted for using peyote during the course of their religious ceremonies.[31] The court pointed out that the church was a small Indian group in an isolated area of the Southwest desert which had a long-standing ceremonial use of the drug central to their beliefs and a corresponding taboo against its use at any other time. By contrast, a group of whites led by one Alan Birnbaum who styled themselves as "The Native American Church of New York" had their claim that they were entitled to a broad exception to the Controlled Substances Act of 1970 rejected. Birnbaum claimed that all psychedelic drugs were "deities." Noting that the group contained few, if any, Indians, the court held that Birnbaum would have to demonstrate a sincere, bona-fide religious belief and purpose in using peyote before the court would consider his desire for a limited statutory exception.[32] Timothy Leary's claim for a religious exemption from prosecution for marijuana possession[33] and the arguments of the *Cannabis*-smoking "Ethiopian Zion Coptic Church" that their use and distribution of the drug was divinely inspired[34] were given short shrift by skeptical courts. In the latter case, the court held that the "easy access to *Cannabis* for a child who had absolutely no interest in learning the religion, coupled with the indiscriminate use of the drug by members. . . , clearly warrants intervention by the state."

The most widespread use of "sincerity" tests for religious beliefs have been in military draft-exemption cases. In order to avoid the difficult constitutional question of whether a religious exemption to the draft is constitutionally mandated (or constitutionally appropriate) the Supreme Court has given an extremely broad definition to religion in draft cases.[35] Nevertheless, the court has consistently upheld the judiciary's duty and ability to determine sincerity of religious belief.

Although not yet a significant factor in legal battles against the cults, tests and evidence of sincerity may prove valuable in confronting those organizations whose religious aspects may appear to a neutral observer to be merely a protective layer shielding them from inquiries into their business practices and protecting them from many of the taxes, controls, and reporting responsibilities of ordinary corporate enterprises. Surely the financial success of the Reconstruction Church, the efforts of Synanon, the drug treatment and life-style organization, to reclassify itself as a religion, and the notorious financial dealings of Herbert W. Armstrong's Worldwide Church of God are likely to prompt more vigorous legal efforts to penetrate the religious curtain thrown up by many of the cults of recent vintage.[36]

CULTS, CULT VICTIMS, AND THE
MENTAL HEALTH PROFESSIONAL

Having established the difficulties and complexities of the constitutional relationship of government and religion, let us return to the specific issues of whether the law may be utilized as an aid to treatment or at least not be a threat and detriment to private familial efforts to restore cult victims to reason and mental health.

There is not space here to dwell upon the rights of parents and their chosen treating professionals with regard to children. Suffice it to say that parents retain substantial control over the activities of their unemancipated offspring, despite the Supreme Court's recognition that children do possess constitutional rights compatible with their maturity and with society's interest in supervising their development through the institutions of schools and family.[37]

As Mr. Justice Stewart put it, "A state may permissibly determine, at least in some precisely delineated areas, a child, like someone in a captive audience, is not possessed of that full capacity for individual choice that is the presupposition of First Amendment guarantees."[38]

Most importantly, the Supreme Court recently ruled that where parents sought to "voluntarily" commit their child to a state mental hospital, formal legal procedures involving an attorney for the child were not required and that an inquiry by a neutral "factfinder," presumably a hospital official, would be sufficient to protect the child's interests. Justice Burger stressed the importance of "the family as a unit with broad parental authority" and that "parents' traditional interests in and responsibility for" their children is of primary concern.[39]

In the light of such language, it is not surprising that a New Hampshire federal jury awarded $30,000 in damages to a parent whose 16-year-old daughter was recruited by the Unificiation Church. The plaintiff had alleged that the church used "mind control" over his daughter.[40] The case was unusual in that the juvenile had actually joined her mother who was a member of the church, and Unification officials claimed they were unaware that the girl was in her father's custody.

Far more typical of the kind of recruit who is attracted by the cults is the young adult college student, recent dropout, or graduate who is particularly vulnerable to the propaganda and blandishments of groups offering friendship, support, and eternal love in the form of like-minded followers of an all-protective father-figure. The anguished families of these young people are most likely to seek legal redress as well as aid from mental health professionals. What practical recourse is available to them?

Despite the occasional legal successes of deprogramers and parents in defending against civil and criminal actions for assault, false imprisonment, kidnapping, and the like as exemplified by *Weiss v Patrick* and *Peterson v Sorlien*, obviously no responsible mental health worker should encourage or participate in involuntary deprograming in the absence of clear judicial authorization. The potential losses in damage suits, suspension or revocation of licensure, and criminal prosecution are so clear that only a lunatic fringe would actively engage in such conduct. Even Delgado, the legal writer most strongly opposed to the cults, cautions that "involuntary deprograming should not proceed unless there has been a prior judicial determination that the individual is incompetent or under mind control" and that it should only be carried out "pursuant to a court order and with periodic reporting to the court."[41] Even if sympathetic prosecutors, grand juries, judges, and petit juries may make criminal conviction or large civil damages problematic, the costs of defending against such actions are in themselves prohibitive. Thus, unless the patient is cooperative, an unlikely circumstance and one which should be carefully checked, evaluated, and substantiated before treatment proceeds, some degree of legal coercion through guardianship, conservatorship, or in the most serious circumstances, involuntary commitment must be resorted to.

What are the chances for the practical success of such drastic remedies? Unless and until courts are convinced that the "mind control" and "brainwashing" techniques allegedly utilized by the cults are substantively different than mere propaganda and persuasion, courts may be expected to reject most such petitions as well as criminal charges based on similar evidence. At least until now, most courts appear to agree with Dr. Thomas Szasz's characterization that "brainwashing" and "mind control" are metaphors to express disapproval of the way in which someone has been influenced by someone else."[42]

In *People v Murphy*[43] a New York City trial court dismissed criminal charges of kidnapping against the International Society for Krishna Consciousness. The court discussed the potential for the utilization of the criminal process to suppress religion and concluded that in a pluralistic society the freedom of a religion to attempt to proliferate its views was essential and that in the absence of the most substantial evidence of intentional physical and mental impairment, charges could not be sustained.[44]

In *Helander v Salonen*,[45] a District of Columbia court denied a habeas corpus petition by parents seeking to compel the Unification Church to produce their 18-year-old daughter for examination. After considering the evidence, the court found that she was not being detained by the use of impermissible psychological methods or pressures.

Even if a habeas corpus procedure is successful in forcing the production of a missing or unapproachable individual in court, unless the individual was really being held against her will or is in obvious physical or mental distress or danger, the likelihood is that she will be immediately released to return to the cult.

The nature of the evidence needed to convince a court that a cult member has in fact been rendered incompetent by "brainwashing" is beyond the scope or expertise of this chapter, although Delgado does offer some helpful, if overly sanguine, legal guidance.[46]

Certainly, what is minimally necessary is psychiatric testimony that the cult member has lost his or her grasp of reality and the ability to rationally deal with the problems of life as opposed to testimony that the religious faith in the cult itself is irrational.

It is important to note that guardianship[47] is primarily intended as a vehicle for the supervision and protection of an individual who is incompetent and impaired

> . . . by reason of mental illness, mental deficiency, physical illness or disability, advanced age, chronic use of drugs, chronic intoxication or other cause. . . to the

extent that he lacks sufficient understanding or capacity to make or communicate responsible decisions concerning his person.[48]

Most cult members do not fit within the traditional judicial view of the kind of enfeebled and incompetent person who is so lacking in the essential tools of survival that he requires the appointment of another person to supervise and control his person and his finances.

The Vermont guardianship statute was recently revised after extensive legislative hearings into the practices of cults.[49] This statute specifically limits the use of guardianships to those instances where they are necessary to "protect the individual from violations of his human and civil rights." The statute does cite "gross mismanagement, as evidenced by recent behavior, of one's income and resources" and defines mental illness broadly to include a "substantial disorder of thought, mood, perception, orientation, or memory, any of which grossly impairs judgment, behavior, capacity to recognize reality, or ability to meet the ordinary demands of life. . . "[50] Other sections of Vermont's codes provide for the drastic remedy of involuntary treatment upon certification by a physician of mental illness for an initial period of 90 days, preferably in a nonhospital setting with specific rights to hearing and counsel for the patient.

This modern statute and others like it have flexibility in the degree and nature of the guardianship or treatment imposed. And the relative broadness of definition of incapacity and mental disability obviously provides a framework for families and mental health professionals to gain access to and provide treatment for those severely disoriented cult members who are not amenable to other less drastic forms of persuasion. Yet in the one appellate case in which a temporary conservatorship was tested under a modern statute, *Katz v Superior Court of San Francisco*,[51] the court ultimately held the granting of temporary conservatorships to the parents of two young adults was improper and a violation of the cult members' right to freedom of religion. Three other cult members voluntarily consented to the appointment of the temporary conservators but the result probably would have been the same had they appealed.

Psychiatric testimony established that techniques of food deprivation, sleep deprivation, isolation, and fear tactics were utilized to break down the will and intellect of the cult inductees who were described by a psychiatrist as exhibiting a limited vocabulary, an emotionally frozen wide-eyed appearance, and a childlike inappropriate smile in response to all stimuli and who were further described as being paranoid, defensive, and regressed. Nevertheless, the court observed that the proposed conservatees were very articulate and were not psychotic or hypnotized.

The court noted "If an adult person is less than gravely disabled, we find no warrant for depriving him or her of liberty or freedom of action." The Katz court concluded by citing the words of Justice Jackson of the Supreme Court dissenting in the Ballard case:

> The way of these things, as I see it, is not in the money the victims part with half so much as in the mental and spiritual poison they get. But that is precisely the thing the Constitution put beyond the reach of the prosecution, for the price of freedom of religion or of speech or of the press is that we must put up with, and even pay for, a good deal of rubbish.[52]

One could go on with other examples leading, depending upon the particular commentator's point of view, to the conclusion that a variety of largely untested civil rights theories or restructured traditional tort actions will either make it easier for parents and deprogramers to resist the cults or vice versa. This is not the place for such speculation. What can be firmly concluded at this point is that without a showing of grave physical danger, most courts are unlikely to license parents and their cooperating psychiatrists or psychologists to take control over young adult cult members for the purpose of deprograming them. On the other hand, habeas corpus petitions and petitions for temporary conservatorship under the appropriate state laws may be useful tools in assuring the physical safety and determining the mental state of such individuals. That is, if the family will risk the heartbreak of the voluntary return to the cult and the ensuing further estrangement which often follow such efforts.

For the future, there is hope that liberal guardianship and conservatorship statutes properly limited by understanding courts will provide more practical tools. In this context the familiarity of psychiatrists and psychologists with the techniques and results of cult indoctrination is crucial, as is the ability of such professionals to convince the courts that there really is a kind of mental illness and incapacity in cult members which does not manifest itself in traditionally recognized psychotic behavior but which nevertheless leads to the conclusion that the victims are not truly exercising their rights of religious freedom.

Finally, as the courts themselves confront the uneradicable horror of Jonestown, the ever more obvious fiscal manipulations of some cult leaders, and the evidence of a continued lack of rationality by cult members, it is likely that some evolutionary change in the interpretation of constitutional requirements as applied to the most destructive cults will be manifested in the judicial consciousness. Indeed this seems to have happened in Minnesota. For as Justice Sutherland of the Supreme Court once put it:

> While the meaning of constitutional guarantees never varies, the scope of their application must expand or contract to meet the new and different conditions which are constantly coming within the field of their operation. In a changing world, it is impossible that it should be otherwise. . . . A degree of elasticity is thus imparted, not to the meaning, but to the application of constitutional principles. . . .[53]

FOOTNOTES

[1]"Anti-cult worker sentenced." *Philadelphia Inquirer,* September 28, 1980, p 4a. Patrick was sentenced to one year in jail, placed on five years probation, and fined $5000 for his part in "the kidnapping of a 25-year-old Tucson waitress whose family feared she was controlled by a religious zealot."

[2]*Id.*

[3]453 F. Supp. 717 (D.R.I. 1978), aff'd. 588 F.2d 818 (1st Cir. 1978) *cert.* denied, 442 U.S. 929 (1979). Cf *Baer v Baer,* 450 F. Supp. 481 (N.D. Calif. 1978), in which federal civil rights actions brought by an adult member of the Unification Church against his parents and a deprogramming group, the Freedom of Thought Foundation, were rejected as not applying to "private religious controversies."

[4]Min 299, _____ N.W.2d 123, (1980), *cert.* denied, 450 U.S. 1031 (1981). Discussed in greater detail in: Novel deprogramming case, *The National Law Journal,* November 17, 1980, p 19. The opinion was by Chief Justice Robert Sheran.

[5]James C. Otis and Rosalie Wahl.

[6]*Alexander v Unification Church of America,* 634 F.2d 673, 49 Law Week 2331 (2d Cir. 1980). See also *Church of Scientology v Siegelman and Conway,* 79 Civ. 1166 (S.D.N.Y.), a suit filed in federal court by two writers of a book critical of the Church of Scientology. A

companion suit for malicious prosecution was voluntarily dismissed. See Book authors drop one suit against Church of Scientology, *The National Law Journal*, November 17, 1980, p 11.

[7]See, for example, *Rader v California* (Calif. Sup. Ct. 7/5/79) *cert.* denied 444 U.S. 916 (1979) in which the Supreme Court refused to interfere with California's audit of all church records and expenditures of the Worldwide Church of God. Cf *Church of Scientology of Calif. v United States*, 591 F.2d 553 (9th Cir. 1979) denying the return of thousands of church records seized under search warrants.

[8]For an extensive optimistic explanation of the potential for future cooperation between the legal and mental health professions in dealing with cults see Delgado R, *Religious totalism: Gentle and ungentle persuasion under the First Amendment*, 51 S.CAL.L.Rev 1, 1–98(1977).

[9]See, in particular, Madison's "Memorial and Remonstrance" to the Virginia legislature (1785). The issue of religious freedom and government tolerance of minority sects has important international ramifications. For an enlightening discussion of United Nations efforts to draft a universal declaration in intolerance and religious discrimination, see Clark, The United Nations and religious freedom, *N.Y.U.J. Int'l Law & Politics* 11:197–225 (1978).

[10]*Torcaso v Watkins*, 367 U.S. 488 (1961).

[11]*School District v Schempp*, 374 U.S. 203 (1963).

[12]*Engel v Vitale*, 370 U.S. 421 (1962).

[13]*Lemon v Kurtzman*, 403 U.S. 602 (1971).

[14]*Tilton v Richardson*, 403 U.S. 672 (1971).

[15]*Meek v Pittinger*, 421 U.S. 349 (1975).

[16]*Wolman v Walter*, 433 U.S. 229 (1977).

[17]592 F.2d 197 (3d Cir. 1979).

[18]98 U.S. 145, 164 (1879).

[19]*Davis v Beason*, 133 U.S. 333, 342–43 (1890). See also, *The Late Corporation of the Church of Jesus Christ of Latter Day Saints v United States*, 136 U.S. 1, 49–50 (1890). As recently as 1955, the Supreme Court dismissed an appeal from a Utah decision which held that custody of children could be removed from parents who taught the religious necessity of polygamy. In re State in Interest of Black, 3 Utah 2d 315, 283 P.2d 887 (1955), *appeal dismissed*, 350 U.S. 923 (1955).

[20]*Jacobson v Massachusetts*, 197 U.S. 11 (1905).

[21]*Braunfeld v Brown*, 366 U.S. 599 (1961). Sunday closing laws were held not to be an establishment of religion because of the secular interests in a day of rest, peace, and quiet. *McGowan v Maryland*, 366 U.S. 420 (1961).

[22]*Prince v Massachusetts*, 321 U.S. 158 (1944).

[23]*Hill v State*, 38 Ala. App. 404, 88 So. 2d 880 (1950); State ex rel *Swann v Pack*, 527 S.W.2.d 99 (1975), *cert.* denied 424 U.S. 954 (1976).

[24]*Cantwell v Connecticut*, 310 U.S. 296 (1940).

[25]*West Virginia State Board of Education v Barnette*, 319 U.S. 624 (1943).

[26]*Heffron v International Society for Krishna Consciousness*, 452 U.S. 640 (1981).

[27]See the discussion of these precepts in *Sherbert v Verner*, 374 U.S. 398 (1963).

[28]*Id.*

[29]406 U.S. 205 (1972).

[30]332 U.S. 78 (1944). See also *Fowler v Rhode Island*, 345 U.S. 67 (1953).

[31]*People v Woody*, 61 Cal.2d 716, 394 P.2d 813 (1964).

[32]*Native American Church of New York v United States*, 468 F. Supp. 1247 (S.D.N.Y. 1979).

[33]*Leary v United States*, 383 F.2d 851 (5th Cir. 1967).

[34]*Town v State* ex rel Reno, 377 So. 2d 648 (1979).

[35]See, eg, *United States v Seeger*, 380 U.S. 163 (1965).

[36]See cases cited *supra* note 7.

[37]See *Tinker v Des Moines School District*, 393 U.S. 503 (1969); *Planned Parenthood of Central Missouri v Danforth*, 428 U.S. 52 (1976).

382

[38]*Ginsberg v New York,* 390 U.S. 629, 649–50 (1968).

[39]*Parham v J.R.,* 442 U.S. 584 (1979).

[40]*Kieffer v Unification Church,* as reported in the August 29, 1980, *Philadelphia Inquirer.*

[41]See the guidelines for deprogramming in Delgado, supra note 8 at 85–88.

[42]*The Nation,* Feb. 26, 1977, p 241, quoted in Note: Deprogramming Religious Cultists, *Loy. L.A.L. Rev.* 807, 811 (1977).

[43]98 Misc. 2d 235 (S. Ct. N.Y. 1967).

[44]See the discussion of this and other cases in Note. *supra* note 42.

[45]No. H C 7-75 (D.C. Super. Ct. Sept. 23, 1975).

[46]See Delgado, *supra* note 8.

[47]The two terms are largely interchangeable although *guardianship* usually refers to the person, while conservatorship, the estate or finances.

[48]Uniform Probate Code, Art. V., § 5-304 (1977).

[49]Delgado, *supra* note 8, p 5, note 16.

[50]Vt. Stat. Ann. tit. 14, S. 3060 et seq.

[51]73 (Calif. App. 3d 952, 141 Cal. Rptr. 234 (1977).

[52]*Ballard v United States,* 322 U.S. at 95. See generally, Note: To Keep Them Out of Harm's Way—Temporary Conservatorship and Religious Sects, *Calif. L Rev.* 845, 845–859 (1978).

[53]*Village of Euclid v Ambler Realty Co.,* 272 U.S. 365 (1926).

I N D E X